READINGS

TOTAL QUALITY MANAGEMENT

READINGS IN

TOTAL QUALITY MANAGEMENT

HARRY IVAN COSTIN

THE DRYDEN PRESS

HARCOURT BRACE COLLEGE PUBLISHERS

*Fort Worth Philadelphia San Diego New York Orlando Austin San Antonio
Toronto Montreal London Sydney Tokyo*

Acquisitions Editor	Ruth Rominger
Project Editor	Doug Smith
Art Director	Melinda Huff
Production Manager	Kelly Cordes
Marketing Manager	Lisé Johnson
Publisher	Elizabeth Widdicombe
Director of Editing, Design, and Production	Diane Southworth
Copy Editor	Dee Salisbury
Indexer	Anne Leach
Compositor	Thompson Type
Text Type	10/12 pt Meridien
Cover Image	Tim Lewis

Address for Editorial Correspondence
The Dryden Press, 301 Commerce Street, Suite 3700, Fort Worth, TX 76102

Address for Orders
The Dryden Press, 6277 Sea Harbor Drive, Orlando, FL 32887
1-800-782-4479, or 1-800-433-0001 (in Florida)

ISBN: 0-03-097301-5

Library of Congress Catalog Card Number: 93-072495

Printed in the United States of America

5 6 7 8 9 0 1 2 090 9 8 7 6 5 4

The Dryden Press
Harcourt Brace College Publishers

Dedicated to Y.S. Chang

Brief Table of Contents

———

vii

Table of Contents

Preface

———

This book is intended for both professional and academic use. The 37 readings included provide a broad overview of the main concepts, tools, and processes of Total Quality Management (TQM). Over the last decade TQM has attracted the attention of managers, engineers and academics due to its early success record in increasing the efficiency of manufacturing and service delivery processes.

TQM is rooted in various disciplines and approaches like Quality Control, Quality Assurance, Total Quality Control, Organizational Development and Strategy. It is therefore an interdisciplinary management system, and many of its concepts and tools can be traced back to various other disciplines and applications ranging from engineering to anthropology. TQM has integrated these different approaches in a unique way and emerged over the last decade as a major paradigm of participatory decision making that focuses on the continuous improvement of production and service delivery processes. The synthesis of concepts, tools and processes found in TQM has occurred over time as a need- and experience-based continuous process of improvement.

For professional use the book provides insight into diverse ways of understanding and applying Total Quality. These approaches range from Statistical Process Control to Hoshin Planning and Quality Function Deployment. Also included are a general overview of the Quality Control and the Management and Planning tools, and specific readings addressing teambuilding, training, and evaluation of quality programs.

For academic use the book is suitable as a textbook or complementary reading for undergraduate and graduate courses in engineering, general management, strategy, operations management, and organizational behavior since Total Quality thinking has been drawn from and has affected each one of these conceptual and academic areas.

Structure of the book

The book has been divided into eight parts and two appendices, which to a certain degree overlap in terms of their content. For example, the classic readings selected specifically address the question: What is Total Quality Management? Nevertheless, it is useful to distinguish the early definition of Total Quality Control of Feigenbaum or the Statistical Process Control concepts of Deming from the more recent Strategic Quality Planning of Garvin or the Learning Organization of Senge.

Part I addresses basic concepts and definitions related to Total Quality and provides a historic overview of the quality movement. The introduction by the editor draws heavily on the readings included in the book and provides a general conceptual framework for the entire book.

Part II includes representative selections from the best-known founding fathers of the quality movement.

Part III provides an overview of the Seven Basic Quality Control Tools and the Seven Management and Planning Tools. These tools, used extensively by Quality Teams ranging from top management to line workers, combine analytical and creative approaches in problem solving and comprehensive planning.

Part IV introduces some of the best-known applications in Total Quality, including the classical Statistical Process Control (SPC), Just-in-Time (JIT) applications, and the more recent Hoshin Planning methods.

Part V focuses on "Listening to the Voice of the Customer," the key concept on which Total Quality systems are built. The reading on Quality Function Deployment (which conceptually should also be included with the readings in part IV) provides a specific example of customer-oriented new product design.

Part VI is the most diverse section of the book and includes readings focusing on various applications, an evaluation of an implementation of a large-scale quality program in a steel mill, and a piece that traces the historical origins of current Japanese management practices.

Part VII addresses the implementation of Total Quality from the human perspective. It includes training issues, team-focused quality improvement programs and the need for management-labor cooperation as a prerequisite for successful quality programs.

Part VIII illustrates early implementation efforts of Total Quality in Higher Education.

Appendix I includes the full text of the 1993 Baldrige Award guidelines and factsheets on 1989–1991 Baldrige Award winners. Also included is the European Model for self-appraisal, the practical guideline for companies pursuing the European Quality Award (the European equivalent of the Deming Prize and Baldrige Award), which was awarded for the first time in 1992.

Appendix II includes a database of the authors and organizations specifically contacted by the editor for this text. Most authors expressed a specific interest in interacting with other colleagues engaged in quality research and applications.

The Dryden Press Series in Management Science and Quantitative Methods

————

Costin
READINGS IN TOTAL QUALITY MANAGEMENT

Etienne-Hamilton
OPERATIONS STRATEGIES FOR COMPETITIVE
ADVANTAGE: TEXT AND CASES

Forgionne
QUANTITATIVE MANAGEMENT

Freed
BASIC BUSINESS STATISTICS

Gaither
PRODUCTION AND OPERATIONS MANAGEMENT
Sixth Edition

Glaskowsky, Hudson, and Ivie
BUSINESS LOGISTICS
Third Edition

Hamburg and Young
STATISTICAL ANALYSIS FOR DECISION MAKING
Sixth Edition

Ingram and Monks
STATISTICS FOR BUSINESS AND ECONOMICS
Second Edition

Lapin
STATISTICS FOR MODERN BUSINESS DECISIONS
Sixth Edition

Lapin
QUANTITATIVE METHODS FOR BUSINESS
DECISIONS WITH CASES

Sixth Edition

Lee
INTRODUCTION TO MANAGEMENT SCIENCE
Second Edition

Mason, Lind, and Marchal
STATISTICS: AN INTRODUCTION
Fourth Edition

Miller and Wichern
INTERMEDIATE BUSINESS STATISTICS

Weiers
INTRODUCTION TO BUSINESS STATISTICS
Second Edition

Zikmund
BUSINESS RESEARCH METHODS
Fourth Edition

THE HARCOURT BRACE COLLEGE OUTLINE SERIES

Lapin
BUSINESS STATISTICS

Pentico
MANAGEMENT SCIENCE

Rothenberg
PROBABILITY AND STATISTICS

xix

Tanis
STATISTICS I: DESCRIPTIVE STATISTICS AND
PROBABILITY

Tanis
STATISTICS II: ESTIMATION AND TESTS OF
HYPOTHESIS

READINGS IN

TOTAL QUALITY MANAGEMENT

1

What Is
Total Quality
Management?

Introduction

The readings in Part I address the basic question: What is Total Quality Management (TQM)? An attempt is made to provide an answer from a historic perspective and by examining the key current concepts related to the quality field.

Historically, it should be noted that quality as a concept has evolved from the focused definitions of quality as inspection and quality control to the almost all-encompassing concept of "quality" of the 90s. Today, "quality" implies product and service quality as perceived by the customer, quality of processes, and even the societal and environmental impact of products and business activity.

As quality concepts have become generalized, two reasons for concern have developed. A first danger is that "quality" is becoming such an overused concept as to become vague and unfocused, the very criticism the quality movement has applied to preceding management approaches. A second danger lies in taking a particular "quality guru" or "party line" as an exclusive interpretation of what TQM is or is not. The key benefits of the diverse writings included under the generic heading of TQM lie in the diversity of approaches used and the emphasis on a "reality check" of our activities, i.e. learning from our mistakes and experiences. In other words, our understanding of quality should evolve with our ongoing learning as we implement diverse quality programs.

Conceptually, current definitions and processes related to "total quality" can be interpreted as an interplay of three fields and approaches:

1. Efficiency concerns rooted in process analysis, related to such traditions as Process Engineering, Operations Management, Operations Research, and Statistical Process Control.

    Here, the key concept is **efficient and continuously improving processes** for product and service delivery.

2. Concerns about quality of work life, collaborative management-labor relations, and synergy through team work. This approach is closely related to the Human Relations school of management thought and the fields of Organizational Behavior and Organizational Dynamics.

    Here, the key concepts are **teamwork, synergy, and empowerment.**

3. Concerns about the goals of any business, i.e. survival, profits, market share and sustainable competitive advantage in an increasingly hostile and competitive global environment. This requires the formulation and implementation of a coherent **strategy** and a **shared vision.** This perspective is the most recent one in the U.S. and European implementation of "total quality" and is closely linked to the field of Strategy or Management Policy.

The key concepts related to this approach are **strategy, mission, vision, and benchmarking.**

Conceptually, and also in its implementation, "total quality" should integrate strategic, human, and operational concerns. In practice though, because of the complexities involved, there are few theorists or practitioners writing about or implementing "total quality" who have enough experience in all three fields to integrate them effectively.

Consequently, several quality efforts under the banner of "TQM" have been criticized over the last two years, e.g. in the Ernst & Young study of quality programs or in the Wall Street Journal.

The shortcomings of specific TQM programs can often be traced back to the professional background and orientation of those involved in their planning and implementation stages. Among the thinkers and practitioners, who often fail to integrate effectiveness, efficiency and motivation concerns in the application of TQM, are:

*   Engineers and other practitioners with experience in process optimization efforts, who are also advocates of teamwork and shared decision making, but have

difficulties grasping the complexities and uncertainties inherent in a strategic approach.

- Other advocates of a human work environment and teamwork, who do not understand the demands of a global competitive environment and do not like to get involved in the details of process analysis.
- Strategists who take efficient working processes for granted.

If "total quality" is to be "total" and live up to the lofty expectations of its advocates, it will have to integrate **strategy, process efficiency, effectiveness, teamwork and shared decision making concerns,** both conceptually and practically. Otherwise "total quality management," will be as its critics argue, "more of the same with a new and more complex jargon."

The next step in terms of the conceptual development of "total quality" lies in extending "total" to include not only the internal and external customers and society at large, but also address specifically the environmental impact of the creation, delivery, and recycling of products. Some companies are beginning to study the full product life-cycle, and to plan ultimate disposal of their products from their very inception and design.

Suggestions in Reading and Study

In case these readings are used in the context of a graduate or advanced undergraduate course the editor suggests that each topic area be complemented by a literature search done by groups of students of recent writings pertinent to each section. Their number is increasing rapidly and the specific concerns of specific fields and industries are being addressed with increasing conceptual richness. For example, students could explore how the concept of TQM is understood in such diverse applications as health care, banking, higher education or government, as well as in various private sector product and service industries.

Exploring the Concepts Underlying Total Quality Management

By Harry Costin

The purpose of this paper is to offer a brief overview of the key concepts underlying the management approach that has come to be known as "Total Quality Management," or, until recently, as "Total Quality Control." The main themes of the quality literature will be presented in a historically significant sequence followed by an analysis of a few predominant models. Finally, suggestions will be offered for a conceptual enrichment of the field.

KEY TOTAL QUALITY MANAGEMENT CONCEPTS

Although there is no perfect consensus in terms of what all the key concepts of Total Quality Management are, the following themes pervade the literature (most of the following have been suggested by Marchese (1991) as core ideas of the TQM movement):

1. Excellence is ascribed to customer-driven organizations that systematically integrate customer feedback into their strategic planning and delivery of products and services.

2. Customer-driven organizations have a strong focus on quality, with quality being defined as both the measurable dimensions of products and services and the perceptions of internal and external customers.

3. Continuous improvement is the result of a focus on quality.

4. Improvement means making processes work better.

5. There is a strong need to extend the existing mind-set and shift to paradigms that see organizational and individual success as a result of collaboration rather than cutthroat competition.

7

6. Decisions should be data driven. Previous experience needs to be systematically documented and analyzed to achieve continuous improvement.

7. Teamwork is the practical application of "collaboration." In order to be effective, teams need to be trained in creative and analytical problem-solving techniques.

8. People should be empowered, i.e., have real input and decision-making power in job design and organizational policies that affect them.

9. Training and recognition are essential (according to Ishikawa TQM begins and ends with education).

10. A vision (what Senge has termed a "shared vision," which needs to be known and shared by all employees and managers) is the key to give any organization a unified direction and avoid wasteful duplication of efforts and infighting.

11. Organizational change is only possible through effective leadership by example. Empty promises and speeches only make existing problems worse.

Historical Foundations

This management approach and theory has been strongly influenced by the ideas of a few American and Japanese scholars and practitioners. Among the most widely credited "founding fathers" of the so-called TQM (Total Quality Management) movement we find Feigenbaum, Deming, Juran, Crosby, Ishikawa, Kano, Imai, Mizuno, and others. The core concepts of TQM can be found in the writings of these thinkers, who have made a lasting contribution to management theory and practice worldwide.

The term "Total Quality Control" was first introduced by Armand Feigenbaum in the Nov.-Dec. 1956 issue of *Harvard Business Review.* His original exploration of what he referred to as a "way out of the dilemma imposed on businessmen by increasingly demanding customers and by ever-spiraling costs of quality, . . . a new kind of quality control, which might be called **total quality control**" already integrated some of the key concepts of what today is known as TQM. Quoting Feigenbaum, Ishikawa defined "total quality control" as

> an effective system for integrating the quality development, quality maintenance, and quality improvement efforts of the various groups in an organization so as to enable production and service at the most economic levels which allow for full customer satisfaction. (1985, 90)

Further, for Ishikawa "TQC requires participation of all divisions, including the divisions of marketing, design, manufacturing, inspection, and shipping." This integration was explained by Feigenbaum in the 1956 HBR article in the following terms:

> The underlying principle of this total quality view—and its basic difference from all other concepts—is that, to provide genuine effectiveness, control must start with the design of

the product and end only when the product has been placed in the hands of a customer who remains satisfied.

The reason for this breadth of scope is that the quality of any product is affected at many stages of the industrial cycle:

1. Marketing evaluates the level of quality customers want and for which they are willing to pay.
2. Engineering reduces this marketing evaluation to exact specifications.
3. Purchasing chooses, contracts with, and retains vendors for parts and materials.
4. Manufacturing engineering selects the jigs, tools, and processes for relay production.
5. Manufacturing supervision and shop operators exert a major quality influence during parts making, subassembly, and final assembly.
6. Mechanical inspection and functional test check conformance to specifications.
7. Shipping influences the caliber of the packaging and transportation.

In other words, the determination both of quality and of quality costs actually takes place throughout the entire industrial cycle. This is the reason why real quality control cannot be accomplished by concentrating on inspection alone, or design alone, or reject trouble-shooting alone, or operator education alone, or statistical analysis alone—important as each of these individual elements is.

The breadth of the job makes quality control a new and important business management function. Just as the theme of the historical inspection activity was "they (i.e., bad parts) shall not pass," the theme of this new approach is "make them right the first time." Emphasis is on defect prevention so that routine inspection will not be needed to as large an extent. The burden of quality proof rests, not with inspection, but with the makers of the part—machinist, assembly foreman, vendor, as the case may be. (1956, 94)

What Feigenbaum calls the "industrial cycle" was popularized in the business literature of the 1980s as "value chain" by Porter (1985). In hindsight, the principles expounded by Feigenbaum may not appear as revolutionary, since today they are part of mainstream thinking. But in an era obsessed by "control" and mass production using Frederick Taylor's management approach, they were.

Some of the key concepts that can be recognized in Feigenbaum's early writings and that have profoundly influenced the TQM movement are:

• To perceive the production process (and later, service delivery) as an integrated system that originates with the customer (what the customer wants) and ends with the customer (customer satisfaction).

• The need to redefine the role of the inspection function (defect prevention and line workers' responsibility for quality in order to reduce the need for inspection), the consequent reduction in costs of quality by building quality into the product ("quality by design"), and the usefulness of statistical quality tools (later to be known as "Statistical Process Control").

The idea of translating customer demands and needs and chosen quality levels into a product "by design" is the basic underlying concept of what is likely the second most widely used TQM process after SPC (Statistical Process Control): Quality Function Deployment, or QFD for short. This is a product or service design process using cross-functional teams that often include customers, marketing and purchasing representatives, and design and manufacturing engineers.

- To define quality as a management function. Deming and Juran elaborated further this concept assigning responsibility for quality to everybody in the organization.
- The important role of the purchasing function in the industrial cycle (or value chain). In modern industrial applications, companies implementing TQM programs favor the introduction of "vendor partnership programs" whereby the vendors commit to the delivery of consistent quality (e.g., implementing SPC processes), thus reducing the need for incoming inspection (Just-in-Time systems).

TQM as a Management System

Dr. W. Edwards Deming, the best-known father of the Quality movement, is widely credited with extending the quality concerns to management practice as a whole rather than simply considering them a domain of action of "quality engineers." Two key concepts developed by Dr. Deming, management responsibility and intrinsic motivation of workers and their relationship to statistical process control, deserve attention:

> Competent men in every position, from top management to the humblest worker, if they are doing their best, know all there is to know about their work **except how to improve it.** Help toward improvement can come **only from some other kind of knowledge.** Help may come from outside the company, or from better use of knowledge and skills already within the company, or both. (1975, 6)

According to Dr. Deming, only management has the power to change "systems," which are responsible for 85% of all defects:

> Another roadblock is management's supposition that the production workers are responsible for all trouble: that there would be no problems in production or in service if only the workers would do their jobs in the way they were taught. Pleasant dreams. The workers are handicapped by the system.

Using statistical terminology, he makes further reference to management's responsibility in the reduction of variation:

> It is good management to reduce the variation of any quality characteristic. . . . Reduction in variation means greater uniformity and dependability of product, greater output per hour, greater output per unit of raw material, and better competitive position.
>   Causes of variation and of high cost, with loss of competitive position, may be usefully subsumed under two categories:

- **Faults of the system (common or environmental causes) 85%:**
  These faults stay in the system until reduced by management. Their combined effect is usually easy to measure. Some individual causes must be isolated by judgment. Others may be identified by experiment: some by records on operations and materials suspected of being offenders.

- **Special causes 15%:**
  These causes are specific to a certain worker or to a machine. A statistical signal detects the existence of a special cause, which the worker can usually identify and correct. (1975, 6)

Statistical tools allow workers to keep the process in control, once management has provided them a system capable of running in control. Management's responsibility is to provide adequate training and to continuously strive to improve the existing systems. Supervision and inspection is thereby replaced by training and education.

Dr. Deming is also a firm believer in the workers' intrinsic motivation in a job well done. His "14 points" call for an "elimination of numerical quotas," and throughout his writings he further advocates the need for an educational system that from childhood fosters collaboration rather than competition.

An example of his clearly defined position on this issue can be found in his introduction to Peter Senge's book on the learning organization *The Fifth Discipline:*

> The prevailing system of management has destroyed our people. People are born with intrinsic motivation, self-esteem, dignity, curiosity to learn, joy in learning. The forces of destruction begin with the toddlers—a prize for the best Halloween costume, grades in school, gold stars—and on up through the university. On the job, people teams, divisions are ranked—reward for the one at the top, punishment for the one at the bottom.

JURAN'S QUALITY TRILOGY

Dr. J. M. Juran, whose impact on the quality movement in Japan was second only to Deming's, developed a useful framework to what he referred to as "a universal thought process—a universal way of thinking about quality, which fits all functions, all levels, all product lines." He called it the "quality trilogy": (1986)

> The underlying concept of the quality trilogy is that managing for quality consists of three basic quality-oriented processes:
>
> - Quality planning
> - Quality control
> - Quality improvement
>
> The starting point is quality planning—creating a process that will be able to meet established goals and do so under operating conditions. . . . Following the planning, the process is turned over to the operating forces. Their responsibility is to run the process at optimal effectiveness [this includes corrective action] . . . the zone defined by the "quality control" limits.

Finally, quality improvement is "the process for breaking through to unprecedented levels of performance." But quality improvement

> does not happen of its own accord. It results from purposeful action taken by upper management to introduce a new managerial process into the system of managers' responsibilities—the quality improvement process. This quality improvement process is superimposed on the quality control process—a process implemented in addition to quality control, not instead of it.

Juran's approach is essentially the same as Deming's. Quality is a management responsibility that needs to be performed systematically to achieve "continuous improvement" (when it is performed over time).

This is the same basic idea behind the so-called PDCA or Shewhart cycle, known in Japan as the Deming cycle, considered to be the essence of the Japanese approach to Total Quality Control:

Plan: The basic planning process described by Juran.

Do: The implementation of the plan.

Check: Evaluation of performance according to critical measures.

Act: Quality improvement efforts based on the lessons learned from experience. These experiences feed into the new plan, since PDCA is a cyclical process.

Defining Quality

One of the most widely used terms and concepts in the quality literature is, of course, **quality.** Definitions of quality range from narrowly defined, "primary operating characteristics" of a manufactured product (e.g., acceleration or cruising speed for a car) to customer-defined quality (emphasized as "core" definition of quality by most writers in the field, i.e., it is the customer who defines what quality is).

Ishikawa, one of the best known Japanese pioneers of the Quality movement, makes a distinction between a narrow and a broad definition of quality:

> Narrowly interpreted, quality means quality of product. Broadly interpreted, quality means quality of work, quality of service, quality of information, quality of process, quality of division, quality of people, including workers, engineers, managers, and executives, quality of system, quality of company, quality of objectives, etc. (1985, 45)

Garvin (1988) has identified eight dimensions or categories of quality that apply for the most part to manufactured products:

- *Performance* It refers to the primary operating characteristics of a product (like clarity, color, and the ability to receive distant stations on a color television set).
- *Features* The "bells and whistles" of a product (like a remote control for the television set).

- *Reliability* The probability of a product's malfunctioning or failing within a specific period of time.
- *Conformance* The degree to which a product's design and operating characteristics meet pre-established standards (a definition of quality often used by Phil Crosby, one of the best known US "quality gurus").
- *Durability* A measure of product life that has both economic and technical dimensions.
- *Serviceability* The speed, courtesy, competence, and ease of repair. Attempts have been made to identify "measurable" characteristics of serviceability (like speed of response) as opposed to the more elusive elements of customer satisfaction.
- *Aesthetics* A user-defined, subjective set of attributes, based on individual preferences, of a product—how a product looks, feels, sounds, tastes, or smells according to the customer.
- *Perceived quality* "Consumers do not always possess complete information about a product or a service's attributes. Frequently, indirect measures are the only basis for comparing brands. A product's durability, for example, can seldom be observed directly; it usually must be inferred from various tangible and intangible aspects of a product."

Juran defined quality as "fitness to use," i.e., the users of a product or service should be able to count on it for what they needed or wanted to do with it (March 1986). He further identifies five dimensions of fitness for use: quality of design, quality of conformance, availability, safety, and field use.

A narrower approach to defining quality is used by Crosby:

> Requirements must be clearly stated so that they cannot be misunderstood. Measurements are then taken continually to determine conformance to those requirements. The nonconformance detected is the absence of quality. Quality problems become nonconformance problems; and quality becomes definable. . . . If a Cadillac conforms to all the requirements of a Cadillac, then it is a quality car. If a Pinto conforms to all the requirements of a Pinto, then it is a quality car. Luxury or its absence is spelled out in specific requirements, such as carpeting or rubber mats. (1980, 15)

Crosby also popularized the concept of "zero defects," a further definition of quality to be found in the literature, and the ultimate goal of quality improvement efforts. "Zero defects" were to be achieved through prevention rather than after-the-fact inspection.

It is evident from these definitions, that most of them refer to tangible manufactured products. Definitions of service quality have been mostly derived from definitions of product quality, with specific emphasis on measurable attributes and the translation of vague customer-based notions of service quality into terms that can be expressed through sophisticated instruments of market research, like scales of customer satisfaction that compare consumer perceptions of competing products.

Even though specific attempts are made to render quality measurable, it is ultimately the customer who defines what it is and what it is not. In the TQM literature, the concept of customer embraces both the "internal" and the "external" customers. Internal customers are the next process in the manufacturing or service delivery value-added chain. External customers include the end user (the "key" customer), suppliers, and even society at large. Many uses of the word "customer" in the TQM literature make us think of the concept of "stakeholders," commonly found in the management policy literature. In a broad sense, customers are all those affected by what we do.

Evolution of the Quality Movement

The evolution of quality concepts, including the development of the concept of quality from a narrowly defined set of product attributes to the nearly all-embracing modern definitions of quality, is closely related to the different eras of the modern quality movement.

Garvin has attempted to map the evolution of the quality movement in the United States and described it in terms of four distinct "quality eras": inspection, statistical quality control, quality assurance, and strategic quality management.

The first stage, the introduction of formal inspection in the industrial process, was the necessary consequence of mass production in the early nineteenth century, while the second stage, Quality Control, can be traced back to the early twentieth century:

> Inspection activities were linked more formally to quality control in 1922 with the publication of G. S. Radford's *The Control of Quality in Manufacturing.* For the first time quality was viewed as a distinct management responsibility and as an independent function. (1988, 5)

During the Quality Control era the essential mathematical and statistical tools of the quality movement were developed. These included the Shewhart cycle and analysis of variability, statistical sampling techniques, and Statistical Process Control (SPC). SPC was used extensively during WWII with phenomenal results (this is one of the reasons why it was so well received in Japan in the 1950s) but came into disuse after the war ended.

The third era, Quality Assurance, includes, according to Garvin, the Total Quality Control approach initiated by Feigenbaum:

> During the period of quality assurance, quality evolved from a narrow, manufacturing-based discipline to one with broader implication for management. Problem prevention remained the primary goal, but the profession's tools expanded far beyond statistics. Four separate elements were involved: quantifying the costs of quality, total quality control, reliability engineering, and zero defects. (12)

The fourth era, Strategic Quality Management, implies a new emerging "vision":

It embodies a dramatic shift in perspective. For the first time, top managers at the levels of the presidents and chief executive officers have expressed an interest in quality. They have linked it with profitability, defined it from the customer's point of view, and required its inclusion in the strategic planning process. In the most radical departure of all, many have insisted that quality be viewed as an aggressive competitive weapon. (21)

This author disagrees with Garvin's contention that this is new, at least conceptually. Garvin's description adequately defines the key elements of the modern Total Quality Management movement, but the basic underlying concepts can be traced back to the original writings of the founders of the movement, including Deming, Feigenbaum, and Juran. Nevertheless, it is true that the implementation of the strategic perspective to quality is recent, particularly the integration of quality principles and strategic planning in the United States. In Japan, this integration began in 1962 at Bridgestone Tire (Akao 1991) and is known as **Hoshin Kanri** or "Policy Deployment."

Another interpretation of the role of the quality movement in the context of management and organizational theory has been advanced by Senge (1992):

I believe that the quality movement as we have known it up to now in the United States is in fact the first wave in building "learning organizations"—organizations that continually expand their ability to shape the future.

The roots of the quality movement lie in assumptions about people, organizations, and management that have one unifying theme: to make continual learning a way of organizational life, especially improving the performance of the organization as a total system. This can only be achieved by breaking with the traditional authoritarian command and control hierarchy where the top thinks and the local acts to merge thinking and acting at all levels.

This represents a profound re-orientation in the concerns of management—a shift from a predominant concern with controlling to a predominant concern with learning.

Senge further recognizes three waves in the evolution of learning organizations. While the United States is in the first wave (the quality movement as we have known it), Japan has moved on to the second:

In the first wave, the primary focus of change was frontline workers. Management's job was to

- Champion continual improvement.
- Remove impediments (like quality control experts and unnecessary bureaucracy) that disempowered local personnel.
- Support new practices like quality training and competitive benchmarking that drive process improvement.

In the second wave, the focus shifts from improving work processes to improving how we work—fostering ways of thinking and interacting conducive to continual learning about the dynamic, complex, conflictual issues that determine system wide performance. In the second wave, the primary focus of change is the managers themselves.

The third wave of quality . . . These two ways of thinking will, I believe, gradually merge into a third, in which learning becomes "institutionalized" as an inescapable way of life for managers and workers alike (if we even bother maintaining that distinction).

Senge's analysis is useful to understand potential conceptual shortcomings of existing TQM models and possible ways to enrich them. We will explore three models that are representative of current approaches to Total Quality Management: the TQM Wheel Model, the Baldrige Award Criteria, and the European Model for Quality.

EXHIBIT 1   *The GOAL/QPC TQM Wheel Model*

The Total Quality Management Wheel, shown below, was developed by GOAL/QPC as a holistic model to illustrate the elements of TQM. It depicts the orientation of TQM—customers—and the interrelationship among systems, people, and tools within an organization implementing TQM.

Looking at the top of the wheel, unit optimization is used to describe the "who, what, and how" of daily management. The term encompasses the concept of continuous improvement, the individuals and teams who are involved, and the methods or tools that can be used most effectively. Unit optimization is typically the first phase of TQM implementation, and it refers to the identification, measurement, improvement, and standardization of the processes that make up daily work. This initial step, often summarized by the Deming or Shewhart Cycle (Plan-Do-Check-Act), involves a variety of individuals, working singly and in teams, in using the Seven Basic Quality Control tools to manage their day-to-day responsibilities.

Moving clockwise on the wheel, the TQM practitioner next focuses on the vertical alignment phase of TQM implementation. Vertical alignment is a term used to describe the "who, what, and how" of Hoshin Planning. Hoshin Planning is a method used to ensure that the mission, vision, goals, and annual objectives of an organization are communicated to and implemented by everyone, from the executive level to the "frontline" level. Senior managers use the Seven Management and Planning Tools to facilitate the sharing of critical information among all members of the organization and to assist in the organizational planning process.

After making gains in Daily Management and Hoshin Planning, senior managers generally face the need for Cross-Functional Management, which requires an integration of quality improvement efforts across the functional areas of an organization. Top-level managers use the advanced TQM tool, Quality Function Deployment (QFD) to elicit the involvement of customer/supplier teams. QFD is a method for integrating the "voice of the customer" into the design of services, and provides the means to analyze and prioritize customer demands. QFD clarifies the actions that are most important to meeting or exceeding customer demands. QFD may also be used at earlier stages of implementation as needed. Additionally, managers use a variety of audit tools to assess how well the organization has incorporated TQM principles and broken down departmental barriers. Strategic information systems can be helpful at this phase to integrate all useful data in the effort to improve quality, cost, delivery, and employee morale.

THE TQM WHEEL MODEL

The Wheel Model (Exhibit 1) was developed by researchers of GOAL/QPC, a leading research and publishing organization in the field of Total Quality with significant input from representatives of large organizations implementing TQM, like GM, Ford, and Hewlett Packard. It represents a systematic effort to integrate all dimensions and processes of TQM around a "Customer-Driven Master Plan" (Moran et al., 1991):

> The Customer-Driven Total Quality Master Plan begins by involving all employees in an organization with the identification of their customers' needs. . . . Total Quality Management begins with a long-term plan (commitment) rooted in the organization's customers. This plan emphasizes thorough understanding of the customers and their needs along with continual improvement of customer satisfaction.

EXHIBIT 1   (*continued*)

SOURCE: GOAL/QPC TQM in Health Care Research Report, 1992.

The implementation of the plan occurs along three dimensions or Macro-processes: Daily Management (elsewhere called a "bottom up" approach), Cross-Functional Management ("side-by-side") and Hoshin Planning ("top-down").

Most references made to Total Quality (e.g., Statistical Process Control and Quality Circles) relate to Daily Management (e.g., Kaizen = continuous improvement). Its purpose is the implementation of a daily control, continuous improvement, and standardization system of best practices with the direct involvement of line workers working as teams under the "coaching" of their supervisors, or as self-directed teams. Daily Management involves the identification of critical processes and the use of systematic data collection and group problem-solving methods (definition of key indicators and use of the 7 QC = "Quality Control" tools to do root cause analysis).

The second key element of the wheel model is "Cross-Functional Management":

> Whether establishing a Customer-Driven Master Plan, a Daily Management system, or Hoshin Planning, all require horizontal integration of many persons and teams. This integration across the organization is known as Cross-Functional Management.

Cross-Functional Teams have different roles:

> Teams may establish organization-wide quality systems. Another cross-functional system, Quality Function Deployment, helps the organization utilize customer and competitive data in planning the best possible products and services.

Quality Function Deployment (QFD) has been widely hailed for reducing new product introduction time, translating customer requirements into actual products, and promoting a dialogue among suppliers, design and manufacturing engineers, and marketing analysts. After SPC and the different types of quality teams (e.g., Quality Circles and Quality Improvement Teams), it is the most popular implementation of the TQM processes.

The third element of the model is Hoshin Planning, a strategy planning and implementation process only recently introduced in large U.S. organizations, like FP&L and Hewlett Packard, but in existence in Japan since the 1970s and pioneered by Bridgestone Tire in 1962:

> When the magnitude of a needed process improvement is widespread and permeates the entire organization, a Daily Management system may not be sufficient to bring about the needed major improvement. In this case, a 'breakthrough' planning system may be needed. One such system, Hoshin Planning is defined as a policy management system. . . . Hoshin Planning is directed by top management but may involve teams throughout the organization. . . . The Hoshin Planning system focuses the energy of the entire organization on achieving a major improvement in a specific area of critical importance. The improvement may be needed to ensure long-term competitiveness or even the survival of the organization.

THE MALCOLM BALDRIGE AWARD

A second model, which in this case defines "excellence" in terms of overall quality of an organization (in terms similar to Ishikawa's broad definition of quality), can be found in the guidelines of the Malcolm Baldrige Award. These guidelines are being used extensively by organizations trying to understand and implement "quality" as a key internal driving force to achieve competitive advantage.

The Baldrige Award defines core values and concepts—a "framework" or model establishing the relationships between the "driver, system, goal, and measures of progress"—and an implicit hierarchy of priorities and values (points assigned to each category of the award, which add to a total of 1000).

The guidelines recognize explicitly the following core values and concepts:

Customer-Driven Quality Quality is judged by the customer. All product and service attributes that contribute value and lead to customer satisfaction and preference must be the foundation for a company's quality system. . . . Customer-driven quality is thus a strategic concept.

Leadership A company's senior leaders must create clear and visible quality values and high expectations. Reinforcement of the values and expectations requires their substantial personal commitment and involvement. The leaders' basic values and commitment need to include areas of public responsibility and corporate citizenship. The leaders must take part in the creation of strategies, systems, and methods for achieving excellence.

Continuous Improvement Achieving the highest levels of quality and competitiveness requires a well-defined and well-executed approach to continuous improvement. The term "continuous improvement" refers to both incremental and "breakthrough" improvement. A focus on improvement needs to be part of all operations and of all work unit activities of a company.

Employee Participation and Development A company's success in meeting its quality and performance objectives depends increasingly on work force quality and involvement. The close link between employee satisfaction and customer satisfaction creates a "shared fate" relationship between companies and employees. For this reason, employee satisfaction measurement provides an important indicator of the company's efforts to improve customer satisfaction and operating performance. . . . Companies need to invest in the development of the work force and to seek new avenues to involve employees in problem solving and decision making.

Fast Response Success in competitive markets increasingly demands ever-shorter cycles for a new or improved product and service introduction. Also, faster and more flexible response to customers is now a more critical requirement of business management.

Design Quality and Prevention Quality systems should place strong emphasis on design quality—problem and waste prevention achieved through building quality into products and services and into the processes through which they are produced.

Long-Range Outlook Achieving quality and market leadership requires a company to have a strong future orientation and a willingness to make long-term commitments to customers, employees, suppliers, stockholders, and the community.

Management by Fact Pursuit of quality and operational performance goals of the company requires that process management be based upon reliable information, data, and analysis. Facts and data needed for quality improvement and quality assessment are of many types, including: customer, product and service performance, operations, market, competitive comparisons, supplier, employee-related, and cost and financial.

Partnership Development Companies should seek to build internal and external partnerships to better accomplish their overall goals. Internal partnerships might include those that promote labor-management cooperation such as agreements with

---

EXHIBIT 2   *Baldrige Award Criteria Framework*

The framework has four basic elements:

Driver
Senior executive leadership creates the values, goals, and systems, and guides the sustained pursuit of customer value and company performance improvement.

System
System comprises the set of well-defined and well-designed processes for meeting the company's customer, quality, and performance requirements.

Measures of Progress
Measures of progress provide a results-oriented basis for channeling actions to delivering ever-improving customer value and company performance.

Goal
The basic aim of the quality process is the delivery of ever-improving value to customers.
    The seven Criteria categories shown in the figure are subdivided into Examination Items and Areas to Address. These are described below.

Examination Items
There are a total of 28 Examination Items in the seven Examination Categories. Each Item focuses on a major quality system requirement. All information submitted by applicants is in response to the Item requirements. Item titles and Examination point values are given on page 15.

Areas to Address
Each Examination Item includes a set of Areas to Address (Areas). The Areas serve to illustrate and clarify the intent of the Items and to place emphasis on the types and amounts of information the applicant should provide. Areas are not assigned individual point values, because their relative importance depends upon factors such as the applicant's type and size of business and quality system.

unions. . . . Examples of external partnerships include those with customers, suppliers, and education organizations.

Corporate Responsibility and Citizenship A company's customer requirements and quality system objectives should address corporate responsibility and citizenship. Corporate responsibility refers to basic expectations of the company—business ethics and protection of public health, public safety, and the environment. . . . Corporate citizenship refers to leadership and support—within reasonable limits of a company's resources—of publicly important purposes. . . . Such purposes might include education, resource conservation, community services, improving industry and business practices, and sharing of nonproprietary quality-related information.

EXHIBIT 2   (*continued*)

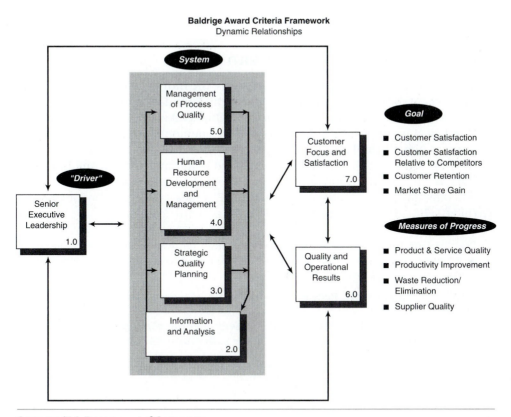

Baldrige Award Criteria Framework
Dynamic Relationships

SOURCE: U.S. Department of Commerce.

These core values and concepts are embodied in the seven categories integrated in the Baldrige Award Criteria Framework (Exhibit 2), which is the quality model of the award:

1.0	Leadership	95 points
2.0	Information and Analysis	75 points
3.0	Strategic Quality Planning	60 points
4.0	Human Resource Development and Management	150 points
5.0	Management of Process Quality	140 points
6.0	Quality and Operational Results	180 points
7.0	Customer Focus and Satisfaction	300 points
		1,000 points

The relative number of points assigned to each category establishes a hierarchy of importance of "quality values." It is to be noted that the category with the strongest weight is "Customer Focus and Satisfaction," the key principle to be found throughout the quality literature.

THE EUROPEAN QUALITY AWARD

Based on both the Deming and Baldrige Awards, the European Community, under the auspices of the Commission and the European Foundation for Quality Management, have recently instituted The European Quality Award, which was awarded for the first time in October 1992 to companies demonstrating excellence in the implementation of Total Quality Management.

The European model, which "was developed as a framework for the European Quality Award, jointly sponsored by the European Commission, the European Foundation for Quality Management, and the European Organization for Quality" (Exhibit 3) has nine elements that link "enablers" with "results":

Processes are the means by which the organization harnesses and releases the talents of its people to produce results. In other words, the processes and the people are the ENABLERS, which provide RESULTS.

Customer Satisfaction, People (employee) Satisfaction, and **Impact on Society** are achieved through
Leadership, which drives **Policy and Strategy, People Management, Resources,** and **Processes** leading ultimately to excellence in **Business Results.**

Each of the nine elements shown in the model is a criterion that can be used to appraise the organization's progress towards Total Quality Management.

The Results aspects are concerned with **what** the organization has achieved and is achieving.

The Enablers are concerned with **how** results are being achieved.

EXHIBIT 3:　*The European Model for Quality*

The European Model

Processes are the means by which the organization harnesses and releases the talents of its people to produce results. In other words, the processes and the people are the ENABLERS, which provide the RESULTS.

Expressed graphically, the principle looks like this:

This model was developed as a framework for The European Quality Award, jointly sponsored by the European Commission, the European Foundation for Quality Management, and the European Organization for Quality. Essentially the model tells us that:

Customer Satisfaction, People (employee) Satisfaction, and *Impact on Society** are achieved through *Leadership* which drives
Policy and Strategy, People Management, Resources, and *Processes* leading ultimately to excellence in *Business Results.*

Each of the nine elements shown in the model is a criterion that can be used to appraise the organization's progress toward Total Quality Management.

The Results aspects are concerned with *what* the organization has achieved and is achieving.

The Enablers aspects are concerned with *how* results are being achieved.

The objective of a comprehensive quality management self-appraisal and self-improvement program is to regularly review each of these nine criteria and, thereafter, to adopt relevant improvement strategies.

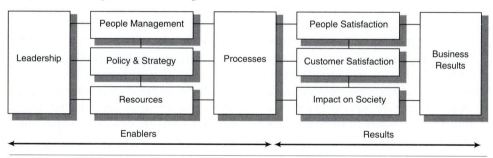

NOTES:
　*In the 1990s it is vital that the organization achieves positive results in terms of the community at large. The criterion "Impact on Society" is included in the Model for this reason.

SOURCE: European Foundation for Quality Management.

A particular feature of the model is also the integration of "Impact on Society" as one of the nine elements:

In the 1990s it is vital that the organization achieves positive results in terms of the community at large. The criterion "Impact on Society" is included in the Model for this reason.

This element includes explicitly an environmental dimension, "the organization's approach to quality of life, the environment, and . . . the preservation of global resources," a consideration largely absent in U.S. quality definitions and models.

Opportunities for Conceptual Enrichment and Model Building

This paper has explored some of the predominant concepts and models of the quality literature. Many of these concepts are key to rethinking the role of management in the 1990s and understand opportunities for cooperative relationship between management and labor, and businesses and society at large.

As the field evolves, the need for further conceptual clarity and model building becomes evident. In most of the current literature, the following conceptual shortcomings, or rather "opportunities for improvement" by building on paradigms of other fields, can be found:

1. The underlying concept of **organization** is not clearly defined. From a point of view of organizational theory, the organization seems largely conceived as a rational unitary decision maker (organizations that succeed or fail) or as a series of interlocking teams (management team, teams of workers, etc.). What is absent is any systematic exploration of the concept of "informal organization" and its implications for the decision-making process. This key concept was already analyzed by Barnard in the 1940s.

   Network theories of organizations would provide useful insights as the quality literature insists on the need to build networks between suppliers, customers, companies, educational institutions, etc. Applications of TQM, like Just-in-Time, are built on the assumption of efficiently working networks.

2. A second perspective largely absent in the literature are political views of organizations. It is insisted (e.g., Baldrige Award) that Management and Labor should collaborate, but the simple insistence on collaboration does not provide adequate guidance to conflict resolution. U.S. unions have been suspicious of TQM implementation efforts, which they have seen as a clear threat to establish labor practices.

   If TQM fails to acknowledge the political realities of organizations and of its models to integrate political concepts, it will continue to provide weak guidelines for implementation in turbulent industrial environments or times of economic distress. Political views of organizations begin addressing questions of values, power, and legitimacy, and at the implementation level, the basic concern expressed by Pfeffer and Salancick in their landmark study on *The External Control of Organizations* (1978): What matters more to organizational success— **efficiency** (largely embraced by the quality definitions) or **effectiveness** (the political maneuvers to co-opt collaboration and resources from the external environment)?

3. One of the key contributions of the writings of quality gurus like Deming and Ishikawa may also constitute one of the potential shortcomings of the litera-

ture—the normative approach to management theory of these writings, i.e., the insistence on value-driven management practices (empowerment, teamwork, and so on). The attempt to construct organizational reality may lead to ignoring reality as it is, a key problem during implementation of TQM programs. We are reminded of Mintzberg (1973), who decided to research what managers "actually do" rather than "what they are supposed to do." The richness of well-designed case analysis may be a prerequisite to design the value-driven organizations hailed in the quality literature.

CONCLUSION

The concepts on which Total Quality thinking is based imply basic values of respect for the individual and a sense of social responsibility. Efficiency is seen as a natural result of our intrinsic motivation and desire to learn. Continuous improvement based on collaboration is a never ending process to be extended to all facets of individual life and societal action.

It is the responsibility of all to make these noble desires a reality, but this can only be achieved through the clear understanding of the complexities inherent in the activities of individuals, groups, and organizations and their interactions in society at large.

Bibliography

Akao, Yoki, ed. *Hoshin Kanri: Policy Deployment for Successful TQM.* Cambridge, MA: Productivity Press, 1991.

Akao, Yoki, ed. *Quality Function Deployment: Integrating Customer Requirements into Product Design.* Cambridge, MA: Productivity Press, 1990.

Barnard, Chester. *The Functions of the Executive.* Cambridge, MA: Harvard University Press, 1968.

Crosby, Philip. *Quality Is Free.* New York, NY: Mentor Books, 1980.

Deming, W. Edwards. "On some Statistical Aids Toward Economic Production." *Interfaces* Vol. 3, N. 4, August 1975.

Deming, W. Edwards. *Out of the Crisis.* Cambridge, MA: MIT Press, 1982.

U.S. Department of Commerce. *Malcolm Baldrige National Quality Award: 1993 Award Criteria.*

Dertouzos, et al. *Made in America.* Cambridge, MA: MIT Press, 1989.

Ernst & Young and American Quality Foundation. *International Quality Study* (1991).

European Foundation for Quality Management. *Total Quality Management: The European Model for Self-Appraisal 1992.* Eindhoven, Netherlands, 1992.

Feigenbaum, Armand V. "Total Quality Control." *Harvard Business Review* Nov.-Dec. 1956, Vol. 34, N. 6.

Feigenbaum, Armand. "Total Quality Control & Customer Satisfaction." *Performance Management* Fall/Winter, 1984.

Hosotani, Katsuya. *Japanese Quality Concepts: an Overview.* New York, NY: Quality Resources, 1992.

Ishikawa, Kaoru. *What Is Total Quality Management: The Japanese Way.* Englewood Cliffs, NJ: Prentice Hall, 1985.

Juran, J. M. "The Quality Trilogy." *Quality Progress,* August 1986, pp. 19–24.

King, Bob. *Better Designs in Half the Time: Implementing QFD in America.* Methien, MA: GOAL QPC, 1989.

Marchese, Ted. "TQM Reaches the Academy." *American Association for Higher Education Bulletin* November 1991, pp. 13–18.

Mizuno, Shigeru, ed. *Management for Quality Improvement: The Seven New QC Tools.* Cambridge, MA: Productivity Press, 1988.

March, Artemis. "A Note on Quality: the Views of Deming, Juran and Crosby." Note 9.687-011. Harvard Business School. Cambridge, MA, 1986.

Mintzberg, Henry. *The Nature of Managerial Work.* New York, NY: Harper & Row, 1973.

Moran, Jack, et al. *Daily Management.* Methuen, MA: GOAL QPC, 1990.

Morgan, Gareth. *Images of Organization.* Newbury Park, CA: Sage Publications, 1986.

Neave, Henry R. *The Deming Dimension.* Knoxville, TN: SPC Press, 1990.

Nemoto, Masao. *Total Quality Control for Management: Strategies and Techniques from Toyota and Toyoda Gosei.* Englewood Cliffs, NJ: Prentice Hall, 1987.

Perrow, Charles. *Complex Organizations,* 3rd Ed. New York, NY: Random House, 1986.

Pfeffer, Jeffrey, and Gerald Salanzick. *The External Control of Organizations.* New York, NY: Harper & Row, 1978.

Porter, Michael. *Competitive Advantage: Creating and Sustaining Superior Performance.* New York, NY: The Free Press, 1985.

Reich, Robert B. *Tales of a New America.* New York, NY: Times Books, 1987.

Schoenberger, Richard J. "Is Strategy Strategic? Impact of Total Quality Management on Strategy." *The Executive* Vol. VI, N. 3, August 1992.

Senge, Peter M. *The Fifth Discipline: The Art and Practice of the Learning Organization.* New York, NY: Doubleday Currency, 1990.

Senge, Peter. "Building Learning Organizations." *Journal for Quality and Participation* March 1992.

Smircich, Linda, et al., eds. "New Intellectual Currents in Organization and Management Theory." Theory Development Forum. Special Issue. *Academy of Management Review* Vol. 17, N. 3, July 1992.

Thompson, James. *Organizations in Action.* New York, NY: McGraw-Hill, 1967.

Young, S. Mark. "A Framework for Successful Adoption and Performance of Japanese Manufacturing Practices in the United States." *Academy of Management Review* Vol. 17, N. 4, October 1992, pp. 647–676.

History and Evolution of the Quality Movement

By David A. Garvin

As a concept, quality has been with us for millennia. Only recently has it emerged as a formal management function. The discipline is still evolving. In its original form, it was reactive and inspection-oriented; today, quality-related activities have broadened and are seen as essential for strategic success. Once the exclusive province of manufacturing and operations departments, quality now embraces functions as diverse as purchasing, engineering, and marketing research, and commands the attention of chief executive officers.

How have these changes come about? Most modern approaches to quality have emerged gradually, arriving through steady evolution rather than dramatic breakthroughs. They are the product of a series of discoveries stretching back over a century. In the United States, these discoveries can be organized into four distinct "quality eras": inspection, statistical quality control, quality assurance, and strategic quality management.[1] The first three are discussed in this chapter; the fourth, a more recent innovation, is reserved for Chapter 2.

THE RISE OF INSPECTION

In the eighteenth and nineteenth centuries, quality control as we know it today did not yet exist. Most manufacturing was performed by artisans and skilled craftsmen or by journeymen and apprentices who were supervised by masters at the trade.[2] Goods were produced in small volumes; parts were matched to one another by hand, and after-the-fact inspection to ensure high quality was conducted informally, if at all. A well-performing product was viewed as the natural outgrowth of reliance on skilled tradesmen for all aspects of design, manufacturing, and service.[3]

Formal inspection became necessary only with the rise of mass production and the need for interchangeable parts. As volumes increased, parts could no longer be fitted to one another by hand: The process required a large pool of skilled labor and was both costly and time-consuming. Prices were often beyond the reach of the average consumer, especially for machinery and equipment. Nor was the federal government able to purchase large quantities of high-quality firearms at low cost.

These pressures gave rise to what has been called the American system of manufacturing: the use of special-purpose machinery to produce interchangeable parts by following a preestablished sequence of operations.[4] Most initial efforts were connected with the military's demand for armaments and were closely coordinated by the United States Ordnance Department, the national armory at Springfield, Massachusetts, and the Harpers Ferry Armory. In consumer products, the Singer Company, which manufactured sewing machines, and the McCormick Harvesting Company, which made farm equipment, later adopted the same techniques.

From a quality control standpoint, the key breakthrough was the development of a rational jig, fixture, and gauging system in the early 1800s.[5] Jigs and fixtures are devices that position tools or hold parts while they are being worked on, keeping them fixed to the equipment so that machining operations can be performed accurately and precisely. Since every part that is worked on is held in place in exactly the same way—all jigs and fixtures having been designed from a standard model of the product to be manufactured—a high degree of interchangeability is assured. Nevertheless, parts may still deviate from one another: They may have been mounted improperly during machining, built from imperfect raw materials, or made on worn tooling. To minimize problems at final assembly, when parts are matched together for the first time, accurate inspection is required during the process of manufacture. A system of gauges is often used for that purpose; like jigs and fixtures, gauges are based on a standard model of the product to ensure uniformity.

By 1819, an elaborate gauging system was in place at the Springfield Armory. It gave inspection a new respectability, for activities that were previously conducted by eye were replaced by a more objective, verifiable process.[6] Two inspectors using a gauge were much more likely to reach the same result than two who were relying on personal judgment alone.

As the American system of manufacturing matured, gauging became more refined, and inspection became even more important. In the early 1900s, Frederick W. Taylor, the father of "scientific management," gave the activity added legitimacy by singling it out as an assigned task for one of the eight functional bosses (foremen) required for effective shop management:

> The inspector is responsible for the quality of the work, and both the workmen and the speed bosses [who see that the proper cutting tools are used, that the work is properly driven, and that cuts are started in the right part of the piece] must see that the work is

finished to suit him. This man can, of course, do his work best if he is a master of the art of finishing work both well and quickly.[7]

Inspection activities were linked more formally to quality control in 1922, with the publication of G. S. Radford's *The Control of Quality in Manufacturing*.[8] For the first time, quality was viewed as a distinct management responsibility and as an independent function. The book even touched on a number of principles regarded as central to modern-day quality control: the need to get designers involved early in quality activities, the need for close coordination among the various departments affecting quality, and the association of quality improvement with increased output and lower costs. Its primary focus, however, was inspection. Nine of the book's twenty-three chapters were devoted to that subject alone. Topics included the purpose of inspection (to "exercise the duty of viewing the work closely and critically so as to ascertain the quality, detect the errors, and present them to the attention of the proper persons in such a way as to have the work brought up to standard")[9]; the evolution of inspection (from visual to dimensional checks); types of inspection (material, office, tool, and process); sampling methods (including 100 percent and random sampling, but without any statistical foundation); gauging techniques; and the organization of the inspection department. Throughout, the emphasis was on conformance and its link with inspection; according to Radford, the purchaser's "principal interest in quality [was] that evenness or uniformity which results when the manufacturer adheres to his established requirements."[10]

Here matters stood for several years. Quality control was limited to inspection and to such narrow activities as counting, grading, and repair. Troubleshooting was considered beyond the reach of the average inspection department.[11] In the next decade, however, the role of the quality professional would be redefined. The stimulus for change was research conducted at Bell Telephone Laboratories; the result was what is today called statistical quality control.

STATISTICAL QUALITY CONTROL

The year 1931 marked a watershed for the quality movement. W. A. Shewhart's *Economic Control of Quality of Manufactured Product* was published that year, giving the discipline a scientific footing for the first time.[12] Much of modern-day quality control can be traced to that single volume. In it, Shewhart gave a precise and measurable definition of manufacturing control, developed powerful techniques for monitoring and evaluating day-to-day production, and suggested a variety of ways of improving quality.

Shewhart was in fact part of a larger group at Bell Telephone Laboratories that was investigating problems of quality. The group's research was prompted by the concerns of engineers at Western Electric, the manufacturing arm of the Bell System, who were seeking greater standardization and uniformity in the nationwide telephone network. Most attention was focused on the complex equipment being built at the company's Hawthorn Works. How, the engineers wondered, could the maximum amount of information about the quality of these units be extracted from the minimum amount of inspection data? And how should that data be presented? In 1924, an Inspection Engineering Department was established at Western Electric to address such questions; it later became the Quality Assurance Department of Bell Laboratories. The group, which included such luminaries as Shewhart, Harold Dodge, Harry Romig, G. D. Edwards, and later Joseph Juran, was largely responsible for creating the present-day discipline of statistical quality control.[13]

Process Control

The initial breakthrough was Shewhart's. He was the first to recognize that variability was a fact of industrial life and that it could be understood using the principles of probability and statistics. Shewhart observed that no two parts were likely to be manufactured to precisely the same specifications. Raw materials, operator skills, and equipment would all vary to some degree. Even the same part produced by a single operator on a single machine was likely to show variation over time. From a management standpoint, this required a rethinking of the problem of quality. The issue was no longer the existence of variation—it was certain to continue at some level no matter what actions were taken—but how to distinguish acceptable variation from fluctuations that indicated trouble.

The entire analysis grew out of Shewhart's concept of statistical control:

> A phenomenon will be said to be controlled when, through the use of past experience, we can predict, at least within limits, how the phenomenon may be expected to vary in the future. Here it is understood that prediction means that we can state, at least approximately, the probability that the observed phenomenon will fall within the given limits.[14]

Shewhart then developed simple statistical techniques for determining these limits, as well as graphic methods for plotting production values to assess whether they fell within the acceptable range. The result, the process control chart illustrated in Figure 1.1, is one of the most powerful tools used by today's quality professionals.[15] By segregating abnormal (assignable) causes of variation from those that are inherent in a production process, it ensures that genuine problems are distinguished from those due purely to chance. Moreover, it does so by drawing samples of output during the course of production, rather than waiting until after a unit has been fully assembled.

At the same time that Shewhart was pursuing his work on process control, other researchers at Bell Laboratories were advancing the practice of sampling, the second critical element in the growth of statistical quality control. Harold Dodge and Harry Romig were the prime movers in this effort.

Sampling

Sampling techniques start from the simple premise that 100 percent inspection is an inefficient way of sorting good products from bad. Checking a limited number of items in a production lot, then deciding on that basis whether the entire lot is acceptable, is clearly an alternative. The process, however, entails certain risks. Because samples are never fully representative, one may occasionally accept a production lot that in reality contains a large number of defective items. A related error is also possible: One may reject a production lot that is actually of perfectly acceptable quality.

Dodge and Romig recognized these problems, called consumer's and producer's risk, and devised plans for dealing with them systematically. They were able to develop sampling plans that ensured that for a given level of defects, the probability of unwittingly accepting an unsatisfactory lot would be limited to a certain percentage.[16] A certain number of items would be checked for a specified lot size. If

FIGURE 1.1   *A Typical Process Control Chart*

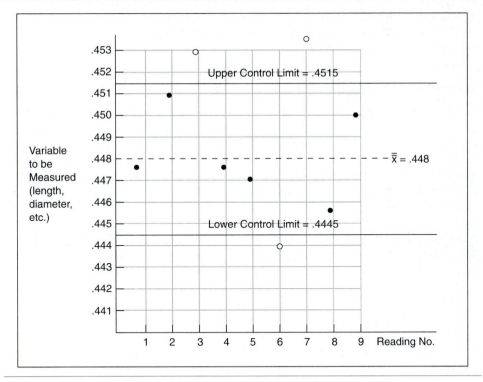

NOTES:

Upper and lower control limits are statistically determined limits of control.
All readings are taken at preset intervals using samples of output (e.g., five parts in a row).
$\overline{\overline{X}}$ = grand average of all readings.
● = readings falling within limits (variations due to chance).
○ = readings falling outside limits (assignable causes to be corrected).

according to the sampling tables the number of defective items in that group exceeded the number allowable, the entire lot would be rejected.

Useful as it was, the method was limited in application. It applied only to individual production lots, rather than to the overall level of quality produced by a manufacturing process. A new concept, the average outgoing quality limit (AOQL), was developed to meet that deficiency. It indicated the maximum percentage of defective units that a process would produce under two conditions: sampling inspection by lots, and the individual separation of good from bad items in all lots that had already been rejected on the basis of sampling.[17] A typical AOQL sampling table, showing the relationship between process quality, lot size, sampling rules, and outgoing quality, is illustrated in Figure 1.2.

These breakthroughs were instrumental in improving the quality of telephone equipment and service. Inspection costs fell, quality improved, and with fewer defects to correct, employees became more productive. Surprisingly, however, neither sampling techniques nor process control charts had much of an immediate impact outside the Bell System. Most of the original research was published in technical journals with limited circulation. Only with the advent of World War II and the need to produce munitions in large volumes did the concepts of statistical quality control gain a wider audience.

The Impact of World War II

In December 1940, a committee was formed by the War Department to draft standards in the area of quality. The standards were published in 1941 and 1942. Their primary focus was the development and use of control charts. At roughly the same time, the Ordnance Department of the U.S. Army was facing the problem of how to get large quantities of arms and ammunition from multiple suppliers at acceptable levels of quality. Two alternatives were under consideration: extensive training of contractors in the use of process control charts and the development of a system of acceptance sampling procedures to be applied by government inspectors. The second approach won out, and in 1942 a Quality Control section was established in the War Department, staffed largely by statisticians from Bell Laboratories.[18]

This group soon developed a new set of sampling tables based on the concept of acceptable quality levels (AQL): The poorest quality (maximum percent defective) that a supplier could maintain over time and still be considered satisfactory. Two kinds of inspection were involved. Normal inspection, which required fewer checks, was used when the products under review had recently proved to have a defect rate lower than or equal to the AQL. Tightened inspection was used when the defect rate had recently exceeded the AQL. The tables also contained rules showing when to switch from one method of inspection to the other.[19]

These techniques were immensely successful. The primary bottleneck slowing the production of war materials had occurred in inspection; it was soon eliminated.[20] In the first eight months after the methods were introduced on a large scale, inspectors were able to process far higher volumes. The number of Ordnance Department

FIGURE 1.2 *A Typical AOQL Single Sampling Table*

AVERAGE OUTGOING QUALITY LIMIT = 0.75%

Process Average %	0–.015			.016–.15			.16–.30			.31–.45			.46–.60			.61–.75		
Lot Size	n	c	P_t%	n	c	P_t%	n	c	P_t%	n	c	P_t%	n	c	P_t%	n	c	P_t%
1–25	All	0	—	All	0	—	All	0	—	All	0	—	All	0	—	All	0	—
26–50	25	0	6.4	25	0	6.4	25	0	6.4	25	0	6.4	25	0	6.4	25	0	6.4
51–100	33	0	5.6	33	0	5.6	33	0	5.6	33	0	5.6	33	0	5.6	33	0	5.6
101–200	39	0	5.2	39	0	5.2	39	0	5.2	39	0	5.2	39	0	5.2	39	0	5.2
201–300	42	0	5.0	42	0	5.0	42	0	5.0	42	0	5.0	42	0	5.0	42	0	5.0
301–400	44	0	4.9	44	0	4.9	44	0	4.9	44	0	4.9	90	1	4.0	90	1	4.0
401–500	45	0	4.8	45	0	4.8	45	0	4.8	90	1	4.1	90	1	4.1	90	1	4.1
501–600	45	0	4.9	45	0	4.9	45	0	4.9	95	1	3.9	95	1	3.9	95	1	3.9
601–800	46	0	4.9	46	0	4.9	100	1	3.8	100	1	3.8	100	1	3.8	100	1	3.8
801–1000	47	0	4.8	47	0	4.8	100	1	3.8	100	1	3.8	100	1	3.8	155	2	3.2
1001–2000	48	0	4.7	48	0	4.7	105	1	3.7	105	1	3.7	170	2	3.1	170	2	3.1
2001–3000	48	0	4.7	110	1	3.5	110	1	3.5	170	2	3.1	170	2	3.1	240	3	2.8
3001–4000	48	0	4.7	110	1	3.5	110	1	3.5	175	2	3.1	245	3	2.7	315	4	2.5
4001–5000	49	0	4.6	110	1	3.6	175	2	3.1	175	2	3.1	245	3	2.7	320	4	2.5
5001–7000	49	0	4.6	110	1	3.6	180	2	3.0	250	3	2.7	325	4	2.5	400	5	2.3
7001–10,000	49	0	4.6	110	1	3.7	180	2	3.0	255	3	2.6	405	5	2.3	560	7	2.1
10,001–20,000	49	0	4.6	110	1	3.7	255	3	2.6	335	4	2.4	495	6	2.1	750	9	1.9
20,001–50,000	110	1	3.7	180	2	3.0	260	3	2.6	420	5	2.2	675	8	1.9	1130	13	1.6
50,001–100,000	110	1	3.7	185	2	2.9	335	4	2.4	590	7	2.0	955	11	1.7	1720	19	1.5

NOTES:

n = size of sample. Entry of "All" indicates that each piece in lot is to be inspected.

c = allowable defect number for sample. If more than this number of defects is found, the lot should be rejected.

P_t = lot tolerance percent defective corresponding to a consumer's risk (Pc) = 0.10. This means that under the given sampling plan, the probability of inadvertently accepting a lot whose quality (measured in percent defective) is P_t, is at most 10 percent.

Process average = the average percentage of defective units produced by the manufacturing process.

SOURCE: H. F. Dodge, "Notes on the Evolution of Acceptance Sampling Plans, Part I," *Journal of Quality Technology*, April 1969, p. 85. Copyright © 1969 American Society for Quality Control. Reprinted with permission.

inspectors per million dollars of accepted material dropped from 42 to 12.[21] Substantial improvements in quality were realized as well.

Meanwhile, additional training programs were being organized by the Office of Production Research and Development (OPRD) of the War Production Board. Researchers at Bell Laboratories again played a leading role, this time in cooperation with major universities. Walter Shewhart, for example, was instrumental in selling the initial proposal to OPRD. At the time, the techniques of statistical quality control had still seen little application outside the telephone company. As one of the early academic participants in the program remarked: "What we professors had at the time was faith—faith that statistical techniques would prove to be widely useful in the control of quality in many different kinds of manufacturing."[22] The aim of the programs that were finally developed was the rapid dissemination of these techniques to other branches of industry.

Courses were first offered at the Carnegie Institute of Technology of 1941 and Stanford in 1942. By the end of the war, institutions in twenty-five states were involved. A total of 8,000 people were trained in courses ranging from one-day executive programs to intensive eight-day seminars for engineers, inspectors, and other quality control practitioners.[23]

Most early trainees made little effort to apply the techniques they had learned. Statistical concepts were still something of a novelty, with only a brief track record. A few companies, however, achieved spectacular gains; these were reported in follow-up seminars and proved instrumental in inducing other companies to experiment with process control and sampling methods.[24]

Soon the students who had attended the courses began to form local societies for quality control. In October 1945, thirteen of these groups banded together to become the Society of Quality Engineers; a year later they merged with another federation to become the American Society for Quality Control (ASQC). Today the ASQC remains the field's dominant professional group. Meanwhile, the first U.S. journal on the subject, *Industrial Quality Control,* was published in July 1944 by the Buffalo Society of Quality Control Engineers. It later became *Quality Progress,* the official magazine of the ASQC.[25]

By the late 1940s, then, quality control was established as a recognized discipline. Its methods were primarily statistical, however, and its impact was confined largely to the factory floor. Little would change until several key works were published in the 1950s and early 1960s. These ushered in the next major quality era, that of quality assurance.

QUALITY ASSURANCE

During the period of quality assurance, quality evolved from a narrow, manufacturing-based discipline to one with broader implications for management. Problem prevention remained the primary goal, but the profession's tools expanded far beyond statistics. Four separate elements were involved: quantifying the costs of quality, total quality control, reliability engineering, and zero defects.

Costs of Quality

Until the 1950s, most efforts to improve quality were based on the unstated assumption that defects were costly. How costly was a matter of conjecture, for few companies had gone to the trouble of tallying up the expenses they incurred because products were not built right the first time. In the absence of such a yardstick, managers accustomed to making decisions on the basis of hard numbers had little to go on. For them, a critical question remained: How much quality was enough?

In 1951 Joseph Juran tackled the question in the first edition of his *Quality Control Handbook,* a publication that would shortly become the profession's bible.[26] Its initial chapter discussed the economics of quality and proposed the now famous analogy to "gold in the mine." Juran observed that the costs of achieving a given level of quality could be divided into avoidable and unavoidable costs. The latter were the costs associated with prevention—inspection, sampling, sorting, and other quality control initiatives. Avoidable costs were those of defects and product failures—scrapped materials, labor hours required for rework and repair, complaint processing, and financial losses resulting from unhappy customers. Juran regarded failure costs as "gold in the mine" because they could be reduced sharply by investing in quality improvement. The payoff from these efforts could be substantial: At the time, Juran estimated that avoidable quality losses were typically in the range of $500 to $1,000 per productive operator per year.[27]

Managers now had a way of deciding how much to invest in quality improvement. Additional expenditures on prevention were likely to be justified as long as failure costs remained high. The concept also illustrated another important principle: that decisions made early in the production chain—for example, when engineers first sketched out a new product's design—had implications for the level of quality costs incurred later on, in both the factory and the field.

Total Quality Control

In 1956 Armand Feigenbaum took this principle a step further by proposing "total quality control." High-quality products, he argued, were unlikely to be produced if the manufacturing department was forced to work in isolation:

> The underlying principle of this total quality view . . . is that, to provide genuine effectiveness, control must start with the design of the product and end only when the product has been placed in the hands of a customer who remains satisfied . . . the first principle to recognize is *that quality is everybody's job.*[28]

Feigenbaum noted that all new products, as they moved from design to market, involved roughly the same activities. From a quality standpoint, they could be grouped into three categories: new design control, incoming material control, and product or shop floor control. The first, for example, involved preproduction assessments of a design's "manufacturability" as well as the debugging of new manufacturing techniques through pilot runs. To be successful, these activities required the cooperation of multiple departments. In fact, as products moved through the three principal stages, groups as varied as marketing, engineering, purchasing, manufacturing, shipping, and customer service had to become involved. Otherwise, mistakes might be made early in the process that would cause problems to appear later—during assembly or, worse yet, after the product was in a customer's hands.

To make the system work, many companies developed elaborate matrices, like the one in Figure 1.3, listing departmental responsibilities across the top and required activities down the left-hand side. The matrices typically showed considerable overlap among functions, for few activities were likely to be error-free if they were assigned to a single department or were pursued seriatim. Interfunctional teams therefore became essential: They ensured that diverse viewpoints were represented and that otherwise autonomous departments worked together. Top management was ultimately responsible for the effectiveness of the system; to maintain its interest, Feigenbaum, like Juran, proposed careful measurement and reporting of the costs of quality.

The two experts also agreed on the need for a new type of quality professional. Statistical methods were still important—both authors devoted large sections of their books to explanations of process control and sampling—as were traditional techniques of inspection and gauging. But the quality system now included new product development, vendor selection, and customer service, in addition to manufacturing control. To deal with these responsibilities, both Feigenbaum and Juran argued that a new function, quality control engineering, was necessary.[29] It would be involved in high-level quality planning, coordinating the activities of other departments, setting quality standards, and providing quality measurements. These activities required a mix of management skills. They implied that a statistics background was no longer enough to guarantee competence as a quality professional.

Reliability Engineering

Yet, at about the same time that Feigenbaum and Juran were making these arguments, another branch of the discipline was emerging that relied even more heavily on probability theory and statistics: reliability engineering, which had as its objective the assurance of acceptable product performance over time.[30] The field was closely aligned with the postwar growth of the aerospace and electronics industries in the United States; as a result, the military was a prime supporter. In 1950 the Department of Defense formed an Ad Hoc Group on Reliability of Electronic Equipment, and in 1957 a major report was issued on the subject.[31] The report eventually resulted in a number of military specifications setting out the requirements for a formal reliability program.

These efforts were stimulated by the plummeting reliability of military components and systems. In 1950 only one-third of the Navy's electronic devices were working properly at any given time. A study by the Rand Corporation at the time estimated that every vacuum tube the military had plugged in and working was

FIGURE 1.3   A Typical Matrix of Quality Responsibilities

	GROUP OR DEPARTMENT							
Activity or Function	General Management	Finance	Marketing	Engineering	Manufacturing	Quality Control	Purchasing	Service
Establish product reliability and quality policies	x	o	o	o	o	o	o	o
Analyze quality costs	o	x				x		
Perform in-process quality audits				o	o	x		
Ensure that new product designs meet the test of manufacturability and ease of service			x	x	o		x	
Establish specifications for purchased parts and materials and qualify vendors				x		o	x	

NOTES:

x indicates the departments primarily responsible for an activity.

o indicates other departments that should be involved in an activity.

SOURCE: Adapted from A. V. Feigenbaum, *Total Quality Control* (New York: McGraw-Hill, 1961), p. 65. Reprinted with permission.

backed by nine others in warehouses or on order. Equally serious problems were encountered with missiles and other aerospace equipment.[32]

Clearly, greater attention needed to be paid to product performance over time. The first step was to define reliability more precisely—as "the probability of a product's performing a specified function without failure, for a given period of time, under specified conditions."[33] Coupled with the tools of modern probability theory, this definition led to formal methods for predicting equipment performance over time. It also resulted in techniques for reducing failure rates while products were still in the design stage.

Much of the analysis rested on the concept of a probability distribution. This was no more than a mathematical relationship specifying a product's reliability (or inversely, its failure rate) as a function of time. Engineers soon found that different operating conditions and different products were better approximated by different mathematical forms. Among the most popular were the exponential life function, which assumed that a product's failure rate remained relatively unchanged over its entire operating life; the Weibull distribution, which allowed failure rates to increase or decrease over time as products improved or deteriorated with age; and the "bathtub curve"—so called because of its distinctive shape—which dropped the assumption that failure rates were constant or changed steadily over time and argued instead for a break-in period (when failure rates were high), a normal operating period (when failure rates were constant and relatively low), and a wear-out phase (when failures rose steadily as the product deteriorated).[34] These relationships were then coupled with careful testing programs designed to simulate extreme operating conditions, to estimate reliability levels even before products reached full-scale production.

Prediction, however, was only the first step. The discipline's real goal was to improve reliability and reduce failure rates over time. To accomplish these ends, a variety of techniques were employed: failure mode and effect analysis (FMEA), which systematically reviewed the ways a product could fail and on that basis proposed alternative designs; individual component analysis, which computed the probability of failure of key components and then tried to eliminate or strengthen the weakest links; derating, which required that parts be used below their specified stress levels; and redundancy, which involved the use of parallel systems to ensure that backups were available whenever an important component or subsystem failed.[35] An effective reliability program also required close monitoring of field failures. Otherwise, engineers would be denied vital information—a product's actual operating experience—useful for planning new designs. Field failure reporting normally involved comprehensive systems of data collection as well as efforts to ensure that failed parts were returned to the laboratory for further testing and analysis.[36]

Like total quality control, reliability engineering was aimed at preventing defects from happening in the first place. It too emphasized engineering skills and attention to quality throughout the design process. Zero defects, the last significant development in the quality assurance era, took a different tack: It focused on management expectations and the human relations side of the equation.

Zero Defects

Zero defects had its genesis at the Martin Company in 1961–62.[37] At the time, Martin was building Pershing missiles for the U.S. Army. Their quality, though generally good, was achieved only through massive inspection. Incentives were offered to workers to lower the defect rate still further; together with even more intensive inspection and testing, these efforts led, on December 12, 1961, to the delivery of a Pershing missile to Cape Canaveral with zero discrepancies.

A defect-free missile could therefore be made, although it was likely to require extensive debugging before shipment. A month later, Martin's general manager in Orlando, Florida, accepted a request from the U.S. Army's missile command to deliver the first field Pershing one month ahead of schedule. He went even further— he promised that the missile would be perfect, with no hardware problems, no document errors, and all equipment set up and fully operational ten days after delivery (the norm was ninety days or more). Two months of feverish activity followed. Since little time was available for the usual inspection and after-the-fact correction of errors, all employees were asked to contribute to building the missile exactly right the first time. The result was still a surprise: In February 1962 a perfect missile was delivered. It arrived on time and was fully operational in less than twenty-four hours.

This experience was an eye-opener for Martin. After careful review, management concluded that the project's success war primarily a reflection of its own changed attitude: "The reason behind the lack of perfection was simply that perfection had not been expected. The one time management demanded perfection, it happened!"[38] Similar reasoning suggested a need to focus on workers' motivation and awareness. Of the three most common causes of worker errors—lack of knowledge, lack of proper facilities, and lack of attention—management concluded that the last had been least often addressed. It set out to design a program whose overriding goal was to "promote a constant, conscious desire to do a job (any job) right the first time."[39]

The resulting program was called zero defects. It was very heavy on philosophy, motivation, and awareness, and much leaner when it came to specific proposals and problem-solving techniques. A key step, in fact—the identification of problems at their source and the design of remedial efforts (called error cause removal)—was developed by the Small Engine Department of General Electric, an early adopter of the program, and not by Martin. Martin's contribution lay primarily in articulating a philosophy—that the only acceptable quality standard was zero defects—and in showing how it could be instilled in the work force through training, special events, the posting of quality results, goal-setting, and personal feedback. That was no small achievement. Since the prevailing quality ethic at the time was acceptable quality levels (AQL)—the idea, associated with sampling techniques, that some non-zero level of defects was good enough—Martin was fighting nearly thirty years of quality control history. Even today, the debate continues. One of the most popular—and controversial—recent books on quality is *Quality Is Free,* written by Philip B. Crosby, an advocate of zero defects who worked at Martin in the 1960s.[40] Crosby's claim that perfect quality is both technically possible and economically desirable has re-kindled many of the old arguments about how much quality is enough.

EVOLUTION AND CHANGE

Zero defects was the last major movement in the quality assurance era. Together with reliability engineering, total quality control, and the costs of quality, it helped expand the boundaries of the quality profession. Design, engineering, planning, and service activities were now as relevant as statistics and manufacturing control. New management skills were required, especially in the area of human relations. Interfunctional coordination became a primary concern, and quality professionals shifted their attention to program design, standard setting, and monitoring the activities of other departments.

Table 1.1 charts the evolution from inspection to quality assurance in more detail. It shows how quality management in the United States has expanded in ever widening circles, each era incorporating elements of the one that preceded it. Quality assurance, for example, acknowledged the role of statistical analysis while placing it in the larger context of the production chain, just as quality control saw gauging and measurement as a small part of the problem of efficient inspection. Early breakthroughs were seldom rejected; rather, they were subsumed within larger categories.

The resulting pattern of change reflects, in microcosm, the evolution of U.S. industry and the escalating demand it faced for technically sophisticated products. When American manufacturing involved only simple fabrication and assembly and low production volumes, informal inspection was enough to ensure high quality. Larger volumes, however, required tighter control and led to separate inspection departments and precise systems of gauging. The nationwide telephone network resulted in a further leap forward. It involved still more complex equipment and even higher degrees of standardization; both enhanced the desirability of statistical methods. Scale effects played a role in the discipline's later evolution as well. The war years were a fertile period for quality control for just this reason.

Quality assurance continued these trends. It was born of necessity: the need to meet the tightened specifications and performance criteria demanded by the country's military, electronics, and space programs. Product design became more exacting, giving rise to reliability engineering and the need for better coordination among departments before new products were released. At the same time, a number of new ideas were emerging in American thinking about human resource management. Such concepts as Theory Y and the Scanlon Plan encouraged companies to offer greater autonomy to workers.[41] The zero defects movement, with its emphasis on motivation and employee initiative, was remarkably similar in spirit.

Yet, in spite of these changes, approaches to quality remained largely defensive throughout this period. The main objective of the quality department was still the prevention of defects. Even though a proactive approach was not being pursued, quality was still viewed negatively—as something that could hurt a company if

TABLE 1.1 *From Inspection to Quality Assurance*

Identifying Characteristics	Stage of the Quality Movement		
	Inspection	Statistical Quality Control	Quality Assurance
Primary concern	Detection	Control	Coordination
View of quality	A problem to be solved	A problem to be solved	A problem to be solved, but one that is attacked proactively
Emphasis	Product uniformity	Product uniformity with reduced inspection	The entire production chain, from design to market, and the contribution of all functional groups, especially designers, to preventing quality failures
Methods	Gauging and measurement	Statistical tools and techniques	Programs and systems
Role of quality professionals	Inspection, sorting, counting, and grading	Troubleshooting and the application of statistical methods	Quality measurement, quality planning, and program design
Who has responsibility for quality	The inspection department	The manufacturing and engineering departments	All departments, although top management is only peripherally involved in designing, planning, and executing quality policies
Orientation and approach	"Inspects in" quality	"Controls in" quality	"Builds in" quality

ignored—rather than as a possible basis for competition. That view finally changed in the 1970s and 1980s, when the strategic aspects of quality were recognized and embraced.

Notes

1. A number of authors have divided the history of the quality movement into distinct periods, although they have frequently used only two categories, quality control and quality assurance. See Robert A. Abbott and David C. Leaman, "Quality Control and Quality Assurance," in Carl Heyel, ed., *The Encyclopedia of Management*, Third Edition (New York: Van Nostrand Reinhold, 1982), pp. 998–1009; Everett Adam, Jr., "Quality Assurance Broadens the Concept of Quality Control," *The Pulse Report*, American Productivity Center, January 1984, p. 4; "ASQC: 40 Years of Growth and Change," *Quality Progress*, May 1986, pp. 56–67; Lawrence R. Dorsky, "Management Commitment to Japanese Apple Pie," *Quality Progress*, February 1984, pp. 14–18; Debra A. Owens, "QA/QC and ASQC History," unpublished paper, American Society for Quality Control, undated; and Jack Reddy, "Incorporating Quality in Competitive Strategies," *Sloan Management Review*, Spring 1980, pp. 53–60.

2. Alfred D. Chandler, Jr., *The Visible Hand* (Cambridge, Mass.: Belknap Press, Harvard University Press, 1977), pp. 50–64.

3. J. M. Juran, "Consumerism and Product Quality," *Quality Progress*, July 1970, p. 20, and Debra A. Owens, Director, Technical Programs, American Society for Quality Control, personal communication, April 18, 1984.

4. William J. Abernathy and John E. Corcoran, "Relearning from the Old Masters: Lessons of the American System of Manufacturing," *Journal of Operations Management*, August 1983, pp. 155–68; David A. Hounshell, *From the American System to Mass Production, 1800–1932* (Baltimore: Johns Hopkins Press, 1984), pp. 15–17; and Merritt Roe Smith, *Harpers Ferry Armory and the New Technology* (Ithaca, N.Y.: Cornell University Press, 1977), esp. chs. 3–5. While the initial breakthroughs involving interchangeable parts have often been associated with Eli Whitney, recent research suggests that his role has been overstated. See Robert S. Woodbury, "The Legend of Eli Whitney and Interchangeable Parts," *Technology and Culture*, Summer 1960, pp. 235–53, as well as the above sources.

5. Hounshell, *From American System*, pp. 6, 34–35.

6. *Ibid.*, p. 34.

7. Frederick Winslow Taylor, *Shop Management* (New York: Harper & Brothers, 1919), p. 101. See also Chandler, *Visible Hand*, pp. 275–77, and Frank Barkley Copley, *Frederick W. Taylor: Father of Scientific Management* (New York: Harper & Brothers, 1923), I:324.

8. G. S. Radford, *The Control of Quality in Manufacturing* (New York: Ronald Press, 1922). The book is predated by an earlier article on the subject by the same author. See G. S. Radford, "The Control of Quality," *Engineering Magazine*, October 1917.

9. Radford, *Control of Quality in Manufacturing*, p. 36.

10. *Ibid.*, p. 5.

11. Charles A. Bicking, "The Technical Aspects of Quality Control," *Industrial Quality Control*, March 1958, p. 7.

12. W. A. Shewhart, *Economic Control of Quality of Manufactured Product* (New York: D. Van Nostrand Company, 1931).

13. Abbott and Leaman, "Quality Control" (note 1), p. 1000, and Harold F. Dodge, "Notes on the Evolution of Acceptance Sampling Plans, Part I," *Journal of Quality Technology,* April 1969, p. 77.

14. Shewhart, *Economic Control of Quality,* p. 6.

15. Shewhart in fact developed two charts: the X or average chart, and the σ or standard deviation chart. The former measured the average level around which dispersion was to be controlled; the latter, the degree of dispersion itself. Standard deviations, however, proved to be difficult to compute and were shortly replaced by range charts (R), developed in England by Leonard Tippett. See Abbott and Leaman, "Quality Control," pp. 1000–1001, for further discussion of this development. For more on the application of process control charts, see such standard texts as J. M. Juran and Frank M. Gryna, Jr., *Quality Planning and Analysis* (New York: McGraw-Hill, 1980), esp. chs. 12, 13, and 14, and E. L. Grant and R. S. Leavenworth, *Statistical Quality Control,* Fifth Edition (New York: McGraw-Hill, 1980), chs. 2–11. For a more succinct treatment, see *Constructing and Using Process Control Charts* (Boston: Harvard Business School Case Services 9-684-073, 1984).

16. These plans were based on two technical concepts: operating characteristic (OC) curves and lot tolerance percent defective (LTPD). For further discussion, see Dodge, "Notes, Part I," pp. 78–81; Juran and Gryna, *Quality Planning and Analysis,* ch. 17; and Grant and Leavenworth, *Statistical Quality Control,* chs. 12 and 13.

17. Dodge, "Notes, Park I," pp. 82–84, and Harold F. Dodge and Harry G. Romig, *Sampling Inspection Tables* (New York: John Wiley & Sons, 1944).

18. H. F. Dodge, "Notes on the Evolution of Acceptance Sampling Plans, Part II," *Journal of Quality Technology,* July 1969, pp. 155–56.

19. *Ibid.,* pp. 156–59. After years of refinement and revision, these techniques led to Military Standard 105D (MIL-STD-105D), the most widely used acceptance sampling plan in the world. See H. F. Dodge, "Notes on the Evolution of Acceptance Sampling Plans, Part III," *Journal of Quality Technology,* October 1969, pp. 229–32.

20. Abbott and Leaman, "Quality Control," p. 1001.

21. H. F. Safford, "The U.S. Army Ordnance Department Use of Quality Control," *Industrial Quality Control,* January 1946, p. 4. W. Edwards Deming, who would later play a leading role in introducing statistical quality control in Japan, was involved in this effort as Adviser in Sampling to the Chief of Army Ordnance.

22. Eugene L. Grant, "Industrialists and Professors in Quality Control: A Look Back and a Look Ahead," *Industrial Quality Control,* July 1953, p. 31.

23. Holbrook Working, "Statistical Quality Control in War Production," *Journal of the American Statistical Association,* December 1945, pp. 425, 433, 439.

24. One initiator of the OPRD programs has observed that had it not been for the early successes of the Ontario Works of General Electric in applying the techniques of statistical quality control, he might have recommended that the program be curtailed. See Grant, "Industrialists and Professors," p. 33.

25. Abbott and Leaman, "Quality Control," pp. 1001–2; Dodge, "Notes, Part III," p. 228; *Industrial Quality Control,* July 1944; Owens, "QA/QC" (note 1).

26. J. M. Juran, ed., *Quality Control Handbook* (New York: McGraw-Hill, 1951).

27. *Ibid.,* p. 37.

28. Armand V. Feigenbaum, "Total Quality Control," *Harvard Business Review,* November–December 1956, pp. 94, 98 (italics in original). See also Armand V. Feigenbaum, *Total Quality Control* (New York: McGraw-Hill, 1961).

29. Feigenbaum, *Total Quality Control,* pp. 54–57, and Juran, *Quality Control Handbook,* pp. 170–72, 174–77, 281–82.

30. Thomas A. Budne, "Reliability Engineering," in Carl Heyel, ed., *The Encyclopedia of Management,* Third Edition (New York: Van Nostrand Reinhold Company, 1982), p. 1023, and George A. W. Boehm, "'Reliability' Engineering," *Fortune,* April 1963, pp. 124–27, 181–82, 184, 186.

31. *Reliability of Military Electronic Equipment,* Report by the Advisory Group on Reliability of Electronic Equipment, Office of the Assistant Secretary of Defense (Research and Engineering) (Washington, D.C.: U.S. Government Printing Office, 1951). This was the so-called AGREE report.

32. Boehm, "'Reliability' Engineering," p. 127.

33. Budne, "Reliability Engineering," p. 1024. For reasons of clarity, Budne's definition, which parallels that of the AGREE report, has been slightly reworded. See Grant and Leavenworth, *Statistical Quality Control* (note 15), pp. 536–37, for a number of similar definitions.

34. Boehm, "'Reliability' Engineering," pp. 181–82; Budne, "Reliability Engineering," pp. 1024–25; Juran and Gryna, *Quality Planning and Analysis* (note 15), ch. 8; and J. M. Juran, *Quality Control Handbook,* Third Edition (New York: McGraw-Hill, 1974), pp. 22-26–22-27. For an introduction to probability distributions, see any basic statistics text, e.g., Richard I. Levin, *Statistics for Management* (Englewood Cliffs, N.J.: Prentice-Hall, 1978), pp. 136–38.

35. Boehm, "'Reliability' Engineering," pp. 182, 184; Budne, "Reliability Engineering," p. 1026; and Juran and Gryna, *Quality Planning and Analysis,* pp. 182–84.

36. Budne, "Reliability Engineering," p. 1028.

37. The discussion of zero defects is based on James F. Halpin, *Zero Defects* (New York: McGraw-Hill, 1966). At the time the book was written, Halpin was Director of Quality at the Martin Company. He had been one of the founders of its zero defects program.

38. *Ibid.,* p. 15.

39. *Ibid.,* p. 5. See also Captain E. R. Pettebone, "'Zero Defects' Type Programs: Basic Concepts," in Office of the Assistant Secretary of Defense (Installations and Logistics), *Zero Defects: The Quest for Quality* (Washington, D.C.: U.S. Government Printing Office, 1968), pp. 45–60.

40. Philip B. Crosby, *Quality Is Free* (New York: Mentor/New American Library, 1979). For an interesting comparison of Crosby's approach with those of other quality experts, see Charles H. Fine and David H. Bridge, "Managing Quality Improvement," Working Paper 1607–84, Sloan School of Management, Massachusetts Institute of Technology, November 1984, mimeographed.

41. See, for example, Douglas McGregor, *The Human Side of Enterprise* (New York: McGraw-Hill, 1960), and Frederick G. Lesieur, ed., *The Scanlon Plan* (Cambridge, Mass., and New York: Technology Press, John Wiley & Sons, 1958).

Continuous Incremental Improvement: An Operations Strategy for Higher Quality, Lower Costs, and Global Competitiveness

By Harold L. Gilmore

Conventional wisdom holds that product and service quality is costly and that the relevant activities behave in an interdependent manner. Their behavior for a particular organization depends to a great extent on the mission, objectives, and ultimately, the operational strategy pursued by management in an effort to achieve its objectives.

This paper presents the notion that under certain operating conditions improving product or service quality can lead to steep short-run reductions in quality expenditures and to substantial long-run reductions in total operating costs. Concurrently, higher levels of product and service quality and customer satisfaction will be achieved. An operations strategy of continuous incremental improvement is suggested as the way to establish the appropriate operating conditions.

DEFINITIONS

Two important terms are defined next as an aid to this discussion. The first insert defines the concept of continuous improvement. It is important to recognize that this concept is comprehensive and therefore not restricted to a specific activity or function in an organization. Operating improvements can be implemented in office

Reprinted from the Winter 1990 issue of *SAM Advanced Management Journal* with the permission of the author.

and support activities as well as on the production line. Identifying improvements need not be restricted to management or supervision but should be an important part of everyone's responsibility.

Given an organizational philosophy and structure equipped with appropriate improvement techniques, the opportunity for improving operations is infinite.

Improved quality is a major source of increased competitiveness and quality expenditure reduction. Traditionally, quality control activities focused on the conformance of products or services to preestablished standards. The degree to which this is achieved is called conformance quality.

CONTINUOUS IMPROVEMENT

The integration of organizational philosophy, techniques, and structure to achieve sustained performance improvements in all activities on an uninterrupted basis.

CONFORMANCE QUALITY[1]

The degree to which a specific product or service conforms to a design or specification.

The continuous incremental improvement concept represents a significant extension of the traditional concept of conformance quality since it includes product and service design in addition to production, delivery, and end use. The concept is not constrained by the idea of standards. While standards are likely to exist, they are viewed as merely a temporary guide to present activity. Over time, standards will yield to the changes introduced as a result of continuous improvement and therefore, will always be changing. Improvements may come from anywhere, internally or externally to the organization. Irrespective of the source, improvements have a significant and measurable effect on an organization's quality assurance activities.

QUALITY ASSURANCE ACTIVITIES

Quality assurance can be viewed as a subsystem of operations composed of three main activities: prevention, appraisal and defect/failure correction. Total quality expenditures are the sum of organizational expenditures on these interrelated and interdependent activities. The quality control subsystem is depicted in Figure 1.

Some research has focused on the extent to which management resource allocations conform with theory, i.e., are in line with the optimum allocation of prevention, appraisal, and defect and failure correction activity to insure product or service conformance to preestablished quality levels.[2] These activities and their associated "costs" have the following widely accepted definitions (Figure 2).

Interestingly quality cost research to date has been limited in quantity and scope.[1] Researchers have found that, for proprietary reasons, organizations utilizing quality costs for managerial purposes are reluctant to disclose cost data. However, it is even more likely that organizations do not have a complete picture of their quality expenditures, and what data they do have are of limited use for decision making.

FIGURE 1   *Quality Assurance Subsystem*

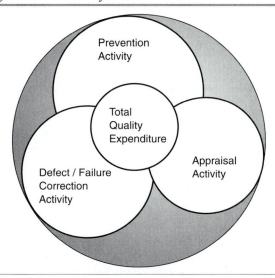

ALLOCATION MODEL

The traditional economic model for the allocation of resources to quality activities assumes that the objective of management is to achieve conformance quality (at a given quality level) at minimum total conformance quality expenditures. Management achieves or approaches this minimum through the prudent commitment of resources to prevention, appraisal, and defect/failure correction activities.

FIGURE 2   *Quality Activity Definitions*

Prevention Activities or actions undertaken to provide a product or service which meets with customer satisfaction and organizational standards of quality. Included here are quality engineering, process planning and design of equipment for quality assurance purposes, training, delivery system and equipment maintenance to assure proper performance.

Appraisal Activities or actions undertaken to determine the actual level of quality achieved relative to desired levels of customer satisfaction and organizational standards of quality. Specifically included are all inspection and tests costs, such as product destruction, utilities consumed, audits, external evaluation.

Defect/Failure Correction Activities or actions undertaken to correct products or services that fail to satisfy the customer or do not conform to organizational standards of quality. Included are refunds, recalls, scrap, rework, vendor produced defects, customer complaints and adjustments, customer service costs due to defects.

FIGURE 3   *Prevention and Appraisal Expenditure Model (Quality Level Fixed)*

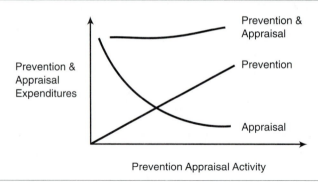

Most people believe that the emphasis in achieving product or service quality should be on prevention rather than appraisal or defect/failure correction activities. As the old adage suggests, "An ounce of prevention is worth a pound of cure." Others have suggested building quality in or doing the job right the first time.

Figures 3 and 4 depict, for the purpose of discussion, nonparametric quality expenditure models based on the foregoing concepts. They diagram the interrelated activities of prevention, appraisal, and defect/failure correction.

Figure 3 shows prevention and appraisal expenditure behavior as a function of prevention appraisal activity. Prevention expenditures are shown rising linearly as prevention activity is increased. The appraisal cost curve illustrates that as prevention activity is increased, the expenditure can be expected to decrease, but at a decreasing rate. This curve is asymptotic as prevention activity increases, which reflects the reality that the complete elimination of appraisal activity (expenditures) is highly unlikely. There will always be some measurement required to determine the extent to which the product or service meets specifications and satisfies customers. In addition, this curve indicates that some finite amount of appraisal activity

FIGURE 4   *Conformance Expenditure Model (Quality Level Fixed)*

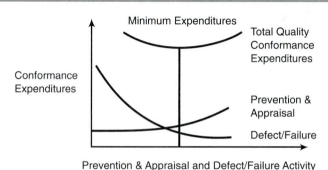

(expenditure) exists even when little or no prevention activity is performed. In that situation, the firm would be engaged in determining what the quality level of the output actually was.

The sum of the prevention and appraisal expenditure curves results in a curve depicting the cost of assuring that the desired quality or customer satisfaction has been achieved.

Figure 4 illustrates conformance quality control total expenditures as a function of prevention, appraisal, and defect/failure correction activity. The prevention and appraisal cost curve as depicted in Figure 3 is duplicated in Figure 4, along with the resulting expected relationship to defect/failure correction expenditures.

Defect/failure correction expenditures are shown decreasing and asympotically approaching the abscissa as the combination of prevention and appraisal activities are increased. The defect/failure correction curve is shown as an asymptote in order to reflect the idea that the complete elimination of defects is unlikely. There are bound to be some scrap, rework, or customer service "call backs" in any operation, for a variety of personnel and material-related causes. The curve also indicates that some finite value of defect/failure correction expenditure exists when little or no quality assurance (prevention or appraisal) activity is performed.

The total conformance quality control expenditure curve is the sum of the two other cost curves. It takes the familiar U-shape of the cost curves depicted by economic theorists—technically a quadratic cost function. The bottom point of the curve indicates the minimum cost combination of prevention, appraisal, and defect/failure correction activity. It should be noted that a firm may have to operate at a quality cost level higher than the minimum cost point due to customer requirements. However, a firm seeking to maximize profits would not be justified in operating at any lower prevention and appraisal level. To do so would result in larger expenditures than necessary at a lower level of conformance quality (higher defect/failure expenditures).

Maximizing profits from a conformance quality control point of view is equivalent to minimizing total conformance quality control expenditures. According to Figure 4, this occurs approximately where the prevention, appraisal, and defect/failure correction cost curves intersect. A firm operating at minimum total conformance quality control expenditure should employ the indicated mix of prevention, appraisal, and defect/failure correction activity. In terms of minimum conformance quality control cost, the combined cost of prevention and appraisal activity should approximately equal defect/failure correction related activity.

Having reviewed popular views and the assumptions associated with the behavior of quality assurance activities and related expenditures, let's review some recent strategic management developments and their likely impact on the foregoing.

CONTINUOUS INCREMENTAL IMPROVEMENT

It is no secret that American industry is experiencing competitive difficulty. The story has been presented by the media time and again. Even in the face of overwhelming evidence, domestic businesses cling to the ways of the past. However, some noteworthy companies such as Nucor Steel, Nashua Corporation, AT&T, Campbell Soup, Ford Motor Company and General Motors, to name a few examples, have brought themselves back from the brink of disaster and to a state of global competitiveness. In fact it was the sense of impending disaster that motivated them to undertake organization-wide change to alter the direction they were traveling. By implementing strategic and systemic changes via continuous incremental improvements these troubled firms sought to improve customer satisfaction, raise quality, lower operating costs, and regain a competitive advantage.

The philosophy of continuous incremental improvement differs significantly from the programmatic management approaches taken in the past. Over the years, American business has been the scene of one technological love affair after another. Commencing in the 1930s with the Human Relations movement and more recently with such programs as Statistical Quality Control (SQC), Zero Defects (ZD), Management by Objectives (MBO), Quality Circles, Job Enrichment, Job Enlargement, Just in Time (JIT), Material Requirements Planning (MRP II), Computer Aided Design (CAD), Computer Aided Manufacturing (CAM), Computer Aided Inspection (CAI) and various other participatory management schemes, the search has been on to find a road map to world class competition. The most recent popular approach is Statistical Process Control (SPC).[2]

The organizations mentioned earlier seem to have found the way. A study of their practices discloses they have skillfully and innovatively crafted total organizational change processes which involve relevant facets of the above.[3,4] These processes focus on management philosophy, the dignity of the individual, close attention to customer needs and to process details. Such a comprehensive and enduring approach has significant impact on quality assurance activities, especially with respect to who does them and for what reason. Several notable characteristics of these organizations are:

- Customer driven
- Employee involved
- Continuous improvement oriented

FIGURE 5   *Quality Expenditure Reduction Relationships*

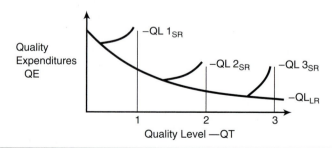

- Process focused
- Internationally sensitive

A moment of reflection on these characteristics reveals a substantial shift from a *primary concern for output* to one that is directed toward 1) the *recipient* of the goods or services; 2) the process which generated them; and 3) a *sustained* concern for *improving the level of satisfaction and value* the goods and services provided. A more subtle characteristic of continuous improvement is a redefinition of the customer. The most advanced organizations have defined the customer as the next person or step in the *process*—again reflecting a focus on the total process rather than exclusively on output or an external customer.

From a quality expenditure allocation perspective, the impact is clearly a stress on prevention activity and an enhancement of appraisal activity so as to continuously raise the level of customer satisfaction, value, and quality. Thus, the earlier discussion of predetermined fixed quality levels achieved via a combination of prevention, appraisal, and failure activity appears passé. The process focus coupled with continuous improvement suggests a significant change in management philosophy and emphasis.

Where prevention and appraisal activities are still practiced they are becoming far more pervasive in the work force. The search for continuous improvement is not the purview of a select few individuals. Nor is some predetermined level of quality established and maintained for all time. The new objective is to seek ever higher levels of quality, value, and customer satisfaction by analyzing process capability and eliminating the causes and amounts of process variation. The ultimate objective is *perfection*, a state previously thought unattainable due to the general acceptance of defects and the widely held view that you cannot please everyone.

How is the continuous incremental improvement strategy reflected in quality expenditure behavior? Figure 5 depicts the familiar total quality expenditure relationships discussed earlier but reflects the concept of continuous incremental improvement over time. The assumption that product or service imperfections are removed by appraisal activity no longer pertains. Continuous improvement is brought about by identifying breakthroughs (e.g., process controls, improved raw materials, training, equipment improvements) that permit incremental changes in product or service performance, added value, and customer satisfaction. Every step of the process must add value from a customer perspective. Failure to do so results in change or elimination. If the customer will not pay for it, do not do it.

The quality expenditure behavior depicted in Figure 5 is based on many examples. One of the 1988 National Quality Award Winners, Motorola, has reported a $250 million reduction in appraisal expenditures as a result of their management's quest for quality improvements. Motorola's quality improvements focused on "six sigma quality." Statistically this measure translates into a benchmark of no more than 3.4 defects per million products, customer services included. The company found that, contrary to conventional thinking, as the number of defects during production were reduced the cost of manufacture decreased to less than one percent. No longer was there a need to maintain production capacity for rework and repair activity. In addition, failures in use were found to be closely associated with products that had undergone repair or rework. Another source of both tangible and intangible cost was eliminated by discontinuing repair and rework activity.

Similarly, Globe Metallurgical adopted a statistical process control strategy in 1985 which has resulted in their becoming the nation's lowest cost, highest quality producer of feroalloys and silicon metal. Like Motorola, Globe's achievement was recognized with the National Quality Award.

Many more success stories could be recounted, all of which would have the same characteristics: predisposition to change for the better, willingness to tap heretofore unused capacity, and a sense of urgency. Robert H. Schaffer[5] recounts the experiences of numerous other companies which have used the strategy of continuous incremental improvements to achieve the behavior reflected in Figure 5.

The family of short run curves illustrates the behavioral relationship of quality expenditures to the level of quality. The short run curves ($QL1_{sr}$, $QL2_{sr}$, $QL3_{sr}$) rise as the limit of existing technology is reached and incremental expenditures exceed quality level gains. But at this point, breakthroughs occur, and the opportunity exists for incremental gains to exceed the inputs. The cycle begins again. Since the search is continuous, there is no end to this cycle of improved quality, value, and customer satisfaction. Of additional importance is the long run phenomena of lowered total quality expenditures (QL_{lr}), increased level of quality, and reallocation of quality resources to prevention and away from appraisal and defect/failure correction activities. This ability to focus increased resources on incremental improvement (prevention) facilitates additional breakthroughs and sustains the process.

CONCLUSION

We have outlined the impact on total quality expenditures and customer satisfaction of a continuous improvement operating strategy. Implementation of this strategy promises to usher in a new era of organizational behavior—one that holds out the promise of world market preeminence once again for American businesses.

The quality assurance professional should emphasize process capability and control rather than output and continuous improvement rather than the setting and maintaining quality standards. Quality expenditures should be increasingly allocated to prevention-related activities, not appraisal. As perfection is approached, the need for defect/failure correction activity will be extinguished. The measure of corporate success will not be simply an acceptable quality level but increased customer satisfaction, improved process capability, decreased process variation, and lowered operating costs. The widespread adoption of continuous improvement philosophy offers American businesses the opportunity to return to global competitiveness.

Notes

1. Gilmore, Harold L., Herbert C. Schwartz, *Integrated Product Testing and Evaluation: A Systems Approach to Improved Reliability and Quality.* Rev. Ed., Marcel Dekker, Inc., New York and Basel; ASQC Quality Press, Milwaukee, 1986.

2. Walton, Mary, *The Deming Management Method.* Dodd, Mead & Company, New York, 1986.

3. Peters, Thomas J., Robert H. Waterman, Jr., *In Search of Excellence: Lessons from America's Best-Run Companies,* Harper & Row Publishers, New York, 1982.

4. Takeuchi, Hirotaka, John A. Quelch, "Quality Is More Than Making a Good Product," *Harvard Business Review,* (July–August 1983) pages 139–145.

5. Shaffer, Robert H., *The Breakthrough Strategy,* Ballinger Publishing Company, Cambridge, MA, 1988.

Additional Sources

Buetow, Richard C. Director of Quality, Motorola Inc., Address 1989 ASQC Quality Congress, Toronto, Canada, May 9, 1989.

Garvin, David A., "Quality on the Line," *Harvard Business Review,* (September–October 1983) pages 65–75.

Gitlow, Howard S., Paul T. Hertz, "Product Defects and Productivity," *Harvard Business Review,* (September–October 1983) pages 131–141.

Leach, Kenneth E., Vice President, Administration and Chief Quality Officer, Globe Metallurgical Inc., Address to 1989 ASQC Quality Congress, Toronto, Canada, May 9, 1989.

Managing for High Productivity and Quality

——

By Ronald D. McNeil

Many buzz words zip through the business world. However, TQM, TOC, and Benchmarking are more than buzz words. If implemented in your business, these words can transform your operation from ordinary to the head of the class.

Total Quality Management (TQM), Theory of Constraints (TOC), and Benchmarking are all terms which employ process improvement as core beliefs. The questions are: What are each one of these, how do they work, what do you need to know about them, and, most importantly, what will each do for you and your business?

What is Total Quality Management? TQM is a philosophy which holds that any organization, large or small, is a system of interconnected processes which must be managed as a whole by using continuous feedback of performance to constantly improve each process so that the quality of products and services as a whole always increases.

At first this definition may seem too complicated to be useful to a small business; however, as we seriously consider this definition, we may see that the concepts it employs can help you and your business. For example, your business is a series of processes that end in a product or service for which you receive payment. Your business is often evaluated by your weakest process.

A rather commonplace example illustrates the point. When someone calls for information about your service, the response to that call is a process that may not directly involve the service or product you offer. However, if the customer's call is not answered as soon as the customer expects it to be answered, you have lost the caller and, perhaps, a customer. No matter what your capability is in the processes

---

Reprinted from the July-August 1992 issue of *Spotting the News* with the permission of the author.

for providing the service or product, the weak phone answering process means that the potential customer will never know the quality of the service or product.

Many of us were once specialists: that is, we could do page layouts or operate a press better than almost anyone. We tend to hold our specialty in high esteem. In fact, we favor our specialized world by devoting resources such as attention, time, and money to the areas that we know about and are comfortable with. It is, therefore, only natural that if we see new equipment or a potential employee which will help our area of interest, we will invest more resources in that equipment or employee than we will in those areas which are somewhat foreign to us.

As an illustration, you may invest a great deal of money in the very latest, hi-tech printing equipment, but the use of that investment depends on other processes that must occur before that printing investment is utilized. The TQM philosophy is that management evaluates and improves all processes as well as the relationship among the processes themselves.

Why would a critical process in a business become the weakest link? One possible reason is that a manager's or owner's attention is elsewhere. In the illustration given of the phone system, it may be the weakest chain of business processes because your attention, interest and experience is in another area. So, while you can outprint any competitor, the printing capability is underutilized because you do not have the capability to respond to phone calls appropriately.

In TQM, a team (if you are a sole proprietor, the team in one) makes a flow chart of all processes that a product or service undergoes including the process for putting the customer's payment in the bank. In short, the TQM manager focuses on the business as a whole, evaluates each step that leads to payment, and constantly improves each of those steps or, in TQM language, processes.

A TQM business owner or manager is careful not to allow any process to get out of step with another interrelated step. Most of all the TQM owner or manager does not allow the business as a whole to get out of step with the customer's expectations.

The Theory of Constraints, as discussed in a previous article, also views a business as a series of processes. Eli Goldratt in his book, *Theory of Constraints,* states that every business was designed for a purpose. For instance, you may have started your own business so that you could have more control over and satisfaction in you life. The business has to make money or you have little control since it is given to creditors and satisfaction simply disappears.

Most entrepreneurs firmly believe that they can improve on the products or services offered by a former employer or competitors. Great satisfaction comes from operating your own successful business; and that success is dictated by customers who are satisfied and pay their bills. Therefore, whatever your purpose for your business or work might be, that purpose is only accomplished long term through highly satisfied customers.

What Goldratt proposes is that customers can best be served by having the fastest service. From the instant a customer places an order to when the satisfied customer pays for the service or product is the most important thing for the business. Goldratt calls this total process throughput.

If the phone is not answered when a customer calls, then throughput does not occur and the unanswered call is a constraint which must be broken (i.e., improved upon). Throughput is only as fast as the slowest process and that slowest process defines the capacity of the business. To improve throughput, the slowest process, or in Goldratt's terms constraint, needs to be broken. When one constraint is broken so that it is no longer the weakest link in a chain, then a new constraint appears.

Which constraint is broken first? The constraint which impedes the system the most should be improved first. In simple terms, the constraint which has the most negative impact on the system is the first one to address.

As previously discussed in the article on benchmarking, benchmarking is the continuous process of measuring products, services, and practices against a corporation's toughest competitors and industry leaders. In fact, benchmarking is a tool for TQM and TOC. It is a method that management can use to improve a process or discover the best way to break a constraint.

Other tools for TQM and TOC include statistical process control, pareto charts, histograms, flowcharts, fish bone diagrams, and a host of other tools. These tools may appear to be overwhelmingly complicated at first, but they are not.

Statistical Process Control may alarm some, but SPC does not take a math degree to use. In many plants, hourly workers with a high school education or less use SPC every day to evaluate what they are doing. The same is true of the other tools mentioned.

Several excellent books on the subject of TQM, TOC, and tools are readily available. A few of these are: *Managing the Total Quality Transformation* by Thomas Berry (McGraw Hill, 1991), *The Memory Jogger Plus +* by Michael Brassard (GOAL/QPC, 13 Branch Street, Methuen, MA 01844), and *Theory of Constraints* by Eliyahu Goldratt (North River Press, Box 309, Croton-on-Hudson, NY 10520).

Another source for help is your local library, technical school, college, and a host of publicly offered training programs. Simply call the nearest school, Chamber of Commerce, trade association, or other resource to find the help you need to have a more successful business.

Building Learning Organizations

——

BY PETER SENGE

Why do many leaders of the so-called "quality movement" hate the term "the quality movement"? The man most often identified as the father of total quality management, Dr. W. Edwards Deming, takes offense at the assumed parentage. "The term is counterproductive," says Dr. Deming, the man who first taught the Japanese statistical quality control. "My work is about a transformation in management and about the profound knowledge needed for the transformation. Total quality stops people from thinking."

"Neither 'total quality' nor 'total quality management' describes what this approach to management is all about," says Dr. Edward Baker, director of Ford's corporate quality office. "It's about improving the total behavior of organizations, about developing the capability of a system to do what its members actually want it to do—anywhere in life."

Without a unifying conceptual framework, the quality movement in the United States risks being fragmented into isolated initiatives and slogans. *The voice of the customer, fix the process not the people, competitive benchmarking, continuous improvement, policy deployment, leadership*—the more we hear, the less we understand.

"Trying to put together the alphabet soup coming out of Japan of SPC, JIT, QIP, QFD, and so on can be hopelessly confusing without a unifying theme," says Analog Devices CEO Ray Stata.

It is not surprising that, for many, it doesn't add up to much more than management's latest *flavor of the month* that must be endured until the next fad comes along.

Even those firms where there has been significant commitment to quality management for several years are encountering slowing rates of improvement. "We've picked all the low hanging fruit," as one Detroit executive put it recently. "Now, the difficult changes are what's left."

Excerpt from "Building Learning Organizations" from *Journal For Quality and Participation,* March 1992, by Peter Senge. Reprinted with the permission of Innovation Associates.

The "difficult changes" are unlikely without a coherent picture of where we are trying to take our organizations through the quality management process.

Our global competitors   Equally troubling, the best of our international competitors are not fragmenting, they are building—steadily advancing an approach to improving quality, productivity, and profitability that differs fundamentally from the traditional authoritarian, mechanical management model.

"Total quality [TQ] is not a closed-ended methodology; its an open-ended methodology," says Shoji Shiba, of Japan's Tsukuba University. "TQ continues to develop according to the needs of society."

The tools American corporations are racing to master today, the frontier of the quality movement in Japan in the 1960s, are no longer the frontier. The "thought revolution in management," as quality pioneer Ishikawa called it, is still evolving.

Learning organizations   I believe that the quality movement as we have known it up to now in the United States is in fact the first wave in building *learning organizations*—organizations that continually expand their ability to shape their future.

The roots of the quality movement lie in assumptions about people, organizations, and management that have one unifying theme: to make continual learning a way of organizational life, especially improving the performance of the organization as a total system. This can only be achieved by breaking with the traditional authoritarian, command and control hierarchy where the top thinks and the local acts, to merge thinking and acting at all levels.

This represents a profound reorientation in the concerns of management—a shift from a predominant concern with controlling to a predominant concern with learning. Failure to come to grips with this shift plagues the efforts of many U.S. firms eager to jump on the quality bandwagon.

Learning organizations in Japan   Our Japanese competitors have no trouble with this shift. "Japan's greatest long-term comparative advantage is not its management system, Japan Inc., or quality," says C. Jackson Grayson Jr., of the American Productivity and Quality Center in Houston. "It's the Japanese commitment to learning."

More specifically, as management practices in Japan have evolved over the past 40 years, there has been a steady spread of the commitment to learning—starting with statistical process control (SPC) for small groups of quality experts, to teaching quality improvement tools to frontline workers throughout the organization, to developing and disseminating tools for managerial learning.

> *"If we fail to grasp the deeper messages of the quality movement, we will one day awake to discover ourselves chasing a receding target."*

Learning waves   The evolution of learning organizations can be best understood as a series of waves. What most managers think of as quality management focuses on improving tangible work processes. This is the first wave.

The first wave of quality   In the first wave, the primary focus of change was frontline workers. Management's job was to:

- Champion continual improvement
- Remove impediments (like quality control experts and unnecessary bureaucracy) that disempowered local personnel
- Support new practices like quality training and competitive benchmarking that drive process improvement.

The second wave of quality   In the second wave, the focus shifts from improving work processes to improving how we work—fostering ways of thinking and interacting conducive to continual learning about the dynamic, complex, conflictual issues that determine system wide performance. In the second wave, the primary focus of change is the managers themselves.

The third wave of quality   These two ways will, I believe, gradually merge into a third, in which learning becomes *institutionalized* as an inescapable way of life for managers and workers alike (if we even bother maintaining that distinction).

We are still in the first wave   American industry is, with a few exceptions, primarily operating in the first wave. "Despite all our improvements, the basic behavior of our managers, especially our senior managers, hasn't really changed much," laments the head of a major corporation's quality office.

Japan and the second wave   By contrast, the second wave is well under way in Japan, driven by their *seven new tools for management,* as distinct from their traditional *seven quality tools* that drove the first wave.

America's challenge   The challenge today, as American companies endeavor to master the basic tools and philosophy of quality management, is not to be caught short-sighted with mechanical "quality programs."

If we fail to grasp the deeper messages of the quality movement, we will one day awaken to discover ourselves chasing a receding target.

THE ROOTS OF THE QUALITY MOVEMENT

A close look at the roots of the quality movement shows that it has always been about learning.

"The prevailing system of management has destroyed our people," says Dr. Deming. "People are born with intrinsic motivation, self-esteem, dignity, curiosity to learn, joy in learning."

Intrinsic versus extrinsic motivation   Intrinsic motivation lies at the heart of Deming's management philosophy. By contrast, extrinsic motivation is the bread and butter of Western management.

The holiest of holy for the American manager, "People do what they are rewarded for," is actually antithetical to the spirit of quality management. This doesn't imply that rewards are irrelevant. Rather, it implies that no set of rewards, neither carrots nor sticks, can ever substitute for intrinsic motivation to learn. A corporate commitment to quality that is not based on intrinsic motivation is a house built on sand.

Motivate *them* or loose *their* own motivation?   Consider, for example the goal of continuous improvement, which remains an elusive target for most American corporations.

Motivate them   From an extrinsic perspective, the only way to get continuous improvement is to find ways to continually motivate people to improve, because people only modify their behavior when there is some external motivation to do so. Otherwise, they will just sit there—or worse, slide backwards. This leads to what workers perceive as management continually raising the bar to manipulate more effort from them.

Loose their motivation with information and appropriate tools   However, from an intrinsic perspective, there is nothing mysterious at all about continuous improvement. If left to their own devices, people will naturally look for ways to do things better. What they need is adequate information and appropriate tools.

From the intrinsic perspective people's innate curiosity and desire to experiment, if unleashed, creates an engine for improvement that can never be matched by external rewards.

Learning and intrinsic motivation to learn have always been the roots of quality   A management system based on intrinsic motivation to learn is as befuddling to Western economists as it is to Western managers.

Princeton economist Alan Blinder recently cited an impressive list of Japanese "violations" of economic orthodoxy—tolerated monopolies and cartels, single suppliers, salary scales that do not differentiate adequately between ranks, keeping promising young managers waiting too long for promotion, and "almost nothing gets you fired."

"We did the opposite of what American economists said," Blinder quotes a top Ministry of International Trade & Industry (MIT) official. "We violated all the normal rules." But the puzzle of how a nation that does so many things *wrong* can get so many things right dissolves when we realize that Western economic theories, from Adam Smith on, are based solely on extrinsic motivation.

The way we thought it was   Adam Smith's *homo economicus* is presumed to maximize his income, not his learning. The following are some maxims of *U.S. homo economicus:*

- If there is no opportunity for significant salary increase by climbing the corporate ladder, he will have little motivation to do his best or to improve.

- If there is no fear of dismissal, there will be nothing to drive him to be productive.

- If his company, made up of lots of greedy little buggers just like him, does not have to compete against other companies, they will have no motivation to continually lower costs of production, nor to improve their products.

In short, no competition, no innovation. But, if the drive to innovate comes from within, all this changes—especially if a management system can nurture and harness this drive.

Shewhart's and Dewey's roots to quality   But we don't have to look just to subtleties like intrinsic motivation to see that the quality movement has always been about learning.

PDCA   The famous PDCA cycle is evidence enough. No one ever gets far into any introduction to total quality management without learning about Plan-Do-Check-Act, the never-ending cycle of experimentation that structures all quality improvement efforts. Deming called it the *Shewhart cycle* when he introduced it to the Japanese in 1950, in honor of his mentor Walter Shewhart of Bell Labs. Eventually the Japanese called it the *Deming cycle*.

Of John Dewey, learning and quality   But the roots of the PDCA cycle go back further than Deming or Shewhart, at least as far as the educator, John Dewey.

Dewey posited that all learning involves a cycle between four basic stages:

- Discover: the discovery of new insights, invent, creating new options for action.
- Produce: producing new actions.
- Observe: seeing the consequences of those actions, which leads to new discoveries, continuing the cycle.

This is how we learned to walk, to talk, to ride a bicycle, to act skillfully wherever we have achieved some proficiency. The young child first must discover that they want to walk, invent ways of getting started, act, and observe the consequences of her or his action.

Interrupting the cycle interrupts the learning. If the toddler is supported so they do not fall, they also do not learn.

Learning is moving from thought to action   In effect, Dewey canonized the simple fact that all real learning occurs over time, as we move between the world of thought and the world of action. Learning is never simply an intellectual exercise. Nor is it a matter of changing behavior. It is an interactive process linking the two, in a spiral of continually expanding our capabilities.

It is not altogether irrelevant to note that this is a far cry from the common image of *learning* inculcated in the schoolroom, where most of us conclude that learning is synonymous with *taking in information* and being able to produce the *right answer* on cue—little wonder that for most adults, the word *learning* does not quicken the pulse.

The PDCA cycle takes Dewey's theory of learning one step further, saying, in effect, that in an organization it is often wise to distinguish *small actions* from widespread adoption of new practices.

The *do* stage then becomes pilot tests from which new data can be collected and analyzed (*checked*). Gradually, a series of such pilots results in more general learnings and the *act* stage moves to broader and broader application of new practices.

PDCA American style   While simple in concept, the PDCA cycle is often practiced quite differently in the U.S. and in Japan.

Impatient for quick results, American managers often jump from *plan* to *act*.

The rush to act undermines efforts   We conceive new programs and then begin rolling them out throughout the organization. In fact, that's exactly what many U.S. firms are doing with their total quality programs.

While rolling out new programs makes us feel good about doing something (*acting*) to improve things in our business, in fact we are actually undermining possibilities for learning. Who can learn from an experiment involving thousands of people that is only run one time?

PDCA Japanese style   By contrast the Japanese are masters of organizational experimentation. They meticulously design and study pilot tests, often with many corporations participating cooperatively.

Through repeated cycles, new knowledge gradually accumulates. By the time for organization-wide changes, people adopt new practices more rapidly because so many more have been involved in the learning.

For Americans, this whole process often seems unnecessarily time consuming and costly. As one manager pointed out to me recently, the statement "I'm running an experiment" in most American companies is a code word for "Don't hold me accountable for the results." Consequently, while we may go through the motions of quality improvement, we often get the facade without the substance. At best, we get limited bursts of learning.

IMPROVING HOW WE WORK

The first wave   Improving tangible work processes (from the production line, to order entry, to responding to customer inquiries or coordinating the typing queue) was the predominant theme of the first wave in building learning organizations.

The initial tools were derived primarily from statistics, including SPC, and related methods for diagraming, analyzing, and redesigning work processes to reduce variability and enable systematic improvement.

As the first wave was unfolded, the focus has broadened to include more complex processes like product development. By and large, the customer was outside the system of production and the system was designed to meet customer needs.

First wave strength   The strength of the first wave lay in achieving measurable improvements in cost, quality, and customer satisfaction through rigorous and reproducible processes of improvement.

First wave limitation   The limitation lay in the relatively passive role of management and the limited impact on the larger *systems* whereby processes interact—for example, how sales, order entry, manufacturing and customer satisfaction interact.

The second wave unfolds   The initial profile of the second wave could be seen in Japan as early as the 1960s when leading firms began to undertake mass deployment of quality tools. Previously, only small groups of quality control experts learned how to analyze work processes, reduce variation, and improve quality and cost.

Japanese quality circles and learning   "Beginning with quality circles," says Massachusetts Institute of Technology's Alan Graham, "that changed. Everyone began to participate in quality improvement." This was the time when *kaizan* (organization-wide commitment to continuous improvement) was born. This also was the time when Japanese organizations began extensive training in team learning skills, to develop the norms and capabilities needed if quality circles were to be effective.

U.S. quality circles and a lack of emphasis on learning   Interestingly, when U.S. firms began to organize production workers in quality circles, 10 to 15 years later, the emphasis was on forming teams, not on developing team learning skills. Consequently, "The skills and practices, both among workers and managers, necessary for QC circles to be effective," according to Graham, "were not present in the introduction of QC circles in the United States. This has been typical of the general underemphasis here on skills and practices, as opposed to official programs and management goals."

The result was that many initial efforts at quality control circles in the United States failed to generate lasting commitment or significant improvement. "Mid-level managers," says USC's Ed Lawler, "saw QC circles as a threat to their authority, and workers saw them as a gimmick to elicit increased effort and undermine union influence."

The second wave arrives   In Japan, the second wave arrived in full force with the introduction of the *seven new tools for management* in 1979.

The seven new tools   These tools, the work of a committee of the Society for QC Technique Development that operated from 1972 to 1979, focus specifically on how managers think and interact. They particularly emphasize developing better communication and common understandings of complex issues, and relating that understanding to operational planning.

"There are a lot of methodologies for measuring, analyzing, and testing quantitative data," says the leader of the group that developed the new tools, Professor Shiba, "but the area of qualitative methodologies, how to create hypotheses, is very weak. Professor Jiro Kawakita, a Japanese anthropologist, developed methods for analyzing non-numerical data and making sense of that data."

For example, the *KJ method* or affinity diagram, as taught by Professor Shiba and other experts on the *seven management tools*, helps teams gather large amounts of non-quantitative data and organize it into groupings based on natural relationships or affinities. Other tools help to clarify interrelationships, establish priorities, and think through and plan the complex tasks required for accomplishing an agreed upon goal.

A new perspective of the customer   Along with these new tools for thinking and interacting, a new orientation toward the customer has gradually emerged. The new perspective moved from *satisfying the customer's expressed requirements* to *meeting the latent needs of the customer*.

The Miata as a second wave example   As one Detroit executive put it, "You could never produce the Mazda Miata from market research. You have to understand what the customer would value if he experienced it." In the second wave, the customer becomes part of the system. There is an interplay between what the firm seeks to produce and what the customer desires.

The second wave in America   Today, a small number of American companies are starting to experiment with the seven new management tools.

They are discovering a whole new territory for increasing organizational capabilities—how we think and interact around complex, potentially conflictual issues. This is the real message of the second wave—leverage ultimately lies in improving us, not just improving our work processes.

Engelbart's *A, B* and *C* work   "There are three levels of work in organizations," says computer pioneer and inventor of the *mouse* Douglas Engelbart, who has spent the better part of 20 years studying the nature of collaborative work.

"The most obvious level, *A work,* involves the development, production, and sale of a firm's products and services. Most of a company's people and resources are focused at this level.

Effective *A work* would be impossible, however, without the next level, *B work,* which involves designing the systems and processes that enable a company to develop, produce, and sell its products and services.

But, the subtlest and potentially most influential level is *C work,* improving how we think and interact. Ultimately, the quality of *C work* determines the quality of systems and processes we design and the products and services we provide."

The first wave and B work   The major contribution of quality management in the first wave was to focus time and energy systematically on Engelbart's *B work,* especially on improving processes, and to provide tools for the task.

The second wave and C work   The major contribution of the second wave will be to systematically focus on Engelbart's *C work.* This, too, will require appropriate tools. But, before such tools can be developed, we must first understand the *core competencies of learning organizations,* those distinctive capabilities in thinking and interacting which will enable us to "continually improve the total behavior of organizations."

Core competencies for learning organizations   The seven new tools point in the right direction. But our work suggests that they are only a start to developing an organization's capabilities in:

Building Shared Vision There is no substitute for organizational resolve, conviction, commitment, and clarity of intent. They create the need for learning and the collective will to learn. Without shared visions, significant learning occurs only when there are crises, and the learning ends when the crises end.

Personal Mastery Shared vision comes from personal visions. Collective commitment to learning comes from individual commitment to learning. An organization that is continually learning how to create its future must be made up of individuals who are continually learning how to create more of what truly matters to them in their own lives.

Working with Mental Models Organizations become frozen in inaccurate and disempowered views of reality because we lack the capability to *see our assumptions,* and to continually challenge and improve those assumptions. This requires fostering managerial skills in *balancing inquiry and advocacy* in organizations that have been traditionally dominated by advocacy.

Team Learning Ultimately, the learning that matters is the learning of *groups of people who need one another to act* (the real meaning of team). The only problem is that we've lost the ability to talk with one another. Most of the time we are limited to *discussion,* which comes from the same roots as percussion and concussion and literally means *to heave one's views at the other*. What is needed also is dialogue, which comes from the Greek *dia logos* and literally means when a group of people talk with one another such that the meaning *(logos)* moves through *(dia)* them.

Systems thinking   It's not just how we learn, but what we learn. The most important learning in contemporary organizations concerns gaining shared insight into complexity and how we can shape change. But, since early in life, we've been taught to break apart problems.

The resulting fragmentation has left us unable to see the consequences of our own actions, creating an illusion that we are victims of forces outside our control and that the only type of learning that is possible is learning to react more quickly. Systems thinking is about understanding wholes, not parts, and learning how our actions shape our reality.

Creating an organizational symphony   The intrinsic limitations to each of these capabilities is only overcome if they are developed in concert:

- Empowering people (an organization-wide commitment to personal mastery) empowers the organization, but only if individuals are deeply aligned around a common sense of purpose and shared vision.

- Shared vision will energize and sustain an organization through thick and thin, but only if people think systemically: once people are able to see how their actions shape their reality, they begin to understand how alternative actions could create a different reality.

- Individual skills in reflection and inquiry mean little if they cannot be practiced when groups of people confront controversial issues.

- Systems thinking will become the province of a small set of **systems experts** unless it is tied to an organization wide commitment to improving mental models, and even then nothing much will change without shared visions.

- A commitment to seeing the larger system only matters when there is a commitment to the long-term. In the short run, everyone can just fix their piece. Only with a long term view can an organization see that optimizing the parts, one at a time, can lead to sub-optimizing the whole.

A SHORT STUDY ON LEARNING AS A WAY OF ORGANIZATIONAL LIFE

In 1970, Royal/Dutch Shell was arguably the weakest of the *big seven* oil companies. Today, it is one of the strongest. A key to Shell's ascent has been reconceiving *planning as learning,* a conscious process of bringing operating managers' mental models to the surface and challenging those models.

Shell's scenario planning   This conceptual shift has been operationalized by tools like scenario planning. Through its use of scenarios, Shell's planners help managers continually think through how they would manage under multiple possible futures. Today, it is hard for a Shell manager to do business planning without engaging in a conscious learning process.

Shell has become perhaps the first global corporation to realize the leverage the institutionalizing learning as the most effective approach to strategy in a turbulent world. "The corporate one-track mind," says former planning chief Arie de Geus, "is the single primary reason why so many once successful corporations fail to survive beyond their infancy."

From a foreboding view to a new form of planning   Shell's innovations in institutional learning were driven by necessity. As early as 1971, Shell's planners became convinced that major shocks in supply and price were becoming a possibility in world oil markets. But, they were unable to convince managers conditioned by the stability of world markets in the 50s and 60s.

This led the planners to develop scenario planning *exercises,* wherein managers thought through how they would manage if there were a shift from a buyer's market to a seller's market, where sudden changes in price would be a part of life, regardless of whether or not they expected such a change.

Prepared for change in the 70s   When OPEC did become a reality and the first oil shocks hit in the winter of 1973 and 1974, Shell responded differently than any other big oil company. It increased local operating company control rather than increasing corporate control. It accelerated development of reserves, especially in its North Sea fields. While the other major oil companies saw a sudden, unexpected crisis and acted accordingly, Shell's managers perceived a sea change in the basic nature of the business, and acted differently.

Shell's scenario planning and the 80s   The discipline of thinking in terms of alternative futures served Shell equally well in the 80s. Shell planners created a *$15 a barrel oil scenario* in 1983, at a time when prices averaged around $30. They considered two alternative futures:

Alternative future one: As managers considered how they would manage in a depressed price world, they quickly concluded that many of their present production processes would have to be shut down because they were too costly.

Alternative future two: A few engineers suggested that radical redesign of their oil platforms using new miniaturization technologies could make them operable at prices as low as $11 per barrel.

As they considered the plan, it soon became obvious that such a redesign was in fact more desirable under any possible scenario.

Their production people went ahead with the new design concepts. And when prices did fall, hitting an unbelievable $8 per barrel in 1984, Shell was, once again, one step ahead of its competitors.

Organizational learning alternatives   Institutionalizing learning as part of the planning process is one of many possible approaches. It's clear that many

Japanese companies have institutionalized learning around quality improvement teams and related innovations.

There is no shortage of ways by which learning may become an inescapable aspect of organizational life, once the nature of the commitment to learning is understood, and once appropriate tools are available.

Institutionalized experimentation "Institutionalizing experimentation can make an enormous difference," says Harvard's Dave Garvin. "For example, Allegheny Ludlum, one of the most profitable American steel companies, treats its entire production process as a laboratory for experimenting with new processes and technologies. Production managers can designate experiments they want to conduct and an entirely different set of measures and standards are used to evaluate their efforts."

Managerial microworlds Another means to institutionalizing learning, the focus of our research at MIT, involves developing *managerial microworlds*, practice fields for management teams.

A financial services microworld For example, in a microworld designed for a leading property and liability insurance company, managers discover how many of their most trusted practices, when they interact in the larger systems of which they are a part, actually contribute to runaway settlement and litigation costs.

Using a computerized *management flight simulator*, they are then able to freely experiment, in ways that would be difficult in real insurance offices, with a wide range of alternative personnel, workflow and quality management practices to find where there may be leverage in reversing the growing insurance crisis.

Eventually, we envision such microworlds being as common place in organizations as meeting rooms. There will be places where we gather to think through complex issues and learn through experimentation when trial and error learning is impossible in the real system.

Activity based cost accounting Another potential breakthrough lies in changing managerial accounting practices to reinforce learning rather than controlling.

"Managers and manufacturing engineers," says Harvard's Robert Kaplan "frequently comment that considerable operating improvements they achieve go unrecognized in their financial results."

If the emphasis is on continuous, system wide improvement, how can we have accounting practices based on historically determined standards? "Traditional cost accounting measures fail when they focus on small, local (but not system wide) measures of efficiency and productivity."

WHY BECOMING A LEARNING ORGANIZATION MATTERS

Seeing quality management as part of a deeper and even more far reaching shift leads to several realizations into why the unfolding changes in American management practices may not produce an enduring transformation.

First wave quality is still not well understood in the U.S. Despite enormous attention, public commitment by prominent corporations, and even a national award, there is a distinct possibility that American management still does not understand what the quality movement is really all about.

Specifically, we lack understanding of what is required for even first wave quality management practices to take root, and why they often fail to take root in American firms.

Confusion over the connections between learning, teams, standards, motivations and innovation   The total quality management task force at one of America's most successful high-tech manufacturing firms recently came unglued around a question of standards.

The external consultant brought in to help develop and implement the TQM strategy argued that standards and standardization were vital to gain better control of the organization's production processes, so that they could be improved. But, to some of the firm's managers, standardization meant rigidity, and a loss of freedom and respect for workers' creativity and individuality.

"Everything becomes vanilla," argued one manager. "We will kill the spark of individual creativity that has made this company what it is."

"If you're not operating in a learning orientation," observed MIT's Dan Kim, "you hear *standardization* differently than if you are. People internalize the need to improve as, *I must be deficient.* Naturally, they then resist what they perceive as an effort to make their deficiencies in public and *fix them.*"

Confusion over the meaning of continuous *and* control   The same happens with continuous improvement. Within a learning culture, continuous improvement is a natural by-product of people's commitment and empowerment. Within a controlling culture it is an admission of deficiency. "Why must I improve, unless I'm not good enough now?"

From such a view point, continuous improvement is about becoming less deficient. It is not about learning. This is why it is so deeply resisted by workers in many U.S. companies.

In response to this resistance, managers with good intentions resort to exhortation and to driving *highly mechanized* quality programs through their organizations. This creates a vicious cycle of increasing exhortation and increasing resistance. What is needed is understanding and changing the source of the resistance, which stems from bringing tools for learning into a managerial system based on controlling.

We still believe controlling people is more important than creating a learning environment   The second realization is that there is nothing in the American bag of quality tools today that will cause the shift to a learning orientation. And causing such a shift is exactly what is needed in most American corporations. Without a shift of mind from controlling to learning, or as Kim puts it, from "protect and defend" to "create and learn," we "get the tools for quality management without the substance."

Learning cannot be switched on   Creating such a shift is an organic process, not a mechanical one. It demands penetrating to deep levels of the corporate psyche and unearthing and examining deep fears.

What will it take to change?   To put it bluntly, the shift will not occur if it is not within us. It cannot be faked. It cannot be achieved by public declarations. If at some basic level, we do not genuinely value and truly desire to live life as learners, it will not happen.

My experience is that it can only be caused by small groups of thoughtful leaders who truly desire to build an organization where people are committed to a larger purpose and to thinking for themselves.

Such thoughtful groups then must be willing to become models of continually learning, with all the vulnerability and uncertainty that implies. They become lead users of new learning tools and approaches.

Public and organizational learning/education are linked   The last, and potentially most important, realization is that the transformation in corporate and public education may be linked.

''Humans are the learning organism *par excellence*'' according to anthropologist Edward T. Hall. ''The drive to learn is as strong as the sexual drive—it begins earlier and lasts longer.''

If the drive to learn is so strong, why is it so weak in our corporations?   What happened to our ''intrinsic joy in learning,'' as Dr. Deming puts it. The answer according to Deming, Hall, and many educators lies, surprisingly, as much in the classroom as on the factory floor. ''The forces of destruction begin with toddlers,'' says Deming, ''. . . a prize for the best Halloween costume, grades in school, gold stars—and on up through the university.''

Performing versus learning   The young child in school quickly learns that the name of the game is not learning it is *performing*. Mistakes are punished, correct answers rewarded. If you don't have the right answer, keep your mouth shut.

If we had operated under that system as two-year olds, none of us would have ever learned to walk. Is it any wonder the manager or worker shows little intrinsic motivation to *learn*—that is, to experiment and discover new insights from *mistakes*, outcomes that don't turn out according to plan.

If the conditioning toward performing for others rather than learning is so deeply established in schools, it may not be possible to reverse it on the job. If knowledge is always something somebody else has and I don't, then learning becomes embedded in deep instincts of self-protection not free experimentation.

If the identification of *boss* with *teacher*, the authority figure who has the answers and is the arbiter of our performance is so firmly anchored, we may never be able to roll up our sleeves and all become learners together.

Today, there is no lack of corporate concern for the erosion in our public education. But, there is a lack of vision as to what is truly needed. It is not enough to go back to the 3R's. We must revolutionize the school experience so that it nurtures and deepens our love of learning, develops new skills of integrative or systemic thinking, and helps us learn how to learn, especially together.

FINAL THOUGHTS

I recently asked Dr. Deming if he thought it was possible to fully implement his philosophy of management without radical reform in our schools, as well as in our corporations. ''No'' was his answer.

However, if we come to a deeper understanding of the linkage between school and work in the 21st century, we may be able to generate a wholly new vision and commitment to the vital task of rethinking both. This may be the real promise of the *learning organization.*

2

Total Quality Management Classics

Introduction

Readings in Part II are selections from some of the best known founding fathers of the modern quality movement. The first reading by Armand Feigenbaum introduced the concept of "Total Quality Control" in a systematic way in 1956. It is striking, from a 1990s perspective, how insightful and comprehensive Dr. Feigenbaum's ideas were at such an early period of evolution of the quality movement.

The readings by Deming, Juran and Crosby illustrate some of the original ideas of the three best known American representatives of the quality movement. Over time their ideas have evolved and been extended to new fields of application.

Japanese quality thinking is represented by Kaoru Ishikawa, whose book "Total Quality Control" remains one of the most lucid, clear, and comprehensive texts in the field. A further reading by a well known Japanese quality expert, Mizuno, can be found in Part III, which is dedicated to the quality tools. Many names are still missing. Among these are Shingo, Taguchi, Kano, Ouchi, etc. Their writings are often highly technical and focused on specific applications (e.g. Taguchi's writings on experimental design) and beyond the scope of this book. Ouchi's analysis of Theory Z is widely known, and readily accessible.

Suggestions in Reading and Study

The readings in this section should be complemented by recent writings of both American and Japanese quality "gurus." Some books like Deming's "Out of the Crisis" go beyond the narrow field of manufacturing quality applications and examine broad societal issues. Other, focus on highly technical applications. A literature review of this sort is useful to understand the historic development of quality concepts, practical applications of the different quality concepts, and discover fruitful areas for applied research. Such effort is best undertaken in the context of teams who survey a particular field or set of readings and provide the larger group with annotated bibliographies and executive summaries.

Total Quality Control

———

By Armand V. Feigenbaum

To design, process, and sell products competitively in the 1956 market place, American businessmen must take full account of these crucial trends:

Customers—both industrial and consumer—have been increasing their quality requirements very sharply in recent years. This tendency is likely to be greatly amplified by the intense competition that seems inevitable in the near future.

For example, the electrical relay that could command the lion's share of the 1950 industrial market is no longer acceptable for 1956 operating needs. Consumers are progressively more minute in their examination of the finish of appliances, or in their judgment of the tone of a radio or television set. Even for military products on which quality has always been the major consideration—e.g., jet engines, airborne electronics, and ordnance—specifications are continually being made more rigorous.

As a result of this increased customer demand for higher quality products, present in-plant quality practices and techniques are now, or soon will be, outmoded.

Thus, the machined part that could once be checked with a pocket scale or a pair of micrometers must now be carefully measured with an air gauge; and material that could once be visually accepted if it were "reddish brown and shiny" must now be carefully analyzed both chemically and physically to assure that it is beryllium copper instead of phosphor bronze. At the same time, automation, in which rapid quality evaluation is a pivotal point, has magnified the need for mechanization of inspection and test equipment—much of which is now in the hand-tool stage. Indeed, the quality control content of the manufacturing equipment investment dollar may well double in the next decade to purchase the benefit of this mechanization.

Quality costs have become very high. For many companies they may be much too high if these companies are to maintain and improve their competitive position over the long run.

In fact, quality costs (inspection, testing, laboratory checks, scrap, rework, customer complaints, and similar expenses) have crept up to become a multimillion-dollar item. For many businesses they are comparable in degree with total direct labor dollars, with distribution dollars, or with purchased material dollars! While I can find no documented research on the subject, evidence points strongly to the fact that many businesses have quality-cost expenditures representing 7%, 8%, 10%, and even more of their cost of sales!

Taken together, these three trends spell out the twin quality objective that 1956 competitive conditions present to American business management: (a) considerable improvement in the quality of many products and many quality practices, and, at the same time, (b) substantial reductions in the over-all costs of maintaining quality.

Under these conditions, if quality must be not only maintained but upgraded, the wave of the future looks like an expensive one to ride. How many of the frailer business craft will be able to avoid getting swamped?

BROAD SCOPE

Fortunately, there is a way out of the dilemma imposed on businessmen by increasingly demanding customers and by ever-spiraling costs of quality. This "way out" seems to lie in a new kind of quality control, which might be called "total quality control."

The underlying principle of this total quality view—and its basic difference from all other concepts—is that, to provide genuine effectiveness, control must start with the design of the product and end only when the product has been placed in the hands of a customer who remains satisfied.

The reason for this breadth of scope is that the quality of any product is affected at many stages of the industrial cycle:

1. Marketing evaluates the level of quality which customers want and for which they are willing to pay.
2. Engineering reduces this marketing evaluation to exact specifications.
3. Purchasing chooses, contracts with, and retains vendors for parts and materials.
4. Manufacturing engineering selects the jigs, tools, and processes for relay production.
5. Manufacturing supervision and shop operators exert a major quality influence during parts making, subassembly, and final assembly.
6. Mechanical inspection and functional test check conformance to specifications.
7. Shipping influences the caliber of the packaging and transportation.

In other words, the determination both of quality and of quality cost actually takes place throughout the entire industrial cycle. This is the reason why real quality control cannot be accomplished by concentrating on inspection alone, or design alone, or reject trouble-shooting alone, or operator education alone, or statistical analysis alone—important as each of these individual elements is.

The breadth of the job makes quality control a new and important business management function. Just as the theme of the historical inspection activity was "they (i.e., bad parts) shall not pass," the theme of this new approach is "make them right the first time." Emphasis is on defect prevention so that routine inspection will not be needed to as large an extent. The burden of quality proof rests, not with inspection, but with the makers of the part—machinist, assembly foreman, vendor, as the case may be.

Like traditional inspection, the quality control function in this total quality view is still responsible for assurance of the quality of products shipped, but its broader scope places a major addition on this responsibility. Quality control becomes responsible for quality assurance *at optimum quality costs.*

The total quality view sees the prototype quality control man, not as an inspector, but as a quality control engineer—with an adequate background of the applicable product technology and with training in statistical methods, in inspection techniques, and in other useful tools for improving and controlling product quality.

Compared with other Views

It may serve further to clarify the character of the total quality view if we compare it with other quality control concepts. Actually, there have been and are today a great many different concepts both of the meaning of the term "quality control" and of what the principal elements of the quality control activity are. The two most widely accepted of these concepts may be described as the "modern inspection view" and the "statistical view."

Historically, quality control meant nothing more than the activity of traditional factory inspection, which was intended to protect the customer by screening bad material from good prior to shipment. In the *modern inspection view*, quality control means this traditional inspection function updated and made more efficient by the use of certain statistical methods and work-in-process inspection routines. Thus:

Statistically verified sampling plans assure the quality of outgoing lots better and more economically than do the older 100% inspection or hit-or-miss spot check procedures.

In-process sampling inspections detect quality errors before too many bad parts have been produced, and are consequently more effective than concentration on final inspection with its risk of producing a large number of bad parts.

An impressive weight of dollars-and-cents evidence demonstrates that such techniques represent a great improvement over old-fashioned practices. Probably most systems of quality control in American business today are examples of this modern inspection point of view. That is, they see the prototype quality control man as a well-grounded inspection specialist who has had training in useful statistical methods.

The *statistical view*, in turn, reflects the major and increasing contributions which probability methods are making to the improvement of industrial decision making. It is a view that predominates both in the literature of quality control and in professional meetings on the subject. It sees the prototype quality control man as an industrial statistician, who works on problems ranging from the design of laboratory experiments, through the establishment of control charts for production processes, on to the analysis of manufacturing rejects. It sees him, in other words, as capable of making contributions in fields not directly connected with product quality, such as time study and safety.

These modern inspection and statistical concepts of quality control have been and are highly useful in the areas of product quality which they cover. But, compared with total quality control, their scope is much too limited; they are able to provide only a partial grasp of the over-all quality problem that faces American businessmen. They simply are not geared to the fact that quality considerations are involved in every phase of industrial activity, and are not equipped to keep over-all costs of quality at a minimum.

Effect of Cost Accounting

If the burden and sharp upward trend of these quality costs—and the need for genuinely broad quality control effort—are only now becoming recognized in some businesses, part of the reason must be ascribed to traditional industrial cost accounting practices. Cost accounting methods often have not identified and grouped quality costs in a form suitable for the development of adequate controls. The magnitude of the quality cost sum has tended to be obscured by the piecemeal identification of certain individual quality cost elements: for example, scrap and spoilage, or field complaint expense. Most often, quality cost has been conceived as the cost of the company inspection activity—actually just a fraction of over-all quality cost—and controls have been established on this fragmentary basis.

Regardless of the source of the fault, the only clear answer to the quality cost problem seems to lie in the new concept of total quality control.

Operation of the Function

The work of this total quality control function may be classified into four broad categories, as follows (see Exhibit 1 for elaboration):

1. New design control, or the planning of controls for new or modified products prior to the start of production.
2. Incoming material control, or the control of incoming purchased parts and materials.

EXHIBIT 1 *Quality Control in the Quality Activity Cycle*

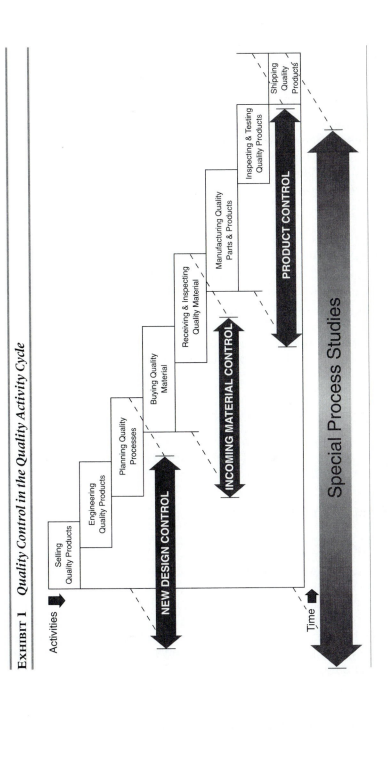

3. Product control, or the shop floor control of materials, parts, and batches from machines, processes, and assembly lines.

4. Special process studies, or the conducting of special analyses of factory and processing problems.

In this work, the two basic responsibilities of the quality control function are: (1) to provide quality assurance for the company's product—i.e., simply, to be sure that the products shipped are right; and (2) to assist in assuring optimum quality costs for those products. It fulfills these responsibilities through its subfunctions: *quality control engineering, inspection,* and *test,* which operate a continuous feedback cycle:

1. Quality control engineering does *quality planning;* this establishes the basic framework of the quality control system for the firm's products.

2. Inspection and test do *quality measuring;* this determines, in accordance with the quality plan, the conformance and performance of parts and products with engineering specifications.

3. There is rapid feedback to quality control engineering for *quality analysis,* which results in new quality planning, thus completing the cycle. (This analysis also fosters corrective action for product quality deviations.)

ENGINEERING COMPONENT

The true nerve center of the total quality control function is the engineering component. Its activities in each of the four broad quality control jobs deserve examination in some detail.

New Design Control

In this area, quality control engineering provides three main activities:

1. *Preproduction service to design engineering and manufacturing engineering in analyzing the quality-ability of new products and production processes, and in de-bugging quality problems*—This assures a product which will be as defect-free as possible *prior* to the start of production. Among the new technical tools which the quality control engineer brings to this effort are process quality capability studies, tolerance analysis technique, pilot run practice, and a wide variety of statistical methods.

2. *Planning of inspections and tests to be carried on when production is under way on the new product*—This is to establish continuous control of in-process quality. It involves determining the following:

   • Dimensions and characteristics of the parts to be checked.

   • Degree to which they are to be checked.

- In-process and final production points at which checks are required.
- Methods and procedures to be used—including statistical sampling plans, control charts, and so on.
- Personnel who will make the checks—that is, production operators or people from the inspection and test subfunctions.

3. *Design of genuinely modern inspection and testing equipment, which, to the fullest possible extent, is physically integrated with manufacturing equipment to permit the machine to check its own work*—The aim of this activity is economical investment expenditures, maximum equipment utilization, and fullest practical mechanization and automation both of operations and of quality control paper work.

Incoming Material Control

In this area, quality control engineering must assist in the establishment of good quality relationships with suppliers. It contributes to this objective in the following ways:

By planning the periodic rating of the quality performance of present suppliers, it provides facts which assist the purchasing function in quickly bringing satisfactory or unsatisfactory quality performance to the attention of vendors.

By evaluating the quality capability of potential suppliers, it provides facts which assist purchasing to select good quality vendors.

By working with the vendors, it assists them in understanding the quality control requirements of the purchase contracts they have won.

By establishing quality certification programs, it places the burden of quality proof on the vendor rather than on an extensive, expensive in-plant incoming inspection effort.

Product Control

In this area, quality control engineering carries on the cost measurement and quality cost reduction project activity required for over-all quality cost control and reduction, and it works closely with the inspection and test subfunctions which perform the actual measuring work. It also performs process quality capability studies to determine the quality limits within which a machine or process may be expected to operate. The aim is to make sure that parts will be routed to equipment which is capable of economically maintaining engineering specifications.

Special Process Studies

In this area, the job of quality control engineering is to analyze complex, in-process quality problems which have been fed back to it by inspection and test. These studies are directed both to the elimination of defects and to the development of possible improvements in present quality levels.

SPECIALIZED ACTIVITY

Certain elements of this quality control engineering work have previously been performed on a sporadic or divided basis. But the quality control engineer himself is something new under the sun. For quality control engineering is not merely a new label for the inspection planning package, nor a fresh designation for the test equipment engineer, nor yet a technologically flavored title for the industrial statistician. It is, instead, a specialized activity with a character all its own, calling for a unique combination of skills.

Quality control engineering work is the product of the cross-fertilization of modern developments in several fields—in statistical methodology, in fast-response high-precision inspection and testing equipment, in management understanding of the nature of the control function in modern business. Altogether, it has the attributes of a genuinely new sector of the engineering profession.

In experience, education, aptitude, and attitude, the man entering quality control engineering work today is, in fact, not very different from the man entering other longer established major technical fields as, for example, product engineering or manufacturing engineering. He must possess, or have the capacity to acquire, the necessary product and process background. He must have the personal characteristics to work effectively in a dynamic atmosphere with people of diverse interests. He must possess the technical background which will enable him to acquire, if he does not already have it, a growing body of quality control engineering knowledge. Finally, he needs the analytical ability to use this knowledge in solving new and different quality problems.

Inspection and Test

The planning and analysis work of the quality control engineer makes a new, more positive type of inspection and test both possible and necessary in the modern quality control function. Instead of policing the manufacturing process, this type of inspection and test becomes a direct *part* of that process by assisting in the production of good quality products.

Thus, during incoming material control and product control, the inspection and test subfunctions are responsible not only for fully establishing that the materials received and the products in-process and shipped are of the specified quality, but also for thoroughly and promptly feeding back facts for preventing the purchase and production of poor quality material in the future.

This positive quality measuring requires only a very minimum of routine hand-sorting inspection and test. In product control, for example, this result is made possible through a continuous sequence of engineering work to assure that with the facilities provided production operators can make parts right the first time, know that they can, and have the necessary equipment and gauges to check their own work. On this basis, then, inspection and test can provide genuine assistance in the production of the right quality by:

- Becoming auditors of the good quality practices that have been established.
- Providing as much as possible on-the-spot, shop floor analysis of defects.
- Feeding back facts about these defects for corrective analysis and action elsewhere.

Such quality assurance effort has been termed *control-audit* inspection and test. Inevitably it means the upgrading of traditional inspection and test; it requires considerably fewer but much more highly qualified and more specialized personnel—those who have genuine ability to be helpful in making the right quality. An instance in point is the arc-welding inspector who now not only knows whether or not weld penetration on a part is satisfactory but also, in the case of defective welds, may be able to counsel the shop on the reasons why the penetration has been unsatisfactory.

ORGANIZATIONAL PROBLEM

In organizing a modern quality control function, the first principle to recognize is *that quality is everybody's job*.

In defiance of this principle, there have been many business experiments over the years which have attempted to make the quality activity cycle less of a decentralized, Tinkers-to-Evers-to-Chance sequence. Often these attempts have taken the form of centralizing all quality responsibility by organizing a component whose job was handsomely described as "responsibility for all factors affecting product quality."

These experiments have had a life span of as long as six months—when the job incumbent had the advantage of a strong stomach, a rhinoceros hide, and a well-spent and sober boyhood. Others not similarly endowed did not last even that long.

The simple fact of the matter is that the marketing man is in the best position to evaluate adequately customer's quality preferences; the design engineer is the only man who can effectively establish specification quality levels; the shop supervisor is the individual who can best concentrate on the building of quality. Total quality control programs therefore require, as a first step, top management's re-emphasis on the responsibility and accountability of *all* company employees in new design control, incoming material control, product control, and special process studies.

The second principle of total quality control organization is a corollary to the first one. It is *that because quality is everybody's job, it may become nobody's job*. Thus the second major step required in total quality programs becomes clear. Top management must recognize that the many individual responsibilities for quality will be exercised most effectively when they are buttressed and serviced by a well-organized, genuinely modern management function whose only area of specialization is product quality, and whose only area of operation is in the quality control job.

Location of the Function

In view of these two organizational principles, where should the quality control function be placed in the larger structure of company organization? Should it be part of marketing, of engineering, of manufacturing? Should it report direct to general management?

While these are crucial questions, they are not susceptible to categorical answers. Certainly, quality control in any company should report high enough so that it can implement its responsibilities for quality assurance at optimum costs. Certainly, also, it should be close enough to the firing line so that it will be able to fulfill its technological role. However, companies vary widely in their objectives, their character, their philosophy of organization structure, and their technology. The answer to the question of where to locate quality control will necessarily vary also.

It may be worthwhile, however, to report one firm's approach to this issue. In the General Electric Company's product departments, each of which operates as a decentralized business with profit and loss accountability reposing with the department general manager, the cycle of basic quality responsibility is as follows:

The marketing component is responsible for evaluating customers' quality preferences and determining the prices these customers are willing to pay for the various quality levels.

The engineering component is responsible for translating marketing's requirements into exact drawings and specifications.

The manufacturing component is responsible for building products to these drawings, and for knowing that it has done so.

Within this structure of responsibility, quality control clearly emerges as a *manufacturing* function. Thus, in the General Electric product department, the quality control manager reports to the chief manufacturing executive in that department—the manufacturing manager—and operates at the same organization level as the production superintendents, the managers of materials, and the managers of manufacturing engineering.

THE RESULTS

Experience in an increasing number of companies shows that operation of a total quality control program has paid off in six ways:

1. Improved product quality.
2. Reduced scrap, complaint, inspection, and other quality costs.
3. Better product design.
4. Elimination of many production bottlenecks.
5. Improved processing methods.
6. Development of a greater spirit of quality-mindedness on the production shop floor.

Certainly our experience with this program has been highly satisfactory in the General Electric Company, where we have been developing the concept and procedure for some years.

Total quality control has thus, in actual practice, been successful in meeting the dual objective of better quality at lower quality costs. The reason for the satisfactory better-quality result is fairly clear from the very nature of the prevention-centered, step-by-step, technically thorough program. But the explanation may not be nearly so obvious for the accompanying by-product of lower over-all quality cost. This needs to be spelled out, especially since it includes, in the long run, lower expenses for the quality control activities themselves as compared with the costs of traditional inspection and test.

Costs of Quality

The reason for the favorable cost result of total quality control is that it cuts the two *major* cost segments of quality (which might be called failure and appraisal costs) by means of much smaller increases in the third and *smallest* segment (prevention costs). Why this is possible can be seen as soon as the character of these three categories is considered:

1. Failure costs are caused by defective materials and products that do not meet company quality specifications. They include such loss elements as scrap, spoilage, rework, field complaints, etc.
2. Appraisal costs include the expenses for maintaining company quality levels by means of formal evaluations of product quality. This involves such cost elements as inspection, test, quality audits, laboratory acceptance examinations, and outside endorsements.
3. Prevention costs are for the purpose of keeping defects from occurring in the first place. Included here are such costs as quality control engineering, employee quality training, and the quality maintenance of patterns and tools.

In the absence of formal nationwide studies of quality costs in various businesses, it is impossible to generalize with any authority about the relative magnitude of these three elements of quality cost. However, I believe it would not be far wrong to assert that failure costs may represent from one-half to three-quarters of total quality costs, while appraisal costs probably range in the neighborhood of one-quarter of this total. Prevention costs, on the other hand, probably do not exceed one-tenth of the quality cost total in most businesses. Out of this 10%, usually 8%–9% are directed into such traditional channels as pattern and tool maintenance and the specification-changing or interpreting work of product engineering. This leaves only 1% or 2% that is spent for elements of quality control engineering work.

It is a significant fact that, historically, under the traditional inspection function, failure and appraisal costs have tended to move upward together, and it has been difficult to pull them down once they have started to rise. The reason for this relationship is that:

As defects increase—thus pushing up failure costs—the number of inspectors has been increased to maintain the "they shall not pass" screen to protect the customer. This, in turn, has pushed up appraisal costs.

For the reasons mentioned earlier in this article, screening inspection does not have much effect in eliminating the defects, nor can it completely prevent some of the defective products from leaving the plant and going into the hands of complaining customers.

Appraisal costs thus stay up as long as failure costs remain high. In fact, the higher these failure and appraisal costs go, the higher they are likely to go without successful preventive activity.

Once these two main elements of quality cost have started to rise—as they seem to have throughout industry generally today—the one best hope for pulling them to earth again seems to be spending more on the third and smallest element, namely, prevention cost. The 10% now spent may well need to be doubled, much of the increase going for quality control engineering as well as for improved methods of inspection and test equipment automation.

At first glance such increases in prevention costs may not seem to be in the interest of quality cost improvement, but this objection is rapidly dispelled as soon as results are considered. Translated into quality cost terms, the operation of total quality control has the following sequence of results:

1. A substantial cut in failure costs—which has the highest cost reduction potential of all quality cost elements—occurs because of the reduced number of defects and the improvements in product quality brought about by modern quality control practice.
2. Fewer defects mean somewhat less need for routine inspection and test, causing a reduction in appraisal costs.
3. Better inspection and test equipment and practices, and the replacement of many routine operators by less numerous but more effective *control audit* inspectors and testers, bring about additional reductions in appraisal costs.

4. Because the new *control-audit* inspection and test is effective in preventing de-fects, appraisal dollars for the first time begin to exercise a positive downward pull on failure costs.

The ultimate end result is that total quality control brings about a sizable re-duction in overall quality costs, and a major alteration in the proportions of the three cost segments. No large, long-term increase in the size of the quality control function is required as a necessary condition for quality cost improvement. Instead, quality control expense, as a proportion of total company expense, will be down in the long run. Improvements of one-third or more in over-all quality costs are not unusual.

Quality Dollar Budgeting

It is worth noting that this identification and analysis of quality costs permits a major forward step in the business budgeting process. That is, it makes feasible determin-ing the dollars needed for quality control, not on the basis of historical inspection cost experience, but on the basis of current company objectives in product quality and quality costs.

Quality needs and problems differ so much from company to company that it is not realistic to generalize about the specific mix of quality costs that should be budgeted under total quality control. But the direction of budgetary trends may be suggested by an example, which embodies current industrial experience in this area. Exhibit 2 shows how one company expects to cut its quality costs by switching from a mild version of the inspection view to total quality control. The company anticipates that total quality expenses will drop from the current high of 7% of sales to 5%, with declines achieved both in failure and appraisal costs while prevention costs increase from only 0.70% of sales to a still modest 1.25%. In this example, the cost savings budgeted are rather moderate, owing to the presence of complicating factors such as the following:

EXHIBIT 2   *Budgeted Quality Costs and Savings under Total Quality Control (Assuming sales increase from $50 million to $75 million)*

Quality Cost Element	Total Dollars Present	Total Dollars 5-Year Goal	Percent of Sales Present	Percent of Sales 5-Year Goal	Percent of Total Quality Cost Present	Percent of Total Quality Cost 5-Year Goal
Failure	$2,275,000	$2,062,500	4.55%	2.75%	65%	55%
Appraisal	875,000	750,000	1.75	1.00	25	20
Prevention	350,000	937,500	0.70	1.25	10	25
Total	$3,500,000	$3,750,000	7.00%	5.00%	100%	100%

- An anticipated 50% increase in sales over the next five years—from $50 million to $75 million.
- Planned additions to a product line that is already highly technical and diversified, hence accompanied by major quality problems.

Such a planned 30% improvement in quality cost ratios is feasible, indeed conservative, with a successful total quality control program—even with a 50% business expansion and even with counterbalancing quality cost increases brought about by the introduction of new products. While the company in the example may not be typical (probably there is no such thing as a typical business enterprise), it is at least illustrative of the good results that can be achieved even when circumstances pose unusual difficulties.

CONCLUSION

Total quality control thus represents another forward step in management science. Its integration of design-through-shipment control of the many elements in the quality picture makes it much more effective than the unlinked fragmentary controls of the past. As a major new business management activity, it provides professional effort in meeting the objective of assured product quality at minimum quality cost.

With this concept, inspection and test have a chance to develop in the direction that conscientious inspectors and testers have always sought; that is, into an activity with a positive role in assisting other members of the manufacturing, engineering, and marketing team toward quality improvement and quality cost control. No longer are inspection and test confined to essentially a negative, fist-shaking role in sorting bad parts from good, a role placing them continually on the defensive and evoking the hostility of other managers.

Further, those tools of statistical methodology that have proved practical and useful can now be brought to their fullest effectiveness. With the quality control engineers as tool builders, and the control-audit inspectors as tool users, statistical techniques can be put to work in a down-to-earth fashion that welds them into regular day-by-day controls. No longer will these techniques be treated—as too often in the past—merely as curiosities, to be employed in special situations on a pinch-hitting basis.

With equipment for inspection and test a direct and major responsibility of the quality control function, more use can be made of equipment specialists who wish to concentrate their skills on the great needs, opportunities, and unique complexities of today's quality control equipment field.

Total quality control thus welds this new technology into a strong yet flexible weapon, capable of successfully coming to grips with the three major quality problems that modern business must face and solve: the upward customer pressure on quality levels, the resulting rapid obsolescence of quality practices, the very high level of quality costs.

While delivery and other factors may sell a product the first time, it is usually quality which keeps the product sold and which keeps the customer coming back a second and a third time. Quality cost—perhaps 8% or more of cost of sales—is one of the major elements of product cost that must be made right to permit the setting of the right price to the customer. Helping to assure this right quality at this right quality cost is the way the new *total quality control* can serve its company in the years ahead.

Reading 7

On Some Statistical Aids toward Economic Production[1]

By W. EDWARDS DEMING

ABSTRACT

This paper covers management's responsibility for (1) design of product; (2) specification of service offered; (3) measurement by simple statistical methods of the amount of trouble with product or with service that can be ascribed to causes that only management can act on; (4) action on the causes so indicated. It shows by principle and by example how management may observe week by week the effects of guided effort toward reduction of trouble. The paper upsets a number of commonly accepted principles of administration. For example, a job description, for best economy, should require the production worker to achieve statistical control of his work; to meet specifications without paying the high cost of inspection, rework, and replacement. Statistical evidence of performance replaces opinion of foreman and supervisor.

As a second principle, it is demoralizing and costly to call the attention of a production worker to a defective item when he is in a state of statistical control. The fault for the defective item is not chargeable to the worker, but to the system. Fewer defectives can come only from a change in the system, not from efforts of the production worker.

Third, it is better to shift to a totally different job a worker that has developed statistical control of bad habits in his present job.

All variation in quality characteristics (dimension, hardness, color) causes loss, whether the variation results in defective product or not. Economies in manufacture are a natural consequence of reduction in the variation of a quality characteristic. The author divides causes of variation into two sources: (1) the system (common causes), the responsibility of management; (2) special causes, which are under the governance of the individual employee. In the author's experience, losses from the system overshadow losses from special causes. The same principles apply to sales and to service.

PURPOSE AND SCOPE OF THIS PAPER

One purpose of this paper is to present a number of new principles of training and administration that upset generally accepted conventions. The new principles had their origin in the author's work in Japan, which commenced in 1950 [1], [2].

Another purpose is to point out to management that most of the trouble with faulty product, recalls, high cost of production and service, is chargeable to the system and hence to management. Effort to improve the performance of workers will be a disappointment until the handicap of the system is reduced.

The principles explained here will apply to any company, large or small, whether engaged in production of manufactured items or in service (hotel, hospital, restaurant, retail store, wholesale, railway, motor freight, delivery service, communication, including the postal service), agricultural or industrial, whether owned by private investment or by the government, and in any country, whether it be developed, underdeveloped, or overdeveloped.

Many causes have contributed to devaluation of the dollar and to our precarious balance of payments, but one contributor, steadfastly avoided by economists, is that the quality of many American products is no longer competitive, here or abroad. Statisticians have failed in America to explain to people in management the impact that statistical methods could make on quality, production, marketing, labor-relations, and competitive position. Schools of business teach words and goals, but not methods.

The reader will note, I hope, that I write as a statistician, working with management on problems in industry and in research in many disciplines. I am not a consultant in management. I am not an economist.

ROADBLOCKS TO QUALITY IN AMERICA

An obstacle that ensures disappointment is the supposition all too prevalent that quality control is something that you install, like a new Dean, or a new carpet, or new furniture. Install it and you have it. This supposition is unfortunately force-fed by the common language of quality control engineers, some of whom offer to install a quality control system. Actually, quality control, to be successful in any company, must be a learning-process, year by year, from the top downward and from the bottom up, with accumulation of knowledge and experience, under competent tutelage.

Another roadblock is management's supposition that the production workers are responsible for all trouble: that there would be no problems in production or in service if only the workers would do their jobs in the way that they were taught. Pleasant dreams. The workers are handicapped by the system.

In my experience, it is something new and incomprehensible to a man in an executive position that management could be at fault in the production end. Production and quality, in the view of management, are the responsibilities of the production worker. Research into faults of the system, to be corrected by management, is not what a manager is trained for. Result: The faults of the system stay put, along with rejections and high costs of production.

Management usually discharges its responsibilities (sweeps them under the rug) by turning the job over to a department of quality control. This would be a happy solution and good administration if it solved anything, but it seldom does: the job lands on people that try hard but have not the necessary competence, and the management never knows the difference.

As a result, one finds in most companies not quality control, but guerrilla sniping—no provision nor appreciation for the statistical control of quality in the broad sense of this paper.

People in management need to know enough about quality control to be able to judge whether their quality control departments are doing the job.

Statements by management of aims desired in quality and production are not quality control, nor are they action on improvement of the system. Neither are periodic reviews and evaluations of quality and production. They are necessary but not sufficient.

Exhortations, pleas, and platitudes addressed to the rank and file in an organization are not very effective instruments for the improvement of quality. Something more is required.

I should mention here also the costly fallacy held by many people in management that a technical man (a statistician, for example) must know all about a process and all about the business in order to work in the company. All evidence points to the contrary. Competent men in every position, from top management to the humblest worker, if they are doing their best, know all there is to know about their work *except how to improve it*. Help toward improvement can come *only from some other kind of knowledge*. Help may come from outside the company, or from better use of knowledge and skills already within the company, or both.

LOSS FROM VARIATION: TWO SOURCES OF VARIATION

It is good management to reduce the variation of any quality characteristic (thickness, or measure of performance), whether this characteristic be in a state of control or not, and even when no or few defectives are produced. Reduction in variation means greater uniformity and dependability of product, greater output per hour, greater output per unit of raw material, and better competitive position [5], [7].

Causes of variation and of high cost, with loss of competitive position, may be usefully subsumed under two categories:

Faults of the System (Common or Environmental Causes)
85%

These faults stay in the system until reduced by management. Their combined effect is usually easy to measure. Some individual causes must be isolated by judgment. Others may be identified by experiment: some by records on operations and materials suspected of being offenders (see reference to Juran).

Special Causes
15%

These causes are specific to a certain worker or to a machine. A statistical signal detects the existence of a special cause, which the worker can usually identify and correct.

Both types of cause require attention of management. Common causes get their name from the fact that they are common to a whole group of workers: they belong to the system [2].

No improvement of the system, nor any reduction of special causes of variation and trouble, will take place unless management attacks common causes with as much science and vigor as the production-workers and engineers attack special causes [3].

The percentages shown, are intended only to indicate that, in my experience, problems of the system overshadow special causes. The percentages will fluctuate as special causes are eliminated one by one, and as faults of the system are reduced or eliminated.

Confusion between the two types of cause leads to frustration at all levels, and leads to greater variability and to higher costs—exactly contrary to what is needed.

Fortunately, this confusion can be eliminated with almost unerring accuracy. Simple statistical techniques, distributions, run-charts, Shewhart control charts, all explained in many books, provide signals that tell the operator when to take action to improve the uniformity of his work. They also tell him when to leave it alone. Results of inspection, without signals, lead to frustration and dissatisfaction of any conscientious worker.

What is not in the books, nor known generally amongst quality-control engineers, is that the same charts that send statistical signals to the production worker also indicate the totality of fault that belongs to the system itself, correction of which is management's responsibility [2]. The production worker can observe from his charts whether attempts by management to improve the system have had an effect. Management can give themselves the same test. Examples appear further on.

Removal of a special cause of variation, important though it be, is not improvement of the system: it merely reduces the variation to a level that identifies the system, but leaves it unimproved.

Mechanical feed-backs that hold dimensions and other quality characteristics within bounds are sometimes helpful but may be wasteful of material and of machine-time. They do not improve the system. Better understanding of the function of feed-back systems, so as to use them effectively, and to supplement them, will be an important step for management.

"We rely on our experience," is the answer that came from the manager of quality in a large company recently, when I inquired how he distinguishes between the two kinds of trouble, and on what principles. This answer is self-incriminating: It is a guarantee that this company will continue to pile up about the same amount of trouble as in the past. Why should it change?

"Bill," I asked of the manager of a large company engaged in motor freight, "how much of this trouble (shortage and damage, 7911 examples in one terminal alone in 1974) is the fault of the drivers?" His reply, "All of it," is again a guarantee that this level of loss will continue until statistical methods detect some of the sources of trouble with the system for Bill to work on.

The QC-Circle movement in Japan (3 million members; 4 to 8 workers to a circle) gives employees the chance to study and revise the system of production at the local level, for greater output and better quality. Japanese workers are not handicapped by the rigidity of the American production line. The QC-Circles represent partial decentralization of management's responsibility to find local faults in the system, and to take action on them. The QC-Circles in Japan bear no relationship to suggestion boxes, common everywhere.

The boost in morale of the production worker, if he were to perceive a genuine attempt on the part of management to improve the system and to hold the production worker responsible only for what the production worker is responsible for and can govern, and not for handicaps placed on him by the system, would be hard to overestimate. It has not been tried, I believe, outside Japan.

It is now clear that the term zero defects can only be a theatrical catchword, a nostrum. The management of many concerns have adopted it outright or in equivalent form and have posted it all over the plant for everyone to see, especially visitors, expecting magic. Empty words they are till the management acknowledges responsibility toward reduction of common causes. One company that I know of reduced their defects by eliminating 8 inspectors out of 10. This is a successful approach until the defectives start coming back with claims attached.

THUMBNAIL SKETCH OF THE STATE OF STATISTICAL CONTROL

Some understanding of the concept of statistical control, invented by Shewhart [6] is necessary as background. A state of statistical control is a state of randomness. Simple tests of randomness are the Shewhart charts—run charts, $\bar{x}$-charts, R-charts. The up and down movements on a chart are to be disregarded by the production-worker unless there is indication of a special cause. A point that falls outside the control limits is a statistical signal that indicates the existence of a special cause of variation. This the production worker can almost always identify readily and correct.

Control limits are not specification limits. Control limits are set by simple statistical calculations from the output itself. What the control limits do is to send out signals that if heeded will minimize the net loss from the two kinds of mistakes that the production worker can make:

1. Adjust his work process when it would be better to leave it alone.
2. Fail to adjust his work process when it needs adjustment. The only rational and economic guide to minimum loss is statistical signals.

The production worker himself may in most cases plot the statistical charts that will tell him whether and when to take action on his work. He requires only a knowledge of simple arithmetic. But the production worker cannot by himself start his own chart, and still less a movement for use of charts. Management must start the movement, and stay on the job.

Some processes in nature exhibit statistical control. Radioactive disintegration is an example. The distribution of time to failure of vacuum tubes and of many other pieces of complex apparatus furnish further examples. But a state of statistical control is not a natural state for a work process. It is instead an achievement, arrived at by elimination one by one, by determined effort, of special causes of excessive variation.

Figure 1 shows the results of inspection from a process that is not in statical control. The upper panel ($\bar{x}$) average of 5 successive items indicates the existence of special causes. There are points below the lower control limit and too many points on the border of the upper control limit. The lower panel (range (R) shows a downward trend, which, although it may indeed be a trend toward greater uniformity, indicates nevertheless also the existence of one or more (possibly additional) special causes, which again the worker must discover and correct. The charts thus indicate the existence of special causes, elimination or reduction of which is the responsibility of the operator. The reader may turn to Figures 2 and 4 to see a state of statistical control.

A process has an identity only if it is in a state of statistical control. The control limits, and the size of the sample, then enable management to predict rationally the level and range of variation of product that will be produced tomorrow. The same principles and rules are applicable to service organizations.

Statistical control thus provides a basis for doing business in a rational way. The manufacturer knows what quality he can produce, and at what cost. He will not walk into heavy loss by taking a contract for uniformity that he cannot meet, or can meet only by inspection and rework, always costly and unsatisfactory. He can make no rational prediction about his product and costs when his processes are not in statistical control.

Results of inspection are too often unreliable—worse, are sources of strife—because of mistrust of the measurements whether made by use of instruments or by

FIGURE 1   *A Control Chart Showing the Existence of Special Causes of Variation*

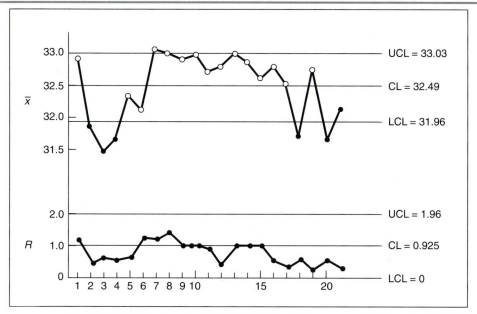

visual inspection. Measurement must be viewed as a process, the product of which is figures. A method of measurement cannot be dignified as a method, unless, with some operators at least, it shows a state of statistical control. A control chart is a powerful scientific tool.

The first step is to achieve reasonably good statistical control of some of the main operations, including inspection. The next step is for management to work on the common causes of variation and of defective products.

Textbooks on quality control (except for Juran [3]) teach only detection of special causes (Shewhart's assignable causes) and acceptance sampling (for disposition of product already on hand). These are important statistical methods, but acceptance sampling does not build quality that is not already there; and removal of special causes stops short of the main part of the problem, namely, faults of the system.

The explanation is simple. The usual terminology, following Shewhart [6] himself, is that the remaining sources of variation, lumped together, once control is established, constitute "chance causes," variation to leave to chance. This is the correct view for the production-worker in a state of control: he should indeed leave the remaining variation to chance. Likewise for a group of workers, or a line, or a process: ups and downs in a state of control are not a basis for action on the process.

The contribution that I am trying to make here is that management must take a different view: Management *must not* leave the remaining variation to chance.

FAMILIAR CONSEQUENCES OF FAULTS OF THE SYSTEM

Recalls of automobiles, electrical apparatus, and of other items, familiar enough to people in America, for possible hazards from failure of components and assemblies, or from contamination, are signs of faults in design. Failure to carry out adequate tests of components and assemblies over the ranges of jolt, stress, dust, speeds, voltages, corrosion, likely to be met in practice, or failure to heed the results of such tests, is chargeable to the system; hence to management. Or, as sometimes happens, management sometimes goes ahead with production, test or no test, to beat a competitor to the marketplace. No amount of care and skill on the part of the production worker can overcome a fault in design. Where is the statistician's report on the performance of parts and assemblies that give rise to trouble and to recalls?

  If one enquires whether more experimentation in advance would have overpaid its cost, or whether it is better business to rush into the marketplace and take a chance, I would offer the following remarks: (a) no dollar value can be placed on the unhappiness of a customer and the loss of future business over a defective item of an unsatisfactory service call; (b) the costliest experimentation on the performance of a product is the tests the customer caries out for himself; and (c) cost-benefit analysis has important uses, but also serious limitations. If the Japanese manufacturers had depended on cost-benefit analysis in 1949 to decide whether to learn and use the statistical control of quality, they would, I surmise, have given it a negative vote, or would still be studying the matter.

PARTIAL LIST OF USUAL FAULTS OF THE SYSTEM (COMMON OR ENVIRONMENTAL CAUSES OF VARIATION)

The reader may make additions and subtractions to suit his own situation.

1. Hasty design of component parts and assemblies. Inadequate tests of prototypes. Hasty production.
2. Inadequate testing of incoming materials. Specifications that are too stringent, or too loose, or meaningless. Waiving specifications.
3. Failure to know the capabilities of processes that are in a state of statistical control, and to use this information as a basis for contracts, both for quantity and quality.
4. Failure to provide production workers with statistical signals that will tell them how they are doing and when to make some change.
5. Failure to use these charts as a measure of the faults of the system, and of the effect of action taken by management to reduce them.
6. Failure to write job descriptions that take account of the capability of the process.
7. Inadequate training of workers, with the help of statistical controls.

8. Settings of machines chronically inaccurate (fault of the crew responsible for settings).

9. Instruments and tests not reliable. Consequent demoralization and loss from false reports and false signals. Loss from needless retesting.

10. Smoke, noise, unnecessary dirt, poor light, humidity confusion.

The production worker is helpless to reduce any of these causes of trouble. Economic considerations must of course govern the decision of management to reduce or eliminate a fault of the system. An easy way out is to say that it would cost too much.

A WORD ON DUE CARE

Statistical control and its consequences, if explained by statisticians to the legal profession in industry and in government, would clear up many problems about safety and reliability. The most that a manufacturer can put into the uniformity and dependability of a device is (a) to achieve and maintain statistical control, at the right level and spread, of the most important quality characteristic of the main outgoing components and assemblies, and incoming ingredients, and (b) to be able to demonstrate by adequate statistical records and charts, along with action taken on special causes and on common causes, that he has done so.

In spite of scrupulous care and intelligent use of statistical controls, it is inevitable that a defective item will get out now and then. An unfortunate freak of this kind cannot be viewed as an act of carelessness on the part of the manufacturer. He can do no more than to exercise due care.

SOME NEW PRINCIPLES IN ADMINISTRATION

This paper upsets some well-accepted principles of administration, which when examined under the logic of statistical inference turn out to be bad practice—that is, demoralizing to the rank and file of production workers, and costly. For example, it turns out to be bad practice to draw the attention of a production worker to a defect in his work when he is in a state of statistical control. Why? The production worker is helpless: He cannot do better. It is as if he were drawing blindfolded handfuls from a mixture of black and white beans. The number of black beans in a handful may be 0, or it may be 1, or 2, or more. The laws of chance apply. He cannot alter these laws, once he achieves statistical control. He will only make things worse (increase the proportion of black beans) if he tries to adjust his work except on statistical signal. To draw his attention to an error or to hold him on the job until he corrects it is to charge him with a fault of the system.

Yet it is common practice in industry, whether it be production or service, to bring to the attention of a man any output that is discovered to be defective. In an example

---

FIGURE 2 *Average Scores in Golf for an Experienced Golfer, before and after Lessons*

Before Lessons	Lessons	After Lessons

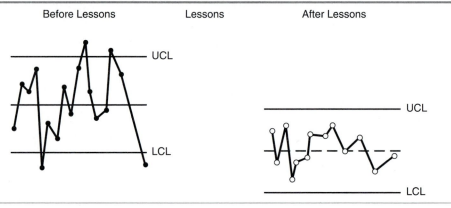

Upper Control Limit

Lower Control Limit

---

that I could cite, a production worker, whether in a state of statistical control or not, reworks on his own time, all the defectives that inspection discovered in the product that he turned out during his shift. This is what some people call quality control. The reason given to me upon enquiry is that this procedure is a continual reminder to the production worker that defectives will not be tolerated; that he is responsible for the work that he turns out. How can he improve if he doesn't know about his mistakes?

Like so many obvious solutions to problems, this one is also wrong. The fallacy in this principle is demonstrated by dependable day-to-day figures on rejections.

A job description, for best economy, should require achievement of statistical control of a dimension [4]. Under this requirement, the production worker is in charge of his own process, and can achieve in his work maximum economic uniformity and output. This is very different from asking a production worker to force a dimension of individual pieces to stay within specified limits.

FIGURE 3 *Average Weekly Scores in Golf for a Beginner Who Took Lessons before He Reached a State of Statistical Control*

Before Lessons	Lessons	After Lessons

UCL

LCL

UCL

LCL

An economic level and spread of the control limits would produce a distribution for individual pieces that rarely if ever extends beyond the specification and produces a defective item. It is the responsibility of the foreman or higher supervision to remove obstacles to an economic level and spread. This might mean better setting of the machine, or better maintenance, or incoming materials better suited to the right spread. None of this refinement in job descriptions will take place without understanding and action on the part of management (see Example 1).

A state of statistical control can exist in a climate of mild but uniform carelessness. This degree of carelessness is part of the system, the climate. In my experience, workers seldom know the cost of carelessness nor the cost of a mistake (see Example 2). Only management can teach them.

To call to the attention of a worker to a careless act, in a climate of general carelessness, is a waste of time and can only generate hard feelings, because the condition of general carelessness belongs to everybody and is the fault of management, not of any one worker, nor of all workers.

A general reminder, posted in a factory so that everyone can see it, to explain to the workers the cost of a defective item, or the cost of a mistake, may be helpful in improving the system. Meetings illustrated with moving pictures to show how defects are made, caught in the act, are also helpful.

Continuing education on the job to rehearse principles of the job and the cost of defective work belong in the system. This is management's job: workers cannot institute it.

A worker who is in a state of control but whose work is unsatisfactory presents a difficult problem. It is usually uneconomical to try to retrain him on this same job. It is more economical to put him into a new job in which the training may be more expert than it was in his present job.

Figure 2 provides an illustration. An experienced man in golf hoped to improve his score by taking lessons. The chart shows that the lessons accomplished nothing. His techniques were engrained: his teacher was unsuccessful in dislodging them and replacing them with better ones.

Curiously, so long as a man has not reached a state of statistical control, there is hope. Figure 3 shows average scores ($\bar{x}$) in golf for a beginner. His scores, before the lessons, were obviously not in a state of control, there are points outside the control limits. Then came lessons. His scores thereupon showed a state of statistical control with the desired results, viz., an average score considerably below what his average was before the lessons. Here, lessons changed the system.

Ten production workers may all be in statistical control as individuals, all at different levels. Their combined output will also be in control. *Improvement comes about by studying the individual workers, transferring to another job with a fresh start anyone that is out of line on the side of poor performance.*

It is my observation that training in industry is deplorable. A new employee simply goes to work. Written instructions for the job, if they exist, are in many cases incomprehensible. What happens is that the new worker gives up on the instructions for fear of being further confused. His co-workers come to the rescue, instructions or no instructions, and in a few days he is running along with the herd. The service industries (restaurants, hotels, laundries, etc.) provide horrible examples. The argument is that instruction and training are too costly, and that it is all lost if an employee quits the job.

In contrast, a girl that runs a lift in Japan, or is conductor on a bus, spends two months in training on how to handle people, this in spite of her genteel background of culture.

Training or the lack of it is part of the system. Training can be improved only by management, certainly not by the workers.

Example 1

This example illustrates how a small change in the system could virtually eliminate the possibility of defective items. The ordinates in Figure 4 are the means ($\bar{x}$) of samples of $n = 3$ for tests of uniformity of finished wheels. The test is the running balance of the wheel. Observations:

1. The production worker is in a state of control with respect to his own work (which is the only work that he is responsible for). No point falls outside the control limits.

2. He is under the handicap of the system. He cannot beat the system and the capability of his process: He will once in a while produce a defective wheel, even though he is a good worker and in a state of control.

3. He is meeting the requirements of his job. He can do no more. He has nothing further to offer.

4. The main trouble lies in the system. The central line in Figure 4, which fall at about 125 gram-cms, represents the contribution of the system to the total trouble. This handicap is built in. If the faults of the system were reduced to 75% of their present level, the upper tail of the distribution of individual pieces would drop well below the specification limit, and the entire production would be accepted; economies in production would be realized.

The reaction of management on the above paragraphs was the usual one, namely, that they did not have in mind this kind of quality control when they went into it. They were looking for everything to clear up, once the production workers put their best efforts into the job. Eventually, however, patience paid off.

Charts like Figure 4 are to be seen almost anywhere, but interpretation of them in terms of a quantitative measure of the faults of the system are rare.

Example 2

The second example deals with a service industry, motor freight. Drivers of trucks pick up shipments and bring them into a terminal for reload and onward movement. Other drivers deliver. A large company in motor freight may have anywhere from ten to forty terminals in or near large cities. There is a long chain of operations

FIGURE 4   Chart for x̄ for Test of Uniformity of Wheels Turned Out by a Production Worker

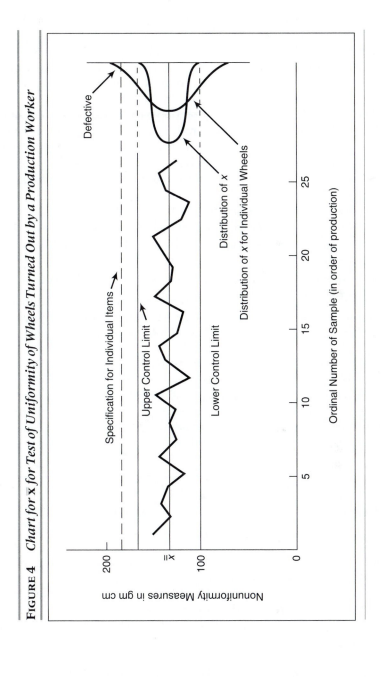

between the request of a shipper to the carrier (usually by telephone) to come and pick up a shipment, and placement of the shipment on the platform of the carrier, ready for reload and line haul to the terminal that serves the destination of the shipment. Every operation offers a chance for the driver to make a mistake. The table shows 6 types of mistakes, plus all others. Although the frequency of mistakes is low, the total loss is substantial.

In mistake No. 1, the driver signs the shipping order for 10 cartons, but someone else finds, later on in the chain of operations, that there are only 9 cartons; one carton missing. Where is it? There may have been only 9 cartons in the first place; the shipping order was written incorrectly; or, more usual, the driver left one carton on the shipper's premises. Let us list some of the sources of loss from mistake No. 1:

1. It costs about $25 to search the platform for the missing carton, or to find the truck (by now out on the road) and to search it.

2. It costs $15 on the average to send a driver back to the shipper to pick up the missing carton.

3. It costs $10 to segregate and hold the 9 cartons for the duration of the search.

4. If the carrier does not find the carton, then the shipper may legitimately put in a claim for it. The carrier is responsible for the 10th carton. Its value may be anywhere from $10 to $1,000, with the possibility of an amount even greater.

It is obvious that mistake No. 1 may be costly. Any one of the 7 mistakes will on the average lead to a loss of $50. There were a total of 617 mistakes on the record, and they caused a loss of $31,000 for claims alone. Multiplied by 20, for 20 terminals, the total loss from the 7 mistakes was $620,000. (This amount is a minimum. It does not include the expenses of searches nor administration. Moreover, some mistakes are not included in the total of 617, but they nevertheless cause loss.)

THE 7 TYPES OF MISTAKES	
Type of Mistake	**Description**
1	Short on pick up
2	Over on pick up
3	Failure to call in (by telephone) on over, short, and damaged cartons on delivery
4	Incomplete bill of lading
5	Improperly marked cartons
6	Incomplete signature on delivery-receipt
7	Other

There were 150 drivers that worked all year long. Figure 5 shows the distribution of the 150 drivers by number of mistakes, all 7 mistakes combined.

We postulate the following mechanism, which will distribute errors at random to drivers. We imagine a huge bowl of black and white beads, thoroughly mixed. Each

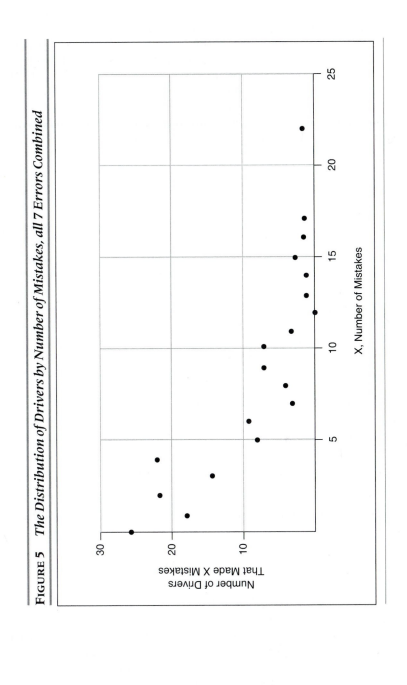

FIGURE 5   *The Distribution of Drivers by Number of Mistakes, all 7 Errors Combined*

driver scoops up a sample of 1,000 or more (the number of trips that an average driver makes in a year), and returns the beads to the bowl for more mixing. The number of black beads in a scoop will be a random variable, following the Poisson distribution. The total number of mistakes in Figure 5 is 617, and there were 150 drivers. An estimate of the mean number of mistakes per driver would be is seen in Figure 5.

The upper and lower 3-sigma limits for these samples would be easy to calculate by use of the square-root-transformation, by which

$$(\sqrt{4.1} + 1.5)^2 = 12 \text{ [Upper Limit]}$$
$$\text{and}$$
$$(\sqrt{4.1} - 1.5)^2 = 0 \text{ [Lower Limit]}$$

One may perform the same calculations instantly by use of the Mosteller-Tukey double square-root paper [8].

We interpret the upper limit to mean that a driver that made 12 or more mistakes in the year is not part of the system. He contributes more than his share. He is a special cause of loss. I may add here that other statistical models that I have tried lead to about the same conclusions.

Drivers that made 0, 1, 2, 3, or 4 mistakes are far more numerous than the Poisson distribution would allow. I accordingly consolidate the drivers that made 0, 1, 2, 3, or 4 mistakes, and postulate that they too form a separate group. There are then three groups of drivers:

A. Drivers that made 12 or more mistakes.

B. Drivers that made between 5 and 11 mistakes.

C. The extra careful group, drivers that made 0, 1, 2, 3, or 4 mistakes.

What have we learned from this simple statistical model?

1. The 7 drivers with 12 or more mistakes accounted for 112/617 or 18% of the mistakes. They could reduce their rates of mistakes to average if they knew that they were outliers.

2. Drivers that made 5 to 11 mistakes measure the losses that arise from the system itself. They make the system what it is. They account for $(425 - 112)/617$ or about 51% of the mistakes. Clearly, about half the losses from the 7 types of mistake arise from the system as it is.

3. The 102 drivers of Group C accounted for only $192/617 = 31\%$ of the mistakes. This Group C is worth studying: how do they do it? Did they have easy routes or easy conditions (e.g., day-time pick-ups, inside pick-ups), or do they have a system of their own? These are questions to pursue. If these men have a system of their own, then they should teach the others. (Enquiry turned up no evidence of easy routes.)

No problem with people is simple. It would be wise for the management to defer criticism of Group A, to determine first whether these drivers worked unusually difficult routes, or whether they had achieved excessive mileage (high productivity). As it turned out, they had.

Here we encounter an important lesson in administration. This company had been sending a letter to a driver at every mistake. It made no difference whether this was the one mistake of the year for this driver, or the 15th: the letter was exactly the same. A letter sent to a driver in Group B or C is demoralizing: the driver's interpretation thereof—and he is absolutely correct—is that he is blamed for faults of the system.

The management had failed to see that they face three distinct types of problem. What was needed was a separation of responsibilities for improvement—special causes, to be corrected by the drivers of Group A; the system itself, to be improved by the management; study of Group C; and examination of the accuracy of their records of mistakes.

One might pause here in passing to ask two questions: (1) what does the manager of the terminal think of the driver to whom he has sent in one year 15 warnings of disciplinary action? More important, (2) what does the driver think of the manager?

Example 3

A small manufacturer of shoes was having trouble with his sewing machines, rent of which was very costly. The operators were spending a lot of their time rethreading the machines, a serious loss.

The key observation was that the trouble was common to all machines and to all operators. The obvious conclusion was that the trouble, whatever it was, was common, environmental, affecting all machines and all operators. A few tests showed that it was the thread that caused the trouble. The owner of the shop had been purchasing poor thread at bargain prices. The loss of machine-time had cost him hundreds of times the difference between good thread and what he had been buying. Bargain prices for thread turned out to be a costly snare.

Better thread eliminated the problem. Only the management could make the change. The operators could not go out and buy better thread, even if they had known where the trouble lay. They work in the system. The thread was part of the system.

Prior to the simple investigation that found the cause, pedestrian but effective, the owner had supposed that his troubles all came from inexperience and carelessness of the operators.

Example 4

The work of every one of 50 production workers on a certain production line is in statistical control. The manager of personnel came forth with a plan, immediately hailed by the management, to award monthly a prize and half a day off to the operator on this line whose production the month before showed the smallest proportion of defective product.

Was this a good idea? What was wrong? Why should the statistician advise the management to drop the idea? The answer is that it would not improve the performance of the workers, nor improve quality.

Why not? Every operator has already put into the job all that he has to offer: the work of each one is in a state of control.

This award would not be an award of merit. What harm would come from it? It would produce frustration and dissatisfaction amongst conscientious workers. Their efforts to find out what they are doing that is wrong, and why their work is not as good as that of the man that won the prize, would be a fruitless chase. They would try out changes in their operations, the only effect of which would be greater variability, not less.

The award would be a lottery. There would be no harm that I know of in introducing a lottery for excitement, provided management calls it a lottery, not an award of merit.

This is an example of administration without statistical judgment. The plan seemed to be a great idea until examined by the theory of probability, with reference to special causes and common causes.

What the personnel man could do, if he wishes to offer a prize and be effective, is to reward a man that contrives ways to improve the system, to decrease the per cent defective for the group by some stated amount of economic importance.

Management could make good use of the figures on defectives for the 50 workers, but not to award a prize. The 50 proportions of defectives furnish a basis, by use of the simple statistical technique called chart for fraction defective, to discover which worker if any ought to be transferred and trained in other jobs. The same chart, even if the 50 workers were not in statistical control with each other, would indicate how much of the overall fraction defective arises from the system itself, beyond reach of the workers, and correctible only by management.

CONCLUDING REMARKS

The principles expounded here, and the examples of application, are all simple, yet the economic gains from corrective action by management are considerable. The examples all belong to the statistical control of quality. Did the solutions require a statistician? Couldn't other people have done as well? One answer is that other people had their chance.

Some people would call this work operations research. Some would call it systems analysis, others, industrial engineering. To me, it is just a statistician trying to be positive and helpful in the use of statistical methods.

When will schools of business and other academic departments get into the business of teaching modern principles of administration and management? Without statistical logic, management learns words and goals, but not methods by which to reach these goals, nor meaningful language by which to describe a goal or to measure advancement toward it or away from it.

References

1. W. Edwards Deming, *Elementary Principles in the Statistical Control of Quality,* Union of Japanese Scientists and Engineers, Tokyo, 1950.

2. W. Edwards Deming, "On the use of theory," *Industrial Quality Control,* vol. xiii, No. 1, July 1956. "On some statistical logic in the management of quality," *All India Congress on Quality Control,* New Delhi, 17 March 1971.

3. J. M. Juran, *Quality Control Handbook,* McGraw-Hill, New York, 1951, 1962; pages 11, 4–5; 26, 10–11, and other pages in this book listed under Pareto. (The pages cited belong to the 3rd edition.) I strongly recommend the whole book for people of all responsibilities and disciplines. See also Hy Pitt, "Pareto re-visited," *Quality Progress,* vol. vii, No. 2, pp. 29–30.

4. This procedure was first described, so far as I know, by J. M. Juran in a meeting of the American Society for Quality Control in New York at least 20 years ago. It was formalized by Irving Burr. "Specifying the desired distribution rather than maximum and minimum limits," Industrial Quality Control, vol. 24, No. 2, 1967: pp. 94–101.

5. Kenichi Koyanagi, *"Statistical Quality Control in Japanese Industry,"* Proceedings of the American Society for Quality Control, Rochester, 1952.

6. Walter A. Shewhart, *The Economic Control of Manufactured Product,* Van Nostrand, New York, 1931. *Statistical Method from the Viewpoint of Quality Control,* The Graduate School, Department of Agriculture, Washington, 1939.

7. An easy reference for the nonstatistician is my chapter entitled, "Making things right," in the book, Judith Tanner, et al., *Statistics, Guide to the Unknown,* Holden-Day, 1972.

8. See almost any textbook in statistical methods. The original reference is Frederick Mosteller and John W. Tukey, "The uses and usefulness of binomial probability paper," *Journal of the American Statistical Association,* vol. 44, 1949: pp. 174–212. The double square-root paper is manufactured by the Codex Book Company of Norwood, Mass.

Notes

1. This paper is based on principles taught in Japan since 1950. I am indebted to the editor and to referees, and to students at New York University, for many helpful suggestions in presentation.

The Quality Trilogy: A Universal Approach to Managing for Quality

BY J. M. JURAN

Several premises have led me to conclude that our companies need to chart a new direction in managing for quality. These premises are as follows.

1. There is a crisis in quality. The most obvious outward evidence is the loss of sales to foreign competition in quality and the huge costs of poor quality.

2. The crisis will not go away in the foreseeable future. Competition in quality will go on and on. So will the impact of poor quality on society. In the industrialized countries, society lives behind protective quality dikes.

3. Our traditional ways are not adequate to deal with the quality crisis. In a sense, our adherence to those traditional ways has helped to create the crisis.

4. To deal with the crisis requires some major breaks with tradition. A new course must be charted.

5. Charting a new course requires that we create a universal way of thinking about quality—a way applicable to all functions and to all levels in the hierarchy, from the chief executive officer to the worker in the office or the factory.

6. Charting a new course also requires extensive personal leadership and participation by upper managers.

7. An obstacle to participation by upper managers is their limited experience and training in managing for quality. They have extensive experience in management of business and finance but not in managing for quality.

8. An essential element in meeting the quality crisis is to arm upper managers with experience and training in how to manage for quality, and to do so on a time scale compatible with the prevailing sense of urgency.

9. Charting a new course also requires that we design a basis for management of quality that can readily be implanted into the company's strategic business planning, and that has minimal risk of rejection by the company's immune system.

A company that wants to chart a new course in managing for quality obviously should create an all-pervasive unity so that everyone will know which is the new direction, and will be stimulated to go there. Creating such unity requires dealing with some powerful forces which resist a unified approach. These forces are for the most part due to certain non-uniformities inherent in any company. These non-uniformities include:

- The multiple functions in the company: product development, manufacture, office operations, etc. Each regards its function as something unique and special.
- The multiple levels in the company hierarchy, from the chief executive officer to the nonsupervisory worker. These levels differ with respect to responsibility, prerequisite experience and training, etc.
- The multiple product lines: large and complex systems, mass production, regulated products, etc. These product lines differ in their markets, technology, restraints, etc.

Such inherent non-uniformities and the associated beliefs in uniqueness are a reality in any company, and they constitute a serious obstacle to unity of direction. Such an obstacle can be overcome if we are able to find a universal thought process—a universal way of thinking about quality—which fits all functions, all levels, all product lines. That brings me to the concept of the "quality trilogy."

(Let me add parenthetically that my colleagues in Juran Institute have urged me to let them call it the "Juran Trilogy." Their reasons are purely mercenary. I have yielded to their wishes. In Juran Institute we also need unity.)

The underlying concept of the quality trilogy is that managing for quality consists of three basic quality-oriented processes.

- Quality planning.
- Quality control.
- Quality improvement.

Each of these processes is universal; it is carried out by an unvarying sequence of activities. (A brief description of each of these sequences appears in the box on page 116.) Furthermore, these universal processes are interrelated in ways we can depict on a simple diagram. (See Figure 1.)

The starting point is quality planning—creating a process that will be able to meet established goals and do so under operating conditions. The subject matter of the planning can be anything: an office process for producing documents; an engineering process for designing products; a factory process for producing goods; a service process for responding to customers' requests.

Following the planning, the process is turned over to the operating forces. Their responsibility is to run the process at optimal effectiveness. Due to deficiencies in the original planning, the process runs at a high level of chronic waste. That waste has been planned into the process, in the sense that the planning process failed to plan it out. Because the waste is inherent in the process, the operating forces are unable to get rid of the chronic waste. What they do instead is to carry out ''quality control''—keep the waste from getting worse. If it does get worse (sporadic spike), a fire fighting team is brought in to determine the cause or causes of this abnormal variation. Once the cause(s) has been determined, and corrective action is taken, the process again falls into the zone defined by the ''quality control'' limits.

Figure 1 also shows that in due course the chronic waste falls to a much lower level. Such a reduction does not happen of its own accord. It results from purposeful action taken by upper management to introduce a new managerial process into the system of managers' responsibilities—the quality improvement process. This quality improvement process is superimposed on the quality control process—a process implemented in addition to quality control, not instead of it.

We can now elaborate the trilogy descriptions somewhat as follows.

Process: Quality planning—the process for preparing to meet quality goals.

End Result: A process capable of meeting quality goals under operating conditions.

FIGURE 1 ***The Quality Triology***

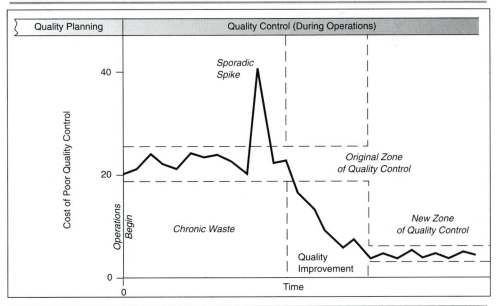

Basic Quality Processes
Quality Planning:

Identify the customers, both external and internal.

Determine customer needs.

Develop product features that respond to customer needs. (Products include both goods and services.)

Establish quality goals that meet the needs of customers and suppliers alike, and do so at a minimum combined cost.

Develop a process that can produce the needed product features.

Prove process capability—prove that the process can meet the quality goals under operating conditions.

Control:

Choose control subjects—what to control.

Choose units of measurement.

Establish measurement.

Establish standards of performance.

Measure actual performance.

Interpret the difference (actual versus standard).

Take action on the difference.

Improvement:

Prove the need for improvement.

Identify specific projects for improvement.

Organize to guide the projects.

Organize for diagnosis—for discovery of causes.

Diagnose to find the causes.

Provide remedies.

Prove that the remedies are effective under operating conditions.

Provide for control to hold the gains.

Process: Quality control—the process for meeting quality goals during operations.

End Result: Conduct of operations in accordance with the quality plan.

Process: Quality improvement—the process for breaking through to unprecedented levels of performance.

End Result: Conduct of operations at levels of quality distinctly superior to planned performance.

The trilogy is not entirely "new." If we look sideways at how we manage finance, we notice some interesting parallels, as shown in Figure 2. (I have often used the financial parallels to help explain the trilogy to upper managers. It does help.)

FIGURE 2   *Quality and Finance: Parallels*

Trilogy Processes
Quality planning
Quality control
Quality Improvement

Financial Processes
Budgeting
Cost control; expense control
Cost reduction; profit improvement

In recent seminars, I have been collecting upper managers' conclusions on their companies' performance relative to the basic processes of the trilogy. The results are quite similar from one seminar to another, and they can be summarized as shown in Figure 3.

These summarized data point to several conclusions.

1. The managers are not happy with their performance relative to quality planning.

2. The managers rate their companies well with respect to quality control, i.e., meeting the established goals. Note that since these goals have traditionally been based mainly on past performance, the effect is mainly to perpetuate past performance—the very performance which is at the root of the quality crisis.

3. The managers are decidedly unhappy with their performance relative to quality improvement.

My own observations of company performance (during consultations) strongly confirm the above self-assessment by company managers. During my visits to companies I have found a recurring pattern of priorities and assets devoted to the processes within the trilogy. This pattern is shown in Figure 4.

As Figure 4 shows, the prevailing priorities are not consistent with the managers' self-assessment of their own effectiveness. That assessment would suggest that they should put the control process on hold while increasing the emphasis on quality planning and especially on quality improvement.

To elaborate on the need for raising the priority on quality improvement, let me present several baffling case examples.

FIGURE 3   *Quality Process Performance*

UPPER MANAGERS' RATINGS OF THEIR COMPANIES' PERFORMANCE			
Trilogy Processes	**Good**	**Passing**	**Not Passing**
Quality planning	13%	40%	47%
Quality control	44	36	20
Quality improvement	6	39	55

FIGURE 4 *Priorities for Quality Processes*

Trilogy Processes	Self-Assessment by Upper Managers	Prevailing Priorities
Quality planning	Weak	Limited priority
Quality control	Very strong	Top priority, by a wide margin
Quality improvement	Very weak	Very low priority

1. Several years ago the executive vice president of a large multinational rubber company made a round-the-world-trip with his chairman. They made the trip in order to visit their major subsidiaries with a view to securing inputs for strategic business planning. They found much similarity with respect to productivity, quality, etc., except for Japan. The Japanese company was outperforming all others, and by a wide margin. Yet the Americans were completely mystified as to why. The Americans had toured the Japanese plant, and to the Americans' eyes the Japanese were using the same materials, equipment, processes, etc., as everyone else. After much discussion the reason emerged: The Japanese had been carrying out many, many quality improvement projects year after year. Through the resulting improvements they made *more and better products from the same facilities.* The key point relative to "ignorance" is that the Americans did not know what to look for.

2. A foundry that made aluminum castings had an identical experience. The foundry was losing share of market to a Japanese competitor, mainly for quality reasons. Arrangements were made for a delegation of Americans to visit the Japanese factory. The delegation came away completely mystified. The Japanese were using the same types of equipment and processes as were used by the Americans. Yet the Japanese results in quality and productivity were clearly superior. To this day the Americans don't know why.

3. A few years ago I conducted research into the yields of the processes that make large scale integrated circuits. To assure comparability, I concentrated on a single product type—the 16K random access memory (16K RAM). I found that Japanese yields were two to three times the Western yields despite similarity in the basic processes. It came as no surprise to me that the Japanese have since become dominant in the market for 64K RAMs and up.

4. My final example relates to the steel industry. The managers of American steel companies report that their cost of poor quality (just for factory processes) runs at about 10–15% of sales. Some of these steel companies have business connections with Japanese steel companies, and the respective managers exchange visits. During these visits the Americans learn that in Japanese steel mills, which use comparable equipment and processes, the cost of poor quality runs at about 1–2% of sales. Again the American managers don't know why. Some of them don't even believe the Japanese figures.

My own explanation is that the Japanese, since the early 1950s, have undertaken to improve quality at a pace far greater than that of the West. The slopes of those two lines (Figure 5) are an index of the rate of improvement. That rate is in turn dependent on the number of quality improvement projects completed. (A project is a problem scheduled for solution.) My estimate is that in terms of numbers of improvement projects completed, the Japanese pace has been exceeding that of the West by an order of magnitude, year after year.

It seems clear that we must change our priorities with regard to the three quality processes. This change in priorities represents a new course. Underlying this new course is the quality trilogy. As a universal way of thinking about quality, the trilogy offers a unified approach for multiple purposes. Let us look at two of these purposes: training in managing for quality, and strategic quality planning.

With respect to training, many of our companies have decided to break with tradition. In the past, their training in managing for quality has been limited to managers and engineers in the quality department. The break with tradition is to extend such training to all functions. Since this is a sizeable undertaking, the companies have set up corporate task forces to plan the approach.

These task forces have run into serious obstacles due to those same systems of variables mentioned earlier. It is hopeless to establish numerous training courses in managing for quality, each specially designed to fit specific functions, specific levels in the hierarchy, specific product lines, etc. Instead, the need is for a universal training course that will apply to all audiences, but with provision for plugging in special case examples as warranted. The trilogy concept meets that need.

The training courses then consist of fleshing out the three sequences of steps described in the box on page 116. Those sequences have been field tested and proven to be applicable to all functions, levels, and product lines.

We have already seen that the trilogy parallels our approach to strategic business planning. Our companies are experienced in business planning; they are familiar and comfortable with the concepts of financial budgets, cost control, and cost reduction. We can take advantage of all that experience by grafting the quality trilogy onto the existing business planning structure. Such a graft reduces the risk that the implant will be rejected by the company's immune system.

The usual starting point is to set up a quality planning council to formulate and coordinate the activity companywide. The council membership consists of high ranking managers—corporate officers. The chairman is usually the chief executive officer or an executive vice president. The functions of this council parallel closely the functions of the company's finance committee, but apply to quality instead of finance.

The council prepares a written list of its responsibilities. These typically involve the following:

- Establish corporate quality policies.
- Establish corporate quality goals; review quality goals of divisions and major functions.

Figure 5　*World Competition in Quality*

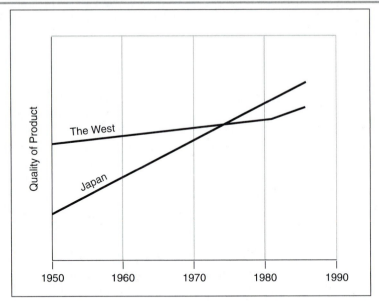

- Establish corporate quality plans; review divisional and functional plans.
- Provide the infrastructure and resources needed to carry out the plans.
- Review quality performance against plans and goals.
- Revise the managerial merit rating system to reflect performance against quality goals.

It is all quite logical, and some companies are already securing gratifying benefits from going into strategic quality planning. However, other companies are failing to get results, and the main reasons for these failures are becoming evident. They relate to some areas which I will now discuss: goal setting; providing the infrastructure; providing resources; upper management leadership.

Setting goals. Goal setting has traditionally been heavily based on past performance. This practice has tended to perpetuate the sins of the past. Failure-prone designs were carried over into new models. Wasteful processes were not challenged if managers had met the budgets—budgets which had in turn assumed that the wastes were a fate to be endured.

All this must change. Goals for parameters that affect external customers must be based on meeting competition in the marketplace. Goals for parameters that affect internal customers must be based on getting rid of the traditional wastes.

Infrastructure. Strategic quality planning requires an infrastructure to be set up. The nature of this is evident when we look sideways at the infrastructure needed for strategic business planning: a budgetary process; an accounting system to evaluate performance; associated procedures, audits, etc.

Much of this structure has long been in place to serve various local needs: divisions, functions, factories, etc. This structure must now be supplemented to enable it to meet strategic quality needs as well. This is especially the case in large corporations which traditionally have delegated matters of quality to the autonomous divisions. The quality crisis has caused some large corporations to revise this delegation. They now require corporate review of divisional quality goals, plans, and reports of performance. The new approach has required revision of the infrastructure.

Resources. It takes resources to carry out plans and meet goals. To date, companies have exhibited a selective response to this need. Let us look at several areas that require such resources.

- Training. Here the response of companies has generally been positive. Companies have invested heavily in training programs for special areas such as quality awareness, statistical process control, and QC circles. To go into strategic quality planning will require extensive training in the trilogy—how to think about quality. One can hope the response will continue to be positive.

- Measurement of quality. The quality crisis has required a major change in the basis for goal setting—the new basis requires measurement of market quality on an unprecedented scale. For example, some companies now have a policy that new products may not go on the market unless their reliability is at least equal to that of leading competitive products. Such a policy cannot be made effective unless resources are provided to evaluate the reliability of competing products.

Beyond the need to expand quality-oriented marketing research, there are other aspects of measurement which require resources: establishing the scorekeeping associated with strategic quality planning (the quality equivalent of the financial profit statements, balance sheets, etc.); extending measures of quality to the non-manufacturing processes; and establishing means for evaluating the quality performance of managers, and fitting these evaluations into the merit rating system.

- Quality improvement. Here we have some puzzling contradictions. An emerging data base tells us that quality improvement projects provide a higher return on investment than virtually any other investment activity. Yet many companies have not provided the needed resources.

To be specific, that data base comes mainly from the companies that have presented papers at the annual IMPRO conferences—conferences on quality improvement. Those published papers and related unpublished information indicate that in large organizations—sales of $1 billion or more—the average quality improvement project yields about $100,000 of cost reduction.[1]

The same data base indicates that to complete a project requires from $5,000 to $20,000 in resources. These resources are needed to diagnose the cause of the problem and to provide the remedy. The return on investment is obviously attractive. Nevertheless, many companies—too many—have failed to provide the resources and hence have failed to get the results.

To go into strategic quality planning will require companies to create, for the quality function, a new role—a role similar to that of the financial controller. In all likelihood this new role will be assigned to the quality managers.

In part this new role will involve assisting the company managers to prepare the strategic quality goals—the quality equivalent of the financial budget. In addition the new role will involve establishing the continuing means of reporting performance against quality goals. This role parallels the financial reporting role of the financial controller.

Collateral with those two new responsibilities will be others, also of a broad business nature.

- Evaluation of competitive quality and of trends in the marketplace.
- Design and introduction of needed revisions in the trilogy of processes: quality planning, quality control, and quality improvement.
- Conduct of training to assist company personnel in carrying out the necessary changes.

For many quality managers such a new role will involve a considerable shift in emphasis: from technology to business management; from quality control and assurance to strategic quality planning. But such is the wave of the future. Those quality managers who choose to accept that responsibility, if and when it comes, can look forward to the experience of a lifetime. They will be participating fully in what will become the most important quality development of the century.

References

1. Eighteen case examples are cited in "Charting the Course," *The Juran Report*, Number 4 (Winter 1985).

J.M. Juran is chairman of Juran Institute, Inc., Wilton, Conn. The Institute offers consulting and management training in quality. An ASQC Honorary Member, Juran is the editor in chief of *The Quality Control Handbook*, author of *Managerial Breakthrough*, and coauthor with Frank Gryna of *Quality Planning and Analysis*.

Quality Is Free:
The Art of Making Quality Certain

———

By Philip B. Crosby

COST OF QUALITY

Let's eavesdrop on the Management Monthly Status Review of our favorite company. The comptroller is providing his overview:

"Inventory increased $270,358 this month for a total of $21,978,375.18. This is still $9,981 below budget, but I think it requires a good look because the rate of increase is getting steeper."

"Good point," says the boss, who then directs purchasing to see if they are bringing material in quicker than needed and asks material control to give him a detailed report on in-process versus finished-goods inventory.

"Sales are directly on budget except for the hotel operation, where occupancy is falling off. During the week occupancy is running 98 percent, but this is dragged down by the weekend rate of 35 percent."

"Hmmm," says the boss. "Marketing better get hopping on putting together some weekend specials. 'Take the little lady away from it all' sort of thing. Give them a special rate and a bottle of bubbly. That should take care of it."

"Employee compensation is overbudget. We've been paying too much overtime in the foundry and electronic test operations. This is caused by delinquent schedules in the assembly group. They got two days late last month and haven't been able to catch up."
"Production," frowns the boss, "hasn't been paying enough attention to scheduling. I think it's all due to that new and expensive computer operation. Set up a task team to find out what's wrong and give me a daily report."

"Our quality is falling off—we've had several customer complaints."

> "There's no excuse for low quality. The quality department has to get on the ball," growls the boss. "Maybe we need a new quality manager. I want high quality. Meeting adjourned."

Now you'll notice that everything in the above report is quite precise, even down to the last 18 cents of inventory. All things are measured, evaluated calmly, and dispositioned. All, that is, except quality, which is merely "falling off." How come that portion of the company is not reported in numbers? Why is it left dangling in midair? Why is the quality manager suddenly considered inadequate when the other functional managers who have troubles are not? Why wasn't he there?

How come there wasn't a report on *quality*? Something like this:

> "Our receiving inspection rejection rate has climbed from 2.5 to 4 percent in the last month. This is due to purchase orders on standard hardware not calling out the proper plating requirements. Printed circuit board rejections have risen from 4 to 6 percent due to untrained assemblers being placed on the line. Production has pulled them back for training. Customer returns have dropped from 3 to 1.2 percent, but this has cost us $35,491 in overtime due to the additional testing required. An engineering error was responsible for the defect. Changes have been issued and the problem will be corrected by the 18th of next month. The cost of quality is running at 6.1 percent of sales, and we plan to meet the year-end objective of 5.9 percent."
>
> "Great," beams the boss. "As long as we can find these situations early and take action, we will be able to have confidence in our conformance. Quality is doing a fine job."

Quality is free, but no one is ever going to know it, if there isn't some sort of agreed-on system of measurement. Quality has always suffered from the lack of an obvious method of measurement in spite of the fact that such a method was developed by General Electric in the 1950s as a tool for determining the need for corrective action on a specific product line. I remember a case history in a course I took that compared two product lines using the cost of quality as the basis of comparison.

The quality profession, however, clings to the very management concepts that allow them to be inadequate, so cost-of-quality measurement was never really implemented except by a radical here and there. The first instance of using a companywide quality measurement, actually calculated and reported by the comptroller was probably in the ITT program we instituted in the mid-1960s.

By bringing together the easily assembled costs like rework, scrap, warranty, inspection, and test, we were able to show an accumulation of expense that made the line management listen to us. This led us to install more sophisticated quality management programs, which uncovered costs in areas such as change notices, installation, and supplier in-plant operations. At present we are learning how to measure "service" costs of quality. This applies not only to operations like insurance or hotels, where there are no milling machines or printed circuit assembly areas, but to manufacturing plants themselves. It took a long time to get around to the realization that half the people in the most manufacturing of manufacturing plants never touch the product. And of course, as individuals we are all service people. Unless we are blood donors—then we are manufacturing plants.

A detailed explanation of how to use the cost of quality to get an improvement team moving is given in Chapters 10 and 11. Here I cover some general details on the things that go into the cost of quality (hereafter often referred to as COQ).

All you really need is enough information to show your management that reducing the cost of quality is in fact an opportunity to increase profits without raising sales, buying new equipment, or hiring new people. The first step is to put together the fully loaded costs of (1) all efforts involved in doing work over, including clerical work; (2) all scrap; (3) warranty (including in-plant handling of returns); (4) after-service warranty; (5) complaint handling; (6) inspection and test; and (7) other costs of error, such as engineering change notices, purchasing change orders, etc. It is normal to obtain only one-third of the real cost the first time you try it.

Many quality management people start out with the thought that it is a good thing for them personally if the company has a very low figure for cost of quality. They tend to come up with readings like 1.3 percent of sales. Then they run to the boss for applause. A few years later their successor finds that it is really 12.6 percent of sales and embarks on a well-rewarded campaign to reduce this needless waste. The first person just refused to understand that the cost of quality has little to do with the operation of the quality department.

To make the total calculation more understandable to other managements it is a good idea to relate it to a significant base. Most people use a percent of sales. However, if you are in a company where there are unusually high costs of distribution like the food industry, you may want to measure COQ as a percentage of cost of sales, or just plain manufacturing costs. In insurance, banks, hotels, and similar businesses the cost of operations makes a good base. What is really important is that the number be something that quality management can use to communicate the importance of the concept. That is what the whole business of COQ is all about.

Many managers wait, and fiddle, and never really do get a workable COQ system installed. They collect endless lists and classifications of things that should be considered. They are too concerned with trying to obtain an exact cost figure, and don't really understand the reason for doing the calculation in the first place.

All this just delays the rest of their program. As I said, the purpose of calculating COQ is really only to get management's attention and to provide a measurement base for seeing how quality improvement is doing. If managers spend all their time getting ready and attending endless conferences searching for the secret, they will be disappointed.

Once an operation knows its COQ, or a good approximation, goals for reducing that cost can be set. Ten percent a year is a good, attainable goal that people can relate to. As you go along, and become more adept in determining things that belong in the COQ, you will find the base number growing. This means that you must go back and apply this information to figures obtained in the past if you want apples to look like apples.

All calculations should be produced by the accounting department; that ensures the integrity of the operation. Naturally, they are going to ask you for a list of those costs which must be included. The following list should be of some help, although you will have to add any items that are unique to your business. These three categories should be sufficient at first; don't search for additional details until you absolutely need them. That is what creates bureaucracy.

PREVENTION COSTS

Prevention costs are the cost of all activities undertaken to prevent defects in design and development, purchasing, labor, and other aspects of beginning and creating a product or service. Also included are those preventive and measurement actions conducted during the business cycle. Specific items are:

Design Reviews

Product Qualification

Drawing Checking

Engineering Quality Orientation

Make Certain Program

Supplier Evaluations

Supplier Quality Seminars

Specification Review

Process Capability Studies

Tool Control

Operation Training

Quality Orientation

Acceptance Planning

Zero Defects Program

Quality Audits

Preventive Maintenance

APPRAISAL COSTS

These are costs incurred while conducting inspections, tests, and other planned evaluations used to determine whether produced hardware, software, or services conform to their requirements. Requirements include specifications from marketing and customer, as well as engineering documents and information pertaining to procedures and processes. All documents that describe the conformance of the product or service are relevant. Specific items are:

Prototype Inspection and Test

Production Specification Conformance Analysis

Supplier Surveillance

Receiving Inspection and Test

Product Acceptance

Process Control Acceptance

Packaging Inspection

Status Measurement and Reporting

FAILURE COSTS

Failure costs are associated with things that have been found not to conform or perform to the requirements, as well as the evaluation, disposition, and consumer-affairs aspects of such failures. Included are all materials and labor involved. Occasionally a figure must be included for lost customer credibility. Specifics are:

Consumer Affairs

Redesign

Engineering Change Order

Purchasing Change Order

Corrective Action Costs

Rework

Scrap

Warranty

Service after Service

Product Liability

Once you and the comptroller have calculated the COQ for your operation, the next step is to figure out what to do with it. This calculation is the only key you will ever have to help your company properly implement quality management. Seize an opportunity and make a speech like the following:

> A prudent company makes certain that its products and services are delivered to the customer by a management system that does not condone rework, repair, waste, or non-conformance of any sort. These are expensive problems. They must not only be detected and resolved at the earliest moment, they must be prevented from occurring at all. To give you an idea of how expensive these problems are, let me show you some of the actual costs we are incurring at this moment. (At this point, show them.)
> To remove these costs and to prove that quality is free, we must implement our quality management system to its fullest. That way we can turn what is sometimes considered a necessary evil into a profit center. Our cost of quality is now X percent of sales. It only needs to be Y percent of sales. The difference is pretax profit.
> Thank you.

Used as a management tool for the purpose of focusing attention on quality management the COQ is a positive blessing and serves a unique purpose. Used as an accounting measurement, like the calculation of nuts-and-bolts inventory, it becomes a useless pain. When the concern becomes which operation has come up with the most accurate figures, the purpose of keeping the figures gets lost. It is like someone on a tight budget keeping neat records of overspending. Make certain you keep your eye on the true reason for the calculation. Don't get lost in statistical swamps.

QUALITY IMPROVEMENT PROGRAM

The most difficult lesson for the crusader to learn is that real improvement just plain takes a while to accomplish. The urgency of the need, the obviousness of the cause, and the clarity of the solution have little to do with getting things straightened out.

That is why government programs almost always fail and are scrapped whenever a new administration takes over. The disappointment and disillusionment of the previous administrator are all too obvious. The administrator blames a lack of funds, cooperation, timing, or whatever for the failure. Yet no matter what the program was, or however well it was directed, its success potential hinged on events entirely separate from the executive's efforts.

Quality improvement programs have similar problems. Because quality improvement sounds like such a great idea, and because it is usually so necessary, managers often feel that merely announcing its conception is the signal for arranging a victory dinner.

I have yet to attend a quality meeting where someone didn't comment to me that they had been unable to "really reach their management," or "get the people motivated," in order to put quality improvement over the top. They claim that they have taken the actions any well-oriented professional would expect, and yet they are disappointed. Those colleagues who have faithfully implemented the fourteen-step quality improvement program worry about an inevitable falloff in "enthusiasm," and search for new means of keeping the program on a high intensity level.

Each time I hear these things I am shocked. I am always surprised that they are surprised. Why should quality be different from the real world? After all, the method of preventing smallpox had been discovered and tested many years before the devastation of plagues ceased. Why wouldn't people take the necessary steps to protect themselves from such a painful and ugly disease? Why did they ignore the simple and inexpensive act of vaccination in the face of absolute evidence that it worked? Why do people continue to smoke tobacco when even the tobacco companies admit it is a clear danger? I smoked for thirty years, enjoying every puff, before being forced to quit. Now that I am free I recognize what a truly messy business smoking is and am not tempted to return to it. But that may be hindsight. Basically, we are slow to change because we reject newness. The world is a complicated and unsettled place. Each individual treasures the few things he or she can depend upon. "Perhaps it is better to take my chances on the pox rather than go over and let these strange people scratch me." If you think this is old-fashioned, just consider how much difficulty the government has had in getting people to take flu shots. Why? Well, for one thing we know for a fact that the flu shot is going to make us ill for a while. And we might not catch the flu even if we don't get the shot (particularly if everyone else takes it).

Take another example: urban redevelopment. It has cost more money than any domestic program in the history of the United States except defense. However, you could say that both operations have similar effects: the subjugation of cities and their populations. The difference is in the location of the cities.

Obviously the goals of urban redevelopment are above reproach. Tear out the old and inefficient and replace it with the new and different. Create jobs in the process and improve our way of life. Very rarely has that happened. Poor people have been uprooted, middle-class people have fled the cities, and the urban patterns built up by centuries of slow development and real living have been destroyed in a few years. Whose fault has it been? Not the politicians—they really didn't have time to do it right because they had to get reelected or they had to spend this year's budget this year.

There is always some reason given for failure, but it is rarely the real one. The real one is that you have to lead people gently toward what they already know is right. Otherwise they just will not cooperate. If you have any doubts, ask those who have tried to stamp out the "adult entertainment" sections in cities, assuming that the population is against such things. But the basic assumption is wrong. The population isn't against adult entertainment. It just doesn't want it next door. After all, nothing lives unless the people support it. It is not the "kooks" who support such enterprises, it is real people with real money.

The most practical way to establish your frame of reference when you decide to start an improvement program is to put it in very personal terms. Pretend that you are a company. Presumably you know yourself well enough to know how you will react under certain circumstances. Then announce to yourself that for your own good you must take up a new sport. Let us say that you have selected golf. Millions of people play the game, there are courses everywhere, and there is probably more information available about the details of this sport than any other. Perhaps someone has even written a book on the fourteen steps of golf improvement through defect prevention. In that case it is only necessary to announce your commitment, agree upon the measurement criteria, and go forth to meet your goals. Maybe you can even have some banners made in order to "motivate" yourself.

You could set up goals based on improvement, and could reward yourself for achievement. But it is going to take a while. There is a lot more to golf than having the equipment and the intent. You must work hard at it, and you must stay at the wheel for a long time, if you ever want to play a really good game of golf.

A company quality improvement effort has a lot of the same elements. It must be well thought out, and it must be implemented according to a plan, over a long period of time. It requires a "culture" change; it must become part of your life-style. And it requires that you never relax your attention. You have to stay at it continually.

You as a manager have an obligation to demand continual quality improvement from your operation, whether you are in the accounting business or a machine shop. You as a manager have an obligation to provide thoughtful and imaginative leadership. What you put out is what you get back.

It is not possible to take shortcuts in an attempt to keep from involving yourself. Everyone can tell whether or not you are being sincere. Experiments in "job enrichment" have shown this clearly. The technique of having one group of individuals completely assemble a car, in order to build their pride in their work, did not noticeably improve quality, interest, or productivity. The people knew they were being used.

People who have to put improvement programs of any kind into their company always feel that others are not for it. This is entirely normal, and reflects the natural shyness of the organization bird. We don't really like to get out front with too much unless we are absolutely certain it will be properly received. But my experience has been that improvement efforts, properly explained, are always received correctly. It's the "proper explanation" that takes some effort. So in searching for a way to convince the quality manager at ITT, I came up with the Quality Management Maturity Grid. The Grid has its own uses, as described in the previous chapters. But in the case of the quality improvement program it is even more important just for itself. The question you have to ask yourself is: "What would the boss, and the rest of the managers who report to him or her, have to do to convince you that they really want a quality improvement program?" The answer, of course, is that they would have to convince you that they personally feel the need for improvement in the operation. And that is what you use the Grid for. Send them a copy, ask them to read it, and then go see them to discuss it. Have each of them rate the company as they see it according to the Grid. Don't be too heavy with them. If they think something is Wisdom and you think it is Awakening, don't argue too much. Just leave room for improvement.

Once you have discussed all their judgments on an individual basis, you can bring them together to discuss the overall program (which is spelled out in the case history presented in Chapters 10 and 11, which thoroughly covers the installation of a quality improvement program). And if anyone is reluctant, you can point out that their personal evaluation showed the need for improvement.

At this time it is a good idea to move right into the basics of quality. Help them to understand what real quality means, emphasizing the absolutes of quality management:

- Quality means conformance, not elegance.
- There is no such thing as a quality problem.
- There is no such thing as the economics of quality; it is always cheaper to do the job right the first time.
- The only performance measurement is the cost of quality.
- The only performance standard is Zero Defects.

Explain the Zero Defects concept (see Chapter 10). Have them take the test, and leave out nothing. Answer all their questions, and keep it all simple and untechnical. Tell them again that quality is free.

They really want to believe, and they really want it to happen. But their life is one continual scene of people bringing them plans and schemes that will help them succeed, cut costs, fly to the moon, and a thousand other things. Like you, they know that most things don't work like they are supposed to work.

The main task you have at this key moment is to show them that the program has worked for other companies and it will work for yours, if they participate. But you also have to help them understand that although there will be instant improvement as soon as you start the effort, it will be a long while before it becomes permanent. It is hard and rewarding work. It will bring recognition to all of them.

As for yourself, remember that the product that you are selling, and they are buying, is quality improvement. The result of quality improvement is improved everything else, from sales to absenteeism. But it is a result. So don't tie in a bunch of marketing motivation activities, the blood bank, the savings bond drive, or the annual barbeque. Keep quality improvement in the front of your mind each time a decision has to be made.

THE FOURTEEN STEPS

Step One: Management Commitment

Action. Discuss the need for quality improvement with management people, with an emphasis on the need for defect prevention. There are plenty of movies, visual aids, and other material available to support this communication. (Do not confuse "communication" with "motivation." The results of communication are real and long-lasting; the results of motivation are shallow and short-lived.) Prepare a quality policy that states that *each individual is expected to "perform exactly like the requirement or cause the requirement to be officially changed to what we and the customer really need."* Agree that quality improvement is a practical way to profit improvement.

Accomplishment. Helping management to recognize that they must be personally committed to participating in the program raises the level of visibility for quality and ensures everyone's cooperation so long as there is some progress.

Step Two: Quality Improvement Team

Action. Bring together representatives of each department to form the quality improvement team. These should be people who can speak for their department in order to commit that operation to action. (Preferably, the department heads should participate—at least on the first go-around.) Orient the team members as to the content and purpose of the program. Explain their role—which is to cause the necessary actions to take place in their department and in the company.

Accomplishment. All the tools necessary to do the job now are together in one team. It works well to appoint one of the members as the chairman of the team for this phase.

Step Three: Quality Measurement

Action. It is necessary to determine the status of quality throughout the company. Quality measurements for each area of activity must be established where they don't exist and reviewed where they do. Quality status is recorded to show where improvement is possible, where corrective action is necessary, and to document actual improvement later on.

Nonmanufacturing measurements, which are sometimes difficult to establish, might include the following:

Accounting:
  Percentage of late reports
  Computer input incorrect
  Errors in specific reports as audited

Data Processing:
  Keypunch cards thrown out for error
  Computer downtime due to error
  Reruntime

Engineering:
  Change orders due to error
  Drafting errors found by checkers
  Late releases

Finance:
  Billing errors (check accounts receivable overdues)
  Payroll errors
  Accounts payable deductions missed

Hotel Front Desk:
  Guests taken to unmade rooms
  Reservations not honored

Manufacturing Engineering:
  Process change notices due to error
  Tool rework to correct design
  Methods improvement

Marketing:
  Contract errors
  Order description errors

Plant Engineering:
   Time lost due to equipment failures
   Callbacks on repairs

Purchasing:
   Purchase order changes due to error
   Late receipt of material
   Rejections due to incomplete description

There are innumerable ways to measure any procedure. The people doing the work will respond with delight to the opportunity to identify some specific measurements for their work. If a supervisor says her area is completely immeasurable, she can be helped by asking how she knows who is doing the best work, how she knows whom to keep and whom to replace.

Accomplishment. Formalizing the company measurement system strengthens the inspection and test functions and assures proper measurement. Getting the paperwork and service operations involved sets the stage for effective defect prevention where it counts. Placing the results of measurement in highly visible charts establishes the foundation of the entire quality improvement program.

Step Four: Cost of Quality Evaluation

Action. Initial estimates are likely to be shaky (although low), and so it is necessary now to get more accurate figures. The comptroller's office must do this. They should be provided with detailed information on what constitutes the cost of quality. The cost of quality is not an absolute performance measurement: it is an indication of where corrective action will be profitable for a company. The higher the cost, the more corrective action that needs to be taken.

Accomplishment. Having the comptroller establish the cost of quality removes any suspected bias from the calculation. More important, a measurement of quality management performance has been established in the company's system.

Step Five: Quality Awareness

Action. It is time now to share with employees the measurements of what nonquality is costing. This is done by training supervisors to orient employees, and by providing visible evidence of the concern for quality improvement through communication material such as booklets, films, and posters. Don't confuse this with some get-motivated-quick scheme. It is a sharing process, and does not involve manipulating people. This is an important step. It may be the most important step of all. Service and administrative people should be included just like everybody else.

Accomplishment. The real benefit of communications is that it gets supervisors and employees in the habit of talking positively about quality. It aids the process of changing, or perhaps clarifying, existing attitudes toward quality. And it sets the basis for the corrective-action and error-cause-removal steps.

Step Six: Corrective Action

Action. As people are encouraged to talk about their problems, opportunities for correction come to light, involving not just the defects found by inspection, audit, or self-evaluation, but also less obvious problems—as seen by the working people themselves—that require attention. These problems must be brought to the supervision meetings at each level. Those that cannot be resolved are formally passed up to the next level of supervision for review at their regular meeting. If a specific functional area does not hold such meetings, the team should take action to establish them in that department.

Accomplishment. Individuals soon see that the problems brought to light are being faced and resolved on a regular basis. The habit of identifying problems and correcting them is beginning.

Step Seven: Establish an Ad Hoc Committee for the Zero Defects Program

Action. Three or four members of the team are selected to investigate the Zero Defects concept and ways to implement the program. The quality manager must be clear, right from the start, that Zero Defects is *not* a motivation program. Its purpose is to communicate to all employees the literal meaning of the words "zero defects" and the thought that everyone should do things right the first time. This must be transmitted to every member of the team. In particular, the ad hoc group should seek out ways to match the program to the company's personality.

Accomplishment. Improvement comes with each step of the overall program. By the time ZD day is reached, as much as a year may have gone by and the initial improvement will be flattening out. At that point the new commitment to an explicit goal takes over, and the improvement begins again. Setting up the ad hoc committee to study and prepare the implementation ensures that the goals of the program will be firmly supported by the company's thought leaders.

Step Eight: Supervisor Training

Action. A formal orientation with all levels of management should be conducted prior to implementation of all the steps. All managers must understand each step well enough to explain it to their people. The proof of understanding is the ability to explain it.

Accomplishment. Eventually all supervision will be tuned into the program and realize its value for themselves. Then they will concentrate their action on the program.

Step Nine: Zero Defects Day

Action. The establishment of ZD as the performance standard of the company should be done in one day. That way, everyone understands it the same way. Supervisors should explain the program to their people, and do something different in the facility so everyone will recognize that it is a "new attitude" day.

Accomplishment. Making a "day" of the ZD commitment provides an emphasis and a memory that will be long lasting.

Step Ten: Goal Setting

Action. During meetings with employees each supervisor requests that they establish the goals they would like to strive for. Usually, there should be 30-, 60-, and 90-day goals. All should be specific and capable of being measured.

Accomplishment. This phase helps people learn to think in terms of meeting goals and accomplishing specific tasks as a team.

Step Eleven: Error Cause Removal

Action. Individuals are asked to describe any problem that keeps them from performing error-free work on a simple, one-page form. This is not a suggestion system. All they have to list is the problem; the appropriate functional group (e.g., industrial engineering) will develop the answer. It is important that any problems listed be acknowledged quickly—within twenty-four hours. Typical inputs might be:

- This tool is not long enough to work right with all the parts.
- The sales department makes too many errors on their order entry forms.
- We make a lot of changes in response to telephone calls, and many of them end up having to be done all over again.
- I don't have any place to put my pocketbook.

Accomplishment. People now know that their problems can be heard and answered. Once employees learn to trust this communication, the program can go on forever.

Step Twelve: Recognition

Action. Award programs are established to recognize those who meet their goals or perform outstanding acts. It is wise not to attach relative values to the identification of problems. Problems identified during the error-cause-removal stage should all be treated the same way because they are not suggestions. The prizes or awards should not be financial. Recognition is what is important.

Accomplishment. Genuine recognition of performance is something people really appreciate. They will continue to support the program whether or not they, as individuals, participate in the awards.

Step Thirteen: Quality Councils

Actions. The quality professionals and team chairpersons should be brought together regularly to communicate with each other and to determine actions necessary to upgrade and improve the solid quality program being installed.

Accomplishment. These councils are the best source of information on the status of programs and ideas for action. They also bring the professionals together on a regular basis.

Step Fourteen: Do It over Again

Action. The typical program takes a year to eighteen months. By that time turnover and changing situations will have wiped out much of the education effort. Therefore, it is necessary to set up a new team of representatives and begin again. ZD day, for instance, should be marked as an anniversary. Nothing more than the notification may be necessary. Or a special lunch for all employees might be given. The point is that the program is never over.

Accomplishment. Repetition makes the program perpetual and, thus, "part of the woodwork." If quality isn't ingrained in the organization, it will never happen.

A Note on Quality: The Views of Deming, Juran, and Crosby

By Artemis March

During the 1980s, concerns about American competitiveness steered many U.S. companies to a new interest in quality. Most were likely to be introduced to quality concepts by one of the three leading "quality gurus"—W. Edwards Deming, Joseph Juran, and Philip Crosby. Each was an active consultant, lecturer, and author, with years of experience. Deming and Juran were in their eighties, and had been enormously influential in Japan; Crosby was in his sixties, and had worked previously at ITT as vice president of quality. Each of the three had developed his own distinctive approach to quality management.

DEMING

W. Edwards Deming was widely credited with leading the Japanese quality revolution. The Japanese began to heed his advice on statistical process control and problem-solving techniques (SPC) in 1950, but it was another thirty years before American businesses began to respond. By then, Deming's message to managers was blunt: "The basic cause of sickness in American industry and resulting unemployment is failure of top management to manage."[1] Known to dismiss client companies that did not change, he stated, "I give 'em three years. I've got to see a lot happen."[2] Best efforts were not enough; a program was needed, and it had to be adopted wholeheartedly:

> Everyone doing his best is not the answer. It is necessary that people know what to do. Drastic changes are required. The responsibility for change rests on management. The first step is to learn how to change.[3]

What Deming then expected from his clients was summarized in a 14-point program (see Exhibit 1).

EXHIBIT 1   *Deming's 14 Points*

---

1. *Create Constancy of Purpose for Improvement of Product and Service.*[a] Management must change from a preoccupation with the short run to building for the long run. This requires dedication to innovation in all areas, to best meet the needs of customers.

2. *Adopt the New Philosophy.* Shoddy materials, poor workmanship, defective products, and lax service must become unacceptable.

3. *Cease Dependence on Mass Inspection.* Inspection is equivalent to planning for defects; it comes too late and is ineffective and costly. Instead, processes must be improved.

4. *End the Practice of Awarding Business on Price Tag Alone.* Price has no meaning without a measure of the quality being purchased. Therefore, the job of purchasing will change only after management establishes new guidelines. Companies must develop long-term relationships and work with fewer suppliers. Purchasing must be given statistical tools to judge the quality of vendors and purchased parts. Both purchasing and vendors must understand specifications; but they must also know how the material is to be used in production and by the final customer.

5. *Constantly and Forever Improve the System of Production and Service.* Waste must be reduced and quality improved in every activity: procurement, transportation, engineering, methods, maintenance, sales, distribution, accounting, payroll, customer service, and manufacturing. Improvement, however, does not come from studying the defects produced by a process that is in control, but from studying the process itself. Most of the responsibility for process improvement rests with management.

6. *Institute Modern Methods of Training on the Job.* Training must be restructured and centered on clearly defined concepts of acceptable work. Statistical methods must be used for deciding when training has been completed successfully.

7. *Institute Modern Methods of Supervising.* Foremen must be empowered to inform upper management about conditions that need correction; once informed, management must take action. Barriers that prevent hourly workers from doing their jobs with pride must be removed.

To begin, managers had to put aside their preoccupation with today to make sure there was a tomorrow. They had to orient themselves to constant improvement of products and services to meet customers' needs and stay ahead of the competition. They had to innovate constantly, and commit resources to supporting innovation and continuous quality improvement. They had to build quality in. They had to break down department and worker–supervisor barriers. They had to rid themselves of numerical targets and quotas, and concentrate instead on improving

---

EXHIBIT 1 *(Continued)*

---

8. *Drive Out Fear.* Because of the tremendous economic losses caused by fear on the job, people must not be afraid to ask questions, to report problems, or to express ideas.

9. *Break Down Barriers between Departments.* Members of the research, design, procurement, sales, and receiving departments must learn about problems with raw materials and specifications in production and assembly. Each discipline must stop optimizing its own work, and work together as a team for the company as a whole. Multidisciplinary quality-control circles can help improve design, service, quality, and costs.

10. *Eliminate Numerical Goals for the Work Force.* Targets, slogans, pictures, and posters urging people to increase productivity must be eliminated. Most of the necessary changes are out of workers' control, so such exhortations merely cause resentment. Although workers should not be given numerical goals, the company itself must have a goal: never-ending improvement.

11. *Eliminate Work Standards and Numerical Quotas.* Quotas focus on quantity, not quality. Therefore, work standards practically guarantee poor quality and high costs. Work standards that state percentage defective or scrap goals normally reach those targets, but never exceed them. Piecework is even worse, for it pays people for building defective units. But if someone's pay is docked for defective units, that is unfair, for the worker did not create the defects.

12. *Remove Barriers That Hinder the Hourly Workers.* Any barrier that hinders pride in work must be removed, including not knowing what good work is, supervisors motivated by quotas, off-gauge parts and material, and no response to reports of out-of-order machines.

13. *Institute a Vigorous Program of Education and Training.* Because quality and productivity improvements change the number of people needed in some areas and the jobs required, people must be continually trained and retrained. All training must include basic statistical techniques.

14. *Create a Structure in Top Management That Will Push Every Day on the above 13 Points.*

NOTES:

[a]Italicized headings are in Deming's words. The remainder of each paragraph paraphrases his discussions.

processes, giving workers clear standards for what constitutes acceptable work, plus the tools needed to achieve it. And, they had to create a climate free of fingerpointing and fear, which block cooperative identification and solution of problems.

If management committed itself to this new order, Deming argued, it would improve productivity as well as quality. Contrary to conventional wisdom in the United States, quality and productivity were not to be traded off against each other. Rather, productivity was a by-product of quality, and of doing things right the first time:

> Improvement of the process increases uniformity of product, reduces rework and mistakes, reduces waste of manpower, machine-time, and materials, and thus increases output with less effort. Other benefits of improved quality are lower costs, . . . happier people on the job, and more jobs, through better competitive position of the company.[4]

Because management was responsible, in Deming's view, for 85% of quality problems, management had to take the lead in changing the systems and processes that created those problems. For example, consistent quality of incoming materials and components could not be expected where buyers were told to shop for price, or were not given the tools for assessing a supplier's quality. Management had to take the lead in developing long-term relationships with vendors, working with vendors to improve and maintain quality, training its own purchasing department in statistical quality control, requiring statistical evidence of quality from vendors, and insisting that specifications be complete, including an understanding of how the material actually worked in manufacturing. Only when management had changed purchasing systems and procedures could buyers be expected and able to do their job in a new way. Once top management was seriously committed to quality, lower-level personnel would be more likely to take action on problems that were within their control.

Accordingly, Deming delineated two means of process improvement: changing the "common causes" that were systemic (and were thus shared by numerous operators, machines, or products), and removing the "special causes" that produced nonrandom variation within systems (and were usually confined to individual employees or activities). Common causes included poor product design, incoming materials not suited to their use, machines out of order, improper bills of materials, machinery that would not hold tolerances, poor physical conditions, and so on. Special causes included lack of knowledge or skill, worker inattention, or a poor lot of incoming materials. Common causes were the responsibility of management and special causes the responsibility of operators:

> The discovery of a special cause of variation and its removal, are usually the responsibility of someone who is connected directly with some operation. . . . In contrast, there are common causes of defectives, of errors, of low rates or production, of low sales, of accidents. These are the responsibility of management. . . . The worker at a machine can do nothing about causes common to all machines. . . . He can not do anything about the light; he does not purchase raw materials; the training, supervision, and the company's policies are not his.[5]

The key tool Deming advocated to distinguish between systemic and special causes—and indeed, the key to quality management in general—was statistical process control. Developed by Walter Shewart while at Bell Labs in the 1930s and later refined by Deming in a well-known paper, "On the Statistical Theory of Errors," SPC was an inevitable fact of industrial life. It was unlikely that two parts, even when produced by the same operator at the same machine, would ever be identical. The issue, therefore, was distinguishing acceptable variation from variation that could indicate problems. The rules of statistical probability provided a method for making this distinction.

Probability rules could determine whether variation was random or not—i.e., whether it was due to chance. Random variation occurred within statistically determined limits. If variation remained within those limits, the process was a stable one, and said to be in control. As long as nothing changed the process, future variation could be easily predicted, for it would remain indefinitely within the same statistical limits.

Data of this sort were normally collected and plotted on control charts kept by the operators themselves. Such charts graphically plotted actual performance readings (e.g., the outside diameters of pistons) on graphs that also depicted the upper and lower control limits for that characteristic, which were statistically determined (see Figure 1). As long as the readings, taken on a small sample of units at predetermined intervals (such as every half-hour), fell between limits or did not show a trend (or "run"), the process was in control and no intervention was required, despite the obvious variation in readings. Readings that either fell outside the limits or produced a run indicated a problem to be investigated.

The practical value of distinguishing random from nonrandom variation was enormous. Operators now knew when to intervene in a process and when to leave it alone. Further, because readings were taken during the production process itself, unacceptable variation showed up early enough for corrective action, rather than after the fact.

Once a process was in control, readings that fell outside the limits indicated a special cause. When the cause of such nonrandom variation was found and removed, the system returned to its stable state. For example, if a particular lot of goods showed yields that were below control limits, further analysis might determine that raw materials peculiar to that lot were the cause. The removal of such special causes, however, did not improve the system (i.e., raise yield levels), but simply brought it back under control at the preexisting yield.

To improve the system itself, common causes had to be removed. Simply because a system was in statistical control did not mean it was as good as it could be. Indeed, a process in control could produce a high proportion of defects. Control limits indicated what the process was, not what it should or could be. To move the average (yield, sales, defects, returns, etc.) up or down—and thus also move the control limits up or down—typically required the concerted efforts of engineering, research, sales, manufacturing, and other departments. To narrow the range of variation around the target point could consume even more effort. In both cases, control charts would readily document the improvements in the process.

FIGURE 1   *A Typical Control Chart*

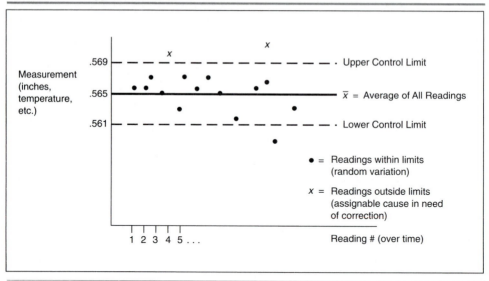

Deming viewed training in the use of control charts as essential if workers were to know what constituted acceptable work. He was adamant that quotas, piece-work, and numerical goals be eliminated. Instead, workers had to be shown what good work was, and given the tools to do it. Such tools would also allow them to monitor their own work and correct it in real time, rather than find out about problems days or weeks later.

Control charts were but one part of the statistical approach to quality. Because 100% testing was inefficient, sampling techniques had been developed to provide a scientific basis on which to accept or reject production lots based on a limited num-ber of units. Although sampling and control charts could indicate problems, they could not by themselves identify their causes. For that purpose, other statistical techniques were needed, such as Pareto analysis, Ishikawa ("fishbone") cause-and-effect diagrams, histograms, flowcharts, and scatter diagrams.

By 1986, Deming's lectures concentrated more on management than SPC, but SPC remained the core of his approach. Many U.S. firms had sought him out, and some, such as the Ford Motor Company, had adopted his approach throughout the company, with great success. Deming, who still worked out of the basement of his home with his secretary of thirty years, was hardly sanguine about the prospects of American business. He believed it would take thirty years for Americans to match what the Japanese had done, and that the United States was still falling behind. With the spectre of a lower standard of living, he concluded, "We should be pretty scared."[6]

JURAN

Joseph M. Juran's impact on Japanese quality was usually considered second only to Deming's. At 82, he had enjoyed a varied and distinguished career, including periods as a business executive, government administrator, lecturer, writer, and consultant. After years of independent activity, he established the Juran Institute in 1979 to serve as a base for the seminars, consulting, conferences, and videotapes long associated with his name. In recent years, clients had included Texas Instruments, Du Pont, Monsanto, and Xerox.

Juran defined quality as "fitness to use," meaning that the users of a product or service should be able to count on it for what they needed or wanted to do with it. For example, a manufacturer should be able to process a purchased material or component to meet the demands of its customers while achieving high yields and minimal downtime in production; a wholesaler should receive a correctly labeled product, free from damage during shipment and easy to handle and display; and a consumer should receive a product that performed as claimed and did not break down—or, if it did, receive prompt and courteous adjustment of his claim.

Fitness for use had five major dimensions: quality of design, quality of conformance, availability, safety, and field use.[7] Quality of design was what distinguished a Rolls Royce from a Chevrolet; it involved the design concept and its specification. Quality of conformance reflected the match between actual product and design intent; it was affected by process choices, ability to hold tolerances, work-force training and supervision, and adherence to test programs. Availability referred to a product's freedom from disruptive problems; it reflected both reliability (the frequency or probability of failure) and maintainability (the speed or ease of repair). Safety could be assessed by calculating the risk of injury due to product hazards. And field use referred to a product's conformance and condition after it reached customers' hands. It was affected by packaging, transportation, storage, and field service competence and promptness.

To achieve fitness for use, Juran developed a comprehensive approach to quality that spanned a product's entire life—from design through vendor relations, process development, manufacturing control, inspection and test, distribution, customer relations, and field service. Each area was carefully dissected, and approaches were proposed to specify and quantify its impact on the various elements of fitness for use. A broad range of statistical techniques was included to assist in the analysis.

Juran's approach to reliability provides a representative example. His reliability program began by establishing reliability goals. It then apportioned these among product components; identified critical components, identified possible modes, effects, and causes of failures; and developed solutions for those most critical to successful product operation and safety. Juran also discussed the setting of realistic tolerances, design reviews, vendor selection, and testing of designs. Statistical methods for improving reliability included analysis of various types of failure rates, analysis of relationships between component and system reliability, and setting of tolerance limits for interacting dimensions. The aims of these activities were quantified reliability goals, a systematic guide for achieving them, and a measurement and monitoring system for knowing when they had been achieved.

Although Juran's analytical methods could identify areas needing improvement and could help make and track changes, they were in the language of the shop floor: defect rates, failure modes, not within specification, and the like. Juran recognized that such measures were not likely to attract top management attention; for this reason, he advocated a cost of quality (COQ) accounting system. Such a system spoke top management's language: money. Quality costs were costs "associated solely with defective product—the costs of making, finding, repairing, or avoiding defects."[8] They were of four types: internal failure costs (from defects discovered before shipment); external failures costs (from defects discovered after shipment); appraisal costs (for assessing the condition of materials and product); and prevention costs (for keeping defects from occurring in the first place). See Exhibit 2A. In most companies, external and internal failure costs together accounted for 50–80% of COQ. When these were converted to dollars, or presented as a percentage of sales or profits, top management usually took notice.

COQ not only provided management with a dollar cost for defective products, it also established the goal of quality programs: to keep improving quality until there was no longer a positive economic return. This occurred when the total costs of quality were minimized. (See Exhibit 2B). Two assumptions were built into this analysis: that failure costs approached zero as defects became fewer and fewer, and that prevention and appraisal costs together approached infinity as defects were reduced to lower and lower levels. COQ minimization therefore occurred at the point where additional spending on prevention and appraisal was no longer justified, because it produced smaller savings in failure costs.

This approach had important practical implications. It implied that zero defects was not a practical goal, for to reach that level, prevention and appraisal costs would have to rise so substantially that total costs of quality would not be minimized. As long as prevention and appraisal costs were cheaper (on a per-unit basis) than failure costs, Juran argued that resources should continue to go to prevention and testing. But when prevention activities started to pull COQ unit costs up rather than down, it was time to maintain quality rather than attempt to reduce it further.

To reach and maintain this minimum cost of quality, Juran proposed a three-pronged approach: breakthrough projects, the control sequence, and annual quality programs. In the early stages, when a firm's failure costs greatly exceeded its prevention and appraisal costs, there were significant opportunities for breakthrough projects, aimed at chronic problems. Such problems were adverse situations of long standing, such as the need to revise tolerances, ignored because they were neither dramatic nor thought to be solvable. The "breakthrough sequence" involved identifying the "vital few" projects, selling them to management, organizing to analyze the issues and to involve the key people who were needed for implementation, and overcoming resistance to change (see Exhibit 3). Juran claimed that most breakthrough analyses found that over 80% of the problems (e.g., defect rates, scrap rates) were under management control and less than 20% were caused by operators.

EXHIBIT 2A   *Categories of Quality Costs[a]*

Internal Failure Costs = Costs from product defects prior to shipment to customer. They include:

- *Scrap*—Net losses in labor and material resulting from defective goods that cannot economically be repaired or used.
- *Rework*—Cost of correcting defective products to make them usable.
- *Retest*—Cost of reinspection and retesting of products that have been reworked.
- *Downtime*—Cost of idle facilities, equipment, and labor due to defective products.
- *Yield Losses*—Cost of process yields lower than could be attained through improved process control.
- *Disposition*—The time of those involved in determining whether nonconforming products are usable and what should be done with them.

External Failure Costs = Costs associated with defects found after shipment to customer. They include:

- *Complaint Adjustment*—Costs of investigating and responding to complaints due to defective product, faulty installation, or improper instructions to users.
- *Returned Material*—Costs associated with receiving and replacing defective product returned from the field.
- *Warranty Charges*—Costs of services and repairs performed under warranty contracts.
- *Allowances*—Income losses due to downgrading products for sale as seconds, and to concessions made to customers who accept substandard products as is.

Appraisal Costs = Costs associated with discovering the condition of products and raw materials. They include:

- *Incoming Materials Inspection*—Costs associated with determining the quality of vendors' products.
- *Inspection and Test*—Costs of checking product conformance throughout design and manufacture, including tests done on customer's premises.
- *Maintaining Accuracy of Test Equipment*—Costs of operating and maintaining measuring instruments.
- *Materials and Services Consumed*—Costs of products consumed in destructive tests; also materials and services (e.g., electric power) consumed in testing.
- *Evaluation of Stocks*—Costs of testing products in storage to assess their condition.

EXHIBIT 2A *(Continued)*

Prevention Costs = Costs associated with preventing defects and limiting failure and appraisal costs. They include:

- *Quality Planning*—Costs of creating and communicating plans and data systems for quality, inspection, reliability, and related activities; includes the costs of preparing all necessary manuals and procedures.
- *New Products Review*—Costs of preparing bid proposals, evaluating new designs, preparing test and experimentation programs, and related quality activities associated with launching new products.
- *Training*—Costs of developing and conducting training programs aimed at improving quality performance.
- *Process Control*—Costs of process control aimed at achieving fitness for use, as distinguished from productivity (a difficult distinction to make in practice).
- *Quality Data Acquisition and Analysis*—Costs of operating the quality data system to get continuing data on quality performance.
- *Quality Reporting*—Costs of bringing together and presenting quality data to upper management.
- *Improvement Projects*—Costs of building and implementing breakthrough projects.

NOTES:

[a]This is a summary and rewording of Juran and Gryna, pp. 14–16.

After successive breakthrough projects, a firm reached the point of optimal quality—in Juran's formulation, the bottom of the COQ curve. It then needed to employ the control sequence to preserve its gains. This sequence was actually a large feedback loop. One first chose an objective to control, then defined a unit of measure, set a numerical standard or goal, created a means of measuring performance, and mobilized the organization to report the measurements. After these preparatory steps, an action cycle was repeated over and over: actual performance was compared with standard, and action was taken (if needed) to close the gap.[9]

The control sequence was also used to attack sporadic problems—sudden, usually dramatic changes in the status quo, such as a worn cutting tool. Eliminating sporadic problems only returned processes to their historical levels; to improve them to optimum levels, breakthrough teams were needed because chronic problems were involved. Juran's contrast between these two types of problems is illustrated in Figure 2.

Both the control and breakthrough processes demanded sophisticated analysis and statistics. The comprehensiveness of Juran's program—it ran from vendor relations through customer service, and covered all the functions in between—required high-level planning and coordination as well. For this reason, Juran argued that a new group of professionals—quality control engineers—was needed. This department would be involved in high-level quality planning, coordinating the activities of other departments, setting quality standards, and providing quality measurements. But Juran also believed that top management had to give overall leadership and support to quality improvement if it were to succeed.

Juran's major vehicle for top-management involvement was the annual quality program. Akin to long-range financial planning and the annual budget process, this program gave top management quality objectives. It was especially important for internalizing the habit of quality improvement and insuring that complacency did not set in.

CROSBY

Philip B. Crosby had started in industry as an inspector; eventually he rose through the ranks at several companies to become vice president of quality at ITT. In 1979, he left ITT to found Philip Crosby Associates, Inc. and with it, the Crosby Quality College, which by 1986 had been attended by some 35,000 executives and managers. General Motors owned over 10% of Crosby stock, and had set up its own Crosby school, as had such companies as IBM, Johnson & Johnson, and Chrysler.

EXHIBIT 2B   *Minimizing the Costs of Quality*[a]

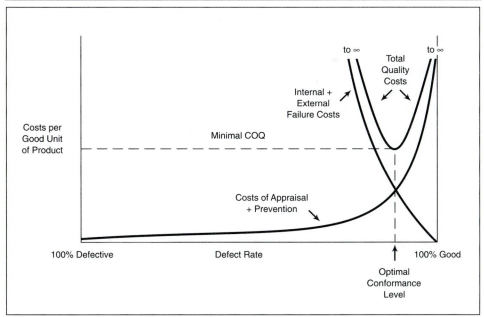

EXHIBIT 3   *Juran's Breakthrough Sequence*[a]

---

1. *Breakthrough in Attitudes.* Managers must first prove that a breakthrough is needed, and then create a climate conducive to change. To demonstrate need, data must be collected to show the extent of the problem; the data most convincing to top management are usually cost-of-quality figures. To get the resources required for improvement, expected benefits can be monetized and presented in terms of return on investment.

2. *Identify the Vital Few Projects.* Pareto analysis is used to distinguish the vital few projects from the trivial many, and to set priorities based on problem frequency.

3. *Organize for Breakthrough in Knowledge.* Two organizational entities should be established—a steering group and a diagnostic group. The steering group, composed of people from several departments, defines the program, suggests possible problem causes, gives the authority to experiment, helps overcome resistance to change, and implements the solution. The diagnostic group, composed of quality professionals and, sometimes, line managers, is responsible for analyzing the problem.

4. *Conduct the Analysis.* The diagnostic group studies symptoms, develops hypotheses, and experiments to find the problem's true causes. It also tries to determine whether defects are primarily operator-controllable or management-controllable. (A defect is operator-controllable only if it meets three criteria: operators know what they are supposed to do, have the data to understand what they are actually doing, and are able to regulate their own performance.) Theories can be tested using past data and current production data, and by conducting experiments. With this information, the diagnostic group then proposes solutions to the problem.

5. *Determine How to Overcome Resistance to Change.* The need for change must be established in terms that are important to the key people involved. Logical arguments alone are insufficient. Participation is therefore required in both the technical and social aspects of change.

6. *Institute the Change.* Departments that must take corrective action must be convinced to cooperate. Presentations to these departments should include the size of the problem, alternative solutions, the cost of recommended changes, expected benefits, and efforts taken to anticipate the change's impact on employees. Time for reflection may be needed, and adequate training is essential.

7. *Institute Controls.* Controls must be set up to monitor the solution and see that it works, and to keep abreast of unforeseen developments. Formal follow-up is provided by the control sequence used to monitor and correct sporadic problems.

NOTES:

[a]This summary adapted from Juran and Gryna, pp. 100–129, and Juran, 1964.

Crosby's message was directed at top management. He sought to change their perceptions and attitudes about quality. Typically, top managers viewed quality as intangible, or else to be found only in high-end products. Crosby, however, spoke of quality as "conformance to requirements," and believed that any product that consistently reproduced its design specifications was of high quality. In this sense, a Pinto that met Pinto requirements was as much a quality product as a Cadillac that conformed to Cadillac requirements.

American managers must pursue quality, Crosby argued, because it would help them compete. In fact, he believed that if quality were improved, total costs would inevitably fall, allowing companies to increase profitability. This reasoning led to Crosby's most famous claim: that quality was "free."[10]

Ultimately, the goal of quality improvement was zero defects, to be achieved through prevention rather than after-the-fact inspection. Crosby had popularized the zero defects movement, but it had actually originated in the United States at the Martin Company in the 1960s, where Crosby was employed. The company had promised and delivered a perfect missile, with limited inspection and rework, and its managers had concluded that perfection was possible if it was in fact expected. The company then developed a philosophy and program to support that goal.

Crosby elaborated on this approach. He believed that the key to quality improvement was changing the thinking of top management. If management expected imperfection and defects, it would get them, for workers would bring similar expectations to their jobs. But if management established a higher standard of performance, and communicated it thoroughly to all levels of the company, zero defects was possible. Thus, according to Crosby, zero defects was a management standard, and not simply a motivational program for employees.

FIGURE 2   *Juran's Sporadic and Chronic Problems[a]*

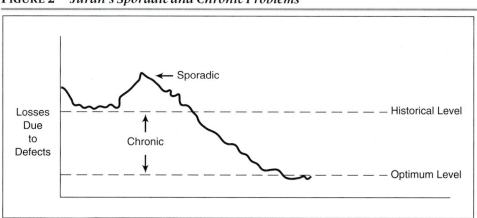

NOTES:

[a]This figure adapted from Juran and Gryna, p. 100.

EXHIBIT 4 *The Quality Management Maturity Grid*[a]

Measurement Categories	Stage I: Uncertainty	Stage II: Awakening	Stage III: Enlightenment	Stage IV: Wisdom	Stage V: Certainty
Management Understanding and Attitude	Fails to see quality as a management tool.	Supports quality management in theory, but is unwilling to provide the necessary money or time.	Learning about quality management and becoming supportive.	Participates personally in quality activities.	Regards quality management as essential to the company's success.
Quality Organization Status	Quality activities are limited to the manufacturing or engineering department, and are largely appraisal and sorting.	A strong quality leader has been appointed, but quality activities remain focused on appraisal and sorting, and are still limited to manufacturing and engineering.	Quality department reports to top management and its leader is active in company management.	Quality manager is an officer of the company. Prevention activities have become important.	Quality manager is on the board of directors. Prevention is the main quality activity.
Problem Handling	Problems are fought as they occur and are seldom fully resolved; "firefighting" dominates.	Teams are established to attack major problems, but the approach remains short term.	Problems are resolved in an orderly fashion and corrective action is a regular event.	Problems are identified early in their development.	Except in the most unusual cases, problems are prevented.

Cost of Quality as Percent of Sales	Reported: unknown Actual: 20%	Reported: 5% Actual: 18%	Reported: 8% Actual: 12%	Reported: 6.5% Actual: 8%	Reported: 2.5% Actual: 2.5%
Quality Improvement Actions	No organized activities.	Activities are motivational and short term.	Implementing the 14-step program with full understanding.	Continuing the 14-step program and starting Make Certain.	Quality improvement is a regular and continuing activity.
Summation of Company Quality Posture	"We don't know why we have quality problems."	"Must we always have quality problems?"	"Because of management commitment and quality improvement programs, we are identifying and resolving our quality problems."	"We routinely prevent defects from occurring."	"We know why we don't have quality problems."

Notes:

[a] This chart is adapted from Crosby, pp. 32–33.

EXHIBIT 5   *Crosby's 14-Point Program*ᵃ

---

1. *Management Commitment.* Top management must become convinced of the need for quality improvement, and must make its commitment clear to the entire company. This should be accompanied by a written quality policy, stating that each person is expected to "perform exactly like the requirement, or cause the requirement to be officially changed to what we and the customers really need."

2. *Quality Improvement Team.* Management must form a team of department heads (or those who can speak for their departments) to oversee quality improvement. The team's role is to see that needed actions take place in its departments and in the company as a whole.

3. *Quality Measurement.* Quality measures appropriate to every activity must be established to identify areas needing improvement. In accounting, for example, one measure might be the percentage of late reports; in engineering, the accuracy of drawings; in purchasing, rejections due to incomplete descriptions; and in plant engineering, time lost because of equipment failures.

4. *Cost of Quality Evaluation.* The controller's office should make an estimate of the costs of quality to identify areas where quality improvements would be profitable.

5. *Quality Awareness.* Quality awareness must be raised among employees. They must understand the importance of product conformance and the costs of non-conformance. These messages should be carried by supervisors (after they have been trained) and through such media as films, booklets, and posters.

6. *Corrective Action.* Opportunities for correction are generated by Steps 3 and 4, as well as discussions among employees. These ideas should be brought to the supervisory level and resolved there, if possible; they should be pushed up further if that is necessary to get action.

7. *Zero Defects Planning.* An ad hoc zero defects committee should be formed from members of the quality improvement team. This committee should start planning a zero defects program appropriate to the company and its culture.

8. *Supervisor Training.* Early in the process, all levels of management must be trained to implement their part of the quality improvement program.

9. *Zero Defects Day.* A Zero Defects day should be scheduled to signal to employees that the company has a new performance standard.

10. *Goal Setting.* To turn commitments into action, individuals must establish improvement goals for themselves and their groups. Supervisors should meet with their people and ask them to set goals that are specific and measurable. Goal lines should be posted in each area, and meetings held to discuss progress.

EXHIBIT 5   (*Continued*)

11. *Error Cause Removal.* Employees should be encouraged to inform management of any problems that prevent them from performing error-free work. Employees need not do anything about these problems themselves; they should simply report them. Reported problems must then be acknowledged by management within 24 hours.

12. *Recognition.* Public, nonfinancial appreciation must be given to their quality goals or perform outstandingly.

13. *Quality Councils.* Quality professionals and team chairpersons should meet regularly to share experiences, problems, and ideas.

14. *Do It All over Again.* To emphasize the never-ending process of quality improvement, the program (Steps 1–13) must be repeated. This renews the commitment of old employees and brings new ones into the process.

NOTES:

[a]This summary is adapted from Crosby, pp. 132–139, 175–259.

To help managers understand the seriousness of their quality problems, Crosby provided two primary tools: cost of quality measures, and the management maturity grid (see Exhibit 4). Costs of quality, which Crosby estimated to be 15–20% of sales at most companies, were useful for showing top management the size of their quality problem and the opportunities for profitable improvement. The management maturity grid was used for self-assessment. It identified five states of quality awareness: uncertainty (the company failed to recognize quality as a management tool); awakening (quality was recognized as important, but management put off taking action); enlightenment (management openly faced and addressed quality problems by establishing a formal quality program); wisdom (prevention was working well, problems were identified early, and corrective action was routinely pursued); and certainty (quality management was an essential part of the company, and problems occurred only infrequently). For each of these five stages, Crosby also examined the status of the quality organization, problem-handling procedures, reported and actual costs of quality as percentages of sales, and quality improvement actions.

Once companies had positioned themselves on the management maturity grid, Crosby offered a 14-point program for quality improvement (see Exhibit 5). It emphasized prevention over detection, and focused on changing corporate culture rather than on analytical or statistical tools. The program was designed as a guide for securing management commitment and gaining employees' involvement through actions such as Zero Defects day. Crosby believed every company should tailor its own defect-prevention program; nevertheless, the goal should always be zero defects. In this process, top management played a leadership role; quality professionals played a modest but important role as facilitators, coordinators, trainers, and technical assistants; and hourly workers were secondary.

Notes

1. W. Edwards Deming, *Quality, Productivity, and Competitive Position*, Cambridge: Massachusetts Institute of Technology, Center for Advanced Engineering Study, 1982, p. i.

2. Jeremy Main, "The Curmudgeon Who Talks Tough on Quality," *Fortune*, June 25, 1984, p. 122.

3. Deming, 1982, p. ii.
   This note has been prepared by Associate for Case Development Artemis March, under the supervision of Associate Professor David A. Garvin, as the basis for class discussion.

4. Ibid., p. 1.

5. Ibid., p. 116.

6. Main, 1984, p. 122.

7. The key parameters of fitness for use, as well as their dimensions, vary somewhat in Juran's writings over a 35-year period. Their comprehensiveness and their spanning the entire product life cycle, however, are constants. The present discussion draws most heavily on Joseph M. Juran and Frank M. Gryna, Jr., *Quality Planning and Analysis*, New York: McGraw-Hill Book Company, 1980.

8. Juran and Gryna, p. 13.

9. This description of the control sequence is based on Joseph M. Juran, *Managerial Breakthrough*, New York: McGraw-Hill Book Company, 1964, pp. 183–187.

10. Philip B. Crosby, *Quality Is Free* (New York: McGraw-Hill Book Company, 1979).

What Is Total Quality Control?
The Japanese Way

By Kaoru Ishikawa

I. WHAT IS TOTAL QUALITY CONTROL?

Companies and individuals may give different interpretations, but broadly speaking, total quality control means management control itself.

The concept of "total quality control" was originated by Dr. Armand V. Feigenbaum, who in the 1950s variously served as company manager of quality control and company-wide manager of manufacturing operations and quality control at General Electric staff headquarters in New York City. His article on total quality control was published in the May 1957 issue of *Industrial Quality Control* and was followed by a book in 1961, entitled *Total Quality Control: Engineering and Management.*

According to Feigenbaum, total quality control (TQC) may be defined as "an effective system for integrating the quality development, quality maintenance, and quality improvement efforts of the various groups in an organization so as to enable production and service at the most economical levels which allow for full customer satisfaction." TQC requires participation of all divisions, including the divisions of marketing, design, manufacturing, inspection, and shipping. Fearing that quality which is everybody's job in a business can become nobody's job, Feigenbaum suggested that TQC be buttressed and serviced by a well-organized management function whose only area of specialization is product quality and whose only area of operation is in the quality control jobs. His Western-type professionalism led him to advocate TQC conducted essentially by QC specialists.

The Japanese approach has differed from Dr. Feigenbaum's approach. Since 1949 we have insisted on having all divisions and all employees become involved in studying and promoting QC. Our movement has never been an exclusive domain of QC specialists. This has been manifested in all of our activities, including the basic QC course for engineers, Dr. Deming's seminars for top and middle management (1950), the course for foremen broadcast in 1956, and the advocation of QC circle activities in 1962. We have promoted these under various names, such as integrated quality control, total quality control, all member participation quality control, and the like. The term "total quality control" has been the most frequently used. Yet when this term is used overseas, people may think that we are imitating Dr. Feigenbaum's approach, which we are not. So I have called ours Japanese-style total quality control, but found it too cumbersome. At the 1968 QC symposium, we agreed to use the term company-wide quality control to designate the Japanese approach.

Quality Control Participated in by All Divisions

What do I mean by company-wide or total quality control? It simply means that everyone in every division in the company must study, practice, and participate in quality control. Merely to assign QC specialists in every division as suggested by Feigenbaum is not enough. In Japan the vertical line authority relationship is too strong for staff members such as QC specialists to have much voice in the operation of each separate division. To counter this situation, our approach has always been to educate everyone in every division and to let each person implement and promote QC. Our QC courses are now well defined, and separate courses are available for different divisions. For example, there are QC courses for the marketing divisions and for the purchasing divisions. After all, "QC begins with education and ends with education."

Quality Control Participated in by All Employees

Our own definition of company-wide quality control has undergone certain changes. Initially total participation extended only to the company president, directors, middle management, staff, foremen, line workers, and salesmen. But in recent years, the definition has been expanded to include subcontractors, distribution systems, and affiliated (*keiretsu*) companies. This system, developed in Japan, is quite different from what is being practiced in the West. In China, Chairman Mao spoke of the inadequacy of control through specialists and advocated combining efforts of the workers, specialists, and leaders. This approach is closer to that of ours. There seems to be a common thread in the way of thinking in the Orient.

Integrated Quality Control

In effecting integrated quality control, control of quality is central, but at the same time cost control (profit control and price control), quantity control (amount of production, of sales, of stock), and control of delivery date are to be promoted. This method is based on the fundamental assumption of QC that a manufacturer must develop, produce, and sell commodities that satisfy the needs of consumers. In conducting QC, unless one knows the cost no quality planning and design can be effected. If cost control is tightly managed, one can know how much profit could be realized if certain trouble spots were eliminated. In this manner, the effects of QC can also be easily anticipated.

As to quantity, unless the exact amount is known, neither the percent defective nor the rate of reworks can be obtained and QC cannot progress. Conversely, unless QC is actively promoted—and unless standardization, the standard yield rate, standard rate of operation, and a standard workload are determined—there can be no way of finding standard cost, and consequently no cost control can be effected. Similarly, if percent defective varies too widely and if there are many rejected lots, neither production control nor control of the delivery date can be effected. In short, management must be done on an integrated basis. QC, cost (profit) control, and quantity (delivery date) control cannot be effected independently of one another. We do our integrated quality control at the core of all efforts, and that is the reason we also call this method integrated quality control. When each of the divisions (design, purchasing, manufacturing, and marketing) engages in QC activities, it must always follow this integrated approach.

In the West the definition of "quality control" has always included control of the quality of both products and services. Thus QC has been practiced in department stores, airlines, and banks. This is a sound approach. In Japan, by translating the term "quality control" into *hinshitsu kanri*, with the term *hin* connoting products, we may have unwittingly created quality control primarily for our manufacturing sector. In the past three decades Japan has emphasized quality of products, manufacturing them inexpensively and exporting them successfully, resulting in a rise in the level of Japan's living standards. In retrospect, then, it has been good to have the term *hin* (products) placed in the word designating quality.

However, I want to emphasize that the term quality means quality, and that the term extends to the quality of work in offices, in the service-related industries and in the financial sector.

I often use a diagram to explain this concept. (See Diagram V-1.) The essence of TQC is found in the central ring, which contains quality assurance narrowly defined, which means doing QC well for the company's new products. In the service industry where no manufactured goods are involved, quality assurance means assuring the quality of services rendered. In developing new services, such as new deposit accounts or new insurance contracts, quality must be assured.

Once the meanings of QC and of good quality and good services become clear, the second ring comes into play. The ring represents control of quality that is defined more broadly, including the questions of how to bring about good sales activities, how to make salesmen better, how to make office work more efficient, and how to deal effectively with subcontractors.

If the meaning is broadened even further, the third ring will be formed. This ring stresses that control of all phases of work is to be done effectively. It utilizes the

DIAGRAM V-1   *Company-wide Quality Control*

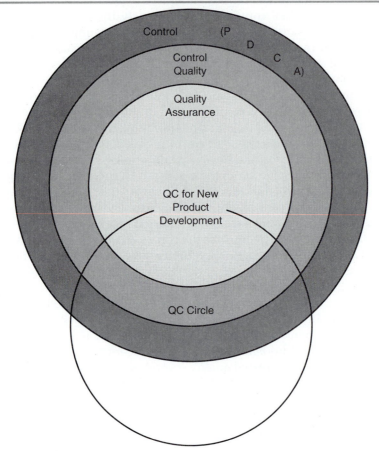

PDCA (plan, do, check, action) circle, turning its wheel over and over again to prevent recurrence of defects at all levels. This work involves the entire company, each division and each function. Each individual must also be actively involved.

Japanese QC has been fortunate in that in its history, once quality has been improved, control has been done effectively by turning the wheel of the PDCA circle. This has contributed effectively to the prevention of recurrence.

How far can a company's QC go in relation to the above three rings? That determination must be made by the chief executive officer taking into account the nature of the company. He must then communicate his decision to the entire company. Otherwise, within the company people may start debating unnecessarily about the QC definition. Some companies in Japan use the second and third rings with broader definitions. Other companies are confined to the central ring with quality assurance as the core. These can still claim to practice total quality control. One note of caution to those companies that use the broader definitions. Whatever you do, you must not forget the very essence of QC, which is found in quality assurance and in QC for development of new products.

Incidentally, QC circle activities must always be conducted as part of company-wide quality control activities. The QC circle is to be regarded as a ring that intersects all other rings. QC circle activities alone will not bring about TQC. Without participation by top and middle management and by the staff, QC circle activities cannot last. All over the world many companies are following the Japanese example in instituting QC activities. I fear many of them will not last unless they take the concept of company-wide quality control seriously and involve their top and middle management and their staff members in QC.

The above is what we call company-wide quality control or total quality control. The two terms can be used interchangeably.

II. ADVANTAGES OF TOTAL QUALITY CONTROL

Why do companies decide to institute TQC? I have given my answers in the April 1980 issue of *Engineers*, in a report entitled "Management Ideals of Companies Receiving the Deming Prize." The companies that have received the Deming Application Prize are all in the forefront of total quality control in Japan. Reproduced below is a summary of my report, outlining the reasons these companies decided to engage in TQC:

- To make our company recession proof, with true sales and technological capabilities (Ricoh Co., Ltd., recipient of the prize, 1975).

- To secure profit for the benefit of our employees, and to secure quality, quantity, and cost to obtain the confidence of our customers (Riken Forge Co., Ltd., 1975).

- To build quality into products that can always satisfy our customers. As a means of doing this, we engage in QC with (1) full employee participation, (2) emphasis on problem solving that can contribute to our profit picture, and (3) utilization of statistical approaches and methods (Tokai Chemical Industries, Ltd., 1975).

- To establish a company whose corporate health and character allow its steady growth by combining the creative energies of all of its employees, with attainment of the highest quality in the world as our goal. To develop the most up-to-date products, and to improve our quality assurance system (Pentel Co., Ltd., 1976).

- To create a cheerful workplace and show respect for humanity through QC circles with all-member participation. To supply in Japan and abroad automatic transmissions of impeccable quality, superior to the international standards but lower in cost, which takes into account fully the requirements of customers and users. To bring about prosperity of the company through improvement in management control, and thus contribute to the welfare of regional society (Aisin-Warner Limited, 1977).

- To improve the corporate health and character of our company, to upgrade quality of our products, and to raise our profit picture (Takenaka Komuten Co., Ltd., 1979).

- To establish a company whose corporate health and character are competitive and viable in any business environment change (Sekisui Chemical Co., Ltd., 1979).

- To attain the following goals: (a) Securing quality control development—To implement product goals according to company policy in a timely manner, the efforts of all employees are to be combined and organized; (b) Strengthening of control—Everyone must put into practice what he has learned about the methods and approaches of quality control and bring about improvement in the quality of control in every aspect of company activities; and (c) Nurturing human resources—To show respect for each employee as an individual, the company is to create a workplace that is worthy of everyone's labor through the nurturing and utilization of human resources and through teamwork (Kyushu Nippon Electric, 1979).

Space does not permit me to go on with other individual examples. In general, companies that have received the Deming Prize—including those not mentioned above—have the following purposes in common:

1. *Improving the corporate health and character of the company*—Almost all companies are serious about this point. Japan has entered a period of steady but less accelerated economic growth. So most companies feel that they must begin again from the beginning and utilize TQC to strengthen the corporate health and character of the company. Some set specific goals. Others do not spell them out. As I have often said, QC is not an act of cheerleading. Employees cannot act if they are given nothing but abstract instructions. Top management must make clear the goals it has in mind, pointing out which part of the company's character requires modification, or which aspect must be improved.

2. *Combining the efforts of all employees, achieving participation by all, and establishing a cooperative system*—As discussed in Chapter 2, control by specialists does not work in Japan. All employees in all divisions must be actively involved and combine their efforts.

3. *Establishing the quality assurance system and obtaining the confidence of customers and consumers*—Quality assurance being what it is, the very essence of QC, most companies announce such assurance to be their goal or ideal. The difference between new-style QC and old-style management is that QC does not seek short-term profit. Its primary goal is "quality first." By doing quality assurance well, QC can gain customer confidence, which will eventually lead to long-term profit.

4. *Aspiring to achieve the highest quality in the world and developing new products for that purpose*—As a corollary to this, many companies speak of development of creativity, or of improvement and establishment of technology. Japan is a resource-poor country. For Japan to be able to survive in international competi-

tion, it must in a short period of time develop highly reliable products with the highest quality.

5. *Establishing a management system that can secure profit in times of slow growth and can meet various challenges*—After the two oil shocks, many Japanese companies attempted a number of new approaches. They included saving resources and energy, casting off debt financing of the company, and encouraging belt-tightening management. To these companies, adoption of QC brings very desirable results. Do not go through the motion of observing perfunctory QC, but consider QC to be your ally in making money. If QC is carried out effectively profit is always assured.

6. *Showing respect for humanity, nurturing human resources, considering employee happiness, providing cheerful workplaces, and passing the torch to the next generation*—A company is no better or no worse than the employees it has. All of the goals presented here can be accomplished through active pursuance of QC activities in the workplace, where respect for humanity must prevail. As for middle management and staff members, delegate to them as much authority as you can. Let them become "managers" in their own right. Proven competence in QC circle activities opens the way for performing well in other management roles.

7. *Utilization of QC techniques*—Some people are mesmerized by the term "total quality control" and do not fully utilize the statistical methods. That is a mistake. Statistical methods form the basis of QC. Whether they be those seven simple QC tools or advanced techniques, people in the appropriate divisions must be able to master them and use them.

These seven items are the goals and accomplishments of those companies that undertook total quality control and accepted the challenge of the Deming Application Prize. I cannot be sure if they all reached 100 percent of the goals they set for themselves—the passing grade for the Deming Prize is seventy out of a possible 100—but I trust that these companies did reach 70 percent of their goals.

III. WHAT IS MANAGEMENT?

Goals of Management

My view of management is as follows. (See Table V-1.)

1. People

In management, the first concern of the company is the happiness of people who are connected with it. If the people do not feel happy and cannot be made happy, that company does not deserve to exist.

The first order of business is to let the employees have adequate income. Their humanity must be respected, and they must be given an opportunity to enjoy their

TABLE V-1   *Objectives and Techniques of Management*

Techniques	Goals	People	
	Quality	Price Cost & Profit	Quantity Date of Delivery
Physics			
Chemistry			
Electrical Engineering			
Mechanical Engineering			
Civil Engineering			
Architecture			
Metallurgy			
Mathematics			
Statistical Methods			
Computer			
Automatic Control			
Production Engineering			
Industrial Engineering			
Time Study			
Motion Study			
Market Survey			
Operation Research			
Value Engineering/Value Analysis			
Standardization			
Inspection			
Education			
Material Control			
Equipment Control			
Measurement Control			
Metallurgical Tool Control			

work and lead a happy life. The term "employees" as used here includes those employees of subcontractors and affiliated sales and service organizations.

Consumers come next. They must feel satisfied and pleased when they buy and use goods and services. If a television just bought breaks immediately, or if an electric heater is the cause of fire and injury, then the company that sold it has done enormous disservice. Also, if at the time of purchase the salesman does not treat the customer with courtesy or fails to explain fully how the merchandise is supposed to work, the customer will not be satisfied.

The welfare of shareholders must also be taken into consideration. Japan is a capitalist society, and each company must make sufficient profit to provide stock dividends for shareholders.

Companies exist in a society for the purpose of satisfying people in that society. This is the reason for their existence and should be their primary goal. We must now deal with the question of how to reach this goal.

There are three basic means which enable us to reach this primary goal. They are quality, price (including cost and profit), and quantity (including the date of delivery). I shall call these three our secondary goals. Controlling these three must be considered the goal of a given company, a process I shall call goal control.

2. Quality

I have discussed quality repeatedly. Defective products will not only inconvenience consumers but also hinder sales. If a company makes too many products that cannot be sold, it will waste raw materials and energy. This waste will also be a loss for society. A company must always supply products with the qualities the consumers demand. Consumers' requirements usually get higher and higher year after year as society advances. What was good last year may not be adequate the following year. In QC narrowly defined, QC means controlling carefully the supplying of quality products that have good sales points.

3. Price, Cost, and Profit

Everything has to do with money. No matter how inexpensive a product, if its quality is poor, no one will buy it. Similarly, no matter how high the quality, if the price is too steep, again no one will buy it. The consumer's main demand is for a just quality at a just price.

It is said that in a capitalist society, making profits is the goal of a company. On the other hand, there are some people who say that profit is sinful. These two statements represent extreme positions and both of them are wrong. If there is no profit, there can be no development of new products and new technology. Nor can there be investment in equipment modernization. Without profit, no salaries can be paid, and good people will not come to work for the company. In the end the company will be bankrupt, inconveniencing the very society it is supposed to serve.

Profit is actually the means to maintain a company permanently. A company without profits cannot even pay its fair share of taxes, and cannot fulfill its social obligations.

To raise profits, cost control must be practiced effectively. First, there must be a cost plan. At each stage of the development of a new product, the wheel of the PDCA circle must be turned in the right direction.

Generally, if QC is conducted effectively, defectives will decrease, and waste of materials and time will also decrease. This will lead to a rise in productivity and as a result will bring cost down. Through this process, products can be supplied to consumers at just prices. Incidentally, the price of a product is not determined by the cost but rather by value of true quality.

4. Quantity and Date of Delivery

A company must manufacture products in the amount required by the consumers and it must supply them to the consumers prior to the specified delivery date.

Quantity control includes control of the following: amount purchased, amount of production, amount of materials and products in stock (including amount of products in the production process), amount of sales, and date of delivery. If the company is overstocked with a certain commodity, a lot of resources and capital are not being utilized. Not only are they wasted, but they also push up the production cost. Of course if the amount of stock is too low, the company will not be able to meet adequately the requirements of consumers. The famed *kanban* (just-in-time delivery) system at Toyota takes this factor into account. It is a system that has been completed after effective implementation of QC and various forms of quantity control have taken place. Without these safeguards and effective control, a premature introduction of the *kanban* system can spell disaster, causing a complete shutdown of a factory.

On the other hand, if people, quality, cost, and quantity are effectively controlled, management can proceed smoothly.

Techniques and Tools of Reaching Management Goals

There are many techniques and tools that can be used to reach management goals. The items listed vertically in Table V-1 are these techniques or tools.

For example, physics, chemistry, mathematics, and mechanical engineering are all tools. At the annual convocation of my Institute, I often say to my students, ''You are going to study many subjects, such as physics, chemistry, mathematics, electrical engineering, and mechanical engineering. You are engineering students, but to study these subjects must not in itself be the purpose of your entering this institute. You are to study these subjects as a means of serving society, the nation, and the world. In your learning, never make the mistake of confusing the true goal with the means.''

Misperceptions are found not only among students but also among their professors. They study statistical methods and computers, but the study becomes the end in itself. In the case of quality control, when it was first introduced in Japan, there was a similar tendency. Some people thought quality control existed for the sake of statistical methods, while others thought that it existed for standardization. They confused the goals with the tools. Japan's quality control has become what it is today only after it has learned to correct past mistakes.

The tools of quality control are often divided into two categories, proper techniques and control techniques. I do not particularly like this differentiation. In Table V-1, items such as mechanical engineering, electrical engineering, architecture, civil engineering, metallurgy, physics, and mathematics are proper techniques, and statistical methods and the items listed below are considered control techniques. In my view, they are proper techniques as well.

To attain the four goals described earlier, we must utilize all proper techniques at our disposal and produce high quality goods inexpensively to serve our society.

I ask all applied scientists and engineers to acquire technology which is more like A. than B. in Diagram V-2. I call B. the well-type technology and A. the cone-shaped technology. When products become complex and technology becomes highly spe-

DIAGRAM V-2

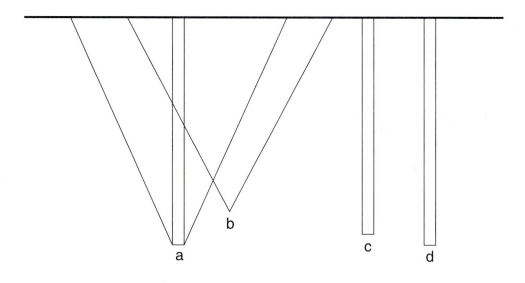

cialized as in today's world, the well-type technology becomes structurally frail. It dries up too quickly and cannot contribute to true technical development or to the development of new products. One must acquire cone-shaped technology, which develops a greater width as one digs in deeper. For example, a mechanical engineer must possess a general knowledge of electrical engineering, electronics, metallurgy, chemistry, statistical methods, and computers. If an engineer has only well-type knowledge he cannot move from project *c* to project *d*. However, if he has cone-shaped knowledge, once he succeeds in new product development in *a*, he can transfer that knowledge to new product development in *b*.

Let us try another example. What makes good engine specialists? Obviously engine specialists must be good mechanical engineers, but they must also know metallurgy and casting to appreciate how raw materials for the engine are made. They must be familiar with the principle of engine operations and must be able to utilize some degree of technical knowledge in the following areas: machine processing technique, fuel and lubricants, packing, ignition, electronics, statistical methods, computers, standardization, etc.

Similarly, to create the highest quality products, we must utilize all tools and proper techniques available to us.

I am often asked, "What is the relationship between quality control, industrial engineering, and operation research?" My answer is simple: "To create a quality product, we utilize all tools at our disposal, including industrial engineering and operation research." The so-called QC techniques (statistical methods) are, of course, the tools. However, QC itself must be treated as one of the basic objectives of the company. "Do not confuse objectives with the tools."

Total Quality Management Tools

Part III describes the so-called "Total Quality Management Tools." These tools are commonly divided into the *Seven Basic Quality Control Tools* and the *Seven Management and Planning Tools.* Their origin lies in fields and applications as diverse as Engineering, Psychology, Anthropology, and Project Management. In the U.S. and Japan the fourteen tools presented here are complemented by other creative and analytical tools like brainstorming and force field analysis.

Use of the tools is one of the essential components of TQM training for line workers and managers alike. Most of the tools are particularly well suited for team-based problem solving and planning. They allow teams to gather, develop and organize significant amounts of information using creative and analytical approaches.

The tools are easy to understand conceptually but not always easy to use. The mechanics of teamwork is complex and the role of a trained facilitator is a key in team-based problem solving. Herein lies one of the greatest difficulties related to the use of tools in problem solving. The tools do not provide answers in and of themselves. They are to be carefully chosen depending upon various factors like the task at hand, the amount and kind of information that can be accessed, the number and experience of the group members, the time available, and the culture of the organization.

Nevertheless, the tools remain one of the most appealing practical features of TQM approaches: the systematic effort to integrate creativity and analysis in team-based problem solving and planning.

Going with the Flow(chart)

By John T. Burr

- Before you try to solve a problem define it.
- Before you try to control a process, understand it.
- Before trying to control everything, find out what is important.
- Start by picturing the process.

Making and using flowcharts are among the most important actions in bringing process control to both administrative and manufacturing processes. While it is obvious that to control a process one must first understand that process, many companies are still trying to solve problems and improve processes without realizing how important flowcharts are as a first step.

The easiest and best way to understand a process is to draw a picture of it—that's basically what flowcharting is. There are many styles that can be used to draw a flowchart. Some people use pictures, some use engineering symbols, and others just use squares or rectangles for the whole diagram. There really is no right or wrong way to display the information. The true test of a flowchart is how well those who create and use it can understand it.

CONSTRUCTING FLOW DIAGRAMS

Every process is supplied with services and products from some supplier(s). Likewise, every process provides products or services to some other process—its customer(s). Figure 1 shows a generic process. Using this figure as a guide, making a flowchart is simple as long as the designer(s) follows these roles:

Rule 1. The most important rule is that the right people must be involved in making the chart. This includes those who actually do the work of the process, suppliers to the process, customers of the process, the supervisor of the area within which the process functions, and an independent facilitator.

Rule 2. All members of the group must participate. To that end, the use of an independent facilitator will be a great benefit for several reasons. There will be less chance of one member of the group having undue influence on the outcome. Second, a facilitator is trained to ask the right questions, seek input from everyone, and resolve any conflicts that arise. Finally, a facilitator can save the group members from the drudgery of writing down all the information. Their time is better spent discussing and charting the process.

Rule 3. All data must be visible to all the people all the time. I have found that the use of newsprint and masking tape is imperative for a good flowcharting session. As one sheet is completed, it is taped on the wall in sequence with previous work. Rarely is a session completed without at least some rework of previous parts of the flowchart as the group members reflect on the information in front of them.

Avoid using transparencies, because that allows only a segment of the chart to be displayed at one time. This reduces the opportunity for the group to rethink earlier decisions. The use of a chalkboard or white board also limits the space available and requires that someone keep a running record of the diagram on paper as it is made.

Rule 4. Enough time must be allotted. Experience shows that much more time is required to make a flowchart than is usually expected. More than one session might be required. It might even be desirable, since group members will have more time to obtain more information on the functioning of the process.

Rule 5. The more questions everyone asks, the better. Questions are the key to the flowcharting process. There are many questions that can be asked by both the facili-

FIGURE 1   *Generic Process/Product Improvement Model*

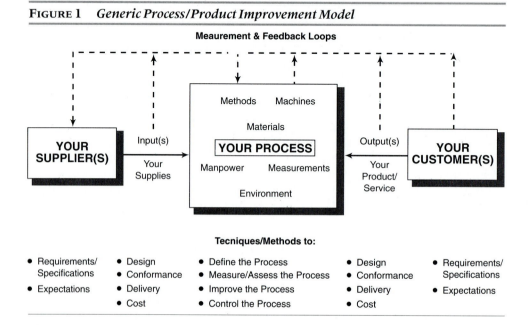

tator and the group members. What is the first thing that happens? What is the next thing that happens? Questioning should continue throughout the process. Questions that will be helpful at certain times during the process include:

- Where does the (service, material) come from?
- How does the (service, material) get to the process?
- Who makes the decision (if one is needed)?
- What happens if the decision is "yes"? What happens if the decision is "no"?
- Is there anything else that must be done at this point?
- Where does the (product, service) of this operation go?
- What tests are performed on the product at each part of the process?
- What tests are performed on the process?
- What happens if the test is out of tolerance?

Even more questions will arise during the session(s). One caution, however: it's usually not a good idea to ask the question "Why?" This question might make one of the team members feel defensive. In very specific situations it might be helpful to ask that question, but only if the team needs the information.

FIGURE 2   *Manufacture of Photographic Film and Paper*

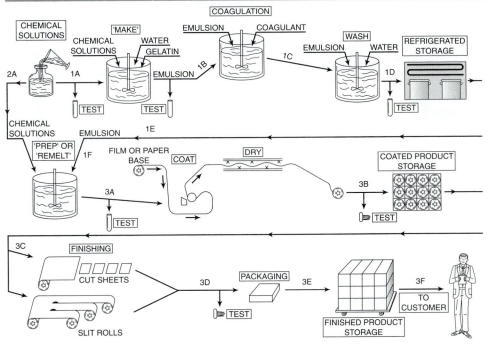

APPLICATIONS

There are many ways to use flowcharts on the factory floor—for example, for equipment diagrams, pipe diagrams, etc. Figure 2 shows one example. Employees should get used to working with flowcharts. The charts can be even more helpful if employees ask the questions listed earlier, particularly the questions about what could be measured.

FIGURE 3   *Getting to Work in the Morning*

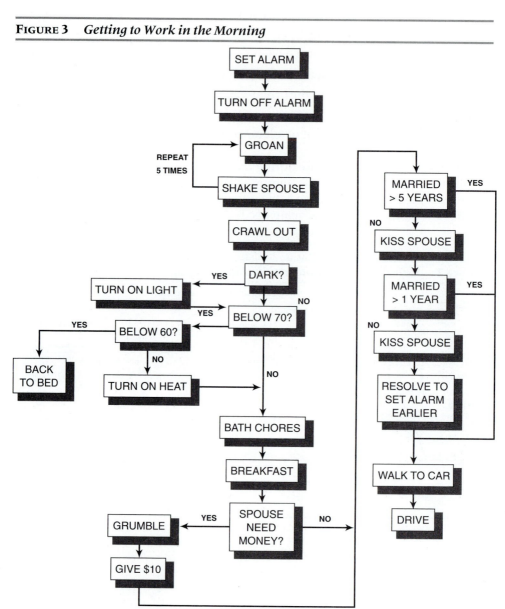

While flowcharts are important in manufacturing, the most substantial improvements can be made by using them in staff or administrative functions. One company I visited recently had almost every staff function flowcharted—including traffic control, billing, accounting, and purchasing. The employees were excited about their jobs; they controlled the process.

One process flowchart with which I've had a lot of fun teaching is shown in Figure 3. If a process as mundane as getting to work can be flowcharted, any process can be flowcharted!

THE BENEFITS OF FLOWCHARTS

Companies that use process flowcharting reap many benefits, including the following:

- The people who work in the process understand the process. They begin to control it—instead of being victims of it.
- Once the process can be seen objectively in the flowchart, improvements can be easily identified.
- Employees realize how they fit into the overall process, and they visualize their suppliers and customers as a part of that overall process. This leads directly to improved communication between departments and work areas.
- The people who participate in flowcharting sessions become enthusiastic supporters of the entire quality effort. They will continue to provide suggestions for even further improvement.
- Process flowcharts are valuable tools in training programs for new employees.

In short, perhaps the most important benefit of using process flowcharts is that the people in the process will all understand it in the same terms. That understanding leads to happier employees who can control their destinies, more economical processes, less waste in administrative functions, and better customer-supplier relationships between departments.

Cause-and-Effect Diagrams

———

BY J. STEPHEN SARAZEN

"Quality begins with education and ends with education." These words, attributed to the late Kaoru Ishikawa, sum up a principle philosophy of quality. To improve processes, you must continuously strive to obtain more information about those processes and their output.

One unique and valuable tool for accomplishing this goal is the cause-and-effect diagram. This tool was first developed in 1943 by Ishikawa at the University of Tokyo; he used it to explain to a group of engineers from the Kawasaki Steel Works how various factors could be sorted and related.

The cause-and-effect diagram is a method for analyzing process dispersion. The diagram's purpose is to relate causes and effects. It is also known as the Ishikawa diagram and the fishbone diagram (because the completed diagram resembles the skeleton of a fish). Whatever it's called, the tool is certainly one of the most elegant and widely used of the so-called seven QC tools.

It has been my experience that this tool is not only invaluable for virtually any issue requiring attention, but can be easily learned by people at all levels of the organization and applied immediately.

There are three basic types of cause-and-effect diagrams: dispersion analysis, production process classification, and cause enumeration. Figure 1 depicts the basic format for the cause-and-effect diagram. Note the hierarchical relationship of the effect to the main causes and their subsequent relationship to the sub-causes. For example, Main Cause A has a direct relationship to the effect. Each of the sub-causes is related in terms of its level of influence on the main cause.

While a cause-and-effect diagram can be developed by an individual, it is best when used by a team. (Considering how well-suited this tool is for team applications, it is not surprising that Ishikawa is the father of quality circles.) One of the most valuable attributes of this tool is that it provides an excellent means to facilitate

---

Figure 1   *The Basic Cause-and-Effect Diagram*

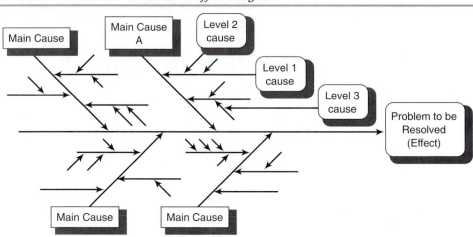

a brainstorming session. It will focus the participants on the issue at hand and immediately allow them to sort ideas into useful categories, especially when the dispersion analysis or process classification methods are used.

DISPERSION ANALYSIS

Let's assume you are having difficulties with customer complaints. Let us further assume that you are able to pull together about seven individuals from various functions throughout the organization. Each of these individuals has sound knowledge of the overall business as well as an area of specific expertise. This team will

Figure 2   *The Main Cause Headings*

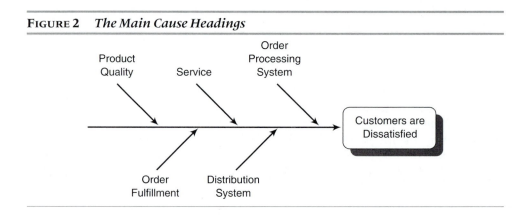

provide a good example of the way to construct a cause-and-effect diagram using the dispersion analysis methods. There are three steps:

Step 1. It is quite simple to construct the diagram. First, determine the quality characteristic you wish to improve—perhaps customer satisfaction. You must be certain there is consensus when you write the problem statement. For example: "Customers are dissatisfied."

Write this brief statement of fact on a large sheet of paper, a white board, or similar area. Write it on the right side, center of the page, and draw a box around it with an arrow running to it. This problem statement constitutes the effect.

In a manufacturing process, you might use a specific characteristic of a product as the effect, such as a problem with paste thickness in a surface mount line, poor paint coverage, or welding errors. In an administrative or service area, you might use customer complaints, decreased sales volume, or increased accounts receivable past due.

Step 2. Now the team must generate ideas as to what is causing the effect, contributing to customer dissatisfaction. The causes are written as branches flowing to the main branch. Figure 2 shows the main cause headings resulting from an actual session in a service/distribution business. In this case, the team determined five areas—product quality, service, order processing system, distribution system, and order fulfillment—as the main potential causes of dissatisfied customers. If there is difficulty in determining the main branches or causes, use generic headings—such as method, machine, people, materials, environment, or training—to help start the team.

Step 3. The next step is to brainstorm all the possible causes of problems in each of the major cause categories. These ideas are captured and applied to the chart as sub-causes. It is important to continually define and relate causes to each other. It is acceptable to repeat sub-causes in several places if the team feels there is a direct, multiple relationship. This effort will ensure a complete diagram and a more enlightened team.

Returning to Figure 2, you can see that the team identified five main causes of customer dissatisfaction. Now the team members must ask themselves, "What could contribute to each of these five main causes?" Once several sub-causes have been identified, the team continues asking the same question until the lowest-level causes are discovered.

Figure 3 shows the completed portion of the diagram for one of the main causes: service. The team identified reliability issues, carrier issues (e.g., a trucking company), poor communications, and lack of, or poor, training.

The next level of causes is identified by asking the question "What could cause a problem in these areas?" In the case of the poor communications, the team focused on functions and jobs—sales people, field representatives, and managers—as potential causes. You can see that lack of knowledge of the customer can cause managers to communicate poorly. Subsequently you can see that inexperience and training can be two key contributors to a manager's lack of customer knowledge. Thus, there are six levels of causes in this example.

FIGURE 3   *A Detailed Look at One Main Course*

Version 1

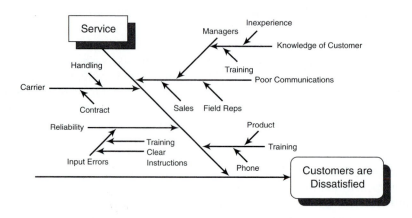

Version 2

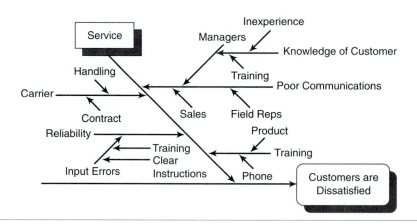

PROCESS CLASSIFICATION

Another type of diagram is known as the process classification diagram. I prefer to eliminate the word "production" from the chart title because it has a manufacturing ring to it. From my experience, this tool is as valuable in service-based businesses as it is in manufacturing companies. After all, every product or service is the result of a process.

Although the basic process for constructing this type of diagram is similar to the one used for dispersion analysis, there are some differences. These differences are driven by the application. For the process classification method, you identify the flow of the process you wish to improve and then list key quality-influencing characteristics at each of the steps.

Step 1. Identify the process and develop a flow diagram of the primary sequential steps. For example, in a generic selling process, the following steps might be identified: make initial customer contact, develop an understanding of customer needs, provide information to the customer, follow up, close the sale, and follow up on the sale.

Step 2. Now add all the things that might influence the quality of each step. Use the method described in the previous section. Brainstorming with a team of knowledgeable people will make the finished diagram more like the actual process.

Figure 4 is an example of a completed process classification diagram. As you can see, the intent is to take the cause and effect to the lowest level to understand all the contributing factors to improve the process.

It is also advisable to consider the connecting steps from process step to process step. Everywhere there is a handoff from one step to the next, there are likely to be possible causes of dispersion. Many opportunities for improvement can be found in these areas.

CAUSE ENUMERATION

The cause enumeration method involves simply brainstorming all possible causes and listing them in the order they are offered. Once the brainstorm has exhausted itself, the team begins the process of grouping the causes as it did for the dispersion analysis diagram. The end result looks exactly the same.

FIGURE 4   *A Completed Process Classification Diagram*

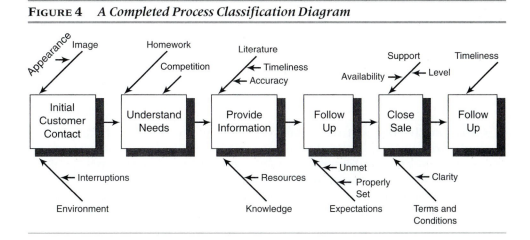

I have found this process can be enhanced dramatically using the affinity diagram process. It is a valuable method for gaining insight and organization of ideas. Basically, the brainstorm is conducted by capturing all ideas on cards or those handy little notepads with the gum on one end. Each card should contain only one idea. The cards are then arranged in groups and subgroups. Cards that have an affinity for one another are placed together. Once it is completed, the affinity diagram provides the basis for the cause-and-effect diagram.

FILLETING THE FISH

Understanding processes, using teams, and identifying areas of opportunity are excellent ways to move toward continuous improvement while solving some of today's tough issues. But they are only the beginning. To obtain the full value from the cause-and-effect diagram, it must be turned into action. It is therefore wise to quantify the problem and as many of the causes as possible. Once this has been done, the business can determine the priority areas to be addressed and can track improvements.

In the earlier example, the business was able to quantify the problem of customer dissatisfaction by measuring several key parameters, including number of calls about problems, number of requests to return material for specific reasons, and receivables aging.

In the areas where sub-causes were identified, various parts of the organization were surveyed to determine the primary areas of opportunity for addressing the causes identified by the cause-and-effect diagram. For example, one need was for training in simple statistical problem-solving methods. This need was quantified not only by the number of people needing training, but also by the results of the training applications.

As the team and business move to quantify the causes, other tools play key roles. Pareto analysis, histograms, control charts, scatter plots, and multivariate analysis might be particularly valuable.

HINTS AND CREATIVE USES

Here are some helpful hints for facilitating or participating in a cause-and-effect exercise.

1. **Consider the big picture.** When constructing a cause-and-effect diagram, think about the issue at hand in its broadest sense. Consider the environment, inside the business and externally; politics, including government policies if appropriate; employee issues; and external factors, such as the local or national economy. Granted, some of these areas are well beyond the control of the team. Nevertheless, there is a benefit to understanding the impact of such factors.

2. **Facilitation.** Facilitating a cause-and-effect session is very challenging. It is similar to facilitating any brainstorming session except that the thoughts must be written in a particular place as opposed to being listed. The facilitator must listen to the ideas of the participants, capture those thoughts in only one or two words, and write them in the appropriate position on the chart. This last step is the tricky part. My recommendation is to have the participants decide where the cause should be written. This approach helps ensure that the correct location is chosen and removes some of the burden from the facilitator.

The Benefits and Weaknesses of Each
Cause-and-Effect Diagram

- Diagram Type: Dispersion analysis
  Key Benefits:
  1. Helps organize and relate factors.
  2. Provides a structure for brainstorming.
  3. Involves everyone.
  4. It's fun.

  Potential drawbacks:
  1. Might be difficult to facilitate if developed in true brainstorming fashion.
  2. Might become very complex; requires dedication and patience.

- Diagram Type: Process classification
  Key Benefits:
  1. Provides a solid sequential view of the process and the factors that influence each step.
  2. Might help determine functional ownership for the work to be done in improvement.

  Potential drawback:
  1. It is sometimes difficult to identify or demonstrate inter-relationships.

- Diagram Type: Cause enumeration
  Key Benefits:
  1. Easy to facilitate.
  2. Provides in-depth list of all possible causes.

  Potential drawbacks:
  1. The added step of creating an affinity diagram might add time to the process.
  2. The final diagram might be difficult to draw because of the random output of the brainstorming session.

---

3. **Review and embellishment.** To ensure that the diagram is complete, have each member of the team review it the next day or have them show it to one or two additional people to obtain their opinion. Use your discretion in deciding whether to use second parties on very technical issues or problems unique to a particular job or area.

4. **Broad-based participation.** If you want to add a creative flair to your development effort and, at the same time, encourage broad-based participation from your group or organization, try this. Hang a large white board or sheet of butcher paper in an accessible location. Ask the group or a manager to identify a problem that needs to be addressed. Write that problem statement in the "head of the fish" and draw the arrow to it. Now invite the entire organization to participate in developing the diagram over a certain time frame—say two weeks. You will be amazed how many people will really get into working and understanding the process.

   The obvious drawback to this approach is that you miss the brainstorming opportunity. However, reading what others have written in the diagram will generate ideas. The commitment that must be made is to take the input and act on it.

   While this might sound a little out of the ordinary, I can tell you from firsthand experience that it works. I trained a vice president's staff in the use of cause-and-effect diagrams several years ago and suggested this approach. We hung a large white board outside his office and began writing a new issue on it every couple of weeks. Some of his people had been trained in the technique; many had not. The end result was that more than 100 people contributed to the first few diagrams and his staff was provided with invaluable information, insight, and suggestions for improving processes.

5. **Working toward the desired result.** I have found it very useful to state the desired result—rather than a problem—in the head of the fish. For example, instead of writing "Customers are dissatisfied," write "100% customer satisfaction." The exercise now focuses on finding means to achieve this goal rather than working the problem. Many of the findings will be the same but some unique approaches might find their way onto the chart.

   The work could also be stated as "how to" arrive at some desired result. A few years ago, I trained a group of elementary teachers in the use of cause-and-effect diagrams. They needed to get students to perform as a team. Rather than trying to solve the problem of why students didn't perform as a team, we developed a cause-and-effect diagram using the statement "What makes an effective/winning team?"

   Many of the teachers returned to their classes and used this exercise with students. The students wanted to be winners. Now they were asked to identify all the attributes of a winning team, and they were able to do so. They learned that it takes a lot of hard work and dedication.

   The teachers then posted the completed diagram every day and when the students did not demonstrate the behavior required to be a winner (in their own words), the diagram served as a reminder. This process had also worked for business issues such as how to improve competitiveness and how to ensure SPC applications will follow training.

UNDERSTANDING PROCESSES

In the past decade, quality has gained recognition as the competitive imperative for all businesses. The root of all quality improvement lies in understanding processes. Many existing tools assist managers, engineers, and others in this work. You need not always look for the newest tool, software, or management theory to construct a sound foundation on which to build improvements. If you are looking for a tool that fosters team work, educates users, identifies lowest-level issues on which to work, helps show a true picture of the process, guides discussion, can be used for virtually any issue your business might face, and is fun, look no further than this 46-year-old tool called the cause-and-effect diagram.

Bibliography

Ishikawa, Kaoru, *Guide to Quality Control* (Tokyo: Asia Productivity Organization, 1986).

Wadsworth, Harrison M., Kenneth S. Stephens, and A. Blanton Godfrey, *Modern Methods for Quality Control and Improvement* (New York: John Wiley & Sons, Inc., 1986).

Control Charts

By Peter D. Shainin

Even the best automatic machine tools cannot make every unit exactly the same. Better tools are followed by new product designs offering lower cost, better performance, or both; both these improved designs often require tighter tolerances. Thus, the luxury of improved machine capability soon becomes the necessity. So, the ability to operate to a tight tolerance without producing defects becomes a major business advantage.

A diligent operator, adjusting the machine settings often to stay within this tight tolerance, will make many scrap pieces. The more diligent the operator, the worse the result—proof of Murphy's law.

W. Edwards Deming does a very dramatic demonstration of this phenomenon using a funnel and a marble as shown in Figure 1. The funnel, mounted on a stand, is placed so its spout is directly over a target. The marble is dropped through the funnel, hits the target, and rolls some distance to one side. The target represents the nominal value (halfway between the tolerance limits), and the final resting place of the marble represents the value of the final product. The direction and distance the marble rolls represents random variation from the manufacturing process. The diligent operator now measures the distance by which the marble missed the target and moves the funnel that distance in the opposite direction. The marble is dropped a second time and again the operator measures the distance by which it missed the target and adjusts the funnel position.

After several drops of the marble, it becomes obvious that the final resting place of the marble is actually moving farther from the target rather than closer. The operator's diligence is making the variation worse!

If we collect all the pieces that could ever be made with this process, this machine, and its specific settings, tooling, raw material, etc. and we measure an important characteristic (such as a dimension) on each piece, we could arrange these numbers

FIGURE 1

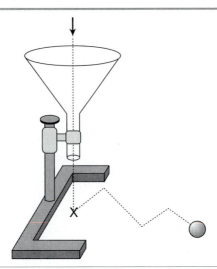

in a frequency plot like Figure 2. The vertical axis is the value of the dimension. The horizontal axis is the number of pieces that have each value. The frequency plot in Figure 2 is the distribution of the dimension produced by this particular process. The distribution gives us a picture of the random variation represented by the rolling marble.

Statistical process control (SPC) uses statistics to tell the operator when to adjust the process and when to leave it alone. SPC recognizes that some random variation always exists. It helps us control the distribution rather than the individual piece dimensions. Control charts are a method of SPC.

FIGURE 2

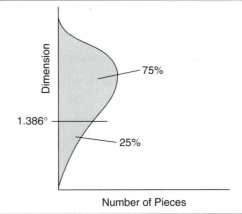

PROBABILITIES AND CONTROL

The shaded area in Figure 2 represents all pieces that will ever be made by this process. Because 75% of the area is above 1.386 inches, three-quarters of the time a piece made by this process will be larger than 1.386 inches. Said another way, the probability of producing pieces larger than 1.386 inches is 0.75. If the distribution is normal or Gaussian shaped and we know its mean and standard deviation, we can find the probability of producing pieces beyond any specific dimension. We could pick a dimension on each side of the distribution with only a very small probability of being exceeded and call them control limits. If the process makes pieces beyond these control limits, we can be quite confident the distribution has changed.

CONTROL CHARTS

In about 1926, Walter Shewhart of Bell Labs worked out a way to take data from a process that allows us to tell if the process variation is from a stable distribution, to transform that distribution into a normal shape, and to estimate its mean and standard deviation. We usually set control limits so that pieces from the stable distribution will exceed them only 0.26% of the time. Any pieces made beyond these control limits indicate the distribution has changed. Shewhart was successful in finding the causes that changed the distribution but was unable to discover the causes of variation within the distribution. He theorized that variation within the distribution was from chance or undiscoverable causes and that changes in the distribution were from assignable causes.

Since Shewhart completed his work, a number of techniques have been developed that will discover both chance and assignable causes of variation. The most universally useful of these is Multi-Varied. Although control charts are no longer useful to decide when a process can or cannot be improved, they can reduce over-adjustment by telling an operator when to adjust the process and when to leave it alone. They can also tell us when a process is good enough that we should direct our improvement resources to more pressing needs.

In general, if the distribution is narrower than the tolerance and within the tolerance, the process should not be adjusted. If the distribution changes so at least some portion of it is out of tolerance, the process must be adjusted immediately or defective work will be produced, as shown in Figure 3. To define the distribution and sense any changes, Shewhart relied on the central limit theorem, central to statistics, which was codified by Pierre Simon Laplace in about 1800. There are three aspects of the theorem relevant to control charts:

1. If samples are taken from a distribution in groups, called subgroups, and the individual items are averaged, the distribution of the averages will approach a normal or Gaussian shape as the subgroups become larger.
2. The distribution of averages will have the same mean as the distribution of individuals.

3. The standard deviation of the distribution of averages will be narrower than the distribution of individuals. In fact, their relationship will be:

$$\sigma_{\overline{x}} = \sigma_x / \sqrt{n}$$

Where $\sigma_{\overline{x}}$ is the standard deviation of a distribution of averages, σ_x is the standard deviation of a distribution of individuals, and n is the number of individuals used to make up each average.

The distribution of averages can be treated as normal for the purposes of control charts provided each subgroup consists of at least four pieces. If we take at least 25 subgroups, we can use the average of all their ranges to estimate $\sigma_{\overline{x}}$. The preceding formula allows us to calculate σ_x and compare the distribution of individual pieces to the tolerance limits.

Making Control Charts

The upper and lower control limits for averages are customarily set at the mean ± 3 standard deviations. Because this includes 99.74% of the area to the left of the distribution, the probability of obtaining a subgroup average from this distribution, which is outside the control limits, is only 0.26%. Occasionally, ± 2 standard deviation limits are used. In that case, the probability of an average falling beyond the control limits is about 5%. We find control limits by taking 25 subgroups consisting of a minimum of four pieces each. We calculate the average and range of each subgroup, then the grand average, $\overline{x}$, and the average range, $\overline{R}$. Figure 4 is a spread sheet convenient for this purpose. The grand average, $\overline{x}$, will be the central line of our $\overline{x}$ chart.

FIGURE 3

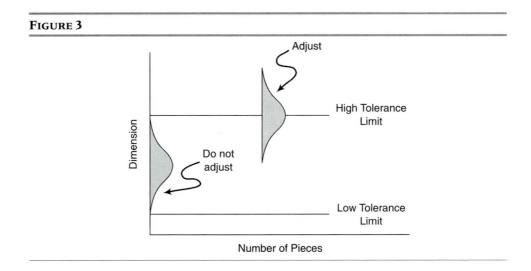

FIGURE 4

SAMPLE #	1	2	3	4	5	6	7	8	9	10	11	12	13
	14.5	13.5	10.5	11.5	12	9	12	17	17	11	19	16	15
	10	12.5	10.5	16	9	9.5	11.5	14.5	12	10	14	12	18
	10.5	16	10.5	15	11	8	8	12	11	14	13.5	14.5	14
	14	9	11	16	10.5	12	9	16	19	16	17	11	11
$\bar{x}$	12.25	12.75	10.63	14.63	10.63	9.63	10.13	14.88	14.75	12.75	15.88	13.38	14.50
R	4.50	7.00	0.50	4.50	3.00	4.00	4.00	5.00	8.00	6.00	5.50	5.00	7.00

SAMPLE #	14	15	16	17	18	19	20	21	22	23	24	25
	15	17	17	15.5	14	13.5	15	19	15	14	11.5	15
	19	15	14.5	19	19	15	19	18	11.5	17	14	13
	10	14	9.5	18	18	18	18.5	14	9	16	15	14
	12	16	14.5	19	16.5	14.5	18	13	17	12	10	17
$\bar{x}$	14.00	15.50	13.88	17.88	16.88	15.25	17.63	16.00	13.13	14.75	12.63	14.75
R	9.00	3.00	7.50	3.50	5.00	4.50	4.00	6.00	8.00	5.00	5.00	4.00

For $\bar{x}$:
Upper control limit $= \bar{x} + A_2 \times \bar{R}$
Lower control limit $= \bar{x} - A_2 \times \bar{R}$
$\bar{R}$ will be the central line for the R chart.

For R:
Upper control limit $= D_4 \times \bar{R}$
Lower control limit $= D_3 \times \bar{R}$

A_2, D_3, and D_4 are factors that depend on subgroup size, n. Values for some typical subgroup sizes are given in Table 1. We draw the charts for $\bar{x}$ and R as shown in Figure 5. The central line and control limits for the data shown in Figure 4 are:

Central line for $\bar{x}$ chart $= \bar{x} = 13.96$
Upper control limit for $\bar{x} = 13.96 + 0.73 \times 5.14 = 17.7$
Lower control limit for $\bar{x} = 13.96 - 0.73 \times 5.14 = 10.2$
Central line for R chart $= \bar{R} = 5.14$
Upper control limit for R $= 2.28 \times 5.14 = 11.7$
Lower control limit for R $= 0 \times 5.14 = 0.0$

TABLE 1

n	A_2	D_3	D_4
4	0.73	0	2.28
5	0.58	0	2.11

All the average and range values used to calculate the control limits must be plotted on their respective charts. If any points fall outside either set of control limits, the distribution was not stable and the control limits are inflated. The reason for this instability must be discovered and controlled or eliminated. A new set of 25 subgroups must be taken and a new set of control limits calculated. The X bar chart of Figure 5 has three points beyond the control limits. The assignable cause must be discovered and these 100 data points retaken. Figure 6 is a plot of the individuals from Figure 4. Overlaid arrows show the shifts in the distribution. Notice, the distribution changed both its mean and standard deviation several times while the control limits were being calculated. If the assignable causes of this shift and width

FIGURE 5

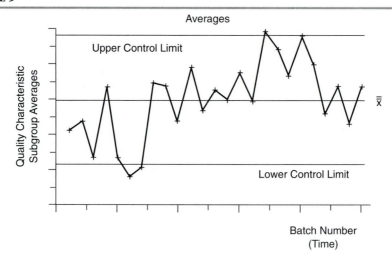

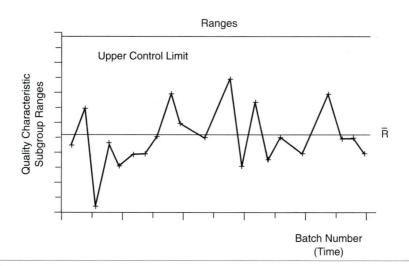

FIGURE 6

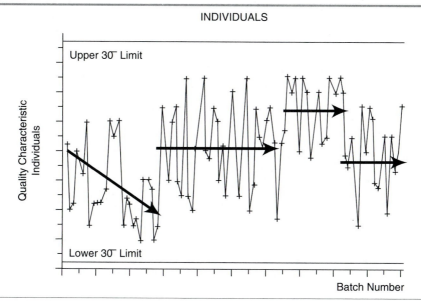

change were discovered and eliminated or controlled, this process could be held to a much narrower variation.

The time and effort required to retake all 100 data points is often so burdensome that many practitioners just delete the subgroups that fall outside of the control limits and recalculate the control limits. Figure 4 demonstrates just how unsatisfactory that practice really is.

INTERPRETING THE RESULTS

After obtaining a good set of control limits, we can take subgroups periodically and plot their average and range on the appropriate chart. If an average falls outside either control limit, the distribution has either moved or gotten wider. If a range falls outside either control limit, the distribution has changed width. In either case, the process is not stable and is said to be out of control. The assignable cause must be discovered and eliminated or controlled in order to control this distribution. Control charts can only warn us of an assignable cause of variation. They are not very good at finding the cause and they cannot eliminate or control it. Process engineers and operators must use other tools to do that.

PROCESS CAPABILITY

A process distribution that stays stable and within control limits is satisfactory only if the control limits are inside the tolerance. The control limits apply to the distribution of averages, and the tolerance applies to the distribution of individuals. These distributions are in terms of two different scales. Their relationship is given by the central limit theorem above. If we wish to compare the tolerance to the control limits, we must first divide the tolerance by the square root of n; so, if the subgroup size is four, we will first divide the tolerance by two. Process capability, Cp, is the scaled tolerance width divided by the width of the control limits. Most processes can be operated satisfactorily if their Cp is 1.33 or greater.

CAUTIONS

I want to issue two cautions. The first involves tolerance limits. It is not a good idea to show scaled tolerance limits on the averages chart. Points beyond the control limits require action even if they are beyond the tolerance limits. Operators are likely to become confused and use tolerance limits instead of control limits. After all, only work outside of tolerance is unsatisfactory.

My second caution involves stability. Many processes do not remain stable for very long. A change in raw material, tooling, or any number of process operating conditions can change the process distribution. New control limits must be calculated for each such change if the control charts are to maintain their effectiveness. Process capability can change as often as several times a day. Management efforts to catalog process capability for all processes in a facility are, therefore, a waste of resources.

Reference

1. Leonard Seder, "Diagnosis with Diagrams," *Industrial Quality Control,* January 1950.

Bibliography

A more complete treatment of control charts, including different types of charts and alternative methods of SPC, can be found in *Juran's Quality Control Handbook,* Fourth Edition, McGraw-Hill Book Company, 1988, chapter 24. Peter D. Shainin, along with Dorian Shainin, are the co-authors of that chapter.

Histograms

ADAPTED FROM THE QUALITY IMPROVEMENT TOOLS WORKBOOK SET PUBLISHED BY THE JURAN INSTITUTE, INC.

A histogram is a graphic summary of variation in a set of data. The pictorial nature of the histogram enables us to see patterns that are difficult to see in a simple table of numbers.

The development of the histogram is credited to the French statistician A.M. Guerry. In 1833 Guerry introduced a new kind of bar graph to describe his analysis of crime data. Guerry's bar graphs were unique in that he arranged the bars to show the number of crimes corresponding to various categories of continuous variables such as the age of the criminal. Since Guerry presented the data pictorially, rather than as simple columns of numbers, it was easier for his readers to "see" his conclusions about crime in France. Guerry's work won him the medal of the French Academy, and his histograms became a standard tool for summarizing, analyzing, and displaying data.

THE CASE OF "COULDN'T HEAR"

We stress the importance of using data and facts in our problem-solving and quality improvement efforts. But sometimes the data can seem overwhelming or of little value to us as we tackle the problem at hand. Consider the following example.

A manufacturer of electronic telecommunications equipment was receiving complaints from the field about low volume on long-distance connections. Aunt Millie in California couldn't hear Cousin Bill in Florida.

A string of amplifiers manufactured by the company was being used to boost the signal at various points along the way. The boosting ability of the amplifiers (engineers call it the "gain") was naturally the prime suspect in the case.

The design of the amplifiers had called for a gain of 10 decibels (dB). This means that the output from the amplifier should be about 10 times stronger than the input signal. This amplification makes up for the natural fading of the signal over the long-distance connection. Recognizing that it is difficult to make every amplifier with a gain of exactly 10 dB, the design allowed the amplifiers to be considered acceptable if the gain fell between 7.75 dB and 12.2 dB. These permissible minimum and maximum values are sometimes called the specification (or spec) limits. The expected value of 10 dB is the nominal value. Because there were literally hundreds of amplifiers boosting the signal on a long connection, low-gain amplifiers should have been balanced by high-gain amplifiers to give an acceptable volume level.

The quality improvement team investigating the "couldn't hear" condition arranged to test the gain of 120 amplifiers. The results of the tests are listed in Figure 1.

This table of data is certainly formidable; there are 120 numbers to examine. More important, since the gain of all the amplifiers fell within the specification limits, the team was tempted to conclude, based on a quick glance at the numbers, that the data were of little value. The testing and data gathering done by the team obviously represented a dead end in their investigation of the case. Or did it?

The team decided to construct a histogram to give them a better "picture" of the 120 data point. They divided the specification range into nine intervals of 0.5 dB each and counted the number of data points that fell in each interval. They found that there were 24 amplifiers whose gain reading fell between 7.75 dB and 8.24 dB, 28 amplifiers between 8.25 dB and 8.74 dB, and so on.

This histogram of the data is shown in Figure 2. The height of each bar on the histogram represents the number of amplifiers with gain readings that fell within the dB range that the bar covers on the horizontal axis. For example, the histogram indicates that 19 amplifiers had a gain reading between 9.25 dB and 9.74 dB.

The histogram of the data gave the team a very different view of the situation. While all the amplifiers fell within the specification limits, the readings were cer-

FIGURE 1   *Data on Amplifier Gain*

GAIN OF 120 TESTED AMPLIFIERS									
8.1	10.4	8.8	9.7	7.8	9.9	11.7	8.0	9.3	9.0
8.2	8.9	10.1	9.4	9.2	7.9	9.5	10.9	7.8	8.3
9.1	8.4	9.6	11.1	7.9	8.5	8.7	7.8	10.5	8.5
11.5	8.0	7.9	8.3	8.7	10.0	9.4	9.0	9.2	10.7
9.3	9.7	8.7	8.2	8.9	8.6	9.5	9.4	8.8	8.3
8.4	9.1	10.1	7.8	8.1	8.8	8.0	9.2	8.4	7.8
7.9	8.5	9.2	8.7	10.2	7.9	9.8	8.3	9.0	9.6
9.9	10.6	8.6	9.4	8.8	8.2	10.5	9.7	9.1	8.0
8.7	9.8	8.5	8.9	9.1	8.4	8.1	9.5	8.7	9.3
8.1	10.1	9.6	8.3	8.0	9.8	9.0	8.9	8.1	9.7
8.5	8.2	9.0	10.2	9.5	8.3	8.9	9.1	10.3	8.4
8.6	9.2	8.5	9.6	9.0	10.7	8.6	10.0	8.8	8.6

FIGURE 2 *Histogram of Amplifier Gain Data Figure*

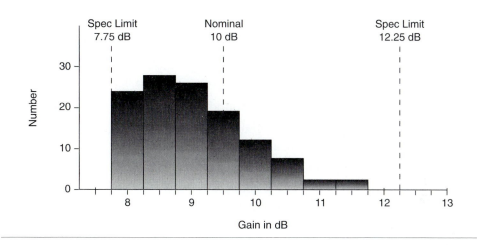

RESULTS OF AMPLIFIER GAIN TESTING

Part Number: AN898   120 Units Tested

tainly not evenly distributed around the nominal 10 dB value. Most of the amplifiers had a lower-than-nominal value of gain. This pattern was hard to see in the table of data, but the histogram clearly revealed it.

If most of the amplifiers in the series on a long-distance connection boost the signal a little bit less than expected, the result will be a low volume level—Aunt Millie in California won't be able to hear Cousin Bill in Florida.

The histogram gave the team a clearer and more complete picture of the data. Their testing, data gathering, and analysis were not a dead end. They could now concentrate their investigation in the factory to find out why the manufacturing line was not producing more amplifiers closer to the nominal value.

HISTOGRAMS IN PROBLEM SOLVING

As this example illustrates, the histogram is a simple but powerful tool for elementary analysis of data. Let us look again at the example and summarize some key concepts about data and the use of histograms in problem solving.

CONCEPT 1: Values in a set of data almost always show variation. Although the amplifiers were designed for a nominal value of 10 dB gain, very few of them actually had a measured gain of 10 dB. Furthermore, very few amplifiers had exactly the same gain. This variation is due to small differences in literally hundreds of factors surrounding the manufacturing process—the exact values of the component parts, the nature of the handling that each amplifier receives, the accuracy and repeatability of the test equipment, even the humidity in the factory on the day the amplifier was made.

Variation is everywhere. It is inevitable in the output of any process: manufacturing, service, or administrative. It is impossible to keep all factors in a constant state all the time.

Consider these examples of variation. Will the measurement be a constant or will there be some variation in the data?

- The height of 10-year-old boys
- The number of pieces of candy in a 1-pound bag
- The exact weight of a 2-foot-by-2-foot piece of sheet steel
- The exact volume of product in a container
- The time required to repair an appliance for a customer
- The number of passengers on a 747 airplane
- The number of minutes required to process an invoice

In each case, the measurement will show some variation; few values will be exactly the same.

CONCEPT 2: Variation displays a pattern. In the amplifier example, the pattern of variation shown in Figure 2 and a number of characteristics. For example:

- All values fell within the specification limits.
- Most of the values fell between the nominal and the lower specification limit.
- The values of gain tended to bunch up near the lower specification limit.
- More values fell in the range of 8.25 dB to 8.75 dB than in any other 0.5 dB category.
- The number of values in each 0.5 dB category decreased uniformly for values of gain greater than 8.75 dB.

Different phenomena will have different variation, but there is always some pattern to the variation. For example, we know that the height of most 10-year-old boys will be close to some average value and that it would be relatively unusual to find an extremely tall or extremely short boy. If we gathered the data on the time required to repair an appliance for a customer, or the time required to process paperwork, or the time required to complete a transaction at a bank, we would expect to see some similar pattern in the numbers.

These patterns of variation in data are called "distributions." There are books available with good introductory discussions on distributions.[1,2]

For our purposes, we simply want to point out that there are usually discernible patterns in the variation and that these patterns often tell us a great deal about the cause of a problem. Identifying and interpreting these patterns are the most important topics discussed here. There are three important characteristics of a histogram: its center, width, and shape.

CONCEPT 3: Patterns of variation are difficult to see in simple tables of numbers. Again, recall the amplifier example and the table of data in Figure 1. Looking at the table of numbers, we could see that no values fall outside the specification limits, but we cannot see much else. While there is a pattern in the data, it is difficult for our eyes and minds to see it. It is easy to conclude erroneously, as the team almost did, that the data represent a dead end in the problem-solving effort.

CONCEPT 4: Patterns of variation are easier to see when the data are summarized pictorially in a histogram. The histogram in Figure 2 gave the team more insight into how to improve the quality of long-distance telecommunications service and made it easier for the team to draw conclusions.

The histogram is a useful tool when a team is faced with the task of analyzing data that contain variation. We know intuitively that the variation will usually follow some pattern, but the pattern is often hard to see from the table of numbers. Because it is a "picture" of the data, a histogram enables us to see this pattern of variation.

TYPICAL PATTERNS OF VARIATION

Figure 3 shows common patterns of variation. The following list contains general explanations of each type and provides suggestions for further analysis.

The bell-shaped distribution: a symmetrical shape with a peak in the middle of the range of data. This is the normal, natural distribution of data from a process. Deviations from this bell shape might indicate the presence of complicating factors or outside influences. While deviations from a bell shape should be investigated, such deviations are not necessarily bad. As we will see, some non-bell distributions are to be expected in certain cases.

The double-peaked distribution: a distinct valley in the middle of the range of the data with peaks on either side. This pattern is usually a combination of two bell-shaped distributions and suggests that two distinct processes are at work.

There is more than one possible interpretation for this pattern. Trying various stratification schemes to isolate the distinct processes or conditions is one method of further analysis.

The plateau distribution: a flat top with no distinct peak and slight tails on either side. This pattern is likely to be the result of many different bell-shaped distributions with centers spread evenly throughout the range of data.

Diagram the flow and observe the operation to identify the many different processes at work. An extreme case occurs in organizations that have no defined processes or training—everyone does the job his or her own way. The wide variability in process leads to the wide variability observed in the data. Defining and implementing standard procedures will reduce this variability.

The comb distribution: high and low values alternating in a regular fashion. This pattern typically indicates measurement error, errors in the way the data were grouped to construct the histogram, or a systematic bias in the way the data were rounded off. A less likely alternative is that this is a type of plateau distribution.

Review the data collection procedures and the construction of the histogram before considering possible process characteristics that might cause the pattern.

The skewed distribution: an asymmetrical shape in which the peak is off-center in the range of data and the distribution tails off sharply on one side and gently on the other. The illustration in Figure 3 is called a positively skewed distribution because the long tail extends rightward, toward increasing values. A negatively skewed distribution would have a long tail extending leftward, toward decreasing values.

FIGURE 3   *Common Histogram Patterns*

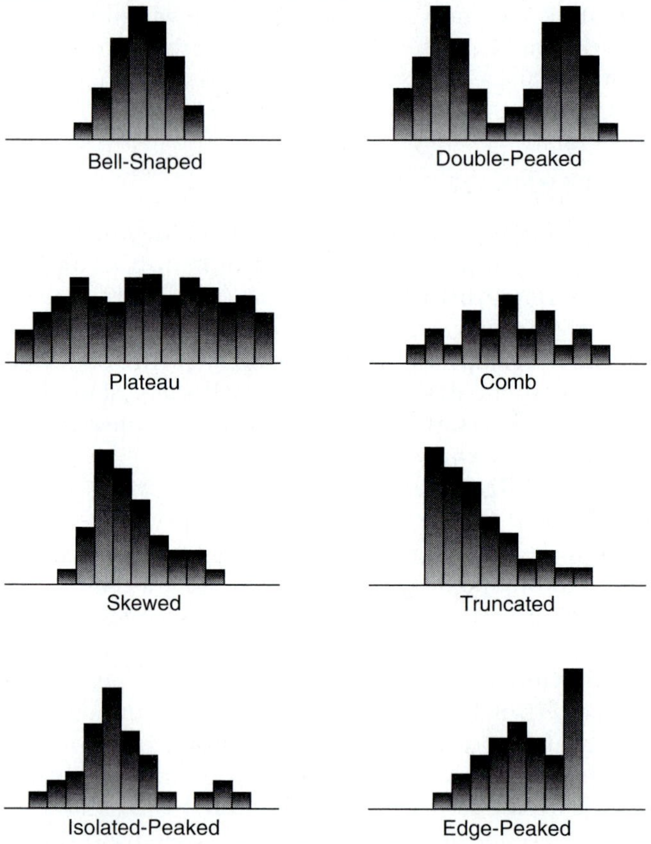

Bell-Shaped

Double-Peaked

Plateau

Comb

Skewed

Truncated

Isolated-Peaked

Edge-Peaked

The skewed pattern typically occurs when a practical limit, or a specification limit, exists on one side and is relatively close to the nominal value. In these cases, there simply are not as many values available on one side as there are on the other. Practical limits occur frequently when the data consist of time measurements or counts of things.

For example, tasks that take a very short time can never be completed in zero or less time. Those occasions when the task takes a little longer than average to complete create a positively skewed tail on this distribution of task time.

The number of weaving defects per 100 yards of fabric can never be less than zero. If the process averages about 0.7 defects per 100 yards, then sporadic occurrences of three of four defects per 100 yards will result in a positively skewed distribution.

One-sided specification limits (a maximum or minimum value only) also frequently give rise to skewed distributions.

Such skewed distributions are not inherently bad, but a team should question the impact of the values in the long tail. Could they cause customer dissatisfaction (e.g., long waiting times)? Could they lead to higher costs (e.g., overfilling containers)? Could the extreme values cause problems in downstream operations? If the long tail has a negative impact on quality, the team should investigate and determine the causes for those values.

The truncated distribution: an asymmetrical shape in which the peak is at or near the edge of the range of the data, and the distribution ends very abruptly on one side and tails off gently on the other. The illustration in Figure 3 shows truncation on the left side with a positively skewed tail. Of course, one might also encounter truncation on the right side with a negatively skewed tail. Truncated distributions are often smooth, bell-shared distributions with a part of the distribution removed, or truncated, by some external force such as screening, 100% inspection, or a review process. Note that these truncation efforts are an added cost and are, therefore, good candidates for removal.

The isolated peaked distribution: a small, separate group of data in addition to the larger distribution. Like the double-peaked distribution, this pattern is a combination and suggests that two distinct processes are at work. But the small size of the second peak indicates an abnormality, something that doesn't happen often or regularly.

Look closely at the conditions surrounding the data in the small peak to see if you can isolate a particular time, machine, input source, procedure, operator, etc. Such small isolated peaks in conjunction with a truncated distribution might result from the lack of complete effectiveness in screening out defective items. It is also possible that the small peak represents errors in measurements or in transcribing the data. Re-check measurements and calculations.

The edge-peaked distribution: a large peak is appended to an otherwise smooth distribution. This shape occurs when the extended tail of the smooth distribution has been cut off and lumped into a single category at the edge of the range of the data. This shape very frequently indicates inaccurate recording of the data (e.g., values outside the "acceptable" range are reported as being just inside the range).

POTENTIAL PITFALLS IN INTERPRETATION

There are three important pitfalls that a quality improvement team should be aware of when interpreting histograms:

1. Before you state your conclusions from the analysis of a histogram, make sure that the data are representative of typical and current conditions in the process. If the data are old (i.e., the process has changed since the data were collected), or if there is any question about bias or incompleteness in the data, it is best to gather new data to confirm and enhance your conclusions.

2. Don't draw conclusions based on a small sample. As we pointed out earlier, the larger the sample, the more confidence we have that the peaks, spread, and shape of our histogram of the sample data are representative of the total process or group of products. As a rule of thumb, if you intend to construct before-and-after or stratified histograms to examine differences in variability or the location of peaks, use a sample large enough to give you 40 or more observations for each histogram you intend to construct. For example, if you plan to stratify the data into three groups, your minimum sample size should be around 120 (3 × 40). If this is not practical, consult a statistical adviser to design an appropriate sampling and hypothesis-testing scheme.

3. It is important to remember that your interpretation of the histogram is often merely a theory that must still be confirmed through additional analysis and direct observation of the process in question. The first conclusion and interpretation might not be correct—even if it sounds perfectly reasonable. Always take time to think of alternative explanations for the pattern seen in the histogram.

WHAT DO WE DO NEXT?

The key accomplishments of our analysis of a histogram are:

1. We have quantified some aspect of the process; we are managing by facts, not opinions.

2. We have a better understanding of the variability inherent in the process; we have a more realistic view of the ability of the process to produce acceptable results consistently.

3. We have new ideas and theories about how the process operates or about the causes of a problem; we have set the stage for additional investigative efforts.

Because histograms almost always provide eye-opening information in a format that is easy to explain to managers and co-workers, there is a certain exhilaration that team members feel as they explain their theories and conclusions.

Unfortunately, this feeling of exhilaration tends to make one think that the work is over, the problem is solved. It is not, of course. Usually, all we have are theories that must still be confirmed before we can be sure that any proposed solutions would be effective.

Our next steps should be to:

- clarify and agree on what we have learned.
- acknowledge that all we have at this point are theories to guide subsequent investigative efforts.
- plan for direct observation of the process and additional collection, stratification, and analysis of data to confirm our theories before we begin implementing remedies.
- continue the diagnostic and remedial journeys.

References

1. J.M. Juran and Frank M. Gryna Jr., *Quality Planning and Analysis,* second edition (New York: McGraw-Hill Publishing Co., 1980), Chapter 3.
2. Harrison M. Wadsworth, Kenneth S. Stephens, and A. Blanton Godfrey, *Modern Methods for Quality Control and Improvement* (New York: John Wiley & Sons, 1986), Chapter 3.

Check Sheets

ADAPTED FROM THE QUALITY IMPROVEMENT TOOLS
WORKBOOK SET PUBLISHED BY THE JURAN INSTITUTE, INC.

Quality improvement is an information-intensive activity. We need clear, useful information about problems and their causes to make improvements. In many cases, the absence of relevant information is the major reason why problems go unsolved for so long.

Most organizations have vast stores of data and facts about their operations. However, when quality improvement teams begin working on a project, they often find that the information they need does not exist. To resolve this apparent paradox, we need to understand some basic concepts about the difference between data and information:

- Data = facts.
- Information = answers to questions.
- Information includes data.
- Data does not necessarily include information.

Quality improvement teams are seeking the answers to questions: "How often does the problem occur?" or "What is causing the problem?" In other words, they are seeking information. But, while good information is always based on data (the facts), simply collecting data does not necessarily ensure that a team will have useful information. The data may not be relevant or specific enough to answer the question at hand.

The key issue, then, is not "How do we collect data?" but rather "How do we generate useful information?" Figure 1 presents a model for generating useful information.

Information generation begins and ends with questions. To generate information, we need to:

- formulate precisely the question we are trying to answer.
- collect the data and facts relating to that question.
- analyze the data to determine the factual answer to the question.
- present the data in a way that clearly communicates the answer to the question.

Learning to ask the right questions is the key skill in effective data collection. Accurate, precise data collected through an elaborately designed statistical sampling plan are useless if they do not clearly address a question that someone cares about.

PLANNING TO COLLECT DATA

Planning for good data collection should proceed along the following lines:

- What question do we need to answer?
- How will we recognize and communicate the answers to the question?
- What data analysis tools (Pareto diagram, histogram, bar graph, etc.) do we envision using, and how will we communicate the results?
- What type of data do we need in order to construct this tool and answer the question?

FIGURE 1   *Generating Information*

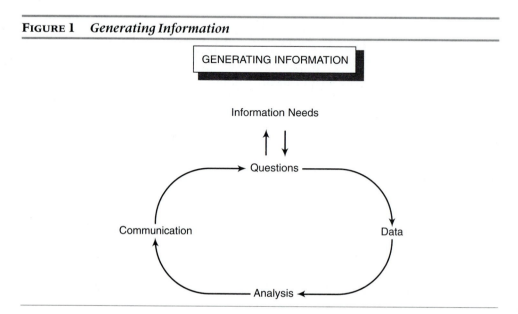

- Where in the process can we get these data?

- Who in the process can give us these data?

- How can we collect these data from these people with minimum effort and chance of error?

- What additional information do we need to gather for future analysis, reference, and traceability?

Notice how this planning process essentially works backward through the model in Figure 1. We start by defining the question. Then, rather than diving into the details of data collection, we consider how we might communicate the answer to the question and what types of analysis we will need to perform. This helps us define our data needs and clarifies what characteristics are most important in the data. With this understanding as a foundation, we can deal more coherently with the where, who, how, and what else issues of data collection.

Of course, like most planning processes, some iteration might be required to complete the design of a good data collection system. For example, the discussion about where in the process to collect the data might require going back and restating the question more precisely.

We will look at the elements of this data-collection planning process in more detail later. First, we will look at some examples of when data collection is necessary and how it is used.

TYPES OF DATA COLLECTION

Three types of data collection forms are commonly used by quality improvement teams: check sheets, data sheets, and checklists. While these three types of forms are quite different, the similarity in their names often leads to confusion.

A check sheet is a simple data recording form that has been specially designed to readily interpret results from the form itself. Figure 2 shows an example of a simple check sheet for recording temperatures in a manufacturing process. Notice that the form was designed to allow the operator to enter the temperatures on a time vs. temperature grid. Because of this, the form does more than simply provide a record of the data—it allows the simultaneous analysis of trends in the data.

Data sheets are also used to gather data. They differ from check sheets, however, in that data are recorded in a simple tabular or columnar format. Specific bits of data—numbers, words, or marks (e.g., X)—are entered in spaces on the sheet. As a result, additional processing is typically required after the data are collected to construct the tool needed for analysis. Figure 3 shows an example of a data sheet for collecting temperatures.

A checklist contains items that are important or relevant to a specific issue or situation. Checklists are used under operational conditions to ensure that all important steps or actions have been taken. Although completed checklists might be analyzed by a quality improvement team, their primary purpose is for guiding

FIGURE 2   A Check Sheet

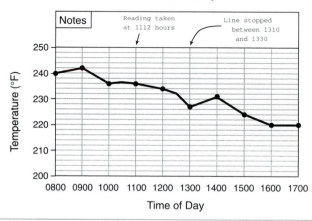

SOLDER BATH TEMPERATURE

- Read temperature to nearest degree off meter number 5.
- Plot the temperature and time on the grid using a dot (●). Connect the dots with a line.
- Reading should be taken on the hour (± 5 minutes).
- Use the "Notes" section to record anything unusual.

Date: ___6-7-88___

Line #: ___13___

Inspector: ___Ginny Smith___

* Questions? Contact Larry Fine x2222

operations, not for collecting data. Checklists are therefore more commonly used in the remedial journey and holding-the-gains phases of problem solving; they are part of the solution. The preflight checklist that a commercial airline pilot must complete is a good example.

Much of the material in this article focuses on check sheets for two reasons: data sheets and checklists are straightforward and need little explanation; and check sheets are typically not used that often.

OBTAINING GOOD DATA

Collected data must be accurate. Inaccurate data might give the wrong answer to information questions. Most collected data are not perfect, but there are techniques that keep inaccuracies to a minimum. The most serious types of data inaccuracies are called biases.

Biases can come from many sources, including the design of the data collection instrument, the collection procedures, and the perceptions of the persons collecting the data. For some types of bias, it is helpful to conduct an audit of the data collection process while the data are being collected. As you study the following examples, notice how some of the teams considered and dealt with issues of bias.

FIGURE 3   *A Data Sheet*

SOLDER BATH TEMPERATURE

- Read temperature to nearest degree off meter number 5.

- Record the temperature in the table below.

- Reading should be taken on the hour (± 5 minutes).

- Use the "Notes" section to record anything unusual.

Date: _____6-7-88_____

Line #: _____13_____

Inspector: _____Ginny Smith_____

* Questions? Contact Larry Fine x2222

Time of Day	Temperature (°F)	Time of Day	Temperature (°F)
0800	240	1300	227
0900	242	1400	230
1000	236	1500	224
1100	236	1600	220
1200	234	1700	220

Notes: – 1100 hours reading taken at 1112

– The line was stopped between
1310 and 1330

REDUCING WARRANTY COSTS

A few years ago, a television manufacturer introduced a line of television sets that was a big commercial success. The style of the cabinet was attractive, the price was competitive, and the set offered a number of features that the public appreciated. As time went by, however, the company discovered that reliability was poor. A high percentage of television sets came back to be repaired within the 12-month warranty period.

A quality improvement project team was chartered to determine the causes of this problem, which was increasing warranty costs for the company to an unacceptable level. The team formulated the following information questions to guide the analysis of the symptoms:

- How many total components are replaced under warranty in each of the three existing models of the set (model numbers 1013, 1017, and 1019)?
- How many integrated circuits, capacitors, resistors, transformers, commands (i.e., switches), and CRTs are replaced under warranty in each of the three models?

How to Collect Data

Data collection is a type of production process itself and, like any process, needs to be understood and improved. Generally speaking, 10 points must be addressed when collecting data:

1. Formulate good questions that relate to the specific information needs of the project. It is much easier to get others to help collect data if they believe those in charge know precisely what they are looking for and that they are going to do something with the collected information.

2. Use the appropriate data analysis tools and be certain the necessary data are being collected. Whenever practical, collect continuous variable data. A few minutes of thought before gathering data can often prevent having to recollect data because they are incomplete or answer the wrong question.

3. Define comprehensive data collection points. The ideal is to set the collection point where the job flow suffers minimum interruption. An accurate flowchart of the work process can help immensely.

4. Select an unbiased collector. The collector should have the easiest and most immediate access to the relevant facts.

5. Understand data collectors and their environment. The training and experience of the collectors determine whether they can handle this additional assignment.

6. Design data collection forms that are simple; reduce opportunities for error; capture data for analysis, reference and traceability; are self-explanatory; and look professional. The KISS (keep it simple, stupid) principle applies here.

7. Prepare the instructions for use. In some cases, a special training course might be necessary for data gatherers. In other cases, a simple sheet of instructions will suffice.

8. Test the forms and instructions. Try out the forms on a limited basis to make sure they are filled out properly. If they aren't, the forms or instructions might need revision.

9. Train the data collectors. Training should include the purpose of the study, what the data will be used for, a properly completed form, and a discussion about the importance of complete and unbiased information.

10. Audit the collection process and validate the results. Randomly check completed forms and observe data collection during the process. Look for missing or unusual data, and be wary of variations in the data that might result from biases in the data collection process.

These questions could be answered with a bar graph or Pareto diagram if the team had simple tallies of the number of each type of component replaced in each model during a typical week. The repair shop where all the sets came for warranty repairs was the obvious data collection point. Since the repair technicians were the closest to the facts of each repair and had no reason to bias the data, they were selected as the data collectors. The team designed a check sheet, showed it to two of the technicians, made some modifications based on their comments, spend 15 minutes describing the study and the final form to the entire group, and then implemented the data collection system. Figure 4 is an example of the check sheet given to each workshop technician to record the components replaced during a one-week period.

It was immediately evident that there was a problem with capacitors. This problem was present in all three models. Model 1017 also had a specific problem associ-

---

FIGURE 4 *Check Sheet for TV Component Failures*

COMPONENTS REPLACED BY LAB
Enter a mark for each component replaced. Mark like the following: / // /// //// ⫫⫫
TIME PERIOD: *22 Feb to 27 Feb 1988*
REPAIR TECHNICIAN: Bob

TV SET MODEL 1013

Integrated circuits	⫫⫫
Capacitors	⫫⫫ ⫫⫫ ⫫⫫ ⫫⫫ ⫫⫫ //
Resistors	//
Transformers	// //
Commands	
CRT	/

TV SET MODEL 1017

Integrated circuits	//
Capacitors	⫫⫫ ⫫⫫ ⫫⫫ ⫫⫫ ⫫⫫ //
Resistors	/
Transformers	//
Commands	⫫⫫ ⫫⫫ ⫫⫫ //
CRT	/

TV SET MODEL 1019

Integrated circuits	/
Capacitors	⫫⫫ ⫫⫫ ⫫⫫ ⫫⫫ ///
Resistors	/
Transformers	//
Commands	
CRT	/

ated with its command components. The on-off switch for that model failed much more often than did the switch in the other two models.

USING A LOCATION PLOT

When the data to be recorded refer to positions on the surface of an item, a variation of the check sheet called a location plot (or concentration diagram) is ideal in terms of ease of use and ability to transform data into information (Figure 5).

This check sheet was designed by a quality improvement project team to answer the question "Are certain areas on our household range more prone to chipped enamel damage during transportation?" It is clear from Figure 5 that the corners were the areas most prone to damage. This information was invaluable in indicating that certain corners of the appliances required more protection for safe transportation.

INTEGRATED CIRCUIT YIELD

The manufacture of integrated circuits begins with silicon slices that, after a sequence of complex operations, will contain hundreds or thousands of chips on their surfaces. Each chip must be tested to establish whether it functions properly. During slice testing, some chips are found to be defective and are rejected. To reduce the number of rejects, it is necessary to know not only the percentage but also the locations and the types of defects. There are normally two major types of defects: functional and parametric. A functional reject occurs when a chip does not perform one of its functions. A parametric reject occurs when the circuit functions properly, but a parameter of the chip, such as speed or power consumption, is not correct.

FIGURE 5   *Location Plot of Chipped Enamel on Range*

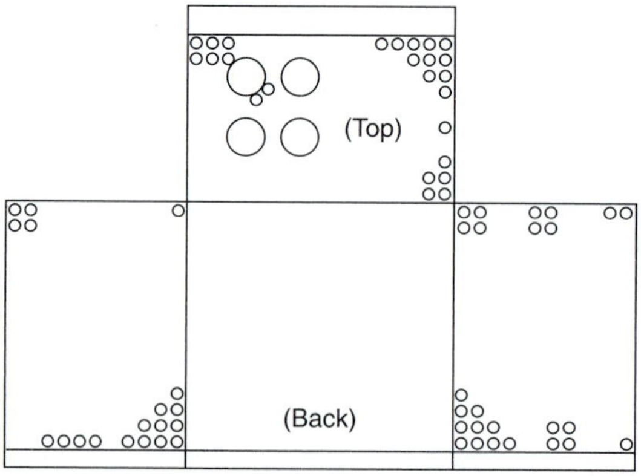

FIGURE 6   *Location Plot of Chip Rejects*

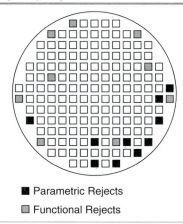

■ Parametric Rejects
□ Functional Rejects

Figure 6 is an example of a check sheet showing the location of rejected chips within the integrated circuit. Only those chips that had five or more defects during the testing of 1,000 circuits are colored in. The information shows that parametric rejects are mostly concentrated on the lower right of the slice, while functional rejects are distributed toward the edges.

This is an unusual check sheet because it takes advantage of the automated testing equipment. Chip failures are recorded by the test equipment for each circuit and displayed on the video screen attached to the test equipment. In addition, the results of each test are stored in the test computer, and the results of hundreds or thousands of tests can be quickly summarized in the form shown in Figure 6. Such computerized applications, when available, should not be overlooked.

PROCESSING PURCHASE ORDERS

When a company wants to buy raw material, piece parts, services, or other items from an outside supplier, a purchase requisition form must be filled out. After management approves the purchase, this request goes to the purchasing department. It will obtain offers from several different potential suppliers before one is selected and a purchase order is used. At this point, with all the internal processing steps completed, the purchase order is sent to the selected supplier and a copy of it to the originator of the order.

A quality improvement project team was appointed to speed up this process. The team analyzed the time required to process purchase orders. The question of interest was "How many working days elapse from the date of the originator's signature to the date the purchase order is sent?" The team used a histogram to analyze the distribution of the total processing time in order to obtain insight into the structure of the process. (See the September issue of *Quality Progress* for the article about histograms.) The needed set of data was the elapsed time in days for 40 or more purchase orders.

Asking purchasing clerks to record when they send out purchase orders is the obvious, ideal approach. However, it raises the issue of potential bias because the clerks might fear they would be blamed for delays. In this case, great care was taken to explain to the clerks that no blame was being placed. Furthermore, it was carefully explained that, unless they followed their normal routines during the study period, the data would be biased and things would never get better permanently. To make sure that this was understood, one of the clerks was enlisted to conduct casual interviews with her peers. These interviews confirmed that the study could be conducted using the clerks as collectors. The clerk was also relieved of some of her normal workload so that she could observe and audit the data collection process during the study period. A completed check sheet from the study is shown in Figure 7.

The design of the check sheet makes the distribution of times immediately obvious, and the distribution can be analyzed as discussed in the section on histograms without any additional processing. Note one nice feature of this check sheet: by providing boxes to mark in, the results will be easier to interpret. If the horizontal lines had not been provided, variations in the size and placement on the x's might make interpretation less exact.

While the use of a check sheet in this case was a good, quick way to obtain some initial insight, the team members realized that the check sheet had limitations when compared to a complete data sheet. For example, they would not be able to differentiate among the times required for different types of materials being purchased.

INTERPRETING DATA, VALIDATING RESULTS

Before starting to draw conclusions from collected data, the team should verify that the data are appropriate. It is helpful to review the questions that were originally asked. Does the data collected still appear to answer those questions?

Look at the results of any audits of the data collection phase. Is there any evidence of bias in the collection process? Is the number of observations collected the number specified? If not, why not?

Are there any missing observations or responses? These can be a major source of error. Identify missing data for special treatment. In a survey of customers, for example, dissatisfied customers who are taking their business to your competitor might be the least likely to respond. But their views are vital. Never assume that missing data will, on average, look like the collected data. Generally, it will not.

Do some comparative tabulations of the data. For example, do the data gathered by each collector look, on average, about the same? If not, why not? Is the variability of the results from each data collector about the same? Excessively high or very low variability by one or two data collectors might indicate problems with the data collection process—or falsified data.

FIGURE 7   *Check Sheet for Elapsed Processing Time*

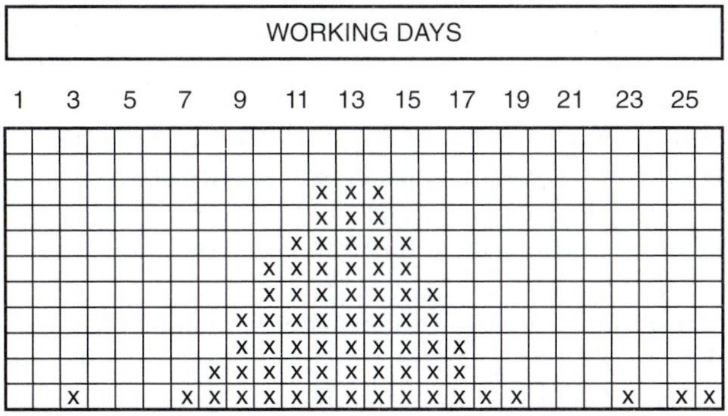

									WORKING DAYS																	

```
WORKING DAYS

   1    3    5    7    9   11   13   15   17   19   21   23   25

                              X  X  X
                              X  X  X
                           X  X  X  X  X
                        X  X  X  X  X  X
                           X  X  X  X  X  X
                     X  X  X  X  X  X  X
                        X  X  X  X  X  X  X  X
                  X  X  X  X  X  X  X  X  X  X
     X            X  X  X  X  X  X  X  X  X  X  X  X        X     X  X
```

Enter an X in the lowest unoccupied box under the number of working days from the date of the originator's signature to the date the purchase order was sent out.

GREAT EXPECTATIONS

Do not expect too much from the data. The data should indicate the answer to the question asked during the design of the collection process. It might not be able to answer other unanticipated questions. Do not try to make inferences from the data that they will not support. Usually a check sheet, with its simple collection and analysis format, is intended for a quick answer to a single question. It will not usually support further analysis or stratification. A good complete data sheet, however, will often support many levels of analysis and stratification if they have been anticipated in the design.

For example, the team looking at enamel chips on kitchen ranges might later develop a theory that the location of the chips might also be, in part, related to the shipping method used—a particular railroad or truck line. The data in Figure 5 would not help test that theory.

INTERPRETATION PITFALLS

Most of the interpretation pitfalls relate to the application of specific tools to the data, but a few are generic to all collected data. The following biases might cause problems:

Exclusion bias. The results will be biased if they are intended to represent the entire process and some part of the process being investigated has been left out. Data should be collected from all the places, times, and conditions under which the process operates.

Interaction bias. The process of collecting the data itself might affect the process being studied. For example, a team was trying to improve the speed with which promotions were processed by a personnel office. Team members began to collect data on the process, but while they were collecting the data, the speed of processing increased by a factor of four.

Perception bias. The attitudes and beliefs of the data collectors can sometimes color what they see and how they record it.

Operational bias. Failure to follow the established procedures is the most common operational bias. This bias usually arises because the instructions, training, and/or forms were not adequately prepared and tested in an operational environment. The transcribing and processing of the collected data can create additional errors.

Nonresponse bias. Missing data can bias the results. As we noted above, it is not safe to assume that missing data, on average, look like the collected data. The fact that they are missing is a clue that they are different from the rest in some way.

Estimation bias. The formulas and methods used to calculate statistics from the collected data might give certain types of biases. These biases are beyond the scope of this article; however, estimation bias must be understood when using tools other than the simple ones described here.

KNOW THE QUESTION

Most quality improvement tools depend on reliable, accurate data. If such data are not available, they must be collected. The data collection process must be driven by the information from questions that we formulate based on our needs. In short, know what question is to be answered before collecting data.

Pareto Charts

———

By John T. Burr

The Pareto principle is several things. It is a state of nature, the way things happen around us. It is also a way of managing projects. Finally, it is a process—a way of thinking about problems that affect us.

STATE OF NATURE

The Pareto principle was first defined by Joseph Juran in 1950.[1] During his early work, Juran found that there was a "maldistribution of quality losses." Not liking such a long name, he named the principle after Vilfredo Pareto, a 19th-century Italian economist. Pareto found that a large share of the wealth was owned by relatively few people—a maldistribution of wealth.

Juran found this was true in many areas of life, including quality technologies. In 1975, he published a retraction of his use of Pareto's name in an article called 'The Non-Pareto Principle; Mea Culpa."[2] Nevertheless, the term "Pareto principle" is here to stay.

In simplest terms, the Pareto principle suggests that most effects come from relatively few causes. In quantitative terms, 80% of the problems come from 20% of the machines, raw materials, or operators. Also, 80% of the wealth is controlled by 20% of the people. It is well-known that 80% of the funds contributed to charity come from only 20% of the possible sources. Finally, 80% of scrap or rework quality costs come from 20% of the possible causes.

In the quality technologies, Juran calls the 20% of the causes the "vital few."[3] He originally called the rest of the causes the "trivial many." However, he and other quality professionals came to understand that there are no trivial problems on the manufacturing floor and that all problems deserve management's attention. Juran

---

FIGURE 1   *Generalized Pareto Diagram*

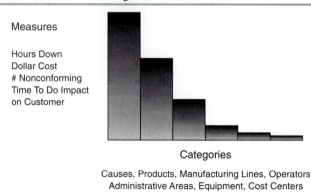

Measures

Hours Down
Dollar Cost
Nonconforming
Time To Do Impact
on Customer

Categories

Causes, Products, Manufacturing Lines, Operators
Administrative Areas, Equipment, Cost Centers

has since renamed the trivial many the "useful many."[4,5] But no matter the labels, the Pareto principle is one of the most powerful decision tools available.

A MANAGEMENT TOOL

Data can be collected on the state of scrap, rework, warranty claims, maintenance time, raw material usage, machine downtime, or any other cost associated with manufacturing a product or providing a service. In the case of providing a service, for example, data can be collected on wasted time, number of jobs that have to be redone, customer inquiries, and number of errors. The data should be organized as illustrated in Figure 1. The most frequent (highest cost) cause is placed on the left, and the other causes are added in descending order of occurrence.

FIGURE 2   *Strut Rod Rejects*

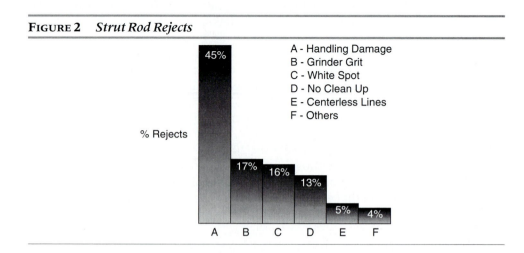

A - Handling Damage
B - Grinder Grit
C - White Spot
D - No Clean Up
E - Centerless Lines
F - Others

% Rejects

45%   17%   16%   13%   5%   4%

A   B   C   D   E   F

FIGURE 3 *Information Systems*

FIRST HALF of 1985

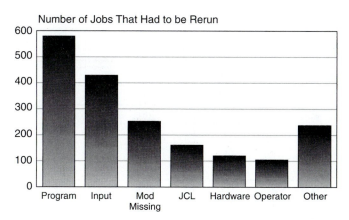

Figures 2 and 3 are examples of the Pareto diagram. It is quite obvious which causes or problems have to be reduced or eliminated to have any real impact on the system.

A double Pareto diagram, as in Figure 4, can be used to contrast two products, areas, or shifts, or to look at a system before and after improvement.

In 1984, Jeffery Kalin, the manufacturing manager of a Hewlett Packard plant in Colorado Springs, stated that no one in his plant worked on a problem until they

FIGURE 4 *Poor Golf Shots*

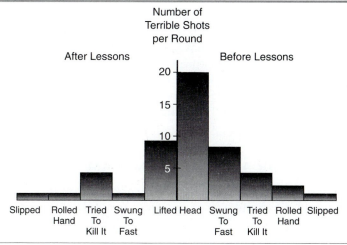

FIGURE 5   *Problems With Supplied Boxes*

			Product					Problem	
		Labels	Liner	Glue	Score	Warp	
A		2		8			10
B		1		4			5
C			1		7	28	36
D			2			4	6
E		3		11			14
F		1				1	2
G		1					1
H					2		2
I		2					2
		10	3	23	9	33	

had developed a Pareto diagram. The diagram had to show that the problem being worked on by the team or the supervisor was the most important one at that time.[6]

A WAY OF THINKING

Figure 5 is not a Pareto diagram, but a set of data on problems encountered with boxes used to package a number of different products. The most frequent problem is on only one of the box types. Talking to the supplier about the specific problem (warping on box style no. 3) will solve almost half of the difficulties. This would also probably lead to less warping of box style no. 4, particularly if the boxes are made on the same line.

The next most frequent problem is glue. The problem occurs over several box types. Are they made on a common line? Is the glue or glue lot the same among these? If so, then a common cause has been identified and should be eliminated. The "mess" of incoming box supply problems will be reduced 80% by solving the two problems that have the most impact on quality. Of course, the improvement process is not stopped. The box manufacturing process should be continually analyzed using the Pareto diagram and the other tools of quality.

GETTING DATA FOR A PARETO DIAGRAM

American industries, manufacturing or service, are some of the greatest collectors of data in the world. Computers store vast amounts of data. Wastebaskets receive data daily. Data are there for the asking. The trick is to recognize what data are useful.

Occasionally data are not available. The situation might come up, for example, when a group must define a problem or look for a cause. With a process flow diagram and a cause-and-effect program visible and understandable to the group, each member must identify what he or she feels are the most important causes of the problem. This can be done in three ways:

1. Each person votes on the major categories in the cause-and-effect diagram. It might also be helpful to have each person explain why he or she is voting for a particular category. Often, consensus can be quickly reached; otherwise, a Pareto diagram of the votes should be made.

2. Each person has five votes and can place them anywhere on the cause-and-effect diagram. It is good to do this in conjunction with a break so that each person has time to come to the diagram to make the marks. By the way, a person could give all five votes to one cause if he or she felt very strongly about it. A Pareto diagram of the results should be made.

3. There is a nominal technique that is more involved and particularly useful when there is a large number of possible causes and a good deal of uncertainty of which is important. This technique requires a large supply of 3 by 5 cards. All members get 10 cards (or five for shorter lists of causes). They write each of their top 10 choices on separate cards. They then pick the most likely cause. This card gets a 10. Next they pick the least likely cause and give it a 1. Then the next least likely cause is selected, a 2. Then the next most likely cause, a 9. This process is repeated back and forth until all the causes are ranked. (It is easier to select the most and the least likely causes than to distinguish among the ones in the middle.) The numbers are then compiled for each cause and a Pareto diagram is constructed. This same technique can be used giving each person 100 points to distribute among the ranked cards. The seam process of compiling is then used.

The Pareto principle describes the way causes occur in nature and human behavior. It can be a very powerful management tool for focusing personnel's effort on the problems and solutions that have the greatest potential payback.

References

1. Joseph M. Juran, "Pareto, Lorenz, Cournot, Bernoulli, Juran and Others," *Industrial Quality Control,* October 1950, p. 5.

2. Joseph M. Juran, "Then and Now in Quality Control," *Quality Progress,* May 1975, p. 8.

3. Joseph M. Juran, editor, *Quality Control Handbook,* 4th edition, McGraw-Hill Book Co., 1989.

4. Joseph M. Juran, *Juran on Planning of Quality* (New York: The Free Press, 1988).

5. Joseph M. Juran, *Juran on Leadership for Quality* (New York: The Free Press, 1989).

6. Jeffery Kalin, Presentation to the Rochester Section, ASQC, on September 6, 1984.

Scatter Diagrams

By John T. Burr

In many situations we have data that might be related to some product characteristic or to other data. These data might come from manufacturing, service, or administrative sources. For example, we might want to know whether the thickness of paperboard will predict its ability to withstand punctures when used, or whether work backlog affects the error rate of computer data entry. These relationships can be nonmathematically evaluated by using a scatter diagram. The data are plotted on graph paper; each axis is used for one of the two sets of data being compared. The y axis is usually reserved for the characteristic we would like to predict, e.g., burst strength of paperboard and error rate. The x axis is used for the variable that we are using to make the prediction, e.g., thickness of the paperboard and the work backlog.

To show how this works, let us review an example from a recent publication.[1] The color of the bread (how well it is toasted) is what we want to predict, so it is assigned to the y axis. The number 1 equals uncooked and 9 equals burnt. The age of the bread is what will be used to predict the color, so it is assigned to the x axis. The data pairs (one number for the color and another for the age) are plotted on the graph paper as a scatter diagram (Figure 1). Is there a relationship? Does it require statistical calculation to see the relationship? There is variability in the measurement or in other process parameters because bread that is the same age does not always have the exact same color. In Figures 2–4, we can see that there are various degrees to which data can be related to each other.

However, it is important to note that, just because two variables appear to be related, it does not mean they are. There might be other reasons why two variables seem to be related. In Figure 5, it would appear that food and housing prices are related to each other, but they are, in fact, both related to inflation or the rising cost of production.

FIGURE 1 *Toast Color*

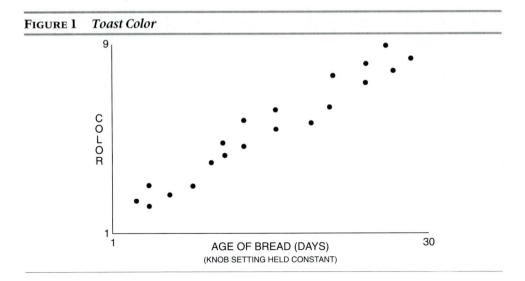

Also, just because there is an apparent graphical relationship between two variables, it does not mean that one causes the other to change. For example, one such diagram related the Dow Jones Index to the height of Lake Superior from 1925 to 1965. There is obviously no relationship between the two, but data can be much more subtle. Don't fall into this trap.

FIGURE 2 *Example of a Scatter Diagram between Variable Numbers 8 and 9 of a Recent Experiment on Plastic Sheeting*

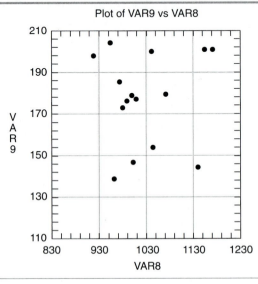

FIGURE 3   *Example of a Scatter Diagram between Variable Numbers 6 and 7 of a Recent Experiment on Plastic Sheeting*

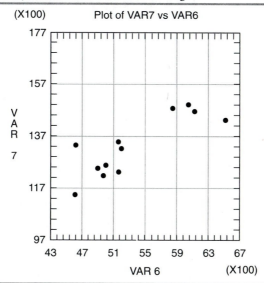

FIGURE 4   *Example of a Scatter Diagram between the Flow Rate of a Liquid and the Voltage Applied to a Valve*

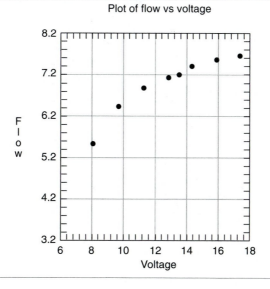

FIGURE 5   *Relationship between Food and Housing Prices*

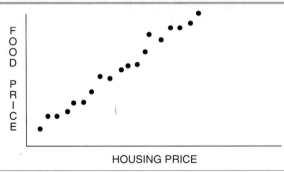

FIGURE 6   *Height vs. Age of Seventh Graders*

FIGURE 7   *Gas Mileage vs. Fuel Additive*

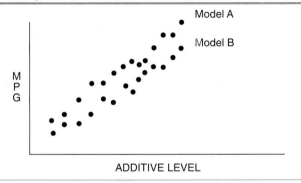

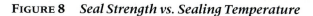

FIGURE 8   *Seal Strength vs. Sealing Temperature*

SEALING TEMPERATURE

If the data do not appear to have a relationship, it does not mean they are not related. There might be a variety of reasons for this, as seen in Figures 6–8. In Figure 6, we have taken data from too small a range of persons; we need to find some children from other grades in the school. In Figure 7, there might be more than one model of automobile used to obtain the data. We would need to make several diagrams, one for each automobile used in the study. In Figure 8, a large measurement error is concealing the relationship.

Like any of the SPC tools, the scatter diagram is very powerful, but it can easily be misused. The diagram must be evaluated by those who know most about the product or the process, e.g., the operators, engineers, supervisors, and maintenance personnel.

Reference

1. John T. Burr, *SPC Tools for Operators* (Milwaukee, WI: Quality Press, 1989).

Seven New QC Tools

———

EDITED BY SHIGERU MIZUNO

OVERVIEW OF THE SEVEN METHODS

This section will introduce only the fundamentals of each method.

The Relations Diagram Method

This is a technique developed to clarify intertwined causal relationships in a complex problem or situation in order to find an appropriate solution.

The Method   In order to analyze problems with a complex network of cause-and-effect relationships, a relations diagram is constructed by indicating the logical relationships that exist between the causal factors (Fig. 2.1). Such a diagram facilitates solutions to problems by allowing the whole problem to be viewed from a broad perspective.

To solve problems using the relations diagram method, a team composed of as many members as necessary should draft diagrams several times. By constructing diagrams in this way, the team generates new ideas that may lead to an effective solution.

Uses   The relations diagram method can be used to

- Determine and develop quality assurance policies
- Establish promotional plans for TQC introduction

Excerpt from *Management for Quality Improvement: The Seven New QC Tools,* edited by Shigeru Mizuno. Copyright © 1979 by QC Shuhou Kaihatsu. English translation copyright © 1988 by Productivity Press, Inc. Reprinted by permission of Productivity Press, Inc.

FIGURE 2.1   *Abstract Relations Diagram*

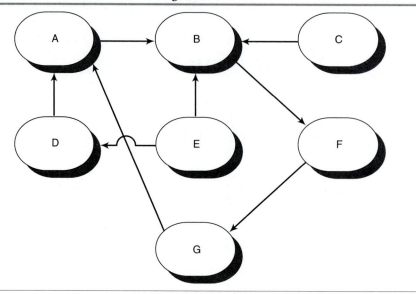

- Design steps to counter market complaints
- Improve quality in the manufacturing process (especially in planning to eliminate latent defects)
- Promote quality control in purchased or ordered items
- Provide measures against troubles related to payment and process control
- Effectively promote small group activities
- Reform administrative and business departments

Applications
   Example 1. At the first symposium on quality control, a survey was conducted on the major items necessary for the introduction and promotion of total quality control. The items obtained from this study are presented in the relational diagram pictured in Fig. 2.2. This diagram clarifies the important items that companies might consider in their promotion of total quality control.
   Example 2. Company U investigated the causes of a chronic deficiency in its assembly line of a certain product by using a relational diagram (Fig. 2.3). As a result of drawing the relational diagram, the staff's preconceptions regarding the causes of the deficiency were corrected and countermeasures were taken that result in a drastic reduction in the defective rate.

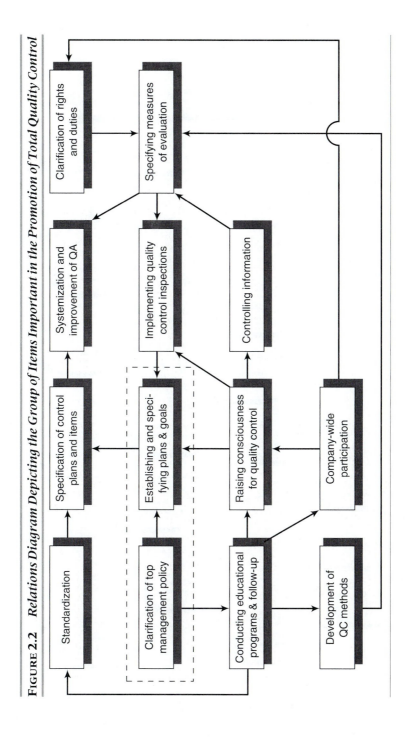

FIGURE 2.2 *Relations Diagram Depicting the Group of Items Important in the Promotion of Total Quality Control*

FIGURE 2.3   *Relations Diagram Examining the Causes of a Deficiency in*
Assembly-Line Production

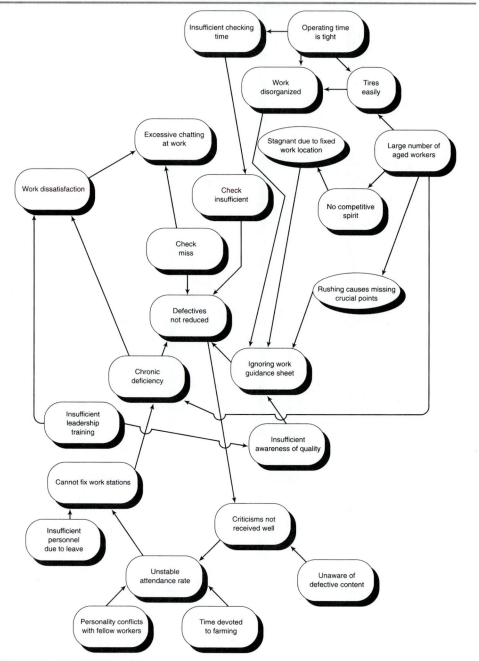

TABLE 2.1 *KJ Method versus Statistical Techniques*

Statistical Techniques	The KJ Method
1. Oriented for testing hypotheses	1. Oriented for discovering problems
2. Quantifies and transforms an event into numerical data	2. Expresses data in language and symbols without quantifying
3. Capable of analytic understanding; ability to stratify	3. Overall understanding possible; harmonizes heterogeneous elements
4. Can grasp by reasoning	4. Can grasp through feeling
5. Western way of thinking introduced through translation	5. Thinking based on Japanese language (said not to be amenable with language written horizontally)

The KJ Method*

This technique clarifies important but unresolved problems by collecting verbal data from disordered and confused situations and analyzing that data by mutual affinity.

The Method   The KJ method attempts to clarify the nature, shape, and extent of problems that affect the near and distant future in fields where there is little or no prior knowledge and/or experience. This technique consists of gathering ideas and opinions in the form of verbal data and drawing a complete diagram based on the common relationships and similarities found among the data.

The KJ method is an organizational technique based on "participatory group formation." Problems are solved through the creation of teams that gather the opinions, ideas, and experiences of diverse people and then coordinate and organize those data in terms of mutual affinity.

The KJ method was originally conceived, developed, and promoted by Kawakita Jiro. Mr. Kawakita attempts to solve all problems by cumulatively using the affinity diagram, which is further explained in Chap. 5. Contrasting the KJ method with statistical techniques (Table 2.1 and Fig. 2.4) highlights its effectiveness as one of the seven new tools in solving problems in conjunction with other methods.

Uses   The KJ method can be used to

- Establish a QC policy for a new company or a new factory and to implement that plan
- Establish a QC policy concerning new projects, new products, or new technology and to implement that plan
- Conduct quality assurance market surveys when entering a new untested market

---

*The KJ method is a trademark registered by the founder of the Kawayoshida Research Center. The trademark is still held by the center. We gratefully acknowledge the center's permission to use its materials in this chapter.

FIGURE 2.4 *Similarities between Statistical Quality Control and the KJ Method*

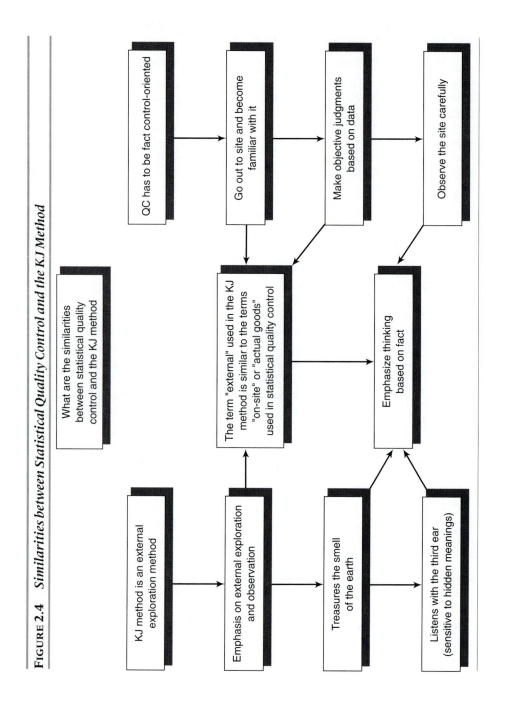

- Find a starting point for TQC promotion by creating a consensus among people with varying opinions regarding the problems that arise within each department
- Invigorate project teams and QC circles and promote team work within various groups.

Applications
Example 1. Shown in Fig. 2.5 is a portion of the affinity diagram obtained from the second round of cumulative KJ method discussions on the topic of "Where and how should our research and development proceed from here?" This discussion was conducted by a 10-member team of engineers and research managers from heterogeneous fields. Since the members were from different fields, the synthesis of their opinions led to a conclusion that will have wide applicability.

The Systematic Diagram Method

This technique searches for the most appropriate and effective means of accomplishing given objectives.

The Method   The systematic diagram method searches for techniques that will be most suitable for attaining established objectives by systematically clarifying important aspects of the problem. Such systematic diagrams enable workers to have an overview of the whole situation at one glance, effectively delineating the means and measures necessary for achieving the desired objectives (Fig. 2.6).

Systematic diagrams can be divided into two types: The *constituent-component-analysis* diagram breaks down the main subject into its basic elements and depicts their relationships to the objectives and means of attaining those objectives. The *plan-development* diagram systematically shows the means and procedures necessary to successfully implement a given plan.

Uses   The systematic diagram method can be used to

- Deploy a design-quality plan in the development of a new product
- Depict the relationship between a QC production process chart and the development of certified levels of quality designed to improve the accuracy of quality assurance activities
- Create a cause-effect diagram
- Develop ideas in order to solve problems dealing with quality, cost, and delivery that arise in new businesses
- Develop objectives, policies, and implementation steps
- Pursue the specification of increased efficiency in parts and control functions

Applications
Example 1. A systematic diagram of the plan-development type is shown in Fig. 2.7. This diagram illustrates the development of design-quality and implementation steps necessary for production of a UHF tuner for a television.

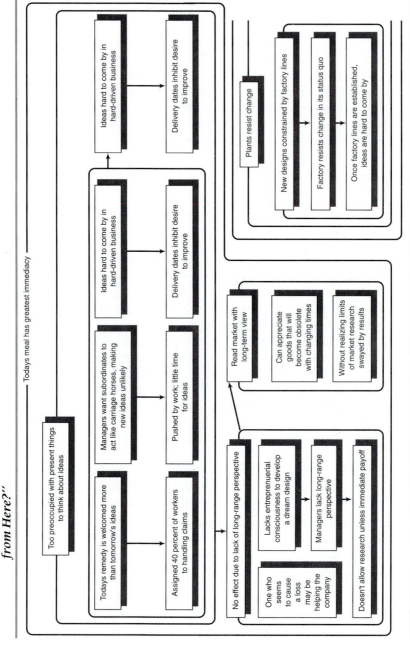

FIGURE 2.5 *Portion of Affinity Diagram Depicting the Discussion of "Where and How Should R and D Proceed from Here?"*

FIGURE 2.6   *Conceptual Systematic Diagram*

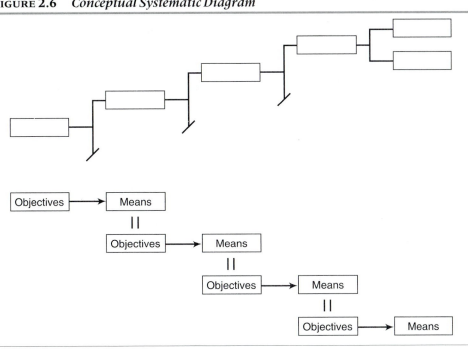

The Matrix Diagram Method

This technique clarifies problematic spots through multidimensional thinking.

The Method   The matrix diagram method identifies corresponding elements involved in a problem situation or event. These elements are arranged in rows and columns on a chart (Fig. 2.8) that shows the presence or absence of relationships among collected pairs of elements. Hopefully, this method will assist in specifying (with a two-way layout) the nature and/or location of problems, enabling idea conception on the basis of two-dimensional relationships. Effective problem solving is facilitated at the intersection points, also referred to as "idea conception points."

Matrix diagrams are classified on the basis of their pattern into five different groups: (1) the L-type matrix, (2) the T-type matrix, (3) the Y-type matrix, (4) the X-type matrix, and (5) the C-type matrix.

Uses   Matrix diagrams can be used to

- Establish idea conception points for the development and improvement of system products
- Achieve quality deployment in product materials
- Establish and strengthen the quality assurance system by linking certified levels of quality with the various control functions

FIGURE 2.7 *Systematic Diagram for Design Quality for a Television UHF Tuner*

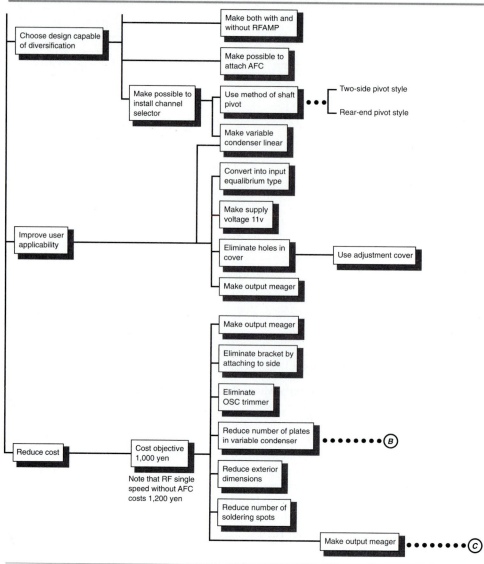

- Reinforce and improve the efficiency of the quality evaluation system
- Pursue the causes of nonconformities in the manufacturing process
- Establish strategies about the mix of products to send to market by evaluating the relationships between the products and market situations
- Clarify the technical relationships among several projects

FIGURE 2.8 *Conceptual Matrix Diagram Method*

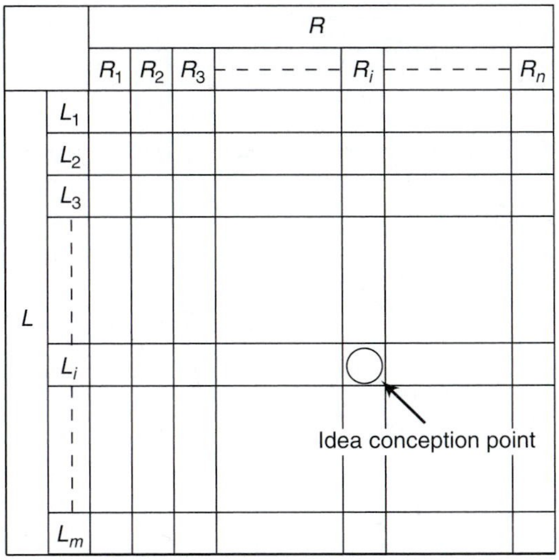

- Explore the application potential of currently available technology and raw materials

Applications   As Fig. 2.9 indicates, a T-type matrix was constructed in the investigation of smearing during the production of printed cloth. The matrix helped to clarify the relationships between nonconformities and their causes. Bases on the results of this matrix, a list of countermeasures was produced, and their implementation considerably reduced smears.

The Matrix Data-Analysis Method

This technique arranges data presented in a matrix diagram so that the large array of numbers can be visualized and comprehended easily.

The Method   The matrix data-analysis method quantifies and arranges matrix diagram data so that the information is easy to visualize and comprehend. The relationships between the elements shown in a matrix diagram are quantified by obtaining numerical data for intersection cells.

Of the seven new QC tools, this is the only numerical analysis method. The results of this technique, however, are presented in diagram form. One major technique that this method also utilizes is known as principal-component analysis, one of the multivariate analysis techniques. The matrix data-analysis method has been included as one of the seven new QC tools so that managers and staff can become more familiar with multivariate analysis techniques.

FIGURE 2.9   *T-type Matrix Searching for Causes of Smears in Printing of Cloth*

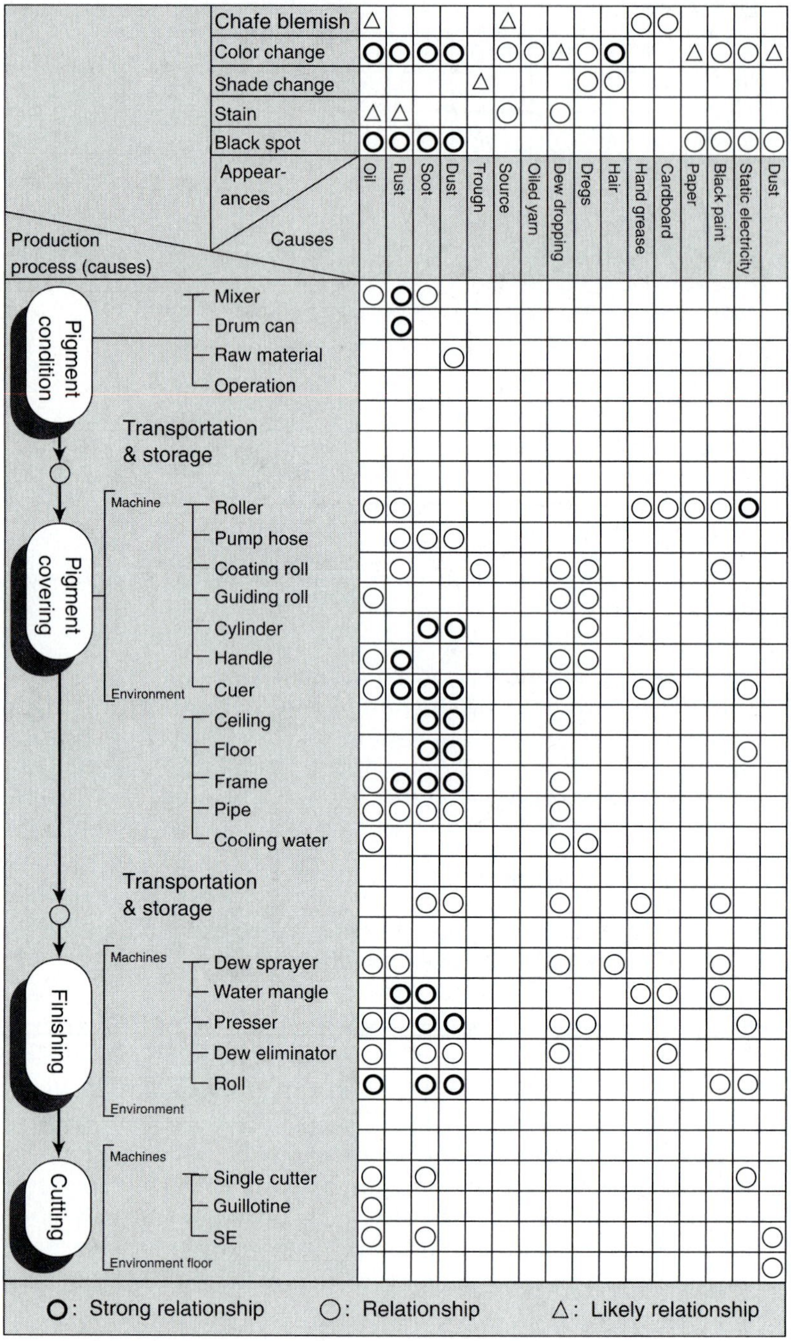

Legend: ◎ = Strong relationship   ○ = Relationship   △ = Likely relationship

Appearances vs. Causes

Appearances	Oil	Rust	Soot	Dust	Trough	Source	Oiled yarn	Dew dropping	Dregs	Hair	Hand grease	Cardboard	Paper	Black paint	Static electricity	Dust
Chafe blemish	△				△						○	○				
Color change	◎	◎	◎	◎		○	○	△	○	○			△	○	○	△
Shade change					△						○	○				
Stain	△	△				○		○								
Black spot	◎	◎	◎	◎									○	○	○	○

Production process (causes) vs. Causes

Process	Element	Oil	Rust	Soot	Dust	Trough	Source	Oiled yarn	Dew dropping	Dregs	Hair	Hand grease	Cardboard	Paper	Black paint	Static electricity	Dust
Pigment condition	Mixer	○	◎	○													
	Drum can		◎														
	Raw material				○												
	Operation																
Transportation & storage																	
Pigment covering (Machine)	Roller	○	○									○	○	○	○	◎	
	Pump hose		○	○	○												
	Coating roll		○					○	○	○					○		
	Guiding roll	○							○	○							
	Cylinder			◎	◎					○							
	Handle	○	◎						○	○							
(Environment)	Cuer	○	◎	○	○					○			○	○		○	
	Ceiling			◎	◎					○							
	Floor			◎	◎											○	
	Frame	○	○	○	○					○							
	Pipe	○	○	○	○					○							
	Cooling water	○							○	○							
Transportation & storage				○	○					○		○			○		
Finishing (Machines)	Dew sprayer	○	○						○		○				○		
	Water mangle		◎	◎								○	○		○		
	Presser	○	○	◎	◎				○	○						○	
	Dew eliminator	○		○	○					○			○				
	Roll	◎		○	○										○	○	
(Environment)																	
Cutting (Machines)	Single cutter	○		○											○		
	Guillotine	○															
	SE	○		○													○
Environment floor																	○

○: Strong relationship   ○: Relationship   △: Likely relationship

As an example of how this technique is used, Table 2.2 is presented as a data matrix showing the relationships between 40 uses of cloth and their desired qualities. Suppose that a new material, material *A*, is developed. The data in Table 2.2 does not readily provide information about the potential uses of material *A*; however, the matrix data-analysis method does offer answers by analyzing the data in Table 2.2.

Uses   The matrix data-analysis method can be used to

- Analyze production processes where factors are complexly intertwined
- Analyze causes of nonconformities that involve a large volume of data
- Grasp the desired quality level indicated by the results of a market survey
- Classify sensory characteristics systematically
- Accomplish complex quality evaluations
- Analyze curvilinear data

Applications   A principal-component analysis is performed on the matrix data provided in Table 2.2. The resulting first and second principal components are shown graphically in Fig. 2.10. This figure reveals that the new material *A* would probably be better suited for skirts and trousers than for sports wear, work uniforms, or gloves.

The PDPC Method

This technique helps determine which processes to use to obtain desired results by evaluating the progress of events and the variety of conceivable outcomes.

The Method   Implementation plans do not always progress as anticipated. When problems, technical or otherwise, arise, solutions are frequently not apparent.

The PDPC (process decision program chart) method, in response to these kinds of problems, anticipates possible outcomes and prepares countermeasures that will lead to the best possible solutions. By anticipating potential outcomes of events, this technique allows process adjustments in light of actual progress.

If an unanticipated event occurs, then it becomes necessary to rewrite the process decision program chart (PDPC) at once so that adjustive countermeasures can be taken.

The PDPC method[1] is borrowed from the operations research field for use in quality control.

Uses   The PDPC method can be used to

- Establish an implementation plan for management by objectives
- Establish an implementation plan for technology-development themes

TABLE 2.2 *Product Uses and Their Desired Qualities*

	Desirable Qualities						
Uses	1 Resists Fading	2 Washable	3 Resists Perspiration	...	23 Flame Retardant	24 Chemical Resistant	25 Non-irritating to Skin
1. Men's summer suits	X_{1-1}	X_{1-2}	X_{1-3}	...	X_{1-23}	X_{1-24}	X_{1-25}
2. Men's all-season suits	X_{2-1}	X_{2-2}	X_{2-3}	...	X_{2-23}	X_{2-24}	X_{2-25}
3. Ladies' summer dresses	X_{3-1}	X_{3-2}	X_{3-3}	...	X_{3-23}	X_{3-24}	X_{3-25}
4. Ladies' all-season dresses	X_{4-1}	X_{4-2}	X_{4-3}	...	X_{4-23}	X_{4-24}	X_{4-25}
5. Skirts	X_{5-1}	X_{5-2}	X_{5-3}	...	X_{5-23}	X_{5-24}	X_{5-25}
6. Trousers	X_{6-1}	X_{6-2}	X_{6-3}	...	X_{6-23}	X_{6-24}	X_{6-25}
7. Overcoats	X_{7-1}	X_{7-2}	X_{7-3}	...	X_{7-23}	X_{7-24}	X_{7-25}
8. Raincoats	X_{8-1}	X_{8-2}	X_{8-3}	...	X_{8-23}	X_{8-24}	X_{8-25}
9. Office wear	X_{9-1}	X_{9-2}	X_{9-3}	...	X_{9-23}	X_{9-24}	X_{9-25}
10. Work clothes	X_{10-1}	X_{10-2}	X_{10-3}	...	X_{10-23}	X_{10-24}	X_{10-25}
11. Sports wear	X_{11-1}	X_{11-2}	X_{11-3}	...	X_{11-23}	X_{11-24}	X_{11-25}
12. Student wear	X_{12-1}	X_{12-2}	X_{12-3}	...	X_{12-23}	X_{12-24}	X_{12-25}
13. Home wear	X_{13-1}	X_{13-2}	X_{13-3}	...	X_{13-23}	X_{13-24}	X_{13-25}
14. Baby wear	X_{14-1}	X_{14-2}	X_{14-3}	...	X_{14-23}	X_{14-24}	X_{14-25}
15. Dress shirts	X_{15-1}	X_{15-2}	X_{15-3}	...	X_{15-23}	X_{15-24}	X_{15-25}
... :	...	...	...	...	...	...	...
40. Foot warmer blankets	X_{40-1}	X_{40-2}	X_{40-3}	...	X_{40-23}	X_{40-24}	X_{40-25}
Material A	X_1	X_2	X_3	...	X_{23}	X_{24}	X_{25}

FIGURE 2.10   *Searching for Uses of New Material **A***

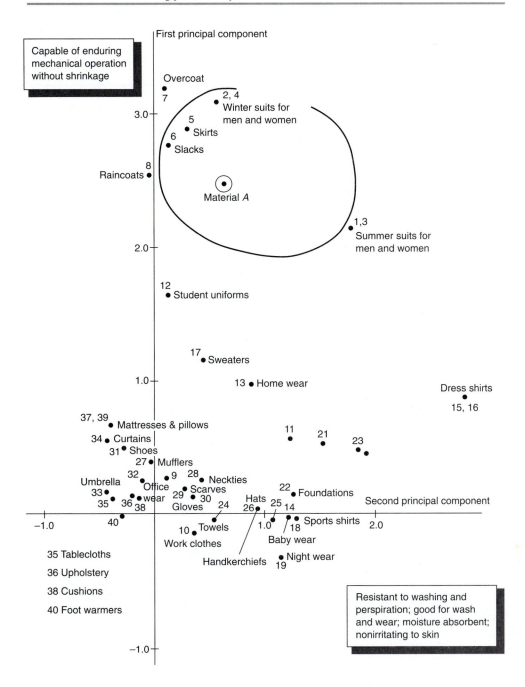

- Establish a policy of forecasting and responding in advance to major events predicted in the system
- Implement countermeasures to minimize nonconformities in the manufacturing process
- Set up and select adjustment measures for the negotiating process

Applications   Suppose that a company's objective is to deliver a fragile item to an addressee in a developing country. The company must anticipate various contingencies from shipment time to delivery, and address all the problems that might arise as a result of transportation and landing. The company must then develop countermeasures to avoid possible mishaps. The PDPC method approach to this hypothetical example and the results are shown in Fig. 2.11.

The Arrow Diagram Method

This technique establishes the most suitable daily plan and monitors its progress efficiently.

FIGURE 2.11   *Delivery of Fragile Item (Pattern II)*

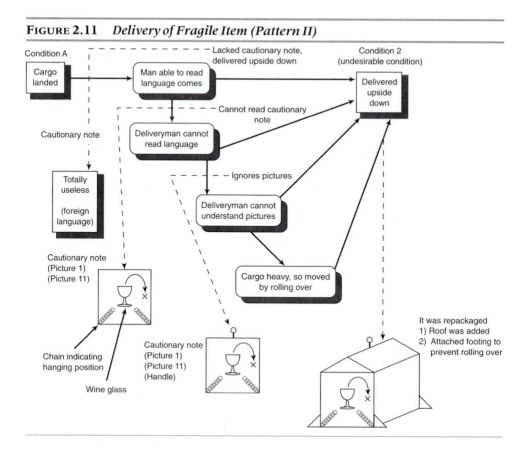

The Method   The arrow diagram method, utilized by PERT and CPM, is a network diagram for daily plans. It illustrates the network of lines that connect all the elements related to plan execution, as shown in Fig. 2.12.

Use of the arrow diagram method in advancing and monitoring daily plans has the following advantages:

1. It establishes a finely tuned plan.
2. It establishes the most suitable daily plan, since changes can be made easily during the early planning stages.
3. It allows one to cope easily with changes that occur in a given situation or during plan execution.
4. It expedites necessary action by quickly providing information on the impact delays in certain subparts will have on the operation as a whole.
5. It is increasingly useful in proportion to the size of the plans.
6. It controls the process efficiently because the progress highlights are easily discernible.

The control of daily plans is extremely important in the promotion of QC activities. An efficient method of constructing and utilizing arrow diagrams that employs cards will be introduced mainly to assist staff members.

Uses   The arrow diagram method can be used to

- Implement plans for new product development and its follow-up
- Develop product-improvement plans and follow-up activities
- Establish daily plans for experimental trials and follow-up activities
- Establish daily plans for increases in production and their follow-up
- Synchronize the preceding plans with QC activities
- Develop plans for a facility move and for monitoring follow-up

---

FIGURE 2.12   *Elements of an Arrow Diagram*

Elements of an Arrow Diagram

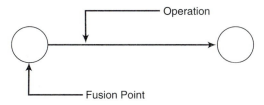

FIGURE 2.13   *Experimental Trials and Quality Confirmation Plan for VE Improvement of Special Resistor Electrodes*

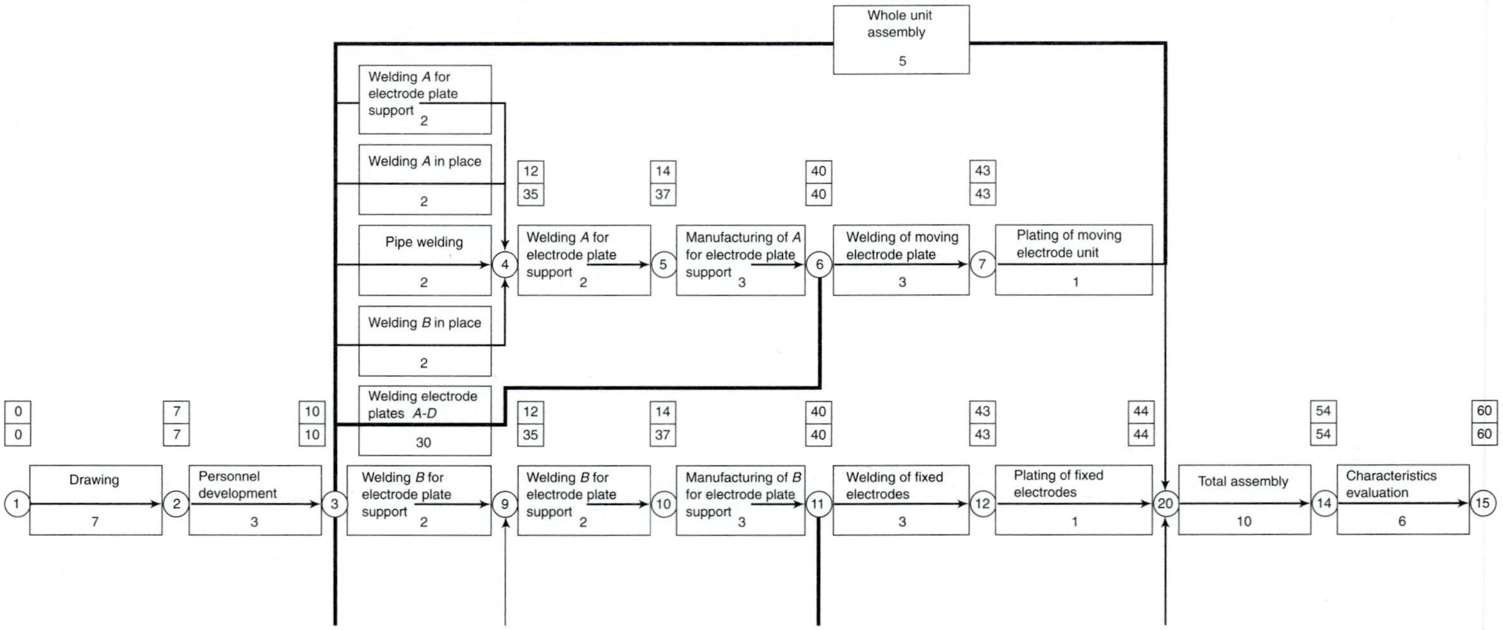

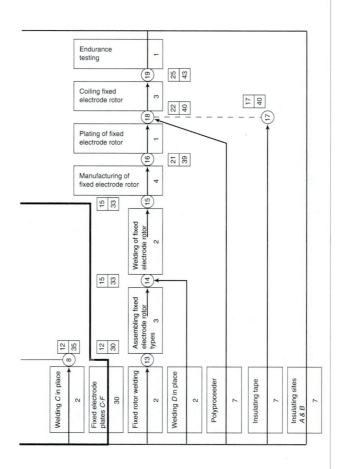

- Implement a periodic facility maintenance plan and its follow-up
- Analyze a manufacturing process and draw up plans for improved efficiency
- Plan and follow up QC inspections and diagnostic tests
- Plan and follow up QC conferences and QC circle conference

Applications   In a low-cost project to produce special resistor electrodes used in a starter for an electric motor, value engineering (VE) experimental trials and quality confirmation tests were implemented based on an arrow diagram (Fig. 2.13) of daily plans constructed using the "card method." This diagram made the trials and tests possible.

THE ROLE OF THE SEVEN NEW QC TOOLS IN QUALITY CONTROL

The seven new tools proposed fulfill the planning steps often mentioned in the "plan, do, check, act" (PDCA) TQC cycle. Figure 2.14 graphically demonstrates the placement of various QC techniques applied in the *plan* and *do* stages to solve an important problem. If an adequate amount of past quantitative data is available, the traditional seven tools would probably suffice; however, as mentioned in Chap. 1, this is not always the case in TQC problem solving. Therefore, Fig. 2.14 should be viewed as relating to a situation where data are relatively scarce.

The plan stage can be divided into the following three phases:

Plan 1: This phase reviews a confusing event and arranges the information so to clarify the underlying nature of the problem.

Plan 2: This phase searches for various means that might be employed to solve the problem and identifies the relationships between the objectives and the means.

Plan 3: This phase establishes an implementation strategy in a time-order sequence in order to increase the chance for success.

During the plan 1 phase, the relations diagram and the KJ methods are used. During plan 2, the systematic diagram and matrix diagram methods, as well as the cause-and-effect diagram and matrix data-analysis methods are used. The plan 3 phase relies on the arrow diagram and the PDPC methods. The arrow diagram method is most often used when the sequence of steps is relatively fixed and predetermined, as in the construction of a building or in shortening the delivery time of a product. However, in QC-related activities, the original readings or plans frequently must be modified because of an unexpected development or occurrence. Whenever there is an unexpected development, information collected up to that point must be analyzed, underlying causes must be understood, and appropriate changes in plans must be made in order to achieve the overall objectives. The PDPC method is an extremely useful technique in such situations, and the PDPC method also can be used to forecast major accidents in such related areas as environmental hazards and product liability.

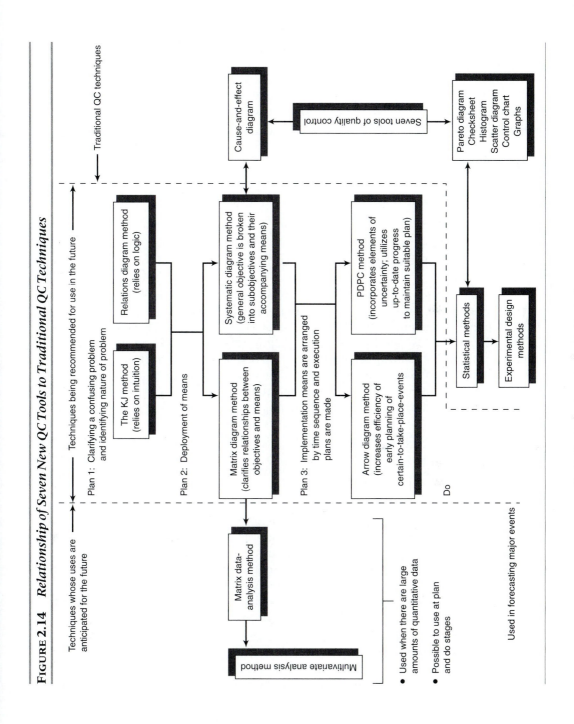

During the *do* stage, other statistical and experimental design methods are selected from the traditional seven tools depending on the particular circumstances of implementation.

Although the *check* and *act* stages of the PDCA cycle are not shown in Fig. 2.14, they proceed from the outcome of the *do* stage. But in Fig. 2.14 it is clear that the following six of the seven new tools should be used in every stage of TQC promotion in the future:

- Relations diagram method
- KJ method
- Systematic diagram method
- Matrix diagram method
- PDPC method
- Arrow diagram method

The matrix diagram method provides a readily comprehensible graphic representation of complex data when each cell in the matrix is given a numerical value. It corresponds to the principal-component analysis method, one of the multivariate analysis methods. Hopefully, the matrix diagram method will be accepted as a tool that can simplify and bring order to numerical or quantitative confusion.

During product planning and process-improvement activities, situations are frequently encountered in which numerous intertwined causes must be untangled. Keeping pace with the development of computers, many businesses have aggressively introduced this method with good results. Even though this technique should be brought to the attention of managers and staff, it should not necessarily be overused.

To prevent misunderstandings about the origin of the seven new QC tools, five points should be highlighted:

1. The seven methods described here do not necessarily exhaust the list. Selection of these seven tools came after much hesitation and thought. Actually, it is hoped that these techniques enrich QC techniques even further. Even people who use the traditional seven tools use them differently over time. Therefore, some modifications and revisions of the seven new tools in response to future developments are necessary. There is also nothing sacred about the number seven. What is essential is that one's toolbox contain all the useful and necessary tools.

2. Most of the techniques described above are already known and were not recently created as QC methods. This also applies to the traditional seven tools, such as the histogram, Pareto chart, scatter diagram, and other statistical methods. Some of these even appear in elementary school textbooks. However, because of their promotion, along with the cause-and-effect diagram, as part of the seven tools for quality control, they have come to be used extensively in QC activities. By christening the preceding methods as the seven new QC tools, it is hoped that

they too will receive the attention necessary to allow the development of diverse applications in fields concerned with quality control.

3. There are two important reasons for using the seven new tools as a group. One is that, as previously mentioned, the seven tools act like an organically integrated set; it would be hard to expect excellent results if they were used independently. The seven new tools should be used in combination, as shown in the second section of Chap. 3, for best results in solving problems. The second reason is that the seven new tools are best used when promoted in all facets of operation under the direction of the company or department head. Effects are limited if the tools are used sporadically in isolated divisions or units.

4. The pioneers who promoted quality control deserve our thanks for having introduced various techniques and for having successfully completed the original seven QC tools, the statistical and experimental design methods for quality control. Unfortunately, however, over the course of the past decade or so, few innovative proposals similar to the ones promoted by the first-generation pioneers have been set forth. As the succeeding generation, though, it is important for us to gather all the seedlings and fruit of the preceding generation, develop them as much as possible in a systematic fashion, and pass them on to the next generation.

5. All the techniques described here have been used previously in various fields and have demonstrated some level of effectiveness. Although not unique to quality control, the requirements for using these tools include a keen awareness of the problem at hand, an incessant desire for improvement, and an enhanced spirit and thought process. Without these kinds of mental preparation, the tools cannot be used effectively. Anyone who expects a tool to do all the work cannot expect good results and cannot really be considered a "user."

THE SEVEN NEW QC TOOLS AND THE BASICS OF GRAPHICS-LANGUAGE THEORY[2]

As discussed earlier, the seven new tools make considerable use of graphics. Table 2.3 presents a classification system developed by T. Kahn[3] that shows the differences between language and graphics as they apply to manner of recognition and relative

TABLE 2.3   *Differences between Graphics and Language*

	Graphics	**Language**
Manner of recognition:	First, the whole is grasped. Next, the elements are analyzed.	First, elements are recognized. Next, whole is constructed.
Ease of understanding:	Understood by almost anybody immediately (pictures).	If rules are not understood, then it is incomprehensible (foreign languages).

ease of understanding. When viewing graphics, we first comprehend the overall structure (pattern, balance, and trends of dots and lines) and then reach out for that which is interesting.

Regardless of nationality and race, any person can understand pictures. Language, however, presupposes an understanding of pre-existing rules, without which the language is totally incomprehensible, for example, when a non-Japanese speaking person tries to make sense of Japanese characters. The understanding of graphics and language is analogous to the human developmental process. Infants start out as "contact beings," whose exchanges of information with others, including their mother, occur through physical contact. These contact beings later grow into "picture beings," who are able to understand information based on pictures, drawings, and graphics of various sorts. Finally, these picture beings turn into "character beings," who are capable of information transmission through written characters. The recent popularity of commercial drawings and comic books may be viewed as an extension of the picture-being stage. In other words, the human capability to understand graphic forms easily seems to be a developmental characteristic. It should be evident that tools anchored in graphics will emerge as powerful techniques in the promotion of company-wide total quality control because of their ready comprehension by all concerned.

Computer graphics theorists distinguish pictures that contain characters, such as the seven new tools, from graphics that contain only drawings by calling them "graphics language." The graphics-language group is further divided into the following four types:

1. Relational system

2. Network system

3. Column-row system

4. Coordinate system

A further explanation of these system types is contained in *Computer Graphics Theory*. However, their names alone suggest their meanings. Of the four types listed, the coordinate system has been in use the longest. Table 2.4 shows the seven new and seven "old" tools classified into the different graphics-language types. Notice that the "old" tools are primarily coordinate-based, while the new tools rely, primarily on the relational or network systems.

Experience has shown that the ease or difficulty involved in constructing graphics for the seven new tools varies from one person to another. The graphics tools used can also be divided into two groups:

Soft graphic tools:	The KJ method, the relations diagram method, and the PDPC method offer a relatively greater degree of freedom in graphics construction.
Hard graphic tools:	The systematic diagram method, the matrix diagram method, and the arrow diagram method have considerably less freedom in graphics construction.

TABLE 2.4   *The Seven New Tools and the Traditional Seven Tools classified by Graphics-language Systems*

Graphics-language System	Seven New Tools	Traditional Seven Tools
Relational system	KJ method	—
Network system	Relations diagram method Systematic diagram method Arrow diagram method PDPC method	Cause-and-effect diagram
Column-row system	Matrix diagram method	Checksheet
Coordinate system	Matrix data-analysis method	Pareto chart Histogram Scatter diagram Control chart Graphs

Even though the former may appear to be the easier to people just starting to use the new tools, they are actually more difficult because they allow a greater degree of freedom. Nevertheless, some beginners have produced outstanding graphics.

A necessary step in company-wide QC activities is for all employees to become thoroughly acquainted with pictorial or graphic thinking. This is accomplished by practicing the construction of various graphics and through the cooperation of everyone involved. All employees should be exposed to a wide variety of graphics so they may identify their own weak areas and learn to construct the diagrams properly. Only this kind of total exposure will make the combined use of all the seven new tools feasible.

Notes

1. Kondo Jiro, *Operations Research* (Tokyo: JUSE Press, Ltd., 1973), pp. 128–136.
2. This section relies heavily on information in Chaps. 2 and 3 of *Computer Graphics Theory,* by Yoshikawa Hiroyuki, published by JUSE Press in 1977. Grateful acknowledgement is due.
3. Yoshikawa Hiroyuki, *Computer Graphics Theory* (Tokyo: JUSE Press, Ltd., 1977).

4

Total Quality Management Processes

T his section of the book introduces some of most widely used TQM processes, which make extensive use of team-based problem solving and planning, and the tools presented in part III.

The five most widely used TQM processes are:

- Daily Management: a systematic approach to document, control, and continuously improve critical processes.

- Just-in-Time (JIT): an inventory management system that links suppliers and customers to minimize total inventory-related costs along the integrated production delivery system. The Japanese also use a more generic definition of JIT as equivalent to "minimizing waste."

- Statistical Process Control: a system design to keep continuous production processes under control and separate special from common causes.
- Hoshin Planning: an integrated planning system which deploys breakthrough objectives throughout the entire organization.
- Quality Function Deployment (covered in part V): a system which systematically translates customer requirements into design and manufacturing specifications.

A sixth, TQM related application, is experimental design, which uses statistical data to study the impact of specific variables on manufacturing processes.

Basic TQM training involves the learning of the tools presented in part III, generally in the context of problem-solving models for the purposes of Daily Management applications. Advanced TQM training focuses usually on the processes described in this and the next section of the book.

As in the case of the tools, the implementation of TQM processes requires a particular set of teamwork-related skills. Experience suggests that the processes can be significantly enhanced if an experienced facilitator is involved in the planning and implementation stages.

Leading the Organization to Perfection through Daily Management

By John W. Moran, Jr.

D aily management can help American businesses capitalize on their human assets in the 1990s. This article explains how an organization can begin a process of
continuous improvement involving everyone in the organization through daily
management supplemented with a customer/supplier mapping process.

The continuous improvement of our daily work processes daily management is
the foundation of any Total Quality Management effort. If all members of an organization constantly work to improve their process elements in a systematic and
focused manner, they will lead the organization closer and closer toward perfection.
The cumulative efforts of these daily management efforts will help an organization
increase its market share and develop loyal and satisfied customers, contented employees, and satisfied shareholders. The most intensive part of the TQM process
involving the greatest number of people in a given organization, daily management
enables all employees to realize their impact and importance within an organization
by measuring and controlling their daily work processes.

THE WHO, WHAT, AND HOW OF DAILY MANAGEMENT

Everyone in an organization—from top to bottom—must be involved in daily management for it to be successful. Daily management can not work where managers
say things like, "I support it; now you do it." Managers must lead by example. Their

Reprinted from Summer 1991 article in *National Productivity Review* with the permission of
the author.

subordinates should see that this example improves their process and shows consistent and sustained improvements focused on customer satisfaction.

If an organization is to prosper and grow in the 1990s, it must become totally customer-focused. To be customer-focused, an organization must

- Involve all its members
- Have strong top-level commitment
- Link its incentive system to customer satisfaction ratings
- Empower employees to solve customer problems on the spot
- Remain in touch with the customer base through ongoing surveys

It is not easy to change an organization's orientation from being quantity-driven to being customer-focused. Doing so requires changing the corporate culture and teaching every employee to be customer-focused.

The first step in reorienting an organization toward its customers is to have all employees view the work they do as a series of processes. The goal of each process must be total customer satisfaction. Everyone in the organization is responsible for establishing a system to define and assess the critical processes that make their job run smoothly. Once employees understand the critical processes, they embark on a never-ending journey of process standardization, continuous improvement, and restandardization of improvements in the process. Each process has three distinct phases of improvement:

Maintenance and Standardization This is how we hold the current gains. If a process gives you a desired output, you must standardize the way you are doing the operation to hold the gains. This is the SDCA cycle (Standardize, Do, Check, and Act) and is shown in **Figure 1.**

Continuous Improvement This is how you change direction when the process output slips or customer needs or expectations change. You then use the PDCA

FIGURE 1

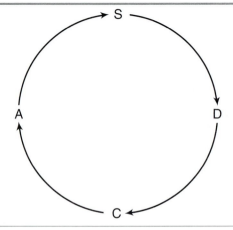

FIGURE 2

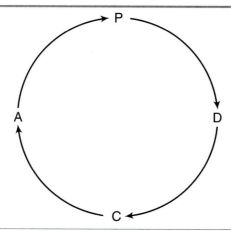

cycle (Plan, Do, Check, and Act), shown in **Figure 2,** to make a plan to change the process, do it, check it, and act if further corrections are needed.

Once you have made a successful change, you standardize it with the SDCA cycle to hold onto the gains (see **Figure 3**).

Innovation and Breakthrough In this phase you develop new approaches to increase the quality level of your process.

THE TOOLS OF DAILY MANAGEMENT

Assessing a process that identifies the critical elements that affect customer satisfaction requires that individuals or teams use some or all of the following tools of daily management. Training in these seven tools is a must.

FIGURE 3

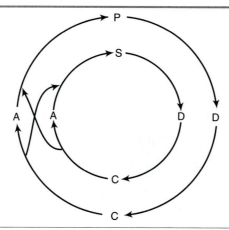

Cause-and-Effect Diagram A graphic depiction showing the relationship between cause and effect. This is an investigative tool, as it organizes randomly connected causes.

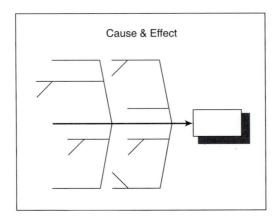

Flow Chart A visual representation of all the steps in a process under study. This tool develops a clear and common group vision of all the elements in a process.

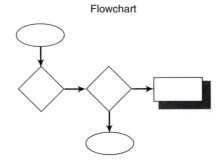

Pareto Chart A graph showing in descending order the major contributors to a problem. It separates the vital few from the trivial many. This tool directs the team to the factors that are the major contributors to the issue being analyzed.

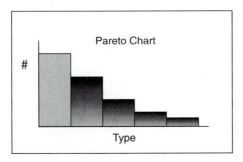

Run Chart A graph of how a parameter of a process is behaving over time. This time is useful in highlighting trends, shifts, and possible cycles.

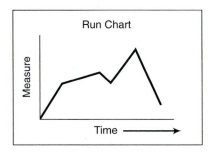

Histogram A bar graph showing the frequency of occurrence of a measured characteristic of a process.

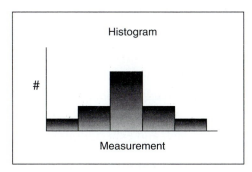

Control Chart A graph of a process characteristic that is used to determine how much process variability is due to random variations and how much is due to unique events. The chart has control limits that point out events that require investigation and correction to aid in achieving and maintaining statistical control.

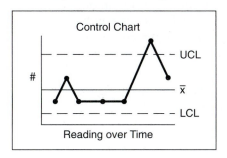

Scatter Diagram A graphical analysis of the relationship between one variable and another. This tool can be used to screen for possible cause-and-effect relationships.

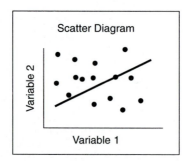

IDENTIFYING CUSTOMERS' AND SUPPLIERS' NEEDS AND EXPECTATIONS

To be effective at daily management, all members of the organization must understand

- Their work process
- Who their customers are
- What their customers' needs and expectations are
- Who their suppliers are
- How to communicate their needs and expectations to their suppliers

The customer/supplier map (© 1990 Moran, Collett, Cote, and Goal/QPC) is a vehicle that clearly displays these items and shows how they interact to produce a product or service for an internal or external customer. As shown in **Figure 4,** the customer/supplier map is a five-part process to help an individual or work team focus on customer-supplier relationships. During this mapping process, an individual or work team must reflect, itemize, and quantify how well they are meeting or exceeding their customer needs and how well their suppliers are meeting theirs.

Step 1: Process Flow Diagram In the center of the map is a flow process diagram completed for the process under consideration. During this step, process elements or sequences of tasks that lead to a particular end are identified. Everyone must recognize that everything they do is a process. Here are some examples of processes:

- Typing a letter
- Producing a part or product
- Registering a hotel guest
- Training a new employee
- Driving a car

FIGURE 4

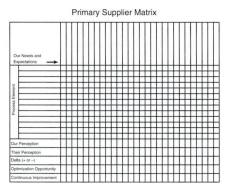

Primary Supplier Matrix

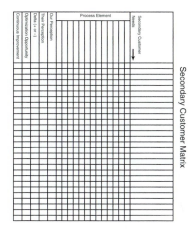

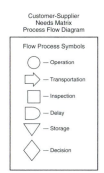

Customer-Supplier
Needs Matrix
Process Flow Diagram

Flow Process Symbols

○ — Operation

⇨ — Transportation

▢ — Inspection

◗ — Delay

▽ — Storage

◇ — Decision

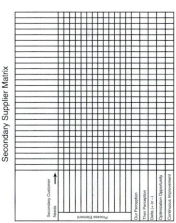

Secondary Supplier Matrix

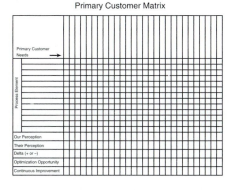

Primary Customer Matrix

Blank - Not Applicable

1 Does not meet
customer needs

3 Acceptable - meets
customer needs

5 Exceeds customer
needs

- Investigating a crime

All these examples have a sequence of tasks that lead to a particular end. Everything we do is a process.

The team graphs out its process, using the following flow process symbols:

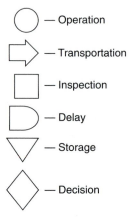

Operation

Transportation

Inspection

Delay

Storage

Decision

Step 2: *Primary Customer Matrix* Once the inputs, outputs, and flow of the process are known, the individual or team needs to develop a list of their customer needs and expectations. The primary customer of a process is whoever gets the product or service directly from the process. This primary customer can be internal or external.

The team fills out the primary customer matrix (bottom of Figure 4) by listing the process elements on the left vertical side and the primary customer needs across the top of the matrix. The next step is to compare each process element against each customer need and attach a score to each comparison as follows:

Blank	Not Applicable
1	Does Not Meet Customer Needs
3	Acceptable—Meets Customer Needs
5	Exceeds Customer Needs

Once all the comparisons are made, you sum up the columns and divide by the number of entries. This is the perception value. The team then has the customer rate the primary customer matrix, using the same rating scale, and fill in their perception value of how well the team is meeting their needs and expectations. The team then subtracts the "our perception value" from "their perception value" and notes whether there is a plus (+) or minus (−) difference under each column.

The plus values are optimization opportunities and should be standardized and improved continuously because they keep customers satisfied. At this point, the SDCA cycle should be used to hold the gains on these customer satisfiers. Too often companies let the satisfiers turn into dissatisfiers through neglect. These satisfiers have to be monitored and improved continuously.

The negative values indicate items that are dissatisfiers. These need to be subjected to the PDCA cycle to identify the continuous improvement opportunities on which the team can work. Continuous improvement plans should be communicated to the customer. The customer needs to be aware of the fact that improvements are taking place and that these positive changes for improvement are a direct result of the shared communication between the customer and the supplier. The team should develop realistic time frames for these improvements. There is nothing worse than to build up the customer's expectations and then not deliver.

Step 3: *Secondary Customer Matrix* The process of Step 2 is repeated for any secondary customers using the secondary customer matrix (left side of Figure 4). A secondary customer is one who receives your output from your primary customer. This step helps you understand how your primary customer uses your output to satisfy their customer. This step leads to an understanding of further continuous improvement and continuous optimization opportunities.

Step 4: *Primary Supplier Matrix* The primary supplier matrix (top of Figure 4) forces the team to examine its relationship with its primary supplier, whether it be internal or external. It is the source from which your process directly receives its inputs. This step forces the team to switch roles and be a customer instead of a supplier, requiring a change in mind-set.

Step 5: *Secondary Supplier Matrix* This is a repeat of Step 4 and the reverse process of the Primary/Secondary Customer Matrix. This matrix is on the right side of Figure 4. Use of a daily management project activity plan sheet, as shown in **Figure 5,** will clarify the sequence that has to happen and determine who is responsible for each activity for successful implementation. This process helps an organization improve its relationship with a secondary or minor supplier.

THE BENEFITS OF CUSTOMER/SUPPLIER MAPPING AND DAILY MANAGEMENT

The customer/supplier map incorporates a series of matrices to empower employees to act on information and take action. Through it, an organization can develop

- Clear understandings of needs and expectations
- A process to communicate them
- Fact-driven teams

Once a work team or individual becomes skilled in the customer/supplier mapping process they begin to understand their pockets of excellence, job functions, areas for immediate improvement, and metrics to track progress, and know how to set a time frame for improvements.

Customer/supplier mapping can be used to move a work team out of management-by-crisis mode and into management by fact. The team will appreciate that the customer's needs and expectations are dynamic and must be monitored continuously; thus the team will meet changes in these needs and expectations proactively—not after the fact. Once the work team has identified continuous optimization and improvement opportunities, it can use daily management tools to discover the root causes of these identified opportunities and plan improvements. The work team can delineate its activities on a daily management project activities plan worksheet (Figure 5), which allows them to understand who is responsible for implementing the desired change and the time it will take to complete the change. The last column on the worksheet is marked "S" for standardization. The team

FIGURE 5

Daily Management Project Activity Plan

Daily Management Project: _____ Team Name: _____ Date: _____

Activity	Primary Responsibility	Secondary Responsibility	PDCA Category	Month												S
				Week	1	2	3	4	5	1	2	3	4	5	

checks off this category once the activity element is incorporated and standardized as part of the ongoing work process.

This intensive process involves everyone in the organization and helps develop a mind-set of continuous improvement that requires everyone to fully understand, measure, control, standardize, and constantly improve their work processes. The benefits to be reaped from it include more streamlined and efficient operations, bolstered by heightened employee and customer satisfaction.

Additional Resources

King, R. *Hoshin Planning: The Developmental Approach*. Methuen, Mass.: Goal/QPC, 1989.

The Memory Jogger. Methuen, Mass.: Goal/QPC, 1988.

Moran, J., R. Talbot, and R. Benson. *A Guide to Graphical Problem-Solving Processes*. Milwaukee, Wis.: Quality Press, 1990.

Just-in-Time: A Production System Built on a Code of Ethics

By Helene S. Fine

ABSTRACT

This paper considers the patterns of industrial behavior that have given rise to Japanese management systems. It draws out a code of ethics from these patterns. The code consists of three imperatives: (1) Consider the person one step further along in the production chain as a valued customer; (2) Deliver, in a timely fashion, a product whose quality is as high and cost is as low as possible; and (3) Help others in the workplace to do the same. It relates the code to the Just-in-Time (JIT) production system and explains, briefly, the JIT pull system of production. It then goes on to show how technological innovation, as well as the application of existing technologies to new situations, flows from the code and the resulting behavior. Statistical Process Control and the use of Order Quantity models within JIT systems are examples of such innovation and application.

INTRODUCTION

In recent years, Japan has become a formidable competitor on the international industrial scene. From automobiles to microprocessor chips, Japanese products command attention. Not surprisingly, the industrial system that spawns the products commands attention as well. In fact, the United States has become a prime customer for both the systems and the products.

As we try to acquire the products and emulate the systems developed in Japan, it is important to keep in mind that they come from a mode of industrial behavior that

1993 report reprinted with the permission of the author.

is very different from our own (Cole, 1979). While there are facets of this behavior that might be feasible for us to try, there are others that are not. Some of these are consistent with our own social values; others clash with them. Before we can decide which features to incorporate, it is important to understand the systems and to become familiar with the underlying patterns of industrial behavior.

This paper will touch only briefly on the Japanese systems while focusing primarily on these patterns of industrial behavior. It will make a case for the fact that the patterns themselves stem from a code of ethics that guide and shape the behavior. It will also suggest that the code is, in turn, consistent with features of the Japanese culture and economy.

JUST-IN-TIME PRODUCTION AND ETHICS

Japanese production systems consist of a range of sophisticated production technologies and innovative organizations to house them (Imai, 1986). Descriptions of these have made it into most Production/Operations Management (P/O M) textbook. Such terms as Just-in-Time (JIT), Kanban, Focused Factories, and Statistical Process Control (SPC) have become part of the ordinary discourse here (Dilworth, 1989; Gaither, 1990).

Since JIT incorporates the behavior that the code of ethics generates and governs, this paper will concentrate on that particular system. It will start with a working definition of JIT and will articulate the code of ethics that seems to govern JIT behavior. It will then elaborate somewhat upon JIT, while indicating how it relates to that code.

JIT itself is a label that is attached to various facets of industrial behavior. Often it refers to an inventory system, to a cellular mode of manufacturing, or to a method of cost accounting. In reality it is a comprehensive philosophy of production that rests on a code of ethics that I believe is implicit in Japanese management systems. It is the code that has given rise to each of these features and more. It is a code that governs behavior at each point in the industrial chain that goes from the purchase of components and materials to the shipping (or sale) of goods and services.

The code consists of these three moral imperatives: (1) Consider the person one step further along in the production chain as a valued customer; (2) Deliver, in a timely fashion, a product whose quality is as high and cost is as low as possible; and (3) Help everyone else in the work unit do the same. Although managers and workers alike are bound by the ethical code, management has a special responsibility to facilitate the process of acting in accordance with it.

The code means that the industrial machine moves forward for the good of particular, easy to identify, people rather than for the good of an abstract construct such as shareholder value or the marketplace. Everyone in it becomes a customer as well as a producer. In each capacity, everyone is assumed to be intelligent, industrious, and better than anyone else at understanding what the tasks are and how best to perform them. Overall production is expected to be lean (this flows from the notion of minimum costs); cooperation rather than competition is the norm; and the style of management is participatory rather than either aloof or authoritarian.

THE CULTURE OF JAPAN AND THE UNITED STATES

There are features of the Japanese economy and culture that foster the sort of thinking outlined above. The Japanese were (and still are) operating in an economy characterized by scarcity. Raw materials and space have been in short supply. The same is true for skilled labor and trained managers. A volatile labor force exacerbated the labor shortage in the post war years (Cole, 1979).

Minimizing waste in general and optimizing the use of labor hours and space in particular became crucial to industrial success. This led to the concern for getting products right the first time (rework wastes material and personhours) and for eliminating inventories (they represent materials and space not being used). The shortage of sophisticated labor and the labor unrest led to the need to center systems on people (contented workers are more likely to stay on the job and perform well), for flexibility in the use of the work force (there isn't labor enough to give everyone a single, narrowly defined job), and for a sharing of managerial tasks with workers. (Again, there aren't enough managers to handle all the tasks, and it's important to keep workers interested in all facets of their work.)

The United States, on the other hand, has had resources to burn, an available pool of labor, and the space of the frontier at its disposal. Although these resources have begun to dwindle, the change has yet to be assimilated and translated into different industrial behavior.

THE PULL SYSTEM OF JIT: THE CODE OF ETHICS AND THE REDUCTION OF INVENTORY

Whatever the cultural and economic features are that give rise to the code of behavior that fosters and sustains the unique JIT system in Japanese industry, there are distinctive features to that system that are worth noting. JIT is a pull rather than a push system of production. Most of the features that we associate with JIT flow from that pull system. Some of the features are: an attitude of viewing inventories— whether of raw materials, work in process, or finished goods—as waste; a comprehensive system for ensuring quality; a constant search for ways to improve the production system; and creativity in the use of existing production techniques and the development of new ones (Dilworth, 1989). An elaboration of each of these will help clarify the system that is JIT.

The pull system itself flows from the ethical code that urges everyone to treat the next person down in the production stream as a respected customer. The end user becomes the customer who starts the production ball rolling by placing an order. This is the stimulus that tells those responsible for delivering the goods or services to begin assembling, packaging, (or in other ways preparing) them for delivery. Those responsible for these functions, in turn, signal the need for subassemblies, and so on, back to the purchase of raw materials. Everyone responsible for delivering a product further down the line is at the same time a customer for a product from the person up the line. In the capacity of producer, each person tries to respond to the signal in accordance with the ethical code. As a consumer, each person demands a similar response from the person passing the product down.

Since a given operator waits for a signal to begin producing his/her particular component, no one accumulates an inventory of those parts. Since that signal represents an immediate need, each operator passes on his/her output immediately. There is, as a result, no pile up of work in process. Since no one completes an item until there is a shipment for it and no one orders materials until an operator demands them, there is no stockpile of either finished goods or raw materials either.

THE TRADITIONAL PUSH SYSTEM: THE GENERATION OF INVENTORY

The push system, which contrasts sharply with this, generates inventory in four ways. A push system begins with intermediate range projections of demand and the purchasing of components and materials to meet the projected demand. The system thus begins with an inventory of purchased goods.

These materials then begin to flow through the plant at a speed and in a direction calculated in advance. Workers perform their operation on the parts that come through their work station as quickly as possible. Some operations and/or operators inevitably take more time than others. This generates bottlenecks where work piles up. This is a second source of inventory.

A third source of inventory stems from the fact that products are generally completed one at a time. The finished first product will wait as inventory while other products that are part of the same order are completed.

Because intermediate range projections lend themselves to error, push systems rely on a stockpile of some inventory as a hedge against production error. This is then a fourth source of inventory.

To summarize, the four sources of inventory in the push system are: materials purchased, work-in-process, finished goods waiting to be shipped, and finished goods that are a hedge against error. By contrast, there are no sources of inventory in the pull system.

THE ETHICAL CODE AND INDUSTRIAL BEHAVIOR AS STIMULUS TO INNOVATION

The ethical code, then, fosters behavior that results in a reduction of inventories. It also fosters behavior that leads to sociotechnological innovation. It does so by placing total responsibility for production on the shop floor. This leads to a pride in workmanship and a search for tools to make the work even better, the systems more effective, and the training more relevant. That search stimulates innovation.

Two sources of innovation are the invention of new techniques and the application of existing techniques to different situations. Kanban is an example of the former. Kanban, the set of cards that signals the need for materials or components and that also requests that these be sent along, is such a technique. The Japanese adaptation and application of American techniques for quality control is an example of the latter—an old technique applied in a new way. Since Japan is now known for the quality of its products, it is worth elaborating a bit on this example.

Statistical sampling techniques had been in use in the United States for over twenty years when the Japanese began their drive to improve quality. They adapted these techniques to their own way of organizing production (Imai, 1986). If each person is a customer for the "product" of a prior operation or process, then it makes sense to use a variation of acceptance sampling on that "product." In this case, however, it is not used to decide whether to accept or reject that lot but whether to accept or reject the performance of the equipment and/or the person that is fashioning it. Thus, Statistical Process Control is born.

There is another way in which the Japanese have adapted existing systems to their own need for improved quality. They borrowed heavily from the job redesign movement that was strong in the United States throughout the sixties (Cole, 1979). They took that movement more seriously than we did and continued to experiment with labor/management teams. Ultimately, they transferred the whole managerial perogative for quality to the teams. Workers became increasingly more responsible for the quality of their own output and more self critical. There were no penalties for speaking out or for spending time working out the bugs in their own operations. Managers then assumed responsibility for training workers and for helping to develop and to use tools for keeping track of the quality of work. In this milieu Demming and others could develop and/or perfect their apparatus for ensuring quality. Control and Flow charts, Pareto Analysis, and Fishbone diagrams came into their own (Cole, 1979; Imai, 1986; Walton, 1986).

As another example of the innovative use of an existing production technique, consider supply ordering models. While an order triggers production, it cannot be the sole mechanism for ordering materials. It is necessary to act on some estimate need. Mathematical order quantity models are, however, inaccurate in the intermediate and long run. As a result, they generally lead to a build of raw materials inventory. Toyota resolved this problem by first searching for ways to reduce overall lot size and then using order quantity models for ordering smaller lots materials where the models are better able to predict need. In the process, they improved die casting equipment to reduce setup times. Small lot production then became even more feasible and order quantity models even more applicable in this situation where they are most accurate—predicting long range need (Ogawa, 1984).

INNOVATIVE ALLOCATION OF RESOURCES

In addition to fostering creativity in the adaptation of existing technologies to their own uses, the Japanese management systems allocate resources in ways different from United States counterparts. They value experience that teaches; they build extensive training into the management function; they allow for a period of trying to understand, in detail, just what a given system can do. They do not, as a result, consider trial and error, learning on the job, and base-line studies to be a waste of time or other resources (Imai, 1986).

SOME PROBLEMS WITH THE CODE AND DRAWBACKS TO THE SYSTEM

There is no system that does not have its costs. The Japanese system is no exception. In general, it is a system where obligations flow upward. As a result, those at the bottom get short shrift.

At the bottom of the economy there are tiers of subsupply establishments whose fortunes rise and fall with fluctuations in the economic cycles. They bear the brunt of the demand of the large corporations and their first tier suppliers for JIT, with its reduction of inventories and high quality. In this part of the economy people are marginally employed. Women, rural workers, and older workers find themselves here. They work part-time, seasonally, and cyclically and thus constitute a dual labor market (Cole, 1979; Pucik and Hatvany, 1988). Such a dual structure would not be acceptable in a democracy such as ours that values equal opportunity.

There is another feature of the Japanese Just-in-Time production system that might conflict with social values in the United States. A society such as ours that values a sense of distance between work and leisure, privacy, and mobility might not want to buy into a system that obliterates all three. The obligation to produce for the "customer" supersedes all other considerations. The search for improvement means opening up every facet of behavior to inspection. The obligation to the group means staying and working within it rather than moving on to further one's own career. It also means commiting all one's energy to group improvement, rather than savoring time away from co-workers, managers, and owners.

CONCLUSIONS

A paper of this scope can do no more than suggest new paths to follow as we try to understand different ways of improving our own production systems. Looking beyond our borders for help in assuring future competitiveness is healthy. Expecting others' systems to transform our own quickly is a mistake. What we can learn from the Japanese experience is a habit of centering a system on a code of acceptable behavior within industry. The code will, however, have to be tailored to our own social values and objectives, not Japan's. Attempting to place responsibility for work in the hands of the workers and to lodge responsibility for facilitating that work in the hands of managers is healthy. The attempt to provide training for handling the responsibility is healthy as well. At the same time, however, we want to avoid some of the costs of doing so that I noted above. The particular route for change will not, in any case, come from a transplant of Japanese techniques from their plants to ours. It will, instead come from our ability to act as they did and allocate resources to the process of change. What this means is allocating resources for baseline studies of what our industry can do and for programs that experiment with change. Only then will we begin to understand what will and will not work here.

References

Cole, Robert E. *Work, Mobility, & Participation: A Comparative Study of American and Japanese Industry*. Berkeley: University of California Press, 1979.

Dilworth, James B. *Production and Operations Management: Manufacturing and Nonmanufacturing*. New York: Random House, 1989.

Gaither, Norman. *Production and Operations Management: A Problem-Solving and Decision-Making Approach*. Chicago: Dryden Press, 1990.

Imai, Masaaki. *Kaizen (Ky'zen): The Key to Japan's Competitive Success*. New York: Random House, 1986.

McMillan, Charles J. *The Japanese Industrial System*. Berlin: de Gruyter, 1989.

Ogawa, Eiji. *Modern Production Management: A Japanese Experience*. Tokyo: Asian Productivity Organization, 1984.

Pucik, Vladimir, and Hatvany, Nina. "Management Practices in Japan and Their Impact on Business Strategy." Quinn, Mintzberg, and James, ed. *The Strategy Process: Concepts, Contexts, and Cases*. Englewood Cliffs: Prentice Hall, 1988.

Walton, Mary. *The Deming Management Method*. New York: Putnam, 1986.

Statistical Process Control: Sophisticated but Simple

By Ellen Domb

Statistical Process Control (SPC) has been evolving over the last seventy years from a mathematical tool of specialists to a family of accessible methodologies to a hierarchy of tools used throughout the manufacturing process by operations workers, industrial engineers, quality specialists, statisticians and managers for process control, process analysis, and process improvement. The understanding gained through this evolution is now being applied to the challenges of quality the service industries.

The sophistication of SPC has been very well documented (see accompanying reading list for some personal favorites). Detailed presentations are available at any level of mathematical complexity to explain how to collect process data, how to calculate all the SPC parameters, how to plot many kinds of charts, and how to interpret the charts in terms of process control and process improvement opportunities.

The simplicity of SPC is less frequently addressed—why use SPC? The answer: so that "how to" knowledge is applied in an environment for success in continuously improving the quality of what is delivered to the customer.

The intuitive appeal of SPC emerges at many levels depending on each user's experience and knowledge. For example:

Inspection is an inadequate method of assuring product or service quality.

Inspection never adds value. At best, it causes rejection of products that don't meet specification before they reach the customer. Since services are created at the time the customer needs them, inspection is even less effective for services, since it only finds problems after the customer has been affected.

1993 report reprinted with the permission of the author.

Inspection never detects all defects. Inspection is a process like any other, with inherent variation.

Analysis of the causes of defects occurs after inspection detects them, which is frequently a considerable time after the defective product was created. Feedback to analyze the process and correct it if appropriate occurs after there has been an opportunity to create many more defective products or deliver more poor service.

The two concepts that move a process from the realm of quality assurance by inspection to quality creation are

Control

Capability

To appreciate both concepts, we need to appreciate the concept of

Variation

A process that is under control is consistent and predictable. Since it may consistently, predictably produce some results that are undesirable, inspection may still be needed after control is established.

Process capability is a measure of how well the control of the process causes its output to match the needs of the customer. A highly capable process produces services or products that consistently, predictably meet the customers' needs.

The objective of SPC is first to get processes under control, next to maintain the control, and then to improve them to increase capability.

Figure 1 is a pictorial view of moving a process from chaos, to control, to continuous improvement. The curves represent the frequency distribution of a process parameter, such as

Number of occasions a customer had to wait (vertical axis) versus length of wait (horizontal axis)

Number of items with a particular diameter versus diameter.

Number of times a particular percentage of defects occurred versus percentage of defects.

The uncontrolled process can be one where the distribution is constant in time but the mean shifts, where the mean is stable but the distribution shifts, or a combination of symptoms (Fig. 1a, 1b, 1c). Fig. 1d represents achieving control.

Why do processes have variation? After all, if we're talking about quality, a thing is either done right or it's not done right! Process variation results from the accumulation of activities that are not controlled or not well understood that influence any process. Examples range from vibration to humidity to wearing of a tool to "the computer is down" to use of many suppliers whose products all meet specification

FIGURE 1 *From Chaos to Control. Time Sequence of Frequency Distributions for a Process*

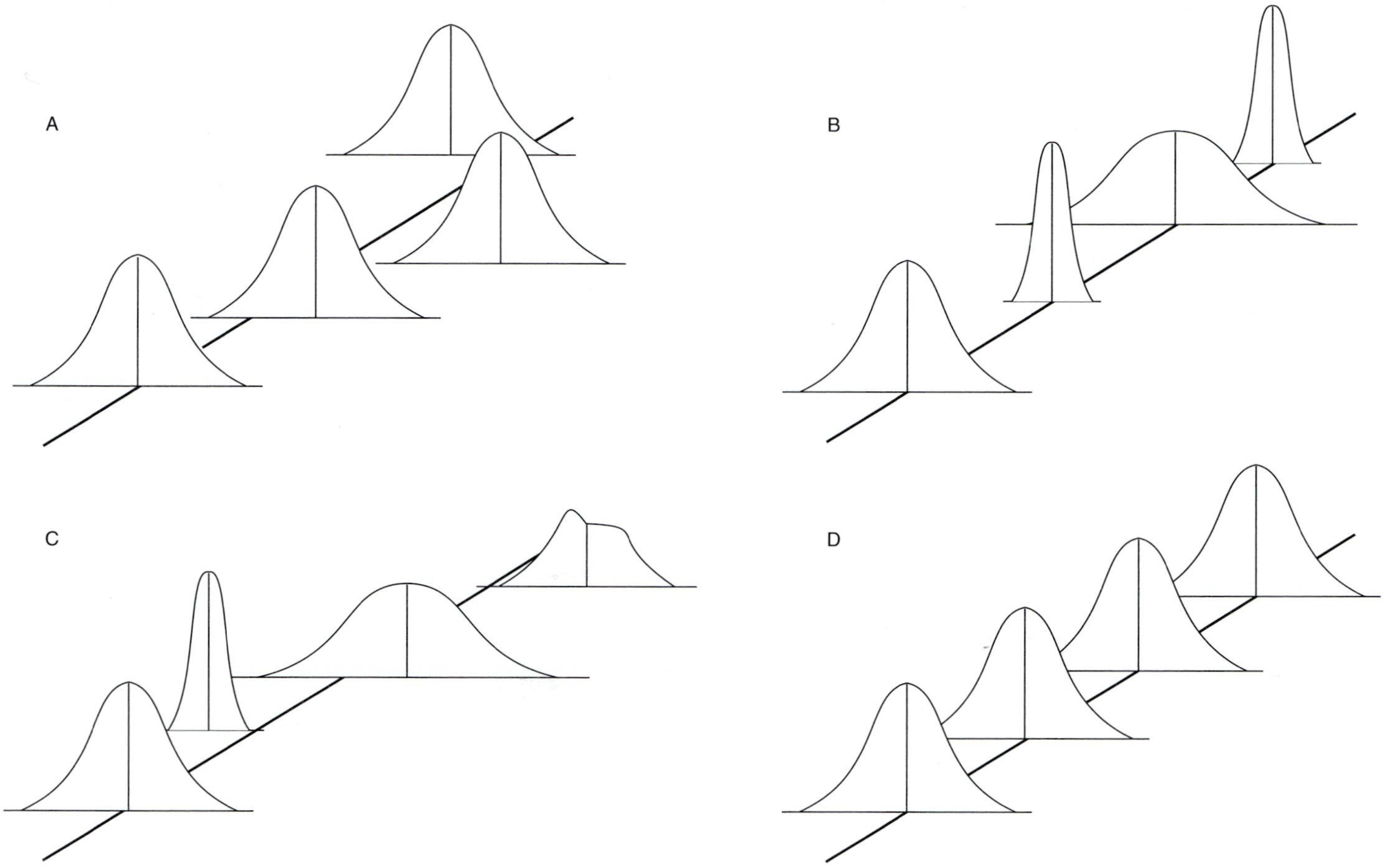

but differ in areas that weren't specified to whether the manager or the employee or the customer had a good breakfast that morning.

SPC identifies two categories of reasons for variation, called special causes and common causes. Special causes are attributable to specific changes from the normal process. Examples include trying to work with broken tools, a new employee told to "try your best" but not given training, new suppliers, and changes in the measuring technique or tools.

Common causes are present every time the process is performed, but combine randomly to create variation in the final result. Work originally done by Shewhart and expanded by Deming and others demonstrates that attempts to identify special causes and common causes are difficult but that the most expensive mistake is to assume that all causes of variation are either special or common. It is best to know that both can be present—and to be wrong part of the time—than to ignore the existence of the two categories.

The most common tool for monitoring process control and for identifying occurrences of special causes is the control chart, Figure 2. There are control charts that deal with variables (length, width, diameter, color intensity, voltage, waiting time, etc.) and those that deal with attributes (number of defects, pass/fail, go/no-go situations.) A simple variable chart is shown.

Significant features of the control chart are

Vertical axis, the value of the variable;

Horizontal axis, time or sample number;

Upper and lower control limits.

The upper and lower control limits are calculated values based on the results of running the process without interference or adjustment. The calculated values are an estimate of three standard deviations from the process mean (see Figure 3). In other words, there is a 99.73% probability that the measured variable will fall inside the control limits, if the process is under control.

FIGURE 2   *A Typical Variable Control Chart*

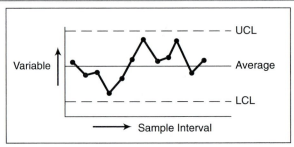

FIGURE 3   *Normal Distribution. Four Percent of Events Have the Value of Parameter X between Two and Three Standard Deviations from the Mean*

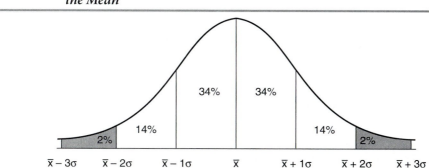

In practical terms, companies using SPC usually teach their workers to gather data, make the charts, and stop the process if a measurement is out of control, or if any of several patterns appear in the data that indicate that the process is no longer functioning normally. This prevents continuation of work when special causes are causing increases in variability. In many companies, the same workers, alone or with a team of colleagues, then diagnose and fix the problems, and resume work, monitoring the process control. In other situations and other company cultures, the worker identifies the situation, but diagnosis, cure, and startup are handled by supervisors, quality engineers, or other specialists.

Throughout this discussion of control, we have not mentioned customer satisfaction. The process can be under control statistically, and still not satisfy the customer. Figure 4 shows two situations:

Fig. 4a. The specification limits (customer requirements) are wider than the control limits. In this case, the process is considered "capable" since staying in control statistically predicts a high probability of satisfying the customer.

Fig. 4b. The specification limits are narrower than the control limits. The process is considered not "capable" since it can be in control and still produce a substantial number of out-of-specification results. Both cases shown here feature symmetrical normal distributions. If distribution is not symmetrical or not normal, the process may be not capable, even if the specification limit width is less than the control limit width.

The use of three standard deviations and the control limits as the defining parameters for capability is based on historical precedent. Organizations that have worked in quality transformation throughout the 1980s and 1990s are setting their own goals at six standard deviations (3.4 defects/million) and even higher.

Once the process is both under control and capable, i.e., predictable and meeting customer requirements predictably, why should you invest in continuing to improve?

FIGURE 4A   *Capable Process*

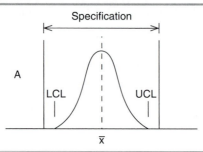

FIGURE 4B   *Not Capable. Shaded Areas Are Measurements in Control but Not Producing Usable Results*

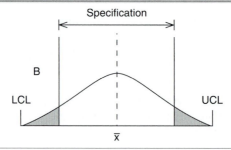

Specifications are frequently not set to optimize the usefulness of the service or product! They are set by tradition, by convenience, by known tooling parameters, or through a combination of perceptions of customer needs. A new view of the loss suffered by the user of high variability products is shown in Figure 5.

Conceptually, the closer the distribution is to the specification limit, the higher the probability that it will not be suitable for use. This is in marked contrast to the earlier view that any result was OK if it was within specification limits. The value to the customer is increased if variation is reduced. In manufacturing, many organizations are now taking steps beyond SPC to create processes that are insensitive to variation in intermediate process steps. These concepts are collectively called robust design or design for producibility. Equivalent concepts apply in service delivery, but are not yet widely known.

Statistical Process Control is the route to continuous improvement for many organizations. The journey from chaos to control to improvement is a learning experience for all participants and rewards those who have the discipline to apply its lessons.

FIGURE 5 *Benefits of Increasing Capability*

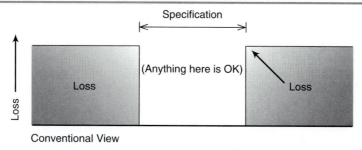

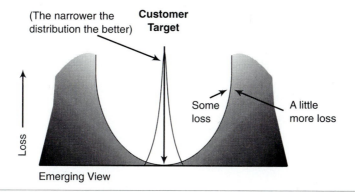

References

D. J. Wheeler and D. S. Chambers. *Understanding Statistical Process Control.* Knoxville, TN: SPC Press, 1986.

W. W. Scherkenbach. *The Deming Route to Quality and Productivity: Road Maps and Roadblocks.* Washington, DC: CEEPress Books, 1986.

R. T. Amsden, H. E. Butler, and D. M. Amsden. *SPC Simplified: Practical Steps to Quality.* White Plains, NY: Quality Resources, 1989.

K. Hosotani. *Japanese Quality Concepts: An Overview.* English Translation 1992. Quality Resources, White Plains, NY.

W. E. Deming. *Out of the Crisis.* MIT Center for Engineering, Cambridge, MA, 1986.

Hoshin Planning: A Planning System for Implementing Total Quality Management

GOAL QPC RESEARCH REPORT

TQC Education Levels/Functions
Hoshin Planning/Management by Policy
Quality Function Deployment
Strategy: TQC Master Plan

Researched and edited by

GOAL/QPC Research Committee
MBP/Hoshin Planning Team

Donald Andrews	*Dow Chemical/Canada*
Michael Brassard	*GOAL/QPC*
Jack Brown	*Procter & Gamble*
James Cuddy	*Spectra Incorporated*
Lois Gold	*Hewlett-Packard*
David Lord	*Procter & Gamble*
Alberto Pardo	*Apollo Division of Hewlett-Packard*
James Riley	*IBM*

Excerpt from *GOAL/QPC Research Report* #89-10-03. Contributed by Copyright © GOAL/QPC, 13 Branch Street, Methuen, MA 01844-1953.

HOSHIN PLANNING RESEARCH TEAM

WHAT IS TOTAL QUALITY MANAGEMENT (TQM)?

TQM (used interchangeably with the Japanese term TQC) is a *system* for meeting and exceeding customer needs through company-wide continuous improvement based upon the implementation of the Plan-Do-Check-Act Cycle supporting *processes, organization,* and *tools* by every manager and employee.

Note that TQM is simply a *system* to better serve the customer. TQM is just a means to an end. Unless this view is maintained, it is very easy to focus more on the "what" of TQM (Models and Methods) rather than on the "why" of TQM.

WHAT IS HOSHIN PLANNING?

As in the case of TQM, Hoshin Planning is a system. It is a component of the TQM system that allows an organization to plan and execute strategic organizational breakthrough.

Its key elements are:

- A planning and implementation process that is continuously improved throughout the year (P-D-C-A)
- Focus on key systems that need to be improved to achieve strategic objectives
- Participation and coordination by all levels and departments as appropriate in the planning, development, and deployment of yearly objectives and means
- Planning and execution based upon facts
- Goals and action plans which cascade through the organization based upon the true capability of the organization

HOW DOES HOSHIN PLANNING INTEGRATE WITH TQM?

When all is said and done, TQM is a system to achieve the following organizational objectives:

Daily Control can be viewed as the application of Plan-Do-Check-Act (PDCA) to daily *incremental* continuous improvement. Hoshin Planning is simply PDCA applied to the planning and execution of a few critical (strategic) organization objectives. Cross-functional management concerns the systems by which functions and departments work together to achieve common organizational targets such as quality, cost, and delivery/productivity. Hoshin Planning is related to daily control and cross-functional management as follows:

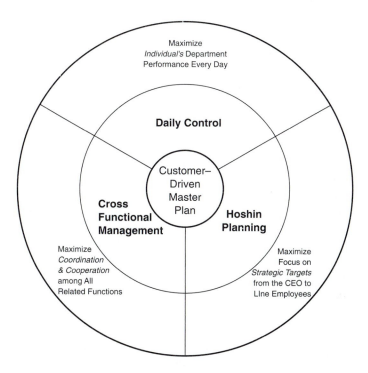

1. **Daily Control**
   (a) Hoshin Planning draws information from the ongoing data collection and analysis of the Daily Control process to identify broad system problems in which breakthrough is needed.
   (b) Once breakthroughs have occurred they can then become the focus of daily continuous improvement.

2. **Cross-Functional Management**
   (a) Quality Function Deployment (QFD), a key system for listening to and incorporating the "voice of the customer," can identify areas for planning breakthrough.
   (b) The Hoshin Planning process often requires cooperation across functions as well as vertical alignment.

WHAT ARE THE BENEFITS OF HOSHIN PLANNING?

- Creates an Established Process to Execute Breakthrough Year after Year
- Creates Commitment to Both the Direction and Implementation Paths Chosen
- Increases Interdepartmental Cooperation
- Draws upon and Reinforces the Plan-Do-Check-Act Cycle (PDCA) in Monthly Progress Reviews

- Creates a Planning and Implementation System that is Responsive, Flexible, Yet Disciplined
- Gives Leadership a Mechanism to Understand the Key Problem Areas in a Company
- Creates Quicker and More Accurate Feedback Loops
- Provides a Common Focus throughout the Organization

HOW DOES THE HOSHIN PLANNING PROCESS WORK?

In TQM *how* a process is implemented is as important as *what* that process includes. It is not enough to have a defined, disciplined set of process steps. TQM depends on predictable implementation. Traditional management approaches accept the fact that some managers will execute well and others will not. Hoshin Planning provides methods that eliminate at least some of the natural manager to manager variability. This combination of process and methods can be summarized in the following equation:

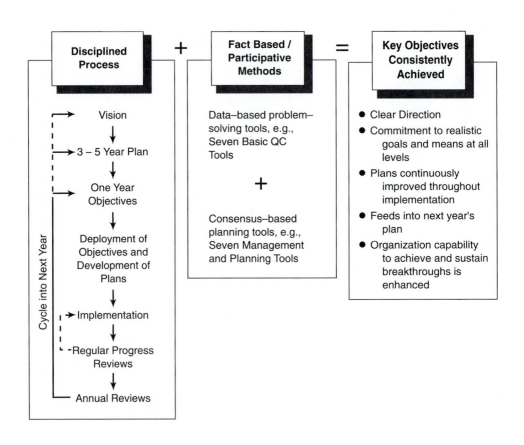

THE HOSHIN PLANNING PROCESS

The steps in the previous graphic describe the evolution of achievable objectives and plans that flow from any organization's long term vision. The vision results from a complete understanding of the outside world and how the organization plans to fit into it long term. The 3–5 year plan is based on an analysis of the broad areas for improvement that will block the attainment of the vision. The one year plan refines these broad areas into *a few key objectives* that must be achieved *this* year. The *key* departments/functions are then identified and involved in the development of sub-objectives and plans to achieve the one year plan. Each appropriate level within these departments/functions identifies areas of improvement that would help achieve the objective. These plans are then implemented. Each level reviews its own performance regularly (monthly or quarterly) and makes necessary changes to the plan. The overall progress for the year is reviewed 9–10 months into the fiscal year to determine whether the plans will be achieved and should be replaced with new objectives for next year or continued into the next year.

THE HOSHIN PLANNING METHODS

The process above is simply a *procedure* for planning and implementation. In order to ensure that the execution of this process is consistent with TQM, there are two sets of methods which participants utilize*:

7 Basic QC Tools	7 Management and Planning Tools
• Check Sheet	• Affinity Diagram
• Pareto Chart	• Interrelationship Digraph
• Run Chart	• Tree Diagram
• Cause & Effect Diagram	• Prioritization Matrices
• Scatter Diagram	• Matrix Diagram
• Histogram	• Process Decision Program Chart (PDPC)
• Control Chart	• Activity Network Diagram

WHAT IS THE STATE OF DEVELOPMENT OF HOSHIN PLANNING IN THE UNITED STATES?

Even though Hoshin Planning (under the name Hoshin Kanri, Policy Deployment, or Management By Policy) has been developed and refined in Japanese companies

---

*These tools are indispensable in surfacing breakthrough ideas out of chaos and converting them into implementable plans. This closely resembles the core of Hoshin Planning. More information is available in *The Memory Jogger Plus*, GOAL/QPC, © 1989.

for nearly 25 years, it is still in its infancy in the United States. The most mature application dates back to 1984, but widespread interest has only occurred in the last two years. Although there is a handful of companies that are truly serious about Hoshin Planning implementation, Florida Power & Light and Hewlett-Packard are the most visible U.S. examples. Both have initiated and customized their own Hoshin Planning models. FP&L, using the term Policy Deployment, incorporated it in their Total Quality model that allowed them to win the coveted Deming Prize in Japan. They are the first non-Japanese company to win the Prize. Hewlett-Packard *has* initiated Hoshin Planning in most of its 50+ operating divisions.

The results in this country have been very encouraging but it remains to be seen whether Hoshin has the needed staying power. One fact should be highlighted, however. Hoshin Planning is the one element of TQM that is most consistently *applied* in Japanese companies of all sizes and in all industries.

WHAT SHOULD BE IN PLACE TO MAKE HOSHIN PLANNING WORK?

HOSHIN PLANNING PREREQUISITES			
Knowledge and Experience	**Manager's Role**	**Motivation**	**Organization**

• Widespread understanding of the basics of TQM including where Hoshin Planning fits
 	
• Understanding of PDCA model
 	
• Widespread knowledge and use of the Seven Basic QC Tools
 	
• Some specialized knowledge of the appropriate Seven Tools for Management and Planning
 	
• Widespread understanding of
	• Set direction
	  –Provide a clean focus
	  –Establish priorities
	  –Communicate it to everyone
	
	• Support for people's efforts
	  –Provide resources
	  –Create horizontal coordination
	  –Remove system barriers
	  –Teach and coach
	
	• Provide a focus on the process
	  –Practice PDCA
	  –Demand data
		• Clear and compelling answer to the question "Why do Hoshin Planning?" (Find a burning issue)
		
		• Desire on management's part to narrow and/or coordinate the focus
			• Leadership demand from the top
			
			• Develop steering teams at different levels of deployment to coordinate problem solving
			
			• Facilitators (preferably bosses) in place
			
			• Champion/sponsor in a highly visible, influential management slot
			
			• A coordinating mechanism (team, committee, or individual)

HOSHIN PLANNING PREREQUISITES *(continued)*			
Knowledge and Experience	**Manager's Role**	**Motivation**	**Organization**
Daily Management/Control	• Reinforce and recognize employees' efforts		to integrate plans across functions and departments
			• A system for making Daily Management/Control work

CONCLUSION

It's difficult to predict the future of Hoshin Planning in the United States based upon the limited sample of implementations thus far. One thing does appear clear. If U.S. companies are serious about adapting and adopting a TQM model that works, a key ingredient is the ability to consistently identify, plan for, and achieve strategic objectives. It is not enough to have everyone doing better everyday in every way.

There is only one remaining question that must be answered by each American CEO: Are you satisfied with your present ability to consistently achieve strategic objectives? If not, then Hoshin Planning deserves serious consideration as an alternate implementation system.

HOSHIN PLANNING OVERVIEW

HISTORY OF HOSHIN PLANNING IN JAPAN

The modern quality movement began in Japan with Dr. W. Edwards Deming teaching statistical values and tools in 1950 and Juran teaching management of quality in 1954. The quality movement has progressed steadily ever since.

1965   The Japanese company Komatsu developed the flag system, an elementary form of Hoshin Planning, to speed the transition from Statistical Quality Control to Total Quality Control.

1970s   Yoji Akao of Tamagawa University improved this system by introducing the target/means matrix as a way of clarifying measures, control items, and control points.

1980s   Nayatani expanded the use of the system by enhancing it with the Seven New Tools for Management and Planning. In Japan during the 1970s and 1980s, MBO was replaced by Hoshin Planning because of Hoshin Planning's flexibility in dealing with quickly changing economic situations.

In its most recent study mission in Japan (October 1988), GOAL/QPC found that Hoshin Planning has become one of the most widely recognized and implemented TQM/TQC systems (along with well established systems such as Quality Circles and the Basic Quality Control (QC) tools, e.g., check sheet, pareto chart).

Hoshin Planning is known by various names: Hoshin Kanri (in Japan), Policy Deployment, Management by Policy, Hoshin, and Management by Planning (MBP).

IN THE UNITED STATES

Hewlett-Packard

In 1983 John Young, the CEO of Hewlett-Packard, announced a set of ambitious company-wide improvement targets: In 10 years Hewlett-Packard would increase its quality measures ten fold. Within five years they had made dramatic strides, but it was clear that the company was not "on the curve" to make the projected time line. They turned for guidance to Yokagawa Hewlett-Packard, a Japanese jointly owned subsidiary that won the Deming Prize in 1982. One of the primary components of YHP's success was its Policy Deployment/Hoshin Planning system. Hewlett-Packard learned from this and has been refining the version (referred to simply as "Hoshin") in a number of operating and service divisions.

Florida Power and Light

FP&L has been on its TQM journey since 1981. In 1986 it introduced Policy Deployment (Hoshin Planning). Under the guidance of Dr. Noriaki Kano of Tokyo Science University and the Japanese Union of Scientists and Engineers (JUSE), FP&L developed a system which now is the primary means by which the top management (chairman, CEO, and vice presidents) develops its improvement focus for the year. This is the core activity of an intensive three week annual executive planning process. In addition, the system presently involves about 20–25% of all FP&L managers and employees in the targeted breakthrough areas.

Other U.S. Users

Other well-known companies that are involved in Hoshin Planning are Procter & Gamble, 3M Corporation, and Omark Corporation.

WHAT IS HOSHIN PLANNING?

Hoshin Planning is a system. It is a component of the TQM system that allows an organization to plan and execute strategic organizational breakthrough. According to Dr. Kano, "It is a marriage between the strengths of the East and the West: The strong leadership exercised by Western top management with the organization-wide consensus of traditional Japanese organizations." Therefore, in Hoshin Planning, *direction/focus flows down while organizational capability/commitment flows up*. (See Figure 1.)

Notice that the "bubble-up" has a direct effect on the direction that is then moved down through the organization. Hoshin Planning also involves coordination of all plans across departments and functions to prevent counter-productive and misdirected individual activities. Figure 2 shows how Kenzo Sasaoka, the President of Yokogawa Hewlett-Packard (YHP), graphically depicts this coordination.

Figure 2 also illustrates "catchball," which is the Japanese term describing the process of give and take across levels of management. Catchball includes:

1. What top management proposes as the key areas of the Hoshin Planning focus for the next year.
2. Identification by managers at various lower levels of other key areas upon which the organization should focus.
3. What these departments/functions could do about the areas that both top management and lower levels have identified.

Mr. Sasaoka admits that during the first year of YHP's Hoshin Planning implementation, what was sent down through the organization came back intact

---

FIGURE 1

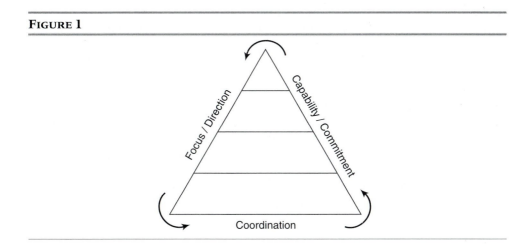

FIGURE 2   *The YHP Hoshin Planning Cycle*

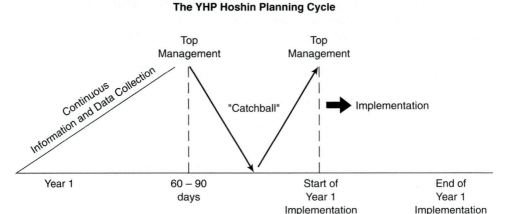

The YHP Hoshin Planning Cycle

(nothing changed or added). He estimates that today, 60% of what is implemented is proposed by management. The remainder has been added or modified by lower level management input.

WHAT IS THE "BEST" METHOD?

In trying to find the "best" process model, the Research Committee considered a half dozen different models that detailed specific process steps. It was decided that rather than detail the pros and cons of each process model, the Committee's job was to find the common features of each model that fit U.S. applications. Actually this wasn't that difficult even when comparing U.S. and Japanese models. The Japanese models tended to be more elaborate, but the core remained surprisingly consistent. The Committee integrated the Seven Management and Planning Tools with each of the models considered. These tools, indispensable in surfacing breakthrough ideas out of chaos and converting them into implementable plans, closely resemble the core of Japanese Hoshin Planning. More information is available in *The Memory Jogger Plus,* GOAL/QPC, © 1989.

The one key difference that we consistently found in the Japanese models was a stronger ongoing link between Hoshin Planning and performance data generated through Daily Control. Daily Control is the day-to-day process by which incremental improvement happens in TQM. It generates constant data that pinpoints performance strengths and weaknesses. The Japanese feed this into the Hoshin Planning priorities. (A detailed explanation of Daily Control is beyond the scope of this paper.)

The following is the Committee's summary of the Hoshin Planning process.

The Core Hoshin Planning Process

The Core Hoshin Planning Process

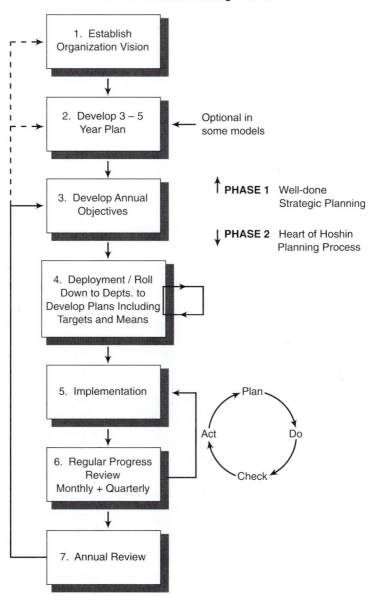

Identified on the following pages are the key steps, elements, and tools necessary to make Hoshin Planning work. This is intended as a generic model against which any company can benchmark or compare its present planning process.

	HOSHIN PLANNING PROCESS	
Step	**Key Elements**	**Key Tools**
1. Establish Organization Vision	• Data input from internal and external performance • Customer focused • Includes all environmental factors, e.g., social, regulatory, economic • Draft of vision reviewed with the organization for reality check • Finalized vision communicated clearly to everyone at all levels	• **Brainstorming** around issues in the external environment • **Affinity Diagram** to identify patterns among seemingly unrelated factors • **Market research** technology to obtain data on the external environment • **Interrelationship Digraph** to identify bottleneck factors in the environment
2. Develop three to five year objectives* *In some models this step is eliminated with the process shifting to a one year focus immediately	• Focus on the "gap" between present organizational capability and required performance to reach the vision • Accurate data from past performances determines the present capability of the organization and the means that should be pursued over the next three to five years • Three to five year objectives communicated clearly to everyone at all levels	• **Market research technology** to gather data in order to identify midterm environmental issues • **Broad internal performance reports and analysis,** e.g., customer complaints, market share • Data collection and analysis using the **7 Basic QC Tools** • **Interrelationship Digraph** to identify the most serious problem areas • **Matrix Diagram** to compare potential action plans with vision statement and criteria

HOSHIN PLANNING PROCESS *(continued)*		
Step	**Key Elements**	**Key Tools**
3. Develop annual objectives	• Completely integrated with three to five year objectives and vision • Small number of focus points, "Fewer more important efforts vs. more, more, more . . ." • Accurate data, minimally filtered is the basis for selecting the one year objective • "Reason for Improvement" must be compelling; convincing case must be made to work on any selected objective rather than on something else • Use data to identify broad patterns among problem areas. Identify the truly "broken" systems	• **Market research technology** to identify key short term external environmental factors • **Data collection and analysis** to identify broad internal performance problems, e.g., customer complaints, profit center information • **Seven Basic QC Tools** to analyze and summarize key problem areas. In a mature TQM organization, these would be in use everywhere. • **Tree Diagram** to explore all of the possible means to address key problem areas • **Matrix** of all of the possible means with the broad target areas for the year to choose the best means to pursue
4. Deployment/Roll down to departments to develop plans (including targets and means)	• Clear, disciplined action plans with direction of improvement, what is to be measured, and the process that is to be improved • Continuous give and take (catchball) between levels around the chosen targets and the organization's capabilities • Emphasizes the plans of departments/units vs. just individuals	• **Matrix Diagram** to match key departments/ functions with chosen objectives and means • **Seven Basic QC Tools** and problem solving models at all involved levels to identify more specific problem areas to address • **Tree Diagram** to identify all the possible actions at all involved levels

HOSHIN PLANNING PROCESS *(continued)*		
Step	**Key Elements**	**Key Tools**
	• A team coordinates plans across departments • Responsibilities clearly designated • A team also ensures that the sum of the plans really reaches the target	• **Matrix Diagram** to match possible actions with the overall objectives in order to choose the best options
5. Implementation	• Disciplined data collection and measurement system implemented "in-process," not after the fact • Visible process (targets and means) allows for recognition and reinforcement in "real time" • Standardized methods reduce some manager to manager variability in outcomes • Problems visible, therefore management can put support where needed	• **Seven Basic QC Tools** in use to collect data as the year's plan progresses • **Process Decision Program Chart (PDPC)** to anticipate likely implementation problems and prepare reasonable means to prevent them • **Arrow Diagram** to create an implementation timetable against which to monitor results
6. Progress Review (Monthly and Quarterly)	• Strong emphasis on self diagnosis of targets and process • Standardized review format and language • Simple analysis emphasized • Builds Plan-Do-Check-Act continuously into the process • Problems are seen as opportunities to be surfaced, not skeletons to be buried • Emphasizes recognition, support, and corrective action, not punishment	• **Seven Basic QC Tools** to define why a target and plan were not met. Emphasize the Cause and Effect Diagram, Run, and Pareto Charts • Simple **documents** to record any changes to the plan • **Tree Diagram** to develop revised plans with complete implementation detail

HOSHIN PLANNING PROCESS *(continued)*		
Step	**Key Elements**	**Key Tools**
	• System problems not directly related to plan have a place to surface	
7. Annual Review	• Data collection and review done all year providing accurate and relevant diagnosis of missed targets and poor processes • Examine plans even when the target is hit, in order to show correlation. The emphasis must be on understanding which plans led to the achievement of which targets so that the resulting process can be standardized • Review Hoshin Process itself, aiming to improve it for the next year	• **Seven Basic QC Tools** as the format used to summarize the results of all of the plans for the entire year. The emphasis is on answering the question: Why did we miss any of our targets or plans? • **Affinity Diagram** to help identify all of the reasons for success or failure and any pattern which may emerge that can improve next year's planning

FOCUS POINTS AMONG LEADING JAPANESE HOSHIN PLANNING EXPERTS

Kano

- Don't spend too much time on the vision step
- Keep vision flexible and responsive to the market
- Don't over-formalize Hoshin Planning—becomes paper system
- Incomplete policies from the previous year may not roll over into following year's activities—must compete
- Focused deployment—not everyone needs to be involved in every policy
- Must prioritize department contribution to policy success—therefore deploy accordingly
- Presidential reviews (not audits) should occur throughout the year, not just one year
- Emphasize "synthesis" of results—examine all policies thoroughly even when target is achieved

- Stresses very strong top management leadership in medium to long term policy setting
- Strong emphasis on Daily Control (PDCA in daily job tasks) as needed in addition to Hoshin Planning
- Stresses using basic QC concepts (e.g., Q I Story) as means to establish and implement policies

Akao

- Can "bubble up" over 1-½ to 2-½ years
- Ultimate goal is company-wide involvement in policies
- Stresses importance of "catchball" at the medium term policy and vision steps
- Formal analysis of critical factors that caused organization to miss targets from the previous year
- Formal "stages" of development criteria for each Hoshin Planning effort

Nayatani

- Very close to Akao except:
    1. Emphasizes even more strongly the need for all departments to be involved in the formulation of all policies (including the work of the Quality Circles)
    2. Stresses the use of the Seven Tools for Management and Planning at every step of the MBP process

5

Listening to the Voice of the Customer

P art V focuses on the most important of all TQM principles, "the customer is king," and its practical applications.

In TQM writings this concept applies to both the internal and external customer. The internal customer is the next process in the value chain. The external customer includes both the end user and, increasingly, any other significant stakeholder, including society at large.

The key concern is how to grasp and better understand customer wants and needs, and how to translate these into cost-efficient, maximum quality processes and services. The key difference with traditional marketing analysis is that a systematic effort is made to use customer inputs to do strategic planning and new product design. In other words, TQM customer-based analysis has a profound, cross-functional impact. Nevertheless there are still many opportunities to benefit from marketing analysis in order to understand the customer, as suggested by the introductory reading in this section.

One of the most powerful customer-focused applications in Total Quality Management is the process known as *Quality Function Deployment (QFD)*. QFD systematically translates vague customer needs and wants into detailed design and manufacturing specifications. QFD, a cross-functional new product design process, has dramatically decreased the time and increased the effectiveness of the new product introduction cycle of companies in industries as diverse as automobile manufacturing and software. QFD is likely to be the most popular TQM application of the 90s as Statistical Process Control was in the early 80s.

Becoming Customer Oriented

———

By Mary Lou Roberts

In the late 1960s and early 1970s American automobile makers ignored the desire of their customers for economical, reliable cars and thus triggered a decades-long decline in market share.

Mass-market retailers including Sears and Montgomery Ward ignored changing consumer demographics, lifestyles, and tastes and opened the way for the success of new entrants such as K-Mart and later Wal-Mart.

Federal Express created a new industry by offering customers guaranteed overnight delivery of small packages even though the founder was assured that this business concept was not viable.

McDonald's revolutionized the fast food industry by promising that customers would always receive "Quality, Service, Cleanliness, and Value" beneath the golden arches.

These and many other examples highlight the importance of being attuned to not only what the customer demands of today's products and services but also what the customer will want and need in the marketplace of tomorrow. Meeting customer wants and needs is one of the cornerstones of the quality approach. Simple as this may sound, it is difficult to do on a consistent basis. The larger the company becomes, and the further management is removed from direct customer contact, the harder it is. Becoming—and remaining—customer oriented requires effort and discipline just like any other aspect of TQM. In this chapter we will discuss both the philosophy and the techniques required to be truly customer oriented.

A FEW WORDS ABOUT TERMINOLOGY

Before we look at a formal definition of the concept of "customer orientation," it is important to clarify the meaning of a number of terms that will be used in the chapter. Many of them are used inconsistently in the literature of marketing and quality, and confusion results.

In this chapter the term *customer* is used in its broadest sense. It encompasses both internal and external, consumer and industrial, product and service, purchaser and user, intermediary and final. Or to put it another way, everyone who produces any kind of economic good has customers who either add value and pass the good on to the next customer or who are final consumers or users of the good. By the same reasoning, virtually all workers are suppliers to one or more customers, either internal or external. In this chapter we will focus primarily on the external customer, but virtually everything that we say also applies to understanding and satisfying internal customers.

In discussions of marketing and quality there is some controversy over whether the terms *customer orientation* and *market orientation* are the same, or whether *market orientation* has a broader meaning. In this chapter we will use them synonymously.

The term *product* can be another source of confusion. Here again we will use the broadest interpretation. Unless otherwise specified, *product* will be used to mean both tangible goods and intangible services. In this context, it is irrelevant whether the goods and services are produced by for-profit or not-for-profit organizations.

Another term that we will use broadly in this chapter is *research*. In a business setting the term *research* usually implies a formal process with an outcome that is frequently expressed in quantitative terms, although qualitative research is recognized as appropriate in many circumstances. In discussions of quality we frequently hear the term *listening to the customer*. While there is no formal definition of this term, it is often inclusive of formal research, both quantitative and qualitative, and of a variety of less formal techniques for obtaining customer feedback. Consequently, it is really the preferred term, but it can lead to some very awkward sentences. In this chapter, we use the word *research* to include any method of obtaining feedback from the customer.

With these issues of terminology in mind, let's begin by looking at what it means to be customer oriented.

WHAT IS "CUSTOMER ORIENTED"?

For many years marketers have been exhorting businesses to base their activities on a thorough understanding of the wants and needs of their customers. Levitt (1960, 1975) was among the first. He faulted businesses for unjustified reliance on the belief that constantly increasing population or decreased costs achieved through cost-cutting and economies of scale or lack of substitute products would assure continuous growth and profits. He argued that an industry is "a customer-satisfying process, not a goods-producing process" (1975, p. 174).

More recently the consulting firm McKinsey & Company set out to study the strategies and management practices of successful firms. According to Peters and Waterman,

> When we started our survey, we expected to find the excellent companies putting stress on cost or technology or markets or niches. In other words, we felt some would have strategies oriented to one thing, and some to another, but we weren't expecting any particular bias. But that is not what we found. While there are differences among industries, we did find a striking commonality: The excellent companies tend to be more driven by close-to-the-customer attributes than by either technology or cost (p. 186).

Being customer oriented is critical to the success of any business in any industry at any time. While technology or fad may seem to take precedence at some points in time, over the long term the business must create products and services and market them in a way that satisfies their customers.

Customer orientation plays an additional role in a firm that is actively engaged in a TQM program. Improving internal processes is a critical part of TQM. It can all too easily become the central focus of the program. A genuine customer focus, one that has become institutionalized within the organization, continually draws attention back to the customer's wants and needs. Without the constant pressure to meet marketplace needs, businesses are in danger of improving a product or process that no one wants!

Granted then, customer orientation is critical. A formal definition is still needed. A recent definition by Kohli and Jaworski seems to capture the essence, even though they use the term *market orientation*. They describe it as:

> The organization-wide **generation** of market intelligence pertaining to current and future customer needs, **dissemination** of the intelligence across departments, and organization-wide **responsiveness** to it (p. 6).

This definition has three key aspects that cause it to tie in very well with TQM practices. First, it speaks of **market intelligence,** a broad term that includes not only data from formal research but also a variety of less formal techniques for listening to the customer that will be discussed in the third section of this chapter. Second, it highlights the importance of **dissemination** of intelligence findings throughout the organization. A necessary prerequisite for TQM success is that information be shared widely within the organization, not hoarded by one person or department. Third, this definition requires organizational **responsiveness** to information about customer wants and needs. Information is not produced for its own sake. Research reports are not written to gather dust on some office shelf. Customer views are not solicited and then ignored as the firm continues doing what it prefers to do. Instead, the customer and the market environment are the focal point of organizational decision making.

For this to be accomplished most firms must make two changes in the way they have typically operated. First, the monitoring of the customer and the market environment must be **continuous.** Most firms view formal marketing research from a project perspective. A project is specified, executed, and a report is made to management. Management acts or doesn't act, but the project is completed. Perhaps it is followed up with another project in a few months. Perhaps it is even repeated (or in research terms replicated) at a later time to see what has changed. However frequently or infrequently research is conducted, the basic orientation is that of discrete projects.

The market intelligence that drives the quality process must be viewed differently. It must be a continuous process of listening, documenting, analyzing, sharing, and acting. It must be an integral part of the manner in which the firm operates. It must be considered a necessity, not a postponable discretionary item or a luxury.

Second, the customer-oriented firm must make decisions cross-functionally in a spirit of cooperation, not competitiveness (Shapiro, 1988). Integrated decision making allows various viewpoints and types of expertise to be incorporated into the decision. It goes a long way toward achieving buy-in on the part of all persons and departments that have a stake in the decision outcome. It also accomplishes something else that is increasingly important in today's globally competitive economy. Cross-functional decision making is necessary to speed products and services to market. It helps to avoid redesign, rework, and more generally the NIH (Not Invented Here) syndrome that can make the introduction of new products and processes agonizingly slow. In an age of ever-shorter product life cycles the organizational disunity that stems from narrow functional perspectives cannot be tolerated.

Before looking at, first, the process of becoming customer oriented and then research and listening techniques that are necessary to achieve and maintain customer orientation, it is important to recognize the danger of becoming bogged down in technique. **Customer orientation is first and foremost a business philosophy**—a way of looking at the world. It requires focusing outward, not inward. It requires always keeping customer wants and needs at the center of decision-making activities. It demands a genuine commitment to satisfying the customer no matter how much effort is required. Without this kind of outlook, focus—and perhaps even obsession—a firm cannot be customer oriented, no matter what techniques it employs.

THE PROCESS OF BECOMING CUSTOMER ORIENTED

Few businesses are really customer oriented. Therefore the assumption is that we must take an existing firm and transform it. At the same time we make this assumption, it is important to point out that these same principles apply to starting a business that is customer oriented from the beginning. This is one of the few areas in which the entrepreneur has an easier task than the manager in an existing business. It is easier to create a new organization than to turn around an existing culture. However, most of us are faced with the job of instilling customer orientation where it does not now exist. We need to recognize this task as a process of organizational change, one that requires great thought and effort and that will undoubtedly encounter resistance along the way from people who simply do not want to change the way in which they are accustomed to doing things. A planned process, not an overnight transformation, must be undertaken.

Figure 1 is a fishbone model that specifies the steps that are necessary to drive the process of becoming customer oriented. This process begins with management commitment, requires training and customer research, continues by establishing standards and benchmarks, empowers employees, provides technology if necessary, and gives rewards and recognition in order to achieve a customer oriented organization. Let's take a brief look at each step in the process.

Management Commitment and Actions

Being customer oriented is not easy. It isn't always neat and structured because it introduces people with their hopes, fears, and aspirations into the business equation. Perhaps most important of all, it is often in conflict with the training and preferred modes of behavior of people educated in narrow technical specializations in management, engineering, and the sciences. To overcome all these barriers

FIGURE 1 *The Process of Becoming Customer Oriented*

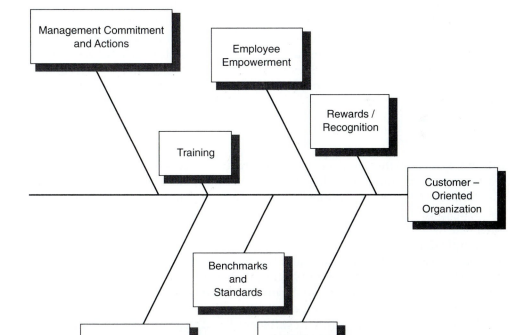

strong and persistent support from management, especially those at the very top, is essential.

As in all aspects of the TQM process, management must be genuinely committed and must demonstrate its commitment by actions, not by words alone. In the next section you should recognize that there are a number of the "research" activities in which management can be actively involved. Managers can take a turn on customer service telephone lines and can, and should, participate in customer visits. When formal research is involved, upper management can demonstrate concern by attending presentations. Most important of all, however, managers from top to bottom must see that information about customers is available and used in all decision making. No amount of customer data can take the place of constant pressure from management to make satisfaction of customer wants and needs the primary criterion for all decisions.

Training

Training in all aspects of TQM is a vital part of the process. In addition to training in group dynamics and problem-solving techniques, most groups of employees need training in customer research techniques. Again, it should be clear from the wide variety of techniques described in the third section that some techniques require more training than others. Some of the sophisticated techniques such as quantitative research or analysis of a customer database require the use of specialists. Many of the others, however, require lower levels of skills and training and can be made available to all employees. It is desirable for front-line employees to collect as much customer data as possible themselves. Not only does that data have great credibility to these same front-line personnel but it is also more likely to be available in a timely fashion.

Customer Research

Customer research must begin early in the process. It seems obvious that customer wants and needs cannot be satisfied if decision makers do not have a clear understanding of what they are. Continuous data is required, however, to keep decisions focused on *real* wants and needs, not what decision-makers *think* customers want and need.

A perplexing problem, to which we will return in the third section, is how to anticipate customer's *future* wants and needs. This problem is compounded when the satisfaction of future wants and needs involves products or technologies which may not yet be available or may not be understood by prospective customers. Conventional research techniques, especially quantitative ones, are not particularly helpful in illuminating the future in sufficient detail to guide decision making. Insight-generating techniques and creative applications are required. This is another good reason to engage as many minds as possible—including those of front-line personnel—in the search for the successful products and services of the future.

Benchmarks and Standards

The activity of benchmarking is a commonly accepted part of TQM. It involves locating the best practices in the industry or in performing a particular business function and measuring performance against them. Benchmarking against the best is a powerful stimulus to improved performance. Benchmarks can range from length of time required to produce a specific product to number of acceptable rings before a telephone call is answered. They are useful operational measures, but some have little direct impact on the satisfaction of customer wants and needs. Production cycle time is invisible to many customers. Number of telephone rings may be only a minor point; more important is whether the person who answers can deal with the caller's issue.

Standards are objectives that are set by the firm on the basis of customer expectations and behavior. They come into play in two instances. One is when the firm cannot find best practices that are similar enough to use as benchmarks or when competitors will not release the data. The second is when the issue is more closely related to customer expectations than to operational feasibility. It is theoretically possible to answer all telephone calls on the first ring. It is almost certain, first, that answering all calls on the first ring would be prohibitively expensive and, second, that it would not make much difference in overall customer satisfaction. The answers to questions like "how many rings are too many" and "how long are customers willing to wait for the shipment of a particular product" can be obtained, although often not by a single direct question. When customer expectations are measured, they can be used to establish standards. It then becomes a business decision as to whether setting standards that simply satisfy customer expectations is sufficient or whether it is worthwhile to exceed expectations and thereby delight the customer.

Employee Empowerment

In the last few years empowerment has become a fashionable term, one that is often used loosely. Yet, we should not let this trendiness mask the potential of the concept. Empowerment implies pushing decision making down to the lowest possible level. More specifically it means giving teams or individual employees power to make customer-satisfying decisions. In a production setting this can mean giving every employee on the assembly line the authority to stop the line if quality is outside acceptable boundaries. In a service setting, it can mean giving frontline personnel the authority to satisfy most customer requests or solve problems on the spot without recourse to a supervisor.

It has become a truism that employees "on the line" have ready answers to many problems that elude management because they deal with those problems on a daily basis and often are frustrated by their lack of resolution. Giving the people who know best the power to resolve problems, again, sounds rather easy. In practice it is incredibly difficult. It means that managers and supervisors must relinquish decision-making power, which previously has been their prerogative.

To say that managers and supervisors are often reluctant to do this is a gross understatement.

TECHNOLOGY AND OTHER ORGANIZATIONAL RESOURCES

Empowered employees must also have the resources they need to perform their tasks effectively. Many of the resources that lead directly to the satisfaction of customer wants and needs do involve use of the latest technology. Production workers may need automated equipment or on-line access to computerized information at their own work stations. Customer service workers often require direct access to multiple databases of customer and product information. This may call for large up-front investments in technology. Sometimes the technology is unproven. Often its payback is difficult to quantify. Even so, thoughtful investments in technology can make workers more productive and can provide customer-pleasing products and levels of customer service that are difficult for competitors to duplicate.

At the same time, management should not overlook the possibility that decidedly low-tech resources may better meet requirements. There is no substitute for a trained, empowered, and genuinely concerned human being to help customers identify and solve problems. Anyone who has become entangled in an endless web of automated telephone instructions with no human intervention in sight can attest to the fact that technology, though it is vital in many applications, is not always an unmixed blessing. The greatest customer frustrations occur when technology is mindlessly substituted for human concern and judgment.

Rewards and Recognition

Rewards and recognition of both individuals and teams are also standard operating procedures in TQM. They should be used to acknowledge increased productivity and also to acknowledge "softer," less easily measurable successes in achieving satisfied customers. Quality planning should deal with two issues; what to reward and what kinds of rewards to bestow.

It is wise to begin with the premise that everyone who participates in the quality process should be recognized in some manner. This is easy to do in the beginning; as time goes on and numbers grow it may take a little more effort. The approach here is to celebrate the firm's quality progress and to thank all who have contributed. It presents an excellent opportunity to gather people together and to involve top management in not only celebrating achievements but also reinforcing the vision and the momentum of the quality process. While there should be a definite social aspect to this gathering, there should also be a clear linkage to the quality process. Many firms use the occasion to present awards to teams or individuals and to have presentations based on award-winning efforts.

Very different from the celebratory approach is the increasingly frequent practice of encouraging employees at all levels to acquire stock in the firm and take a proprietary attitude toward its success. Employees in firms from Wal-Mart to Polaroid to

Avis have significant ownership stakes. Avis has used this in advertising to give credibility to their claims of excellent customer service. The merits of this approach seem obvious, but by itself employee ownership may not be sufficient to motivate excellent performance. In addition, many organizations do not have the ability to provide for employee ownership. Many, in fact, complain that they have little in the way of tangible (translate that monetary) awards to give.

All organizations can, however, recognize excellence. The recognition can be a certificate, a reserved parking space, a letter of commendation, time off, being singled out for additional training, or something more creative. If the tribute is genuine and sincere, it will be effective. Quality planning must treat reward and recognition as an important strategic issue, no matter how large or how small the pool of resources devoted to it.

These, then, are the activities necessary to create a customer-oriented firm. Each may receive more or less emphasis at various times but they are all essential. Again, however, their focus will be inappropriate if the customer is not always at the center of both planning and execution. We must, then, provide an overview of the techniques that will help accomplish that customer centrality.

RESEARCH APPROACHES

In deciding what kind of research activity is best to meet a particular need, quality planners should use several criteria. These include the cost and time required by the techniques under consideration and the expertise required to collect the data, analyze it, and prepare a presentation. Whether team members are doing the research themselves or whether they can use staff members or external service bureaus to conduct the research is also important. These considerations can become complex and are clearly beyond the scope of this chapter, but the references provided at the end will be helpful to the neophyte. In this chapter we will approach the subject of research only from the perspective of how it can contribute to the quality process.

Figure 2 presents a comprehensive listing of research techniques that are useful in the context of TQM. They are loosely grouped into three categories that reflect the timeliness of the data gathered by each technique. It is also worth remembering that the more complex the technique the longer it may take to analyze the data and therefore the greater the time before it can be incorporated into the decision-making process.

Early Signals and In-Depth Understanding of the Customer

The first category has been labeled "insight generating." The techniques in this group can produce useful ideas or insights. These ideas or insights are rarely quantified, at least at this point. They are sometimes vague and in need of refinement through further data gathering and analysis. However, the insights produced by this set of techniques probably would not be achieved by the exclusive use of approaches in the other two categories.

FIGURE 2 *Overview of Customer Research Approaches*

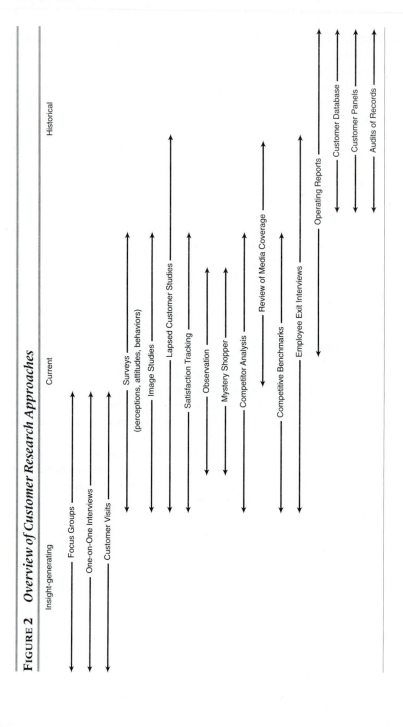

It is extremely important to recognize that these "insights" are a type of leading indicator. They may provide a warning of looming customer dissatisfaction or competitive activity long before marketplace indicators such as market share or other research techniques would uncover them. They may also alert the firm to potential opportunities in time to achieve a head start over competitors. Their importance cannot be overstated even though they are open to criticism for lack of methodological rigor. These techniques often provide signals that warrant action by the firm. They are also frequently used as input to large-scale quantitative research.

The three research approaches that fall completely into this category are focus groups, one-on-one interviews, and customer visits. Focus groups and one-on-one interviews are the qualitative techniques of conventional marketing research. Much has been written about their ability, when professionally conducted, to probe for deeply held but not easily verbalized customer attitudes and perceptions (see, for example, Goldman and McDonald, 1987). Focus groups are especially highly regarded for the effect of group interaction in encouraging customers to reveal thoughts and feelings that they might otherwise keep to themselves. Recent research, however, suggests that one-on-one interviews may be even better for specific uses such as eliciting ideas for new products (Griffin and Hauser, 1992).

Customer visits, on the other hand, have only recently been recognized as a research technique (McQuarrie, 1991). Their value, however, is well known to "close to the customer" firms such as Hewlett-Packard and Du Pont. Customer visits should not be delegated to research suppliers or considered a by-product of sales activities. Instead they should be viewed as an opportunity to involve top managers and cross-functional teams directly with customers. They are not just a "fishing expedition"; they should be carefully planned and executed (McQuarie and McIntyre, 1992).

Other techniques sometimes produce important insights or early signals. Customer surveys of many types and competitor analyses can generate useful ideas. Surveys of lapsed customers and employee exit interviews can be especially important for obtaining early indications of dissatisfaction.

All these techniques, whether purely qualitative or whether relying for insight on the interpretation of quantitative data, are dependent on thoughtful questioning and careful, nonbiased analysis to produce valid indicators of marketplace sentiment. Even then, their sample sizes are usually too small to permit generalizing their results to nonstudied populations.

Obtaining Data about the Current State of Affairs

The second category is labeled "current." It includes techniques that provide descriptions of the current status of many indicators and that can provide diagnostics or "reasons why" these conditions exist. They provide opportunities to study the customer's verbalizations of thoughts, feelings, and behaviors. There are also techniques that focus on competitors and the competitive marketplace. Many of the techniques in this group are readily quantifiable. Some lend themselves to sophisticated quantitative analysis. They are invaluable current indicators, but few of them have much to offer in the way of generating insights about future wants and needs.

The applications of traditional survey research fall into this category. Almost by definition, a survey is conducted at one point is time and is often likened to a snapshot of conditions at that time. When repeated, or replicated, it can illuminate trends. This is often referred to as a tracking study. Surveys, whether of customer attitudes, images, or satisfaction with a particular product, are very good at answering "what" types of questions. They also can be designed to get at "whys" although they are usually open to criticism of the depth of response to "reasons why" questions. Surveys of lapsed customers can be especially revealing, but it is important to remember that these customers have already been lost, and the best research can do is to prevent further damage.

Surveys of all kinds lend themselves to carefully chosen samples. If sufficient funds are available, these samples can be large enough to permit statistically valid generalization of results to the population from which the sample was drawn. In addition, large and carefully constructed samples permit the analysis of data by segment.

Observational research techniques also fall squarely into the current category because, by definition, a researcher can only observe current behavior. Simple observation, in the hands of knowledgable collectors and users of data, can be very powerful. Potential customers' reactions to both exterior features and the interior design of automobiles are carefully observed during the design process. Small children cannot effectively verbalize their reaction to toys, but observation of their play activities is very revealing. The "mystery shopper" is an old retailing technique revived by quality personnel to obtain first-hand, and therefore difficult to refute, data about how customers are treated.

Analyses of secondary data generally fall into the current category but lean toward the historical. Just how far they learn depends on the age of the data. Activities like competitor analysis and documented reviews of media coverage add another, potentially important, dimension to a firm's assessment of its current standing in the broad marketplace.

Competitive benchmarks can be thought of as a type of secondary data that is unique to TQM activities. It is true that for years trade associations have been disseminating to their members many industry-specific operating statistics such as sales per square foot for a certain type of retail store or percent of scrap in a particular operating process. However, these are usually aggregate figures, made up of both the best and the worst. Quality experts argue that using these measures causes firms to set objectives that are lower than excellence demands. Competitive benchmarks are preferred. Benchmarks, however, tend to deal with operating parameters which may or may not have a direct relationship to customer satisfaction.

The final technique that has been placed in this category is the employee exit interview. Relatively few firms do exit interviews on a regular basis, and that is an unfortunate oversight. Many things can be learned as employees exit the firm. Simple structured surveys can shed light on major problems. Open-ended questions administered by skilled interviewers can uncover more subtle but potentially more revealing issues.

This group of research techniques can be very powerful. Alone, however, they are rarely sufficient to provide all the data required for effective TQM planning and implementation.

Records of Actions and Activities

The third category is called "historical." The techniques in this group are primarily reports of customer actions or internal operations of the firm. This data is often captured on line, for example, by the computerized cash registers in a retail store or as the by-product of computerized sales activities or service requests. It has the advantages of being very detailed and complete; i.e., not for just a sample of customers or activities but for all of them. On the other hand, by its very nature this data reports on behaviors or activities that have already occurred—on mistakes that have been made or on customers that have been left unsatisfied. This category might be thought of as containing lagging indicators, ones that are only available after the fact. This can be dangerously late when customer satisfaction is at stake. The customer may have already been lost by the time the data becomes available.

Operating reports on any relevant activity of the firm seem to fall into this category. In many firms they do, because reports reach decision makers so slowly that they are of only historical interest. However, by using appropriate information technology these data can be collected on-line and transmitted immediately to the relevant users. When this is done operating results become much more than historical artifacts.

Databases that contain records of sales and service plus descriptive information about the household or business firm can be a rich source of data about the firm's entire customer base. Customer panels can add data about product and media use but usually only for a sample of customers.

Finally, audits of internal records such as warranty repairs or customer complaints can yield important information. Such audits can be immensely valuable in the early stages of TQM when the organization is looking for the 20 percent of the activities that typically generate 80 percent of the problems. Properly used, internal records then become an important way of tracking progress toward resolving these problems.

These measures of past activity should not be overlooked or undervalued. They contain vital information. They should also be readily available, and some have little incremental cost from a TQM perspective because they are necessary to everyday operations. These data are important, but they are not sufficient. They rarely reveal the "whys" behind the "whats" they report. They do not generally lead to insights about how the customer might be delighted in the present or what he or she might want and need in the future. Data about past actions and activities can only be one part of the critical base of customer information in an effective TQM environment.

SUMMARY

The overall theme of this chapter has been that a customer orientation is critical to the success of TQM. The overriding objective of all businesses must be to at least meet—and preferably to exceed—customer wants, needs, and expectations. Without this focus on the customer, firms are likely to spend a great deal of time and effort improving internal processes that make only marginal differences in customer satisfaction.

This chapter has described customer orientation in two ways. First, it is a business philosophy that puts customer wants and needs at the center of all decision making activities. Second, it is a process, like TQM itself, that requires committed top managers, empowered employees, and data on which to base customer-centered decisions.

There are many techniques that can be used to collect data for the TQM process. The appropriate technique depends on many factors including the type of data required, the speed with which it is needed, and the resources available for collection, analysis, and reporting.

Above all, this chapter has stressed that becoming—and remaining—customer oriented requires an organization-wide commitment. The entire organization, from top management to front-line personnel, must recognize the importance of keeping customer satisfaction as its central focus. Even more important, *actions* of personnel from top to bottom of the organizational ladder must consistently put customer satisfaction first. Then the organization can consider itself truly customer oriented.

References

Customer Orientation

Howe, Roger J., Dee Baekkert, and Maynard A. Howe. *Quality on Trial* (St. Paul, MN: West Publishing Company, 1992).

Kohil, Ajay K., and Bernard J. Jaworski. "Market Orientation: The Construct, Research Propositions, and Managerial Implications," *Journal of Marketing*, April 1990, pp. 1–18.

Levitt, Theodore. "Marketing Myopia," *Harvard Business Review*, July/August 1960, pp. 45–56; September/October 1975, pp. 26–44, 173, 181.

Narver, John C., and Stanley F. Slater. "The Effect of a Market Orientation on Business Profitability," *Journal of Marketing*, October 1990, pp. 20–35.

———. *Becoming More Market Oriented: An Exploratory Study of the Programmatic and Market-Back Approaches* (Cambridge, MA: Marketing Science Institute Report No. 91–128, October 1991).

Peters, Thomas J., and Robert H. Waterman, Jr. *In Search of Excellence: Lessons from America's Best-Run Companies* (New York: Warner Books, Inc., 1982).

Shapiro, Benson, P. "What the Hell Is 'Market Oriented'?" *Harvard Business Review*, November/December 1988, pp. 119–125.

Slater, Stanley F., and John C. Narver. *Market Orientation, Performance, and the Moderating Influence of Competitive Environment* (Cambridge, MA: Marketing Science Institute Report No. 92–118, July 1992).

Whiteley, Richard C. The Customer Driven Company: *Moving from Talk to Action* (Reading, MA: Addison-Wesley Publishing Company, 1991).

Customer Research Techniques

Bitner, Mary Jo, Bernard H. Booms, and Mary Stanfield Tetreault. "The Service Encounter: Diagnosing Favorable and Unfavorable Incidents," *Journal of Marketing,* January 1990, pp. 71–84.

Blankenship, A. B., and George Edward Breen. *State-of-the-Art Marketing Research* (Lincolnwood, IL: NTC Business Books, 1993).

Eccles, Robert G. "The Performance Measurement Manifesto," *Harvard Business Review,* January/February 1991, pp. 131–137.

Goldman, Alfred E., and Susan Schwartz McDonald. *The Group Depth Interview* (Englewood Cliffs, NJ: Prentice-Hall, 1987).

McQuarrie, Edward F., "The Customer Visit: Qualitative Research for Business-to-Business Marketers," *Marketing Research,* March 1991, pp. 15–28.

———— and Shelby H. McIntyre. *The Customer Visit: An Emerging Practice in Business-to-Business Marketing* (Cambridge, MA: Marketing Science Institute Report No. 92–114, May 1992).

Griffin, Abbie, and John R. Hauser. *The Voice of the Customer* (Cambridge MA: Marketing Science Institute Report No. 92–106, March 1992).

Parasuraman, A., Leonard L. Berry, and Valarie A. Zeithaml. "Guidelines for Conducting Service Quality Research," *Marketing Research,* December 1990, pp. 34–44.

———— Valarie A. Zeithaml, and Leonard L. Berry. "SERVQUAL: A Multiple-Item Scale for Measuring Consumer Perceptions of Service Quality," *Journal of Retailing,* Spring 1988, pp. 12–40.

Smith, Daniel C., Jonlee Andrews, and Timothy R. Blevins. "The Role of Competitive Analysis in Implementing a Market Orientation," *The Journal of Services Marketing,* Winter 1992, 23–36.

Smith, R. P. "Research and Other Data in the Monitoring of Product Quality," *Journal of the Market Research Society,* July, 1979, pp. 189–205.

Urban, Glen L., and John R. Hauser. *Design and Marketing of New Products* (Englewood Cliffs, NJ: Prentice-Hall, 1980).

Westbrook, Robert A. "A Rating Scale for Measuring Product/Service Satisfaction," *Journal of Marketing,* Fall 1980, pp. 68–72.

Quality Function Deployment: A Process for Translating Customers' Needs into a Better Product and Profit

GOAL QPC RESEARCH REPORT

This report is a product of the Quality Function Deployment Team.
Prepared by:

Doug Daetz	Hewlett-Packard
Thomas K. Flaherty	Rockwell International
Mary Lou Kotecki	Deere & Company
Glen Mazur	Japanese Business Consultants
Stan Marsh	GOAL/QPC
Jack Moran	Polaroid Corporation
Jack B. ReVelle	Hughes Aircraft Company

ABSTRACT

Quality Function Deployment was first introduced in the United States in an article by Dr. Yoji Akao in the October 1983 issue of *Quality Progress*, a monthly publication of the American Society for Quality Control. In November 1983 the Cambridge Corporation of Tokyo, under the leadership of Masaaki Imai, conducted a Total Quality Control (TQC) and Quality Function Deployment (QFD) workshop in Chicago.

Quality Function Deployment is a structured process that provides a means to identify and carry the customer's voice through each stage of product and service development and implementation. QFD is achieved by cross-functional teams which collect, interpret, document, and prioritize customer requirements. Through the use of charts and matrices, quality responsibilities are effectively deployed to any needed activity within a company to ensure that appropriate quality is achieved.

QFD relies on easy to understand techniques supported by analytical tools. QFD, though structured, is a flexible planning tool which allows organizations to react quickly in developing or improving products and services and which also allows for creative and innovative thinking.

Application of QFD is growing at a rapid rate as product and service industries have begun to understand the need for customer-driven management and systems to continuously improve their competitive position.

INTRODUCTION

The evolution of a quality philosophy in Japan began with the visits of Dr. W. Edwards Deming and Dr. Joseph Juran from 1950 through 1954. The influence of these two individuals resulted in quality becoming the distinguishing characteristic that led to Japan's significant market successes. In the 1960s employee involvement at all levels within a Japanese organization became standard procedure. This quality philosophy and participative environment evolved in the 1970s into what is now called Total Quality Management.

Total Quality Management (TQM) begins with listening to the voice of the customer. TQM threads this voice throughout the product and service development process. As illustrated in Figure 1, the TQM concept can be represented by a wheel containing various supporting elements.

The hub of the wheel is the Customer-Driven Master Plan. This central plan describes fundamental improvements that an organization needs to make and how the improvements will be accomplished. The second level of detail in the TQM Wheel includes cross-functional management, which focuses on the horizontal activities in an organization. Quality Function Deployment is a subset of this element. QFD is a system for understanding what the customer wants and for assigning the responsibility of achieving appropriate quality to all the parts of an organization.

QFD, as a formalized approach, started in 1972 at the Kobe Shipyard, a division of Mitsubishi, with the introduction of product planning using a matrix. Dr. Yoji Akao expanded the basic concept from the Kobe exercise into a coordinated set of matrices and charts that looked into planning, cost, reliability, new technology, and production. This activity developed into many of the basic QFD approaches that are in use today. Appendix A provides a detailed history of the development of QFD.

In June 1987, *Business Week* stated that the typical American factory spends 20% to 50% of its operating budget to find and fix mistakes and that as many as 25% of factory employees do not produce anything. These people rework things that were

FIGURE 1   The TQM Wheel

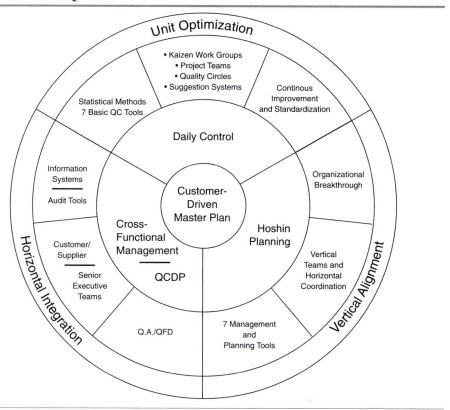

not done right the first time. The same article stated some 80% of quality related problems occur during the design phase of product development or during outsourcing as the result of purchasing policies that value low price over the quality of purchased parts and materials. All of these behaviors add cost and ultimately affect a product's market position.

Many major companies have decided that if they are to remain competitive in the global marketplace, they must listen to their customers and develop products and services that satisfy customer needs. The October 1988 issue of *Quality Progress* reinforced that position with a set of articles written by top executives from prestigious companies. Colby H. Chandler, Chairman and CEO of Eastman Kodak Company, expressed his view by saying, "We must take quality beyond customer satisfaction to customer delight. Customer delight is the delivery of products and services that exceed expectations." Roberto C. Goizueta, Chairman of the Coca-Cola Company, reemphasized the thought with, "Make the consumer someone special to you, and your products will become something special to him or her." In the current economic environment, *listening to the customer* is a necessity if companies aspire to satisfy or exceed customer needs.

Quality Function Deployment is a planning tool and a process for translating customer requirements into products or services. It enables prioritization of needs, innovative responses to those needs, and coordinates implementation for maximum effect. When instituted, QFD leads to process or product efforts that enable a company to exceed the expectations of the customer. QFD works best within a company when there is organizational commitment and a disciplined approach to implementation. Fundamental changes in company culture may also be required.

Quality Function Deployment encompasses every phase of development and delivery of products and services. QFD involves the functions of marketing, research, design, manufacturing, quality, purchasing, sales, and service. The QFD discipline provides both a framework and a structured process to enhance an organization's ability to communicate, document, analyze, and prioritize. The documentation and analysis steps lead to breakthroughs which illuminate understanding and enhance competitiveness.

QFD AND THE VOICE OF THE CUSTOMER

Obtaining and clarifying the voice of the customer is an important task. Sources of customer input are market surveys, focus groups, warranty claims, and interviews.

FIGURE 2   *Voice of the Customer*

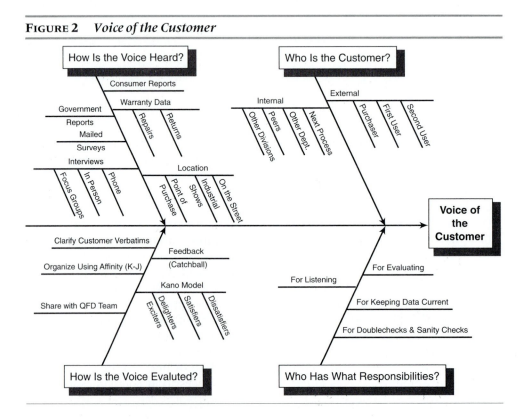

Regardless of the methods chosen, it is imperative to obtain the voice of the customer. Figure 2 is a cause and effect diagram which illustrates the complexity involved in capturing customer wants and needs.

It is unlikely that customers will define all of their preferences even with a very efficient method of gathering customer data. Through a graphical model, Dr. Noriaki Kano, a Japanese professor and consultant, clarified why customer input can be insufficient. This model shows relationships between product and service attributes and customer satisfaction. (See Figure 3.)

The arrow in the middle of the diagram labeled "one dimensional quality" illustrates instances where customers express what they want and where their satisfaction depends on product/service conformance to the expressed requirement. The arrow on the bottom represents details that customers expect. Because these characteristics are taken for granted, customers are less likely to mention them. Safety features are an example of this category. Products are expected to be safe. If they are not safe, customers are unhappy.

The arrow on the top represents "exciting" quality. Features which fall into this category can provide customer satisfaction, but not dissatisfaction. The customers do not know about them in advance and do not expect them. As a result, customers will not ask for them in an open-ended focus group. This category includes items that the producer or service provider often develop themselves. Generally, they result from talent resident within the producer or service organization and can represent significant competitive opportunities.

FIGURE 3   *Kano Model of Customer Satisfaction*

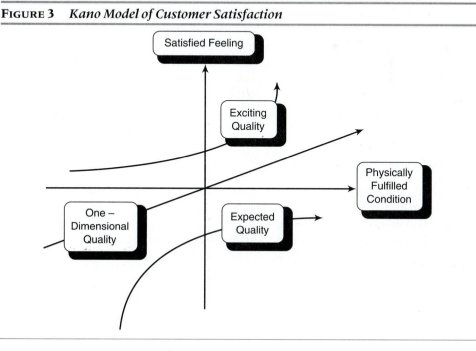

Features which contribute to exciting quality do not stay in this category very long. As customers become accustomed to them, the attraction level of the features moves toward the bottom and to the right on the Kano model. Eventually, customers will view these features as one dimensional or expected.

QFD IMPLEMENTATION

Implementation of QFD should be considered in terms of four phases:

1. **Organization Phase**: Management selects the product or service to be improved, the appropriate cross-functional team, and defines the scope of the QFD study. Initial QFD projects should address improvement on products or services that already exist and are well understood. This makes it possible to concentrate on the QFD techniques. Later projects can focus on new product or service introductions.
2. **Descriptive Phase**: The selected team defines the products/services from several viewpoints: customer demands, quality characteristics, functions, new technology, reliability, and cost. QFD uses a matrix system to array the various viewpoints, to assess current and competitive positions, and to establish and plan for target values. QFD matrices are often shown in literature as illustrated in Figures 4 and 5. A more complete approach is depicted in Appendix B.
3. **Breakthrough Phase**: The team selects areas for improvement and competitive advantage through investigation of technology, new concepts, better reliability, and cost reduction and monitors the bottleneck engineering process.
4. **Implementation Phase**: The team defines the product or service and how it will be produced. Using QFD, the team carries the development of the product or service through preparation for production, production, delivery, and confirmation of customer satisfaction. Appendix C is an outline for a focus course on implementing QFD.

USERS OF QFD

In 1986 Dr. Yoji Akao, past chairman of the QFD research committee of the Japan Society for Quality Control (JSQC), conducted a survey of QFD usage among the larger member companies of the Union of Japanese Scientists and Engineers (JUSE). The study showed that although QFD was not being used in some Japanese companies, it had grown significantly and was used with great success at many Japanese companies. (See Figure 6.)

Currently, many U.S. companies are using QFD. In the automotive industry, Ford, Chrysler, and General Motors, users of QFD themselves, are involving their supplier bases in QFD studies. In the electronics field, Digital Equipment Corporation and Texas Instruments have been QFD pioneers. Numerous other companies

FIGURE 4   *Basic House of Quality*

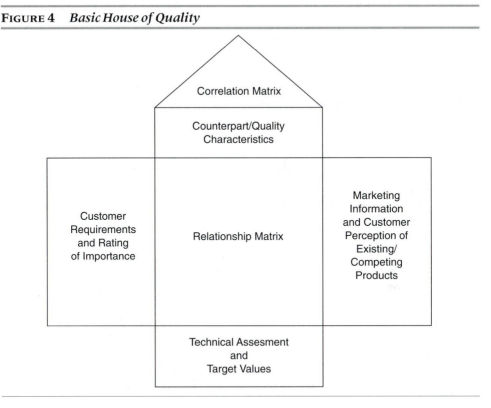

use QFD including: Procter & Gamble, Deere & Company, The Kendall Company, Polaroid, Rockwell International, Hughes Aircraft, and Hewlett-Packard.

Because use of QFD in the United States is so recent, there are few documented success stories for a wide variety of industries. A further difficulty in obtaining detailed case studies which describe successes lies in the reluctance of companies that have had major successes to broadcast those activities to their competition. Refer to Appendix D for a partial list of U.S. QFD applications.

THE BENEFITS OF QFD

The results of the 1986 JSQC survey conducted by Dr. Yoji Akao and others were published with details on the status of QFD in Japanese companies. Companies which used QFD reported the following benefits:

- Decreased start-up problems
- Competitive analysis became possible
- Control points clarified

FIGURE 5 *QFD Requirements Carry through the Development Process*

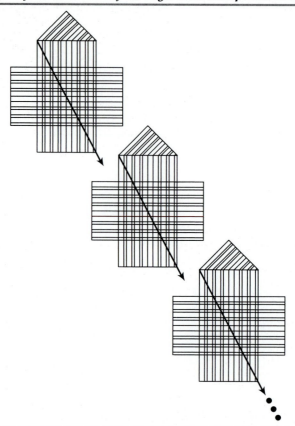

FIGURE 6 *Results of JSQC Question: Do You Use QFD?*

Industry Answer	Electronics	Precision Machines	Transportation	Process Industry	Metal/steel	Construction	Other Manufacturing	Service	Total
Yes	24	14	13	10	1	9	2	7	80
No	14	7	2	15	2	2	11	15	68
Number of replies	38	21	15	25	3	11	13	22	148

- Effective communications between divisions
- Design intent carried through to manufacturing

Additional information gathered from translations of Japanese reports as well as U.S. company presentations and publications highlights other benefits:

- Better communication
- Fewer product/service changes
- Better reliability of key elements
- Improved market research
- Quality is built in "upstream"
- Reduced product/service development time
- Lower start-up costs
- Increased understanding of complex relationships
- Greater clarity of organizational and program priorities
- Better designs
- Identification and resolution of conflicting requirements

Quality Function Deployment provides a tracking system for development efforts and preserves knowledge for future reference. QFD helps companies determine where to invest time and money, ensure that cost-oriented quality is achieved, and differentiate their products/services from those of the competition. QFD ensures that each phase of the development cycle is rooted in customer needs and, within the development process, serves to facilitate the use of other tools, techniques, and in-house expertise at the appropriate time.

CONCLUSION

Each year various conferences bring together speakers to describe a wide variety of continuous improvement tools that will enable companies to achieve "*world class*" status. These tools are important and certainly have their place in the quality improvement process. The tools alone, however, cannot provide a solution to needed quality improvement. Fundamental changes to planning and listening to customers must occur if a company is to become a strong competitor.

This paper has presented one of the TQM planning tools—Quality Function Deployment. QFD provides activities that bring together all required disciplines to work and plan the product or service development efforts in a highly disciplined, communicative, and effective manner. QFD's focus on the voice of the customer contributes to a company's ability to attain quality levels that provide a cost competitive position in the world marketplace.

TQM-related Frameworks and Implementation Issues

Readings in this section address diverse implementation issues and TQM-related frameworks like benchmarking and concurrent engineering. Benchmarking, pioneered by Xerox, and lately also Reengineering, have profoundly affected the process of strategy formulation. They are other examples, besides QFD and Hoshin Planning, of how companies attempt to become increasingly customer-focused and increase efficiency.

During the decade of the 50s American pioneers like Deming, Juran and Feigenbaum profoundly influenced the quality movement, and delineated systems that were widely implemented in Japanese industry. During the 60s, 70s and 80s the quality movement became strongly influenced by Japanese thinking and experience, and the so-called "Japanese management style," which is based on participative decision-making. One of the readings focuses on the historic origins of Japanese practices like life-long employment and management-labor cooperation. The author addresses the question of whether these practices are contemporary, post WWII developments, or deeply rooted in Japanese culture. This question is key to the problem of crosscultural transfer of management experience.

The final reading in this section explores the perspectives of those affected by a TQM change process. TQM is often plagued by an all too prescriptive approach to organizational change. The reading assumes a descriptive perspective and allows the different levels of the organization, from top management to line workers, to express their views regarding how a particular TQM organization-wide program affected their work life.

Integrating TQM into Daily Worklife

By Joann DeMott

Before people can work effectively in a system, there must be an effective system to work in.
  Roger H. Stayer
  Johnsonville Foods, Inc.

Today's customers buy thousands of products and services each year. Leaders and managers of companies, divisions, departments, organizations, and agencies work to help produce and supply the world with goods and services and then supply them to the world.

For consumers, the message is clear. They no longer want to pay for products that break or for insufficient services. Consumers are reluctant to duplicate their names, addresses, phone numbers, social security numbers, credit card numbers, and other vital information for a single service. They will not pay to be treated as an inconvenience by cashiers. With many businesses to choose from, consumers no longer have to take only goods that are available.

As managers, the message is also clear. We know that daily management of quality is tough work. And because we thoroughly understand how discriminating customers can be, we know that our methods for leading operations that either support or ignore quality are essential to the survival of business.

Though we understand both sides of the matter, we may not know what to do about the situation or how to go about it. Making quality the baseline of operations takes thorough and disciplined planning and an engaged, leading-edge-thinking work force to follow through on plans. Quality also takes attention on a daily basis to know what is being done, who is doing it, and how it is working. It takes daily

---

management of an efficient system to consistently deliver products and services that delight customers.

NEW PATTERNS OF BEHAVIOR FOR THE NEW STYLE MANAGER

Structuring an organization to manage quality efficiently is the primary focus of this text. The framework includes identifying critical processes that recognize:

- Managing is a process
- The old process doesn't work anymore
- The patterns of behavior that supported the old process have to change

Often one hears about an excited CEO or university president who has come back to the office from a conference, inspired by a presentation made about "quality," who shifts the responsibility for implementing a quality system onto everyone else by saying, "I like this quality stuff. Go out, do it, and tell me how it all turns out." The CEO or president may make an inspirational speech or two about how things are going to change and get better, but will not back up his/her words with appropriate action.

But Quality, as W. Edwards Deming is quick to point out, cannot be delegated. A commitment to quality is a commitment to action, a different kind of action than has previously been taken. Literature on the role of the new manager coins such words as "coach" and "guide" and "counselor." Although these titles indicate something about the new role, specific behaviors are rarely delineated. During the transition from the old management paradigm to the new, it is helpful to contrast beliefs and behaviors exhibited by managers in both paradigms to study the differences.

These are seven behavior patterns a new-style manager must possess:

1. **Rather than hiding or avoiding problems, the manager actively seeks to know the parts of all processes that are not working so the parts can be fixed or improved.**

    In many organizations, admitting to the existence of a problem or a mistake can be a career decision for the unfortunate manager. It has been assumed that those with problems are not capable of managing the responsibilities of their jobs and therefore are not appropriate for promotion to a higher level.

    In order to avoid being publicly chastised or passed over for promotion, such managers might hide a problem until they have time to get it fixed or might avoid a problem entirely, hoping it will work itself out and go away. In the new system, managers recognize that, at the outset, there will be problems in most every process examined. The manager consciously seeks out the problems and brings process co-operators together to examine and improve the process. It takes courage to look for the things that are not working in the system.

2. **When a problem emerges, the modern manager looks first for problems in the process, not with the people.**

   "Everything would be so much better if I could just get people to do things right," cries the old-style manager. How quick we blame and shame our work force. The new-style manager's philosophy is quite different. Having learned from Dr. Deming that 94 percent of problems occur as a result of poor process, while only six percent are controlled by the worker, the manager looks at improving the process as the first course of action. Work stress is reduced, and both managers and workers can move faster to fix the problems experienced.

3. **The new style manager brings the process co-operators to the table to solve problems, rather than assuming the role as the sole or primary problem-solver.**

   Most managers have successfully risen to their positions by being quick-thinking, individual problem-solvers. In the past, they have assessed a given situation, made a decision, and then told the work group how they were to proceed. Resenting this system, workers held onto valuable information and kept their good ideas to themselves.

   In today's complex environment, where there is a vast amount of available information, it has become essential to use the brain power and creative talents of the entire work force. Responsibility for decision making and problem solving is given to those at most appropriate level rather than simply given to the individual with the highest position.

   Process co-operators—those who operate the process and can change the process steps—are brought together to examine and improve processes. Cross-functional teams of owners also integrate interdependent processes into a single system. New-style managers encourage individual thinking, choose and sponsor teams, remove barriers that deter improvement efforts, and actively communicate among groups.

   During the transition, sharing responsibility for decision making can be very threatening for some managers.

   As one new manager stated, "I'd been working on a problem for several weeks. I'd observed both the process and the workers in action. There had been unfortunate results. I'd thought and fretted about it, but just couldn't seem to come up with a sound idea. I finally mentioned my dilemma to one of the workers, who, after talking with several others, came to me with a simple, inexpensive, and easy-to-install solution. I felt ridiculous, as though I should have come up with that solution myself. He had touched upon my greatest fear; what if workers who report to me turn out to be smarter than I am?"

   Managers must put aside their egos and draw without fear on the intellectual skills and experience of all those around them. Ideas are actively sought from process co-operators. When significant changes are to be made, requests for information must be more than just asking for input; the decision-making process is shared. In this way, the work force becomes far greater than hands to do the work. The minds of those closest to the processes are actively engaged in thinking of better and better ways of operating. With personal and professional investment comes a sense of ownership of the system and the outcome and a genuine interest in the efficiency of the operation.

When people want to work together, nothing can stop them—they'll work in large groups of 35 or small groups of six; they'll stay after the formal session is over, reluctant to leave the team; they'll talk together during breaks to continue the work; they'll willingly implement the process they've created even when it has not yet been proven; they'll make commitments to share information without being required to do so. The energy created when workers are challenged and given control over their processes is enormous.

4. **Making decisions solely on "guts" is no longer admired by the new manager; rather, the gut is verified with data.**

"Gut," in this case, is not bravado. Here, the gut is a combination of intuition, wisdom, and experience. Although wisdom and experience are most certainly not discarded, data are used to verify what is and is not working with a process or what a customer does and does not want or need. Process performance data are extremely helpful in seeing what is needed and deciding what action, if any, should be taken. A thoroughly developed strategy for data collection ensures that only useful data will be obtained. Once the data are collected, it is then used in the decision-making process.

5. **Continuous process improvement is the norm for the new style manager.**

During the old days, new ways of operating were not encouraged until disaster struck; otherwise, workers were expected to leave a working system alone. Today, "If it ain't broke, don't fix it," is as antiquated a way of thinking as, "We've always done it this way," and "We tried that once, and it didn't work." These tired phrases have been replaced by, "Just because it's not broken, doesn't mean we can't improve it."

Tracking—that is, data collection and analysis—allows a manager to know when a given process needs to be fixed, improved or left alone. With the quality control tools and the management and planning tools, individuals or teams of process co-operators can create, fix, improve, and track any process needed by a business, university, or organization. Being better today than yesterday is a living value in the new system.

6. **The manager improves processes to improve results.**

A fixation with results is a malady of the American system. As a company increases its return to stockholders, it increases its value in the market, and everyone is thrilled. When the numbers begin to sink, however, threat of losing its preferred status on the quality stock list can throw a company into a panic.

Of course, results matter. We would not be in business, operating our college or university or school, or keep our organization open if we were not productive, did not meet our deadlines, or satisfy customers. It is tempting for some boards of directors, managers, or supervisors to push harder on the system already in place. "Try harder," is a common command indicative of the old system.

When not happy with the results produced, managers can view the situation in one of several ways. They may believe their work force is lazy, unmotivated, and uncaring. To remedy this situation, they may place higher demands on the employees, driving them to do better. Fear is used as a motivator and in the very short term, it can work. Fear of failure can push a staff to work overtime to deliver a rush order or finish writing a last-minute grant or wait on an extra three tables after the restaurant doors close. In the longer term, however, fear wears the body down and erodes the creative, enthusiastic, cooperative spirit.

Viewing the situation differently, managers can take long-term action. If an organization knows exactly what its customers want and need, the processes necessary to deliver the product or service can be systematically and incrementally improved to reduce waste, rework, delays, waits, and unnecessary complexity. These same managers can bring process co-operators together to fix the immediate problems and make longer-term improvements. If the situation is urgent, processes critical to the operation may have to be blown apart and reconstructed in a new way.

Whether taking the slower or the faster path, managers know that hitting the process with a bigger stick will not produce significantly better results. Change the process, however, and the results will follow.

7. **The modern manager's reviews are frequent, educational, and supportive.**

When reviews—of people, processes, goals, plans—occur only at year end, one either lives for the pat on the back if the results are good or else fears the beating that will occur if the expected results are not good. Modern managers hold frequent reviews. Once important processes are identified and tracked, managers must review the processes within their area of responsibility.

Reviews are constant. Process reviews by managers should be both an educational and supportive experience for the process co-operators so they will be comfortable telling what is and is not working about the process. It is certainly gratifying—to both managers and process co-operators—to know when operations are moving as planned and processes are performing well. However, it is essential to know which processes are not working so corrective action can be taken. The more complex the process, the more critical communication and coordination are to achieving and report deadlines, obtaining the results desired, and satisfying customers.

BEING A MANAGER IS A TALL ORDER!

Exhibiting these seven behaviors our efforts are focused like a laser beam—clear, clean, concentrated, and sure. Energy is neither wasted nor diffused. As managers, we must exhibit an alertness, a readiness, a discipline, a pride. Managers, like the organizations they serve, must be nimble, flexible, able to move swiftly in response to customers' needs and wants. There is no longer room for complacency. Respect for managers is gained by the quality of their work performance, not as a result of trying to be respected. Managers do not always know the ways to make things better, so they work together with those closest to our processes to find better ways. They must coordinate their efforts with those of others to meet objectives.

CHOSEN THOUGHT, CONSCIOUS SPEECH, AND CONSISTENT ACTION

As we begin to identify the behaviors needed in the new management style, there is a difference between what we know intellectually and how we behave. Most of us, at one time or another, have found huge discrepancies between what we say and what we do. Though we have learned the tools used to manage quality and have begun to implement their behaviors, we tend to forget Daily Management's concepts in the heat of the day's crises. We revert back to the familiar ways of doing things. At those moments, Daily Management seems like an "add-on" to our "real" work.

Especially throughout the implementation stage of Daily Management, staff will watch their leaders, managers, and supervisors to see how serious they are about living the Daily Management concepts. Tom Mosgaller, training manager for the City of Madison, Wisconsin, puts it succinctly:

Listen to what they say.
Watch what they do.
If there is a contradiction,
Watch what they do.

Staff will listen to and watch management, from the top executive to their closest supervisor. They will see the inconsistencies between talk and action, and, given the choice, will believe the actions taken by management. Management talk is cheap. It is necessary to link what we think with what we say and with what we do.

The following chart provides a list of factors for managers involved in choosing patterns of thoughts about work, consciously speaking the words that support those thoughts, and exhibiting consistent behavior in line with the Total Quality Management paradigm. Linking thought, speech, and action together will help integrate TQM into daily work life and make managing quality a reality.

Integrating TQM into Day-to-Day Worklife

Think	Speak	Act
• What are the issues surrounding the processes for which I'm responsible? What is working? What is not working?	• Talk to others about processes, not people.	• Sponsor and serve on teams for improvement.
• Do I have data or information about the problems in the processes?	• Talk about solving problems, not fixing people.	Choose the "right" team members, facilitators, leaders.
• What would things be like if they were perfect? What would I have to do to move things closer to "perfect."	• Talk to the owners of the process when you have concerns.	Use the seven Quality Control tools. Use the seven Management and Planning tools.
• What are my plans? What have I done? What are the differences between what I planned to do and what I did? What could I do about the differences?	• Talk to others about information you have or need. Keep information flowing rather than holding it.	• Collect information and data on processes.
• What information do other people need to know that I already know?	• If you are a visionary thinker, talk to those who are detailed thinkers. Ask what could go wrong and what the potential barriers might be.	• Make thoughtful plans and follow them through.
• Who would benefit from knowing what I know?	• If you are a detailed thinker, talk to those who are visionary. Ask how to enhance the idea(s) so the effort is far-reaching and "ideal."	• Listen to the answers given to you.
		• Identify critical processes for each position and track performance measures.
		• Map the process BEFORE beginning a new project or activity. Add countermeasures to avoid problems before they occur.

Integrating TQM into Day-to-Day Worklife (continued)

Think	Speak	Act
	• Ask questions to encourage thought: What isn't working? What barriers are in the way to doing one's best work? What is needed to make processes better?	• Recognize individuals for their work, and reward teams for their contributions.
	• Ask about the critical processes of the individual. Ask about the performance measures and what the person has already learned about the health of their processes.	• Conduct reviews which are both educational and supportive.
	• Ask individuals about the process improvement teams on which they serve. What process are they improving? What have they learned so far? What were the problems from the customer's point of view?	• Conduct internal customer surveys specific to your own processes.
	• Ask individuals about their "breakthroughs."	• Change, change, change—constantly and at every turn—*in order to better satisfy the customers of your processes.*

Historical Sources of
Japanese Management Practices

———

By Jan C. Knakal

Introduction

The goal of this paper is to present the historical events and the cultural traditions that according to our belief have shaped the current Japanese management practices. We will accomplish this by first identifying some distinctive attributes of Japanese management, using *The Art of Japanese Management* from Pascale and Athos as our guide.[1] We will turn next to the historical events which other authors credit with helping to create these distinctive management practices. Then, we will examine ancient Japanese cultural traditions which may also be at work in contemporary management techniques. Our last step will be to bring all these ideas together and draw some conclusions.

In their work, *The Art of Japanese Management,* Pascale and Athos note the emphasis managers place on so-called soft factors. These include: *staff* (a focus on personnel), *skills* ("things which the organization and its key personnel do particularly well") and *style* ("patterns of behavior of the top executive and the senior management team").[2]

Drawing a distinction between American and Japanese management practices, the two authors say the Japanese approach allows great corporations to "successfully persist in harmony with their culture's deepest values."[3]

Because Japanese managers take the *"whole* of human needs"[4] into account when dealing with their workers, according to Pascale and Athos, Japanese behavior and performance in the work place closely reflects their ideals and values.

Again making a comparison with the West, Pascale and Athos point to the Matsushita company, whose founder "fundamentally believes that people can be

---

1992 report reprinted with the permission of the author.

trusted." One high-level manager at Matsushita said this faith turns the "individual" into the "drive" of the system.[5]

"The Japanese," say Pascale and Athos, "see each individual as having economic, social, psychological, and spiritual needs, much as we do when we step back and think about it. But Japanese executives assume it is *their* task to attend to much more of the whole of the person, and not leave so much to other institutions (such as government, family, or religious ones). And they believe it is only when the individual's needs are well met within the subculture of a corporation that they can largely be freed for productive work that is in larger part outstanding."[6]

Crediting the Japanese for doing a better job in human resource development, they add that "the essence of Japanese success in these areas is rooted in assumptions that are rather fundamental to life."[7]

We will explore this connection between Japanese management and traditional values in more detail later. Our purpose at this point is only to establish the link the Japanese themselves see between management and their system of values.

Another student of the Japanese character in the corporate environment is William Ouchi, author of "Theory Z." He defines the key to successful Japanese management as: trust, subtlety and intimacy.[8] He says these are at the core of corporate interactions. Thus, Japanese in the work place relate as whole human beings and do not overly concentrate on each other's "productive" or "business" functions.

The father of the Total Quality Management concept, Dr. Kaoru Ishikawa, insists that "all the employees participate in its implementation."[9] Through his work and others which we will refer to later, there emerges a pattern of strong involvement between the Japanese employee and his company. Workers and companies seem linked both in terms of giving and receiving. These ties of dedication and expectation—for example, life-time employment—take place in the unique context described by Pascale and Athos in the aforementioned book.

According to Pascale and Athos Japan has not made many of the mistakes of the Occident because their nation has not separated the social or spiritual being from the "productive" being. Unlike the West, the Japanese have not decided "one's spiritual and social life should reside *outside* the workplace."[10] They have not been overly influenced by the separation of Church and State or Machiavelli's belief that management is separate from moral law.[11]

REBORN FROM THE ASHES

Now we will explore the historical aspects of this issue and consider the special development of Japanese industry in the aftermath of World War II, according to the author Kenichi Ohmae.[12]

Ohmae, a management consultant, contends that much of the interpretation of Japanese business practices is "mystifying and misleading,"[13] discarding the theoretical elements as real factors.

Ohmae says much of Japanese management has its roots in the poverty and turmoil which followed World War II. He writes:

Nearly everyone was jobless. Virtually all factories had been burned to ashes. Money had become nearly worthless, with inflation exceeding 100 percent per annum. The capitalists—the Big Five as well as many smaller companies—were broken up by zaibatsu kaitai, because General MacArthur was convinced that some sort of military-industrial complex had pushed Japan into war.

There was virtually nothing there with which to start a corporation. Fortunately, the technology that had been devoted to the creation of tanks, airplanes, and ships was preserved in the heads of trained engineers, and some of these got together with a handful of managers from the prewar *zaibatsu* companies to start small factories producing rice cookers, clothing, and other necessities. These enterprises welcomed skilled labor but lacked money to pay wages, and so most of them paid in food, which in those days was more important than money.[14]

Thus, it was out of necessity, says Ohmae, that Japanese firms became more like communes than corporations. He notes, "People shared their lives, hardships, and toil. If anyone tried—and some did—to organize and run a company in the old way, seeking to exploit the hungry laborers, strikes would break out."[15]

Born of hardship, this spirit would have shaped future Japanese management practices, creating special ties more like a family bond than a society getting together for a common economical end. According to Ohmae, the hard circumstances were the ones that generated the special "esprit de corps" in Japanese companies.

Other Japanese historical analysts consider traditional values to have had an important role in the shaping of management styles and social behavior in general. The author of the book *Why Japan Has ''Succeeded''* Michio Morishima[16] describes what he sees as a strong national ethos combining religious, social, and technological influences, at the core of this success.

Morishima says that Japan had her own special way to assimilate the influence of China: "Chinese Confucianism is, at all events, humanistic, whereas Japanese Confucianism is remarkably nationalistic."[17]

He adds that "Japan has perpetually been in the position where she has felt herself under pressure from a strong world empire and has, as a result, perhaps become excessively defensive. She has instinctively perceived that to continue to exist in her corner of East Asia she has to be both frugal and courageous."[18]

Morishima describes the process of how the values rooted in the Samurai class spread to the rest of the society during the Meiji revolution (1867–1868): "In the process of 'taking off,' a most important part was played by the secularization of Confucianism and Japanese chivalry. This began in the closing of the Tokugawa Shogunate and accelerated as the Meiji government spread Confucianism, which had not yet become generally popular among ordinary people in the Tokugawa era, by means of compulsory education."[19] In the process of modernization—he says— the old spirit was conserved as expressed in the slogan of the post Meiji revolution period: "Wa-kon Yo-sai" (Japanese spirit with Western ability) as an inspiring principle in importing occidental technology.[20]

As an economist and lecturer at Cambridge University, Morishima offers later a more complete explanation of how the Code of Chivalry got into the general population: "In those days (Tokugawa period, 1603–1867) samurai were expected to excel in the moral virtues of loyalty, righteousness, and propriety; they gained honor as the ruling class because of their moral training. But their material lives were poor, sometimes miserably so, especially those of the lower samurai. The populace, on the other hand, were despised because they did not need to practice Confucian ethics. . . . Farmers and tradesmen were also called upon to be loyal to their bosses and faithful to their friends and customers. It should be noted that in the mid-Tokugawa period large landowners and large-scale shops emerged, while many people became tenant farmers, shop boys, and servants. They were soon taught that they should devote themselves to their masters in the same way as the samurai did to their lords. The 'secularization' of *bushido* (that is, samurai ethics) had started."[21]

In regard to the strong influence of the Shinto religion to "maintain" the social system, Morishima says: "Because of the influence of Shintoism and Confucianism, the Japanese people set much value on ancestor worship, self-sacrifice for the bene-fit of one's master, and concord with other members of society."[22]

Morishima also contends that part of the strength of the Japanese people stems from their feeling toward their land, grounded on religious, mainly Shinto, values: Japan is the land where "the gods settled, the land of the gods."

He also says that "the growth of the 'land of the gods' doctrine resulted in a corresponding increase in the emphasis on the deity of the Emperor."[23]

SOURCES

Let us look at some traditional sources in order to explore more fully those ideas and values. In describing the Ancient Japanese character of the samurai, Inazo Nitobe, author of the book *Bushido, the Soul of Japan*,[24] states that the Bushido, the ethical code of the warrior class, indeed became a common spirit for the whole nation, reaching beyond the limits of this group. He says that this spirit, being deeply rooted in the people, permeated the centuries.

> Nitobe speaks also about the ancient feudal lord's concept of authority: A feudal prince, although unmindful of owing reciprocal obligations to his vassals, felt a higher sense of responsibility to his ancestors and to Heaven. He was the father to his subjects, whom Heaven entrusted to his care. According to the ancient Chinese *Book of Poetry,* 'Until the house of Yin lost the hearts of the people, they could appear before heaven.' And Confu-cius in his *Great Learning* taught: 'When the prince loves what the people love and hates what the people hate, then he is what is called the parent of the people.'[25]

The sense of commitment has often been mentioned by different scholars as something essential in explaining the behavior of Japanese employees. This ap-proach to their work is almost "sacred," as shown in Pascale's explanation that the separation between the spiritual and productive life did not take place in Japan.

In A. L. Sadler's translation of the work of the samurai Daidoji Yuzai, published as *The Code of the Samurai*,[26] it explains the commitment of the samurai as being based upon the consideration of life as temporal and the soul as eternal:

For existence is impermanent as the dew of evening, and the hoarfrost of morning, and particularly uncertain is the life of the warrior, and if he thinks he can console himself with the idea of eternal service to his lord or an unending devotion to his relatives, something may well happen to make him neglect his duty to his lord and forget what he owes to his family. But if he determines simply to live for today and take no thought for the morrow, so that when he stands before his lord to receive his commands he thinks of it as his last appearance and when he looks on the faces of his relatives he feels that he will never see them again, then will his duty and regard for both of them be completely sincere, while his mind will be in accord with the path of loyalty and filial duty.[27]

This idea of life as a service to others for a samurai implied the understanding that the most important thing in his life was his mission. This sense of mission is reinforced by Ohmae when he writes that after setting a strategy, it has to be executed with a sense of mission.

This dedicated attitude arises from the myth of the origins of Japan as being the "Land of the Gods." It says that the gods Izanami and Izanaghi chose the beautiful island of Awasi to live and procreate beautiful children that would play in the nice valleys. But, when the children began to grow up sadness fell over the parents.

The divine couple could not ignore that everything that lives on the earth will sooner or later die. And the sweet Izanami trembled in imagining that she would have to close the eyes of their children and to keep enjoying immortality. Indeed, she would prefer to go down with them to the grave. Izanaghi resolved to put an end to the situation and persuaded his companion to go up to the heavenly dwelling before the spectacle of death would sadden his domestic happiness. 'Truly,' he said to his wife, 'our children cannot follow us to the mansion of the immutable happiness, but in abandoning them I will sweeten the separation by leaving for them a legacy that will enable them to approach us as nearly as their mortal condition will allow.'[28]

That is the origin of one of the most important symbols and great inspirations for Japan: That "legacy," "left by the gods," is symbolized in the mirror that stands in the shinto shrines, the most ancient creed of Japan. In that mirror they are told they should look upon themselves and remember their divine origin. . . . As the moon reflects the sun, so the mirror reflects what is behind the eyes, the soul, albeit, imperfectly.

As we will see later, the "know thyself" is present as a central and key element in the Japanese tradition and religion. In looking at that mirror they are supposed to see the painful effects of the earthly life upon their faces and to imagine the harmony of the heavenly life of their ancestors. That is what Izanaghi said in the ancient shinto myth when he left the mirror. Their legacy, though painful, is with them.

"Shinto theology," says Nitobe, "has no place for the dogma of 'original sin.' On the contrary, it believes in the innate goodness and God-like purity of the human soul, adoring it as the adytum from which divine oracles are proclaimed. Everybody has observed that the Shinto shrines are conspicuously devoid of objects and instruments of worship, and that a plain mirror hung in the sanctuary forms the essential part of its furnishing. The presence of this article is easy to explain: it typifies the human heart, which, when perfectly placid and clear, reflects the very image of the

Deity. When you stand, therefore, in front of the shrine to worship, you see your own image reflected on its shining surface, and the act of worship is tantamount to the old Delphic injunction, 'Know Thyself.'"[29]

To Know Thyself in this way enabled the worshipers to "recognize" themselves as sons of the gods, to increase their virtues by seeing them in the image of their ancestors. Also in contemplating the mirror, the 'human sons of the gods' could perfect themselves by becoming aware of their passions and managing them, thus, some day, to join their divine parents again.

So, a special sense of loyalty is related to keeping a certain attitude and harmony as something owed to their ancestors. That implies a path of achievement, as a gradual realizing of that harmony that has to be discovered.

THREE SOURCES

Inazo Nitobe speaks about three main sources of the Bushido: Buddhism, Shinto, and the teachings of Confucious. They shaped from ancient times the "Soul of Japan." Buddhism furnished a "sense of calm trust in Fate, a quiet submission to the inevitable, that stoic composure in the sight of danger or calamity, that disdain of life and friendliness with death."

The author continues: "A foremost teacher of swordsmanship, when he saw his pupil master the utmost of his art, told him, 'Beyond this, my instruction must give way to Zen teaching.' 'Zen' is the Japanese equivalent for the Dhyâna, which 'represents human effort to reach through meditation zones of thought beyond the range of verbal expression.' Its method is contemplation, and its purport, so far as I understand it, is to be convinced of the principle that underlies all phenomena, and, if it can, of the Absolute itself, and thus to put oneself in harmony with this Absolute. Thus defined, the teaching was more than the dogma of a sect, and whoever attains to the perception of the Absolute raises himself above mundane things and awakes 'to a new Heaven and a new Earth.'"[30]

The Shinto, explains Nitobe, inculcated into the Japanese people the sense of family and strong ties between the different classes of the society, especially toward the emperor, whose image was a sort of cornerstone of the social system.[31]

Also, in regard to the social ties and commitments, the Chinese philosopher Confucius was a great influence. Nitobe says: "As to strictly ethical doctrines, the teachings of Confucius were the most prolific source of Bushido. His enunciation of the five moral relations between master and servant (the governing and the governed), father and son, husband and wife, older and younger brother, and between friend and friend, was but a confirmation of what the race instinct has recognized before his writings were introduced from China. The calm, benignant, and worldly-wise character of his politico-ethical precepts was particularly well suited to the samurai, who formed the ruling class."[32]

Nitobe states that the writings of Confucius and Mencius were the principal textbooks for youth and the highest authority in discussions among the old. A common proverb ridicules a person that possesses an intellectual knowledge but doesn't act accordingly. To be studious is not to be wise. Another saying points out: "A man who has read little smells a little pedantic, and a man who has read much smells yet more so; both are alike unpleasant." The writer meant thereby that knowledge becomes really such only when it is assimilated in the mind of the learner and shows in his character. The doctrine is summarized by the Chinese philosopher Wan Yang Min: "To know and to act are one and the same."[33]

Work ethics and commitment to performance appears to be as something with very deep roots. These teachings combined with the experiences and special circumstances shaped the special character of the Japanese work force. A very traditional symbol, the sword of katana, symbolizing the power of the will, is of tantamount influence upon the Japanese. The Japanese character is pragmatic in that it insists upon applying what has been learned.

Nitobe later explains that "whatever the sources, the essential principles that *Bushido* imbibed from them and assimilated to itself, were few and simple."[34]

Life, then becomes a work of art. Through daily practice, one gets nearer to the achievement of that harmony that reflects itself in beauty. This is symbolized in the Tea Ceremony or Cha-No-Yu.

CONCLUSIONS

To support our thesis about the important role of the traditional elements in the Japanese management, recall the comments of Pascale and Athos.

The authors explain the importance in management of the capacity to deal with human nature—the complexities of human reactions—and to be able to reach to other human beings by going beyond our own uniqueness and overcoming the differences of views.

They point out the necessity to overcome the routine and mechanical patterns of behavior. They present concepts that help us to reach further into the subtlety and richness of human nature via attitudes related to those of old.

The Japanese believe, say Pascale and Athos, that by removing yourself from the picture you gain greater insight into what is truly there. We are blinded by our own egos from seeing the full possibilities of life. If we discipline ourselves to adopt periodically a 'no-ego' state, we can perceptively drink in the full meaning of a situation without imposing ourselves upon it.[35]

In talking about this capacity of mastering psychological states, they mention Zen Buddhism and its insistence upon "emptying ourselves" before looking into something in order to fully appreciate it. That concept of emptying ourselves is related to the way that they conceive of the universe. In it the "emptiness" has a great value, because as seen in the philosophy of Lao Tse, the emptiness is much more than just that. It becomes a kind of metaphysical source of everything, like a sort of mythological mother goddess, containing everything essential within her.

The space in-between things, the undefined, is what gives meaning to and unites the defined things. Pascale and Athos explain the importance of seeing the big picture in management. Thus going beyond the personal vision of the manager, of being able to integrate the complexities of human relationships. In this way, the manager should not always be "assertive," and defined in his opinions. Rather he should, within the context of his strategy and vision, be flexible and open enough to deal with complex situations. These require understanding of the various factors involved before taking a stand. They mention the need of ambiguity as a management skill and the necessity to sometimes "decide" to "proceed": "As proceeding yields further information, the best course may be to move toward the goal through a sequence of tentative steps rather than by bold stroke actions."[36]

Well, that's very much what Lao Tse meant when he spoke in an even more obscure language. He said that the "weak wins over the strong and the small is more than the big, and from the emptiness is where things really can be managed" such as in the "eye of the storm." What makes a cup of coffee useful? The emptiness inside it.[37] (*Note:* As Morishima explains, the teachings of the Chinese philosopher Lao Tse became part of the Shinto religion. This integrated new form served as a rational and social bond for all the people.)

So, we find an approach that enables us to experience the following concepts; in the tides of life, the interaction of the "Yin and Yang"; the positive and negative, active and passive. This approach then leads us to the identification with the "Tao," the ultimate wholeness that is beyond those tides. Thus, an understanding would be created in us that helps us to deal with the uniqueness of others.[38]

There are many examples that we could use if space would allow. We definitely suggest the work of Pascale and Athos as a reference in this aspect. They present many concrete examples that we cannot enumerate here and show useful attitudes in daily management which are definitely rooted to those characteristic of the Japanese of old. They are drawn from vital and metaphysical sources, integrated with technical aspects.

In Japan many people attend and draw inspiration equally from Shinto, Buddhist and Confucian services and rituals. This practice helps the people at large to participate more deeply in their work. This process of inner transformation becomes a kind of art form that was highly developed by the samurais. Actually a samurai was supposed to read and hopefully even write poetry.

As we stated at the beginning of this work, it is not the philosophical elements alone, but the way in which they were combined that finally shaped the Japan that we admire today. To more fully understand the historical development, such as the Meiji period of reform in the VI c., the slogan "occidental technology and Japanese spirit" and the "secularization of the samurai" processes, we recommend to the reader the quoted work of *Why Japan Has "Succeeded."*

We would state that, according to traditional thought, they believe that their performance is a part of their spiritual development and not something separate.

There were and will be other countries destroyed by war. There are others, some of which are islands, that lack natural resources. Many countries were also rebuilt with the help and the technological aid from the United States, but there is only one country of the rising sun.

Without doubt, what we see operating in Japan is unique. The historical forces that have shaped her are complex. We do not pretend to explain it here. It is, however, our wish to give the reader some "appetizers" to rouse his further interest in those ancient sources of inspiration that, although they have been changed, adapted, and mutated, still remain basically entrenched in modern Japan. The samurai of old and current Matsushita are different in many ways, yet they have much in common as well. The same light of the legendary Amateratsu, the goddess of the sun, shines forth from the soul of each, though in different manners and degrees. Equally present is the mythical hero SusunaHo, who re-instated the rituals that link man to the sacred, and thus returning the meaning to music and the arts.

In Japan today, the sun may not be rising as it once did. However, the same intrinsic elements that were present in antiquity are also found to some degree in the Japanese management. Some of these elements are the sense of family, the concept of a nation as a large integrated family, commitment to the land, and the need to have a motivating and unifying bond that is higher and far broader than a monetary profit.

Due to the fact that these same social values exist in other cultures around the world, we may speculate that they constitute a forgotten legacy of Mankind. A Mankind which is currently falling into diversification, self-absorption, and has lost the ability to see the "whole picture." We can indeed learn much from the example set by Japan by understanding and appreciating its ancient and current history. Perhaps, it may inspire us as a nation to achieve more, to unite as a people, and to become better human beings and in this way to be more competitive in business. So, let's look for and develop in ourselves values that would enable us to embrace the whole spectrum of human needs. And that is not "Japanese"; or is it?

Notes

1. Richard Tanner Pascale and Anthony G. Athos *The Art of Japanese Management* (New York: A Warner Comm. Co., 1979).

2. Ibid., p. 124.

3. Ibid., p. 129.

4. Ibid., p. 31.

5. Ibid., p. 59.

6. Ibid., p. 132.

7. Ibid., p. 135.

8. William G. Ouchi *Theory Z* (New York: 1981).

9. Dr. Kaoru Ishikawa, "Total Quality Management."

10. Richard Tanner Pascale and Anthony G. Athos *The Art of Japanese Management* (New York: A Warner Comm. Co., 1979) p. 29.

11. Ibid., p. 28.

12. Kenichi Ohmae *The Mind of the Strategist* (New York: Penguin Group, 1982).

13. Ibid., p. 217.

14. Ibid., p. 217.

15. Ibid., p. 217.

16. Michio Morishima *Why Japan Has ''Succeeded''* (Cambridge University Press, 1982).

17. Ibid., p. 15.

18. Ibid., pp. 15, 16.

19. Ibid., p. 17.

20. Ibid., p. 23.

21. Ibid., pp. 49, 50.

22. Ibid., p. 51.

23. Ibid., p. 63.

24. Inazo Nitobe *The Soul of Japan* (Tokyo: Tuttle Co., 1969).

25. Ibid., pp. 38, 39.

26. Daidoji Yuzan (by A. L. Sadler translator) *The Code of the Samurai* (Tokyo: Tuttle Co., 1988).

27. Ibid., pp. 15, 16.

28. *Ankh* Magazine, (Madrid: Nueva Acropolis, 1991).

29. Inazo Nitobe *The Soul of Japan* (Tokyo: Tuttle Co., 1969) pp. 12, 13.

30. Ibid., pp. 11, 12.

31. Ibid., p. 12.

32. Ibid., pp. 15, 16.

33. Ibid., pp. 17, 18.

34. Ibid., p. 20.

35. Richard Tanner Pascale and Anthony G. Athos *The Art of Japanese Management* (New York: A Warner Comm. Co., 1979) p. 143.

36. Ibid., pp. 144, 145.

37. Lao Tzu Tao Teh Ching (Boston: Shambhala Pub., Inc., 1989) p. 23.

38. Ibid., pp. 9, 33, 25, 87, 89.

Organizational Impact of Introducing Concurrent Engineering

———

By Ellen R. Domb, Robert C. Culver, and
Richard H. Rawcliffe

Abstract

The introduction of concurrent engineering as the primary method of new product development stimulates organizational change. An existing model is examined which integrates all elements of the organization, not just the structure and strategy. This "7-S" model draws attention to the issues which must be addressed effectively to institutionalize the formal tools of concurrent engineering. Key formal methods include Quality Function Deployment (QFD) to help the planning for a quality product; Robust Design, including Taguchi methods, to desensitize the product to manufacturing and user environments; and Statistical Process Control (SPC) to help manufacture the quality product. Products that combine hardware, software, and field support elements present particular challenges but demonstrate significant benefits from the concurrent engineering approach.

INTRODUCTION

The benefits of concurrent engineering in both the commercial and the government contracting environments have been demonstrated repeatedly.[1,2] New products and improvements to old ones are conceived, developed, produced, and in the customers' hands 25 to 45% faster than with conventional serial product development.

Successful pilot projects have shifted the emphasis in many companies from the question, "Will concurrent engineering work for us?" to, "How do we make concurrent engineering our only way of doing business?"

Multifunctional product development teams are the most common first approach, as documented by Ancona and Caldwell,[3] and recommended in the widespread concurrent engineering courses given by the GOAL/QPC, the American Supplier Institute, and the Juran Institute.[4,5,6] Teams attempt to replace the serial structured communication of the conventional product development process ("toss it over the wall") with continuous communication among team members from many specialty fields. Teams are formed to overcome the communication and coordination problems of serial product development. Techniques for communication in concurrent engineering teams range from informal, ad hoc techniques through the highly structured use of quality function deployment (QFD).

Typical cross-functional teams include people from marketing, program management, systems engineering, design engineering, production, distribution, and field support, and may include suppliers and customers. The team may also draw on a larger pool of specialists in reliability, quality assurance, contracts, human factors, process design, packaging, finance, etc. Just making the list demonstrates why simply forming the team will not solve the problems of communication; the complexity of product development requires the application of many kinds of knowledge, while the pressure to get better products to market faster requires something much more difficult: that all these specialists understand each other.

Reorganization is the trite solution to changing communication patterns. Frequently the new organizational structure is derived from the old, or is designed to overcome perceived weaknesses and preserve perceived strengths of the previous structure. The new structure may be no more effective than the old, but because of resistance to the stress of further change, or the failure to measure the effectiveness before and after the change, or the considerable time it takes for new communication patterns to be established, the first new structure tried may become the only new structure tried. The progress of concurrent engineering from the occasional pilot project stage to organization-wide acceptance as the normal way of business will then be set back by the perception that the organization's management is not committed to concurrent engineering, to Total Quality Management, and to customer service since it is not providing structural support to the product development teams.

It is necessary to find a model for organizational change that will enhance the probability of success for the concurrent engineering teams, a model that is flexible enough to deal with existing and new products, and that can be a vehicle for continuous improvement so that the organizational structure itself is seen as part of the TQM process. One useful model for alignment of structure with strategy and a full network of support is the set of organizational factors described by Waterman, Peters, and Phillips in their "7-S" model[7,8] (Fig. 1).

To demonstrate the application of the 7-S paradigm to concurrent engineering, we will step through the elements of the 7-S model, showing how each of the "S" elements supports the others and supports the effectiveness of the emerging con-

FIGURE 1   *The 7-S Framework for Effective Organizational Change*

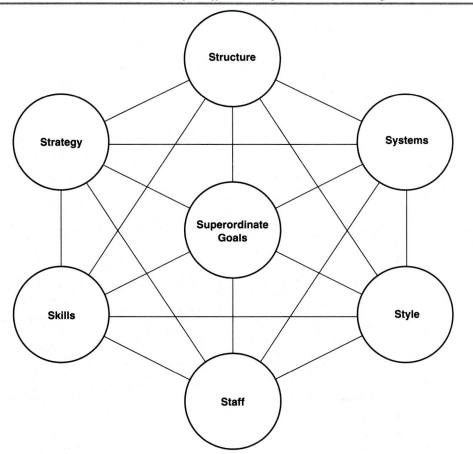

current engineering organization. The concentric wheel model of concurrent engineering (Fig. 2), derived by Rawcliffe from the work of Winner,[1,4] will be used as a general catalog of concurrent engineering attributes that require support.

APPLYING THE 7-S MODEL

Structure

Organizations have formal structures in order to divide tasks and coordinate effort. As businesses have grown, functional organizations have largely been abandoned in favor of decentralized structures. The linear increase in the number of people or activities drives a geometric increase in the number of interactions; beyond some

FIGURE 2 *The Concentric Wheel Model of Concurrent Engineering*

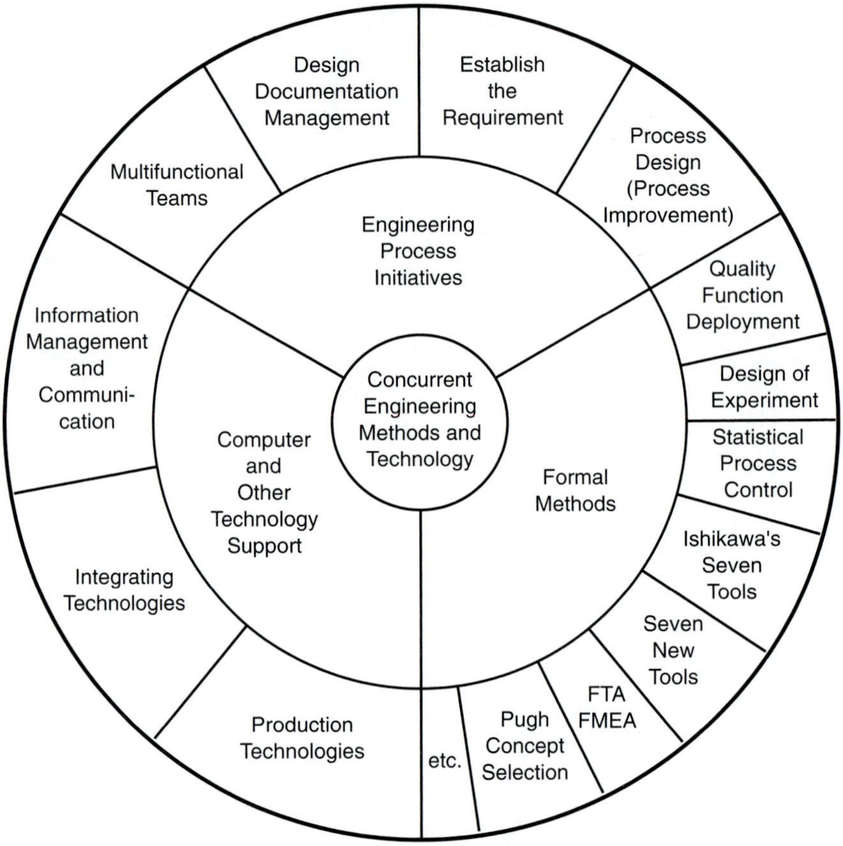

SOURCE: Reprinted from *Business Horizons,* June 1980. Copyright 1980 by the Foundation for the School of Business at Indiana University. Used with permission.

threshold of size and complexity, centralized functions must give way to decentralized operations to reduce the number of interactions to a manageable level. Matrix organizations are frequently the next step in evolution, to keep some central control while minimizing the coordination complexity. In the aerospace/defense community, matrix organizations have been used since the mid-1950s, and have developed new vocabulary to describe their evolution, ranging from the "strong" (program management oriented) to the "weak" (functional organization dominated) to the "balanced" matrix.

The product development teams which implement concurrent engineering have either "strong" or "balanced" matrix forms. A team can be flexible in membership, depending on the skills needed at each stage of product development, and can use the resources of the matrix to respond quickly to changing customer environments. The functional organizations provide the basis of standards and tools, and of education and training, for team members. On the concentric wheel, a team uses all the elements of the outer ring at various times in the development process, while the functional organization maintains and improves the processes, methods, and technologies. Companies as diverse as Hewlett Packard, Boeing, General Motors, and Aerojet use a combination of central standards organization and flexible product development teams as the practical solution to the problems of complexity and speed.

Strategy

Strategy is what a company does in response to or in anticipation of changes in its external environment—its customers, its competitors, or its regulatory agencies. Strategy is the company's concept for providing unique value to its customers. Many companies articulate clear strategies but they fail to implement them; the flaw may not be in the strategy or the structure, but in other elements of the organizational design. The decision to implement concurrent engineering is a strategy to provide customer satisfaction through quality services and products delivered quickly to market; actually implementing this strategy needs the full use of the other five elements of the 7-S model.

Systems

Systems are the procedures and processes, both formal and informal, that are the foundation of how the work in the organization gets done. Extensive systems development is required to support the evolution of concurrent engineering. Many companies find it necessary to change the system of design documentation and design release, since the design is now shared by people from many specialties, and from supplier and customer organizations. A large industry of CAD/CAE/CAM/CIM has developed to provide tools to automate these information exchange processes. A strong theme at many recent conferences on TQM and concurrent engineering[9,10] has been the need to simplify processes before you automate them, to get the maximum advantage of speed and simplicity. The supporting systems of the organization—particularly planning and budgeting systems—must be brought into the conversion to concurrent engineering, to be sure that they help to keep the product development teams flexible and responsive while retaining the financial controls needed to protect the business.

Style

Management style is, to many people in changing organizations, like pornography—"I can't define it, but I know it when I see it." The patterns of management's actions are the manifestations of a management style, and are used to convey a manager's values to the organization.

One key element of a manager's style is choosing among all the issues that demand his or her time. If quality improvement is the last item on management's agenda and is frequently dropped for lack of time, all the motivational efforts in the catalog won't be effective in developing quality awareness.

If management solicits employee involvement in policy development but implements few of the policies, the response to future involvement invitations will be small.[11,12] Many organizations have top management TQM Councils, or Quality Planning Councils, as a way of using a visible style to convey the message that quality is the management's concern.[6,11]

In the early stages of implementing concurrent engineering, management must educate itself to use the communication tools of the product development teams, and must develop the styles that support those teams. For example, if QFD and design of experiments (robust design, Taguchi methods) are primary tools of product development, management must cultivate the style of conducting reviews based on the vocabulary and mathematical structures of these tools. The style then shows that the managers know the difficulty of learning new communication and design modalities, but also appreciate the benefits enough to take the time to learn the techniques themselves, and make the effort to combine traditional management techniques with the new philosophies.[13]

Popular catch phrases express the importance of style in delivering the messages of change:

> "Don't talk the talk unless you walk the walk."
> "Watch their feet, not their lips."
> "If you always do what you always did, you'll always get what you always got."

Staff

In the 7-S model, "staff" encompasses all the "people" issues, especially those that involve preparing people for future leadership in the company. In the context of introducing concurrent engineering, the staff issues include systems issues, such as the development of performance evaluation and career planning assistance, pay and promotion policies that reward both team and individual contributions and skills, and training and education in use of new skills and new communication methods. In virtually all concurrent engineering introductions, formal training programs are needed as well as on-the-job training (frequently provided by team facilitators).

A company's style greatly influences the way it handles staff issues under the stress of a new strategy like concurrent engineering, but successful implementations have been observed in both very rigid and very loose cultures.[1,3,7]

Skills

We characterize companies by what they do best. The dominating attributes, or capabilities, are the "skills" of the 7-S model, and range from financial control to marketing, to technological innovation. To implement a new strategy, it may be necessary for a company to develop new skills. The classic success story of the past decade has been the "Baby Bell" companies developing speed, flexibility, and marketing skills after the AT&T divestiture. Skills can drive strategy several ways; both Xerox and Hewlett Packard realized that their strong skills in field service had developed in response to low product reliability, and with different techniques developed quality strategies to reduce the need for field service.

The attributes of a company that has successfully deployed concurrent engineering are visibly different from those of competitors which have not. These company skills depend on integrating the technical and management skills of people throughout the company with the company's technical resources, to support the customer-oriented organization. The customers' appreciation of new skills can be there ahead of the company's own deployment schedule. At Aerojet, our Air Force Space Systems Division customer appreciated the benefits of concurrent engineering in improved system requirements development after exposure to our first pilot project, and asked for our help teaching their staff the techniques of QFD, and providing facilitators for their staff on other new projects.

A challenge to any organization developing new skills is weeding out old skills and the systems, structures, and styles that support them. If we try to implement concurrent engineering while maintaining all our old product development methods, the contradictions will stall the system, and neither the old nor the new methods will work.

Superordinate Goals

The values, aspirations, and guiding concepts of an organization are the fundamental ideas around which the business is built. They are the broad concepts of future direction and present activity. A technical paradigm for superordinate goals is that they are the postulates of the system. They are not logically derived from anything, but if they are not logically consistent the system, structure, skills, staff, strategy, and style will not work as a coherent whole. The recognition in many TQM processes that the organization's vision and mission must be stated clearly so that all can work on making it a reality reflects the importance of superordinate goals. The rewards to the companies that have persevered in defining their superordinate goals and fully integrating their actions with their goals have been documented extensively, at this conference and throughout the literature of TQM.[7,9]

CONCLUSION

Implementing Total Quality Management challenges all seven "S" attributes of any company (Table 1). Because concurrent engineering requires the simultaneous implementation of new skills and new support mechanisms in many areas, it challenges severely an organization's ability to deal with change.

The networked nature of the 7-S model invites continuous iteration and continuous improvement. For companies implementing concurrent engineering, it can be an excellent tool to balance all the elements of company organization.

TABLE 1   *Organizational Factors in Introducing Concurrent Engineering*

"S" Factor	Concurrent Engineering Manifestation
Structure	The TQM team structure can be either a "strong" or a "balanced" matrix, drawing on the strengths of functional organizations.
Strategy	The *decision* to implement concurrent engineering is a strategy.
Systems	Systems must change to support concurrent engineering communication, planning, budgeting, and "traditional" product development systems, such as configuration management, information sharing, design reviews, and production reviews.
Style	When management does take concurrent engineering seriously, it shows in their style and the company follows.
Staff	Introducing concurrent engineering requires training, and affects compensation and evaluation policies.
Skills	Concurrent engineering may require building new skills, and unlearning old ones.
Superordinate Goals	Concurrent engineering must be introduced in a way that keeps it consistent with the company's vision and mission.

References

1. R. I. Winner, J. P. Pennell, H. E. Bertrand, and M. M. C. Slusarczuk, "The Role of Concurrent Engineering in Weapons System Acquisition," Institute for Defense Analysis (IDA) Report R-338, December 1988.

2. R. H. Rawcliffe and R. L. Randall, "Concurrent Engineering Applied to an SDIO Technology Program," *AIAA/ADPA/NSIA First National TQM Symposium,* 89–3191, (November 1989).

3. D. G. Ancona and D. Caldwell, "Improving the Performance of New Product Teams," *Research Technology Management,* March–April 1990, 25–29.

4. R. King, *Better Designs in Half the Time,* GOAL/QPC, Massachusetts, 1987.

5. American Supplier Institute (ASI), "Quality Function Deployment Workshop," Michigan, 1987.

6. Juran Institute, Inc., "Juran on quality Planning," Connecticut, 1988.

7. R. H. Waterman, Jr., *The Renewal Factor,* Bantam Books, New York, 1988.

8. R. H. Waterman, Jr., T. J. Peters, and J. R. Phillips, "Structure is not Organization," *Business Horizons,* 484–017, June 1980, 1–13.

9. AIAA, Second National Total Quality Management Symposium, Maryland (November 1990).

10. D. Clausing, "Concurrent Engineering," Presented at the Concurrent Engineering Design Clinic Sponsored by the Society of Manufacturing Engineers (June 1990).

11. R. King, *Hoshin Planning,* GOAL/QPC, Massachusetts, 1989.

12. A. R. Shores, *Survival of the Fittest,* ASQC Quality Press, Wisconsin, 1988.

13. R. L. Randall, ''Results of Quality Function Deployment as Applied to Focal Plane Arrays,'' to be presented at 1991 Conference on the Producibility of Infrared Focal Plane Array Assemblies, sponsored by the Environmental Research Institute of Michigan (February 1991).

Benchmarking: Staying at the Head of the Pack!

By Ronald D. McNeil

This article defines and gives a brief history of benchmarking. The next article in this series looks at success stories in benchmarking. The final article gives specific steps for implementing the benchmarking process.

Benchmarking has emerged as a popular topic in American business conversations. Why? It is a criterion for the Malcolm Baldrige National Quality Award. More importantly, it is a process by which a company, large or small, can become more competitive locally, regionally, nationally and internationally. It is a means for becoming and staying world-class.

What is benchmarking? Benchmarking is the search for the best practices that will lead to superior performance. It is continuous, has measurement as it fundamental basis, and compares against the best.

In layman's terms, what is benchmarking? For example, if you are a golfer, your role model might not be the highest dollar winner on the PGA tour. In fact, you probably will have a number of role models, not simply one. Rather, you would analyze your own game and, for instance, if you had more trouble with putting than any other part of the game, you would search out the best putter in the world. Your benchmark would be the technique of that world-class putter and you would implement that technique into your putting game. You would then proceed through your golfing game and prioritize areas which require improvement. Next, you would find the best golfer in each area of deficiency and then systematically bring each superior

Reprinted from the January-February 1992 issue of *Spotting the News* with the permission of the author.

standard into your golfing game. In theory, you would become the best of the best.

In business, you are not limited by only one industry for benchmarks. While financial performance of a company should be at or above the average for its industry, other areas of performance can be benchmarked outside the industry. For example, the company which has the best collection methods in the world may be in an entirely different business. In benchmarking, it is quite acceptable to go outside one's industry and adopt the very best process in any given area. If your company has a poor collection procedure, then going to the company with the very best collection process and adopting that process is benchmarking.

Why? Benchmarking is the search for the best practices that will lead to the superior performance of a company. Benchmarking is continuous, has measurement as its fundamental basis, and compares against the best.

It is the formal process of measuring and comparing a company's operations, products and services against those of top performers both within and outside that company's primary industry. One of the hallmarks of benchmarking is capitalizing on the experiences and success of other firms even if the firm is in another industry.

Who popularized this process of sharing information and benchmarking best practices? The Japanese embraced benchmarking by sharing information across companies with Japan. For example, when one electronics firm in Japan discovered a marketing practice which yielded increased market share abroad, this information was shared with other Japanese industries. The industry might not have been in the electronics business, but the automobile industry.

By sharing processes and procedures which yielded the best products or methods, each Japanese company could quickly become world-class in a particular area. As companies in Japan had success after success, the shared information allowed each Japanese company to become world-class in many areas.

The system of implementing the best process by importing it from another company is benchmarking. The standard of benchmark is the best practice for a given process, procedure or policy worldwide. As each benchmark of excellence is imported, a company becomes increasingly the best in each area. With adaptations and improvements, each imported benchmark may become a benchmark for another company elsewhere. Understanding the Japanese practice of benchmarking may explain their success in world markets.

Why and how did benchmarking arrive in the United States? It was popularized in the United States by Xerox. Xerox was highly successful until the mid-1970s, when Japanese camera makers entered the low end of the light-lens copier market. By 1980, it became obvious that Xerox had to evolve rapidly into a world-class organization if it were to compete effectively in the global market. Xerox began assessing its corporate strengths and weaknesses, as well as those of its competitors. In 1981, the company instituted a formal benchmarking process to identify the successful practices of top competitors in each of Xerox's operations. It learned that it took too long to develop new products, that the products cost too much, and that the products failed to satisfy customers' requirements.

After a decade of effort to develop the strategies and put in place the systems for Xerox to be a world-class competitor, it has significantly narrowed the advantage held by Canon, Richo, Sharp, and Minolta, stemming their advance on Xerox's market share. Xerox won the coveted Malcolm Baldrige National Quality Award in 1989. As Xerox's Robert C. Camp points out, the success of Xerox can be attributed to employee involvement and benchmarking.

David T. Kearns, former chairman of Xerox, introduced a total quality process as a weapon in the competitive global market. He introduced the process of competitive benchmarking in which every aspect of the business is rated against the best competitor. Kearns has said that a quality process was needed to give people the tools necessary to compete. The benchmarking process should not just focus on where competitors are, but also on how they are getting there. Kearns called customer satisfaction the number one benchmark. Because of increasing customer expectation levels, Xerox is setting higher goals. The quality thrust enabled Xerox to compare itself with the very best and use the resulting information to build the future. As others have said, and Xerox discovered, benchmarking is a dynamic process that requires constant rechecking of performance standards.

Benchmarking—Developing the Competitive Edge

Benchmarking is a significant tool since it allows you to measure your company's performance in meeting your customers' expectations as compared to your competitors. Your customers have alternatives—your competitors—and you have to be as good as or better than those competitors in the eyes of your customers.

While the list of companies and organizations using benchmarking as a method for attaining competitive advantage is growing and almost endless, a few notable examples serve as role models. AT&T, IBM and Alcoa are significant leaders in employing benchmarking: however, Xerox stands as the originator of benchmarking. Therefore, a close look at why and how the most oft cited benchmarking company embraced this practice may help you to introduce benchmarking into your company. Also a brief review of why AT&T, IBM and Alcoa benchmark will be given.

First, why did Xerox turn to benchmarking? By necessity is the answer. In the late 1970s, disciplined and determined Japanese competitors operated so efficiently that they were able to sell many copiers for what it cost Xerox to produce a similar product. Some business leaders predicted that without radical change, Xerox's long term survival was in question.

Second, what were some of the major problems which handicapped Xerox's ability to compete? Rework, scrap, excessive inspections, lost business and other similar items were estimated to cost Xerox 20 percent of revenues. This equated to almost $2 billion dollars in gross income. These were major areas which demanded immediate attention and were high potential areas to apply benchmarking.

To find what to benchmark, Xerox involved its workforce to scrutinize its operations and then to compare itself to competitors. Some serious shortcomings were discovered. For example, Xerox had nine times as many production suppliers as competitors. This led to complex relationships and increased systems and personnel to deal with suppliers. Xerox had twice as many employees as their Japanese counterparts. This led to increased costs without increased productivity. Production lead times were twice as long as the best in the field. This hindered timely product improvements and development. Xerox had 10 times as many parts rejected and seven times as many manufacturing defects as their Japanese counterparts.

These priority deficiencies illustrated why Xerox was not a world class competitor. More importantly, these constraints had to be broken if Xerox was to remain a dominant force in its marketplace. Xerox first committed itself to meeting customer requirements. In short, the commitment was to become the best in the marketplace.

Third, where did Xerox go for benchmarks? Xerox went to AT&T to benchmark research and development, to American Express to benchmark billing processes, to Milliken and Company to benchmark employee suggestion systems, and so on. In short, Xerox used benchmarking as part of the solution by measuring products, services and practices against its toughest competitors and against industry leaders. Xerox employees benchmarked their performance in over 250 different areas.

Fourth, what were some of the specific benefits of benchmarking? The outcome was fewer parts-rejected, no inspection on suppliers parts, product-development time reduced by 60 percent, suppliers cut from 5,000 to 500, inventory reduced from three months to 20 days, cost of purchased parts reduced by 45 percent, six out of seven parts inspectors reassigned to other jobs, manufacturing costs reduced 20 percent, and overall product quality improved by 93 percent.

Xerox implemented benchmarking because it had to. It evaluated its competition and found itself non-competitive in several key areas. Xerox then went to those companies which were the best at those things where Xerox lacked expertise. It then implemented those benchmarks at Xerox. The story is one of success: that is, a story of how Xerox became better than its competitors so that its customers had only one place to go and that was to Xerox.

Other well known companies have followed the lead of Xerox. IBM is also viewed as a leader in benchmarking techniques. It rates itself not only against competitors in its own markets, but against leaders in other industries. It compares itself to DEC in the workstation business and Canon in the photocopier market. IBM went to L.L. Bean to find out how to improve its own warehousing operations; to John Deere to find the best service parts logistics system; and to Ford to discover the best assembly automation process. IBM has even studied the United States Federal Reserve's bill-scanning procedures and Citicorp's document-processing activity to learn better methods.

Why did AT&T's Material Management Service Division go into benchmarking? It saw that it had to improve its business and culture so that it could remain competitive. The MMS Division of AT&T provides distribution services for AT&T's business units.

Why did Alcoa embrace benchmarking? It became involved in benchmarking to improve processes and to add value. Alcoa uses benchmarking to understand what level of performance is really possible and to understand why the gap exists between its current performance and that optimum performance. Alcoa felt it had to be the best of the best or its customers would go to competitors. At best Alcoa, without improving, could not capture greater market share in its businesses nor be at the cutting edge of introducing new products for future growth.

Benchmarking to Break Constraints and Bottlenecks

In previous articles, the history and applications of benchmarking have been discussed. For instance, the Xerox example illustrated the power of the benchmarking process. Xerox was no longer competitive in the market place because competitors were selling products for what it cost Xerox to manufacture its products. Xerox lost market share and profits were eroded.

At first glance, the major problem facing Xerox was in the market. It could not sell its machines at competitive prices and still make a profit. Xerox could have decided to wait until competitors' costs rose; however, the decision was made to make Xerox competitive now. This decision led to asking why costs were high and it became apparent that Xerox's processes from order taking to payment for products or services were not the best in the business and probably did not compare favorably with higher standards of companies outside the industry.

Xerox examined all its processes from orders to payment and determined which processes were below competitors' or industry practices. They found rework, scrap, number of employees and number of suppliers much higher than competitors and world class organizations. The cost of these inferior practices to Xerox was in terms of time to design, manufacture, and receive payment for its products and services.

Time has a significant relationship to lost opportunities and costs; and, in Xerox's case, time directly related to lost market share and lost income. It takes time to rework products, hold inventory, deal with an excessive number of suppliers, and the like. All of these add up to slower processes which impede new product introduction and add to costs.

What Xerox discovered were bottlenecks in its processes, prioritized those bottlenecks according to how far off the mark they were (i.e., the mark is the standard of the best in the industry or world), and then used the benchmarking process to improve deficiencies. As each constraint to profits was broken, another constraint rose to head the list of profit robbers.

While Xerox did not formally view their problems in terms of constraints to profits, they did approximate the process of identifying constraints and breaking those constraints. They broke constraints by determining the best practices available and then using the best of the best to improve the Xerox system.

The concepts, constraints, and bottlenecks were introduced by Eli Goldratt in his book. *The Goal* and further explained in *Theory of Constraints.* Both books are published by and available from the North River Press, Box 309, Croton-on-Hudson, New York 10520. The goal for a business, according to Goldratt, is to make a profit or add value to a product or service. In any organization, bottlenecks or constraints exist which adversely affect profits. Many companies address constraints and bottlenecks myopically and fail to appreciate the impact of each constraint on the total process from order receipt to the receipt of payment for the product or service.

For example, a printer may determine that a new, high tech, high capacity press will increase profits. So, a new press is purchased. The press has all the capacity required to take care of every order generated by sales. In fact, the new higher quality and more versatile press allows sales to bring in a high volume of business. So far so good, or is it? The press has such high capacity that, for example, a process upstream (i.e., preceding it) cannot keep up with the orders and the press. Maybe typesetting cannot keep up with the volume and is a constraint to the flow. How do you know it's a constraint? Simply by looking at the mainly idle new press and then physically seeing all the work backed up in front of typesetting. The constraint is obvious and you learn that the new press is only as fast as typesetting.

As one constraint is broken, a new one appears in the process. Acquiring new typesetting equipment may lead to a high volume of orders which may emerge as the new constraint. Break the order processing constraint and the constraint may move to sales. That is, our capacity is greater than our orders or sales.

One method for breaking a constraint is benchmarking. Benchmarking is a means to discovering the best way of improving the process which is constraining the organization. The best methods or technology for improving a process may be within or outside the industry. Innovation may become necessary so that a novel and original world standard or benchmark is developed.

But why break constraints? What are the effects of constraints or bottlenecks on the goal of profits? Goldratt introduced the concept of *throughput.* Businesses exist to receive orders and process those orders as quickly as possible in order to receive payment from the customer. Whatever prolongs the processing of that order from time it is known until the time payment is received is a constraint on the profits of the business.

What are some of the things that can affect "throughput"? One popular notion today is poor quality. A customer may not pay or may delay payment for a product or service that does not meet expectations or requirements. In this example, why doesn't the product or service meet the expectations of the customer? As processes are studied from the order to the delivery of the product or service, bottlenecks and constraints to quality can be determined. Find the most critical constraints and benchmark. Find the best methods to address the constraint from other companies and then improve the deficient process.

Does improvement ever end? No! Continuous improvement is a condition of survival. Processes which most adversely impede ''throughput'' should be examined first. Remember, time is money. The more time it takes to deliver a customer's order and be paid for it, the higher the cost. The higher the cost, the less competitive the business, and the higher the probability the business will not make profits now and in the future.

Basic TQM Tools and the Management of Multiple Personality Disorder

By Elizabeth Power

ABSTRACT

The correlation of TQM (Total Quality Management) to the management of Multiple Personality Disorder (MPD) parallels external and internal organizations and the management systems applied to each. Teaching multiples (those with MPD) the use of basic TQM tools as part of the process of healing increases functionality and health through encouraging leadership and reduces fear by increasing focus on gathering and considering data that can be used as a support for the healing process.

TQM AND MPD: THE RELATIONSHIP

According to W. Edwards Deming, the goal of the transformation brought about by embracing TQM is to "improve constantly and forever the system of production and service, to improve quality and productivity, and thus constantly decrease costs."[1] TQM focuses on managing processes through the use of theory of variation, or statistics, rather than trying to manage the results at the end of the process. It is more efficient to adapt the process than to fix the result.

Multiple Personality Disorder (MPD) is a psychiatric condition caused by chronic overwhelming childhood trauma and abuse in which the child is able to step back and let another part self manage a traumatic situation. If not resolved, this manifests

1992 report reprinted with the permission of the author.

in adulthood through the presence of two or more relatively enduring personalities or selves (alters) which take control of the body. Persons with MPD, called multiples, identify the internal selves, learn to manage the process of "switching" (changing who has control of the body), resolve the traumas that caused the selves to come into being, apply different styles of internal management to the selves, and resolve to one of several treatment outcomes. These outcomes may be either integration (fusion of all selves into one), forms of business organizations such as corporation or partnership, or as a committee working together to accomplish common goals while sharing one body. As a *process,* it would be far more efficient to prevent child-hood trauma than to attempt to fix the *result* of MPD. Since, however, the result is what is diagnosed, the process under consideration *begins* with diagnosis.

To connect Deming's work to a person with multiple personalities, the "*system* of production and service" may be defined as those interactions among selves internal to the multiple and with the self most often presenting (frequently called the host). The nature of these interactions, a form of services, involves "quality and productiv-ity" in the form of control of the body, and development of the skills and abilities contained within the entire group of selves sharing one body. These skills include those used in work, recreation, and functions necessary to sustain and maintain life.

Variation that increases "costs" occurs among the alters in cognitive (thinking), kinesthetic (physical), and affective (emotional) skills as well as in value systems, beliefs and accuracy of thinking based on the developmental level and experience of the alter. Each personality or alter, for example, may have very different PET scans, EEGs, EKGs and even different allergies.

"Costs" to be decreased are the amount of mental and emotional energy required to manage internal interactions, the amount of conflict among selves based on excess variation in values and preferences such as food and clothing, and the time, trauma and fiscal cost of healing.

PERSONAL TQM: SELECTED POINTS AND TREATMENT PROCESS

Deming's transformation is accomplished through refocusing on processes instead of results (points 1,3,5), driving out fear (point 8), breaking down barriers (point 9), ceasing dependence on inspection (point 3), and taking on leadership for change (point 2).[2]

Result focused treatment may manifest in pressure early in the treatment pro-cess to integrate (combine all alters into one personality) or to commit to this as an outcome by clinician or client, resistance to pacing of the process to preserve daily functioning, and definition of health as integrated.

The **presence of fear** is evidenced by adoption of belief in stereotypes of those with MPD: fear of the alters, resistance to sharing roles and responsibilities among alters (the internal community), refusal to develop awareness of and foster healthy communication with selves, resistance to developing internal community-based expectations that foster intrinsic motivation for required performance, maintaining a rating system of selves designed to punish and reward, refusal to develop operational expectations of selves, and inability to foster and develop conscious choice and shared control among selves.

Barriers between selves exist in the form of amnesia required initially for management of selves driven by external sources of motivation (to prevent harm to physical self or contain violent selves); barriers are also required between developmental groups for healthy protection of younger selves from age-inappropriate inputs until (1) traumatic information is somewhat resolved and less damaging and (2) younger selves have matured developmentally or coalesced into more mature groups.

The requirement for **inspection** results in compulsive requirements for knowing by clients, the adoption of double standards for multiples/others by clients and clinicians, and the demand for an account for every moment of time.

Absence of leadership for change is obvious in the dependency-based relationships where the clinical or institution external to the multiple becomes responsible for the multiple in the resistance of the multiple to becoming an active participant with selves for the purpose of reducing inappropriate variation and increasing system (the internal community of selves) functioning and in the failure of clinician or client to recognize and capitalize assets of selves (even those presenting as hostile or destructive) as well as the failure to recognize that effective internal process management dramatically decreases requirement for external interventions and frees more clinical time for trauma work.

BARRIERS TO ACCOMPLISHMENT: EVIDENCE OF DEMING'S DISEASES

The **"diseases"** which Deming[3] says prevent this are lack of constancy of purpose, emphasis on the short-term, personal review systems, mobility of management, use of visible figures only for management, and excessive medical and liability costs. While Deming states these in terms of external organizations with profit and loss ratios that show up in terms of dollars, considering them in the multiple in terms of functional versus dysfunctional makes them equally applicable.

Evidence of these diseases is readily available at the individual, clinical, and social level. Consider the evidence offered for each of the seven diseases.

Lack of Constancy of Purpose   Lack of consciously chosen and adopted healthy central values by multiples that are incorporated into the growing system (such as "all for one and one for all") results in the evident (and opposite) value of "whoever's up front runs the show by their own values." Resistance to the effort required to offer increasingly consistent presentation of self externally increases reactive interventions that increase variation. Both cases are forms of tampering with the system.

Emphasis on the Short-Term   Reliance on instant gratification, "fast-food" mentality and resistance to teaching selves about interrelationships and delayed gratification keeps the focus on short term effects. Resistance to adopting a less linear view of life also does this by reinforcing only immediate stimulus-response situations. No linkages to intermediate or long-term results are evident in either style.

Personal Review Systems   Internalized judgement systems where selves denigrate each other, operate from conflicting value systems, or use information as ammunition are forms of personal review systems. One self may harshly judge another that has assumed responsibility for child rearing or work, when the judging self has in no way contributed. This fosters fear, increases barriers, and decreases quality of life for all.

Mobility of Management   Lack of adoption of protocol by which management team created results in "whoever's up front chooses for everyone" without commitment to common values.

Use of Visible Figures Only   Emphasis on number of alternate selves met ("numbers Olympics") creates the risk of increasing alters for the sake of having the biggest group. Reliance on psychological testing as sole indicator of functioning is also an erroneous reliance on visible figures only (who was tested?).

Excessive Medical Costs   The cost of treatment to integration averages $500,000 per multiple—after diagnosis.[4] In 1989, the typical multiple had been in treatment 6 years with 3 other diagnoses before diagnosis as a multiple.[5] After diagnosis as a multiple, 5 to 7 years of treatment with an average of 3 hospitalizations in excess of one month and as many as 15 other short-term stays is not atypical.[6]

External organizations (businesses and the visible self of the multiple) and internal organizations (subsets of businesses and the selves inside the multiple as they become known and interrelate) tend to focus on management by feeling instead of by fact, develop errors in thinking patterns that impede optimum functioning, and often distort outcomes to hide shame-based processes.

The application of teaching basic TQM tools to multiples allows clients to move away from the fear associated with their internal systems to the confidence associated with active involvement in leadership. It also provides the basis for long-term developmental thinking about implications and problem solving with less distortion. This is the implementation of the plan-do-check-act continuous improvement cycle. The MPD/DD Resource & Education Center has taught the tools to 12 clients with reports of enhanced functioning by clinicians and clients alike. Specific anecdotal reports focus on increased group health and ability in problem solving, less fear around the process of healing, and increased ability to form appropriate questions about specific patterns that emerge from personal charts.

THE TOOLS AND THEIR APPLICATION

Using the tools creates a common language that can be translated to levels appropriate for most clients and is understood by clinicians in the context of statistical training from graduate school. Tools also offer conceptual frameworks for other processes by focusing on the internal/external customer/supplier relationship for clients, and, for clients with their clinicians, taking responsibility for one's own life is supported. "Customers" are those who receive, "suppliers" those who provide; "internal" means within one body and "external" is outside the body. The multiple is then an external customer of the clinician who has internal customers in the form of alters. Alters are also internal suppliers to the multiple, and the multiple is also an external supplier to the clinician, providing information and revenues.

Fishbone Analysis

Used to examine factors influencing a situation, this technique allows the various selves to input causes of a problem from their perspective. Selves may give input to the host in a variety of ways; the end result is that the group explores its process together without focusing on punishment/reward mechanisms. Instead, the focus is on facts grouped into a set of basic categories. These categories usually are grouped into **methods,** how things have gotten done; **materials,** physical items; **people,** selves or other bodies; and **machines.** Some uses of **communication, selves, procedures** and **policies** has been helpful with multiples who find these groups more useful. Categorization into any four major groups can be effective.

As in any application of the fishbone diagram, the statement of the problem is written in the head of the fish, the four ribs represent the four major categories, and perceived causes flow towards the tail, parallel to the backbone. Causes are written under the category in which they are most likely to belong.

The result is a group (even if a subgroup or if groups change over time) generated graphic record of what happened with as many variables as perceived visible. This visual representation erodes attachment to the cognitive errors that someone else is responsible for everything that happens and that every self has a different physical body. In addition, group responsibility is fostered as well as the development of process-based conscious thinking. By operating from associative instead of trance logic, everyday functioning is enhanced regardless of the number of selves involved.

Scatter Diagrams

Plotting ages of alters met each day of each month on a scatter diagram shows the possible relationship of age groups to date met. The value of this information is in gaining an overview of group developmental level, rate at which age groups are emerging, and trends for age at which trauma occurred. It is interesting to note that the ages not represented may provide as much information as those that are, which age groups might be offering protection for others, and the average age of selves across months or other implications based on presence and absence of specific ages. Considering the relationship between two variables allows more effective planning and more efficient treatment.

Histograms

Since histograms show how frequently something occurs, they can be used to plot when new alters are met over a given period of time (by day, week, month) or which times of day loss of time (amnesia) or switching selves occurs. This information builds a profile of information useful over time. Trends in a complex (over 50 personalities) multiple provides valuable hints about correlation with physical cycles, seasons, or days of week that help the multiple become proactive in creating a safe environment for higher functioning. This counters planning failure into the process by incorporating measures that either accommodate the known situation or change the skills in the host to suppress introduction of new selves until therapy.

Run Charts

The simplest tool, a run chart is used to show data collected over time. Run charts can be used to help multiples become aware of how often they expose themselves to stimuli that may cause a personality switch, how often a switch occurs, at what times of the day or week they are aware of switching, or any other data that can be counted over time.

Control Charts

At the heart of measurement, the control chart can be used in several ways when working with multiples. Bennett Braun's BASK model asserts that people can dissociate or separate from the Behavior, Affect (emotions), Sensations (physical feelings), or Knowledge of an event (cognitive awareness).[7] Since dissociation is a "more or less" phenomenon, it is more accurate to express it as occurring along a continuum ranging from pathological association to pathological dissociation, with a range representing "normal."

Each self will have a control chart that depicts location along the association-dissociation continuum for behavior, affect, sensation, and knowledge. "Will" can also be added to depict degree of association with one's capacity to choose. With the clinician, the client can assess that "normal limits" are for each component of the BASK/W model and for each component for each self. Attention can then be focused on developing operational definitions and attending to meeting the criteria provided by these operational definitions to create more conscious choice about levels of dissociation during daily functioning.

To be sure, the nature of the dissociative process means some data will not be gathered, some will be erroneous, and some uses may be mistaken. In spite of these limitations, the benefits of helping individuals learn to use these tools outweighs the risks of error. Variation is inherent in the association-dissociation continuum; capitalizing on it helps clients regain choice about daily functioning.

CONCLUSIONS AND IMPLICATIONS

Since TQM and continuous improvement processes (CIP) are becoming an integral part of the mental health delivery system, teaching applications pertinent to their own process is timely; it leads to the development of joint determination of requirements and goals that have appropriately higher expectations. Taking TQM and CIP concepts to daily practice levels supports their adoption by clinicians whose practices require TQM for third party payment or the increase of efficiency.

Bibliography

Power, Elizabeth. *Managing Our Selves: Building A Community of Caring.* Nashville: Power & Associates, 1992.

Ross, Colin. *Multiple Personality Disorder: Diagnosis, Clinical Features and Treatment.* New York: John Wiley & Sons, 1989.

Walton, Mary. *The Deming Management Method.* New York: Perigee Books, 1986.

Notes

1. W. Edwards Deming, "A Theory for Management," Transformation through Application of the Fourteen Points.
2. Ibid.
3. Ibid.
4. MPD/DD Resource & Education Center (Nashville, TN) survey and projections based on costs of therapy, time lost from work, social services required, disability payments.
5. Ross, Norton, and Wozney (1980) *Canadian Journal of Psychiatry, 34* (5), pp. 413–418.
6. MPD/DD Resource & Education Center (Nashville, TN) survey of multiples.

The Voices of Implementation: Real Life Perspectives on Implementing TQM

———

By Madelyn Yucht

People make or break an organization's TQM initiative. The level of people's commitment and the quality of their work determines success or failure. Modern SPC (Statistical Process Control) teaches that there are five elements of quality: men, machines, materials, methods, and mother nature. While all these elements affect quality, if the employees of an organization are not on board, no amount of high tech equipment, grade-A materials, or new and improved methods and processes will generate a sustainable quality initiative.

Little happens in an organization that does not require its employees. They are fundamentally responsible for every aspect of a business: Designing, maintaining, and operating the equipment; purchasing and handling the supplies/materials; developing and implementing the methods and processes; selling the products; and providing the customers with service. Organizational impediments that prevent employees from becoming fully engaged and committed in the quality process will undermine if not destroy the TQM effort.

TQM literature seems to ignore or gloss over the fact that TQM affects people. The literature tends to focus predominantly on concepts, tools, and processes. The unspoken assumption is that people will embrace the new tools and concepts with gusto, understand how to integrate them into their jobs, and agree automatically with the implementation strategy. Unfortunately, this scenario does not bear any resemblance to reality. The intent of this article is to provide

———

1992 report reprinted with the permission of the author.

the reader with a "reality check" by providing a glimpse into an actual TQM implementation process. One company that embarked on the quality journey will be examined.

The viewpoints expressed represent the range of employment positions in the organization: The CEO, production supervisors, quality managers, vice-presidents, rolling mill operators, slitter operators, layout and scheduling, production, technical managers, customer service, personnel shipping, information services, claims, material management, sales, and warehousing. The quality process is very real to these individuals who for the last five years have been working hard to translate TQM concepts and tools into concrete results.

ULBRICH STAINLESS STEEL AND SPECIAL METALS (USSM)

Ulbrich Stainless Steel & Special Metals is a re-rolling mill in Connecticut. It was founded during WWII by Fred Ulbrich, Sr., with a second-hand rolling mill and slitter. The finished steel was used for manufacturing the army mess-kits for GI's. Today, the company has a strong presence in the United States and customers worldwide.

In 1988, the U.S. steel and other industries were facing stiff competition from overseas. Ulbrich's customers, mostly manufacturers, were being pressured to improve the quality of their products and processes to be more price competitive. In an environment where customers demanded stringent quality and low prices, Ulbrich was compelled to embark on a Quality Revolution.

Early in 1988, Ulbrich senior executives decided to implement a company-wide TQM program. A change agent and trainer were hired and a half million dollars was allocated to Quality training. A year and a half later, Ulbrich's 400+ employees had received over 10,000 hours of training and had spent thousands of additional hours in meetings learning ways to implement their newly learned skills.

Initially, the energy was intense, the pace fast. There were high expectations, optimism, confusion, skepticism, frustration, and exhaustion—feelings ran the gambit. Five years into the process many lessons have been harvested (some painful, some costly) and numerous rewards realized. The process has involved discussions, arguing, negotiations, meetings, experiments, false starts, long–kept secrets being swept out from under the rugs, innovation, and the emergence of heroes and quality zealots.

The Quality trail has been neither simple nor easy. Not every objective has been achieved, not every time table adhered to. What happened, in no uncertain terms, was that the "Ulbrich Quality Revolution" began a process of organizational change and learning that has Ulbrich Steel positioned to be a competitor in the global economy. The Ulbrich story is worth telling and the voices of the people who keep making it happen worth hearing!

VOICE OF THE INTERNAL CUSTOMER—THE EMPLOYEES

Oral and written survey responses from Ulbrich employees form the core of this article. Looked at individually, the comments show individual perspectives and ideas. Collectively, they reveal the pulse of the organization.

Q 1. *What Was Your Gut Reaction to the Quality Initiative?*

On the positive side my reaction was that we were finally going to try to do things with a specific plan and method in place. On the negative side I had concerns regarding those who were primarily responsible to implement the process. Not the Training & Development staff but the functional staff.

Negative at first, thought to myself, not another waste of money in the process of achieving quality! We had just gotten over a miserable experience with consultants who tried to make us more efficient and that money was spent for almost nothing.

Too much a canned presentation. Needed a more personal type of training for people to buy into the program. Support from the top did not seem intense at the beginning. They were focused on other matters amongst themselves and therefore *did not* give the quality program their all.

I welcomed a systematic approach to solving problems. However, I must point out that I considered myself strictly a layperson when Quality Control was the subject of conversation. I considered myself a technical person, a problem solver. Quality Management was someone else's bag!

My gut reaction was very positive. I have always taken pride in my work. I wanted to produce the best products in order to please the customer so they would continue doing business with Ulbrich. Obviously, the better our company becomes, the more secure my job is, and therefore, the greater the potential for me to move up within the company.

My first reaction was confusion! In my opinion we had good quality already.

No negative reaction, more of a ''wait and see''—hey, they want to send me to school, I'm willing to try any idea to improve the position of myself/company. Why not?

My gut reaction was that it was about time! I felt that most companies I knew about, that were doing well, had implemented a Quality program and that it was necessary for us to have one to survive.

Good, official backing to involve people! But, oh my!!!! There are going to be a lot of questions asked that can no longer be brushed aside, but will require systematic and complete explanations. This is going to be very time consuming as a supervisor.

The pace was too quick and disjointed, particularly considering the ''culture block'' which existed at the company.

My gut reaction was that I knew that I would like to be involved but I honestly thought not many people would really care or try to make it work. My attitude was positive because I had read several articles about Mr. Deming and how General Motors scoffed at him so he went to Japan and the rest is history.

Significance of Comments   A broad spectrum of reactions should be expected when a TQM intervention is introduced into a company. Management should carefully listen to these concerns and be aware that employees will assign credibility to implementation efforts based on the following:

1. Who is implementing the process.
2. Are senior managers demonstrating support? Is support perceived?
3. Relationships between senior staff members are not invisible to people in organizations. Lack of cohesiveness at senior levels can sabotage the effort before it even begins.
4. Past efforts can taint new initiatives. It is important to communicate clearly how the TQM initiative will be different and support this claim with unequivocal actions.
5. Perceptions and reality-based fears (e.g., less power, time commitment required) need to be addressed. Providing support to supervisors is particularly important in that supervisors assume the lions' share of responsibility for implementation.
6. The "Natural" advocates are important to identify to mobilize support. Often, the strongest, most influential allies are found outside the management ranks.
7. Decide up front how are you going to manage individuals with the "sitting on the fence—wait and see" attitude. Not dealing with these individuals sends mixed messages to those fully engaged and often deflates overall commitment.

Q 2. What Changes Have Occurred in the Corporation for the Better as a Result of the Quality Process?

The knowledge of cost of nonconformance has opened people's eyes to the real effects on sales—from the actual cost of a claim to the possible loss of future business. Corrective action has become a very valuable tool within Ulbrich, and during audits our customers expect to see it.

Company employees do have greater awareness of the importance of quality at the micro (personal job) and the macro (shipping a defect free product) levels. With an old company like Ulbrich, this in itself is a significant mental shift to 1990s business conditions.

Problems are talked about! Employees are starting to realize that it is their responsibility not to run bad or questionable material or equipment.

The employees in manufacturing know customers' names now. They look at names and try to understand special requirements. Now that operations has direct contact with customers vs. just the sales people, operations is much more responsive and does a better job at solving problems for the customer.

Deliberate use of training and education for **all** employees. Use of measurement as a tool to focus attention and unify efforts. Goal and objective orientation. Awareness of and attention to the chain of events necessary to deliver a quality product. Use of Quality activities to impact the budget positively. Better understanding of peoples abilities and limitations. Adherence to a quality process makes for an improved manufacturing and sales environment.

There is more awareness of Quality; SPC. Specific-team approaches have worked well.

I believe everyone tries to **do things right the first time.** I believe the process makes them all think in this manner—but I don't know if all of them are aware of how much easier their job is by **doing it right the first time.**

More openness and sharing of goals and objectives and good and poor results. Report cards from our customers as well as other communications showing the way we respond to our customers and vendors on a regular basis.

Significance of Comments   Positive results and attitudes often go unacknowledged. The wins are powerful resources to be leveraged and learned from.

1. Identify the wins and communicate them often to the entire organization to provide credibility and momentum.
2. Provide information about success and failures that occur around the organization. This assists everyone in the organization in learning and making appropriate adjustments.
3. It is crucial to monitor actual results and provide feedback about what is working and what is not working. If this is not done, people in the organization will feel their efforts are going into a ''black hole.''

Q 3. What Changes Have Occurred in the Corporation for the Worse as a Result of the Quality Process?

Disappointment of a large group of employees looking for the ''Big Bang,'' not recognizing quality improvement is normally made in small but meaningful steps.

Some feel that the money spent could have been directed into other areas that **really** would have effected quality: capital expenditures (i.e., new equipment, additional staffing).

PAPER WORK! Minutes, procedures, copies to the world. Quality Improvement demands paperwork and documentation for consistency and repeatability. At the same time, it just seems like there is a downside in that it stops people from being creative or innovative. They seem to begin to follow procedures without question if its an approved ''Quality'' procedure. We must push to keep innovation and change as a part of improvement while at the same time following quality procedures.

In the spirit of getting everyone's opinion, sometimes we have everyone in the company in a meeting just remotely involved with the issue—sometimes it's overkill and a waste of time.

Initial distrust of employees towards company as the motivation for the change was not explained properly or understood by all. Process caused splits within the ranks. Process was perceived to be a cure-all rather than as guidelines or tools. Poor signal to employees as the program lacked continuity of training to immediate implementation which was interpreted as a lack of support/interest by top management.

The only problm I saw was when the employees were given knowledge to solve and measure the problems and made suggestions. It often took a great deal of time to get action or the problem corrected. This had discouraged their attention and they often gave up.

Since everything is being questioned, people sometimes get very defensive attitudes.

Significance of Comments

1. Implementation never goes exactly according to plan and there are always problems or issues that arise. Problems will get solved, but new problems will arise. Let people know in advance that the process is imperfect so they do not interpret stumbling as failure, but rather as a normal part of the process.
2. Develop a mechanism to find problems related to the quality process. Preventing stumbling is impossible, but discovering problems with the process quickly will provide information necessary for adjustments. The TQM process itself has to be subject to continuous improvement.

Q 4. Please Provide Evidence of How Ulbrich's Quality Process Has Either Met, Exceeded, or Did Not Live Up to Your Personal Expectations—Is It Working or Not Working?

Soon after starting the process we set up a Safety Committee. I feel the understanding of the concept *zero defects* was a leading cause in substantially lowering our injury rate.

Communication between departments is up and requirements are better known. Since implementing the process our customer rejects are dramatically lower, and when a reject does occur, people actually care and don't just provide lip service.

As a corporation overall, it appears that some of the Divisions are very committed, while others are not. We could do better.

In my department people were enthusiastic, and the things taught made sense and could be used, but some areas were overwhelmed by pressure to get work out, and these areas failed. There was little support and follow-up with management when that happened.

There have certainly been successes throughout the company, but as a corporation overall we have failed. If the quality process had worked, the service centers would view USSM as their primary source of supply (because the quality is competitive) versus a mandated requirement.

Just being involved in a Quality Process is keeping us competitive with customers who demand that vendors have a quality program.

We are presently going through SPC classes for ISO-9000 certification. The Quality process helped all employees to write procedures and use SPC to measure all phases of our operations. This certification will provide more potential business for Ulbrich.

Specifically focusing the divisional requirements in the Quality Process around the detailed requirements of ISO-9000 certification has pulled everyone into the process with a clear-cut goal; individuals responsibilities, specific work instructions, and own understanding of how everyone contributes to the Total Quality Process.

My personal attitudes and work habits have changed drastically since the inception of the Quality Process. I think I am more effective and others around me are more effective.

The secretarial group made major strides to complete guidelines for written correspondence to make it uniform and standardized internally and outside. Much better written communication.

At the very early stages we had an account that did a quality audit of our mill to Ford standards and we failed. It opened a lot of eyes when we lost the account to how a formal documented program is. This was learning the hard way.

Significance of Comments　　Like the story of the three blind men touching different parts of an elephant and describing different animals, individuals will perceive a TQM initiative dissimilarly, depending on factors such as their job, supervisor, department, division, etc. The most appropriate strategies will be those that take into account the unique nature of different parts of the organization, strategies that make sense to the people in the organization, and strategies that are consistent with the organizational culture.

1. Focus on issues meaningful and visible to employees to establish credibility.
2. Different people interpret quality differently. Therefore, there is no single correct measure to determine how well the effort is going.
3. TQM processes should not be assessed solely by internal standards and expectations. Discovering how other companies are implementing the process will provide perspective on existing expectations and objective information to evaluate the implementation process.
4. It is highly likely that some parts of the organization will experience more success than others. Benchmarking works within the company for best practices. Determine what is working and not working in different areas and begin to have the

organization teach one other. This increases organizational learning and keeps the process vital.

Q 5. *If It Were Up to You and You Had It to Do All over Again, What Would You Suggest?*

Maybe take a more deliberate approach. I think at its inception we inundated everyone with Quality and everyone got very motivated . . . But then, reality set in and people did not see immediate change and consequently did not stay interested.

The training was excellent. There should have been more follow up to find out how the process was working, how people were using what they learned, weekly, monthly. The process fell apart in some areas dragging morale down in other areas.

The training program failed to contain a "loop," or ongoing process. After the initial training program was completed, it was over. I feel that continuing education is very important and would keep the attention to the quality process fresh in the minds of employees. The ongoing process of change never ends, and in Quality the attention must not stop.

We are very fortunate to have a solid base of truly good people in our work force, that have been accustomed to doing their jobs in a positive manner. Our thrust has been, and will remain to further refine, and improve that process. The only change that comes to mind is to have started sooner, as the rewards we find are so vast!

Better definition to intent of process. Precise gant chart of activities to take place, reasons why and anticipated results. Different role for corporate involvement. Methodical and focused plan versus throw it all into the pot—**run like hell**—see what happens. Better preassessment of the potential pitfalls which would be encountered.

More cross-pollination between divisions. Shared successes and shared stumbling blocks. This would encourage team building across geographical "boundaries," which in essence was the goal within each facility.

Pay closer attention to the quality of work departments are sending out. Monitor not just the process but also the products. Then the expectations and goals of all departments are reinforced and people are accountable.

More interaction with customers, so that everyone fully understands the importance of quality to the customer.

There is no question an effective quality system starts at the top of the organization. The company leaders have to understand the basic concepts, agree on their plan of attack, and then make sure middle managers understand that the system must be reinforced and all employees must participate. If upper and middle managers are allowed to "buy in or deal me out"—forget the quality system!!! You will end up with as many ball games being played as you have management personnel.

Much more visible commitment by owners and more importantly, top management, **practice what you preach.** I would take one real concrete problem like packaging or slitting and take it from beginning to end to make the **whole** process zero defects (This would mean make equipment changes necessary, training necessary, process changes—address everything). Work with the people and make them feel important and like they make a difference.

Recruit (not order) help in running the program. Enroll people who have trust and respect.

This process was "something else" to manage, along with the normal productivity and bottom line issues and pressures a middle manager typically has to deal with.

I feel a better selling job to middle management should be done because it doesn't seem that everyone is convinced that it was necessary to implement the program.

A more custom tailored program, not only more specific to our business, but more custom within our business. Office staff should get different training than manufacturing.

We should have established a profit sharing/gain sharing program to reinforce and motivate employees to go that extra step.

Maybe a little better [documented] understanding of what our customers vs. just conversations.

Significance of Comments

1. When people in an organization say something is wrong, it should not be interpreted as resistance. Discovering the points of contention can provide the ideas for transforming a quality initiative from stumbling to soaring.
2. Part of respecting the people participating in the process is making sure there is a mechanism for them to communicate parts of the process that are not working. This should be built into the process **at the outset,** not as an afterthought.

Q 6. What Have You Learned Personally and How Have You Changed Your Behavior and Methods as a Result of Your Company's Quality Process?

Learned not to comment on what the Company was doing or could do without checking it out first. (The difference between what we say we do and then actually doing it). At the beginning we had a quality manual that wasn't being followed and some of us were embarrassed during quality audits.

QUALITY IS A BUZZ WORD—A BIG ONE THAT IS NOT GOING AWAY!

I have learned how important quality is in the present business environment and that it can be a strong selling point.

I'm still struggling with managing other people and trying to (really) take care of things instead of just getting it done: managing by meetings, managing by committee, and the extra time it takes when it's done that way. But I am learning that the gain in worker self-esteem is much more value laden than having the project done my way, *quickly!* Also, a lot of the time they do it as good and even better!

Reinforced an analytical approach to daily tasks.

The persons that I now hire are more trainable and more skillful to perform multiple duties.

I have become more aware of how my work effects fellow employees.

I have learned to be more of a team player and have adjusted my communication techniques accordingly.

I have learned much about myself that I didn't know before. The quality process has changed how I deal with not only customers but my fellow employees. How can you find fault with a product if you don't know what the requirements for that product are, or you have not made your requirement clear? I no longer fault people; I question the process! I feel very confident now when dealing with customers because we have taken quality a step further by saying that our product should not just meet the customer's requirement but also the customer's expectations.

I have learned that to achieve Quality in any aspect of life, work or anything, it takes no longer to do it right than it would to do it wrong. And also to not keep your mouth shut if you think something is wrong. THINGS CAN CHANGE!!!

Company culture is extremely difficult to change. I try to keep up with quality processes and incorporate them in my work, but I do not let it overshadow what my primary responsibilities are.

Awareness of small things that can be caught before they affect the outcome of the product and cost the Company a remake and past due order. A company that has good quality processes will be a survivor at the top.

I have learned that a company that does not address quality day in and day out will rapidly diminish, and in time be replaced.

The quality process cannot be force-fed. It comes from a genuine understanding and desire for change. Organization and well prepared plans are key to success. You must have full support. You must remain singularly focused with one agenda only. You must show up front a clearly defined end which justifies the means. The skill and commitment of key individuals must be thoroughly understood and evaluated before you charge them with a responsibility of this magnitude. You simply cannot "learn as you go."

Everyone needs to feel recognized and know that they can affect change. It is also very important to be objective when defining quality and remove subjectivity.

Significance of Comments   Learning is the engine of the TQM process. The more people have an opportunity to see, read, discover, and try, the more learning occurs. The more learning that occurs, the more each individual is able to contribute and the entire organization is stronger because of it.

Perspectives of Owner, President, CEO

When undertaking a major TQM change initiative, senior executives must balance a complexity of competing demands. The comments made by the president of Ulbrich provide insight into intricacies of leading a TQM effort.

Owner's Vision

My vision for Ulbrich Steel is that of a "world-class" organization. My challenge was to find the way to lead the organization toward that goal. I know that changes have to be made to shift the business from small town thinking to world-class competitor thinking. I had hoped TQM was going to do it.

Implementation Stumbles:

We lost a great deal of money after the first round of TQM training and a total of about one million in the first 3 months. I realize now that it was due to the fact that we hadn't discussed or realized the need to manage the new set of expectations or how we were going to phase the concepts into the mill while keeping business going. Our TQM training emphasized two concepts, the first one was: You are the customer of the previous process, the process before you is responsible for sending quality work and the second was Zero Defects. What happened was that our employees interpreted this to mean that if they didn't get a perfect roll from the previous operation, they sent it back to process preceding them. The mill started getting backed up, nothing was moving. The second, what I will call cross-wire, was the interpretation of what zero-defects means—what happened was that nothing was shipped out to the clients unless it was PERFECT. Again, I don't think as management we did a good job of planning for or explaining how the new quality standards would be integrated into the business. I had to go down to the mill floor and say, "SHIP IT!" I know that this gave the wrong signals, but the business has to say solvent during the transition process.

Creating the Right Environment for Implementation:

If I had it to do over, I would make it a point to learn a lot more and have members of the organization learn more about TQM and high performance before taking action. I'd whet appetites so people become hungry for the change. If it had been done this way, the executives and employees could have gotten more involved in deciding the right approach and the attitude would have been, "Now let's go do it," with full commitment! Just telling the senior staff to do something they didn't trust and didn't believe in had a significant impact on the level of trust and commitment for the overall effort. I think this was my most serious error and my biggest lesson. I would expose the organization to companies that were already world class, suppliers, customers, similar operations. I'd arrange tours of their plants, arrange for Ulbrich employees to meet peers in other companies. I'd create opportunities for them to explore, touch, feel, look, and ask questions. Maybe go work at a suppliers facility, or work at a customers' facility, give employees learning sabbaticals so they could be exposed to other ways of thinking other than Ulbrich. This would also include books, articles, and examples of real life, real-time quality initiatives. I think this should be the first step toward changing a company.

CONCLUSION

Today, Ulbrich is a stronger company than it was five years ago. Employees have a solid commitment to quality products, service, and management, and they have the tools and skills that enable them to take on a new challenge. Ulbrich still contends with disappointments, successes, high hopes, false starts, frustrations, enthusiasm, fatigue, apathy, confusion, elation, I'll wait and see, show me, risk taking, resistance, risk aversion, fear, and power plays—BUT THEY DON'T STOP—they push forward, taking one step at a time.

It is hoped that by hearing the voices of people who have gone beyond the theory and beyond the rhetoric to real life and real-time implementation, you have gained an appreciation for the human element in TQM. Failure to adopt strategies that deal with human issues often accounts for why quality initiatives do not realize the levels of success hoped for. Key questions an organization should ask are:

1. How will the TQM initiative change jobs (tasks, time, skills needed)? What is the plan for communicating these changes and making adjustments to accommodate the changes? Are priorities being set or are people just being given more to do?

2. What is the plan for managing the day-to-day impact the TQM initiative will have on people? (Management and supervisors must be able to answer very specifically the question most often asked by employees, "What exactly do you want me to do differently and how?")

3. What apprehensions, doubts, and expectations are pervasive in the organization?

4. What organizational obstacles must be overcome by employees? (Existing policies, incentive systems, poor supervisors)

5. What organization idiosyncrasies exist that contradict the quality message?

6. What organizational thorns are sticking in people's sides preventing them from "really" committing?

7. Is the implementation process designed to be directly relevant to jobs, and does it make sense to the people doing the jobs?

8. Is the executive team giving a clear consistent message and are they walking the talk? (How do you know, has it been checked out throughout the organization?) Are managers/supervisors giving a clear consistent message?

9. What training is being offered? Is it enough? Is it high quality in the eyes of the employees. Does the training directly increase people's ability to perform.

People make quality happen. People are the most valuable Quality resource. Taking the time to listen to their suggestions, understand their reservations, and address their difficulties should be as fundamental to the Quality process as SPC!

7

Teams and Labor Issues

This section addresses the applications of one of the most important principles of TQM: *cooperation.* In TQM literature cooperation translates into teamwork, a shared corporate Mission and Vision developed with input from all levels of the organization, and labor-management cooperation.

The use of teams for continuous improvement of processes and problem-solving was seen during the late 70s and early 80s as the key to Japanese industrial success. Consequently, many U.S. companies sponsored the forming of *Quality Circles* with varying degrees of autonomy.

Quality Circles fell into disrepute over time as much time and effort was seen as wasted in endless meetings and efforts to solve often trivial problems. But the problem did not lie in the use of teams for problem-solving. The wrong thing with that approach was the prevalent interpretation of what Japanese quality efforts were all about.

Recent research suggests that Quality Circles in Japan work under the banner of coordinated, focused efforts of problem-solving throughout the organization. These teams are never totally independent in their selection of issues to focus on, but work under supervision and in coordination with other quality efforts.

Today, other forms of teams have emerged in organizations. Quality Circles have largely been replaced by Quality Improvement Teams (QITs), also known as Process Improvement Teams (PITs), which usually work on predetermined, clearly focused issues. In the last decade, thousands of companies have organized front line employees into Self Directed Teams (SDTs), which plan, implement and improve the daily work of the organization. Drawing on the experience with autonomous work groups in the field of socio-technical systems, these SDTs are empowered to make many decisions without any direct supervision.

Lessons for a
Learning Organization

———

BY BARRY A. GOFF, BARRY G. SHECKLEY, AND
SANDRA L. HASTINGS

INTRODUCTION

For well over a decade, American business has been responding to a rapidly changing world with fundamental structural and procedural alterations. Companies have
removed employees from every layer of their company and removed whole layers
in some instances. They have introduced Total Quality Management (TQM) and
other management and operational innovations. With less media attention, public
organizations and government also have begun implementing a wide range of
change activities. Meanwhile, most experts project the pace of worldwide change
to accelerate. As the pace accelerates, public and private sector organizations will
have to increase their capacity to respond.

Greater attention to learning must be a part of any future strategy for keeping
pace. At least one expert has concluded that the rate at which an organization learns
will be the most sustainable source of competitive advantage. Companies will compete most effectively by processing the latest information, learning the latest techniques, and providing employees with the skills to respond to changing conditions
and customer needs.

The education and training specialists in many organizations are developing new
approaches that provide education for a highly skilled work force. Trainers base
more training in the workplace than the classroom. Some have introduced distance
learning to reach wider audiences. Others have integrated computers and other
new technologies to develop more flexible and effective training experiences. In
spite of these innovations in learning techniques, few experts have directly addressed the relation between learning activities and the success of TQM.

1992 article reprinted with the permission of the authors.

Two of the many learning issues related to TQM will be the focus of what follows. First we will describe a learning and job classification system that represented a radical change for a state agency. The system was a major support for the overall structural reorganization taking place. In discussing this learning and job classification system, we will address two important issues tying learning to TQM. First, not attending to both unlearning and learning can cause an organization to attempt to build new learning on outdated, inadequate assumptions and attitudes. Using a weak, outdated, and ultimately inadequate foundation endangers the establishment of new ideas and their long-term stability. Second, we will discuss the particular value of developing employees who are self-directed learners. To date, experts have given little attention to ways in which the employee can effect the pace of the process between the time an employee identified a training need and the time he or she completes the learning process. Improving the speed of this process has only been addressed to this point with technological alterations to the delivery systems. Experience suggests that the timeliness of learning is as much a function of how employees participate in the learning process, as it is a function of what technologies deliver the information. Before describing the two aspects of learning and the job and classification system, a brief description of the state agency's overall plan and goals will provide a context.

THE DEPARTMENT OF LABOR MOVES TOWARD TQM

In the spring of 1991, the State of Connecticut's Department of Labor (DOL) under the leadership of Deputy Commissioner Lawrence Fox committed to a major reorganization and to bringing Total Quality Management (TQM) to the agency. At the start of our work with DOL, they were functioning under the burden of nine layers of management. They could not serve the rapidly changing needs of the working people in the state nor the business community. The agency structure that once served them well was now causing delays in some client services and proving inadequate for other business and labor force needs. Numerous hand-offs caused customers to routinely become mired in the bureaucracy. DOL clients seeking employment or unemployment benefits waited in long lines and often felt abused by DOL employees when they finally reached the front of the line for service.

The employees, themselves, were mired in the very bureaucracy of which they were a part. Employees complained that they neither had the information to make decisions for an unemployed client nor the authority. They looked to supervisors or experts in the central office to solve problems. Customers and DOL employees were caught and frustrated by this multi-layered system.

Given these conditions, DOL established these goals to guide their reorganization:

- Ensure highest quality services in the shortest possible time
- Reduce hands-off by reducing layers of management and giving more responsibility for decisions to front-line workers
- Decentralize authority by empowering those closest to the customer

- Provide more responsive administrative support from the central office to local offices
- Be a model agency for state government

Senior management took the first step by developing a reorganization strategy to reduce the nine layers of management to four. This brought the front line worker, who for many years was eight layers away from the commissioner's office to within three. Although only a first step, reorganization reduced the layers, brought decision making closer to the customer, and began the decentralization of the agency. This reduction was accompanied by a complete reorganization of the agency along functional lines.

They did not expect to achieve the appropriate level of responsiveness to local offices and customer service solely from restructuring, however. They knew that TQM was also necessary. TQM incorporated the new skills and attitudes necessary to ensure quality service and reinforce the other goals. Senior management saw learning as the central component of their organizational change. They also recognized that traditional learning methods and strategies would not produce adequate learning and that many strategies were incongruent with the TQM perspective.

FROM TRADITIONAL LEARNING TO LEARNING FOR TQM

While not often emphasized, innovative learning techniques have a long history in TQM. While implementing Quality Control in the 1950s, the Japanese found the use of television programs, workbooks, and manuals ineffective in teaching shop foremen statistical control techniques. As a result, they tried bringing foremen together in study groups. Group discussion proved a highly successful strategy for promoting learning. Later, these groups became known as Quality Circles, part of the foundation of TQM in Japan. As Ishikawa has stated, "QC begins and ends with education." While the educational focus of the original groups diminished in the U.S. versions of many QC groups, it is important to note their original intent. They also represent a part of the quality movement that deserves more attention in this country.

The Department of Labor needed to rethink how employees would learn the skills to perform their jobs. Their traditional training process placed the trainer in front of the class. The trainer, whether called an expert or facilitator, was the focus of the learning experience. The trainer lectured and lead discussions. Training occurred almost exclusively in the classroom. The objectives of the training were based on the amount of knowledge an employee was able to retain, not on their competency or skill on the job. The system promoted employees solely through competitive examination. Those who scored highest on written exams gained the promotion.

Their traditional training matched the traditional approach to doing the job. The trainer defined the rules and procedures, gave examples, gave opportunity for practice, and lead a discussion. The employees applied the rules and procedures to the situation as defined in the training. If the situation was an exception that required problem solving and an independent decision, employees avoided dealing with the situation, refused to deal with it, or passed the customer and the problem along to their supervisor or a specialist with greater authority. Their training did not provide practice in problem solving, decision making, or thinking independently. The organization had functioned well with set procedures in the stable, unchanging environment. The current, rapidly changing world, however, was and would continue to be full of exceptions. To deal with an increasing number of exceptions and changes, DOL needed employees who were independent decision makers with training to match.

A COMPETENCY BASED TRAINING/JOB STRUCTURE

The new training and promotion system is based on skill and knowledge. This competency-based system demands the same level of responsibility and initiative required for the implementation of TQM. Employees receive training for a job classification and receive a diagnostic evaluation at the end of the training to determine competency levels. If employees meet the standards for all levels, they are placed in the classification. If employees do not meet some competencies, they have opportunities for further training. Employees are evaluated on initiative, problem-solving, and decision-making as well as knowledge.

Job training for the system makes extensive use of group learning activities. These groups are designed to promote efficient learning and teamwork. Learning experts have known for some time that adults' learning is effectively increased in cooperative, group environments. Cooperative learning also promotes the teamwork that is so important to TQM. Group learning reinforces this central value and follows in the tradition of the quality circles which were the foundation of Japan's industrial rebirth.

The system promotes employees based on continually gaining new skills to meet new challenges within the established parameters of the job classification and the additional skills to qualify for the next job classification level. Therefore, employees must learn some new skills and information to maintain their current position. Moving to a new classification requires an employee to gain the additional skills associated with performing at an overall higher level.

Two learning principles were essential to supporting the success of this competency-based job and training structure and to achieving the organization's goals:

- Building trust by giving attention to unlearning as well as learning
- Basing continuous learning on the encouragement of adults as self-directed learners

UNLEARNING MISTRUST AND BUILDING TRUST

The Department of Labor dealt with trust by addressing sources of mistrust as well as finding ways to build trust. In the early stages, two types of mistrust were evident: Mistrust of what was being said and mistrust of who was saying it.

The need to unlearn the mistrust of what was being said was evident early in the reorganization around the issue of job security. For most employees the very word, "reorganization," engendered fear and uncertainty. Every DOL employee had heard about the hundreds of reorganizations in Connecticut and other parts of the country that lead to the loss of jobs. Although senior management, including the deputy commissioner, had told all employees that they would have a job in the new organization if they wanted one, early survey results indicated that employees continued to have doubts. Many did not believe any major changes would occur. Others felt that even if major changes occurred, they would not benefit because they might lose their current job or face being shifted to an undesirable alternative job. One individual best expressed these sentiments when she wrote, "I am concerned about my position with the organizational change. Where will I fit in with the new changes coming about?" Clearly this person and many others believed that major changes would include layoffs and, even if there were no lay-offs, they might not fit into the new organization. Their mistrust of what was being said initially held many back from participating.

Employees also mistrusted management's requests for their ideas and opinions. When the Deputy Commissioner asked employees for their ideas on how the reorganization should look, many would only say what they thought management wanted to hear. Even when senior management went through time-consuming and elaborate processes to elicit opinion from all employees, the opinions were guarded and limited in scope. So that only a few nearby could hear, one woman said, "I'll tell you what I really think if you pass out an anonymous survey, but I sure won't tell you anything here." Many years of work had taught her and many others a valuable lesson: Don't say anything openly with which managers may disagree. They heard each request through years of mistrust. Past experience suggested that stating opinions that contradicted senior management could only bring trouble.

Mistrust also extended beyond what was said to who said it. When employees spoke to Larry Fox, they addressed him as "Commissioner." Apart from the title, there was obvious deference to Larry—deference that said, "Whatever you say, goes, sir." Deference is often part of a more general feeling of distance between employees and senior managers. This sense of distance breeds mistrust, because employees do not view senior managers as understanding their needs. They view senior managers as "being above it all."

Such distance can have serious consequences. If employees view managers as distant, employees may suspect that managers will not make decisions in their best interest. As in politics, if the manager appears to be so far from the employees' experiences that he or she is out of touch, the employees don't believe that the manager will understand their needs. When employees say, "Whatever you say, goes, sir," they will really mean whatever you say goes and is likely to go against us.

Reducing mistrust is being accomplished at DOL by deliberately reducing the distance that generates the mistrust. For example, after the initial discussions and opinion gathering about the reorganization, the deputy commissioner began inviting small groups of employees from the local offices to sit and talk with him. He continued these meetings in his office for most of the first year. The meetings had no particular agenda. Employees were free to talk about whatever was on their mind. While employees and management judged the meetings helpful, the employees were generally polite during their talks with the deputy commissioner in his office.

More recently, the deputy commissioner has begun visiting every local office in the state holding two-hour meetings at each office. Unlike earlier meetings where people asked for an anonymous survey, employees have been speaking their mind. Recent encounters have included employees yelling at the deputy commissioner and, in at least one case, an employee walked out of the meeting in protest. The deputy commissioner related these events with a certain pride. It was evident from his descriptions that some of the deference had disappeared. Consequently, distance had been reduced. The deputy commissioner had practiced "management by walking around" with a clear objective, reducing the distance between employees and management.

Building trust takes even longer than reducing mistrust. That the deputy commissioner kept his promise about no layoffs did reduce mistrust. When no one experienced a pay reduction and many had pay increases, mistrust again diminished. Employees abandoned some of their mistrust each time management kept a promise.

Creating trust requires repeating this sequence of behaviors frequently and consistently over a long time. Senior managers, in particular, set the standard. Do they say they want employee participation and, then, dismiss employees' ideas when offered? Do they talk about employee empowerment but make decisions before employees had a chance to voice their preferences? The old ways are very easy to reinforce with only one or two reminders. Establishing a new standard, a new norm, usually means repeating the same approach so often and so consistently that employees began to expect the process to be conducted in the new way. Unlearning mistrust and learning trust is one aspect of TQM that requires long-term planning and commitment. Senior management must continually take a hard, sometimes painful look at what they are doing and how they are doing it. The organization reaps the reward of creating an environment which provides fertile ground for TQM and the learning which supports it.

JUST-IN-TIME-LEARNING FOR ORGANIZATIONS MOVING AT HYPER-SPEED

Most TQM strategies emphasize TQM's value to an organization's ability to succeed amidst rapid change. Most change experts point to employee empowerment within their work as a key feature in responding successfully to change. But, employees also must become empowered as self-directed learners if they are to meet the challenges of a rapidly changing work place. While a focus of adult education experts are meeting this challenge, others have rarely addressed the importance of self-directed learning regarding TQM.

Self-directed learning has many definitions. For our purposes, we use the term to identify learning activities that the employee initiates by identifying the learning need and accessing the necessary resources. The actual learning may involve sitting in a formal classroom, having informal group discussions with coworkers and supervisor, or spending time by oneself in a library, in front of the computer, or using other means of skills or information acquisition. The major feature of self-directed learning, in this definition, is that the employee identifies the learning need and initiates action to resolve the need.

Adult learning theorists such as Stephen Brookfield have noted the importance of self-direction in the adult learning process. He suggests that self-direction is the distinguishing characteristic of the adult learning experience. He also notes that adults are not necessarily self-directed just because of their age. Adults who may have developed adult capacities in many areas may not have developed abilities as self-directed learners. Therefore, any organizational innovation such as TQM should include introducing self-directed learning to employees.

ADVANTAGES OF SELF-DIRECTED LEARNING

Organizational innovation experts such as Rosabeth Moss Kanter and Peter Senge talk about the centrality of learning for employees and managers in the "new organization." Kanter emphasizes the critical role of learning and the manager's role in motivating learning and other activities in a rapidly changing environment. Senge emphasizes the importance of not being caught in old patterns of thinking and learning new patterns. However, neither Kanter nor Senge suggest how organizations can establish new learning perspectives or move to new patterns of thinking quickly enough to handle rapid changes. They both touch on the supervisor's responsibility as facilitator in accomplishing these shifts but provide no clear definition of the learner's responsibilities. Nonetheless, they imply that there must be a change in the locus of responsibility for learning. We contend that just as decision-making responsibility should reside with those who do the work, the responsibility for learning must reside with those who do the learning.

Alvin Toffler provides another reason why the focus of responsibility for learning must shift to the individual learner. He has noted that one of the greatest pressures facing contemporary business and society as a whole is not just change but the rapidity of that change. Toffler talks about organizations moving at "hyper-speeds," and suggests further that those who do not reach "hyper-speeds" will be left behind.

The Japanese are already developing "hyper-speed" manufacturing strategies that radically alter the life cycle of a product. They are compressing the product development cycle so that, as the product reaches the market, its withdrawal is being planned and its replacement developed. Every employee involved in such rapid change must be prepared to identify learning needs as they experience the need and be able to satisfy that need through "just-in-time-learning" (JITL). When employee development cannot keep pace with new product development, errors are made, service suffers, and customers are lost.

JITL also addresses a common training problem, transfer of training from the classroom to the workplace. One reason for the lack of transfer is that rather than training arriving too late, it arrives too early. Employees are trained on a new computer program, but they have no projects with which to use the new program when they return to work. When a project comes along 3 months later, they've forgotten most of what they learned, and valuable training time has been wasted.

Adult learning experts suggest several other advantages in placing responsibility for learning with the learners. First, adults tend to be pragmatic in the sense that they attempt to solve problems or achieve a particular goal when they learn. In their private lives, individuals frequently identify goals that require learning. A woman decides to plant a vegetable garden with the goal of providing fresh vegetables for her family through the summer and fall. She may decide to take a gardening course, consult the extension service, or read books and watch videos. Her goal is fresh vegetables on her table early this summer.

A different dynamic affects a goal structure in the workplace. The same woman works in the Department of Labor's unit that serves the business community in the areas of hiring and training. She notices that something has changed in the business community, because many of her recent placements and training plans have met with strong resistance. Her goal is to improve the quality of her placements so that business will welcome her efforts. She may go to a conference, attend a course, or conduct some personal research by talking to a selection of business people in her area. If she does not trust that her management can see this as a legitimate learning need, she may fear they will see this as a deficiency disqualifying her for future promotion. In that case, she will not acknowledge the need. She is more likely to ignore the problem or blame the employers.

Clearly, this learning goal cannot be driven merely by personal concerns for success. The Department of Labor also has goals regarding their service to the business community. In the best circumstances, where trust fosters the free flow of information, personal and organizational goals mesh and provide a powerful impetus for learning. At a minimum, coordination of a learning goal may be a compromise accomplished at the lowest cost to employee motivation and with the best match to organizational goals.

Placing responsibility for learning in the employee's hands also fosters critical reflection. The same woman will provide more effective service to businesses if she has the habit of stepping back from her work and thinking about the last placement and why it did or did not work for the employer. She may need to give special attention to the placement that did not work in contrast to the four preceding placements that did work. Critical reflection and the analysis, which such reflection generates, are central to the problem-solving and critical thinking skills. Her reflection on her work also increases her potential productivity as a member of any problem-solving or project team.

Finally, self-directed learning compliments and supports the overall empowerment strategy of TQM. If DOL tells employees that they are responsible for making decisions and empowered to serve their customers, the message is reinforced and consistent if they are also made responsible for their learning and development. A TQM approach would say that the woman is responsible for actively pursuing the businessman's satisfaction with each placement. Traditional training procedures would say that the same woman should wait for her manager to identify her training needs. Yet, it may be the need for learning that ensures that customer's satisfaction. The two messages must be consistent.

THE SUPERVISOR'S ROLE IN SELF-DIRECTED LEARNING

By definition, responsibility for self-directed learning must reside with the individual learner. There are numerous reasons, however, why self-directed learning cannot be left completely to the individual. Previous experiences may limit what adults see, what they expect, and what they can ultimately do. Their years of school, sitting in classrooms waiting for the teacher to call on them or give them an assignment, can translate into waiting for the manager to identify how the job should be learned and who will learn what.

Organizational and situational constraints may also keep adults from exercising self-direction. The lack of rewards for exercising self-direction may suggest to employees that the organization does not value self-directed learning. The employees may be so overloaded with work that there is no time to reflect about work or imagine taking time to learn new skills. The organization that tells employees to be self-directed but provides no opportunities to do so will not see self-directed behavior.

There may also be individual reasons why particular adults are not ready to exercise self-direction. Some employees may suffer from low self-esteem. Because they do not believe they can do well, they do not look for ways to improve. Some employees may not have the personal commitment to high achievement in their job. For them, extra learning for higher job performance holds little interest. In addition, personal differences among employees may play a role in the use of self-direction. Those with a number of previous, negative learning experiences may be reluctant to seek out new learning experiences.

Finally, the level of trust in the organization can have a particularly dampening effect on self-directed learning. Employees who mistrust management are likely to maintain a defensive stance at work. They avoid acknowledging any deficits which management might use as a reason for not giving them desired pay raises or promotions. If the woman in the employer services unit mistrusts her management, she will hide her lack of knowledge and avoid discussing problems she encounters. She is more likely to blame the employer for her unsuccessful job placements. She will pay more attention to the weaknesses in the employer's description of a job opening. After all, if he could only be clearer, she could send him the right people. She cannot consider how she could learn more about this new job category or find a way to improve her own procedures. Unless she feels free to acknowledge her deficiencies as the first step in learning, self-directed learning cannot take place.

All of these factors indicate the importance of having supervisors who create trust and encourage self-direction. Supervisors can support, encourage, and guide self-directed learning in a number of ways. They can hold periodic meetings to encourage employees to engage in the critical reflection that is the beginning of the self-directed process. They can create an atmosphere in which all employees treat errors, skill deficits, and customer dissatisfactions as opportunities to problem solve and identify solutions. In such an atmosphere, trust grows and individuals are motivated to admit problems. Once employees are relieved from the fear of being harmed by admitting mistakes and needs, they become open to finding their own solutions and helping others to find theirs.

DOL's plans for addressing this include training for employees in how to identify learning needs and seek opportunities for learning. They also plan manager training in facilitating these activities at least in the short term. What is more important, they plan to train managers in building the trust in a new standard in which employees see mistakes and problems as opportunities. The standard will begin with the managers, themselves, and their ability to see the opportunities in their own mistakes.

The long-term strategy includes a schedule for introducing the tools of TQM. Within that schedule, DOL will weave the continued themes of trust and self-direction. Employees will be trained to make decisions on the job and about what they must learn to grow and develop in their job. As long as trust exists, employees will continue to take the risks that maintain a learning organization.

Implementing TQM with Self-Directed Teams

By Michael J. Brower

ABSTRACT

Teams are highly useful, probably essential, vehicles for implementing TQM. Most companies developing TQM have used temporary Project Teams, also called Process Improvement Teams (PITs) or Process Action Teams (PATs) to study and recommend improvements in critical processes. More recently a large and rapidly growing number of organizations are removing and retraining their first line supervisors, flattening their hierarchies, and building Self-Directed Teams (SDTs) at the base, the frontline, of their organizations. These SDTs serve as the main building block of the organization; they plan, carry out, and improve the daily work of the organization. And they become the main vehicle for implementing TQM in the day to day operations—all without traditional direct supervision. But SDTs are not simple or easy to create, develop, and support. For significant and lasting success, SDTs must be Empowered, which means they must have Authority, Ableness, Accountability, and Alignment. In addition, Empowered Teams depend upon Reinforcing Support from around and above them, on Leadership, at four levels, and on everyone's understanding that this is an Evolutionary process.

INTRODUCTION AND OVERVIEW

Total Quality Management, or TQM, has many different meanings. The definition I choose to work with is the one developed and refined by the Research Committee of GOAL/QPC. TQM is "a structured system for creating organization-wide partici-

---

1992 article reprinted with the permission of the author.

pation in planning and implementing a continuous improvement process to meet and exceed customer needs.''

Fundamental to this definition of TQM, and most others, are the purposes of meeting and exceeding customer needs, a focus on processes, a commitment to continuous improvement, and the importance of involving the whole organization, all employees, in this effort and system.

The most common way of involving employees in most approaches to TQM is through the use of Project Teams, also called, in various organizations, Quality Improvement Teams, Process Improvement Teams, or Process Action Teams. These teams may be formed within a particular function or department. Usually they are cross-functional, involving employees from all of the departments and functions that own a part of the process targeted for improvement. Normally these teams focus only on that single specific topic or issue or process needing improvement. Usually they are temporary, finishing their work in a few weeks or months and disbanding. Often they are led by an appointed Team Leader, typically a manager. In every case their members are representatives of their respective functions and do not include all the employees in any single department.

In some organizations, supervisors are encouraged and trained to form teams of all their employees to work on improving processes. These teams may be more permanent, they may work on many process improvement ideas, and they may involve all employees in a given work area. By definition, they are supervisor led and the traditional role of the supervisor is unchanged.

However, going beyond these common approaches to TQM, a rapidly growing number of organizations are turning to a different kind of team, the Self-Directed Team (SDT), or Self-Directed Work Team, as the basic building block of their organizations for doing and managing the daily work, and as the fundamental group for implementing TQM at the base and on the front line.

SELF-DIRECTED TEAMS: DEFINITIONS, DESCRIPTIONS, AND DIFFERENCES FROM OTHER TEAMS/QUALITY CIRCLES

Self-Directed Teams are:

> On-going teams that plan, perform, and improve their own value-adding work and develop the ableness to do this, all without traditional direct supervision. They also determine their own Direction in interdependence and alignment with customers and other teams and with the Direction of the organizational levels above. They are composed of all the people who work in a given work area,

A typical Self-Directed Team will have anywhere from 5–20 members, including all of the people who work in a given work area. If there are too many people for one team, two or more teams will be formed, with each team taking accountability for a complete value-adding transform process or set of processes. These teams typically will have the authority to plan and schedule their work, to assign work among team members, to schedule their own vacations, to hold regular meetings daily or weekly or both, and to call special meetings as needed. They solve problems and improve processes. But in addition, they manage themselves—all day long, every day—without traditional supervision. They manage their equipment and may even repair it themselves when they have the necessary know-how. They manage their own material inputs and they are responsible for their own quality. They have no supervisor. SDTs are thus different from Quality Circles and Employee Involvement Groups and similar Teams popular a few years ago that typically had little or no authority, that had volunteer membership, and that made very few fundamental changes in how work was structured and managed.

Self-Directed Teams are also different from the Project Teams, or Process Improvement Teams, widely used today for developing process improvements under TQM. These Project Teams may or may not have any clear authority, they have a specific focus and a limited life. They are usually made up of representatives of several departments or functions. These differences are illustrated below.

SOME DIFFERENCES BETWEEN SELF-DIRECTED TEAMS AND PROJECT TEAMS

Project Teams	Self-Directed Teams
Temporary	Permanent
Cross Functional/Cross Departmental/ Cross Unit	Within one department or function or unit
Representatives of Different Departments	Everybody in the Department or unit is on the Team
Focus on a Single Process Improvement	Team Plans, Does, Improves All their Work; focus on customers
Led by appointed Manager, Supervisor, or sometimes, Hourly Employee	Led by elected, or sometimes in the beginning appointed, Team Leader
Team finishes its project and disbands	Team does the daily work, works on many improvement projects; never disbands
Team makes recommendations to upper management or a Steering Committee; usually given little decision authority	Team empowered to make decisions; as scope and depth of Ableness grows, Team given more and more authority
Employees still have supervisor	As team develops readiness, supervisor is phased out

---

THE HISTORY AND BENEFITS OF SELF-DIRECTED TEAMS

SDTs are not new. Although they are only now reaching widespread use as an ideal vehicle for creating continuous improvement at the front line under TQM, their existence in some U.S. companies goes back long before anyone started talking about and implementing TQM in this country.

Those whose national pride is bothered by all of the TQM techniques and tools imported from Japan might be pleased to learn that SDTs were not invented in Japan or imported here from Japan. They were born in England in the late 1940s

(Trist, 1981) and gained some footholds in Norway, Sweden, India, and Australia in the next couple of decades—usually under the title of Autonomous Work Groups, or Semi-Autonomous Work Groups. In this country several companies were already building new plants based on SDTs in the late 1960s, under the name of Technician Systems (Procter & Gamble) and Intact Work Groups or High Performance Teams in General Foods and other companies. Based on the early very impressive results, Procter & Gamble today has many plants with SDTs, and several hundred of our largest and many hundreds more not-so-large companies have at least one plant or office area organized this way.

The roster of U.S. SDT users includes: A. O. Smith, Aid Association for Lutherans, AT&T Credit, Bridgestone, Coors Brewery, Corning, Cummins Engine, Diebold, Inc., DuPont, Frito-Lay, General Foods, General Motors, Harley Davidson, Hewlett-Packard, Honda America, Johnsonville Foods, Loyola University Medical Center, Motorola, Northern Telecom, Alliant Health Care Systems, Rohm & Haas, Saturn Corporation, Skippy Peanut Butter, Tektronix, the Town of Windsor, Connecticut, Xerox, General Electric, Texas Instruments, Quad Graphics, Masland Industries, and many, many more.

Why have so many companies, and the number is expanding very rapidly now, decided to implement SDTs? Because the benefits are enormous when these Teams are well designed, established, and supported. There are many documented quantifiable benefits in terms of improved quality, increased productivity and reduced costs, and improved service to customers. In manufacturing, these SDTs balance the production line by smoothly shifting cross trained team members up and down the line as needed. In any organization, they adapt quickly to replace absent employees with the most qualified possible temporary replacements. In the design world these teams contribute to creating better product and service designs in greatly reduced time.

Major cost savings come not only from increased frontline worker productivity, but also from reduced levels of hierarchy, of bureaucracy, since one level, or even several levels of supervisors or managers are taken out. These flatter organizations, compared to a traditional hierarchical organization, save a great deal of money now being spent on middle managers' salaries, benefits, offices, support staffs, and other perks. This also reduces the time required for decision making. And it improves the quality of decisions, because those with frontline information are making many more decisions themselves, based on real unadulterated information. In traditional hierarchies, the quality of information decreases (decreased signal to noise ratio in technical language) as information is moved across several boundaries upward in a traditional hierarchy (and sometimes across) to the level authorized to make a decision, and again when the decision is moved back down to those on the front lines who will implement it.

Other related benefits of empowered SDTs are improved flexibility and responsiveness to customer requirements—a greater ability to "turn on a dime" and give a situation specific appropriate response, quickly, to individual customers. For the employees, there are benefits of increasing skills and knowledge, and greater understanding of the whole, of how their work fits into and contributes to the ultimate end user of the product or service. This enhances state of being and self-worth, and increases employees' ableness to work in teams, interdependently. Overall, this brings a greater meaning to work, and a greater ownership of the work. All of this, in turn leads to reduced turnover and absenteeism from employment. Finally, it probably leads to improved mental and physical health, although on this I have anecdotal but not published scientific evidence.

THE REQUIREMENTS FOR SELF-DIRECTED TEAMS TO BECOME EMPOWERED AND TO SUCCEED

One does not make changes this significant in the structures and operations of large organizations, and one does not reap such deep and widespread benefits quickly, easily, or cheaply. Establishing and developing Self-Directed Teams, and creating the required organizational support above and around them, is a complex and difficult process.

After years of working with teams, both empowered and not-so-empowered, I have developed a definitional model of Team Empowerment. Put simply, empowerment requires that Teams have the four A's and that they receive Reinforcement, Leadership, and understanding that this is a process of *Evolution* over time. So:

Empowerment means   *Authority* delegated to the Teams,
Accountability accepted by the Teams,
Alignment of the Teams' Direction, and
Ableness development of the Teams.

In addition, for Empowerment to succeed over time, these Teams need

Reinforcement from around and above the teams,
Leadership within, of, and above the Teams, and
Evolution over time.

The remaining sections of this chapter examine these seven requirements in more detail.

AUTHORITY DELEGATION TO THE TEAMS AND ACCOUNTABILITY ACCEPTANCE BY SDTs

Authority to make decisions without checking with "the boss," or his boss above, is what most people think of first when they talk about empowerment. It is basic. If a team can make decisions on its own, without getting specific permission from someone above them in the hierarchy, then they have at least some authority. If the team, or individuals within it, can spend up to a certain amount of money on their own decision, then they have that degree of authority.

Authority is therefore not seamless; it is not "all or nothing," although organizations and managers sometimes make the mistake of acting as though it is. Teams can be, and should be, given specific degrees of authority for specific realms of decision making, with the degree and number of realms or arenas of authority growing as the teams developing Ableness and demonstrated Accountability justifies it.

Here is a generic list of the kinds of decision authority that many Self-Directed Teams have been delegated, in some degree or other, in a wide range of manufacturing and service organizations.

Planning their work; scheduling their work; team member assignment; material input control; quality; equipment management; equipment maintenance; vacation scheduling; dealing with team member absenteeism and tardiness; balancing the production line; writing and upgrading process descriptions; problem solving; process improvement; safety; housekeeping; budgeting; environmental control; expenditure control; service recovery; team ableness development through training and other means; screening, selecting and hiring new members; peer review on knowledge and skills for pay increases; disciplining team members; and firing. (These last two are often specifically *not* taken on by teams in their first few years, except for informal forms of peer pressure and discipline.)

Accountability is the other side of the Authority coin. Accountability means: "I, or we, accept accountability for designated activities, for designated responsibilities, for managing and improving designated processes, and/or for creating designated outcomes." In short, it means: "You can count on me to . . ." People in our society often say they want authority. Some are less eager to accept accountability. It is "where the rubber meets the road," and "where the buck stops." Yet without accountability, authority delegation won't last; it will be pulled back as a result of performance failures. So authority delegation and accountability acceptance must march forward, in parallel, hand-in-hand.

Here is a specific example of this kind of accountability acceptance. For public training workshops we need to have workbooks prepared, printed, and inserted into three-ring binders, with copies ready for each participant at 8:00 A.M. on the opening morning. As the trainer, I am accountable for preparing the master copy of the workbook and turning it in to production people with enough lead time for them to get it ready. Even if I do this, the print shop may be backed up and deliver the copied material late in the afternoon before the workshop to the person who is to assemble the workbook into 25 three-ring binders. He then goes to the stock room and finds only 7 of the correct size binder. It is almost 5:00 P.M. What does he do? If he is a "normal," "unempowered" employee who has not accepted accountability, he (1) blasts the print shop for taking so long; (2) curses (under his breath) the person who let the supply of three ring binders run down so low; (3) packs the few that are available; (4) maybe notifies his supervisor, if she is still around, that she has a problem to solve; and (5) goes home at 5:00 P.M. as always.

But if he is a person who has accepted accountability for his piece, his role, in this value adding stream, as I have defined accountability, he does something like the following, all without having to ask permission, or be told or asked to do this by a supervisor. He: (1) checks around the stock room and the offices to see if anybody has stashed away somewhere enough empty binders. Finding none, he: (2) telephones around to find an office supply store that is open late and that has enough acceptable binders, and he telephones home to warn that he will be late; (3) drives his own car, or gets a friend to drive him or takes a taxi if no car is available; (4) buys the binders with his own cash, check, or credit card; (5) stays late to pack all the necessary binders; (6) checks his work carefully; (7) places one workbook at each person's place in the training room; and (8) scans the room to see if there is anything else missing or to be done (not his job of course); before (9) going home very late. The next day he submits his costs for reimbursement. He also goes to the appropriate team or manager to suggest that a team go to work on improving the critical processes of maintaining adequate stocks of binders and of getting printing orders ready, to the print shop in time, and out of the print shop in time, for he and others to have adequate time for assembling materials into binders and checking their work.

Another example. A hotel employee took a telephone call, receiving a message for an elderly guest who was not in her room. The message was that she should call home and prepare to return home immediately because a close relative was gravely ill. In addition the caller expressed grave concern because the guest was very elderly, was traveling with a tour group on a set ticket, was perhaps too frail to travel alone without the help of her group from the hotel to the plane, and might not have enough money or credit available to buy the special ticket. The hotel employee reassured the worried caller that he would handle everything for the elderly guest, and "not to worry," and that he would report back.

The hotel employee then: (1) found the elderly guest, and in the kindest way he could think of, notified her of the family member's grave illness; (2) reassured the guest that he would handle her airline reservation and get her to the airport and onto the plane; (3) called the airline, reserved a seat, paid for it on his own credit card, and asked the airline to have a flight attendant ready to watch over the passenger and to have a wheelchair available for her at the other end; (4) arranged for hotel personnel to back him up during his time away (because they worked in effective teams this was not difficult); (5) assisted the woman to check out and get her bags down to his car; (6) drove her to the airport and personally escorted her onto the plane; (7) verified with the flight attendant that the message had come through and that the passenger would be taken care of on the flight and at the destination; (8) telephoned back to the relative who had made the initial call and told her of the arrangements and arrival time; and (9) learned how he would be reimbursed for the cost of the ticket.

Sound unlikely? Exaggerated? Utopian? Well, it actually happened. This is the kind of accountability that empowered employees are accepting and demonstrating in those companies that have moved into, or are in transit towards providing world-class quality of product and service.

ABLENESS DEVELOPMENT IN SDTs

Self-Directed Teams require all of the Ableness to plan and do their basic work; to chart, study, control, and improve their processes; to plan and lead effective meetings, to reconcile conflict, and to accept the authority and perform the roles and processes formerly in the job description of the supervisor. This is not simple or easy to accomplish. It is in fact a tall order, and requires a long and difficult and sometimes expensive process of individual and team development.

Ableness is not a common term; it needs defining. Ableness is the state of being Able to perform well in a given role, or in a set or mixture of roles. This includes being capable of handling certain tasks, which means having the knowledge and skills necessary to perform these tasks. Being able to perform also requires a certain state of being, a level of mental energy, a sense of self-worth and self-esteem. Without these, a person, even with all the necessary knowledge and skills, may still not be able to perform the roles. Finally, Ableness requires that there be sufficient Affirming and Receptive Will in the person or team to take on the roles and perform them well. In street language, motivation or determination are terms we use for affirming will. Being a good listener and being open to change are common terms for receptive will.

Back to our SDT. As a whole the team will need to have, or develop, a wide range of job skills plus coordinating, decision making, communicating, and conflict resolution capabilities, plus the whole kit bag of TQM/SPC problem solving and process improvement capabilities. In addition, the Team will need to develop its own identity, its own culture, or norms and values and state of being. Furthermore, the Team will, to be successful, have to develop its own Mission and Vision, and to hold and live out a strong set of values which will serve to pull forth the will and effort of its individual members.

But the team of course is made up of individual members. Those SDTs which have survived the longest and been most effective are those that have done the best job of respecting, nurturing, developing and utilizing the individual Ableness, the self-identity, of its members. In short it is not team development *or* individual development; it is team development *and* individual development. It is not team identity *or* individual identity; it is team identity *and* individual identity that are required.

Call it Ableness, as I do here, or capability, or whatever, SDTs both depend upon, and serve to create, a wide range of knowledge and skill development, a strong and healthy state of being/identity, and a high degree of will or motivation, in its members and itself. The organization embarking on the establishment of Self-Directed Teams, either to support TQM or for whatever other reasons, had best recognize up front that a major investment in training and coaching will be required. Or they might as well not start.

ALIGNMENT OF DIRECTION WITH SDTs

Highly successful SDTs have their own Mission or Purpose, and they have a Vision, whether written or not, that guides and pulls its members together and forward. They develop their own set of guiding principles, either as written principles or as unwritten norms of behavior, that help individual members make difficult decisions on behalf of the team, customers, and the overall business.

This combination of Mission, Vision, and Principles is what I call Direction. Do SDTs set their own Direction? Yes. But not in isolation. We are talking about teams that exist within, and carry out, the basic work of large organizations. So they cannot be totally Self Directed, to the exclusion of taking account the needs, requirements, and expectations of other stakeholders. If every SDT, or for that matter every team of any kind, or every work department or functional unit in a modern organization set its own Direction, and optimized its own performance, in isolation from the others, the result would be sub-optimization of the whole at best, and chaos and anarchy at worst.

The way we reconcile this is to acknowledge, and insist, that Self-Directed Teams determine their own Direction in *interdependence and alignment with* customers and other teams, and with the Direction of organizational levels above. It is important that each SDT develop its own Mission. And it is important that this Mission be aligned with the corporate Mission. It is also important that this not be a one way street. If the corporation, or other large organization, wants its work to be done, improved, and managed by SDTs, then the organization must also learn how to align its Mission, Vision, and Principles with those of its SDTs and with the general requirements for successful SDTs.

But we are left with a bit of unease about terminology. The problem is the same as that facing those SDT ancestors which were called "Autonomous Work Groups." Critics said these Work Groups or Teams were not really autonomous, since they were part of, and interdependent with, larger organizations. So in some companies these came to be called "Semi-Autonomous Work Groups." OK. It satisfied truth in labeling requirements. But it doesn't exactly roll easily off your tongue. So we don't hear so much about them anymore. So what should we call Self-Directed Teams? One organization, I've been told, calls them Shared-Directed Work Teams. More nearly correct, but clumsy. So I will continue to call SDTs Self-Directed Teams, and will continue to try to help all parties understand that we live in an interdependent world and work in interdependent teams, and that Directions must be set interdependently.

REINFORCEMENT AND SUPPORT FOR SDTs FROM AROUND AND ABOVE

There are at least half a dozen different kinds of support that SDTs require from their larger organizations.

1. There need to be several or many SDTs starting at once. If only a couple of SDTs are launched initially, there is a high probability that failure of the one or two will result in cancellation of the whole idea. "Don't put all your eggs in one basket." So one form of reinforcement that the initial SDTs need is that of numbers, to have enough started at once so that even if one or two fail or limp along, the others will still survive.

2. The initial SDTs should not be set up as "pilots" in an "experiment" to decide whether to cancel the whole idea of SDTs, or to expand the concept into additional departments and teams. If SDTs are seen as an experiment, which may be cancelled if the initial teams don't do so well, then those who feel threatened by

them will find ways, subtle or not-so-subtle, to sabotage the pilots and make sure the experiment fails. The support these initial SDTs need is that they be viewed not as a pilot to decide whether or not to go forward, but rather as pilots from which to learn what leadership, training, and other support will be required to insure success of present and future SDTs. The decision to go forward with SDTs should have already been made, up front.

3. Support Functions. SDTs are often, although not always, initially set up in production or other operations departments and groups. If so, they will need reinforcement and support from the other functions and departments. For example, production SDTs cannot succeed without a lot of help from maintenance people, since so many line improvements they will think of will require maintenance help in rebuilding equipment, moving equipment, adding or moving controls and a thousand other ways to improve the production process. Production teams also are greatly dependent upon the Purchasing and Materials Control people, who can make or break a production team by succeeding in supplying the quality and quantity of parts and other inputs which the production team depends upon. Other support functions are from time to time equally important to SDTs—HRD, Engineering, Accounting, Payroll, and Information Systems, among others. Many of these departments, in traditional large organizations, will refuse telephone calls and requests for information from hourly people. They will ask them over and over "who are you?" and tell them "you are not authorized to file a maintenance (engineering, training, purchase order) request" and instruct them to "have your supervisor call us." To succeed, SDTs will need a whole revolution in mind set in these support functions, so that they shift from suspicion and hostility to truly being *support* functions—even to these new, dangerous looking SDTs!

4. Systems. SDTs are based on new paradigm assumptions about people, trust, human development, the importance of processes, and so on. Most of the systems in a large organization were created at various times, for various purposes, and based on various sets of assumptions about people, human nature, the purpose of the organization, etc. Although SDTs can survive and even thrive in an organization with outdated systems, eventually it will become very important to review and revise as necessary all of the important systems of the organization. These include the Management Information Systems, the Absenteeism and Tardiness Control Systems, the Discipline Systems, the Pay and Promotion Systems, the Performance Review System, the Purchasing Systems, and the Materials Control System.

5. Mistakes. Empowerment and Growth require experimentation, taking risks, pushing boundaries, and therefore, inevitably, making mistakes. If we are not making mistakes, we are being too cautious, not taking any risks, not stretching ourselves at all. SDTs will make mistakes, must make mistakes. What will be the attitude and behavior of upper and middle management when the SDTs make their mistakes? Will they scold or worse, at the team and member that made the mistake? Once or twice is all it will take before risk taking, and empowerment,

will be driven out. Or will managers leave the teams alone as they make mistakes, or encourage them to learn from the mistake, and reinforce the expectation that empowered people take risks and occasionally make mistakes?

6. Celebrating Successes. Positive reinforcement means SDTs celebrating their successes, and having lots of management support for, and participation in this.

LEADERSHIP OF AND ABOVE SDTs, AT FOUR LEVELS

Four levels of leadership are required for successful Empowered Teams: (1) The Team Leader (Leader *of* the Team); (2) Distributed Leadership Within the Team (Leaders *in* the Team); (3) The Leader *above* the Team; and (4) Executive Leadership of the organization.

Team Leader

The first level of Leadership is that of Team Leader, the one person (or in some cases two persons) who are selected or elected to be *the* Team leader. Some people argue that a team doesn't need one single designated leader. They say that leadership can float around the team, that the leadership that is needed in any situation will simply come forth as needed, or that the "natural leader" of the team will emerge. No doubt these alternatives can and sometimes do happen. A group of friends who play jazz together for fun and an occasional paid gig certainly don't have to designate one of their members as "the leader" if they don't want to. And they may play, and work, very well together. Even inside an organization the same thing *can* happen. Especially with very stable, mature, and experienced, teams. But the *probability* of a team succeeding, I believe, is greatly reduced if there is no one designated leader. So those of us guiding and leading the conversion of organizations to Self-Directed Teams have some obligation, I think, to strongly recommend that, to increase the probability of success, every team should have one person as the Leader.

Now, having said all that, four other related questions must be addressed. One, should this team leader be permanent, or rotating. Here the benefits of rotation seem very strong. It reduces the probability of turning a team leader into just an old fashioned supervisor with a different title. It gives several, and eventually perhaps all, team members an opportunity to grow into and step up to the requirements of Leadership.

The second question is: How often should leaders be rotated? My recommendation, in most cases, is that the rotation be fairly slow, such as every six to twelve months. This is enough to allow a significant amount of learning and Ableness development by the team leader during her/his term in office before it is passed on to another. However, SDTs in the real world are rotating their leaders every day, every week, every month or six weeks, and all the way up to once a year—or not at all.

The third question to be addressed is whether the Team leader should be elected by the team, or selected by management. On the face of it, the answer should be obvious: a Team, if it is empowered, will have the authority to elect its own leader. So long as the Team leader is appointed by management that is one aspect of authority, of empowerment that has been withheld from the team. However, management, especially in the initial period of transition from a traditional supervisory culture to an empowered team, is often reluctant to let go of the myth that management knows best when it comes to leadership. There is, of course, the legitimate concern that the team, any team, might turn the leadership election into a popularity contest, electing the member most popular but not most qualified to be leader. To reduce this risk I encourage teams, and coach internal facilitators to do the same, to think about and record on a flipchart what characteristics they are looking for in their leader, what qualities of character are important in leadership. This should take place a week or two before there are any actual nominations or election for leader. Managers observing this process are sometimes surprised that very similar qualities of leadership emerge from this process, regardless of whether the team is highly educated professionals or high school dropouts in low-skilled jobs.

Sometimes management still insists on appointing the Team Leader(s), even after being offered this process, and even after accepting the undeniable argument that election increases the leaders' legitimacy with the rest of the team, compared to an appointed leader. Management clings to the security of a more traditional approach in which they exercise their right (i.e. power) and allegedly superior judgment to appoint the team leader. In such cases I strongly recommend that management appoint *only* the first leader, and only for a fixed term of 3 to 6 or 8 or 9 months, that is called a transition period for team formation and development, after which the team will elect its own leaders.

Another question emerges in the case of management appointed team leadership. Should management appoint the existing supervisor to be team leader? Pros: It solves the problem, at least temporarily, of where to place the existing supervisor. It retains the work knowledge and skills of the supervisor in that area which otherwise might be lost. It allows for a transition period that may be less disruptive than if the supervisor were pulled out with very short notice. Cons: Very little may change. The supervisor may—in fact is very likely to—continue to act in the same old way with a new title of Team Leader. Team members may come out more cynical than ever; if the organization is making no real change in authority/empowerment it is better not to make claims (propaganda?) that something is changing.

Reconciliation: If management decides to appoint the existing supervisor, they should make sure that the following six things also happen simultaneously:

1. The supervisor, and team, are told that this is temporary, for a known period of time.
2. A commitment is made that in x months the team will elect its own leader.
3. The supervisor is given, well in advance, a new and different future role in the organization.
4. The supervisor is told, repeatedly, that his/her present temporary assignment is to lead the team, not direct and control it in the old paradigm, and to develop the

team's Ableness, so that in x time the team will no longer need the experience, knowledge, skills, etc. of the supervisor. The performance rating system is changed, and the supervisor is fully informed about this change, to reflect this new transitional role of the supervisor. Her/his next performance review will in large part depend upon how well s/he prepared the team during this transition period.

5. The supervisor is given lots of training and coaching, up front, and on-going, in mind-set and skills, overall Ableness actually, to be a leader-coach instead of the former boss-manager.

6. The manager above the supervisor (see below) not only monitors this process, and steps in to facilitate any needed adjustments; she also learns how to be a leader-coach herself and thereby is able to be a role model. S/he "walks the talk" and "educates by example."

Distributed Leadership within the Team

Even if a company moves, immediately or after a transition period, from appointing a Team Leader to enabling the Team to elect its own Leader, there remains a considerable risk of the Team relying too much on the judgment and decision making of that one person. The result can be, even with an elected Team Leader, that the Team comes to function very little differently than it did under a more traditional Supervisor. One answer is Distributed Leadership within the Team. Not instead of, but in addition to, an elected Team Leader.

This is usually accomplished by having the team define, with help from an experienced facilitator, the main or key processes that it needs to manage well, or have someone manage well for it, to enable it to create and deliver high quality products/ services to its customers. This is the parallel, at the level of an SDT, of a whole organization determining its Critical Processes under a TQM implementation model. The facilitator then puts to the Team questions such as these: Under our prior system, who was responsible for ensuring that these processes, essential for our team success, were managed well? (The typical answer that comes back is: "The Supervisor.") Second question: Under our new system, with a single elected Team Leader, who are we likely to expect will handle all these processes? (Usual answer: "The Team Leader"). This can lead into a full discussion of what Empowerment really means and requires, of the risks of putting too much on the shoulders of one person, and of the importance of all members taking some accountability. This then leads to the idea of Distributed Leadership, under which various team members each take accountability for being a Coordinator for one of these key processes for a given limited time period such as six months.

The actual processes which need to be managed or coordinated are often grouped around a visual structural model, such as a five pointed star, which helps insure completeness and distinctiveness in describing the requirements for a successful on-going entity such as a Team. The star, used first in Procter and Gamble and DuPont team-based plants, originally had the following five general categories, derived by consultant Charles Krone from general systems theory: Managing or Leading

Processes, Site Processes, Operations Processes, Personnel Processes, and Auditing Processes. Today, after many adaptations and copies of copies there are dozens of different versions of this star in use, and in the literature on SDTs.

There are many benefits of having some, or if possible all, team members accepting accountability for one of these processes for a time, and then later for others. These benefits include:

1. It focuses Accountability for each key process with a single person (or in very large teams it is sometimes one Coordinator and an Assistant Coordinator, or Back-up Coordinator, or Coordinator in Training).
2. It avoids overloading Accountability, Authority, and work on one single person—the Team Leader.
3. It enhances participation in team planning and decision making.
4. It provides personal growth and development "stretch" opportunities for many or all team members. I like to call SDTs, with Distributed Leadership, "Schools of Leadership."
5. Overall, it results in enhanced team synergy and in the team becoming a "Learning Organization."

The Leader above the Team

Self-Directed Teams, by definition, do not have a Supervisor. But, except in the most advanced, dynamic, free-form and experimental organizations, SDTs do still fit within a hierarchy and are responsible (Accountable) to a Manager above them. This manager may have three or four or as many as eight or ten SDTs in the organization chart "under" her/him. This manager may in the past have operated very much like a traditional boss-manager. Job description, written or informal: Direct and Control people. Make decisions. Tell supervisors what to do. Hold them accountable. Reward the good supervisors, reform or drive out the weak ones, etc., etc. If this manager continues to operate out of this old mind set, the SDTs below will not thrive nor even survive for long. Such a manager, with no first line supervisors between him and the teams, will be frequently tempted to move into the area of one SDT after another and start behaving like the traditional supervisor would have in the old days. The manager will be tempted into trying to be a substitute himself for the removed supervisors. Of course with several teams, and up to 100 individual employees in those teams, the new span-of-control is so wide that these efforts will inevitably fail. Nobody can give direct supervision, or succeed at directly managing, so many people. That is the virtue of such an extended span-of-control: it makes it evident to all that traditional efforts to manage other people can't work and must be replaced with something better—empowerment. The something better is Leading and Coaching. Space does not allow for a full discussion of the beliefs, styles, and processes used by Leader-Coaches. In short the Leader-Coach creates with others a compelling mission and vision, operates from principle rather than from self-interest or whim, delegates, listens and ask questions a great deal, invests time and effort in evoking and enabling the development of others, and is constantly observing and managing his/her own thoughts, actions and state.

Perhaps one real example will serve to illuminate this significant shift from manager to leader-coach. A manager that I was working with once had been a traditional "direct and control" manager and was then put in charge of starting up a new product line composed of three new SDTs. This manager, who became a friend, asked me one day for advice. He said:

> I really feel unsure of myself in this new role. I'm never sure whether or not I'm dealing with employees in the right way. For example, this morning a member of one of our teams came up to me, explained a problem he was having, and asked me what to do. In the old days I would have told him. But this morning, I caught myself before answering, and instead I started asking him a series of questions. What do you think might work? Have you had a similar situation come up in the past? How did you handle that one? Did it work? What are some alternatives that you might consider? This seemed to work, because he eventually came up with a couple of ideas he wanted to check out. But did I do the right thing? It certainly took longer that just telling him what to do.

I reassured my friend that I thought he had done very well and that I admired two things. First, the way he handled the situation, turning it into an opportunity for the employee's continued growth in Ableness. And I also admired the way he was observing himself, reflecting on what he did, and seeking advice and help in assessing and improving himself. I told him I thought he was right on track, and serving as an excellent role model for other managers, ex-supervisors, and Team Leaders.

Other questions he might have asked the employee include: Who else on your team have you consulted with about this? Who might you go to? Does your team have a formally designated Coordinator for an area or process that includes this situation? Or is there a team member who would be particularly knowledgeable (or creative) about this kind of problem? Did you check this out with your Team Leader? What did he say? Etc., etc.

Executive Leadership

SDTs are sometimes established at the base of an organization, and succeed for a time, to some degree, without top executives' strong support. But rarely. And not for long. For SDTs to be established in more than an isolated department or two, and for them to reach their full evolution and potential, they depend in many ways on top executive strong support. Someone must lead in the creation of a vision of a new style organization based upon SDTs, and in the creation of a clear and compelling overall Mission that SDTs can align with. Someone must find new roles for present supervisors. Someone must insist that middle managers shift or evolve from being boss-managers into being leaders-coaches, and must be role models themselves from this process. Someone must allocate the resources—time and money—for the very significant amounts of training and meeting time required. Someone must make the decision to start sharing information, in understandable formats, about the competitive situation and economic health of the business all the way to the bottom, to the SDTs. Often this is information that until now has not even been shared with middle managers.

In short, establishing and developing SDTs in a way that leads to long term success requires major systemic changes in the whole organization. These changes must be led, can only be led, by top managers.

IT IS AN EVOLUTIONARY PROCESS

All involved should understand this. Three of the most important implications of this are:

1. Time. It takes many years to fully empower a team of employees who have been managed, and limited, in a traditional organization.
2. Development. Individual and team Ableness can evolve over time, if it is planned and supported and the PDCA cycle, or some equivalent structured model or approach, is used.
3. Persistence. Setbacks and difficulties are to be expected. All should be seen as, and turned into, learning opportunities. Teams must be allowed, even encouraged, to take risks. Taking risks means making mistakes, even failing. An evolutionary process is not straight and smooth. There will be failures along the way. Leadership must understand this, take it in stride, learn from it, and process with, in the words of Dr. Deming's First Point: Constancy of Purpose.

Bibliography

Articles

Alster, Norm. "What Flexible Workers Can Do," *Fortune,* February 13, 1989.

Blache, Klaus, M., et al. "Process Control and People at General Motors Delta Engine Plant," *IE,* March, 1988.

Brown, Tom. "Why Teams Go 'Bust,'" *Industry Week,* March 2, 1992.

Dumaine, Brian. "Who Needs a Boss?" *Fortune,* May 7, 1990.

Geber, B. "From Manager into Coach," *Training,* February 1992.

Hammer, Michael. "Reengineering Work: Don't Automate, Obliterate," *Harvard Business Review,* July-August 1990.

Hoerr, John. "The Cultural Revolution at A. O. Smith," *Business Week,* May 29, 1989.

Hoerr, John. "The Payoff from Teamwork," *Business Week,* July 10, 1989.

Holpp, Lawrence. "Making Choices: Self-Directed Teams or Total Quality Management," *Training,* May 1992.

Hughes, B. "25 Stepping Stones for Self-Directed Teams," *Training,* December 1991.

Reid, Peter C. "How Harley Beat Back the Japanese," *Fortune,* September 25, 1989.

Schelder, J. "Productivity," *Personnel Journal*, February 1992.

Semler, Ricardo. "Managing Without Managers," *Harvard Business Review*, September-October 1989.

Zenger, J. H., E. Musselwhite, K. Herson, and C. Perring. "Leadership in a Team Environment," *Training and Development*, December 1991.

Books

Barker, Joel Arthur. *Discovering the Future: The Business of Paradigms*, St. Paul: ILI Press, 1989.

Bothwell, Lin. *The Art of Leadership*, New York: Prentice-Hall, 1983.

Byham, William C. *Zapp! The Lightening of Empowerment*, Pittsburgh: Development Dimensions International Press, 1989.

Cohen, M. H. *The Power of Self-Management*, Oak Park, IL: Canoe Press, 1992.

Covey, Stephen R. *The 7 Habits of Highly Effective People*, New York: Simon & Schuster, 1989.

DePree, Max. *Leadership Is an Art*, New York: Bantam, Doubleday, Dell, 1989.

Emery, Fred E. *Systems Thinking*, Baltimore: Penguin Books, 1969.

Goodman, Paul S. & Associates. *Designing Effective Work Groups*, San Francisco: Jossey-Bass, 1986.

Hackman, J. Richard, Ed. *Groups That Work (and Those That Don't)*, San Francisco: Jossey-Bass, 1990.

Harper, Bob, and Ann Harper. *Skill-Building for Self-Directed Team Members*, Croton-on-Hudson: MW Corporation, 1989.

Harper, Bob, and Ann Harper. *Succeeding as a Self-Directed Work Team*, Croton-on-Hudson: MW Corporation, 1989.

Hicks, R. F., and D. Bone. *Self-Managing Teams: Creating and Maintaining Self-Managed Work Groups*, Los Altos, CA: Crisp Publications, Inc., 1990.

Johnsonville Sausage Co., Harvard Business School, Case Study Number 9–387–103, Revised 6/27/90.

Kelly, Mark. *The Adventures of a Self-Managing Team*, Raleigh, NC: Mark Kelly Books, 1992.

Ketchum, Lyman D., and Eric Trist. *All Teams Are Not Created Equal: How Employee Empowerment Really Works*, Newbury Park, CA: Sage Publications, Inc., 1992.

Lawler, Edward E., III. High-Involvement Management, San Francisco: Jossey-Bass, 1986.

Miller, Lawrence M., and Jennifer Howard. *Managing Quality through Teams*, Atlanta: The Miller Consulting Group, 1991.

Orsburn, Jack D., Linda Moran, Ed Musselwhite, and John H. Zenger. *Self-Directed Work Teams*, Homewood, IL 60430: Business One Irwin, 1991.

Peters, Tom. *Thriving on Chaos*, New York: Knopf, 1987.

Scholtes, Peter R. *The Team Handbook*, Madison, Joiner Associates Consulting Group, 1988.

Scott, C. D., and D. T. Jaffe. *Empowerment: A Practice Guide for Success*, Los Altos, CA: Crisp Publications, 1991.

Senge, Peter M. *The Fifth Discipline: The Art & Practice of the Learning Organization*, New York: Doubleday, 1990.

Trist, Eric. *The Evolution of Socio-Technical Systems,* Toronto: Ontario Quality of Working Life Centre, 1981. Reprinted in Andy Van de Ven and William Joyce, Eds., *Perspectives on Organizational Design and Behavior,* Wiley Interscience, 1981.

Weisbord, Marvin R. *Productive Workplaces,* San Francisco: Jossey-Bass, 1990.

Wellins, Richard S., William C. Byham, and Jeanne M. Wilson. *Empowered Teams,* San Francisco, CA: Jossey-Bass, Inc., 1991.

TQM: Labor–Management Cooperation

By Robert P. Waxler and Thomas Higginson

INTRODUCTION

Why do we need to change the conventional labor–management relationship? Let us begin to answer that question by using Taylorism as a type of metaphor for the problem in the workplace today.

Despite its original intentions, Taylorism today fits well with the tradition of hierarchy and command. It is a style of distance, rigidity, and discrete power. Imagine machines lined up in regimented order, equally distant one from the other. Time clocks bolted to the walls with stiff cards next to them ready to be punched; the plant functioning within specialized compartments: production, personnel, sales—each with its own preconceived definitions. The worker fits within these boundaries: his effectiveness is first controlled from above, and then the final quality of his work is inspected by a manager at the end of the line, after the product is completed for shipping to the marketplace.

Taylorism today is identified with bureaucratic efficiency without a human face, a deadening science that undermines quality rather than creating it. Despite a clear understanding that Taylorism served its purpose and is now outmoded, too many companies refuse to break from it to establish a new approach to achieving quality. Taylorism has slowly led to mistrust in the corporate culture, to the rule of management controls rather than the sense of responsibility that comes with the freedom of mature human creativity.

The pioneers of the revolution in quality—Deming, Juran, Feigenbaum, Crosby—understood that Taylorism could no longer work because people could no longer accept the denial of their human identity nor could they accept an adversarial approach to work itself. And that notion of the need for human identity and the need

1992 article reprinted with the permission of the authors.

for community, it seems to us, is the central one that needs to be considered when thinking about the revolution in quality in the workplace. We cannot have quality products unless they have the human imprint, and we cannot have that human imprint unless we have a corporate culture that has been humanized through meaningful communication.

It is the Total Quality Management (TQM) approach that appears to be at the current forefront of this revolution, a revolution that emphasizes the organic process of change, the importance of long-term commitment, to hope of participating in decision making that always points to the possibility of improvement, and the challenge of the world market itself. When we think of TQM in these terms, we can see its humanistic and communal thrust. Unlike the late stages of Taylorism, TQM is empowering. It offers back to all of us the possibility of cooperation and the rejuvenation of the human face.

Historically, the issue of quality was really not an issue of human identity, but an issue of "quality control." It was, in other words, an issue connected with Taylorism. The primary responsibility for quality rested with the inspection group, not with the makers or producers of the product. In this context, quality was thought about as if it could be approached primarily as a quantitative skill. It was fragmented. Quality was not a human value, but a commodity that could be measured like all other commodities.

To us it is obvious that without the involvement of the makers in the decision-making and judgment-making processes, quality could not be created because the processes lacked that genuine human dimension that we like to think of as the "human spirit." Furthermore, quality could not be achieved because the emphasis was placed on the quantitative results rather than the human processes of creation and decision making.

It is this notion, we believe, (i.e., that quality is primarily a human process rather than an end product) that is at the center of the revolution in thinking about quality. For it is this sense of process that can rejuvenate the meaning of human identity and cooperation in the workplace, a necessity if quality is to be achieved. At the same time, it must be noted that such changes in the perception of the process and achievement of quality cannot occur by chance. The top leaders have to be genuinely committed, training has to be offered, and management itself has to admit that it has been to a large extent the problem. In addition, customers have to be listened to, and attention has to be paid to the human networks that make up this total process of quality. In this context, new relationships between management and labor need to be forged, relationships that emphasize cooperation rather than adversity, flexibility rather than rigidity.

LABOR–MANAGEMENT CULTURE

In the Taylor model, management has too often forgotten that labor is an important human agent in the formulation and control of the production process. This kind of neglect has created, in turn, a profound sense of mistrust that has often led to lower productivity and poor quality at a time when increased productivity and high quality are often the only way for a company to survive. As Lawrence Bankowski, the national president of the American Flint Glass Workers Union, put it at the Conference Board's Third Annual Quality Conference: "Our union represents most of the hourly employees at Corning. We are involved with quality for one reason: survival. We can't survive in the global market unless we produce top quality." For Bankowski, the American worker wants to work in partnership with management, but management must commit to creating a trust culture that supports the human efforts of labor.

At Corning, management and the union, since 1989, have drawn up company goals together, creating a cooperative rather than an adversarial culture. Not only has this type of process significantly increased the number on the bottom line for Corning, but it has encouraged top executives at Corning to build two new factories that were immediately filled with union employees, thus saving the union money by avoiding a costly union organizing campaign and immediately creating an environment of trust. At Corning, the union serves as an important conduit in establishing good labor–management relations, relationships that are good enough, in fact, so that recent compensation packages include significant gain sharing percentages for all employees.

At Corning, the instigation for TQM came from the union, but it never would have worked if management had not demonstrated clearly its good faith by putting up millions of dollars for training. For Bankowski, an early sign of that good faith always comes in any plant from management's early willingness and ability to commit substantial sums to the training effort at all levels of the company. And that commitment must demonstrate management's inclusive approach to the project. If the union detects a "hidden agenda" or if management attempts to exclude parts of the union from segments of the TQM program, then, Bankowski believes, the project will inevitably fail.

It is usually impossible to train everyone at once, especially in a large company. But the financial commitment at the beginning of the process to train everyone is absolutely necessary. At Corning, that training seems to have been successful at least in part because various levels of the organization worked in an atmosphere of mutual respect and various levels were mixed together in much of the training process. To us, that mixture of levels seems important, especially since TQM implies a restructuring of an organization to establish cross-functional activities for all employees. If TQM is to work, it must be a communal effort.

By contrast, however, other companies seem to have met success with different training strategies. Motorola, for example, which invests 1.5 percent of a unit's payroll in training people, has determined that top management must be trained first. As A. William Wiggenhorn, Director of Training at Motorola, explains it: "We wasted $7 million trying to train from the bottom up. By 1984, we realized we had started at the wrong end. In 1985–86, we put the top 2,000 people through 17 days of classroom training."

We believe that the mixture of levels approach used at Corning has more chance for permanent success since such a structure suggests a mutual, team effort consistent with the overall goals of TQM. However, Motorola seems to understand fully that the TQM process is not a quick fix. They have publicly stated that the company's key goals will probably take 20 years to meet, and key initiatives will take three to six years. From a union perspective, training management first may make sense, especially if everyone keeps in mind Juran and Deming's suggestion that as much as 85% of the quality problems are caused by management. In the case of Motorola, only time will tell.

EMPLOYEE INVOLVEMENT AND EMPOWERMENT

In his General Office Accounting Report in May 1991, Allan I. Mendelowitz emphasizes that TQM must include strategies to seek employee involvement and empowerment and that these strategies call for a fundamental shift in the philosophy of senior management. As Mendelowitz reports: "The TQM philosophy is that the work force, given the power to develop and implement new and better business systems, can be a tremendous source of competitive advantage. Successful companies believe that the employees most closely involved with the business systems have the most precise knowledge of how these processes work or how they should work." From the union perspective, a good example of the need for this type of change can be found in the steel industry.

In a recent paper on corporate restructuring in the steel industry, Gordon L. Clark studied five different adjustment strategies aimed at increasing labor productivity and quality: strategies used by USX, LTV, Armco and Inland, National, and Weiton. For our purposes, a few highlights of this study are appropriate. In the case of USX, for example, the strategy has been an adversarial approach to the union. USX's goal in this context has been to achieve lower-than-average hourly labor costs through aggressive concessions bargaining while attempting to increase the pace and tighten the organization of work. According to Clark, the results have been unsuccessful because the strategy has caused disputes that have served only to exacerbate antagonisms between the union and management. As Clark views it: "In these circumstances, labor productivity is unlikely to increase as much as desired by the corporation." In such a situation, there is little hope for genuine gains in quality or long term productivity, we believe.

By comparison to the strategy of global rationalization being used by USX, National Steel has adopted a strategy of cooperative partnerships. In 1986, National Steel and the union (USWA) signed a Cooperative Partnership Agreement that included a profit-sharing program and guaranteed employment linked to the formation of joint problem-solving committees that include teams at the shop-floor level charged with the responsibility of making changes in the day-to-day operation of each plant and, more importantly, the standard operating procedures of the company. In the plant, hourly workers often act as supervisors, and executives share financial information with the workers in regularly scheduled monthly meetings set for that purpose.

In an article on the success at one of the plants, Anthony J. Rutigliano reports significant increases in productivity and a cooperative spirit within the corporate culture measured in part by the dwindling number of employee grievances. The key here seems to be employee involvement and empowerment leading to a quality workplace. Over the long haul, we believe that although National will have weak quarters, its policies will provide for long-term productivity and good quality. As James Howell, vice president at the Great Lakes Division puts it: "Who knows more about the equipment, a worker or a new supervisor? It's amazing when you treat people like people, isn't it?"

ASSETS AND LIABILITIES FOR THE UNION

Most of the gains in labor–management cooperation seem to lead to higher quality, but they often have consequences not only for the conventional structures of management, but for those of unions as well. As Gordon Clark suggests, the changes call for flexibility and leadership from the international unions, but also a willingness, at times, to sacrifice individual plants and workers. Such a situation can obviously lead to tension between the international and the local unions. In addition, such flexibility can undercut the power of the union as suggested by the stance of the International Association of Machinists (IAM) who essentially believe that cooperative programs, including TQM, undermine the efforts of bargaining agents elected to represent workers.

To a large extent, the issue is one of control. Who controls the TQM program? In the conventional setting (our Taylorism metaphor), management was charged with the responsibility and so given the power in the area of production and quality. Unions were charged with the task of protecting workers in terms of wages, hours, and conditions of employment. Their primary goal was not power over management, but power for workers to achieve a good work environment and reasonable satisfaction in the consumer market. Only through the formal structures of collective bargaining could labor be on an equal footing with management to achieve this goal.

Even in the new environment of flexibility, however, unions cannot expect the kind of power reserved for management. In such a context, TQM programs must be established in the form of a separate agreement with management which makes clear that the program will not nullify anything in the existing contract. At Corning, for example, legal counsel is present at the national level during all meetings about TQM procedures. Of course, innovative processes for quality can be negotiated as parts of new contracts.

The legal implications of labor–management cooperation programs under the National Labor Relations Act (NLRA) and the Labor–Management Relations Act (LMRA) are also important in this context. The NLRA, for example, requires that the employer bargain in good faith over wages, hours, and working conditions—a basic ingredient, it would seem, to maintain any kind of protection for workers in collective bargaining. Various court cases have tested the limits of this rule, however, and Congress itself has been asked to consider how deeply employees may be involved in company decisions. Such posturing suggests the tenuous nature of much of the TQM effort and how far we still are from developing a trust culture in the corporate environment.

To some, in fact, the problem is with the unions. Jim Truesdell, in a recent issue of *The Quality Observer*, argues, for example, that TQM programs were being sabotaged by union resistance and NLRB decisions. "It seems," Truesdell said, "that groups such as the AFL-CIO and the Teamsters are arguing that quality groups may be a form of 'dummy' union dominated by employers, especially when the purpose of such committees is to solicit employee complaints and problems . . . workers should not have labor organizations forced on them."

Collective bargaining needs to be respected by both sides if trust is to be established, and critics of unions in this regard often seem to misunderstand the union's position on this important matter. There are many union–management agreements in existence that have for years provided for extensive labor–management cooperation, quality of work life, and employee participation committees—those between Ford, Chrysler, General Motors, and U.A.W., for example. The joint U.A.W.-Chrysler agreement states specifically that it "is a non-adversarial effort supported by both Union and Management. Teams are deliberately limited to activities directly affecting product quality." TQM programs can certainly be negotiated and become part of the contractual language, providing everyone is operating in good faith.

According to a recent study at Carnegie Mellon University, large, multi-plant companies need unions to support programs such as TQM if those programs are to be successful and productive. Non-union factories with employee involvement programs are 34.9% less productive than union factories with no formal programs at all. In part, these results may come from the fact that unions are not only interested in protecting their workers, but also committed to improving the system. When 90% of problems of poor quality in companies is due to the system not the worker, then union philosophy can only enhance TQM efforts. In such a context, management will inevitably make out well too, especially when we realize that poor quality can account for as much as a 30% loss in sales and profits.

CAN TQM WORK FOR UNIONS?

There are numerous examples of successes with labor–management cooperation in both the unionized and open shop sectors of business. The original Scanlon Plan, which is often cited as one of the more successful labor–management models of cooperation, originated in a union shop environment. That plan created in 1938 allows workers to share directly in gains in productivity and acknowledges not only the right but the desirability of union participation in the business. The joint venture between the UAW and General Motors-Toyota at New United Motors Manufacturing in Fremont, California, is another widely acclaimed example of success. But the very fact that so much publicity has been given to plans based on the cooperative approach graphically symbolizes how few in number they have been thus far. In addition, the cooperative approach which undergirds the TQM program is still so incompatible with present-day management value systems that, to date, most of these plans have been implemented only as a last resort when the management is faced with a severe financial crisis.

The TQM revolution suggests in its most radical dimension that a new organizational model for American business to compete in the international market during the next century is absolutely necessary. And that model can be conceived as one that basically turns the old hierarchy upside down. Middle managers and supervisors may very well be squeezed out in such a model, and top management may then serve as a kind of support team for the work force. As Brian Dumaine asked recently in his cover story for *Fortune* magazine: In such a situation, who needs a boss? "Not employees who work in self-managed teams. They arrange schedules, buy equipment, fuss over quality and dramatically boost the productivity of their companies. Many American companies are discovering what may be the productivity break through of the 1990s. Call the still-controversial innovation a self-managed team, a cross-functional team, a high-performance team or, to coin a phrase, a super team. . . . No matter what your business, these teams are the wave of the future." Currently though only about 7% of the work force is working under such a new model. Part of the problem may be that not only are managers stripped of old-fashioned forms of power and given coaches' hats to wear instead, but unions too need to adjust to a world that seems in many ways to privilege workers by empowering them.

Cooperation at this radical level may be simply a utopian dream. If 7% of the companies have begun to move in the direction of TQM, the vast majority are wracked by problems rooted in the old tradition of Taylorism. Under Presidents Reagan and Bush, unions have suffered severe damage as many companies in the spirit of Neo-Conservatism have not worked to empower workers, but to undermine their foundation for protection. Poor communications, lack of faith in top management, the huge pay gap between many CEOs' salaries and the average worker's wages, employee sabotage, and the general tendency on the part of many managers to pass the blame for most failures and disasters on to the shoulders of the workers have all contributed to what Alan Farnham has called "the trust gap."

Furthermore the nature of capitalism itself seems based on an inevitable gap between what labor can get and what it can produce. In this sense, TQM in its most radical conception may be inconsistent with the capitalist social and economic orders. Although labor and management can cooperate, they may always be cooperating inside a system that basically supports management's right and need for a bigger piece of the pie than that given to labor. In such a situation, there appears to be a fundamental contradiction that will not allow for the human face of labor to emerge fully. However, as many business analysts have suggested, a program like TQM still offers considerable hope, not only for immediate survival, but for the long term. TQM replaces "compliance" management with "commitment" management, and that in itself reflects a new kind of cooperative relationship between labor and capital, unions and management.

CONCLUSION

Labor–management cooperation is the key ingredient in the success of any Total Quality Management (TQM) effort. However, that cooperation must not come at the price of sacrificing unions or the collective bargaining process. TQM processes, however, should be negotiated to become part of the contract. Since adversarial relations between unions and management have proven over and over again to create mistrust and an unhealthy working environment, it seems reasonable that management will want to work to implement TQM without attempting to pressure unions into concessions that will produce negative long-term results. Companies that work to build trust may in fact find that unions will actually initiate TQM projects and offer suggestions on a host of ways to save money.

As Aaron Bernstein recently reminded us in his article ''Busting Unions Can Backfire on the Bottom Line,'' the benefits of cooperative relationships with unions far outweigh the liabilities. ''In the 1980s U.S. employers pursued two sharply divergent strategies in dealing with organized labor. Some followed the examples set by President Reagan when he crushed the air-traffic controllers' strike. Others used an approach commonly associated with the Japanese. Ford Motor Co. and Cummins Engine Co. among others, established cooperative relationships with unions hoping that teamwork would boost productivity and quality and hold costs down.'' The results are clear and they augur well for the institution of TQM. ''Employers that tried teamwork—about half the sample—reported a 19% increase over the decade in value added per employee—defined as operating income plus inventory divided by the number of workers. The combative employers reported a 15% decline in the same measure. This cost (34% difference) reflects the huge expense of withstanding a union busting strike plus the lingering effects on employee morale.''

We believe that American companies can no longer assume ''business as usual.'' Given the structural changes in job formation, the increasing development and use of high technology, and the unsettling rhythms of the international marketplace, both unions and management must break the rigidities of the old order of organization, including the assumption that the primary relationship between these groups must be defined in adversarial terms. Both unions and management must adopt a social and political flexibility and a foundation of cooperation defined through TQM initiatives. If such a change is to work, however, management must recognize that labor is a significant human agent in the realm of quality and production, and so it must grant labor increasing power in that realm. At the same time, labor must recognize that management has the right and the need for profits that exceed those that labor gets. In this context, collective bargaining agreements must remain the formal structure for labor to maintain an equal footing with management.

Bibliography

Adam, E. E. Jr., and R. J. Ebert. *Production and Operations Management.* Prentice-Hall, Englewood Cliffs, N.J., 1992.

Allender, Hans D. ''Total Quality Management: A Primer on a New Management Paradigm,'' *The Quality Observer*, February 1992.

Aquayo, Rafael. *Dr. Deming: The American Who Taught the Japanese About Quality.* Simon & Schuster, 1991.

Bass, B. M., and G. V. Barrett. *People, Work and Organizations.* Allyn and Bacon, Inc., Boston, 1981.

Bernstein, Aaron. "Busting Unions Can Backfire on the Bottom Line," *Business Week,* March 18, 1991.

Clark, Gordon L. "Restructuring in the Steel Industry: Adjustment Strategies and Local Labor Relations" in *America's New Market Geography* (edited by George Sternleib and James W. Hughes). Rutgers, 1988.

Cooke, William N. "Factors Influencing the Effect of Joint Union–Management Programs on Employee-Supervisor Relations," *Industrial & Labor Relations Review* (Vol. 43, #5) July 1990.

Dumaine, Brian. "Who Needs A Boss?" *Fortune,* May 7, 1990.

Farnham, Alan, "The Trust Gap," *Fortune,* Dec. 4, 1989.

Frangos, S. "Empowerment: Using People to Achieve Excellence," *The Quality Observer,* Feb. 1992.

Gunderson, Steven. "Archaic Rules Foul Innovative Labor Strategies" "Manager's Journal," *The Wall Street Journal,* Oct. 21, 1991.

Hoerr, John. "The Payoff From Teamwork," *Business Week,* July 10, 1989.

Hoerr, John. "The Strange Bedfellows Backing Workplace Reform," *Business Week,* April 30, 1990.

Keichel, Walter III. "When Management Regresses," *Fortune,* March 9, 1992.

Kirkpatrick, David. "What Givebacks Can Get You," *Fortune,* Nov. 24, 1986.

Kilingel, Sally, and Ann Martin (ed.), *A Fighting Chance,* ILR Press, 1988.

Leap, Terry L. *Collective Bargaining and Labor Relations,* Macmillan Publishing Company, New York, 1991.

Mendelowitz, Allen I., Director. *Management Practices: U.S. Companies Improve Performance through Quality Efforts,* U.S. General Accounting Office (G.A.O.) Washington, D.C., 1991.

Peters, Barbara H., and Jim L. Peters (ed.), *Total Quality Management* Report Number 963 of the Conference Board, 1991.

Rutligliano, Anthony. "Cooperating To Survive at National Steel" in *Management Review,* February 1988—for an updated account of National see Dana Milbank's story in *The Wall Street Journal,* May 2, 1992.

Sloane, A. A., and F. Whitney. *Labor Relations.* Prentice-Hall, Englewood Cliffs, N.J., 1991.

Tank, Andrew G., *Global Perceptives on Total Quality,* Report Number 958 of the Conference Board, 1991.

Truesdell, Jim. "Quality Programs Under Fire As Labor Violations," *The Quality Observer,* March 1992, p. 16.

Walton, Mary. *Deming Management at Work,* Perigree Books, New York, 1990.

Woodruff, David. "They've Made It a Manhood Issue Now," *Business Week,* March 9, 1992.

Zaremba, A., and B. Kittle. "The Value of Organizational Teams: A Study in Team Intervention," *The Quality Observer,* Feb. 1992.

TQM in Higher Education

Readings in this section illustrate efforts to implement TQM principles and processes in Higher Education. These applications are of general interest since colleges and universities are complex organizations with many stakeholders ranging from society at large to local governments, parents, students, faculty, and staff. In other words, a multi-organization institution is responsible for addressing simultaneously a myriad of needs, wants, and claims.

Early efforts to bring TQM to Higher Ed settings have focused on administrative processes, which are largely similar to those of any large service organization. Under increasing cost containment pressures Higher Ed administrative units have to do more with less, and process improvement becomes an overriding priority.

Implementation of TQM principles and processes in the classroom is trickier and requires fundamental paradigm shifts. The shift of the role of the instructor from provider of knowledge to that of facilitator, the shared responsibility in course design and delivery, and the decrease of importance of grades, require new attitudes and skills from both faculty and students. In other words a radical change in organizational culture is required to build learning environments where fear is eliminated (one of Deming's essential requirements for true organizational change) and responsibility shared. It is yet to be seen to what extent such lofty goals will become a reality in the 90s and beyond.

TQM Reaches the Academy

By Ted Marchese

Total Quality Management . . . an American set of ideas, engine behind the Japanese economic miracle, agent for the dramatic turnabouts at Ford and Motorola . . . suddenly it's at work in more than half the Fortune 1000 firms . . . it's the "preferred management style" of the federal government . . . you'll find it in hotels, city government, your local hospital . . . *it's in the air* . . . can the academy be next?

In fact, TQM has *already* arrived in higher education, in dozens of institutions, notably research universities and community colleges. TQM's collegiate practitioners, their zeal and worries on full display, already have networks in place and a literature at hand; their quality-improvement message dominated last spring's AACSB conference of business schools and this month's ABET meeting of engineering educators; next April 5–8, TQM debuts as a major theme of AAHE's National Conference on Higher Education in Chicago.

What's going on here? How relevant can TQM be to the special work of a college or university? Are we about to be shelled again by the latest fad in corporate management?

To get answers to these questions, last July I travelled to Los Angeles for the Second Annual Symposium on the Role of Academia in National Competitiveness and Total Quality Management, hosted by the University of Southern California. A hundred colleges had representatives among the 300 people on hand. Afterwards I met with two dozen of TQM's lead practitioners in higher education; since then, through interviews and document collection, I've pieced together a picture of the movement's first days on campus. This is what I found.

Reprinted from the November 1991 issue of *American Association for Higher Education Bulletin* with the permission of the author.

THE TQM STORY

The saga is triumphalist: W. Edwards Deming, an American statistician whose ideas about quality find little response at home, lectures in1950 to Japan. He excoriates his hosts for their cheap, shoddy goods; he tells them that an emphasis on quality will reap lasting benefits in market share and profitability; he lays out principles—eventually fourteen in number—for making quality a "strategic advantage." They listen to him. They listen also, in 1954, to Joseph Juran ("management for quality"); they devour Armand Feigenbaum's 1951 classic, *Total Quality Control,* and later the writing of Philip Crosby *(Quality Is Free).* They struggle, adapt, develop their own gurus (Ishikawa, Imai), pursue the quality ideal relentlessly. . . . The rest, as they say, is history.

In the early- and mid-1980s, hardpressed American firms take up the message: at Motorola (1982) and Ford (1984), quality becomes "everybody's job" and "Job 1." Soon Xerox, Federal Express, IBM, Westinghouse, Disney, Corning, Hewlett-Packard, and the Hospital Corporation of America are on board; the books, workshops, and consultants multiply; the U.S. Navy coins the phrase "Total Quality Management." In 1987, Congress sets up a Malcolm Baldrige National Quality Award; its seven criteria become a consensus statement of TQM values. In 1988, the Department of Defense mandates TQM for itself and all contractors; a Federal Quality Institute starts to implement TQM across all departments and agencies. Surveys show that buyers—nine of ten in 1990 versus three in ten in 1980—now place a first value on quality (above price and styling); studies demonstrate that quality-oriented firms in fact do better in market share and profits.

In banking and airlines, in manufacturing and services, from microchips to pet food, the word is out: Consumers value *products* that work and last, *service* that's prompt, courteous, and dependable, and *TQM* is the way to deliver it.

With all that, I wondered aloud in Los Angeles why *all* firms hadn't given themselves over totally to the concept. "They haven't," an executive from McDonnell Douglas told me, "because not many companies have felt as hard-pressed as Ford and Motorola did ten years ago. Firms claim to be into TQM, but their implementation is spotty. It's too great a change to make without a big need at your backside."

WHAT IS IT?

What is TQM, this "too great a change"? At one level, it's an approach to management and a set of tools, a coalescing of new and old ideas—from systems thinking and statistical process control, from theories of human behavior, leadership, and planning, plus lessons from earlier, less-than-successful attempts at quality improvement (such as quality circles)—all these brought together in a new orthodoxy.

But at another level, and looking at TQM as a phenomenon, it is a call to leadership for the reform of American enterprise. Its advocates want more than a change in management practice; they want an entirely new organization, one whose culture is quality-driven, customer-oriented, marked by teamwork, and avid about improvement . . . "corporate revolution" and "paradigm shift" are the words one hears. Armand Feigenbaum, now an international consultant, told the Los Angeles conference that American corporate philosophy has been to "make it quick and cheaper, finance it cleverly, and sell it hard. The value of 'making it better' was left out. Firms have to march to an entirely new drumbeat: quality."

From among the many strands of thought and prior experience feeding into TQM, I've teased out a dozen themes that seem at its core.

1. *A focus on quality.* The alpha and omega of TQM is its singular focus on quality as the defining characteristic of an organization. Quality in this view is not just an attribute of products or services; it is a mindset, the soul of the company itself, an all-pervasive drive of such intensity that it defines the corporate culture. Just as geneticist Barbara McClintock's breakthroughs came when she was able to "think like corn," TQM enjoins managers to "imbibe" quality; the corporation that lives for quality, that takes quality as its strategic advantage, is promised long-run gains in market share and return on investment.

2. *Customer-driven.* What is quality? To Juran, it's "fitness for use" by the consumer; to Deming, it's that which "surpasses customer needs and expectations." In TQM companies, a keen sense of customer needs governs all activities. The cardinal rule is to identify explicitly who your customers are, know their needs systematically, and commit to meeting those needs. Why? Because in a competitive environment the customer—not executives, engineers, or inspectors—defines quality. If you don't satisfy the customer, someone else will.

3. *Continuous improvement.* An American adage says, "If it ain't broke, don't fix it." TQM responds, "Wrong!" Customers, markets, technologies change every day; what's good enough now will be suicide tomorrow. Deming preaches "constancy of purpose" on behalf of continuous adaptation and improvement; he and Juran describe quality as a "journey." Education undersecretary David Kearns, former Xerox CEO and a quality champion, proclaims, "In the race for quality, there is no finish line."

4. *Making processes work better.* Every organization is a network of processes. These range from the "single-purpose" (discharging a patient from a hospital) to the "cross-functional" (Federal Express's hub-and-spoke delivery system). The aim is to identify those processes; enable the people who work in them to understand that work in relation to customer needs (Are we doing the right thing? How well?); and set in motion, through problem-solving teams, process improvements.

5. *Extending the mindset.* In the old paradigm, attention to quality began and ended on the shop floor; it was a matter to be "controlled" or "inspected in." In the new, quality concerns reach in all directions. An "absence of defects" isn't enough; goods are followed "out the door," where their quality is judged by how well they fit or exceed customer expectations in actual use. Quality, too, is a function of good, up-front product and process design. And it reaches backward from the shop floor: No longer will it do for automakers to say, "We know

The Baldrige Award

Secretary of Commerce Malcolm Baldrige, a quality advocate, died in a rodeo accident in 1987. Shortly thereafter, Congress authorized a "National Quality Award" in his name, a public-private endeavor administered from the Commerce Department. A distinguished group of quality experts was empaneled to write criteria for the award; the panel's ultimate scheme, derived from TQM, quickly became the accepted template for judging corporate quality-improvement efforts.

The Baldrige criteria categories and their relative values (on a 1,000-point scale) are as follows:

Leadership. The senior management's success in creating and sustaining a quality culture. (100 points)

Information and analysis. The effectiveness of the company's collection and analysis of information for quality improvement and planning. (70)

Planning. The effectiveness of integrating quality requirements into the company's business plans. (60)

Human resource utilization. The success of the company's efforts to utilize the full potential of the workforce for quality. (150)

Quality assurance. The effectiveness of the company's systems for ensuring quality control of all operations. (140)

Quality results. The company's results in quality achievement and quality improvement, demonstrated through quantitative measures. (180)

Customer satisfaction. The effectiveness of the company's systems to determine customer requirements and demonstrated success in meeting them. (300)

The Baldrige application is detailed: The seven categories are broken down into thirty-two subcategories with ninety-nine "areas to address." The award's key values are self-described as customer-driven quality, leadership, continuous improvement, fast response, actions based on facts, and participation by all employees. The criteria ask about results but especially focus on the conditions and processes that led to them.

The guidelines themselves constitute a self-study exercise for applicants, a corporate "examination" (with an accompanying "scoring system") in quality commitment; firms that apply get feedback from the Baldrige judging panels. Because of these diagnostic features (and low entry fees), many companies apply just for the self-study exercise ... Ford, Motorola, and IBM even make their suppliers go through the process. Last year, 200,000 copies of the guidelines were distributed; in a poll, 86 percent of business

> **The Baldrige Award** *(continued)*
> executives claimed to know the criteria; 6 percent of all firms actually applied. This year's winners were announced October 29th from the White House.
>
> In the September/October *Change*, SHEEO director James Mingle proposed that regional accrediting bodies mount a Baldrige Aware competition for higher education. His colleague Peter Ewell, of NCHEMS, doubts the idea would work just now ("It assumes a process within colleges that isn't there yet."); but the idea is alive, with several parties in the country now trying to cook up "higher-ed versions" of the criteria. At the Los Angeles conference, Baldrige director Curt Reimann acknowledged that "if such an award could make a contribution, and educators expressed interest, the Secretary would welcome the suggestion."

our cars aren't very good, but our lowest-bid suppliers sent us so-so goods." With quality precedent to price, TQM companies attempt to develop stable relations with a small set of suppliers who agree to be partners in the quality-improvement process.

6. *The discipline of information.* TQM people always want to see the data, and they want it to be public data, up on the shop or office wall. If you're serious about improving quality, they say, everybody has to know how they're doing. Customers aren't just bowed to; they're systematically surveyed, interviewed, poked, prodded, and begged for suggestions. Process-improvement teams are taught to track meticulously every fault, complaint, breakdown, accident, or shortage that comes their way; "Every process," Wisconsin's George Box teaches, "generates the data to improve it." A variety of statistical tools—ingenious diagrams, charts, matrices, graphs, and checksheets—are deployed in what the Japanese call *Kaizen* (continuous improvement) methods of process control.

7. *Eliminate rework.* An aim of all this attention to work processes is to ferret out the "scrap, waste, and complexity" (Deming) from a system . . . simplify, standardize, get it right the first time. The time spent fixing earlier mistakes (rework), in useless work that has to be done over (scrap), and in extra steps that add no value to a product or service (complexity) can equal 20 percent of all costs, say "findings" in the Baldrige legislation. Service organizations can have an even greater problem: Crosby concludes they spend "35 percent or more of their operating costs doing things wrong and then doing them over."

8. *Teamwork.* From top management to the shop floor, within units and across functions, quality issues are attacked in teams. "Teams" are *not* your familiar committees; they are "self-directed work groups" with their own required competencies and protocols. Unlike committees, teams aren't "representative":

they bring together most or all of the people who work in a process to work on its improvement—no others need apply. TQM wants all persons to share responsibility for the processes they work in and for the whole; it believes in the superiority of collaborative work that achieves "team learning."

9. **Empowering people.** In Deming's view, 85 percent of all problems are traceable to the process itself, just 15 percent to the people in them. Stop attacking people, he admonishes managers, look to your systems: "Drive out fear from the workplace!" Patrick Townsend says management must "believe that its personnel department has been in the habit of hiring adults"; TQM "empowers" people "by trusting all employees . . . to act responsibly and giving them appropriate authority." People *want* to do the right and better thing, TQM urges, they *want* pride in their work; the task of managers is to remove the system barriers that prevent people from doing so. Who, in TQM, reviews work processes? Again, not distant managers or external evaluators but the people closest to the processes, those who do the work itself.

10. **Training and recognition.** So that all employees can understand the corporate vision of quality, have the skills of teamwork and problem solving they need, and relate more effectively to customers, TQM firms invest heavily in human resource development. Across its various units, Motorola spends 2 to 6 percent of its salary budgets on training; IBM-Rochester invests 5 percent across the board. Personnel systems in TQM companies rely less on incentives and rewards directed at the individual than on team-oriented "recognition, honors, and celebration."

11. **Vision.** The TQM world wants stripped-down, plain-English statements of the organization's core values, and it wants these "vision statements" a clear part of every employee's work. A story is told: When Tylenol was recalled a few years back, it wasn't an act of J&J's top management . . . a third-line manager learned of the peril and, with specific reference to J&J's values statement, recalled the product on his own authority. Unlike the lofty piffle of "mission" statements, TQM urges compelling, down-to-earth language that gets all parties focused on the right thing to do.

12. **Leadership.** To achieve all the above, TQM partisans want fewer managers, at least of the old type—powerful figures in sole command of vertical authority structures. Instead, they want leaders, and of a new type—vision-givers, listeners, team-workers, committed to quality and customer needs, avid but patient, for long-term ends, orchestrators and enablers of people-driven improvement. Lehigh University president Peter Likins puts this change more simply: ". . . we'll need to talk to each other more and control one another less."

The book I found TQM practitioners reading last summer was Peter Senge's *The Fifth Discipline* (Doubleday, 1990). In it, Senge (of MIT) describes the "ensemble of disciplines" that lie behind an organizational capacity for innovation: systems thinking, personal mastery, mental models, shared vision, and team learning. Senge barely mentions TQM, even as his "disciplines" capture the movement's values.

STILL NOT SURE?

Did I return from Los Angeles a convert? Not exactly. But I heard on reflection, a lot of good answers to the objections I came with.

"Students aren't customers!" A "student as a customer" analogy, for sure, falls well short of full description; students are important agents for their own learning, indeed the creators of it. All that said, the customer analogy—taken as an attempt to understand the experience of college from a student point of view—should hardly be taken as alien; it provides a useful lens for introspection and improvement. Want to improve registration or a chemistry major or library services? Why not talk with students?

TQM, importantly, does not imply pandering to student satisfaction or every short-term expression of needs. Faculties do well to weigh student views alongside their own professional judgment about the requirements of learning, of society, of future employers, and of a student's own longer-term interests. Some TQM educators entertain a responsibilities-oriented "student as worker" theme.

"We already talk with our students." Let us hope. The objection misses, however, what TQM wants: systematic, across-the-board listening, based on notions of customer importance. But as Kansas business professor Larry Sherr told an AIR audience recently, ". . . very few of our institutions have any idea even of who their customers are."

Customer analysis is one of TQM's fresh ideas, and it doesn't begin or end with students. Indeed, the prime "customer" of most administrative offices turns out to be . . . other administrative offices. While the end-point customer counts (a lot), more often the customer at hand is the in-house individual or unit to whom you supply products, a service, or information; the goal is for the work of each office to meet or exceed the expectations of its internal customers. Thinking in such terms tends to raise a host of new questions for collegiate TQM project teams.

It follows also that each person and unit has *suppliers,* most of them internal, on whom it relies for its work. "How can we be partners in quality-improvement work?" TQM would have teams ask one another.

"Oh, that language!" There are, let it be said, more-technical versions of TQM than I've recounted here; an engineer or statistician's view of the thing would whip you quickly into an exotic work of Pareto charts, cause-and-effect ("fishbone") diagrams, and "Plan, Do, Check, Act" schemes. Initial presentations of TQM to faculty-staff audiences at Wisconsin and Maryland faltered when just such versions were paraded forth . . . reminding one of assessment's rocky road to faculty understanding when first versions of it were presented by psychometricians.

But, just as with assessment, there are plain-English, larger-picture versions of TQM that can make sense to academic ears. Viewed broadly, TQM is a call to quality and a mindset about improvement; it values data, teams, and process; for the many faculty and staff of an institution, it offers respect and a voice. As for its special tools and vocabularies, they come second and are for adaptive use.

"It's okay for corporations but. . . ." In a recent TQM newsletter, Ellen Chaffee described her interview in Tokyo with Prof. Masao Kogure, a revered leader in the

application of quality improvement to the service sector. Kogure told her that every time TQM came to a new industry in Japan it encountered resistance: "We're not like the industry that is already using it."

Pondering Kogure's words, then higher education's special history and character, I came to wonder how different many of our functions really were from those in business—generating a bill, advising a student or client . . . if hospital TQM programs can teach doctors to introduce themselves to patients and listen to their questions, might there not be *something* here for us? Rutgers biologist Lion Gardner phoned in October to tell me of his own new interest in the topic: "We have to do something with the hard, alienating structures of the university," he hold me; "TQM is relevant for its humanistic thrust."

"It's okay for administrators, but . . ." Most faculty members wouldn't mind at all if their institution's administrators used TQM (or anything else) to get a better act together. Indeed, we've all seen and come to appreciate the new customer orientation and service ethic in certain hotel chains, department stores, car-rental companies, and so on, and no doubt wondered why these new standards for service stopped at the campus gate. TQM, its early practitioners have found, finds many targets of opportunity in collegiate administration.

In that sense, its academic applications are, well, academic; let TQM be for administrators. Faculty have their own, more apt set of questions in assessment (which also is about quality, listening to students, and continuous improvement). Winona's Darrell Krueger, for years a national leader in the uses of assessment for academic improvement, is enthusiastic about TQM's arrival on the administrative side: "It brings the whole rest of the university into the quality quest."

Does TQM, though, have anything to contribute on the academic side? I think it might, especially to improving aspects of a department's services and to helping it to a keener sense of who its customers and suppliers are. Also, though most of the early collegiate adopters of TQM have left the academic side alone, a few have used the emphasis to encourage faculty to try the assessment-like techniques of Classroom Research—certainly a plus.

Does TQM have anything to add to assessment itself? Again I think it might. Pat Hutchings and Peter Ewell three years ago taught assessors the importance of getting "behind outcomes," of understanding the crucial processes of learning that contribute to outcomes . . . the process-analysis approaches of TQM are more than a bit suggestive here. Also suggestive is the TQM concept of "benchmarking," which insists that an organization intent on improving quality compare its performance not with industrywide averages but with a corporate "best of class." In educational testing, for example, this might imply comparing student performance not against local norms but against "high, international standards" (as the new National Education Goals will do).

"None of this is new . . . it's just good management." A quick way to dismiss TQM— business professors do this—is to resort to the above, a truism. Indeed, as mentioned earlier, TQM itself is an amalgam of ideas and tools, many of which have been around for quite some time—which is not to say they've been much used. And on

Hoshin Planning

TQM far from ignores "outcomes" (recall "fitness for use") or "inputs" (good design, work with suppliers); but its distinctive contributions center or organizational processes. It's not that process is more important than input or outcome, simply a judgment about where new effort should best be focused. "The crux of the thing is that it forces us to pay attention to a lot of daily processes we've typically ignored," Carnegie Mellon's Richard Cyert told the Los Angeles conference.

What about planning, then? TQM practitioners in Japan evolved their own version of what Americans know as strategic planning, called *Hoshin*, or "breakthrough," Planning. It starts, as you'd expect, with a "vision statement," typically for the next five years. This is followed by goals (which have a customer orientation), work plans (for specific critical processes), deployment and execution, followed by monthly "audits" to monitor progress toward the vision. An important feature in Hoshin is the identification of no more than four "breakthroughs" (fundamental quality improvements), items that all units in the organization will specially pursue in a given time frame.

Hoshin practitioners have developed their own set of planning tools (the matrix and affinity diagrams, for example). They're also prone to put value statements in plans, as a reminder that how things are done can be as important as their direction. In American higher education, at least two institutions—Oregon State and Delaware County C.C.—have used Hoshin Planning.

most campuses, let it be noted, one will find offices and departments that seem perfectly well managed without the grace of TQM. But there are plenty more that aren't, that could sorely use the bursts of insight and energy TQM seems to bring.

"Here we go with another fad." Those of us who've been around long enough have sharp memories of earlier management nostrums—MBO, zero-based budgeting, endless planning schemes. Typically these arrive at higher education's doorstep five years after their trial in business, often just as corporations are discarding them. Let the record note here that first grumblings about TQM have started to appear in the business press, and that one of TQM's star companies—Florida Power and Light, a winner of Japan's Deming Prize, no less—has taken recent steps to deemphasize it.

It's easy to cry "fad," though, and miss the real article—as we saw with assessment. Two management "fads," in my memory, proved valuable and stuck: marketing in the late 1970s, strategic planning in the mid-1980s. They stuck, Michigan's Marvin Peterson reminded me, because they seemed to speak to an environmental need, they found their guru (Kotler, Keller), and they proved adaptable. TQM has yet to find its collegiate guru, but the first and third of the conditions do apply. Given the doldrums many college administrations find themselves in today, maybe it's time for the next "fad" to step up and find its uses.

THE EARLY ADAPTERS

At and since Los Angeles, I've tried to keep track of TQM's campus parties of interest. My best sense is that the number of individuals devoted to the topic runs well up in the hundreds, the number of institutions trying TQM in particular offices might be near one hundred, the number of those that have committed to TQM on an institutionwide basis stands at two dozen, of which the number with deeper experience constitutes a mere handful.

An intriguing observation is that most of the early innovators are from just two institutional types: either prominent research universities of *un*prominent (up to now) community colleges. Among the former are Oregon State, Wisconsin, Penn, and Colorado State, followed by Harvard, Carnegie Mellon, Maryland, Lehigh, Chicago, Minnesota, Wyoming, Clemson, Georgia Tech, and Miami. Interestingly, the TQM initiator in many universities has been the president—several of these presidents have technical or business backgrounds, so they can't help knowing of TQM. Sometimes pressure for TQM adoption comes from community or alumni friends; Ford's Donald Peterson happens to be Oregon State's best-known alum, as Lee Iacocca is Lehigh's. The Lehigh Valley area, not incidentally, is a hotbed of TQM interest; so is the city of Madison, a fact not unrelated to Wisconsin's decision to hire that city's TQM manager as its own in-house facilitator.

Among the two-year colleges, community relatedness and expectation have also clearly played a role in spurring TQM adoption. Within the sector, Fox Valley Technical College (WI) and Delaware County C.C. (PA) are the leaders, having each been at this since 1985; Houston (TX), Jackson (MI), and Lamar (CO) are among the recent adopters. Fox Valley has an especially beguiling story to tell: As it drove TQM concepts deeper and deeper into the institution, it began to reap high, measurable returns in morale, cost reduction, student attainment, and community approbation. As a result, it has become a Mecca of sorts for TQM initiates, the Alverno of the movement, with eighty colleges visiting last year and a new Quality Institute offering publications, training materials, consultation, and workshops (details from Callie Zilinsky at 414-735-5707).

Notably absent from TQM rosters are liberal arts colleges (Samford, Belmont, and Pepperdine come to mind as exceptions) and the regional publics (Winona, Towson, Northwest Missouri, Central Connecticut, and Arkansas Tech are active). North Dakota's board of higher education two years ago mandated TQM for the state's public colleges; last year, the Minnesota state university system adopted a TQM-derived "Q-7" program; both initiatives look to an enhancement of public confidence. Samford, a small Baptist university in Alabama, has built its interest in TQM on thoughtfully developed notions of Christian stewardship and collaboration.

Books, Brains, and Bucks

A huge literature has sprung up around TQM, as you'll see in the business section of any good bookstore. Many authors have their peculiar slant on the thing; more than a few **TQM books** are given over to exhortation and self-help. None of the masters—Deming, Juran, Crosby, Feigenbaum—has on the shelves today a "must read" book for TQM newcomers. Several practitioners recommend starting with journalist Mary Walton's *The Deming Management Method* (Putnam, 1986) or her *Deming Management at Work* (Putnam, 1990). I find in bibliographies at least five published papers on Deming's fourteen points applied to higher education; Tennessee's Trudy Banta heads a **FIPSE project** that will scrutinize corporate quality-improvement ideas for relevance to the academy.

On November 22, ACE/Macmillan releases the first book-length treatment of **TQM in the academy,** *On Q: Causing Quality in Higher Education,* by Daniel Seymour, a contributor to this *Bulletin* ($27.95; for a credit card order, phone 1-800-323-7445). Last month, the Jossey-Bass New Directions for Institutional Research series brought out *Total Quality Management in Higher Education,* edited by Lawrence Sherr and Deborah Teeter, seven good essays plus an annotated bibliography; order it for $13.95. The American Society for Quality Control (310 West Wisconsin Ave., Milwaukee, WI 53203) has a publishing and sales arm called Quality Press Publications that stocks most of the field's essential books, training materials, and so forth; write for a catalogue.

For a free copy of the **Baldrige Award application** guidelines, phone (301) 975-2036.

Most of the colleges and universities mentioned in this article have moved into TQM with a **corporate partner**—Winona State

Abroad, TQM is knocking at the door of higher institutions in the Netherlands and Australia; it's been a non-starter in Japan; in Britain, it's swept the polytechnic sector—Liverpool Polytechnic, for example, is as far along as Fox Valley.

IMPLEMENTATION STRATEGIES

Anything as comprehensive as TQM, so sweeping in its reach (and claims), raises daunting prospects for the adopter. Deming was once asked how to implement his fourteen points. 'What!'' he huffed, "You want me to do your work for you?"

Nothing but admiration should go to the handful of institutions that have dug in and confronted the full TQM agenda—Fox Valley, Delaware County, and Samford, led by their presidents, have pursued nothing less than institutional transformation.

Books, Brains, and Bucks *(continued)*

with IBM-Rochester, Oregon State with training from Hewlett-Packard, Fox Valley with Nashua Paper, and so on. Typically the consultation comes at little or no cost—TQM companies want to spread the gospel. Colleges warn not to rely on corporate people to sell a TQM vision internally; it's better to call them in to learn specific things like team building, statistical tools, or Hoshin.

Within the **consulting world,** a stand-out is the nonprofit GOAL/QPC of Methuen, Mass. Its early research focused on corporate implementation; later came work with hospitals and state and local governments; it now targets help for educators. It has useful publications, notably a 1989 research report (No. 89-10-03) on *Hoshin Planning: A Planning System for Implementing Total Quality Management* ($11.95 each). For information or publications, call (508) 685-3900.

TQM practitioners find one another at the "Role of Academia" conference described in this article, with the next scheduled for July at Lehigh; at the annual GOAL/QPC meeting in Boston, this November 11–13; at meetings of SCUP and AIR; and soon at AAHE **meetings,** including our National Conference next April 5–8 in Chicago and our Assessment Conference next June 21–24 in Miami Beach. People are also linked through a **newsletter,** with lists maintained by W.A. Golomski and Associates, 59 E. Van Buren St., Chicago, IL 60605-1220.

IBM announced October 1st a **major grants program** to promote TQM in colleges and universities—to teach, use, and do research on it. Eight $1 million awards will be made. For guidelines, write Director, Market-Driven Quality Management Systems, IBM Corporation, 208 Harbor Dr., Room 2C-09, Stamford, CT 06904-2501, or call (203) 973-7397.

But many TQM advocates—administrative or faculty champions of the concept—confront difficult situations, which they were candid about in Los Angeles. Obstacle one is often the president—he's a loner, she doesn't trust teams, he relies on intuition (his own) over data, she could never be a provider of vision, and so on. Most administrative cabinets and staff are unpracticed at team work; powerful individuals and offices resist from sheer inertia. Very importantly, there's often no perceived external pressure to take up TQM or the concerns it addresses.

In the circumstance, some converts have set out first to educate colleagues and build a critical mass of support for TQM; they've brought in speakers, engaged consultants, staged retreats. Oregon State began this way, in 1989, then was quickly able to implement a whole array of process improvement projects, ten pilot teams at first, now fifty (the OSU work enjoys full presidential support and has a vice-presidential champion, the energetic Ed Coate). Other TQM advocates, however, have basically decided to ignore for now their president, the faculty, and other offices, to try TQM in their own units and attract attention through results.

Much of the early implementation of TQM falls in this latter category—that is, it is within-unit, addresses single functions, uses TQM techniques selectively, and begs (for now) larger change agendas. The Penn story is a good one here. Activity proceeded within the domain of a single (senior) vice president; a trainer was engaged (from the Juran Institute); criteria were developed for choice of projects; four were run in 1990–91, three of them successfully. One of the latter entailed reducing the cost of trash removal; another sought ways to ensure timely recovery of sponsored research funding (participants in the process uncovered, as they went along, lots of make-work, confusing forms, loose ends in existing procedures, *and* $1.7 million in billable charges!).

This sort of adaptive use of TQM, while it won't please the purists, seems the near-term future of the thing in most institutions. The stories here are compelling: the time spent in generating a student work-study check reduced from sixteen days to three (Kansas); the percentage of faculty grades handed in on time up from 30 percent to 98 percent (Connecticut College—which doesn't use TQM language); transcript request time cut from ninety days to five (Samford); registration and course-availability "greatly improved" (Fordham's business school).

At Oregon State, Coate has already identified 250 internal processes potentially amenable to TQM analysis. Where do you start? According to Coate, "You look first for a screwed up process that's fixable, important to customers, and that can save you money." Penn's Quality Council looked for projects that were of manageable size, had campuswide visibility and impact, and that promised savings. "But if a unit is sick," Coate observes, "TQM can't cure it. In fact, it won't work. You'll need other remedies."

Is TQM a way to cut costs and save money? The party line is *no;* TQM is about quality and putting customers first, *after* which come the market and financial returns. But Coate's university faces major losses in state support; he feels forced to include in the process a hard look for cost savings, including personnel slots (captured by attrition).

Doubtless other institutions will skip Oregon State's careful groundwork and turn directly to TQM as a retrenchment tool, which would seem a mistake. "TQM is not instant pudding!" snorts Deming. Larry Sherr observes, "If resources are being used unwisely, they can't be found on the day you have to retrench." Fordham's Sylvia Westerman, a former NBC News executive, observes that "TQM absolutely can achieve efficiencies, raise morale, show good stewardship of funds, and win public trust. . . . but it's hard to make claims for cost-savings."

The Japanese experience and U.S. research show that it is only when firms attack cross-cutting functions (enrollment management, for example) that they realize major gains in effectiveness and cost-savings. But such functions prove very difficult to address, especially in a collegiate ethos of semi-autonomous units. Samford and UM-Duluth both report disappointment with first attempts at cross-functional projects; Delaware County, on the other hand, brought off a full-blown TQM review of its general-education program. TQM advisors with the Hospital Corporation of America recommend several years of work and learning with single-function projects (which Delaware County indeed had) before pursuing more ambitious targets.

REFLECTION

TQM doesn't speak to some of higher education's toughest problems (like working through the implications of multiculturalism); it is probably less profound a development than assessment (which speaks to the difficult, central issues of student learning); it won't rescue sagging public support or inept administrations; it might not save us any big sums of money.

It's unlikely, too, that TQM will sweep through our full 3,614 campuses soon—many just won't feel the customer or competitive pressure to undertake its difficult tasks. What I'd anticipate is the spread of TQM concepts, selectively deployed, across hundreds of institutions in the years ahead, with many of the resultant benefits and pitfalls described here and in Dan Seymour's article that follows.

The Chinese have an expression for "fad" that translates as "a gust of wind." It's been several years now since we've had a good gust of fresh ideas for college and university administration; TQM seems poised to provide just that. If TQM people will talk us into a greater interest in quality, customers, teamwork, and getting things right the first time, I'm ready to listen.

Implementing Total Quality Management in a University Setting

By L. Edwin Coate

INTRODUCTION

Leadership is not so much the exercise of power itself as the empowerment of others.

Warren Bennis

Total Quality Management (TQM) is a commitment to excellence by everyone in an organization—excellence achieved by teamwork and a process of continuous improvement. TQM means dedication to being the best, to delivering high quality services which meet or exceed the expectations of customers.

As with any significant cultural change, TQM requires strong leadership at all levels. Inspiring people to do things differently takes leaders who can communicate what needs to be done and why. It takes leaders who have a clear goal or vision, can impart that vision to others, and then demonstrate through action how to make the vision a reality.

Most of all, TQM requires leadership that empowers people to work toward achieving their shared vision. No single company or university has successfully implemented and maintained progress in the concepts of Total Quality Management without that leadership by top management.[1]

At Oregon State University, our President, Dr. John V. Byrne, committed himself to lead OSU into a Total Quality Management program. We began about one year ago. Our goal was simple: to implement TQM throughout the university by 1994. This paper is designed to tell the story of that process.

1990 article reprinted with the permission of the author.

A LITTLE HISTORY

The Quality Gurus

W. Edwards Deming was first, the pioneer, the American who believed: "Improve quality and you automatically improve productivity. You capture the market with lower prices and better quality. You stay in business and you produce jobs. It's so simple."[2] Deming was the American who took his message to Japan, in 1950, and was instrumental in turning Japanese industry into an economic world power.

Juran arrived in Japan a few years after Deming and built an equally impressive record around quality planning, quality control, and quality improvement. Crosby became the third "quality guru" in 1979. The message of all three is basically the same:

- Commit to quality improvement throughout your organization.
- Attack the processes, not the employees.
- Strip down the process to find and eliminate problems that diminish quality.
- Identify your customers and satisfy their requirements.
- Instill teamwork and create an atmosphere for innovation and permanent quality improvement.[3]

The Quest for Quality in the United States

The quest for quality took 30 years to catch on in the United States. Organizations such as Ford Motor Company, Hewlett-Packard, Xerox, and Motorola have led the quality movement in the industry.

Ask almost anyone in industry today and they either have or are planning to implement TQM or another quality program. A recent survey by GOAL/QPC of Massachusetts found that about 50 percent of the "1000" Business Week top companies had initiated some form of quality improvement.[4] As each major company implements Total Quality Management, it requires its "vendors" to implement a similar program: hence the movement is growing logarithmically.

WHY USE TQM?

The major underlying principle of the quality movement in industry has been survival. Lost sales and declining profits have forced companies to try anything—even total quality management—to survive. Although public sector problems have not been that severe, across the country, belt tightening is now the rule in the public sector as the growth rate of tax revenues drops and services are shifted from the federal government to state and local levels. States, cities, and universities all hear the same cry: "Do more with less." They are asked to maintain or even increase productivity in spite of budget and staff cuts. (Stanford University recently faced a 20 percent across-the-board cut of administrative staff.)

How can we cope with this pressure? One answer may lie in the total quality management movement. Deming and Juran both say that with TQM we can achieve savings of up to 30 percent, and this has been validated by industry.

TQM in the Public Sector

Several attempts have been made to adapt Total Quality Management to the public sector. Two that have been particularly well documented are Florida Power and Light and the city of Madison, Wisconsin. Several hospitals and states are also implementing TQM. However, comparatively few attempts are under way in the education sector. (See Figure 1 for a partial listing.)

Delaware County Community College and Fox Valley Technical College began their work in TQM in 1986 using the Crosby model. Both started by providing training to business and industry and then expanded the concept to their own service areas. Both are now working to introduce TQM on the academic side.

TQM in Higher Education

In a telephone survey, we contacted 25 colleges and universities who are involved in some way with the TQM process. We found that 17 institutions are implementing a TQM focus in some part of the graduate or undergraduate curriculum, usually in business- or industry-related courses. In Florida, TQM is being implemented in the post-secondary vocational school system with the aim of producing well-trained graduates for industries that follow Total Quality principles and want to meet the criteria that will soon be required by the European common market.

We found that half of the institutions surveyed have significantly implemented TQM, using the process to the point of forming study teams. In five, TQM is used only for instruction or research. Of the 25 schools, 15 have significant efforts going on the service side and 10 have efforts going on the academic side. The most significant work in the academic area appears to be in two-year institutions.

The Big Questions

The big question is: How adaptable are the methods of Deming, Juran, and Crosby to the education industry? Manufacturing processes are far more predictable and controllable than the learning process. However, the service areas of the institution—facilities, billing, registration, security, etc.—all have counterparts in industry and should easily lend themselves to training in precision performance. This side of the educational enterprise can become the beginning point for TQM.

In addition, we do know a great deal about educational processes. Measurements of student achievement, curriculum, and instruction may yield more widely variable results than measurements on an assembly line. Nevertheless, using the principles and techniques of quality improvement, we can learn much.

FIGURE 1   Status of TQM in 25 U.S. Institutions of Higher Education

Status of TQM — Column key:

1. Used in administrative areas
2. Used in academic areas
3. Used in instruction
4. Doing research on TQM
5. Doing TQM consultation
6. Number of TQM teams operating
7. Use external consultants/trainers
8. Have TQM coordinator
9. Have TQM "champion"
10. Use "Guru" model
11. Use other models
12. Have TQM publications
13. Have had training
14. Have had training

Institution	1	2	3	4	5	6	7	8	9	10	11	12	13	14
Carnegie-Mellon U	X											X		
Chicago, Univ of	X	X	X									X	X	
Colorado State U	X	X	X	X		50	X	X	X	X	X	X	X	
Columbia U	X	X	X											
Delaware Co CC	X	X	X		X	@15	X	X	X	X		X	X	
Florida State U	X	X	X	X			X	X	X			X	X	
Fox Valley Tech	X	X	X	X	X	45	X	X	X	X	X	X	X	
Harvard U	X	X	X	X	X	3	X	X	X		X	X	X	
Hawkeye Inst of Tech	X	X	X	X		8		X						
Illinois Inst of Tech	X	X	X	X	X									
Jackson CC	X			X	X	3	X	X	X		X		X	
Lamar CC	X	X		X										
Michigan, Univ of	X	X	X			15-20	X	X	X	X		X		
Milwaukee Sch of Engin	X	X	X				X							
Minnesota, Univ of	X	X	X				X							
North Carolina, Univ of	X		X											
N D University System	X	X			X	2	X	X	X	X		X	X	
Northwestern U	X		X											
Oregon State U	X				X	15	X	X	X	X	X	X	X	
Palm Beach CC	X	X	X		X	3	X	X	X	X	X	X	X	
Pepperdine U	X	X	X		X			X	X	X	X			
Pittsburgh, Univ of	X		X							X				
St. Augustine Tech Cent	X	X	X		X	4	X	X	X	X		X	X	
Wisconsin, Univ of	X	X				5	X	X	X	X		X	X	
Wyoming, Univ of	X			X		9	X	X	X	X		X	X	

We must not, however, apply TQM principles without research, adaptation, training, and pilot testing in the actual university setting. Educators will need to be trained to collect and interpret data on program effectiveness and pupil achievement and to identify patterns that develop over a period of time. When a pattern is having a negative effect on the educational process, changes must be made. The quality improvement tools of TQM are available to do this.

The Purpose of This Paper

The purpose of this paper is to document Oregon State University's attempt to implement TQM throughout its structure, focusing on what we have learned to date in OSU's quest for improved quality. Particular attention will focus on documents developed, lessons learned from mistakes, structural changes, e.g., a reward system, that evolved from the program, and on changes in the behavior and attitudes of the participants.

Methodology

The matrix was derived from an informal telephone survey conducted during June 1990. Twenty-four institutions of higher education known to be involved in some form or Total Quality Management were contacted (Oregon State University is the 25th). Information was supplied by one or more persons knowledgeable about the status of TQM at the institution. A list of the institutions contacted, with their locations, is in Appendix D. The matrix does not represent all U.S. institutions of higher education involved in TQM. The survey was developed with assistance from Samford University, Birmingham, AL, and Fox Valley Technical College, Appleton, WI.

WHAT IS TOTAL QUALITY MANAGEMENT?

Total Quality Management is a system that combines the quality control theory, systems, tools, and organizational models developed over the last 40 years both in the United States and Japan. It is a logical evolution of management by objectives (MBO). Strategic Planning, Quality Circles (QC), Quality Assurance (QA), and many other systems. It builds on the successful components of each and discards the failures.

TQM is a structural system for creating organization-wide participation in planning and implementing a continuous improvement process that **exceeds** the expectations of the customer/client. It is built on the assumption that 90 percent of our problems are process problems, not employee problems.

TQM has three major components:

1. **Breakthrough Planning,** sometimes called Hoshin Planning. (Figure 2 diagrams the full planning process.) The purpose is to:
   - Clarify a vision of where the organization wants to go in the next five or ten years;

Figure 2   *Full Planning Process*

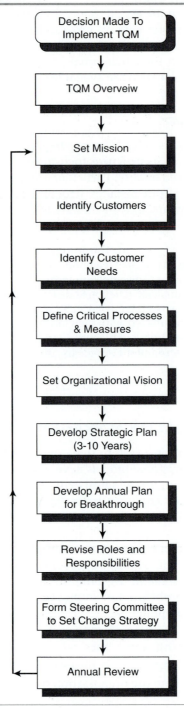

- Identify goals and objectives that move the organization toward its vision;
- Identify critical processes that must deliver the services provided to clients in a way that exceeds their expectations;
- Select a few (no more than 4) breakthrough items that can help the organization reach its vision quickly;
- Communicate this vision and the methods by which it will be met to all employees;
- Provide a structure for monitoring progress toward the vision.

Vision planning allows the organization to identify and focus on key areas of service, and it ensures full development of the methods and pathways by which "breakthroughs," major, fundamental quality improvements, can be implemented. All vertical levels of the organization then participate in the planning, development, and deployment of the identified strategic breakthroughs (see Figure 2).

Breakthrough Planning is an evolution of strategic planning which adds value statements, reminding us that "how we got here" is just as important as where we are going.

2. **Daily Management.** This system shows people what they personally must do, and what they must measure and control, to keep the organization running smoothly. It helps them define and understand the processes they use in producing services to meet customers' needs and expectations. Once these processes are understood, individuals and departments can continuously improve them, then standardize the improvements to ensure that gains are maintained.

   This continuous improvement is achieved by problem-solving teams who engage in identifying customer problems, finding solutions, and then providing ongoing control of the improved process. Use of several basic quality control tests and statistical methods helps people manage with facts, not opinions, and solve the real problems, not just the symptoms. Problem solving requires the collective efforts of everyone in the organization, working in study teams with the 10-step process shown in Figure 5.

   Daily Management is the most revolutionary of the three components of TQM. It empowers employees at all levels of the organization and focuses management improvement efforts on process problems.

3. **Cross-Functional Management.** This is the integration of team activities across divisions/departments to achieve organizational goals. It is the vehicle for breaking down departmental/divisional barriers. Through cross-functional management, top level managers can ensure that all groups in the university—faculty, staff, etc.—are working together for the good of the institution.

   This system leads the institution to listen to the "voice of the customer," identify customer needs, and incorporate those needs into every phase of the university operation.

IMPLEMENTING TQM

In TQM, how a process is implemented is as important as what the process includes. Many organizations still labor under the remnants of a departmentalized Taylor approach in which some employees plan improvements, others carry out the work, and still others inspect to see if procedures and results are correct. In TQM, all employees, every day, commit to improving the quality of their service so that customers' needs are not only met but exceeded.

At OSU, we found the growing TQM literature inundated with techniques, prescriptions, admonitions, and anecdotes. But little attention was devoted to how firms have implemented TQM, the hurdles they encountered, and how they responded and adapted TQM principles to their existing cultures.

FIGURE 3   *The OSU Total Quality Management Implementation Model*

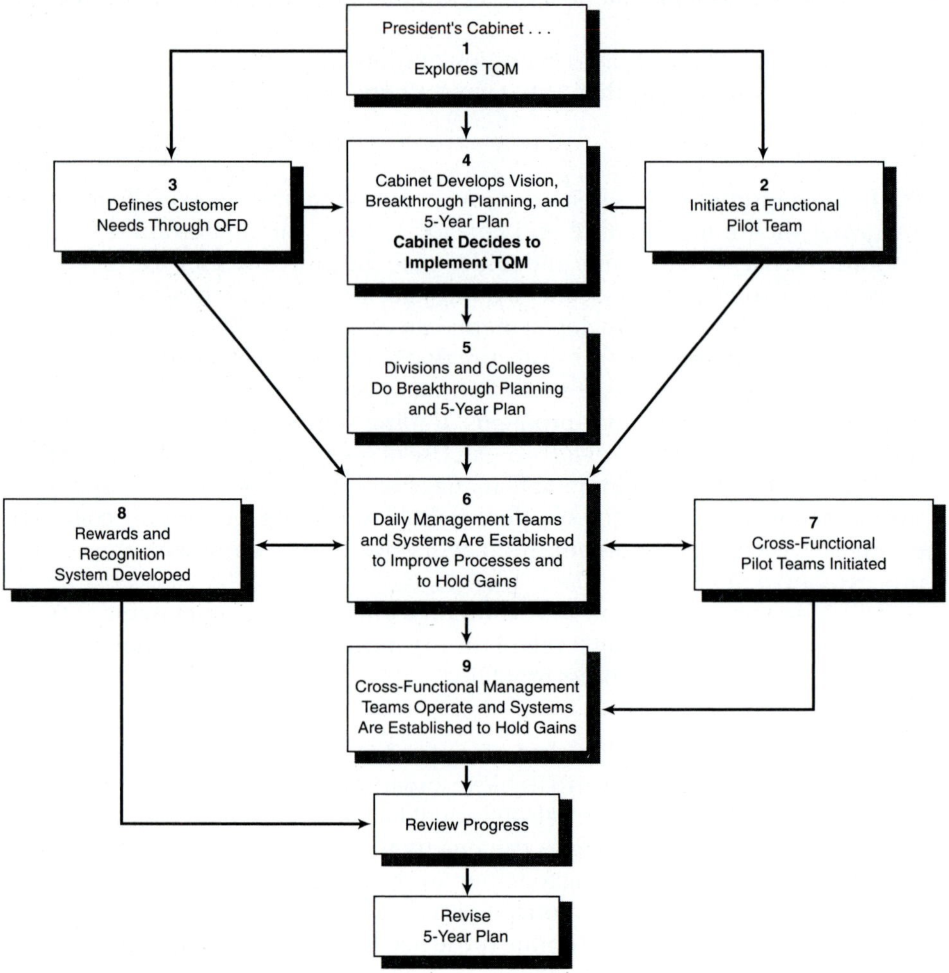

Furthermore, the lack of agreement among the TQM gurus produces contradictions and inconsistent prescriptions that are puzzling to would-be users. Deming says "eliminate slogans," while Crosby uses the slogan of "zero defects." Deming says "drive out fear," while Juran says "fear can bring out the best in people." Deming's process starts at the top and works down, while Juran starts with middle management and works both ways.

A non-profit TQM research company in Massachusetts, GOAL/QPC, found that six implementation models are currently being used.[5]

1. **The TQM Element Approach.** This approach, used in the early eighties, employs elements of quality improvement programs such as Quality Circles, Statistical Process Control, Quality Functional Deployment, etc., rather than full implementation of TQM.

2. **The Guru Approach.** This approach uses writing of a guru such as Deming, Juran, or Crosby, as a benchmark to determine what the organization lacks, then uses the guru's systems to make changes. Use of Deming's 14-point model is an example.

3. **The Japanese Model Approach.** Organizations using this method focused on study of the Japanese "Deming Prize Winners" as a way to develop an implementation master plan. This approach was used by Florida Power and Light.

4. **The Industrial Company Model Approach.** In this approach, people visit a U.S. industrial company using TQM, identify its successes, and integrate this information with their own ideas to create a customized approach. This method was used in the late 1980s by many of the Baldrige National Quality Award winners.

5. **The Hoshin Planning Approach.** This approach, developed by a Japanese firm, Bridgestone, was used successfully by Hewlett-Packard. It focuses on successful planning, deployment, execution, and monthly diagnosis.

6. **The Baldrige Award Criteria Approach.** In this model, an organization uses criteria for the Malcolm Baldrige National Quality Award to identify areas of improvement. The criteria cover seven key components of TQM. As the 1990s begin, this approach is being used by hundreds of industrial companies.

All of these approaches work. At OSU, we developed a model most closely associated with the Hoshin Planning Model used by Hewlett-Packard, and we used the Baldrige Award Criteria to help develop our five-year plan. Figure 3 shows OSU's model.

IMPLEMENTING TQM AT OREGON STATE

Implementation of Total Quality Management at OSU moved through the following phases.

Phase One: Exploring Total Quality Management

Our purpose in exploring TQM was to provide a "critical mass" of top management people who would understand what TQM is and why it might be of use to the university, and who would be willing to try a pilot to test the concept in our culture. This step was initiated because of the positive potential of the quality vision and in response to major challenges such as unhappy customers, lack of resources, and low employee morale.

Activities carried out during Phase One:

- Visited excellent companies with TQM programs, including Ford, Hewlett-Packard, and Dow, whose CEOs were alumni.
- Invited Dr. Deming to visit our university and explain TQM. (OSU awarded him an honorary doctorate in June 1989.)
- Read key books and articles on TQM (see Bibliography).
- The president, two other top managers, the staff development officer, and I attended an OSU continuing education class taught by Hewlett-Packard TQM staff on the seven TQM tools.
- Reviewed Baldrige Award criteria.

What We Learned

At the conclusion of Phase One, the President and Cabinet were enthusiastic about the potential of TQM. However, as word of these activities began to circulate, we perceived skepticism about TQM on the academic side of the university. TQM was seen as the "latest fad" in management style, and there was a severe "language barrier." Faculty members objected to terms like "total quality" and "management," feeling that they might lose control of important academic processes.

Title change. At this point we made the mistake of attempting to change the TQM title to something we felt would be more palatable—System Improvement Process. However, this simply generated suspicion and reinforced the idea that, by any name, this was just another management fad.

Faculty concerns. At a deeper level, faculty members see themselves as emphasizing diversity. To them, the idea of "quality control" suggests uniformity—trying to bring everything to the same level. In addition, faculty members are often accustomed to working alone, to competing, in fact, for limited resources such as grant money. Gaining acceptance for the idea of working together in teams to change processes may be a challenge on the academic side.

"Qualified approval." Some members of the academic community, however, began to give qualified approval to TQM. One said that "the great value I see in this concept is changing our orientation to seeing students as customers. This will require a turnaround in our culture." In fact, we were later able to establish TQM teams in two academic service-oriented areas: international education and continuing education.

Begin with service areas. For many reasons, then, we decided to proceed slowly on the academic side. We realized that our service areas would be the place to begin, as there are many parallels with industry in such areas as physical plant, computing, and business services. Our next step was the initiation of a pilot project in the Physical Plant Department.

Phase Two: Initial Pilot Study Team

In order to apply what we had learned about TQM and to learn more, we formed a TQM study team in the physical plant. We asked them to address a specific, high-priority issue that:

- had a high probability of success,
- management agreed was important,
- no one was working on, and
- was very important to the customer.

Initial Situation

When the TQM study team was formed, OSU's Physical Plant Department was characterized by poor internal communication and low worker morale. The department's image among many of its customers was extremely negative. Its services were seen to be slow, expensive, and delivered with little concern for customers' needs or desires.

The TQM Process

The pilot study team included managers and front-line workers, a team leader, and a training officer/facilitator, for a total of 12. The issue the team developed for study was "To decrease turnaround time in the remodelling process." As they moved through the TQM process, the team opened communication with the entire department, briefing other employees on progress, publishing team minutes, and posting their "process flow diagram" on the office wall for comments and suggestions.

The team found overlaps, time delays, and unnecessary paper flow in the remodelling process. They came to realize that their issue, though solvable, required study of too many facets. (The process flow chart, if laid out in a straight line, would be 17 feet long.) The team also found that a key area, engineering, needed more representation on the team.

To solve these problems, the team leader formed two sub-teams: engineering design, and construction. These groups identified problems in their processes, brainstormed causes, and proposed solutions to the team.

The Result: Change

Solutions implemented through TQM changed the basic structure of the physical plant and shortened the remodelling process by 10 percent, a percentage that continues to increase. Process changes affected worker attitudes and behaviors and delighted many customers. Among the changes were these:

- A new Customer Service Center was formed. Work requests and questions had formerly come to a secretary, who then sought information from several people in different places who were responsible for work scheduling, control, and follow-up. Now these people form a common unit that customers can call to find out what they need to know. The new unit is meeting with tremendous customer satisfaction, improving both project scheduling and the image of Physical Plant.

- To improve communication with customers, the team recommended and management established the position of project manager. Shop supervisors report work progress to the manager, and customers can talk about their needs with one person, face-to-face. The team recommended elements of the position description, criteria for measuring the position's effectiveness, and plans for customer and internal surveys to assess communication improvements.

- Four time-saving changes suggested by subteams are being implemented:
  - A free initial consultation with customers, using a brochure explaining the project process;
  - Hand-carrying of design and project authorization forms to the customer for consultation and completion;
  - Identification of equipment and materials that can be purchased during the design process;
  - A "shop participation walk-through" at the beginning of design to get input from the shops and identify possible problems.

Employee Attitudes

Formation of TQM teams in the physical plant has brought tremendous changes in work relationships and attitudes. The process showed top managers internal problems they had not recognized before and exposed workers to problems managers face in day-to-day operations. The result is cooperation.

Because team members came from all levels of the organization, they were able to improve internal communication. Shortly after the team was formed, word filtered out to the shops that things were changing for the better. Shops began talking with each other, and coordinating projects became much easier.

Physical Plant has become a much better place to work, employees say. Networks are spreading across the whole work force. Spirits are high. Workers are making many suggestions for improvements. With worker cooperation, areas that have had too many or too few employees are being reorganized.

One factor that is not measurable, the TQM team leader says, is a change in the work ethic. People are conscious of possibilities for improvement. They are doing a better job. Even beyond the teams and the TQM process, the result has been more trusting relationships between workers and happier customers.

Customer Satisfaction

A survey of customers showed that, even when the time to completion of a project has not decreased, they are more satisfied and more understanding of delays. Customers see that the Physical Plant Department is concerned and working on its problems. Customers feel that they are important because they've been listened to and are getting more personalized service.

Phase Three: Defining Customer Needs through Quality Function Deployment

Quality Function Deployment (QFD) is an organized system to identify and prioritize customer needs and translate them into university priorities. QFD is also a strategic tool in which customer needs and the characteristics of a service system are pulled into a matrix and compared.

We began QFD by identifying our customers and placing them in major groupings. They included:

External Customers
Students who Attend OSU
Students who Don't Attend OSU

Internal Customers
Supervisors
Staff   Faculty
Co-Workers

Community
Parents
Chancellor

Legislature
Visitors
Alumni

International Communtiy   Grantors
Other Institutions
State Board of Higher Education

Tools such as customer surveys, focus groups, complaints/feedbacks, etc., helped us to identify customer needs. These data sources were pulled together to form a set of customer views that is as accurate and complete as possible. This information helped executive management to understand where the university is and where it should be in its customers' eyes. It also highlighted points where data on customer needs and expectations is incomplete or non-existent.

About Our Customers

Three customer surveys conducted in 1989–90 provided the following data about OSU's customers.

The OSU Image Survey evaluated the perceived images of Oregon State University in the minds of six important customer groups: the general public, college-bound Oregon high school students, OSU alumni living in Oregon, OSU undergraduate students, classified staff, and faculty. Some findings:

- About one-third of the general public, one-sixth of the prospective students, and nearly one half of the alumni are not knowledgeable about OSU, its programs and activities.
- Physical attractiveness of OSU received the highest ratings, and while most groups perceived a friendly atmosphere, students, alumni, staff, and faculty gave low ratings to the concern of the OSU administration in dealing with their needs.
- Customers in the general public gave OSU good ratings in areas of providing service to the state, such as preparing graduates to be useful employees, listening to Oregonians, and helping them solve their problems.
- In general, OSU's academic reputation was rated as average, with recruitment of top students and matters of rigor and requirements rated low.

The Admitted Students Survey gave us additional information about student customers, those who did and did not enroll at OSU. Respondents compared OSU with other institutions they considered. In the basic area of information provided about OSU, they gave lowest marks to financial aid communications, college-sponsored meetings, contact with faculty, and contact with coaches. Contact with students and campus visits were rated highest. The images of OSU most frequently cited were friendly, social, comfortable, and fun.

The 1990 Faculty Survey provided this information about the university's internal academic customers:

- Their highest professional goal is to be good teachers, and their undergraduate teaching goal is to develop students' ability to think clearly.
- Their highest priority issues for the university are promoting intellectual development and conducting basic applied research.
- Job satisfaction centers mainly on having autonomy and independence; time pressures are the greatest source of stress.
- The primary funding priority is salaries, with support services, including facilities repair and library, second.

A survey of classified staff is currently being conducted.

Customer Survey

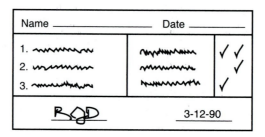

What We Learned

Universities have traditionally shied away from marketing. The idea of designing classes/courses to fit the "market" has been foreign to our university's way of thinking. Faculty know what students need, not the other way around! To begin to deal with this, we created a marketing committee to look at OSU's image and the products we deliver, a first step in beginning to realign classes offered with classes needed.

The marketing committee will become one of our first cross-functional teams. Training will help them to better understand TQM concepts and carry out Quality Functional Deployment activities. Because of the lack of non-industry examples (most QFD "house of quality" matrix examples focus on automobile designs) we are still having problems fully utilizing this concept. Total commitment to developing "customer-driven" systems will not come easily.

Phase Four: Top Management Breakthrough Planning (Hoshin Planning)

There are five major steps in the breakthrough planning process (see Figure 2):

- Mission;
- Customers;
- Critical Processes;
- Vision; and
- Breakthrough.

Step 1: Mission. All universities have a mission of teaching: because we are a land grant and sea grant university, we also have a mission of research and service. Hence:

OSU's mission as a land grant university is to serve the people of Oregon, the nation, and the world through education, research, and service.

Step 2: Customers. Customers are becoming increasingly more value conscious. If we are to be a leader in the future educational marketplace, we at OSU need to firmly establish ourselves as the highest value supplier, most responsive to our customers' expectations.

This means evaluating everything we do in terms of the value it brings to our external customers. It means asking our customers what their expectations are and taking action to meet those expectations. It also means continually surveying our customers for feedback on how we're doing.

Step 3: Critical Processes. Identifying the critical processes of the President of the university builds the foundation for the TQM processes. To do this, we identified the President's principal customers and the services we provide to each customer group. We then identified the key critical processes for these groups. The 12 processes and their performance measures are shown in the box below.

Step 4: Vision. OSU's vision began to take shape with the creation of an affinity diagram.

Affinity Diagram

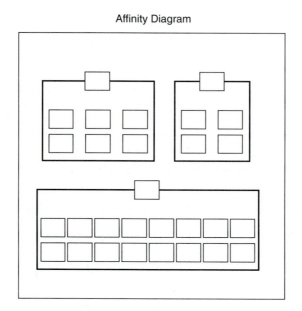

This chart is a TQM tool which collects attributes of the ideal university and organizes them into sets of related information. Discussions around the reasons why senior managers may differ in the desired characteristics of their future university highlighted the uniqueness of our university and its mission. OSU's vision statement was built on the university's mission and values statements (Appendix A).

> "It is OSU's vision to be recognized as a premier international university. We want each student to have at least one additional language, to have at least one quarter's experience in a foreign country, and to be computer literate. We want our faculty to have international experience and to increase our international research programs by 100 percent (from 26 countries now to 52). We want to increase foreign undergraduates from 10 to 15 percent of the student body.
>
> "We also want our university to be the best university in which to study and work. We want to be a university that knows what its clients will want ten years from now and what it will do to exceed all expectations. We want to be a university whose employees understand not only how to do their jobs but also how to significantly improve their jobs on a regular basis; where problems and challenges are met by a team of the most appropriate people, regardless of their level or jobs in the university."

After completing the vision statement, attention shifted to identifying barriers to achieving it. Using the affinity chart process again, we explored characteristics of the barriers, then used another TQM tool, the spider chart, to prioritize them. The purpose was to develop actions to deal with the barriers that might keep us from reaching our vision.

Spider Diagram

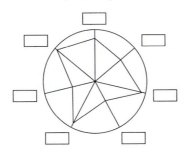

OSU's 12 Critical Processes

Process	Performance Measure
1. Admissions	concordance with enrollment management plan
2. Curriculum Development	peer acceptance
3. Teaching	student teaching evaluation
4. International Development	number of students going overseas
5. Research	number of publications
6. Service Delivery (Extension)	% of community participation
7. Community Relations	number of complaints
8. Information Services	computer-student ratio
9. Long-Range Planning	% objectives met
10. Workforce Hiring and Development	% first choice hires
11. Facilties Development	% of value to money for repairs
12. Funding Development	$ obtained/$ requested

We also integrated the university's goals with our critical processes (see Figure 4). OSU's goals and objectives are listed in Appendix B.

Barriers identified for OSU included:

- deteriorating physical infrastructure,
- increasing costs of doing research,
- deteriorating public image,
- deteriorating staff morale, and
- inadequate information systems (computing, library, telecommunications).

Step 5: Identifying Priority Breakthrough Items. Using our vision statement, our goals and objectives (Appendix B), and the barriers identified in Step 4, the process led us to focus on key breakthrough areas of service. We concluded that TQM's breakthrough planning does not replace the university's strategic plan, but supplements it by:

- Ensuring that employees at all levels understand their role in achieving the vision;
- Deploying the plan to the department level and ensuring that each academic or support department develops targets and strategies for reaching the vision;
- Providing detailed plans for support and measurement of progress toward the vision;
- Providing more operations detail than most traditional plans.

Results. As a result of these activities, three priority breakthrough items were identified:

- Increase computing capability in the university,
- Increase internationalization of the university, and
- Increase administrative efficiency by implementing TQM.

We then developed a preliminary 5-year plan (Appendix C) based upon the assessment and selection of priority breakthrough items and the Baldrige Award Criteria.

What We Learned

Breakthrough Planning is a logical extension of strategic planning, and we found that the planning process went very smoothly. We held four 4-hour sessions with the President and his Cabinet. Originally, we had hoped to use 8-hour sessions on Saturdays, but we found that four hours was the maximum time we could work effectively. We also found that the President's attendance at all sessions was critical.

We realized that all products of planning must be considered "first cut." They are continually modified as the process cascades down. For example, after we developed our critical processes at the vice president's level, we found that we needed to expand the President's critical processes from ten to twelve. We had missed two critical areas.

We also realized that it would take at least five years to implement TQM in all facets of university life. This was a surprise to our President and required him to make a significant, long-term commitment.

(Figure 2 details breakthrough planning process OSU followed.)

Phase Five: Divisions Do Breakthrough Planning

The Vice President and the division directors of Finance and Administration followed the process used by the Cabinet to create a vision statement, revise their unit's mission statement, and identify nine critical processes for Finance and Administration. Directors also identified the critical processes within their divisions.

The goals and objectives previously developed as part of OSU's Management by Objectives process were then distributed among the division directors as shown in Figure 4. Our major breakthrough item was to implement TQM throughout Finance and Administration.

Phase Six: Form Daily Management Teams

Teams are at the very heart of TQM. Better solutions emerge when everyone is given a chance to work on process problems. Just as importantly, solutions are implemented faster and last longer because the people affected have helped to develop them.

Study teams are composed of people who normally work together on the process being reviewed. They are led by someone from the natural work group, typically the supervisor. They usually work on processes that can be improved with resources they control. Teams are kept small (no more than ten) and each has a sponsor, usually the group's division director. The sponsor ensures that the team's work is linked to the critical processes and moves the university toward its vision.

Team Roles

If teamwork is to be successful, roles must be clearly identified and communicated at the outset.

The team leader is responsible for planning meetings, establishes constraints, distributes agendas in advance, keeps minutes, communicates with the sponsor, and ensures that the team completes its action plans.

The facilitator makes problem-solving suggestions, helps the team stay focused, provides "just-in-time" training on the problem-solving process, and ensures that everyone has a chance to participate.

FIGURE 4 OSU Critical Processes: Finance and Administration Detail

PRESIDENT: CRITICAL PROCESSES AND RELATED OSU GOALS

Admissions	Curriculum Development	Teaching	International Development	Research	Service Delivery (Extension)	Community Relations	Information Services	Long-Range Planning	Workforce Hiring & Development	Facilities Development	Funding Development	Safety
Goal 6	Goal 2	Goal 1	Goals 2,7	Goals 1,3	Goal 1	Goal 10	Goal 9	Goals 1–10	Goals 3,4,5	Goal 8		

VICE PRESIDENT FOR FINANCE AND ADMINISTRATION: CRITICAL PROCESSES AND RELATED OSU OBJECTIVES

Fiscal Services	Information Services	Workforce Hiring & Development	Long-Range Planning	Budgeting	Community Relations	Facilities Management	Law Enforcement	Safety
7.4, 9.4	9.3, 9.4, 9.5, 9.7, 9.8	3.1, 4.4, 4.5, 4.7, 4.8, 5.1, 5.2, 5.4, 5.5, 5.6, 5.8	10.1, 10.3, 10.4	1.4, 4.1, 8.4	10.2, 10.5	3.2, 4.2, 5.4, 8.1, 8.2, 8.3, 8.5, 8.6, 9.2		

Business Affairs
Accounting
Property Control
Travel & Transport
Fiscal Services
Telecommunications
Purchasing
Contracting
Risk Management
4.2, 4.4, 7.4, 9.4,
9.5, 9.8

Computing Services
Maintaining Hardware
Computer Purchasing
Networking
Training
Developing Standards
9.3, 9.4, 9.5, 9.7, 9.8

Printing & Mailing
Accounting
Printing
Quick Copy
U.S. Mailing Services
Blank Paper Sales
4.4, 7.4

Human Resources
Hiring
Labor Relations
Staff Development
Position Classification
Personnel Reporting
Benefits
Administration
Workers' Comp.
Claims Management
3.1, 4.4, 4.5, 4.7, 4.8,
5.1, 5.2, 5.4, 5.5, 5.6,
5.8

Radiation Center
Teaching
Research
Technical Services
1.2, 1.3, 1.7, 3.2,
3.3, 3.5

Budgets and Planning
Long-Range Planning
Archiving/Records
Management
Data Analysis
Budgeting
Policy Communication
1.4, 4.1, 4.2, 4.4, 8.4
**Institutional Research
and Planning**
Information Gathering
Information
Dissemination
Long-Range Planning
10.1, 10.3, 10.4

FIGURE 4 *OSU Critical Processes: Finance and Administration Detail (continued)*

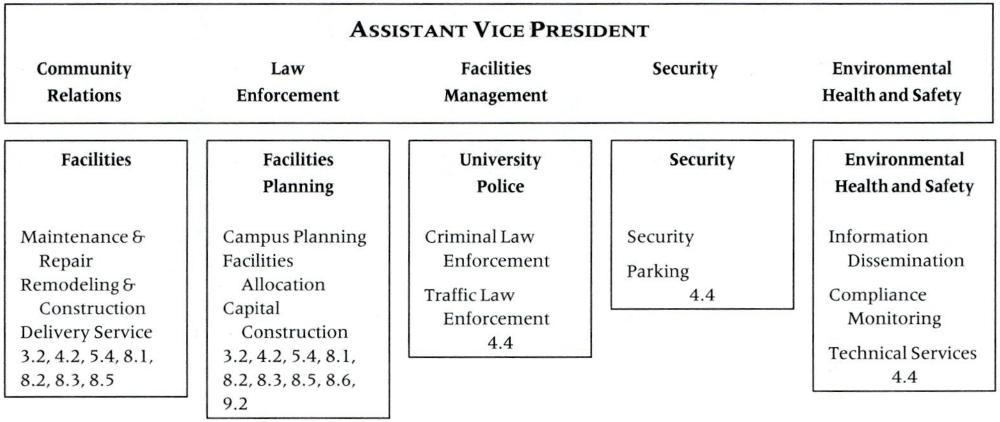

ASSISTANT VICE PRESIDENT

Community Relations	Law Enforcement	Facilities Management	Security	Environmental Health and Safety

Facilities

Maintenance & Repair
Remodeling & Construction
Delivery Service
3.2, 4.2, 5.4, 8.1, 8.2, 8.3, 8.5

Facilities Planning

Campus Planning
Facilities Allocation
Capital Construction
3.2, 4.2, 5.4, 8.1, 8.2, 8.3, 8.5, 8.6, 9.2

University Police

Criminal Law Enforcement
Traffic Law Enforcement
4.4

Security

Security
Parking
4.4

Environmental Health and Safety

Information Dissemination
Compliance Monitoring
Technical Services
4.4

FIGURE 5 *Step Problem Solving Process*

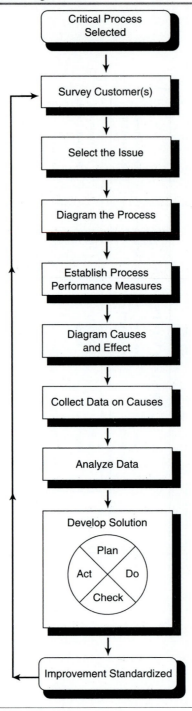

The team member attends all meetings, contributes ideas, collects data, recommends solutions, and helps to implement them.

10-Step Problem Solving Process

How do teams make improvements? They do it by using the 10-step problem solving process (Figure 5). The process is designed to provide a common technique and language for process improvement. It begins with the customer, focuses on root causes/barriers to improvement, and ensures that decisions and actions are based on real data.

ONE. At the "sponsor" level, identify and select the most important opportunities for improvement. We started with our critical processes, especially those that support our goals, objectives, and breakthrough items. Select team members and empower them to make improvements.

TWO. Determine the key customers of the processes and the services we provide them. Then survey the customers, using a standard format, and analyze the survey data using check sheets, Pareto diagrams, etc.

THREE. Select the most important issue and write a clear issue statement.

FOUR. Identify and flow chart the key process or processes. This enables the team to more clearly recognize opportunities for improvement.

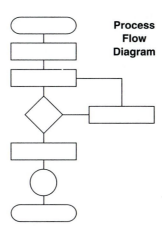

Process Flow Diagram

FIVE. Agree on which aspects of your performance you want to measure and, with your customers, set goals for continuous improvement in meeting or exceeding their expectations. To do this, the team must realistically evaluate current performance and set obtainable goals for improvement.

SIX. Begin to explore probable causes of the problems and barriers to improvement. A fishbone diagram tool is used in this step.

Fishbone Diagram

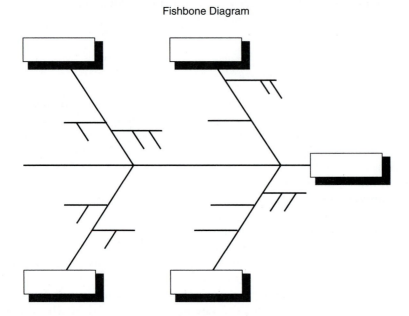

SEVEN. Gather data on the probable causes. The information collected gives the team a benchmark against which to measure its future progress.

EIGHT. Evaluate the data and show it in "pictures"—charts and graphs.

NINE. Brainstorm and develop permanent solutions. Implement solutions; monitor their performance; adopt them if they work.

TEN. If the problem is solved, standardize the fixes as normal operating procedures.

New Teams Being Formed

We are now forming study teams in areas outside the Finance and Administration area in International Education, Continuing Education, Housing, and Development. We have formed a steering committee to begin implementation in the academic area. Ultimately, all OSU employees will have the experience of being on a team. About 400 teams will be required.

What We Learned

In evaluating the Finance and Administration TQM study teams, participants said they liked the fact that teams were formed at all levels of the organization. They believed they had seen process improvements that impact their own and other departments.

Survey, flow chart. The parts of the problem-solving process members found most valuable were the customer survey and the flow chart. Surveys helped them

TQM Teams in Finance and Administration

In Finance and Administration, we formed teams in each division around one of the division's critical processes, if possible, a process that dealt with a university objective. The first ten teams, their processes and issue statements, are shown below

Team	Division	Critical Process	Issue Statement
1A	Physical Plant	Facilities Management	Reduce the amount of time it takes to complete the re-modeling process.
1B	Physical Plant	Facilities Management	Improve servicing of fixed equipment.
2	Printing	Information Services	Reduce the amount of time in the pre-press stage of the printing process.
3	Budgets and Planning	Budgeting	Increase the timeliness of the Budget-Status-at-a-Glance report development process.
4	Computing Services	Information Services	Increase the timeliness and consistent delivery of net-work information.
5A	Business Affairs	Fiscal Services	Increase the availability of information provided by Business Affairs for the monitoring of 050 income and expense projections.
5B	Business Affairs	Fiscal Services	Reduce the time expended in processing grant and contract documents within Business Affairs.
6	Public Safety	Safety	Decrease response time for requests for service.
7	Radiation Center	(President's critical processes: teaching, research, service delivery)	Increase customer demand for the Center's products and streamline response process.
8	Human Resources	Workforce Hiring & Development	Increase the speed of initial response in the informa-tion dissemination process.

get to know their customers as people. The flow chart often helped them visualize their process for the first time. Teams used a standard computer software package called "Easy Flow" to create their diagrams.

Issues. We found that although all ten teams began with the issue/problem suggested by their sponsor, through customer surveys, every team discovered the issue to be different than the sponsor had perceived. All changed their issue statements before moving on. Many teams said they would rather choose their own issues than have one assigned.

Team diversity. Each team used the tools of the TQM process in the way that best fitted their situation. Some moved rapidly, others more cautiously. Some teams felt pushed by their sponsor, leader, and facilitator. They wanted more time to do the process and less pressure to succeed. Other teams felt they were moving too slowly and wanted to rush ahead. We learned that sponsors and other managers needed to accept the uniqueness of each group's functioning, not expecting everyone to reach the same point at the same time.

Time. Many team members said that taking time away from their regular tasks for team meetings and study assignments was a problem. Some felt that they should be released from some duties. Sponsors need to show their commitment to TQM by supporting the team members as they deal with time and job pressures.

Training. The quality of training was an issue, especially for facilitators and team leaders. As consultants gradually withdrew from the process, some facilitators felt unprepared for their role. Some teams asked for more training as well, with a focus on the specific procedures teams need to use.

Phase Seven: Cross-functional Pilot Projects

Frequently, difficult problems and opportunities lie across several functional areas. The purpose of cross-functional teams is to provide advanced skill development within the university, to target team efforts on key projects that cross functional lines, and to evaluate and improve the work of ongoing study teams. Cross-functional teams can integrate study across division lines, often improving systems at the policy level.

Cross-functional teams can also select projects aligned with the priority breakthrough items. These well-educated team members can use their knowledge in selecting study problems and evaluating results.

At OSU, our pilot cross-functional team was composed of Finance and Administration division directors. They selected the issue of improving the study team process.

This team has completed a survey of its customers—the other study team members, sponsors, and facilitators—and is in the process of refining their issue statement. As early evaluations by team members showed ("What We Learned," this page) time required by TQM work and the content of training are problems the cross-functional team will need to address as they continue through the TQM problem-solving steps.

Phase Eight: Cross-Functional Management

The cross-functional pilot project is still under way and results are not yet in. However, we can already see many excellent applications of this process. Universities operate with many committees, most of them composed of faculty, staff, and students.

As the Vice President for Finance and Administration, I have 15 committees advising me in such areas as parking, safety, handicapped access, university computing, etc. Most of these committees have cross-functional responsibility and, with the necessary training, are naturals for implementing TQM at a cross-functional level. Within the next year, we plan to convert these committees to cross-functional study teams.

Phase Nine: Reporting, Recognition, and Awards

Reporting   Each division director reports monthly to the Vice President for Finance and Administration. These monthly reports focus on the performance measures of each division director's critical processes. Each year, the vice president reviews improvements made in each critical process with each division director and sets the goals for the director for the next year. These performance evaluations are also tied to salary setting, with salary increases reflecting improvements.

As study teams finish their efforts on a particular issue, the vice president and the division directors meet as a review committee and hear the team's presentation of their solutions. The team sponsor reports on progress in implementation of the solutions.

Teams also report to the President and his Cabinet. These presentations demonstrate senior management interest in TQM and provide immediate recognition. However, team members have identified implementation of their solutions as the best reward possible, and implementation tracking is an important part of our reporting and recognition program.

Awards   We are also developing an awards program for outstanding team or individual performance based on savings (time and money), uniqueness of solutions, and importance to the university. Three categories of awards will be presented.

Each category is open to any employee; any employee can make nominations; and we are developing specific criteria and a selection process for each award.

- **Quality Award.** This award recognizes employees who have participated in an activity (problem-solving task) that, either through teamwork or outstanding individual effort, has made a significant, measurable impact on the university. The activity must have reached its objectives, have measurable results, and have a daily management plan established.

One or more Quality Awards are presented once a year during University Day and include a personalized plaque, a monetary award, recognition in the staff newsletter, and engraving of the name on a Quality Award Winners plaque that is displayed in the administration building.

- **Beaver Award.** This award, named for OSU's mascot, recognizes and shows appreciation for employees or teams who have sustained continuous, high-quality work performance that goes beyond expectations. For instance, recipients will have completed special projects while maintaining high efficiency in regular duties; repeatedly accepted added responsibilities; continually accomplished major job objectives above expected levels; and shown innovation and initiative.

  Beaver Awards may be given twice a year to any number of recipients and include a pin and certificate and a Beaver Balloon as well as recognition in the staff newsletter and at University Day.

- **Great Performance Award.** This award is used to spontaneously recognize and show appreciation to employees who have exceeded expectations in the performance of a specific activity or action, either unique or routine, showing at least one of the following: initiative, competence, customer service, flexibility, communication, cooperation, or tenacity. Examples: showing good judgment in handling a crisis; developing a procedure, identifying an ineffective system, or correcting an omission that saves money; receiving commendations from customers.

  The Great Performance Award is given at any time, within one month of the employee's action. It can include a small gift, a Great Performance balloon or certificate, and includes recognition in the staff newsletter.

Lessons Learned

Recognition is very important, and presentations to the President are critical. Team sponsors have also participated in the recognition process by purchasing team hats, coffee cups, etc. Everything helps. We are also exploring the possibility of financial awards based solely on savings; awards of up to ten percent of the savings are allowed by state government. In the early going, we found that simply being on a team is a form of recognition, giving the team member special status.

CONCLUSIONS AND RECOMMENDATIONS

In creating Oregon State's vision statement, we identified Total Quality Management as vital, not only for the realization of our vision, but also for OSU's continued survival in the university's world marketplace. Quality is what our customers tell us it is, not what we say it is. Both internal and external customers want to receive the same high-quality service at all times, with no surprises. Progress can only be determined and improved by measurement.

While Total Quality Management is a relatively simple concept, putting it to work in a university was more challenging than many of us realized at first. The language was foreign to us (universities do use different words than industry). The teamwork approach to problem solving was unfamiliar to most of our mid-level managers. But so far, we consider TQM a real success at OSU. We now have 15 teams operating and the results have been spectacular. Time has been saved, costs have been reduced, people have been empowered at all levels, and morale has skyrocketed.

Managers must lead the TQM process. Each manager's job is to continuously demonstrate in both words and action that TQM is a top priority. This means regularly using study teams, reviewing progress in staff meetings, providing training to everyone, and recognizing and rewarding those who use the process.

Six Key Points . . .

Let me conclude by suggesting six key points in the successful implementation of TQM in a college or university:

- **Support from the top.** It is essential to have a firm commitment from the President or Chief Operating Officer of the university. Deming found this to be the single most important step in implementing TQM.

- **Just do it!** Don't study it to death. Learn about the steps the teams go through and get one started. Only then will you understand what TQM is all about and whether it will fit into your culture.

- **The teams are everything!** Focusing teams on process improvement is what it is all about. Make sure they have adequate training before they begin. Then stick to the process. The Hawthorn effect is prevalent at first, but the TQM process will see that solutions get implemented. Team building is almost as important as process improvement.

- **You need a champion.** Implementation of TQM takes a long commitment (five years), a lot of time (up to 20 percent), and costs money (at least 60K/year). Someone has to be the champion to get it going, keep it going, and make sure solutions are implemented.

- **Breakthrough planning helps.** Not all TQM programs include breakthrough planning. But it helps in vertical alignment, integration of strategic planning processes already under way, and in focusing efforts on processes that can really make a difference.

- **Try the service side first!** In a university setting, the service sector is an easier place to start than the academic side. Start with a unit that is having trouble; they know they need help and will appreciate being helped. You need early success to get momentum going.

An Invitation . . .

As we look toward the future, a future of increasing international competition, TQM will be more important than ever. Implemented properly, it can make the difference between success and failure. Is it a fad? Who knows. But I believe it can make a real difference and that it **can** be implemented in a university setting. If you are considering a TQM program at your institution and want more information, please call me at Oregon State University. I'll be glad to help!

Appendix A

OSU's Mission, Values, and Guiding Principles

Oregon State University is among the leading comprehensive teaching and research universities in the nation. Our mission as a land grant university is to serve the people of Oregon, the nation, and the world through education, research, and service. Through our dedicated teaching, through the pursuit of knowledge, and through our extended relationships to the broader society, we seek continually to improve our contributions to the general welfare.

Values

How we accomplish our mission is as important as the mission itself. The following values are fundamental to our success:

People. Our people—students, faculty, staff, and alumni—are our strength. They are the source of our creativity, they determine our reputation, and they provide our vitality.

Respect. All our people are important contributors. Respect, humanity, and integrity are required in our treatment of each other.

Openness. In the classrooms, laboratories, studios, and field stations, our efforts are open to challenge and debate.

Truth and Truths. We seek truths in our pursuit of knowledge. But we know that there is no such thing as "the truth." Understandings in the sciences, arts, and humanities change. We challenge dogma when we encounter it in our classrooms, in our laboratories and studios, and in our role of serving the broader society.

Guiding Principles

Students are our most important clients. The quality and completeness of their education is our top priority.

We have a responsibility to society to contribute to its social, aesthetic, and economic well-being.

Our social responsibility extends to offering informed criticism even when that criticism may not be well received. We maintain an internal environment that will nurture this important contribution.

Flexibility, change, and constant improvement are essential to our continued success.

In instruction, research, and service activities, we honor and impart principles of academic honesty, freedom, and integrity.

Diversity is a key to our success. Not only are our doors open to men and women alike without regard to race, ethnicity, personal belief, disability, age, or sexual preference, but we also have a moral obligation to open the doors wider for any groups that are under-represented or that have suffered from discrimination.

Appendix B

Oregon State University's Strategic Plan Goals and Objectives

GOAL 1   Serve people through instruction, research, and extension.

1.1   Promote and recognize good teaching.
1.2   Adequately staff and support academic programs essential to the university's mission.
1.3   Adequately support essential programs of research and artistic creativity.
1.4   Periodically review programs to shift resources to areas of need.
1.5   Use evening, weekend classes, and Oregon's Ed-Net to make degree programs available to nontraditional students.
1.6   In developing criteria, procedures for assignment of rank, evaluation, and promotion and tenure, continue to recognize the varied roles of faculty in programs.
1.7   Involve faculty and staff in extension programming and cooperation with other agencies to help Oregonians solve problems, develop leadership, and manage resources.

GOAL 2   Help students to achieve their full potential.

2.1   Improve recognition for teaching, academic advising, and student-faculty interaction.
2.2   Improve students' experiences in living groups, orientation, peer relationships, academic learning/assistance centers.
2.3   Streamline and personalize support service rules, procedures.
2.4   Provide child care for children of students.
2.5   Encourage awareness and understanding of cultural diversity by developing international programs and campus interaction between students of different cultures.
2.6   Improve analysis and evaluation of student achievement, advising, academic support services, and overall university experience.
2.7   Regularly review undergraduate curricula not subject to special accreditation.

GOAL 3   Expand research and artistic creativity.

3.1   Recruit and support faculty, staff, and students of high research, artistic capability.
3.2   Improve research facilities and equipment.
3.3   Encourage interdisciplinary studies and research.
3.4   Enable scholarly and creative productivity of faculty in humanities, social sciences, arts, and education.
3.5   Promote, coordinate, and publicize research and artistic achievement.

GOAL 4   Attract, develop, retain excellent faculty and staff.

4.1   Bring faculty salaries to competitive levels.
4.2   Expand facilities and program support as required for a major teaching and research university.

4.3   Strengthen programs and rewards that promote good teaching.
4.4   Provide a work environment that builds cooperation, mutual respect, and high morale.
4.5   Expand programs that promote faculty and staff professional development.
4.6   Establish university day-care services for faculty and staff.
4.7   Promote upward mobility for staff positions.
4.8   Improve faculty/staff recruiting procedures.

GOAL 5   Expand opportunities for minorities, females, disadvantaged, and disabled.

5.1   Intensify recruitment of women and people of color to faculty positions in which they are under-represented.
5.2   Evaluate classified employment processes to increase personnel from under-represented groups; seek external policy change where necessary.
5.3   Improve recruitment of students from under-represented or disadvantaged groups.
5.4   Remove physical barriers for persons with disabilities and increase their representation at management and senior levels.
5.5   Promote retention of students, faculty, and staff from under-represented groups.
5.6   Sustain a campus climate sensitive to the needs of under-represented groups and help to make the Corvallis community more attractive to people of color.
5.7   Diversify curriculum to include courses and materials relevant to the culture and experiences of women and people of color.
5.8   Ensure pay equity for women and people of color.

GOAL 6   Increase enrollments of outstanding students.

6.1   Improve the quality and rigor of academic programs.
6.2   Raise undergraduate admission standards.
6.3   Strengthen the Honors Program and other academic enrichment programs for outstanding students;
6.4   Actively market the highest quality academic programs.
6.5   Expand resources for merit scholarships, awards, and research stipends.
6.6   Target recruitment of outstanding applicants.
6.7   Improve instructional support services.
6.8   Develop a policy on the makeup of the OSU student body.

GOAL 7   Sharpen the university's international focus.

7.1   Strengthen the international dimensions of the curriculum.
7.2   Expand the international perspective of faculty.
7.3   Increase students' global awareness and interest in international educational experiences.
7.4   Support international activities.
7.5   Strengthen liaison with international constituents.
7.6   Support international programs and services in higher education in Oregon.

GOAL 8   Improve facilities and equipment.

8.1   Give fund-raising priority first to library expansion, second to visual and performing arts instructional facilities, third to computer science facilities.
8.2   Upgrade instructional laboratory facilities and equipment.
8.3   Upgrade classroom facilities and equipment and provide more large classrooms.
8.4   Increase funding for facilities repair and remodeling.
8.5   Improve and maintain research facilities and equipment.
8.6   Promote joint use of facilities and equipment.

GOAL 9   Improve library and computing services.

9.1   Qualify for membership in the Association of Research Libraries.
9.2   Review information support services needs and fund a major library facilities expansion to meet them.
9.3   Provide computing services consistent with the university's research and instructional mission.
9.4   Impelement the Student Information System and Financial Information System.
9.5   Continue to expand student access to computing facilities.
9.6   Improve print and non-print collection to meet needs.
9.7   Coordinate decision-making for computing management.
9.8   For library and computing services, expand networking access on campus, statewide, nationally, and internationally and keep pace with new technologies.
9.9   Coordinate collection development, resource sharing, and automated access with other libraries.

GOAL 10   Improve the university's relationships with its constituencies.

10.1   Create and maintain a clear OSU image to emphasize quality of students, instruction, research, and service.
10.2   Motivate OSU's constituencies to increase their support.
10.3   Improve responsiveness of faculty, staff, administrators to their clients.
10.4   Maintain programs to evaluate OSU's effectiveness in meeting constituency needs.
10.5   Maintain close, productive relationships with community citizens and leaders.

Note: Some objectives have been abbreviated for the purposes of this paper.

Appendix C

Oregon State University Total Quality Management

	Aim	Jul	Aug	Sept	Oct	Nov	Dec	Jan	Feb	Mar	Apr	May	Jun
	Items to Accomplish This Year.							F&A Pilot projects — Strategic, daily mgmt systems established, deployed — Executive concensus on TQM direction — Announce TQM to staff — Steering Comm established					
System Changes	Daily Management		Top mgmt team establishes mission. critical processes & measures, vision, strategic plan framework. — F&A mgmt team establishes mission critical processes, and vision.					Deploy ⟶			Review plans		
	Hoshin Planning			Top mgmt team selects Year 1 breakthrough objective and review dates. ⟶ F&A team selects and plans breakthrough objectives in keeping with top mgmt plans. ⟶						Review plans			
	Cross-functional Management				Top mgmt team establishes plans to support daily mgmt ⟶ and Hoshin plans.					Review plans			
	Training and Teams		Top mgmt attends TQM class.		Ten teams, one in each unit of F&A, trained in philosophy, tools of TQM. — Quarterly executive briefings: a. Steering committee b. F&A mgmt team					Ten teams in units other than F&A trained in TQM. — Two teams started in cross-functional processes			

	Aim	Year 2: 1990–91	Year 3: 1991–92
	Items to Accomplish This Year.	Pilot project evaluation; annual review of plans: expand pilot areas and planning systems. Pilot "Presidential Review."	Expand TQ to all areas; establish "Presidential Review" in all areas. (6.1) Plans now based on customer competitive and past performance data.
System Changes	Daily Management	All managers using daily management methods of planning and process control. (5.7) Educate employees on customer/supplier issues.	(5.5) Document TQ systems in Quality manual. (5.7) (7.1) Improve understanding of customer/supplier needs. Daily management system improved and standardized. (7.2) Measure trends in customer data.
	Hoshin Planning	(7.1) (3.2) (2.1) (2.2) Customer, competitive data gathered and fed into plans. (Quality Function Deployment)	All managers trained in planning tools. All managers using breakthrough planning system. Conduct Baldrige Award review.
	Cross-functional Management	(5.6) (5.7) (6.2) Results of QFD shared with all managers. University-wide standing committee established on Quality.	QFD results aid planning processes. University-wide standing committee established on cost.
	Training Teams	(6.3) Require use of QC story to record team results. (4.1) Daily management and hoshin systems include employee education and involvement in TQ.	Interdepartment TQ results sharing/seminars. (4.2) All employees trained in TQ. (4.4) Employee recognition system developed.

Aim		Year 4: 1992–93	Year 5: 1993–94
	Items to Accomplish This Year.	Hoshin, daily management system based on data and well-established. (5.3) (2.3) Systems standardized and prevention-oriented.	
System Changes	Daily Management	Daily management plan based on data; now a continuous system (year-to-year) with small shifts. (7.3) Monitor macro-trends in customer data, "wins - losses.'	WIN BALDRIGE AWARD.
	Hoshin Planning	Address Baldrige Award deficits. (5.1) Vision, strategic plan and breakthrough objective based on data; continuous process with small shifts.	
	Cross-functional Management	(5.2) Standing cross-functional teams. Team results shared cross-functionally.	
	Training Teams	University-wide team seminars. Results well-documented. (4.5) Total Quality includes Quality of Worklife issues.	(1.4) Teams share with other universities.

Appendix D

TQM Survey: Institutions Contacted

Four-Year Institutions
Carnegie-Mellon University, Pittsburgh, PA
Colorado State University, Fort Collins, CO
Columbia University, New York, NY
Florida State University, Tallahassee, FL
Harvard University, Cambridge, MA
Illinois Institute of Technology, Chicago, IL
Milwaukee School of Engineering, Milwaukee, WI
Northwestern University, Evanston, IL
Oregon State University, Corvallis, OR
Pepperdine University, Malibu, CA
University of Chicago, Chicago, IL
University of Michigan, Ann Arbor, MI
University of Minnesota, Minneapolis, MN
University of North Carolina, Chapel Hill, NC
University of Pittsburgh, Pittsburgh, PA
University of Wisconsin, Madison, WI
University of Wyoming, Laramie, WY

Two-Year Institutions
Delaware County Community College, Media, PA
Fox Valley Technical College, Appleton, WI
Hawkeye Institute of Technology, Waterloo, IA
Jackson Community College, Jackson, MI
Lamar Community College, Lamar, CO

Palm Beach Community College, Lake Worth, FL
St. Augustine Technical Center, St. Augustine, FL
Other:
North Dakota University System, Bismarck, ND

Notes

1. W. Edwards Deming, *Out of the Crisis* (Cambridge: Massachusetts Institute of Technology Center for Advanced Engineering Study, 1986): Chapter Two.
2. Joseph Oberle, "Quality Gurus, the Men and Their Message," *Training Magazine* (January 1990): 47.
3. Oberle: 48.
4. *Vision 2000, America's Top 1,000 Companies' Quality Progress,* 1990 Research Report (GOAL/QPC, Methuen, MA).
5. *Competitive Times,* Volume I, 1990 (GOAL/QPC, Methuen, MA).

Bibliography

Aubrey, Charles A., III, and Patricia K. Felkins. *Teamwork: Involving People in Quality and Productivity Improvement.* Milwaukee: Quality Press, 1988.

Block, Peter. *The Empowered Manager.* San Francisco: Jossey-Bass Publishers, 1989.

Bone, Diane, and Griggs, Rick. *Quality at Work.* Los Altos: Crisp Publications.

Bowsher, Jack E. *Educating America.* New York: John Wiley & Sons, Inc., 1989.

Byham, William C., Ph.D., with Jeff Cox. *Zapp! The Lightning of Empowerment.* DDI Press.

Crosby, Philip B. *The Eternally Successful Organization.* New York: McGraw-Hill, 1988.

Crosby, Philip B. *Quality Is Free. The Art of Making Quality Certain.* New York: McGraw-Hill, 1979.

Crosby, Philip B. *Quality Without Tears.* New York: McGraw-Hill, 1984.

Davis, Stanley M. *Future Perfect.* New York: Addison-Wesley Publishing Co., 1989.

Deal, Terrence E., and Allen A. Kennedy. *Corporate Cultures, the Rites and Rituals of Corporate Life.* New York: Addison-Wesley Publishing Co., 1982.

Deming, W. Edwards. *Out of the Crisis.* Cambridge: Massachusetts Institute of Technology Center for Advanced Engineering Study, 1986.

Goldzimer, Linda Silverman. *'I'm First.' Your Customer's Message to You.* New York: Rawson Assoc., MacMillan, 1989.

Hart, Marilyn K. and Robert F. *Quantitative Methods for Quality and Productivity Improvement.* Milwaukee: ASQC Quality Press, 1989.

Imai, Masaaki. *Kaizen, The Key to Japan's Competitive Success.* New York: Random House Business Division, 1986.

Ishikawa, Kaoru. *What is Total Quality Control? The Japanese Way.* New York: Prentice Hall, 1986.

Joiner Associates, Inc. *A Practical Approach to Quality (Selected Readings in Quality Improvement).* Madison, 1985.

Juran, J. M. *Juran on Leadership for Quality, An Executive Handbook.* New York: The Free Press, Macmillan.

Kume, Hitoshi. *Statistical Methods for Quality Improvement.* Tokyo: The Association for Overseas Technical Scholarships (AOTS), 1985.

McLean, Gary N., and Susan H. DeVogel. *Role of Organization Development in Quality Management and Productivity Improvement.* Minneapolis: University of Minnesota & ASTD.

Miller, William C. *The Creative Edge, Fostering Innovation Where You Work.* New York: Addison-Wesley Publishing Co., 1987.

Ray, Michael, and Rochelle Myers. *Creativity in Business.* New York: Doubleday, 1989.

Reddy, W. Brendan, and Kaleel Jamison, eds. *Team Building, Blueprints for Productivity and Satisfaction.* NTL Institute for Applied Behavioral Science & University Associates, Inc., 1988.

Rosander, A. C. *Applications of Quality Control in the Service Industries.* Milwaukee: ASQC Quality Press.

Rosander, A. C. *The Quest for Quality in Services.* Milwaukee: Quality Press, 1989.

Schwarz, Robert A. *Midland City, Recovering Prosperity Through Quality.* Milwaukee: ASQC Quality Press, 1989.

Townsend, Patrick L., with Joan E. Gebhardt. *Commit to Quality.* New York: John Wiley & Sons, 1990.

Tucker, Allan. *Chairing the Academic Department.* 2nd ed. New York: Macmillan, 1984.

Walton, Mary. *The Deming Management Method.* New York: Putnam, 1986.

The Paradigm Shifts Required to Apply TQM and Teams in Higher Education

———

By Michael J. Brower

ABSTRACT

From manufacturing, where it got its major start in this country, TQM has spread recently and rapidly into many service industries, including hospitals and health care organizations. Finally, in the last few years, some institutions of higher educations have begun to study and apply TQM, in one or more of three forms. The largest number are applying TQM philosophy, principles and tools to improve their supporting services and functions that are most like those in industry, such as student registration, housing, financial services, housekeeping, buildings and grounds, etc. Another very large group has approached TQM as new subject matter to be taught, as content, for courses in Business, Engineering and other departments and schools. On the other hand, only a small handful of colleges and universities are now beginning to apply TQM to their heart and core: the education of students. This essay deals with nine of the fundamental concepts used in TQM, and with the shifts in mind set, in mental models or paradigms, that are required if TQM and Teams are to be seriously applied to the core educational processes of colleges and universities. These nine concepts: The Customer, The Product, The Producer, The Process, Teams, The Source of Quality, The Role of Management, Continuous Improvement, and Benchmarking.

INTRODUCTION AND OVERVIEW

Total Quality Management (TQM) and Teams are rapidly becoming the preferred fundamental ways of organizing, planning, and leading for competitiveness in

---

1992 article reprinted with the permission of the author.

manufacturing. They are spreading now rapidly in dozens of service industries, including financial institutions, hospitals, and other health care institutions. Institutions of post-secondary education are also, finally, getting involved with TQM and the use of Teams. (This essay applies to all such institutions, including two and four year colleges and universities, public and private. However for simplicity in writing I will hereafter use the single word universities to apply to any and all institutions of post-secondary or higher education.) There are three general arenas in which universities are applying TQM. First, of the couple of hundred institutions that are known to be interested in and acting in some way on TQM, the vast majority are applying it to their administrative, service and support functions, such as buildings and grounds, student registration and housing, food service, and financial administration (Axland, Marchese, Seymour & Collett). These support activities are most similar to those in private business, they are easiest to start with, and they are least threatening to the traditional power and paradigms of the faculty. The other arena in which TQM is showing up at large numbers of universities is in the curriculum. Faculty in Business Schools and in Engineering and other departments are beginning to teach courses *about* TQM, as though this is just another business or manufacturing topic to be included in the course curriculum. (Axland).

Finally, a far smaller number of universities, perhaps a dozen or two at most, are actually beginning to *apply* TQM and Teams to the core mission of the university, the educational process itself, which is the focus of this essay. The leaders in this process may be Samford University in Birmingham, Delaware County Community College in Media, PA and Fox Valley Technical College in Appleton, Wisconsin. Also on the path are Terra Technical College in Fremont, Ohio, Lakeshore Technical College in Cleveland, Wisconsin, the University of Rhode Island and the Deming Scholars MBA Program at the Fordham University Graduate School of Business. There are of course in addition many hundreds and probably thousands of individual faculty who are experimenting with applying various of these ideas and concepts on their own, within the limits allowed by the requirements of their universities. Some of these individuals that I am aware of include David Porter at the Air Force Academy, Mark Borzi at the University of Hartford, the editor of this book at the University of Massachusetts in Dartmouth, and Merlin Ricklefs during his 1991–92 year as a Visiting Professor at the University of Minnesota—Duluth.

Of course this is not new. Carl Rogers includes some very interesting well-documented examples in his 1983 book, *Freedom to Learn*. Back then we did not use the terminology of TQM, but many of these concepts and approaches have been around a long time, although not part of a comprehensive disciplined system.

I myself was one of those individually experimenting faculty almost thirty years ago. Teaching at the M.I.T. Sloan School of Management during the early 1960s, I was a very traditional lecturer. My lectures were over-prepared, and I was young and insecure and thoughtless about any possible differences between teaching and learning. So I lectured the complete class period, barely tolerating the first student question and almost literally "chopping off the head" of the second student to raise his hand and ask a question. The reasons? I still had too much lecture material prepared *and* I was scared to death that I might not know the answer to the next question. Sometime in my early years as a high speed lecturer I was up all night with sick children and could only prepare half a dozen topic ideas instead of a full lecture. The next morning I walked out of the classroom exhausted and exhilarated. I was the worst prepared I had been in my short academic career, and I had clearly just conducted my best class! Since I couldn't fill the hour with lecturing I was "forced" to ask the students questions, engage their minds, and support full class participation. Surely there was something here I was supposed to learn!

Within a couple of years I had transformed my teaching process into a guiding/ coaching, facilitating process and was using small student teaching teams. Typically, I would teach about the first third of the semester, using that time to lay out some theory and concepts and to lead the organizing process for the remainder of the semester. The students talked about and prioritized what they wanted to learn in the course. Then we used a decision matrix (although I didn't know then what it was called) in which we put down the side the students' top priorities for learning in the class, and then put across the top of the matrix what they wanted to teach. We used the matrix to make sure we had a high correlation. No student taught alone; they were always required to prepare and lead the class in small, two 4-person teams. No team taught any topic that had not been identified by the class as a high priority topic. Most teams used a more creative, comprehensive, interesting, and multi-media teaching approach than I had ever thought of on my own. In the early 1970s I adapted this process to a wide variety of courses first at the Brandeis University Heller Graduate School and later at the University of Massachusetts— Boston, with blue collar working and commuting students. At all three institutions the students learned more content, learned more about learning, and about teaching, and came out with enhanced self-esteem, than if they had sat through my lectures. No, I cannot document that with solid research, but many many students demonstrated that and reported that to me.

There are many definitions of TQM, many gurus, a few "absolutes" (or none, depending on who you listen to or read), many steps, recipes, or components, etc. In the discussion that follows, I do not attempt to be all inclusive. Rather, I have taken nine of the most fundamental concepts of TQM and Teams, and for each I attempt to show the contrast between the "old paradigm" or traditional mindset in higher education, and the new thinking required if higher education is to learn from how industry is thinking about and applying TQM and Teams. The nine concepts are: The Customer; The Product; The Producer; The Process; Teams; The Source of Quality, The Role of Management; Continuous Improvement; and Benchmarking. On each concept, to fully embrace the teachings and learnings of TQM and use of Teams, faculty will have to accept a major shift in perceptions and in mindsets so massive that they truly add up to a whole Paradigm Shift for faculty.

THE CUSTOMER: IDENTIFYING, UNDERSTANDING, AND DELIGHTING YOUR CUSTOMERS

TQM calls for us to be customer focused, led, driven. If Universities are to adopt, learn from, and apply Total Quality Management, they too will have to determine who are their customers, and they will have to develop ways of listening to their customers and meeting and exceeding their requirements. Who are the customers of Universities?

If we define our customers as those who receive our products, or as those who benefit from our existence, or as those who pay for our services, then universities have many customers—a bewildering variety of customers. Let us list some of the more obvious groups of customers, as seen through the eyes of University Administration and/or faculty.

Faculty may be seen as internal to a university, as its employees, or its heart and soul. But faculty are often highly mobile. They move around a lot. So educational institutions compete for attracting and holding faculty, which makes them customers to be sought after and catered to. And faculty themselves often identify less with the university that is providing their temporary home and more with the peers, journals, and organizations of their separate professions that provide periodic peer review, plaudits, and mobility.

Some Universities see their primary mission as developing new knowledge, and many others see this as at least a secondary mission. They compete to attract research funding from *Foundations and federal government agencies,* and provide them in return with basic or applied research and a share in the resulting status. So these groups too are seen as customers.

Businesses hire the graduates and make donations with an eagerness roughly proportional to how they rank a college's quality, so they too must be seen as customers.

Other Universities accept graduates for advanced and professional degree programs based in part on *their perception* of the quality of the undergraduate output. So they are also customers.

Accrediting Agencies must be constantly thought about, understood, and periodically provided with evidence on whatever standards of excellence they use, in order to insure that programs, departments, and schools within the university continue to earn the official stamp of approval.

Alumni receive an on-going stream of status from their alma mater. In exchange they recruit new students and give and raise money. Their effort is proportional to how they feel about good old U. So good old U. must work constantly to impress alumni and those whose opinions the alumni respect.

Public universities provide graduates, research, football and other sports for local pride, and, in general, status to the citizens of their city, state, or region. In return they receive financing, and expectations, from their *citizens and governments,* which are also therefore customers.

Finally, for at least some faculty, the future of society, or the ideal of a good society, or serving the timeless quest for art, beauty, and truth is the customer (god) they cherish.

Hold on! Where and when do the students come in? Aren't they customers too? Certainly the answer is yes, or should be. But have we really come very far since the 1960s when an underground classic pamphlet described student's lack of status and influence in University affairs under the title "The Student as Nigger"? On the whole the student is still taken for granted, and is told what classes to attend, what to study, and what to learn, and in what sequence. The student is even told how to learn: listening to lectures, taking notes, reading and by boring, repetitive study, alone, not in teams. At the end of each course, semester, and year the student is also told whether or not she or he had "learned" (actually memorized) enough information to have passed inspection (examination) with sufficient marks to be allowed to continue. In short, the student is seen, and treated, as anything *but* an important customer.

In the new paradigm, the student is seen as the primary customer of the institution. But many faculty in many universities today still choke on even thinking of the student as one customer among many. On the other hand, the institution that has adopted the new paradigm treats the students with the respect due its most important customers. It is constantly seeking to understand them and their requirements. And, as is happening now in industry, the university and its faculty will seek to build a partnership with the student—a partnership in discovery and learning. This is already the model in our best graduate schools; it is coming in our colleges more slowly. One of the many results of this shift to a partnership is that the role of evaluation shifts from the institution evaluating students to a continuing improvement partnership in which each joins in developing processes for evaluating themselves, the other, and their joint process.

THE PRODUCT

The Product of education is a person empowered to educate herself or himself—an "educating person," not an "educated person." What is the product of education? And how can we specify it with sufficient clarity to give guidance to the processes chosen to produce that product? In the old paradigm the student's growing body of knowledge is seen as the product of education. In the worst cases, this is simply how much knowledge, clearly defined, broken up, isolated into chunks, even atomized, can the student memorize and retain just long enough to pass the exams. (As this is written the newspapers are carrying reports on a National Science Foundation study that is said to show how destructive this process of studying to tests has been to the real education of our people.)

In the best of cases there still is an assumption that the product of higher education is "an educated man or woman." Let's listen in, for example, at the Harvard commencement. Every spring the President of Harvard University tells the graduates at commencement, if memory serves and this hasn't been modernized, that he "takes great pride in admitting you into *the company of educated men and women.*" There you have it. Until the moment of graduation they were uneducated. Then, after four years at Harvard, they are finally educated. Complete. Finished. Now they are educated men and women and can get on with the rest of their lives.

Perhaps you think this is merely a leftover legacy of ancient Harvard. Consider the following recent news from Dartmouth:

> Dartmouth College, in the first revision of its curriculum in 70 years, is replacing required courses in traditional subjects with mandated study of a series of 'intellectual fields' such

as social analysis, and is formalizing a multicultural requirement. The curriculum over-haul, which also includes an interdisciplinary requirement and a required senior-year project, was approved by the Dartmouth faculty Monday night. The effort is an attempt to redefine what it is **to be an 'educated person,'** said Dartmouth president James O. Freedman. (Flint. Emphasis added.)

Now the old paradigm of the product of education being "an educated person" was probably appropriate in former times, when change was slow, when the function of higher education was to help create and certify a leadership elite, and when a hard working reasonably bright person could learn some meaningful fraction of all the scientific and cultural knowledge then available in the world—or at least in the Western world, which was all that mattered to most Western elites.

What has changed in this picture? Everything! Change is continuous—and accelerating. The relevant world is not every culture, every nook and cranny of the planet, in every period of time—and every interpretation of the universe. The total amount of knowledge available is so vast, and increasing so rapidly, that no student in any four-year program could possibly learn even a tiny, tiny fraction of 1% of the total. And whatever the knowledge content the student learns in these four years is inevitably going to be outdated within a few years—or even a few months!

Thus a person cannot possibly be "educated" in four years—or any other given period of time. For the modern world a person is never truly educated. So we need a new concept, a new paradigm, to clarify what our best faculty have long been practicing, which is that the product of higher education is a person "empowered to continue their own education for the rest of their life." Not an *educated* person, but an *educating* person. Not developed, but developing. Put bluntly, if education is completed, or thought to be completed, in four years, it is a failure. Put another way, the *product* of education is not a product at all; it is a *process* of never ending education. To be empowered in this way requires that the student gain from education:

- Knowledge of how to continue learning and developing for the rest of her/his life,
- Skills in continuing to learn and develop,
- A state of mind and being that enables lifelong learning, that sees and feels self-guided learning to be natural, doable, and fun, and
- A strong drive, a will, to continue learning and developing her/himself.

WHO IS THE PRODUCER OF EDUCATION?

This question is not so often raised and addressed in TQM, mostly because the answer is usually clear and obvious. But in education this question is crucial. In the old paradigm, teachers, the faculty, are seen as the producers of education. It is something that they "do to" the student, whenever the student cooperates by paying attention and doing what she is told. In the new paradigm, if the *product* is to be a person enabled, empowered to be a continuously learning, self-developing person, then the *producer* of that education must be, can only be, the *student herself.* This basic truth has been known for thousands of years by our greatest educators and philosophers, and has been equally forgotten and ignored in thousands of universities and schools to this day. Education takes place within a person, not on the outside or the periphery. So it is beyond the direct reach of any outsider and can only be produced by the insider, the person himself. Complete education involves the development of the whole person, of all parts of the person, of the mind, the emotions, the values and the spirit. This can, and should, be undertaken by the person herself. You and I produce our own education—no one else can do it for us or to us.

THE PROCESS OF EDUCATION

A fundamental concept of TQM is that we must focus our attention as much or more on the process as on the product. We must visualize that process, draw it, understand it thoroughly. Then we can find out whether or not it is under control, producing predictable results, and whether or not it is capable of meeting the customers' requirements. And then we can, and must, work on developing continuous improvement of that process.

In the old paradigm, there is little in depth attention to, thinking about, or understanding of, educational process. It is mostly taken for granted, since all the attention is on "getting the content across." There is almost no concern for, and attention to, the process of learning. All the attention is on the process of something called "teaching." The best analogy for our actual old paradigm process of education may be the auto assembly line. The student and his knowledge content play the part of the slowly growing auto body. He is moved slowly and boringly down the four-year "assembly line of education." As the student moves down the long line of teachers, each of them tries to pour in or to attach some fragments and pieces of disconnected knowledge to the student. Periodically he is tested and either held back for another try or passed on to the hands of the next classroom and teacher. The student is mostly passive. The quality of the student's knowledge "assembly" is always suspect, so we inspect (examine) it frequently. And a high proportion of students are tossed aside as they fail along the way and at the end. Many are not even eligible to be reworked in the repair bay, which is what a mediocre auto assembly line does. Instead, they are tossed out of the institution and onto the scrap heap of life with less caring than we show to our machinery mistakes.

In the new paradigm, we start by specifying that the student is simultaneously the customer, the product, *and the producer* of her own educator. We further specify that quality of learning and development is the primary objective, not quantity, and that if students are *not* producing their own education/learning/development now, and throughout the remainder of their life, the system has failed.

THE ROLE OF TEAMS IN HIGHER EDUCATION

TQM relies on Teams and Teamwork. Project Teams work within each department and function to study, plan, carry out, monitor, and learn from improvement efforts. Cross functional teams work on special projects that cut across departmental lines to improve a given critical process, and on continuous cross departmental cooperative efforts to improve quality, cost, and customer service. A rapidly growing number of organizations are redesigning and restructuring themselves around Self-Directed Teams that plan, perform, and improve the basic work of the organization at the base and the front lines, without direct supervision. (See the Chapter on Self-Directed Teams).

In the old paradigm in higher education students work in isolation, or in one to one interaction with the Professor, or more likely, in the larger Universities, with a Teaching Assistant. There is little or no room for Teams and Teamwork. In fact when this happens, it is usually called cheating. The honor system at many universities includes: "I will neither give nor receive help." Yet industry, and life, require skills and attitudes that support working teams. In a study of 20 year alumni of three dozen colleges and universities, Georgetown Vice President Joe Petit found that over 80 percent reported that "can work in groups to accomplish goals" is an important current need, but only 20 percent said their college had helped them learn it (Marchese, 1990 as cited in Porter, "Total Quality Learning" (1991).

In the new paradigm, students are encouraged to study in groups and teams, or are actively organized into learning teams. The Second Report of the Harvard Assessment Seminars came up with the "surprise" finding that "students who get the most out of college, who grow the most academically, and who are happiest, *organize their time to include interpersonal activities with faculty members, or with fellow students, built around substantive work.*" The author, Professor Light, points out that for many students this is difficult. He makes the specific point that it is different from studying alone. Based on research reports by, and input from, many students, he recommends to faculty that they create study groups in large classes and that they have several students share their papers each week, in advance of class, with other members (Light, p. 21). He further recommends that advisors encourage their students to create or join a study group outside of their classes (p. 53). And he adds that these small study groups are especially important for students in the sciences (p. 56).

Have there been any scientific controlled experiments? David Porter reports on one:

> A study at the Air Force Academy compared the performance and satisfaction of students enrolled in classes employing group-oriented projects and grades to those receiving traditional instruction. The 53 students in the group-oriented classes (in sections taught by four different instructors) performed significantly better on four different, common, objective tests than students in the control group. Students' self reports of participation and effort were also significantly higher. The most interesting finding, however, was the extent to which students in the experimental sections attributed their learning to one another rather than to their teacher. Student 'testimonials' from previous similar experiments

illustrate this: 'I noticed an attitude developing in the class I'd never seen anywhere else. Everyone had prepared for the quiz but not just for themselves . . . for each other.

THE SOURCE OF QUALITY

In the old paradigm, a small percentage of students produce really high quality learning. Another large block produce lower, but still acceptable, quality. And another significant number produce unacceptable quality and are failed. How do we know who is in which group? Examinations. We use them to weed out the low quality learning and hold it back or refuse to certify it. Examinations are in higher education what traditional inspection is in industry. A final attempt, in the hands of non-producers, to screen out the errors caused by the system, before they get to the outside world (customers). In fact, in higher education it is even worse; a second purpose of examinations, or at least an unfortunate by-product, is to inculcate and maintain fear in the "workforce" (students).

Many corporations, thanks to TQM, have learned that final inspection: (1) Does not catch all the mistakes of the system, and lets some, sometimes many, slip through to the customer; (2) Takes responsibility for quality out of the hands, and therefore out of the minds, of the producers; (3) Does nothing to raise, and actually lowers, the ableness of the system to produce consistently high quality, since it does nothing to improve the average or reduce the variability; and (4) is very expensive, since it requires a lot of people and time, is not value adding, and actually encourages waste. As a result, industry is rapidly switching (but education is not) to the new paradigm, which includes: specifying the product, studying the process, getting the process under control, improving the process average and variability, improving all the surrounding systems that enable or undermine quality, educating the producers (work force) on what high quality and acceptable quality are, according to measurements, and what they look like (and in some cases sound, feel, smell, taste like). Then, along with all of this, the work force are given the authority, and the accountability is accepted by them, for the quality of the output they are producing. In this process, the old uses of inspection, and the old separate inspector roles, are eliminated. Instead, everyone inspects the product as they receive it, as they work on it, and before it leaves their hands or work area.

The parallels to Higher Education are massive and obvious, if extremely questionable and unpleasant to those "educators" locked in the old paradigm. Students, or student-faculty partnerships together, must develop baseline and milestone measures for how the student's ableness for self-development is progressing and for helping the student, or the partnership, discover what would be helpful and logical paths and next steps for improvement.

THE ROLE OF MANAGEMENT

Under TQM in industry, and especially where on-going empowered Teams are in use, the role of managers is dramatically changing. In higher education, the equivalent of the manager is the teacher, although most teachers will reject this. For TQM to work, the teachers' role must also change dramatically.

As we have said, in the old paradigm, teachers see their role as, and act as though they are, the producers of education. They design curriculum, decide on content within each course and module, decide the teaching process (not usually asking whether it is or is not identical to a learning process), then they teach, and finally they examine. Of course they are still learning this method.

But for the new paradigm, we have said that the students themselves are the producers of their own learning, and that, in fact, they are the only players on the learning stage who can actually produce learning.

What then is the role of teachers in the new paradigm? To become what many great and good teachers have always been doing. Try on the roles below, described in terms of action verbs, and see if they don't sound more like what is needed for the new paradigm than do the older terms of Professor (one who professes?), Instructor (one who instructs), and Teacher (one who teaches). The new paradigm faculty may do some or all of the following:

• Lead	• Enable	• Call forth (educate)
• Inspire	• Empower	• Resource
• Coach	• Evoke	• Guide
• Facilitate	• Support	• Encourage
• Create a vision	• Share a Vision	• Role Model
• Question	• Listen	• Create Context

It is perhaps relevant that many of these are exactly the same new roles that thousands of middle managers are being asked to learn and take on, and are taking on, in industry today. It is difficult, but not impossible, for traditionally trained managers to learn these new roles. Could teachers do the same?

CONTINUOUS IMPROVEMENT

In the old paradigm, continuous improvement is only partially in the faculty mindset. With respect to students, the faculty expects to see improvement of some kind in their ability to take tests and write papers. With respect to themselves, faculty expect to increase their knowledge and skills in their own specialized academic field. But until recently there has been little systemic thinking about, or application of, the idea of continuous improvement of processes, either for the teacher's own development, or for that of the student. (Under the new accreditation guidelines of the American Assembly for Collegiate Schools of Business this may be changing.)

In the new paradigm, the concept of continuous improvement, and the Shewhart-Deming PDCA model is applied to every process, great and small, in the organization, starting with the core educational processes. In Japan and many U.S. companies this model is called the Deming model because they learned it from W. Edwards Deming. But Dr. Deming calls it the Shewhart model, since he learned it from his teacher, Walter Shewhart. Plan something, Do it, Check or Audit what we did (Study it, Deming now says), then Act on what was Learned. That is what the model says.

Shewhart-Deming PDCA Model

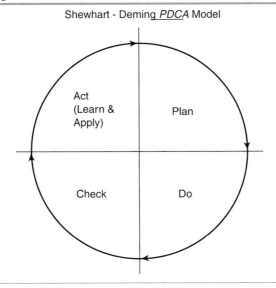

Shewhart - Deming *PDCA* Model

Applied to higher education, the teachers and students Plan some educational process together. They then Do it, carry it out. During the process, and at the end, they audit, or Check on their process. Are we following the plan? Are we accomplishing our objectives? What is working? What needs to be modified? Mid-course corrections are made, so that the Check can result in some immediate process improvements. At the end of the process, a more thorough Check or audit is performed. Student evaluations, both quantitative and qualitative are gathered. Hard data is obtained as much as possible and is carefully analyzed. Non-quantitative information is also obtained and studied.

Then, after all the auditing is completed, the teachers and students step back and carefully evaluate. What did we learn from that effort? What part of the process worked well and is worth using again, worth building on in future learning efforts? How will we save the best of what we just did, institutionalize it, "hold the gain"? What part of our process did not work so well? Why didn't it? What can we learn from that? How will we modify future planning and doing to avoid those mistakes and do better next time? These and dozens of similar questions are asked in the fourth, evaluation, quadrant, which perhaps should be called Evaluation, or Learn and Apply, which seems to be nearer the authors' original intent. And then new Acts of learning are planned, based on this evaluation.

In this way every process is planned, done, checked on, learned from, and the learnings are fed into another round of planning, doing, checking and learning. Can you think of a better way to build in continuous improvement?

BENCHMARKING

In the old paradigm, faculty see no reason to learn from others about how to "teach" (or about how students learn). In fact, at its worse, the concept might be called: "You stay out of my classroom and I'll stay out of yours." This changed years ago in Schools of Education, and is certainly changing in some schools and departments now.

In the new paradigm, since continuous improvement is a fundamental value and goal and since the faculty are not teachers, they, together with the students in partnership, are constantly seeking the best examples, the best methods, the best processes, for learning and development of ableness to learn from. They seek, as does industry today, to learn from any organization, in any industry, in any part of the world, that is doing something well that we might learn from.

With the growing national attention to our national and international deficits and the growing awareness of the relationship of education to quality and productivity, there does seem to be a growing interest in benchmarking as a foundation for continuous improvement. Hopefully faculty everywhere will come to see that different students learn differently, that different courses need different approaches, and that involving the students in designing their own educational processes will pay off doubly: in improved processes now, and in students more empowered to continue their own education for the rest of their lives.

Bibliography

Articles and Speeches

Axland, Suzanne. "Looking for a Quality Education?" *Quality Progress,* October 1991.

Flint, Anthony. "At Dartmouth, 'Educated Person' Redefined," *The Boston Globe,* April 8, 1992, pp. 21, 25.

Marchese, Ted. "A New Conversation about Undergraduate Teaching," *American Association of Higher Education Bulletin,* 1990.

Marchese, Ted. "TQM Reaches the Academy," *American Association of Higher Education Bulletin,* November 1991.

Porter, David B. "Course Critiques: What Students Can Tell Us about Educational Efficacy," *Proceedings of the Human Factors Society, 32nd Annual Meeting, 1988.*

Porter, David B. "Educating from a Group Perspective," *Proceedings of the Human Factors Society, 33rd Annual Meeting, 1989.*

Porter, David B., Megan E. Bird, and Arthur Wunder. "Competition, Cooperation, Satisfaction, and the Performance of Complex Tasks among Air Force Cadets," *Current Psychology: Research & Reviews,* Winter 1990–91, Vol. 9, No. 4, 347–354.

Porter, David B. "Total Quality Leadership," Chapter 11 in K. D. Lam, Frank D. Watson, and Steven D. Schmidt, *Total Quality: A Textbook of Strategic Quality Leadership and Planning,* Colorado Springs: Air Academy Press, 1991.

Porter, David B. "A Perspective on College Learning," *Journal of College Reading and Learning,* Vol. XXIV, Number 1, 1991.

Ricklefs, Merlin. "Total Quality Management in the Academic & Business Life of a University," Presentation at Lehigh University, Third Symposium on Quality in Action in Academe, July 29, 1992.

Books

Baugher, Kathy. *Learn: The Student Quality Team Process for Improving Teaching and Learning,* Birmingham: Samford University, 1992.

Glasser, William. *The Quality School,* New York: Harper and Row, 1990.

John W. Harris and J. Mark Baggett, eds. *Quality Quest in the Academic Process,* Birmingham: Samford University, and Methuen, MA: GOAL/QPC, 1992.

Light, Richard J. *The Harvard Assessment Seminars, Second Report,* Cambridge: Harvard University, 1992.

Ritter, Diane. *Education and Total Quality Management . . . A Resource Guide,* Methuen, MA: GOAL/QPC, November 1991.

Rogers, Carl, *Freedom to Learn for the '80's,* New York: Macmillan, 1983.

Seymour, Daniel T. *On Q: Causing Quality in Higher Education,* New York: Macmillan, 1992.

Seymour, Daniel and Casey Collett, *Total Quality Management in Higher Education: A Critical Assessment,* Methuen, MA: GOAL/QPC, 1991.

Quality Awards

"In business, there is only one definition of quality—the customer's definition. With the fierce competition of the international market, quality means survival."

George Bush

Malcolm Baldrige Quality Award 1993 Award Criteria

THE MALCOLM BALDRIGE NATIONAL QUALITY AWARD: A PUBLIC-PRIVATE PARTNERSHIP

Building active partnerships in the private sector, and between the private sector and government, is fundamental to the success of the Award in improving quality in the United States.

Support by the private sector for the Award Program in the form of funds, volunteer efforts, and participation in information transfer is strong and growing rapidly.

To ensure the continued growth and success of these partnerships, each of the following organizations plays an important supporting role:

The Foundation for the Malcolm Baldrige National Quality Award

The Foundation for the Malcolm Baldrige National Quality Award was created to foster the success of the Program. The Foundation's main objective is to raise funds to permanently endow the Award Program.

Prominent leaders from U.S. companies serve as Foundation Trustees to ensure that the Foundation's objectives are accomplished. Donor organizations vary in size and type, and are representative of many kinds of businesses and business groups. To date, the Foundation has raised approximately $11 million.

National Institute of Standards and Technology (NIST)

Responsibility for the Award is assigned to the Department of Commerce. NIST, an agency of the Department's Technology Administration, manages the Award Program.

NIST's goals are to aid U.S. industry through research and services; to contribute to public health, safety, and the environment; and to support the U.S. scientific and engineering research communities. NIST conducts basic and applied research in the physical sciences and engineering and develops measurement techniques, test methods, and standards. Much of NIST's work relates directly to quality and to quality-related requirements in technology development and technology utilization.

American Society for Quality Control (ASQC)

ASQC assists in administering the Award Program under contract to NIST.

ASQC is dedicated to facilitating continuous improvement and increased customer satisfaction by identifying, communicating and promoting the use of quality principles, concepts, and technologies. ASQC strives to be recognized throughout the world as the leading authority on, and champion for, quality. ASQC recognizes that continuous quality improvement will help the favorable repositioning of American goods and services in the international marketplace.

Board of Overseers

The Board of Overseers is the advisory organization on the Award to the Department of Commerce. The Board is appointed by the Secretary of Commerce and consists of distinguished leaders from all sectors of the U.S. economy.

The Board of Overseers evaluates all aspects of the Award Program, including the adequacy of the Criteria and processes for making Awards. An important part of the Board's responsibility is to assess how well the Award is serving the national interest. Accordingly, the Board of Overseers makes recommendations to the Secretary of Commerce and to the Director of NIST regarding changes and improvements in the Award Program.

Board of Examiners

The Board of Examiners is the body that evaluates Award applications, prepares feedback reports, and makes Award recommendations to the Director of NIST. The Board consists of quality experts primarily from the private sector. Members are selected by NIST through a competitive application process. For 1993, the Board consists of more than 270 members. Of these, 9 serve as Judges, and approximately 50 serve as Senior Examiners. The remainder serve as Examiners. All members of the Board take part in an examiner preparation course.

In addition to their application review responsibilities, Board members contribute significantly to building awareness of the importance of quality and to information transfer activities. Many of these activities involve the hundreds of professional, trade, community, and state organizations to which Board members belong.

Award Recipients

The seventeen recipients of the Award in the first five years have shared information on their successful quality strategies with hundreds of thousands of companies, education institutions, government agencies, health care organizations, and others. By sharing their strategies, Award recipients have made enormous contributions to building awareness of the importance of quality to improving national competitiveness. This sharing has encouraged many other organizations in all sectors of the U.S. economy to undertake their own quality improvement efforts.

INTRODUCTION

The Malcolm Baldrige National Quality Award is an annual award to recognize U.S. companies that excel in quality management and quality achievement.

The Award promotes:
- awareness of quality as an increasingly important element in competitiveness,
- understanding of the requirements for quality excellence, and
- sharing of information on successful quality strategies and the benefits derived from implementation of these strategies.

Award Participation   The Award has three eligibility categories:
- Manufacturing companies
- Service companies
- Small businesses

Up to two Awards may be given in each category each year. Award recipients may publicize and advertise their Awards. In addition to publicizing the receipt of the Award, recipients are expected to share information about their successful quality strategies with other U.S. organizations.

Companies participating in the Award process are required to submit applications that include completion of the Award Examination.

The Award Examination   The Award Examination is based upon quality excellence criteria created through a public-private partnership. In responding to these criteria, each applicant is expected to provide information and data on the company's quality processes and quality improvement results. Information and data submitted must be adequate to demonstrate that the applicant's approaches could be replicated or adapted by other companies.

The Award Examination is designed not only to serve as a reliable basis for making Awards but also to permit a diagnosis of each applicant's overall quality management.

Application Review   Applications are reviewed and evaluated by members of the Board of Examiners in a four-stage process:

Stage 1—independent review and evaluation by at least five members of the Board

Stage 2—consensus review and evaluation for applications that score well in Stage 1

Stage 3—site visits to applicants that score well in Stage 2

Stage 4—Judges' review and recommendations

Board members are assigned to applications taking into account the nature of the applicants' business and the expertise of the Examiners. Assignments are made in accord with strict rules regarding conflict of interest.

Applications are reviewed without funding from the United States government. Review expenses are paid primarily through application fees; partial support for the reviews is provided by the Foundation for the Malcolm Baldrige National Quality Award.

Feedback to Applicants   All applicants receive feedback reports at the conclusion of the review process. The feedback is based upon the applicants' responses to the Award Examination Criteria.

Purpose of This Booklet   This booklet contains the Award Criteria, a description of the Criteria, scoring guidelines, and other information. In addition to serving as the basis for submitting an Award application, organizations of all kinds use the booklet for self-assessment, planning, training, and other purposes.

DESCRIPTION OF THE 1993 AWARD CRITERIA

Award Criteria Purposes

The Malcolm Baldrige National Quality Award Criteria are the basis for making Awards and for giving feedback to applicants. In addition, the Criteria have three other important national purposes:

- to help raise quality performance standards and expectations;
- to facilitate communication and sharing among and within organizations of all types based upon a common understanding of key quality and operational performance requirements; and
- to serve as a working tool for planning, training, assessment, and other uses.

Award Criteria Goals

The Award Criteria are designed to support dual, results-oriented goals:

- delivery of ever-improving value to customers; and
- improvement of overall company operational performance.

Core Values and Concepts

The Award Criteria are built upon a set of core values and concepts. Together, these values and concepts represent the underlying basis for integrating the overall customer and company operational performance requirements.

These core values and concepts are:

Customer-Driven Quality   Quality is judged by the customer. All product and service attributes that contribute value to the customer and lead to customer satisfaction and preference must be the foundation for a company's quality system. Value, satisfaction, and preference may be influenced by many factors throughout the customer's overall purchase, ownership, and service experiences. These factors include the company's relationship with customers that helps build trust, confidence, and loyalty. This concept of quality includes not only the product and service attributes that meet basic customer requirements, but it also includes those that enhance them and differentiate them from competing offerings. Such enhancement and differentiation may be based upon new offerings, combinations of product and service offerings, rapid response, or special relationships.

Customer-driven quality is thus a strategic concept. It is directed toward customer retention and market share gain. It demands constant sensitivity to emerging customer and market requirements, and measurement of the factors that drive customer satisfaction and retention. It also demands awareness of developments in technology, and rapid and flexible response to customer and market requirements.

Such requirements extend well beyond defect and error reduction, merely meeting specifications, and reducing complaints. Nevertheless, defect and error reduction and elimination of causes of dissatisfaction contribute significantly to the customers' view of quality and are thus also important parts of customer-driven quality. In addition, the company's success in recovering from defects and errors ("making things right for the customer") is crucial to building customer relationships and to customer retention.

Leadership   A company's senior leaders must create a customer orientation, clear and visible quality values, and high expectations. Reinforcement of the values and expectations requires substantial personal commitment and involvement. The leaders' basic values and commitment need to include areas of public responsibility and corporate citizenship. The leaders must take part in the creation of strategies, systems, and methods for achieving excellence. The systems and methods need to guide all activities and decisions of the company. The senior leaders must commit to the growth and development of the entire work force and should encourage participation and creativity by all employees. Through their regular personal involvement in visible activities, such as planning, communications, review of company quality performance, and recognizing employees for quality achievement, the senior leaders serve as role models reinforcing the values and encouraging leadership in all levels of management.

Continuous Improvement   Achieving the highest levels of quality and competitiveness requires a well-defined and well-executed approach to continuous improvement. The term "continuous improvement" refers to both incremental and "breakthrough" improvement. A focus on improvement needs to be part of all operations and of all work unit activities of a company.

Improvements may be of several types: (1) enhancing value to customers through new and improved products and services; (2) reducing errors, defects, and waste; (3) improving responsiveness and cycle time performance; (4) improving productivity and effectiveness in the use of all resources; and (5) improving the company's performance and leadership position in fulfilling its public responsibilities and serving as a role model in corporate citizenship. Thus, improvement is driven not only by the objective to provide better product and service quality, but also by the need to be responsive and efficient—both conferring additional marketplace advantages. To meet all of these objectives, the process of continuous improvement must contain regular cycles of planning, execution, and evaluation. This requires a basis— preferably a quantitative basis—for assessing progress, and for deriving information for future cycles of improvement. Such information should provide direct links between desired performance and internal operations.

Employee Participation and Development   A company's success in meeting its quality and performance objectives depends increasingly on work force quality and involvement. The close link between employee satisfaction and customer satisfaction creates a "shared fate" relationship between companies and employees. For this reason, employee satisfaction measurement provides an important indicator of the company's efforts to improve customer satisfaction and operating performance. Improving company performance requires improvements at all levels within a company. This, in turn, depends upon the skills and dedication of the entire work force. Companies need to invest in the development of the work force and to seek new avenues to involve employees in problem solving and decision making. Factors that bear upon the safety, health, well-being, and morale of employees need to be part of the company's continuous improvement objectives. Increasingly, training and participation need to be tailored to a more diverse work force, and to more flexible work organizations.

Fast Response   Success in competitive markets increasingly demands ever-shorter cycles for new or improved product and service introduction. Also, faster and more flexible response to customers is now a more critical requirement of business management. Major improvements in response time often require work organizations, work processes and work paths to be simplified and shortened. To accomplish such improvement more attention should be given to measuring time performance. This can be done by making response time a key indicator for work unit improvement processes. There are other important benefits derived from this focus: response time improvements often drive simultaneous improvements in organization, quality, and productivity. Hence it is beneficial to consider response time, quality and productivity objectives together.

Design Quality and Prevention   Quality systems should place strong emphasis on design quality—problem and waste prevention achieved through building quality into products and services and into the processes through which they are produced. In general, costs of preventing problems at the design stage are much lower than costs of correcting problems which occur "downstream." Design quality includes the creation of fault-tolerant (robust) processes and products.

A major issue in the competitive environment is the design-to-introduction ("product generation") cycle time. Meeting the demands of ever-more rapidly changing markets requires that companies carry out stage-to-stage coordination of functions and activities from basic research to commercialization.

Consistent with the theme of design quality and prevention, continuous improvement and corrective action need to emphasize interventions "upstream"—at early stages in processes. This approach yields the maximum overall benefits of improvements and corrections. Such upstream intervention also needs to take into account the company's suppliers.

Long-Range Outlook   Achieving quality and market leadership requires a company to have a strong future orientation and a willingness to make long-term commitments to customers, employees, suppliers, stockholders, and the community. Planning needs to determine or anticipate many types of changes including those that may affect customers' expectations of products and services, technological developments, changing customer segments, evolving regulatory requirements and community/societal expectations, or thrusts by competitors. Plans, strategies, and resource allocations need to reflect these commitments and changes. A major part of the long-term commitment relates to the development of employees and suppliers, and to fulfilling public responsibilities and serving as a corporate citizenship role model.

Management by Fact   Pursuit of quality and operational performance goals of the company requires that process management be based upon reliable information, data, and analysis. Facts and data needed for quality improvement and quality assessment are of many types, including: customer, product and service performance, operations, market, competitive comparisons, supplier, employee-related, and cost and financial. Analysis refers to the process of extracting larger meaning from data to support evaluation and decision making at various levels within the company. Such analysis may entail using data to reveal information—such as trends, projections, and cause and effect—that might not be evident without analysis. Facts, data, and analysis support a variety of company purposes, such as planning, reviewing company performance, improving operations, and comparing company quality performance with competitors' or with "best practices" benchmarks.

A major consideration relating to use of data and analysis to improve performance involves the creation and use of performance indicators. Performance indicators are measurable characteristics of products, services, processes, and operations the company uses to evaluate and improve performance and to track progress. The indicators should be selected to best represent the factors that lead to improved customer satisfaction and operational performance. A system of indicators tied to customer and/or company performance requirements represents a clear and objective basis for aligning all activities of the company toward common goals. Through the analysis of data obtained in the tracking processes, the indicators themselves may be evaluated and changed. For example, indicators selected to measure product and service quality may be judged by how well improvement in quality correlates with improvement in customer satisfaction.

Partnership Development   Companies should seek to build internal and external partnerships to better accomplish their overall goals. Internal partnerships might include those that promote labor-management cooperation, such as agreements with unions. Agreements may entail employee development, cross-training, or new work organizations, such as high performance work teams.

Examples of external partnerships include those with customers, suppliers, and education organizations. An increasingly important kind of external partnership is the strategic partnership or alliance. Such partnerships might offer a company entry into new markets or a basis for new products or services.

Partnerships should seek to develop longer-term objectives, thereby creating a basis for mutual investments. Partners should address the key requirements for success of the partnership, means of regular communication, approaches to evaluating progress, and means for adapting to changing conditions.

Corporate Responsibility and Citizenship   A company's quality system objectives should address corporate responsibility and citizenship. Corporate responsibility refers to basic expectations of the company—business ethics, and protection of public health, public safety, and the environment. Health, safety and environmental considerations need to take into account the company's operations as well as the life cycles of products and services. Companies need to address factors such as waste reduction at its source. Quality planning related to public health, safety and environment should anticipate adverse impacts that may arise in facilities management, production, distribution, transportation, use and disposal of products. Plans should seek avenues to avoid problems, to provide forthright company response if problems occur, and to make available information needed to maintain public awareness, safety, trust, and confidence. Inclusion of public responsibility areas within a quality system means not only meeting all local, state, and federal legal and regulatory requirements, but also treating these and related requirements as areas for continuous improvement beyond mere compliance.

Corporate citizenship refers to leadership and support—within reasonable limits of a company's resources—of publicly important purposes, including the above-mentioned areas of corporate responsibility. Such purposes might include education, resource conservation, community services, improving industry and business practices, and sharing of nonproprietary quality-related information.

Criteria Framework

The core values and concepts are embodied in seven categories, as follows:

1.0   Leadership
2.0   Information and Analysis
3.0   Strategic Quality Planning
4.0   Human Resource Development and Management
5.0   Management of Process Quality
6.0   Quality and Operational Results
7.0   Customer Focus and Satisfaction

The framework connecting and integrating the categories is given in the figure on page 512.

The framework has four basic elements:

Driver   Senior executive leadership creates the values, goals, and systems, and guides the sustained pursuit of customer value and company performance improvement.

System   System comprises the set of well-defined and well-designed processes for meeting the company's customer, quality, and performance requirements.

Measures of Progress   Measures of progress provide a results-oriented basis for channeling actions to delivering ever-improving customer value and company performance.

Goal   The basic aim of the quality process is the delivery of ever-improving value to customers.

The seven Criteria categories shown in the figure are subdivided into Examination Items and Areas to Address. These are described below.

Examination Items   There are a total of 28 Examination Items in the seven Examination Categories. Each Item focuses on a major quality system requirement. All information submitted by applicants is in response to the Item requirements. Item titles and Examination point values are given on page 525.

Areas to Address   Each Examination Item includes a set of Areas to Address (Areas). The Areas serve to illustrate and clarify the intent of the Items and to place emphasis on the types and amounts of information the applicant should provide. Areas are not assigned individual point values, because their relative importance depends upon factors such as the applicant's type and size of business and quality system.

The Information and Analysis Category— The Basis for Quality System Alignment and Integration

The Information and Analysis Category (2.0) is the focal point within the Award Criteria for all key information to drive improvement of quality and overall operational performance. In simplest terms, the Information and Analysis Category is the "brain center" for the alignment and integration of a quality system—regardless of the system's structure or organization. The Category addresses the key requirements for organizational learning and improvement based upon the improvement of basic processes.

The Information and Analysis Category consists of three Items:

2.1   *Scope and Management of Quality and Performance Data and Information*
This Item calls for information describing how the company selects data and information and the roles of such data and information in improving quality and operational performance. Major emphasis is placed upon the adequacy of data—from customers and processes—to drive process improvement. Though cost and financial data provide useful support, process improvement is driven primarily through nonfinancial indicators—indicators linked to requirements derived from customers and from company operational performance. The Item addresses other key issues in information management. These issues include: data reliability; broad and rapid access; data review and update; and systematic attention to improvement of all aspects of the scope and management of key data and information.

2.2   *Competitive Comparisons and Benchmarking*
This Item addresses external drivers of improvement—data and information related to competitive factors and to best practices. The major premises underlying this Item are: (1) companies need to "know where they stand" relative to competitors and relative to best practices performances for similar activities; (2) comparative and benchmarking information provides a key impetus for improvement, and alerts companies to competitive threats, and new practices; and (3) companies need to understand their own processes and the processes of others, as well as performance levels associated with these processes. The Item addresses the key issues in management of competitive comparisons and benchmarking. These are: criteria for selection; scope, sources and principal uses of the main types of comparative and benchmarking information; how benchmarking and comparative information is used to understand processes, stimu-

late innovation, and elevate expectations; and how the process of obtaining and using competitive comparison and benchmarking information is improved.

2.3 Analysis and Uses of Company-Level Data

Management by fact is a core concept underlying the Award Criteria. These Criteria call for a wide variety of data—nonfinancial and financial—to guide a company's courses of action toward beneficial results. Despite their importance, however, individual facts do not usually provide a sound basis for appropriate action or priorities. Action depends upon understanding cause/effect connections among processes and between processes and results. Process actions may have many resource implications; results may have many cost and revenue implications as well. Given that resources for improvement are limited, and cause/effect connections are often unclear, there is a critical need to provide a sound, analytical basis for decision making. In the Award Criteria, this role is fulfilled by analyses of many types. Item 2.3 plays the key linkage role in an integrated data strategy.

There are three analysis components within Item 2.3:

Area 2.3a calls for the aggregation and analysis of customer-related data (from Category 7.0) and other key data to focus on improving customer-related decision making and priorities. This is the only Area within the Criteria that addresses the understanding of and interrelationships among all customer-related sources of information. Together with product and service quality information (Item 6.1), the data in Category 7.0 provide a basis for identifying key drivers of customer satisfaction, customer retention, and market share gain. Inasmuch as Item 6.1 is linked to key processes (Category 5.0), the analysis carried out in 2.3a translates the "voice of the customer" into internal process improvement requirements. These requirements ensure that priority attention is focused on process improvements that lead to marketplace success, captured in Items 7.5 and 7.6.

Area 2.3b calls for the aggregation and analysis of operations-related data (from Category 6.0) and other key data to focus on improving operations-related decision making and priorities. This is the only Area within the Criteria that addresses the understanding of and interrelationships among operations-related sources of information. It is thus the principal basis for optimizing overall operational improvement consistent with improving customer-related indicators. Inasmuch as the Items of Category 6.0 are tied directly to the key processes (Category 5.0) and to human resource processes and data (Category 4.0), the analyses carried out in 2.3b support all internal process improvement.

Area 2.3c calls for linking overall quality and operational performance improvement data to changes in overall financial performance. This is the only Area within the Criteria that addresses this key linkage at the company level. Thus, it is an important source of information for allocating limited resources among potential improvement projects or initiatives based upon improvement potential and financial impact.

The Pivotal Role of the Quality and Operational Results Category

The Quality and Operational Results Category (6.0) plays a central role in the Award Criteria. This Category provides a results focus for all quality system actions. It represents the link between the customer requirements and the quality system. Through this focus, the dual purpose of quality—superior value of offerings as viewed by the customer and the marketplace and superior company performance reflected in productivity and effectiveness indicators—is maintained. Category 6.0 thus provides "real-time" information (measures of progress) for evaluation and improvement of quality system processes and practices.

The Quality and Operational Results Category consists of four Items:

6.1 Product and Service Quality Results

This Item calls for reporting quality levels and improvements for key product and service attributes—**attributes that truly matter to the customer and to the marketplace**. These attributes are derived from customer-related Items ("listening posts") which make up Category 7.0. If the attributes have been properly selected, improvements in them should show a strong positive correlation with customer and marketplace improvement indicators—captured in Items 7.5 and 7.6. The correlation between quality and customer indicators is a critical management tool. It is a device for focusing on key attributes. In addition, the correlation may reveal emerging or changing market segments, changing importance of attributes, or even potential obsolescence of products and/or services.

6.2 Company Operational Results

This Item calls for reporting performance and improvements in internal operations and productivity of the company. Paralleling Item 6.1, which focuses on attributes that matter to the customer, Item 6.2 focuses on **attributes that best reflect overall company operational performance**. Such attributes are of two types: (1) generic—common to all companies; and (2) business-specific. Generic attributes include cycle time and productivity, as reflected in use of labor, materials, energy, capital, and assets. Indicators of productivity, cycle time, or internal quality should reflect overall company performance. Business- or company-specific effectiveness indicators vary greatly. Examples include rates of invention, environmental quality, export levels, new markets, percent of sales from recently introduced products or services, and shifts toward new segments.

6.3 Business Process and Support Service Results

This Item calls for reporting performance and improvements in quality, productivity, and effectiveness of the business processes and support services. This permits a demonstration of how support units contribute to overall improvement in quality (reported in Item 6.1) and overall improvement in company operational performance (reported in Item 6.2). This Item is thus a useful device in aligning support activities with the company's overall principal quality, productivity, and business objectives. Through this Item, progress in meeting special requirements, which may differ among work units and which define work-unit effectiveness, can be measured.

6.4 *Supplier Quality Results*

This Item calls for reporting quality levels and improvements in key indicators of supplier quality. The term "supplier" refers to external providers of products and services, "upstream" and/or "downstream" from the company. The focus should be on the most critical quality attributes from the point of view of the company—the buyer of the products and services. Trends and levels of quality should reflect results by whatever means they occur—via improvements by suppliers within the supply base, through changes in selection of suppliers, or both.

Key Characteristics of the Award Criteria

1. The Criteria are directed toward results.

The Criteria focus principally on seven key areas of business performance, given below. Results are a composite of:

(1) Customer satisfaction/retention
(2) market share
(3) product and service quality
(4) productivity and operational effectiveness
(5) human resource performance/development
(6) supplier performance/development
(7) public responsibility

Improvements in these seven results areas contribute to overall company performance, including financial performance. In addition, the results indicators recognize the importance of contributions to improving suppliers and to the national well-being. The use of a composite of indicators helps to ensure that company strategies appropriately balance short- and long-term considerations, as well as external and internal goals. The use of a composite of results indicators also helps to ensure that strategies do not inappropriately trade off among important company objectives or responsibilities.

2. The Criteria are nonprescriptive.

The Criteria are a set of 28 basic, interrelated, results-oriented requirements. However, the Criteria imply wide latitude in approaches to meeting the requirements. Accordingly, the Criteria do not prescribe:

• specific quality tools, techniques, technologies, systems, or starting points;

• that there should or should not be within a company a separate quality department or organization; or

• how the company itself should be organized.

The Criteria do require that these and many other basic factors be regularly evaluated as part of the company's improvement processes and activities, as they are important and are very likely to change as needs and strategies evolve.

The Criteria are nonprescriptive for three important reasons:

(1) The Criteria's focus is on requirements that produce results, not on pre-set procedures, tools or organizations. Through this approach, companies are

encouraged to develop and *demonstrate* creative, adaptive, and flexible approaches to meeting basic requirements. The nonprescriptive nature of the requirements thus supports incremental and major ("breakthrough") improvement.

(2) Selection of tools, techniques, systems, and organizations usually depend upon many factors such as business size, business type, the company's stage of development, and employee capabilities.

(3) Focus on common requirements within a company rather than on specific procedures fosters better understanding, communication, and sharing, while encouraging diversity and creativity in approaches.

3. The Criteria are comprehensive.

The Criteria address all internal and external requirements of the company, including those related to fulfilling its public responsibilities. Accordingly, all operations and processes of all company work units are tied to these requirements. New or changing strategies or directions of the company may be readily adapted within the same set of Criteria requirements.

Baldrige Award Criteria Framework

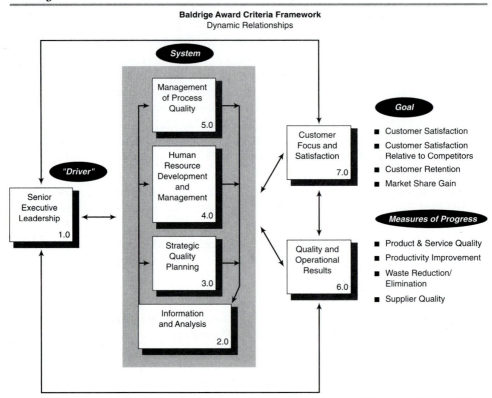

Baldrige Award Criteria Framework
Dynamic Relationships

4. **The Criteria include interrelated (process→results) learning cycles.**
The arrows in the figure on page 512 indicate dynamic linkage among the Criteria requirements. Learning (and action based upon that learning) takes place via feedback among the process and results elements as outlined above (The Pivotal Role of the Quality and Operational Results Category, 6.0).
    The learning cycles have four, clearly-defined stages:
    (1) planning, including design of processes, selection of indicators, and deployment of requirements;
    (2) execution of plans;
    (3) assessment of progress, taking into account internal and external (results) indicators; and
    (4) revision of plans based upon assessment findings.

5. **The Criteria emphasize quality system alignment.**
The Criteria call for improvement (learning) cycles at all levels and in all parts of the company. To ensure that these improvement cycles carried out in different parts of the company support one another, overall aims need to be consistent or *aligned*. Alignment in the Criteria is achieved via interconnecting and mutually reinforcing indicators, derived from overall company requirements. These indicators tie directly to customer value and to company operational performance. The use of indicators thus channels different activities toward agreed-upon, common goals. At the same time, use of indicators avoids the need for detailed procedural prescriptions or unnecessary centralization of decision making or process management. Indicators thus provide a basis for deploying consistent customer and company operational performance requirements to all work units. Such alignment ensures consistency of purpose while at the same time supporting speed, innovation, and empowerment.

6. **The Criteria are part of a diagnostic system.**
The Criteria and the scoring guidelines make up a two-part diagnostic (assessment) system. The Criteria are a set of 28 basic, interrelated, results-oriented requirements (Examination Items). The scoring guidelines spell out the assessment dimensions—approach, deployment, and results—and the key factors used in assessment relative to each dimension. An assessment thus provides a profile of strengths and areas for improvement relative to the 28 requirements. In this way, the assessment directs attention to processes and activities that contribute to the results composite described above.

Linkage of the Award Criteria to Quality-Related Corporate Issues

Incremental and Breakthrough Improvement   Use of nonprescriptive, results-oriented Criteria and key indicators is intended to focus on *what* needs to be improved. This approach helps to ensure that improvements throughout the organization contribute to the organization's overall objectives. In addition to supporting creativity in approach and organization, results-oriented Criteria and key indicators encourage "breakthrough thinking"—openness to the possibility for major improvements as well as to incremental ones. However, if key indicators are tied too directly to existing work methods, processes, and organizations, breakthrough changes may be discouraged. For this reason, analysis of operations, processes, and progress should focus on the selection of and the value of the indicators themselves. This will help to ensure that indicator selection does not stifle creativity and prevent beneficial changes ("re-engineering") in organization or work processes.

Benchmarks may also serve a useful purpose in stimulating breakthrough thinking. Benchmarks offer the opportunity to achieve significant improvements based on adoption or adaptation of current best practice. In addition, they help encourage creativity through exposure to alternative approaches. Also, benchmarks represent a clear challenge to "beat the best," thus stimulating the search for major improvements rather than only incremental refinements of existing approaches. As with key indicators, benchmark selection is critical, and benchmarks should be reviewed periodically for appropriateness.

Financial Performance   The Award Criteria address financial performance via three major avenues: (1) emphasis on quality factors and management actions that lead to superior offerings and thus to better market performance, market share gain, and customer retention; (2) emphasis on improved productivity, asset utilization, and lower overall operating costs; and (3) support for business strategy development, business decisions, and innovation.

The focus on superior offerings and lower costs of operation means that the Criteria's principal route to improved financial performance is through requirements that seek to channel company activities toward producing superior overall value. Delivering superior value—an important part of business strategy—also supports other business strategies such as pricing. For example, superior value offers the possibility of price premiums or competing via lower prices. Pricing decisions may enhance market share and asset utilization, and thus may also contribute to improved financial performance.

Business strategy usually addresses factors in addition to quality and value. For example, strategy may address market niche, alliances, facilities location, diversification, acquisition, export development, research, technology leadership, and rapid product turnover. The Award Criteria support the development, deployment, and evaluation of business decisions and strategies, even though these involve many factors other than product and service quality. Examples of applications of the Criteria to business decisions and strategies include:

- quality management of the information used in business decisions and strategy—scope, validity, and analysis;
- quality requirements of niches, new businesses, export target markets;
- quality status of acquisitions—key benchmarks;
- analysis of factors—societal, regulatory, economic, competitive, and risk—that may bear upon the success or failure of strategy;

- development of scenarios built around possible outcomes of strategy or decisions, including risks and consequences of failures; and
- lessons learned from previous strategy developments—within the company or available through research.

The Award Criteria and evaluation system take into account market share, customer retention, customer satisfaction, productivity, asset utilization, and other factors that contribute to financial performance. However, the Criteria do not require direct reporting of aggregate financial information such as quarterly or annual profits. The Criteria *do encourage* the use of financial information, including profit trends, in analyses and reporting of results derived from quality and operational performance improvement strategies. That is, companies are encouraged to demonstrate the connection between quality, operational performance improvement and financial performance. The exclusion of profit information that does not have a clear connection to quality and operational performance improvement is made for the following reasons—technical, fairness, and procedural:

- Short-term profits may be affected by such factors as accounting practices, business decisions, write-offs, dividends, and investments.
- Some industries historically have higher profit levels than others.
- The time interval between quality improvement and overall financial improvement depends upon many factors. This interval is not likely to be the same from industry to industry or even for companies in the same industry.
- The Award Criteria measure performance relative to rigorous, customer-oriented, company-performance criteria. Though improved quality and productivity are likely to improve a company's overall financial performance, its financial performance depends also on the performance of competitors—which the Award process cannot measure directly. The inclusion of aggregate financial indicators in evaluations would thus place at a disadvantage applicants in the most competitive businesses. Such applicants may have the most to offer from the point of view of quality management strategies.
- Financial performance depends upon many external factors, such as local, national, and international economic conditions and business cycles. Such conditions and cycles do not have the same impact on all types of businesses or on individual companies.
- Some companies would not participate in the Award process if required to provide financial information.

Invention, Innovation, and Creativity   Invention, innovation, and creativity—discovery, novel changes to existing practices or products, and imaginative approaches—are important aspects of delivering ever-improving value to customers and of maximizing productivity. State of technology may play a key role in corporate involvement in research leading to discovery. However, innovation and creativity are crucial features in company competitiveness and can be applied to products, processes, services, human resource development, and overall quality systems at all stages of the technological maturity of products and services.

The Award Criteria encourage invention, innovation, and creativity in all aspects of company decisions and in all work areas. Examples of generic mechanisms used in the Criteria to encourage such activities include:

- Nonprescriptive criteria, supported by benchmarks and indicators, encourage creativity and breakthrough thinking as they channel activities toward purpose, not toward following procedures.

- Customer-driven quality places major emphasis on the "positive side of quality," which stresses enhancement, new services, and customer relationship management. Success with the positive side of quality depends heavily on creativity—usually more so than steps to reduce errors and defects which tend to rely more on well-defined techniques.

- Human resource utilization stresses employee involvement, development, and recognition, and encourages creative approaches to improving employee effectiveness, empowerment, and contributions.

- Continuous improvement and cycles of learning are integral parts of the activities of all work groups. This requires analysis and problem solving everywhere within the company.

- Strong emphasis on cycle time reduction in all company operations encourages companies to analyze work paths, work organization, and the value-added contribution of all process steps. This fosters change, innovation, and creative thinking in how work is organized and conducted.

- Focus on future requirements of customers, customer segments, and customers of competitors encourages companies to seek innovative and creative ways to serve needs.

Examples of specific quality management mechanisms to improve new product and process innovation include:

- Strong emphasis on cycle time in the design phase to encourage rapid introduction of new products and services derived from company research. Success requires stage-to-stage coordination of functions and activities ranging from basic research to commercialization.

- Quality system requirements for research and development units that address: climate for innovation, including research opportunities and career advancement; unit awareness of fundamental knowledge that bears upon success; unit awareness of national and world leadership centers in universities, government laboratories, and other companies; shortening the patenting cycle; effectiveness of services to research and development by other units including procurement, facilities management, and technical support; key determinants in project success and project cancellation; company communication links, including internal technology transfer; key technical and reporting requirements and communications; and key measures of success—such as problem-solving effectiveness and responsiveness—for research and development units. Improvement activities of research and development units should be reported in Items 5.1, 5.2, and 5.3, as appropriate.

Changes from the 1992 Award Criteria

The 1993 Award Criteria are built upon the seven-category framework used in previous years. However, a number of changes have been made to improve clarity and to strengthen key themes and linkages. Major changes are:

- The number of Areas to Address has been increased from 89 to 92. (The number of Examination Items remains at 28.)
- Point values of several Items have been adjusted to improve overall balance.
- More Item Notes have been added to clarify the intent of the Items and to indicate key Item linkages.
- The scoring system has been clarified.
- The Guidelines and Recommendations for Responding to Examination Items have been expanded.
- The Description of the Criteria has been revised and expanded.

Key Themes Strengthened in the 1993 Criteria
  - public responsibility and corporate citizenship
  - employee development/satisfaction
  - analysis to achieve better bases for priorities and for alignment of quality system with customer requirements and operational performance requirements
  - results orientation
  - connection with invention, innovation, and creativity

A summary of the most significant changes from 1992, by Category, follows:

Leadership
  - Item 1.2 (Management for Quality) now includes an Area addressing company communication activities in support of quality improvement. The 1992 Area addressing how a company analyzes its organizational structure is now part of Item 3.1.
  - The title of Item 1.3 has been changed to Public Responsibility and Corporate Citizenship. There are three important changes within the Item: (1) a future orientation; (2) a leadership orientation; and (3) inclusion of corporate citizenship issues expanding

a company's role beyond sharing of quality-related information. Applicants' responses should reflect their circumstances and resources. The point value of the Item has been raised to 25.

Information and Analysis

- Item 2.2 has been clarified to better highlight the purpose and importance of "best practices" information—as more than numerical data. The Item is also more explicit in projecting that benchmarking information should encourage "breakthrough" thinking and innovation. The point value of Item 2.2 has been reduced to 20. It remains an extremely important Item, as its influence extends to many other Items.

- Item 2.3 has been clarified and strengthened as the "central intelligence" Item within the Criteria. The extended Notes included with this Item offer a wide variety of examples that illustrate the crucial role analysis plays in strengthening and aligning a quality system. The major consideration underlying this Item is that analysis is the only tool capable of revealing cause and effect information to guide company decision making.

Strategic Quality Planning

- Item 3.1 seeks to strengthen the focus on productivity and waste reduction, and achieve better integration of customer-related and operational-performance-related goals. The Item now addresses how realignment of work processes ("re-engineering") to improve operational performance is considered. A new Note addresses the meaning of productivity improvement and waste reduction.

Human Resource Development and Management

- Item 4.1 is now titled Human Resource Planning and Management. This Item is now the "central intelligence" for human resource issues. There is clearer linkage to overall planning (Category 3.0) and more of a future orientation. Employee satisfaction and diversity issues are more directly addressed. The Item also places greater stress on employee development and on flexibility in work organization and assignments.

- Items 4.2, 4.3, and 4.4 are now more explicit in seeking better linkages between company activities/actions and hard results reflected in customer, market, and operational performance indicators. Overall, more emphasis is placed on effectiveness indicators than on extent indicators.

- Item 4.5 is now titled Employee Well-Being and Satisfaction. The change reflects the importance of employee satisfaction as a key management tool in improving customer satisfaction.

Management of Process Quality

- Items 5.2 and 5.3 are now more parallel and better focused on process management. Both Items require descriptions of how processes are controlled and improved using information from within and from outside the process.
- Item 5.4 now requires a description of how the company evaluates and improves its procurement activities to make itself "easier to do business with."

Quality and Operational Results

- The point values in two Items have been adjusted to provide better balance. Product and Service Quality Results (Item 6.1) is now 70 points. Company Operational Results (Item 6.2) is now 50 points.

Customer Focus and Satisfaction

- The Items in this Category have been arranged in a more logical sequence. The first Item (7.1) is now Customer Expectations: Current and Future. This Item includes the main requirements of Item 7.6 from the 1992 Examination but, in addition, adds a current focus. This is reflected in the new title of the Item. The remaining Items in the Category retain their titles from the 1992 Examination, but Item numbers are changed.
- The point values of three Items have changed: (1) Customer Satisfaction Results (Item 7.5) is now 85 points; (2) Customer Satisfaction Comparison (Item 7.6) is now 70 points; and (3) Customer Satisfaction Determination (Item 7.4) is now 30 points.

*Applicants and other users of the Award Criteria are cautioned to note that some changes have been made to **all** Items, even though the basic requirements within the Items are substantially the same as in 1992.*

KEY BUSINESS FACTORS AND THE APPLICATION OVERVIEW

Introduction to Key Business Factors and Their Use in Evaluation of Applications

The Award Examination is designed to permit evaluation of any quality system for manufacturing and service companies of any size, type of business, or scope of market. The 28 Items and 92 Areas to Address have been selected because of their importance to virtually all businesses. Nevertheless, the importance of the Items and Areas to Address may not be equally applicable to all businesses, even to businesses of comparable size in the same industry. The specific business factors that may bear upon the evaluation and that are described below must be presented in the Application Overview and will be considered at every stage of evaluation.

Application Overview Addressing Key Business Factors

Applicants are required to submit a four-page Overview that addresses key business factors that must be considered in the Award evaluation process. The Overview is intended to "set the stage" for the Examiners who conduct the evaluation, helping them to understand what is *relevant and important.*

Careful attention should be given to the preparation of the Overview because it directly impacts the Examiners' evaluation of the entire application, at every stage in the review.

An Overview fully responsive to the requirements of the Examiners should include:

- nature of the applicant's business: products and services delivered
- description of the applicant's employee base, including: number, type, and education level
- key quality requirements for products and services
- description of principal customers (consumers, other businesses, government) and their special requirements
- nature of major markets (local, regional, national, or international)
- applicant's position in the industry and the competitive environment
- major equipment, facilities and technologies used
- types of suppliers of goods and services
- importance of suppliers, dealers, and other external businesses to the applicant and the degree of influence the applicant has over its suppliers
- special relationships with suppliers, partners, or customers
- regulatory environment within which the applicant operates, including occupational health and safety, environmental, and other regulatory considerations
- other factors important to the applicant, such as major new thrusts for the company or major changes taking place in the industry

If the applicant is a subsidiary or division, a description of the organizational structure and management links to the parent company should be presented. The Overview should also include information that shows key relationships to the parent company: (1) percent of employees; (2) percent of sales; and (3) types of products and services. (The Overview is not counted as part of the page limit.)

1993 EXAMINATION RESPONSE GUIDELINES

Guidelines and Recommendations for Responding to Examination Items

The guidelines and recommendations given below are offered to assist applicants in preparing responses to the Examination Items:

General Guidelines and Recommendations

1. Read the entire Award Criteria booklet before developing responses to any of the Examination Items.

2. Note that the Criteria are intentionally nonprescriptive. If an Area to Address or portion of an Area seems inappropriate because of the applicant's unique business factors, briefly state the reasoning in the application. This is likely to provide greater insight than an attempt to redefine company practices to suit the Area.

3. The unique business factors of some companies could affect their level of activity in a particular area. For example, a small business' resources might limit its participation in key communities as a corporate good citizen (Item 1.3), in training key suppliers (Item 5.4), or in obtaining some types of competitive comparisons and benchmark data (Item 2.2). It is appropriate to briefly describe these limitations in the application.

4. Applications are scored on the basis of the applicant's quality system approach, deployment and results. Note from the requirements in the Examination Items and from the Scoring System (page 33) that some Items may request information only on approach/deployment, some Items only on results and several Items on all three. Items are classified in terms of kinds of information requested. These classifications are noted below each Item by red check marks in the Approach, Deployment and Results boxes. In responding to Items requiring results, the conclusions drawn should directly relate to the data presented.

5. Report only what is requested in each Item, and include only the types of information requested. Check related Items to determine the distinctions between the types and amounts of information required. Each Item is best interpreted by noting the purposes of its Category. Make responses self-contained and not dependent upon information given in responses to other Items. However, if other Items contain information that directly supports a response, and at the same time avoids significant duplication of information, provide cross references to these Items using their Item and Area designators.

6. **Respond to Items with concise, factual statements. Support statements with quantitative information whenever appropriate. Use of charts, graphs, and tables, properly labeled and compactly presented, is strongly encouraged**. Lengthy narratives not directly responsive to the requirements of Items are discouraged. Also avoid reiteration of the words and phrases of Examination Items.

7. Avoid the use of anecdotal information or information lacking overall context. An example is at times appropriate, but applicants should make clear that the example illustrates the overall system function (i.e., the larger point being made) and is not itself the response to the Item.

8. A quality management system requires consistency and linkages among the components of the system (through proper use of human, informational and operational/capital resources). To describe this system requires consistency and linkages in responses to Items in the Award Examination. For example, there needs to be a consistent set of responses among the special customer requirements and key product/service quality requirements in the Overview, the customer satisfaction response data in Item 7.5, the product and service quality results data in Item 6.1, and the key processes and process designs for producing and delivering products and services described in Items 5.1 and 5.2.

9. Some **Areas to Address** have the word "include" to illustrate the **types of topics applicants should discuss** in response to Examination Items. Applicants should seek to provide a complete response, addressing those topics as well as similar topics **of direct relevance and importance** to the company's business and/or quality system.

10. The information in some Items is supplemented by Item Notes. These **Notes** are intended to **clarify requests for information** made in the Areas to Address. These Notes indicate limitations on requested information, cross-references to other Items and aids in responding to the Item. The **Notes** to some Items include the words "such as," "might involve," or "could include" to illustrate **the types of topics applicants might discuss**. Applicants should address only those topics, or similar topics, **of relevance and importance** to their company.

11. The application of a subsidiary or division must respond to requirements given in all 28 Examination Items, even if some of the activities described are performed by the parent company or a unit of the parent company. Such activities are subject to evaluation, including review during site visits. When these activities are performed by the parent company or another company unit, the applicant should clearly state their own role and the role of the unit that is performing these activities.

12. If acronyms are used, the applicant should include a separate section containing a list of all acronyms, their meanings and the page numbers where they are first described or used.

Data and Results Guidelines and Recommendations

13. There is a critical distinction between data and results; this distinction is frequently misunderstood. Data are numerical information used as a basis for reasoning, discussion, determining status, or further calculation. Results are the consequence of actions. Data could help describe an activity, as well as the outcome of that activity. **Results Items require data to substantiate prog-**

ress. Approach and deployment Items may benefit from data that permit better linkage between action and results. When data are used to support approach/deployment Items, such data should relate directly to approach and deployment and not to the results that may derive from the approach and deployment. Such results data are requested in other Items. For example, the formation of 5 self-directed work teams is datum (giving deployment information to support an approach); these teams reducing scrap by 17% is a result.

14. Note which Items *require* data. These are: 1.3d, 4.2d, 4.3d, 4.4c, 4.5d, 6.1, 6.2, 6.3, 6.4, 7.5, and 7.6. In addition, Item 3.2d calls for a projection of data. Other Items frequently can be supported by data.

15. Trend data are requested to permit applicants to demonstrate progress over a period of time and to show that improvements are sustained. No minimum period of time is specified for trend data. However, Examiner evaluations of trend data do take into account evidence of continuity. Time periods for trend data may span up to five years or more for some product, service, or operational characteristics, but may be much shorter in areas where improvement efforts have been established more recently. Trend data should be presented in graphical, tabular, or other compact form. Integrate charts, graphs, and tables into the body of the text whenever possible.

16. The following graph illustrates data an applicant might present as part of a response to Item 6.1, Product and Service Quality Results. The applicant has indicated on-time delivery as a key business factor in the Overview and in Item 7.1.

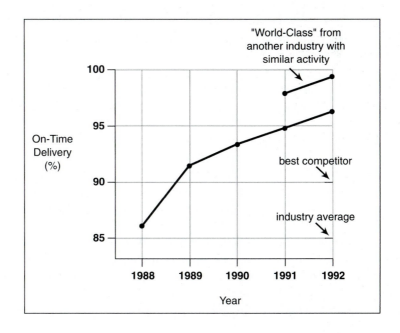

Using this graph as a model, the following attributes of a clear and effective manner of presentation have been illustrated:

- The graph reports results identified as key to the business.
- Both axes have been clearly and quantitatively labeled.
- Results are presented for several years.
- Comparisons to industry average, best competitor and "world-class" are clearly shown.

The comparison with "world-class" is important, both to set stretch goals for the company (encouraging breakthrough improvement) and to document an applicant's position relative to the "best."

17. To help with understanding the scoring matrix on page 34, the following interpretation of the graphed results in the adjacent column would be made:

- excellent improvement trend
- results can be evaluated against relevant comparisons and benchmarks
- current performance is excellent
- strong evidence of industry leadership

Category- and Item-Specific Guidelines and Recommendations

18. **Item 2.3** is a key linkage Item. Applicants should respond with **analyses at the company level**. This Item highlights the importance in setting priorities of analysis of key data from Categories 6.0, 7.0 and elsewhere. The extensive notes to Item 2.3 are intended to give applicants numerous examples of important linkages and correlations that could provide critical cause/effect information to drive improvement at the company level. This Item represents one of the greatest challenges in demonstrating the maturity of an applicant's ability to manage by fact.

19. Items 4.2, 4.3, 4.4, and 4.5 are approach/deployment and results Items. In documenting the effectiveness of these Category 4.0 results, the applicant must show how these results are related to employee satisfaction and performance improvement, as well as to improvements in quality and operational performance.

20. The reporting of results should display consistency and linkages among Categories. Specifically:

- Product and service results in Item 6.1 should address: all product and service features of importance to customers, as expressed in Items 7.1, 7.2 and 7.4; process quality issues presented in Items 5.1 and 5.2; and, key product and service features described in the Overview.
- Company operational results reported in Item 6.2 should derive from process improvements described in Items 5.1 and 5.2. Item 6.2 results also receive input from business and support process improvements, Item 5.3, and supplier improvements, Item 5.4.

- Business process and support service results reported in Item 6.3 should derive from business processes and support services described in Item 5.3.
- Supplier quality results reported in Item 6.4 should derive from supplier quality processes described in Item 5.4.

1993 EXAMINATION ITEMS AND POINT VALUES

1993 Examination Categories/Items	Point Values
1.0 Leadership	95
1.1 Senior Executive Leadership	45
1.2 Management for Quality	25
1.3 Public Responsibility and Corporate Citizenship	25
2.0 Information and Analysis	75
2.1 Scope and Management of Quality and Performance Data and Information	15
2.2 Competitive Comparisons and Benchmarking	20
2.3 Analysis and Uses of Company-Level Data	40
3.0 Strategic Quality Planning	60
3.1 Strategic Quality and Company Performance Planning Process	35
3.2 Quality and Performance Plans	25
4.0 Human Resource Development and Management	150
4.1 Human Resource Planning and Management	20
4.2 Employee Involvement	40
4.3 Employee Education and Training	40
4.4 Employee Performance and Recognition	25
4.5 Employee Well-Being and Satisfaction	25
5.0 Management of Process Quality	140
5.1 Design and Introduction of Quality Products and Services	40
5.2 Process Management: Product and Service Production and Delivery Processes	35
5.3 Process Management: Business Processes and Support Services	30
5.4 Supplier Quality	20
5.5 Quality Assessment	15
6.0 Quality and Operational Results	180
6.1 Product and Service Quality Results	70
6.2 Company Operational Results	50
6.3 Business Process and Support Service Results	25
6.4 Supplier Quality Results	35
7.0 Customer Focus and Satisfaction	300
7.1 Customer Expectations: Current and Future	35
7.2 Customer Relationship Management	65
7.3 Commitment to Customers	15
7.4 Customer Satisfaction Determination	30
7.5 Customer Satisfaction Results	85
7.6 Customer Satisfaction Comparison	70
Total Points	1000

1993 EXAMINATION CRITERIA

1.0 Leadership (95 pts.)

The **Leadership** Category examines senior executives' *personal* leadership and involvement in creating and sustaining a customer focus and clear and visible quality values. Also examined is how the quality values are integrated into the company's management system and reflected in the manner in which the company addresses its public responsibilities and corporate citizenship.

1.1 Senior Executive Leadership (45 pts.)   Describe the senior executives' leadership, personal involvement, and visibility in developing and maintaining an environment for quality excellence.

☑ Approach[1]
☑ Deployment
☐ Results

Areas to Address

a. senior executives' leadership, personal involvement, and visibility in quality-related activities of the company. Include: (1) reinforcing a customer focus; (2) creating quality values and setting expectations; (3) planning and reviewing progress toward quality and operational performance objectives; (4) recognizing employee contributions, and (5) communicating quality values outside the company.

b. brief summary of the company's customer focus and quality values and how they serve as a basis for consistent communication within and outside the company

c. how senior executives regularly communicate and reinforce the company's customer focus and quality values with managers and supervisors

d. how senior executives evaluate and improve the effectiveness of their personal leadership and involvement

---

NOTES:
(1) The term "senior executives" refers to the highest-ranking official of the organization applying for the Award and those reporting directly to that official.
(2) Activities of senior executives might also include leading and/or receiving training, communicating with all employees, benchmarking, customer

---

[1]All Items are designated as Approach and Deployment, and/or Results Items. A discussion of these descriptors is given on page 554.

visits, interactions with suppliers, and mentoring other executives, managers, and supervisors.

(3) Communication by senior executives outside the company might involve: national, state, and community groups; trade, business, and professional organizations; and education, health care, government, and standards groups. It might also involve the company's stockholders and board of directors.

1.2 Management for Quality (25 pts.)   Describe how the company's customer focus and quality values are integrated into day-to-day leadership, management, and supervision of all company units.

☑ Approach
☑ Deployment
☐ Results

Areas to Address

a. how the company's customer focus and quality values are translated into requirements for all managers and supervisors. Summarize: (1) their principal roles and responsibilities within their units; and (2) their roles and responsibilities in fostering cooperation with other units.

b. how the company's customer focus and quality values (1.1b) are communicated and reinforced throughout the company, with all employees

c. how company and work unit quality and operational performance plans are reviewed. Describe: (1) types, frequency, content and use of reviews and who conducts them; and (2) how the company assists units that are not performing according to plans.

d. key methods and key indicators the company uses to evaluate and improve awareness and integration of quality values among managers and supervisors

1.3 Public Responsibility and Corporate Citizenship (25 pts.)   Describe how the company includes its responsibilities to the public in its quality policies and improvement practices. Describe also how the company leads as a corporate citizen in its key communities.

☑ Approach
☑ Deployment
☑ Results

Areas to Address

a. how the company integrates its public responsibilities into its quality policies and practices. Include: (1) how the company determines or sets operational requirements and goals taking into account risks, regulatory, and other legal requirements; (2) a summary of the principal public responsibility areas addressed within the company's quality policies and/or practices and how key operational requirements are communicated throughout the company; and (3) how and how often progress in meeting operational requirements and/or goals is reviewed.

b. how the company looks ahead to anticipate public concerns and to assess possible impacts on society that may derive from its products, services, and operations. Describe briefly how this assessment is used in planning.

c. how the company leads as a corporate citizen in its key communities. Include: (1) a brief summary of the types and extent of leadership and involvement in key communities; (2) how the company promotes quality awareness and sharing of quality-related information; (3) how the company seeks opportunities to enhance its leadership; and (4) how the company promotes legal and ethical conduct in all that it does.

d. trends in key indicators of improvement in addressing public responsibilities and corporate citizenship. Include responses to any sanctions the company has received under law, regulation, or contract.

Notes:

(1) The public responsibility issues addressed in 1.3a and 1.3b relate to the company's impacts and possible impacts on society associated with its products, services, and company operations. They include business ethics, environment, and safety as they relate to any aspect of risk or adverse effect, whether or not these are covered under law or regulation.

(2) Details of the company's process management associated with issues both relevant and important to the company's business should be included in Category 5.0.

(3) Health and safety of employees are not included in Item 1.3. They are covered in Item 4.5.

(4) The corporate citizenship issues appropriate for inclusion in 1.3c relate to contributions by the company to strengthen community services, education, health care, environment or practices of trade or business associations. Applicants' involvement would be expected to be limited by the company's available human and financial resources.

(5) If the company has received sanctions under law, regulation, or contract during the past three years, include the current status in responding to 1.3d.

2.0 Information and Analysis (75 pts.)

The *Information and Analysis* Category examines the scope, validity, analysis, management, and use of data and information to drive quality excellence and to improve operational and competitive performance. Also examined is the adequacy of the company's data, information, and analysis system to support improvement of the company's customer focus, products, services, and internal operations.

2.1 Scope and Management of Quality and Performance Data and Information (15 pts.)   Describe the company's data and information used for planning, day-to-day management, and evaluation of quality and operational performance. Describe also how data and information are managed to ensure reliability, timeliness, and rapid access.

☑ Approach
☑ Deployment
☐ Results

Areas to Address
a. criteria for selecting data and information for use in quality and operational performance improvement. List key types of data and information used and briefly outline the principal roles of each type in improving quality and company operational performance. Include: (1) customer-related; (2) product and service performance; (3) internal operations and performance, including business processes, support services, and employee-related; (4) supplier performance; and (5) cost and financial.

b. how the company assures reliability, consistency, and rapid access to data throughout the company. If applicable, describe how software quality is assured.

c. key methods and key indicators used to evaluate and improve the scope and management of data and information. Include: (1) review and update; (2) shortening the cycle from data gathering to access; (3) broadening access to all those requiring data for day-to-day management and improvement; and (4) alignment of data and information with process improvement plans and needs.

NOTES:

(1) This Item permits the applicant to demonstrate the *breadth and depth* of its quality-related data. Applicants should give brief descriptions of the data under major headings such as "internal operations and performance" and subheadings such as "support services." Note that information on the scope and management of competitive and benchmark data is requested in Item 2.2.

(2) Actual data should not be reported in this Item. Such data are requested in other Items. Accordingly, all data reported in other Items, such as 6.1, 6.2, 6.3, 6.4, 7.5, and 7.6, should be part of the base of data and information to be described in Item 2.1.

2.2 *Competitive Comparisons and Benchmarking (20 pts.)*   Describe the company's processes, current sources and scope, and uses of competitive comparisons and benchmarking information and data to support improvement of quality and overall company operational performance.

☑ Approach
☑ Deployment
☐ Results

Areas to Address

a. how the company uses competitive comparisons and benchmarking information and data to help drive improvement of quality and company operational performance. Describe: (1) how needs are determined; and (2) criteria for seeking appropriate comparison and benchmarking information—from within and outside the company's industry.

b. brief summary of current scope, sources and principal uses of each type of competitive and benchmark information and data. Include: (1) customer-related; (2) product and service quality; (3) internal operations and performance, including business processes, support services, and employee-related; and (4) supplier performance.

c. how competitive and benchmarking information and data are used to improve understanding of processes, to encourage breakthrough approaches, and to set "stretch" objectives

d. how the company evaluates and improves its overall processes for selecting and using competitive comparisons and benchmarking information and data to improve planning and company operations

NOTES:

(1) Benchmarking information and data refer to processes and results that represent superior performance and set a "stretch" standard for comparison.

(2) Sources of competitive and benchmarking information are of several types, and could include: (1) information obtained directly from other organizations through sharing; (2) information obtained from open literature; (3) testing and evaluation by the company itself; and (4) testing and evaluation by independent organizations.

2.3 Analysis and Uses of Company-Level Data (40 pts.)   Describe how data related to quality, customers and operational performance, together with relevant financial data, are analyzed to support company-level review, action, and planning.

☑ Approach
☑ Deployment
☐ Results

Areas to Address

a. how customer-related data and results (from Category 7.0) are aggregated with other key data and analyses, analyzed, and translated into actionable information to support: (1) developing priorities for prompt solutions to customer-related problems; and (2) determining key customer-related trends and correlations to support status review, decision making, and longer-term planning

b. how operational performance data and results (from Category 6.0) are aggregated with other key data and analyses, analyzed, and translated into actionable information to support: (1) developing priorities for short-term improvements in company operations, including cycle time, productivity and waste reduction; and (2) determining key operations-related trends and correlations to support status reviews, decision making, and longer-term planning

c. how the company relates overall improvements in product/ service quality and operational performance to changes in overall financial performance

d. how the company evaluates and improves its analysis as a key management tool. Include: (1) how analysis supports improved data selection and use; (2) how the analysis-access cycle is shortened; and (3) how analysis strengthens the integration of overall data for improved decision making and planning.

NOTES:

(1) Item 2.3 focuses primarily on analysis for company-level purposes. Data for such analysis come from all parts of the company. Other Items in the Criteria call for analyses of specific sets of data for special purposes. For example, the Items of Category 4.0 require analyses to demonstrate effectiveness of training and other human resource practices. Such special-purpose analyses are assumed to be part of the information base of Category 2.0, available for use in Item 2.3. These specific sets of data and special-purpose analyses are described in 2.3a and 2.3b as "other key data and analyses."

(2) "Actionable" means that the analysis provides information that can be used for priorities and decisions leading to allocation of resources.

(3) The focus in 2.3a is on analysis to improve customer-related decision making and planning. This analysis is intended to provide additional information to *support* such decision making and planning that result from day-to-day customer information, feedback, and complaints.

Analysis appropriate for inclusion in 2.3a could include relationships between and among the following: the company's product and service quality improvement and key customer indicators such as customer satisfaction, customer retention, and market share; relationship between customer relationship management strategies and changes in customer satisfaction, customer retention, and market share; cross-comparisons of data from complaints, post-transaction follow-up, and won/lost analyses to identify improvement priorities; relationship between employee satisfaction and customer satisfaction; cost/revenue implications of customer-related problems; and rates of improvement in customer indicators.

(4) The focus in 2.3b is on analysis to improve operations-related decision making and planning. This analysis is intended to *support* such decision making and planning that results from day-to-day observations of process performance.

Analysis appropriate for inclusion in 2.3b could include: evaluation of the productivity and cost impacts of improvement initiatives; rates of improvement in key operational indicators; evaluation of trends in key operational efficiency measures; and comparison with competitive and benchmark data to identify improvement opportunities and to establish improvement goals and priorities.

(5) The focus in 2.3c is on the linkages between improvements in product/service quality and operational performance and overall financial performance for company goal and priority setting. Analyses in 2.3c could incorporate the results of analyses described in 2.3a and 2.3b, and draw upon other relevant data and analyses.

Analysis appropriate for inclusion in 2.3c could include: relationships between product/service quality and operational performance indicators and overall company financial performance trends as reflected in indicators such as operating costs, revenues, asset utilization, and value added per employee; comparisons of company financial performance versus competitors based on quality and operational performance indicators; allocation of limited resources for improvement among possible projects based on cost/revenue implications and improvement potential; net earnings derived from quality/operational performance improvements; and comparisons among business units based upon quality improvement and its impact on financial performance.

3.0 Strategic Quality Planning (60 pts.)

The **Strategic Quality Planning** Category examines the company's planning process and how all key quality requirements are integrated into overall business planning. Also examined are the company's short- and longer-term plans and how quality and operational performance requirements are deployed to all work units.

3.1 Strategic Quality and Company Performance Planning Process (35 pts.)   Describe the company's strategic planning process for the short term (1–2 years) and longer term (3 years or more) for customer satisfaction leadership and overall operational performance improvement. Include how this process integrates quality and company operational performance requirements and how plans are deployed.

☑ Approach
☑ Deployment
☐ Results

Areas to Address

a. how the company develops strategies, goals and business plans to address quality and customer satisfaction leadership for the short term and longer term. Describe how business plans consider: (1) customer requirements and the expected evolution of these requirements; (2) projections of the competitive environment; (3) risks: financial, market, and societal; (4) company capabilities, including human resource development, and research and development to address key new requirements or technology leadership opportunities; and (5) supplier capabilities.

b. how the company develops strategies and plans to address overall operational performance improvement. Describe how the following are considered: (1) realigning work processes ("re-engineering") to improve operational performance; and (2) productivity improvement and reduction in waste.

c. how plans are deployed. Describe: (1) the method the company uses to deploy overall plan requirements to all work units and to suppliers, and how it ensures alignment of work unit plans and activities; and (2) how resources are committed to meet the plan requirements.

d. how the company evaluates and improves its planning process, including improvements in: (1) determining company quality and overall operational performance requirements; (2) deploying requirements to work units; and (3) receiving planning input from company work units

---

NOTES:

(1) Productivity improvement and waste reduction may address a variety of issues including inventories, work in process, inspection, downtime, changeover time and better utilization of resources such as materials, energy, capital and labor.

(2) How the company reviews quality and overall operational performance relative to plans is addressed in Item 1.2.

3.2 Quality and Performance Plans (25 pts.)   Summarize the company's quality and operational performance goals and plans for the short term (1–2 years) and the longer term (3 years or more).

☑ Approach
☑ Deployment
☐ Results

Areas to Address

a. for the company's chosen directions, including planned products and services, markets, or market segments, summarize: (1) key quality factors and quality requirements to achieve leadership; and (2) key company operational performance requirements

b. outline of the company's principal short-term quality and company operational performance goals and plans. Include: (1) a summary of key requirements and key operational performance indicators deployed to work units and suppliers; and (2) a brief description of resources committed for key needs such as capital equipment, facilities, education and training, and personnel.

c. principal longer-term (3 years or more) quality and company operational performance goals and plans, including key requirements and how they will be addressed

d. two-to-five-year projection of improvements using the most important indicators of quality and company operational performance. Describe how quality and company operational performance might be expected to compare with competitors and key benchmarks over this time period. Briefly explain the comparisons, including any estimates or assumptions made regarding the projected quality and operational performance of competitors or changes in benchmarks.

4.0 Human Resource Development and Management (150 pts.)

The **Human Resource Development and Management** Category examines the key elements of how the work force is enabled to develop its full potential to pursue the company's quality and operational performance objectives. Also examined are the company's efforts to build and maintain an environment for quality excellence conducive to full participation and personal and organizational growth.

4.1 Human Resource Planning and Management (20 pts.)   Describe how the company's overall human resource plans and practices are integrated with its overall quality and operational performance goals and plans and address fully the needs and development of the entire work force.

☑ Approach
☑ Deployment
☐ Results

Areas to Address

a. brief outline of the most important human resource plans (derived from Category 3.0). Address: (1) development, including education, training and empowerment; (2) mobility, flexibility, and changes in work organization, processes or work schedules; (3) reward, recognition, benefits, and compensation; and (4) recruitment, including possible changes in diversity of the work force. Distinguish between the short term (1–2 years) and the longer term (3 years or more), as appropriate.

b. how the company improves its human resource operations and practices. Describe key goals and methods for processes/practices such as recruitment, hiring, personnel actions, and services to employees. Describe key performance indicators, including cycle time, and how these indicators are used in improvement.

c. how the company evaluates and uses all employee-related data to improve the development and effectiveness of the entire work force and to provide key input to overall company planning and to human resource management and planning. Describe: (1) how this improvement process addresses all types of employees; and (2) how employee satisfaction factors (Item 4.5) are used to reduce adverse indicators such as absenteeism, turnover, grievances, and accidents.

NOTES:

(1) Human resource plans might include the following: mechanisms for promoting cooperation such as internal customer/supplier techniques or other internal partnerships; initiatives to promote labor-management cooperation, such as partnerships with unions; creation and/or modification of recognition systems; mechanisms for increasing or broadening employee responsibilities; creating opportunities for employees to learn and use skills that go beyond current job assignments through redesign of processes; creation of high performance work teams; and education and training initiatives. Plans might also include forming partnerships with educational institutions to develop employees or to help ensure the future supply of well-prepared employees.

(2) "Categories of employees" refers to the company's classification system used in its personnel practices and/or work assignments and also includes factors such as union or bargaining unit membership. "Types of employees" takes into account other factors, such as work force diversity or demographic makeup. This includes gender, age, minorities, and the disabled.

(3) "All employee-related data" refers to data contained in personnel records as well as data described in Items 4.2, 4.3, 4.4, and 4.5. This includes employee satisfaction data, and data on turnover, absenteeism, safety, grievances, involvement, recognition, training, and information from exit interviews.

4.2 Employee Involvement (40 pts.)   Describe the means available for all employees to contribute effectively to meeting the company's quality and operational performance goals and plans; summarize trends in effectiveness and extent of involvement.

- ☑ Approach
- ☑ Deployment
- ☑ Results

Areas to Address

a. principal mechanisms the company uses to promote ongoing employee contributions, individually and in groups, to quality and operational performance goals and plans. Describe how and how quickly the company gives feedback to contributors.

b. how the company increases employee empowerment, responsibility, and innovation. Briefly summarize principal goals for all categories of employees, based upon the most important requirements for each category.

c. key methods and key indicators the company uses to evaluate and improve the effectiveness, extent and type of involvement of all categories and all types of employees. Include how effectiveness, extent and types of involvement are linked to key quality and operational performance improvement results.

d. trends in the most important indicators of the *effectiveness* and *extent* of employee involvement for each category of employee

---

NOTE:

The company may use different involvement methods, goals and indicators for different categories of employees or for different parts of the company, depending on needs and on the types of responsibilities of each employee category or part of the company. Examples include problem-solving teams (within work units or cross-functional), fully-integrated, self-managed work groups, and process improvement teams.

4.3 Employee Education and Training (40 pts.)   Describe how the company determines quality and related education and training needs for all employees. Show how this determination addresses company plans and needs as well as supports employee growth. Outline how such education and training are evaluated, and summarize key trends demonstrating improvement in both the effectiveness and extent of education and training.

☑ Approach
☑ Deployment
☑ Results

Areas to Address

a. how the company determines needs for the types and amounts of quality and related education and training for all employees, taking into account their differing needs. Include: (1) linkage to short- and long-term plans, including companywide access to skills in problem solving, waste reduction, and process simplification; (2) growth and career opportunities for employees; and (3) how employees' input is sought and used in the needs determination.

b. summary of how quality and related education and training are delivered and reinforced. Include: (1) outline of methods for education and training delivery for all categories of employees; (2) on-the-job application of knowledge and skills; and (3) quality-related orientation for new employees.

c. how the company evaluates and improves its quality and related education and training. Include how the evaluation supports improved needs determination, taking into account: (1) relating on-the-job performance improvement to key quality and operational performance improvement goals and results; and (2) growth and progression of all categories and types of employees.

d. trends in the *effectiveness* and *extent* of quality and related training and education based upon key indicators of each

---

NOTES:

(1) Quality and related education and training address the knowledge and skills employees need to meet their objectives as part of the company's quality and operational performance improvement plans. This may include quality awareness, leadership, project management, teamwork, problem solving, interpreting and using data, meeting customer requirements, process analysis, process simplification, waste reduction, cycle time reduction, and other training that affects employee effectiveness and efficiency. In many cases, this may include job enrichment skills and basic skills such as reading, writing, language, arithmetic, and basic mathematics that are needed to meet quality and operational performance improvement objectives.

(2) Education and training delivery may occur inside or outside the company and may involve classroom or on-the-job delivery.

(3) Trends in the extent of quality and related education and training should provide information regarding coverage of employee categories, including new employees, how much education and training, as well as the basic type and content.

4.4 Employee Performance and Recognition (25 pts.)   Describe how the company's employee performance, recognition, promotion, compensation, reward, and feedback approaches support the attainment of the company's quality and performance plans and goals.

☑ Approach
☑ Deployment
☑ Results

Areas to Address

a. how the company's employee performance, recognition, promotion, compensation, reward, and feedback approaches for individuals and groups, including managers, support the company's quality and operational performance goals and plans. Address: (1) how the approaches ensure that quality is reinforced relative to short-term financial considerations; and (2) how employees contribute to the company's employee performance and recognition approaches.

b. key methods and key indicators the company uses to evaluate and improve its employee performance and recognition approaches. Include how the evaluation takes into account: (1) effective participation by all categories and types of employees; (2) employee satisfaction information (Item 4.5); and (3) key indicators of improved quality and operational performance results.

c. trends in key indicators of the *effectiveness* and *extent* of employee reward and recognition, by employee category

---

NOTES:

(1) The company may use a variety of reward and recognition approaches—monetary and non-monetary, formal and informal, and individual and group.

(2) The evaluation in 4.4b should be segmented by employee category, as appropriate. Employee satisfaction may take into account employee dissatisfaction indicators such as turnover and absenteeism.

4.5 Employee Well-Being and Satisfaction (25 pts.)   Describe how the company maintains a work environment conducive to the well-being and growth of all employees; summarize trends in key indicators of well-being and satisfaction.

☑ Approach
☑ Deployment
☑ Results

Areas to Address

a. how well-being factors such as health, safety, and ergonomics are included in quality improvement activities. Include principal improvement goals, methods, and indicators for each factor relevant and important to the company's employee work environment. For accidents and work-related health problems, describe how root causes are determined and how adverse conditions are prevented.

b. special services, facilities, and opportunities the company makes available to employees

c. how the company determines employee satisfaction. Include a brief description of methods, frequency, and the specific factors for which satisfaction is determined. Segment by employee category or type, as appropriate.

d. trends in key indicators of well-being and satisfaction. This should address, as appropriate: satisfaction, safety, absenteeism, turnover, turnover rate for customer-contact personnel, grievances, strikes, and worker compensation. Explain important adverse results, if any. For such adverse results, describe how root causes were determined and corrected, and/or give current status. Compare results on the most significant indicators with those of industry averages, industry leaders, key benchmarks, and local/regional averages, as appropriate.

NOTES:

(1) Special services, facilities, and opportunities might include: counseling; recreational or cultural activities; non-work-related education; day care; special leave; safety off the job; flexible work hours; and outplacement.

(2) Examples of specific factors for which satisfaction may be determined are: employee views of leadership and management; employee development and career opportunities; employee preparation for changes in technology or work organization; work environment; recognition; benefits; communications; job security; and compensation.

5.0 *Management of Process Quality (140 pts.)*

The *Management of Process Quality* Category examines the systematic processes the company uses to pursue ever-higher quality and company operational performance. Examined are the key elements of process management, including research and development, design, management of process quality for all work units and suppliers, systematic quality improvement, and quality assessment.

5.1 Design and Introduction of Quality Products and Services (40 pts.) Describe how new and/or improved products and services are designed and introduced and how processes are designed to meet key product and service quality requirements and company operational performance requirements.

☑ Approach
☑ Deployment
☐ Results

Areas to Address

a. how designs of products, services, and processes are developed so that: (1) customer requirements are translated into product and service design requirements; (2) all product and service quality requirements are addressed early in the overall design process by appropriate company units; (3) designs are coordinated and integrated to include all phases of production and delivery; and (4) key process performance characteristics are selected based on customer requirements, appropriate performance levels are determined, and measurement systems are developed to track performance for each of these characteristics

b. how designs are reviewed and validated, taking into account key factors: (1) product and service performance; (2) process capability and future requirements; and (3) supplier capability and future requirements

c. how the company improves its designs and design processes so that new product and service introductions and product and service modifications progressively improve in quality and cycle time

---

NOTES:

(1) Design and introduction may include modifications and variants of existing products and services and/or new products and services emerging from research and development. Design also may include facilities to meet company operational performance, and key product and service quality requirements.

(2) Applicants' responses should reflect the key requirements of their products and services. Factors that may need to be considered in design include: health; safety; long-term performance; environment; waste generation/reduction; measurement capability; process capability; manufacturability; maintainability; and supplier capability.

(3) Service and manufacturing businesses should interpret product and service requirements to include all product- and service-related requirements at all stages of production, delivery, and use.

> (4) Results of improvements in design and design process quality should be reported in Item 6.2a.

5.2 Process Management: Product and Service Production and Delivery Processes (35 pts.) Describe how the company's key product and service production and delivery processes are managed to ensure that design requirements are met and that both quality and operational performance are continuously improved.

☑ Approach
☑ Deployment
☐ Results

Areas to Address

a. how the company maintains the quality of production and delivery processes in accord with the product and service design requirements (Item 5.1). Include: (1) the key processes and their requirements; (2) key indicators of quality and operational performance; and (3) how quality and operational performance are determined and maintained, including types and frequencies of in-process and end-of-process measurements used.

b. for significant (out-of-control) variations in processes or outputs, how root causes are determined, and corrections made and verified

c. how the process is improved to achieve better quality, cycle time, and overall operational performance. Include how each of the following is used or considered: (1) process analysis/simplification; (2) benchmarking information; (3) process research and testing; (4) use of alternative technology; (5) information from customers of the processes—within and outside the company; and (6) challenge goals.

Notes:

(1) Manufacturing and service companies with specialized measurement requirements should describe how they assure measurement quality. For physical, chemical, and engineering measurements, describe briefly how measurements are made traceable to national standards.

(2) Variations (5.2b) may be observed by those working in the process or by customers of the process output. The latter situation may result in formal or informal feedback or complaints. Also, a company may use observers or "mystery shoppers" to provide information on process performance.

(3) Results of improvements in product and service production and delivery processes should be reported in Item 6.2a.

5.3 Process Management: Business Processes and Support Services (30 pts.) Describe how the company's key business processes and support services are managed so that current requirements are met and that quality and operational performance are continuously improved.

☑ Approach
☑ Deployment
☐ Results

Areas to Address

a. how key business processes and support services are designed to meet customer and/or company quality and operational performance requirements. Include: (1) the key processes and their requirements; (2) key indicators of quality and performance; and (3) how quality and performance are determined and maintained, including types and frequencies of in-process and end-of-process measurements used.

b. for significant (out-of-control) variations in processes or outputs, how root causes are determined, and corrections made and verified

c. how the process is improved to achieve better quality, cycle time, and overall operational performance. Describe how each of the following are used or considered: (1) process analysis/simplification; (2) benchmarking information; (3) process research and testing; (4) use of alternative technology; (5) information from customers of the business processes and support services—within and outside the company; and (6) challenge goals.

Notes:

(1) Business processes and support services might include activities and operations involving finance and accounting, software services, sales, marketing, public relations, information services, purchasing, personnel, legal services, plant and facilities management, basic research and development, and secretarial and other administrative services.

(2) The purpose of this Item is to permit applicants to highlight separately the quality activities for functions that support the product and service production and delivery processes the applicant addressed in Item 5.2. The support services and business processes included in Item 5.3 depend on the applicant's type of business and quality system. Thus, this selection should be made by the applicant. Together, Items 5.1, 5.2, 5.3, 5.4, and 5.5 should cover all operations, processes, and activities of all work units.

(3) Variations (5.3b) may be observed by those working in the process or by customers of the process output. The latter situation may result in formal or informal feedback or complaints.

(4) Results of improvements in business processes and support services should be reported in Item 6.3a.

5.4 Supplier Quality (20 pts.)   Describe how the company assures the quality of materials, components, and services furnished by other businesses. Describe also the company's plans and actions to improve supplier quality.

☑ Approach
☑ Deployment
☐ Results

Areas to Address

a. how the company defines and communicates its quality requirements to suppliers. Include: (1) a brief summary of the principal quality requirements for key suppliers; and (2) the key indicators the company uses to evaluate supplier quality.

b. methods the company uses to assure that its quality requirements are met by suppliers. Describe how the results of these methods and other relevant performance information are communicated to suppliers.

c. how the company evaluates and improves its own procurement activities. Describe feedback sought from suppliers and how it is used in improvement.

d. current plans and actions to improve suppliers' abilities to meet key quality and response time requirements

NOTES:

(1) The term "supplier" as used here refers to other-company providers of goods and services. The use of these goods and services may occur at any stage in the production, delivery, and use of the company's products and services. Thus, suppliers include businesses such as distributors, dealers, contractors, and franchises as well as those that provide materials and components.

(2) Methods may include audits, process reviews, receiving inspection, certification, testing, and rating systems.

(3) Plans and actions may include one or more of the following: joint planning, partnerships, training, long-term agreements, incentives and recognition, and supplier selection.

5.5 Quality Assessment (15 pts.)   Describe how the company assesses the quality and performance of its systems, processes, and practices and the quality of its products and services.

☑ Approach
☑ Deployment
☐ Results

Areas to Address

a. approaches the company uses to assess: (1) systems, processes, and practices; and (2) products and services. For (1) and (2), describe: (a) what is assessed; (b) how often assessments are made and by whom; and (c) how measurement quality and adequacy of documentation of processes and practices are assured.

b. how assessment findings are used to improve: products and services; systems; processes; practices; and supplier requirements. Describe how the company verifies that assessment findings lead to action and that the actions are effective.

NOTES:

(1) The systems, processes, practices, products, and services addressed in this item pertain to all company unit activities covered in Items 5.1, 5.2, 5.3, and 5.4. If the approaches and frequency of assessments differ appreciably for different company activities, this should be described in this Item.

(2) Adequacy of documentation should take into account legal, regulatory, and contractual requirements as well as knowledge preservation and knowledge transfer to help support improvement efforts.

6.0 Quality and Operational Results (180 pts.)

The **Quality and Operational Results** Category examines the company's quality levels and improvement trends in quality, company operational performance, and supplier quality. Also examined are current quality and operational performance levels relative to those of competitors.

6.1 Product and Service Quality Results (70 pts.)   Summarize trends in quality and current quality levels for key product and service features; compare the company's current quality levels with those of competitors and/or appropriate benchmarks.

☐ Approach

☐ Deployment

☑ Results

Areas to Address

a. trends and current levels for all key measures of product and service quality

b. current quality level comparisons with principal competitors in the company's key markets, industry averages, industry leaders, and appropriate benchmarks

---

NOTES:

(1) Key product and service measures are measures relative to the set of all important features of the company's products and services. These measures, taken together, best represent the *most important factors that predict customer satisfaction and quality in customer use*. Examples include measures of accuracy, reliability, timeliness, performance, behavior, delivery, after-sales services, documentation, appearance, and effective complaint management.

(2) Results reported in Item 6.1 should reflect all key product and service features described in the Overview and addressed in Items 7.1 and 5.1.

(3) Data reported in Item 6.1 are intended to be objective indicators of product and service quality, not the customers' satisfaction or reaction to the products and/or services. Such data may be of several types, including: (a) internal (company) measurements; (b) field performance (when applicable); (c) proactive checks by the company of specific product and service features (7.2d); and (d) data routinely collected by other organizations or on behalf of the company. Data reported in Item 6.1 should provide information on the company's performance relative to the specific product and service features that best *predict* customer satisfaction. These data, collected regularly, are then part of a process for monitoring and improving quality.

(4) Bases for comparison in Item 6.1b may include independent surveys, studies, or laboratory testing; benchmarks; and company evaluations and testing.

6.2 Company Operational Results (50 pts.)   Summarize trends and levels in overall company operational performance and provide a comparison of this operational performance with competitors and/or appropriate benchmarks.

☐ Approach

☐ Deployment

☑ Results

Areas to Address

a. trends and current levels for key measures of company operational performance

b. comparison of performance with that of competitors, industry averages, industry leaders, and key benchmarks

---

NOTES:

(1) Key measures of company operational performance include those that address productivity, efficiency, and effectiveness. Examples should include generic indicators such as use of manpower, materials, energy, capital, and assets. Trends and levels could address productivity indices, waste reduction, energy efficiency, cycle time reduction, environmental improvement, and other measures of improved *overall company performance.* Also include company-specific indicators the company uses to monitor its progress in improving operational performance. Such company-specific indicators should be defined in tables or charts where trends are presented.

(2) Trends in financial indicators, properly labeled, may be included in this Item. If such financial indicators are used, there should be a clear connection to the quality and operational performance improvement activities of the company.

(3) Include improvements in product and service design and production/delivery processes in this Item.

6.3 Business Process and Support Service Results (25 pts.)   Summarize trends and current levels in quality and operational performance improvement for business processes and support services; compare results with competitors and/or appropriate benchmarks.

☐ Approach
☐ Deployment
☑ Results

Areas to Address

a. trends and current levels for key measures of quality and operational performance of business processes and support services

b. comparison of performance with appropriately selected companies and benchmarks

---

NOTE:

Business processes and support services are those as covered in Item 5.3. Key measures of performance should reflect the principal quality, productivity, cycle time, cost and other effectiveness requirements for business processes and support services. Responses should reflect relevance to the company's principal quality and operational performance objectives addressed in company plans, contributing to the results reported in Items 6.1 and 6.2. They should also demonstrate broad coverage of company business processes, support services, and work units and reflect the most important objectives of each process, service, or work unit.

6.4 Supplier Quality Results (35 pts.)   Summarize trends in quality and current quality levels of suppliers; compare the company's supplier quality with that of competitors and/or with appropriate benchmarks.

☐ Approach
☐ Deployment
☑ Results

Areas to Address

a. trends and current levels for the most important indicators of supplier quality

b. comparison of the company's supplier quality levels with those of appropriately selected companies and/or benchmarks

---

NOTES:

(1) The results reported in Item 6.4 derive from quality improvement activities described in Item 5.4. Results should be broken down by major groupings of suppliers and reported using the principal quality indicators described in Item 5.4.

(2) Comparisons could be industry averages, industry leaders, principal competitors in the company's key markets, and other appropriate benchmarks.

7.0 Customer Focus and Satisfaction (300 pts.)

The **Customer Focus and Satisfaction** Category examines the company's relationships with customers and its knowledge of customer requirements and of the key quality factors that drive marketplace competitiveness. Also examined are the company's methods to determine customer satisfaction, current trends and levels of customer satisfaction and retention, and these results relative to competitors.

7.1 Customer Expectations: Current and Future (35 pts.)   Describe how the company determines near-term and long-term requirements and expectations of customers.

☑ Approach
☑ Deployment
☐ Results

Areas to Address

a. how the company determines *current and near-term requirements* and expectations of customers. Describe: (1) how customer groups and/or market segments are determined including how customers of competitors and other potential customers are considered; (2) the process for collecting information, including what information is sought, frequency and methods of collection, and how objectivity and validity are assured; (3) the process for determining specific product and service features and the relative importance of these features to customer groups or segments; and (4) how other information such as complaints, gains and losses of customers, and product/service performance are cross-compared to support the determination.

b. how the company addresses *future requirements* and expectations of customers. Describe: (1) the time horizon for the determination; (2) how important technological, competitive, societal, economic, and demographic factors that may bear upon customer requirements, expectations, or alternatives are considered; (3) how customers of competitors and other potential customers are considered; (4) how key product and service features and the relative importance of these features are projected; and (5) how changing or emerging market segments are addressed and their implications on new product/service lines as well as on current products and services are considered.

c. how the company evaluates and improves its processes for determining customer requirements and expectations. Describe how the improvement process considers: (1) new market opportunities; and (2) extension of the time horizon for the determination.

NOTES:

(1) The company's products and services may be sold to end users by intermediaries such as retail stores or dealers. Thus, determining customer groups should take into account both the end users and the intermediaries.
(2) Product and service features refer to all important characteristics of products and services experienced by the customers throughout the overall purchase and ownership experiences. These include any factors that bear upon customer preference and repurchase loyalty or customer view

of quality—for example, those features that enhance or differentiate products and services from competing offerings.

(3) Some companies may use similar methods to determine customer requirements/expectations and customer satisfaction (Item 7.4). In such cases, cross-references should be included.

7.2 Customer Relationship Management (65 pts.)   Describe how the company provides effective management of its relationships with its customers and uses information gained from customers to improve customer relationship management strategies and practices.

☑ Approach
☑ Deployment
☐ Results

Areas to Address

a. for the company's most important processes and transactions that bring its employees into contact with customers, summarize the key requirements for maintaining and building relationships. Describe key quality indicators derived from these requirements and how they were determined.

b. how service standards that address the key quality indicators (7.2a) are set. Include: (1) how service standards requirements are deployed to customer-contact employees and to other company units that provide support for customer-contact employees; and (2) how the overall service standards system is tracked.

c. how the company provides information and easy access to enable customers to seek assistance, to comment and to complain. Describe the main types of contact and how easy access is maintained for each type.

d. how the company follows up with customers on products, services, and recent transactions to seek feedback and to help build relationships

e. how the following are addressed for customer-contact employees: (1) selection factors; (2) career path; (3) deployment of special training to include: knowledge of products and services; listening to customers; soliciting comments from customers; how to anticipate and handle problems or failures ("recovery"); skills in customer retention; and how to manage expectations; (4) empowerment and decision making; (5) satisfaction determination; (6) recognition and reward; and (7) turnover

f. how the company ensures that formal and informal complaints and feedback received by all company units are aggregated for overall evaluation and use throughout the company. Describe: (1) how the company ensures that complaints and problems are resolved promptly and effectively; and (2) how the company sets priorities for improvement projects based upon analysis of complaints, including types and frequencies of complaints and relationships to customers' repurchase intentions.

g. how the company evaluates and improves its customer relationship management strategies and practices. Include: (1) how the company seeks opportunities to enhance relationships with all customers or with key customers; and (2) how evaluations lead to improvements in service standards, access, customer-contact employee training, and technology support. Describe how customer information is used in the improvement process.

NOTES:

(1) Information on trends and levels in indicators of complaint response time, effective resolution, and percent of complaints resolved on first contact should be reported in Item 6.1.

(2) In addressing empowerment and decision making in 7.2e, indicate how the company ensures that there is a common vision or basis to guide the actions of customer-contact employees.

7.3 Commitment to Customers (15 pts.) Describe the company's commitments to customers regarding its products/services and how these commitments are evaluated and improved.

☑ Approach
☑ Deployment
☐ Results

Areas to Address

a. types of commitments the company makes to promote trust and confidence in its products/services and to satisfy customers when product/service failures occur. Describe these commitments and how they: (1) address the principal concerns of customers; (2) are free from conditions that might weaken customers' trust and confidence; and (3) are communicated to customers clearly and simply.

b. how the company evaluates and improves its commitments, and the customers' understanding of them, to avoid gaps between expectations and delivery. Include: (1) how information/ feedback from customers is used; (2) how product/service performance improvement data are used; and (3) how competitors' commitments are considered.

NOTE:

Examples of commitments are product and service guarantees, warranties, and other understandings, expressed or implied.

7.4 Customer Satisfaction Determination (30 pts.)   Describe the company's methods for determining customer satisfaction, customer repurchase intentions, and customer satisfaction relative to competitors; describe how these methods are evaluated and improved.

☑ Approach
☑ Deployment
☐ Results

Areas to Address

a. how the company determines customer satisfaction. Include: (1) a brief description of methods, processes, and measurement scales used; frequency of determination; and how objectivity and validity are assured. Indicate significant differences, if any, in these satisfaction methods, processes, and measurement scales for different customer groups or segments; and (2) how customer satisfaction measurements capture key information that reflects customers' likely market behavior, such as repurchase intentions.

b. how customer satisfaction relative to that for competitors is determined. Describe: (1) company-based comparative studies; and (2) comparative studies or evaluations made by independent organizations and/or customers. For (1) and (2), describe how objectivity and validity of studies are addressed.

c. how the company evaluates and improves its overall processes, measurement, and measurement scales for determining customer satisfaction and customer satisfaction relative to that for competitors. Include how other indicators (such as gains and losses of customers) and customer dissatisfaction indicators (such as complaints) are used in this improvement process.

NOTES:

(1) Customer satisfaction measurement may include both a numerical rating scale and descriptors assigned to each unit in the scale. An effective (actionable) customer satisfaction measurement system is one that provides the company with reliable information about customer ratings of specific product and service features and the relationship between these ratings and the customer's likely market behavior.

(2) Customer dissatisfaction indicators include complaints, claims, refunds, recalls, returns, repeat services, litigation, replacements, downgrades, repairs, warranty work, warranty costs, misshipments, and incomplete orders.

(3) Company-based or independent organization comparative studies in 7.4b may take into account one or more indicators of customer dissatisfaction as well as satisfaction. The extent and types of such studies may depend upon industry and company size.

(4) The company's products and services may be sold to end users by intermediaries such as retail stores or dealers. Thus, "customer groups" should take into account both end users and intermediaries.

7.5 Customer Satisfaction Results (85 pts.)   Summarize trends in the company's customer satisfaction and trends in key indicators of customer dissatisfaction.

☐ Approach
☐ Deployment
☑ Results

Areas to Address

a. trends in indicators of customer satisfaction. Segment by customer group, as appropriate. Trends may be supported by objective information and/or data from customers demonstrating current or recent (past 3 years) satisfaction with the company's products/services.

b. trends in indicators of customer dissatisfaction. Address the most relevant indicators for the company's products/services.

NOTES:

(1) Results reported in this Item derive from methods described in Items 7.4 and 7.2.

(2) Information supporting trends may include customers' assessments of products/services, customer awards, and customer retention.

(3) Indicators of customer dissatisfaction are given in Item 7.4, Note 2.

7.6 Customer Satisfaction Comparison (70 pts.)   Compare the company's customer satisfaction results with those of competitors.

☐ Approach
☐ Deployment
☑ Results

Areas to Address

a. trends in indicators of customer satisfaction relative to competitors. Segment by customer group, as appropriate. Trends may be supported by objective information and/or data from independent organizations, including customers. This information and/or data may include survey results, competitive awards, recognition and ratings.

b. trends in gaining and losing customers, or customer accounts, to competitors

c. trends in gaining or losing market share to competitors

NOTES:

(1) Results reported in this Item derive from methods described in Item 7.4.

(2) Competitors include domestic and international ones in the company's markets, both domestic and international.

(3) Surveys, competitive awards, recognition, and ratings by independent organizations and customers should reflect comparative satisfaction (and dissatisfaction), not comparative performance of products and services. Information on comparative performance of products and services should be included in 6.1b.

SCORING SYSTEM: APPROACH, DEPLOYMENT, RESULTS

The system for scoring Examination Items is based upon three evaluation dimensions: (1) Approach; (2) Deployment; and (3) Results. All Examination Items require applicants to furnish information relating to one or more of these dimensions. Specific factors associated with the evaluation dimensions are described below. Scoring Guidelines are outlined on pages 556–557.

Approach

''Approach'' refers to the methods the company uses to achieve the requirements addressed in the Examination Items. The factors used to evaluate approaches include one or more of the following, as appropriate:

- the appropriateness of the methods, tools, and techniques to the requirements
- the effectiveness of methods, tools, and techniques
- the degree to which the approach is systematic, integrated, and consistently applied
- the degree to which the approach embodies effective evaluation/improvement cycles
- the degree to which the approach is based upon quantitative information that is objective and reliable
- the degree to which the approach is prevention-based
- the indicators of unique and innovative approaches, including significant and effective new adaptations of tools and techniques used in other applications or types of businesses

Deployment

"Deployment" refers to the extent to which the approaches are applied to all relevant areas and activities addressed and implied in the Examination Items. The factors used to evaluate deployment include one or more of the following, as appropriate:

- the appropriate and effective application of the stated approach by all work units to all processes and activities
- the appropriate and effective application of the stated approach to all product and service features
- the appropriate and effective application of the stated approach to all transactions and interactions with customers, suppliers of goods and services, and the public

Results

"Results" refers to outcomes and effects in achieving the purposes addressed and implied in the Examination Items. The factors used to evaluate results include one or more of the following:

- the performance levels
- the quality and performance levels relative to appropriate comparisons and/or benchmarks
- the rate of performance improvement
- the breadth and importance of performance improvements
- the demonstration of sustained improvement or sustained high-level performance

SCORING GUIDELINES

Score	Approach/Deployment	Score	Results
0%	• anecdotal information; no system evident in information presented	0%	• no data reported or anecdotal data only • data not responsive to major requirements of the Item
10% to 30%	• beginning of a systematic approach to addressing the primary purposes of the Item • significant gaps still exist in deployment that would inhibit progress in achieving the major purposes of the Item • early stages of a transition from reacting to problems to preventing problems	10% to 30%	• early stages of developing trend data • some improvement trend data *or* early good performance reported • data are not reported for many to most areas of importance to the Item requirements and to the company's key performance-related business factors
40% to 60%	• a sound, systematic approach responsive to the primary purposes of the Item • a fact-based improvement process in place in key areas addressed by the Item • no major gaps in deployment, though some areas may be in early stages of deployment • approach places more emphasis on problem prevention than on reaction to problems	40% to 60%	• improvement or good performance trends reported in key areas of importance to the Item requirements and to the company's key performance-related business factors • some trends and/or current performance can be evaluated against relevant comparisons, benchmarks, or levels • no significant adverse trends or poor current performance in key areas of importance to the Item requirements and to the company's key performance-related business factors

SCORING GUIDELINES *(cotinued)*

Score	Approach/Deployment	Score	Results
70% to 90%	• a sound systematic approach responsive to the overall purposes of the Item • a fact-based improvement process is a key management tool; clear evidence of refinement and improved integration as a result of improvement cycles and analysis • approach is well-deployed; with no significant gaps, although refinement, deployment, and integration may vary among work units or system activities	70% to 90%	• good to excellent improvement trends in most key areas of importance to the Item requirements and to the company's key performance-related business factors *or* sustained good to excellent performance in those areas • many to most trends and current performance can be evaluated against relevant comparisons, benchmarks, or levels • current current performance is good to excellent in most areas of importance to the Item requirements and to the company's key performance-related factors
100%	• a sound, systematic approach, fully responsive to all the requirements of the Item • approach is fully deployed without weaknesses or gaps in any areas • very strong refinement and integration—backed by excellent analysis	100%	• excellent improvement trends in most to all key areas of importance to the Item requirements and to the company's key performance-related business factors *or* sustained excellent performance in those areas • most to all trends and current performance can be evaluated against relevant comparisons, benchmarks, or levels • current performance is excellent in most areas of importance to the Item requirements and to the company's key performance-related business factors • strong evidence of industry and benchmark leadership demonstrated

ELIGIBILITY CATEGORIES AND RESTRICTIONS

Basic Eligibility

Public Law 100–107 establishes the three eligibility categories of the Award: Manufacturing, Service, and Small Business. Any for-profit business located in the United States or its territories may apply for the Award. Eligibility for the Award is intended to be as open as possible to all U.S. companies. Minor eligibility restrictions and conditions ensure fairness and consistency in definition. For example, publicly or privately owned, domestic or foreign-owned, joint ventures, incorporated firms, sole proprietorships, partnerships, and holding companies may apply. Not eligible are: local, state, and national government agencies; not-for-profit organizations; trade associations; and professional societies.

Award Eligibility Categories

1. **Manufacturing**
   Companies or subsidiaries (defined below) that produce and sell manufactured products or manufacturing processes, and those companies that produce agricultural, mining, or construction products.

2. **Service**
   Companies or subsidiaries that sell services.
   - Proper classification of companies that perform both manufacturing and service is determined by the larger percentage of sales.

3. **Small Business**
   Complete businesses with not more than 500 full-time employees. Business activities may include manufacturing and/or service. A small business must be able to document that it functions independently of any other businesses which are equity owners. For example, a small business owned by a holding company would be eligible if it can document its independent operation and that other units of the holding company are in different businesses.

   If there are equity owners with some management control, at least 50% of the small business' customer base (dollar volume for products and services) must be from other than the equity owners, or other businesses owned by the equity owners.

Subsidiaries

For purposes of the Malcolm Baldrige National Quality Award application, a subsidiary will be taken to mean an actual subsidiary, business unit, division, or like organization. In the Manufacturing and Service categories, subsidiaries of a company may be eligible for the Award. Small businesses must apply as a whole; subsidiaries of small businesses are not eligible.

The following application conditions apply for subsidiaries:

- The subsidiary must have existed one year prior to the Award application.
- The subsidiary must have clear definition of organization as reflected in corporate literature, e.g., organization charts, administrative manuals, and annual reports.
- The subsidiary must have more than 500 full-time employees, OR
- It must have 25% of all employees in the worldwide operations of the parent company. ("Parent company" refers to the company that owns or controls subsidiaries through the ownership of voting stock.)

Restrictions on Eligibility

The intent of Public Law 100–107 is to create an Award process incorporating rigorous and objective evaluation of the applicants' total quality system underlying its products and services. *Award recipients are to serve as appropriate models of total quality achievement for other U.S. companies.* Customer satisfaction is to play a major role in the Examination. Site visits are required to verify descriptions given in written applications.

The nature of some companies' activities are such that the central purposes and requirements of Public Law 100–107 cannot be fulfilled through their participation in the Award Program; companies or subsidiaries whose businesses cannot fulfill these purposes are not eligible. Specifically, four restrictions apply:

1. A company or its subsidiary is eligible only if the quality practices associated with all major business functions of the applicant are inspectable in the United States or its territories. One or both of the following conditions must apply:
   - more than 50% of the applicant's employees must be located in the United States or its territories, or
   - more than 50% of the applicant's physical assets must be located in the United States or its territories

   Note: *The functions/activities of foreign sites must be included in the Application Report in the appropriate Examination Item.*

2. At least 50% of the subsidiary's customer base (dollar volume for products and services) must be free of direct financial and line organization control by the parent company. For example, a subsidiary is not eligible if its parent company or other subsidiary of the parent company is the customer for more than one-half of its total products and services.

3. Individual units or partial aggregations of units of "chain" organizations (such as hotels, retail stores, banks, or restaurants) are not eligible.

   For purposes of this application, a chain organization is defined as an organization where each unit (e.g., subsidiary or franchise) performs a similar function or manufactures a similar product. Accordingly, a potential applicant is not eligible if the parent company or another unit of the parent company provides similar products or services for substantially the same customer base. Similarly, an individual unit is not eligible if customers would be unable to distinguish easily which unit of the company provides the products or services to them.

4. Subsidiaries performing any of the business support functions of the company are not eligible. Examples of business support functions include: Sales/Marketing/Distribution, Customer Service, Finance and Accounting, Human Resources, Environmental-Health-Safety of Employees, Purchasing, Legal Services, and Research and Development.

Multiple-Application Restrictions

1. A subsidiary and its parent company may not both apply for Awards in the same year.

2. Only one subsidiary of a company may apply for an Award in the same year in the same Award category.

Future Eligibility Restrictions

1. If a company receives an Award, the company and all its subsidiaries are ineligible to apply for another Award for a period of five years.

2. If a subsidiary receives an Award, it is ineligible to apply for another Award for a period of five years.

3. If a subsidiary consisting of more than one-half of the total sales of a company receives an Award, neither that company nor any of its other subsidiaries is eligible to apply for another Award for a period of five years.

Eligibility Determination

In order to ensure that potential Award recipients meet all reasonable requirements and expectations in representing the Award throughout the United States, applicants must have their eligibility approved prior to applying for the Award.

Determination takes into account the following factors:

- small business status
- subsidiary status and subsidiary functions performed
- customer base
- sales to a parent company or another unit or units of the parent company
- status as a U.S. company
- relationship of products and services to those of the parent company or other units of the parent company
- number and type of support services provided by the parent company or other units of the parent company

Potential applicants for the 1993 Award are encouraged to submit their Eligibility Determination Form as early as possible and no later than March 1, 1993. This form is contained in the 1993 Application Forms and Instructions booklet. For information on how to obtain a copy of this booklet, see page 562.

FEES FOR THE 1993 AWARD CYCLE

Eligibility Determination Fees

The eligibility determination fee is $50 for all potential applicants. This fee is nonrefundable.

Application Fees

- Manufacturing Company Category—$4000
- Service Company Category—$4000
- Small Business Category—$1200

These fees cover all expenses associated with distribution of applications, review of applications, and development of feedback reports.

Site Visit Review Fees

Site visit fees will be set when the visits are scheduled. Fees depend upon the number of sites to be visited, the number of Examiners assigned, and the duration of the visit. Site visit fees for applicants in the Small Business category will be charged at one-half of the rate for companies in the Manufacturing and Service categories.

These fees cover all expenses and travel costs associated with site visit participation and development of site visit reports. Site visit fees are paid only by those applicants reaching the site visit stage.

Eligibility Determination Forms due—March 1, 1993
Award Applications due—April 1, 1993

AWARD WINNERS: 1988 TO 1992

1992 Award Winners
Manufacturing
AT&T Network Systems
Group
Transmission Systems Business Unit
Morristown, NJ

Texas Instruments, Inc.
Defense Systems &
  Electronics Group
Dallas, TX

Service
AT&T Universal Card
  Services
Jacksonville, FL

The Ritz-Carlton Hotel
Company
Atlanta, GA

Small Business
Granite Rock Company
Watsonville, CA

1991 Award Winners
Manufacturing
Solectron Corp.
San Jose, CA

Zytec Corp.
Eden Prairie, MN

Small Business
Marlow Industries
Dallas, TX

1990 Award Winners
Manufacturing
Cadillac Motor Car Company
Detroit, MI

IBM Rochester
Rochester, MN

Service
Federal Express Corp.
Memphis, TN

Small Business
Wallace Co., Inc.
Houston, TX

1989 Award Winners
Manufacturing
Milliken & Company
Spartanburg, SC

Xerox Business Products and
Systems
Stamford, CT

1988 Award Winners
Manufacturing
Motorola, Inc.
Schaumburg, IL

Westinghouse Commercial
Nuclear Fuel Division
Pittsburgh, PA

Small Business
Globe Metallurgical, Inc.
Cleveland, OH

HOW TO ORDER COPIES OF 1993 AWARD MATERIALS

Note: The **1993 Award Criteria** and the **1993 Application Forms and Instructions** are two separate documents.

Individual Orders   Individual copies of either document can be obtained free of charge from:

Malcolm Baldrige National Quality Award
National Institute of Standards and Technology
Route 270 and Quince Orchard Road
Administration Building, Room A537
Gaithersburg, MD 20899
Telephone: 301-975-2036
Telefax: 301-948-3716

Bulk Orders   Multiple copies of the **1993 Award Criteria** may be ordered in packets of 10 (Item Number T997):

American Society for Quality Control

Customer Service Department
P.O. Box 3066
Milwaukee, WI 53201-3066
Toll free: 800-248-1946
Telefax: 414-272-1734

Order Item Number T997

Cost: $24.95 per packet of 10 plus postage and handling

Postage and handling charges are:

	U.S.	Canada
1 packet	$ 3.75	$ 8.75
2–4 packets	6.00	11.00
5 or more	12.00*	17.00

For orders shipped outside of the continental United States, there is a fee of 25 percent of order value to cover postage and handling. This fee does not apply to Canada.

Payment   Payment options include check, money order, purchase order, VISA, MasterCard, or American Express.

Payment must accompany all mail orders.

Payment must be made in U.S. currency. Checks and money orders must be drawn on U.S. institutions.

Make checks payable to ASQC.

Shipment   Orders delivered within the continental United States and Canada will be shipped UPS or first class mail.

HOW TO ORDER ADDITIONAL AWARD-RELATED MATERIALS

Each year, the Award Program develops materials for use in training members of the Board of Examiners, and for sharing information on the successful quality strategies of the Award winners. These listed materials and information may be obtained from the American Society for Quality Control (toll free: 800-248-1946). Prices and/or availability dates for all materials are given below.

Case Studies

The case studies are used to prepare Examiners for the interpretation of the Award Criteria and the Scoring System. The case studies, when used with the Award Cri-

*If actual shipping charges exceed $12.00, ASQC will invoice the customer for additional expense.

teria, illustrate the Award application and review process. The case studies are sample applications written for fictitious companies applying for the Baldrige Award. They demonstrate the form and content of an application, providing information requested in the seven Categories of the Award Criteria. Responses are presented for each of the individual Items and Areas to Address. The case studies can provide valuable insights into the Award Criteria and Scoring System for companies interested in making application, as well as for self-assessment, planning, training, and other uses.

1991—Item Number T508: $25.00

Award Winners Video

The Award winners videos are a valuable resource for gaining a better understanding of excellence in quality management and quality achievement. The videos provide background information on the Award Program, highlights from the annual Award ceremony, and interviews with representatives from the winning companies.

1988—Item Number T993:	$10.00
1989—Item Number T502:	10.00
1990—Item Number T992:	15.00
1991—Item Number TA996:	15.00
1992—Item Number TA512:	20.00*

Quest for Excellence V Conference

The annual Quest for Excellence Conference provides a unique opportunity to hear firsthand the Award-winning quality strategies of the past year's winners. Presentations are made by the CEOs and other key individuals who are transforming their organizations. The annual Quest for Excellence Conference is the principal forum for Award winners to present their overall strategies in detail.

The two and one-half day Quest for Excellence V Conference will provide ample opportunities to explore the Award Criteria in depth, network with executive-level individuals from around the country, and view displays of each of the Award-winning organizations.

The Quest for Excellence V Conference will feature:

- AT&T Network Systems Group, Transmission Systems Business Unit

---

*Available February 22, 1993.

- Texas Instruments, Inc., Defense Systems & Electronics Group
- AT&T Universal Card Services
- The Ritz-Carlton Hotel Company
- Granite Rock Company

The Conference dates are February 15–17, 1993. The Conference will be held at the Washington Hilton and Towers, in Washington, D.C. The registration fee is $695.00 until January 31, 1993. Effective February 1, 1993, the fee is $750.00. The registration fee includes conference handout materials and participation in all conference activities. For further information, telephone ASQC (toll free: 800-248-1946 or FAX: 414-272-1734).

THE MALCOLM BALDRIGE NATIONAL QUALITY IMPROVEMENT ACT OF 1987—PUBLIC LAW 100–107

The Malcolm Baldrige National Quality Award was created by Public Law 100–107, signed into law on August 20, 1987. The Award Program, responsive to the purposes of Public Law 100–107, led to the creation of a new public-private partnership. Principal support for the program comes from the Foundation for the Malcolm Baldrige National Quality Award, established in 1988.

The Award is named for Malcolm Baldrige, who served as Secretary of Commerce from 1981 until his tragic death in a rodeo accident in 1987. His managerial excellence contributed to long-term improvement in efficiency and effectiveness of government.

The Findings and Purposes Section of Public Law 100–107 states that:

1. the leadership of the United States in product and process quality has been challenged strongly (and sometimes successfully) by foreign competition, and our Nation's productivity growth has improved less than our competitors' over the last two decades.
2. American business and industry are beginning to understand that poor quality costs companies as much as 20 percent of sales revenues nationally and that improved quality of goods and services goes hand in hand with improved productivity, lower costs, and increased profitability.
3. strategic planning for quality and quality improvement programs, through a commitment to excellence in manufacturing and services, are becoming more and more essential to the well-being of our Nation's economy and our ability to compete effectively in the global marketplace.
4. improved management understanding of the factory floor, worker involvement in quality, and greater emphasis on statistical process control can lead to dramatic improvements in the cost and quality of manufactured products.

5. the concept of quality improvement is directly applicable to small companies as well as large, to service industries as well as manufacturing, and to the public sector as well as private enterprise.

6. in order to be successful, quality improvement programs must be management-led and customer-oriented, and this may require fundamental changes in the way companies and agencies do business.

7. several major industrial nations have successfully coupled rigorous private-sector quality audits with national awards giving special recognition to those enterprises the audits identify as the very best; and

8. a national quality award program of this kind in the United States would help improve quality and productivity by:
   A. helping to stimulate American companies to improve quality and productivity for the pride of recognition while obtaining a competitive edge through increased profits;
   B. recognizing the achievements of those companies that improve the quality of their goods and services and providing an example to others;
   C. establishing guidelines and criteria that can be used by business, industrial, governmental, and other organizations in evaluating their own quality improvement efforts; and
   D. providing specific guidance for other American organizations that wish to learn how to manage for high quality by making available detailed information on how winning organizations were able to change their cultures and achieve eminence.

The Malcolm Baldrige National Quality Award

Managed by:

United States Department of Commerce
Technology Administration
National Institute of Standards and Technology
Route 270 and Quince Orchard Road
Administration Building, Room A537
Gaithersburg, MD 20899

Administered by:

American Society for Quality Control
P.O. Box 3005
Milwaukee, WI 53201-3005

Malcolm Baldrige National Quality Award 1992 Fact Sheet

___

Malcolm Baldrige National Quality Award

Public Law 100–107, the Malcolm Baldrige National Quality Improvement Act of 1987, signed by President Reagan on August 20, 1987, established an annual U.S. National Quality Award. The purposes of the Award are to promote quality awareness, to recognize quality achievements of U.S. companies, and to publicize successful quality strategies. The Secretary of Commerce and the National Institute of Standards and Technology (NIST, formerly the National Bureau of Standards) are given responsibilities to develop and administer the Awards with cooperation and financial support from the private sector.

The Awards

Up to two Awards may be given each year in each of three categories:

- manufacturing companies or subsidiaries
- service companies or subsidiaries
- small businesses

Fewer than two Awards may be given in a category if the high standards of the Award Program are not met. In 1988 three Awards were presented: Motorola, Inc.; Commercial Nuclear Fuel Division of Westinghouse Electric Corporation; and Globe Metallurgical, Inc. In 1989 two Awards were presented: Milliken & Company; and Xerox Corporation's Business Products and Systems. In 1990 four Awards were presented: Cadillac Motor Car Division; IBM Rochester; Federal Express Corporation; and Wallace Co., Inc. In 1991 three Awards were presented: Marlow Industries; Solectron Corporation; and Zytec Corporation. Recipients receive a medal in a crystal base. They may publicize and advertise their Awards provided they agree to share with other American organizations information about their successful quality strategies.

Eligibility

Businesses located in the United States may apply for Awards. Subsidiaries are defined as divisions or business units of larger companies. Subsidiaries must primarily serve either the public or businesses other than the parent company. For companies engaged in both services and manufacturing, classification is determined by the larger percentage of sales. Small businesses are independently owned with not more than 500 full-time employees.

Award Criteria

Seven (7) areas are examined: (1) leadership; (2) information and analysis; (3) strategic quality planning; (4) human resource development and management; (5) management of process quality; (6) quality and operational results; and (7) customer focus and satisfaction. Applicants must address a set of examination items within each of these categories. Heavy emphasis is placed on quality achievement and quality improvement as demonstrated through quantitative data furnished by applicants.

Examination Process

Each written application is evaluated by members of the Board of Examiners. High-scoring applicants are selected for site visits. Award recipients are recommended to the Secretary of Commerce by a panel of judges from among the applicants site visited. Applicants receive a written feedback summary of strengths and areas for improvement in their quality management. The American Society for Quality Control assists in the administration of the examination process.

Examiners

The Board of Examiners is comprised of quality experts selected from industry, professional and trade organizations, and universities. Those selected meet the highest standards of qualification and peer recognition. Examiners must take part in a preparation program based upon the Criteria, the scoring system, and the examination process. Each fall applications are solicited from quality experts to serve as Examiners for the following year. The schedule for the 1993 Board is:

1993 Examiner Applications available	September 1992
1993 Examiner Applications due	November 1992

1992 Award Timetable

Award Applications available	December 1991
Award Eligibility Determination Forms due	March 6, 1992
Award Applications due	April 1, 1992
Award Application review/site visits	April–October 1992
Award Ceremony	Fall 1992

Confidentiality

All applications are confidential. Applicants are not expected to provide proprietary information about products or processes. Examiners are assigned to avoid conflicts of interest. Information on the successful strategies of Award recipients is released only after written approval is received from recipients.

Fees

Fees are set to cover some of the costs of review. Fees for 1992 include a non-refundable payment of $50 that must accompany the Eligibility Determination Form. The written application review fee for manufacturing and service companies is $4000, while the fee for small business review is $1200. There is a separate fee of $1500 if Supplemental Sections are necessary. Separate site visit fees are set at the time the visits are scheduled.

For applications or information, write or call:

Malcolm Baldrige National Quality Award
National Institute of Standards and Technology
Administration Building–Room A537
Gaithersburg, Maryland 20899
TELE: 301-975-2036
 FAX: 301-948-3716

1991 AWARD WINNERS

Marlow Industries

In 1987, Marlow Industries set out to improve a manufacturing and service operation that did not seem to need fixing. Founded in 1973, the Dallas-based company increased its share of the world market to more than 50 percent for customized thermoelectric (TE) coolers—small, solid-state electronic devices that heat, cool, or stabilize the temperature of electronic equipment.

But Marlow chose not to sit tight. Instead, it initiated a structured, yet evolving system of continuous improvement through Total Quality Management, setting ever higher performance standards and challenging itself to exceed ever more demanding customer requirements. The company has worked to strengthen all areas of its business, and again to set new targets for improvement and innovation.

Since 1987, employee productivity has increased at an average annual rate of 10 percent, the time between new product design and manufactured product has been trimmed, and the cost of scrap, rework, and other non-conformance errors has been cut nearly in half. For customers, these and other gains have translated into products that exceed performance specifications by wider margins, on-time deliveries, extended warranties, and prices that have remained stable or decreased. Not coincidentally, Marlow Industries' worldwide market share continues to improve, even in Japan where the company has local competition.

Marlow at a Glance   Marlow Industries is fully vertically integrated. The company processes raw materials into thermoelectric semi-conductors, assembles these devices into TE coolers, and integrates the coolers into heat exchangers for commercial and defense applications. Manufacturing operations consist of three materials "minifactories" and five assembly minifactories organized by market segments. Each is staffed by about 15 employees cross-trained in several jobs and directed by a supervisor, who is empowered to make decisions affecting all facets of production within his or her minifactory.

Commercial customers include makers of laser diodes, such as those used in fiber-optic communication systems, as well as medical instrumentation manufacturers. Marlow products also are used in heat-seeking missiles, inertial navigation systems, satellites, and other defense and space-related technologies.

Started in 1973 as a five-person operation, Marlow Industries now employs 160 people and has total annual sales of $12 million. Exports account for 15 percent of annual sales.

Although the company earns most of its revenues from sales of TE coolers designed to meet one-of-a-kind customer needs, Marlow Industries has set its sights on applying its Total Quality Management philosophy to enter new markets.

TQM System   Marlow describes its Total Quality Management System as a "top-to-bottom" approach to continuous improvement. The emphasis on quality begins with CEO and President Raymond Marlow. As chairman of the TQM Council, which crafts the company's 5-year strategic business plan and oversees efforts to accomplish short- and long-term goals, he has daily responsibility for quality-related matters. A senior-executive team headed by the chief operating officer attends to day-to-day management. Marlow's leadership has provided an environment that encourages all employees to participate and to be involved in the continuous improvement process.

Employee involvement is fostered through a flat organizational structure and a variety of participatory mechanisms. Marlow includes worker representatives in weekly TQM Council sessions. Monthly companywide meetings are held to review company performance, recognize employees for quality contributions, review quality values, and make widespread acknowledgment of teams. In 1990, 88 percent of all personnel—as compared with 44 percent in 1988—participated on "action teams," which focus on attaining corporate and departmental goals, or on "employee effectiveness teams," which concentrate on preventing potential problems in specific work areas. Each team has a senior-executive mentor, and all teams regularly make formal presentations before the TQM Council.

All workers—from CEO to hourly employee—have taken Marlow's voluntary "quality pledge," committing them to the same performance standard: "Do it right today, better tomorrow." Training programs, averaging 32 hours a year per employee, impart the skills needed to achieve the standard. All workers, even temporary employees, receive quality-awareness training, and the entire permanent work force has completed initial courses in statistical problem solving. Three-fifths have undergone the second round of more comprehensive training in the use of quality tools.

An information system consisting of 500 data categories describes all essential elements of company performance—from customer satisfaction to manufacturing process control to supplier quality—and helps Marlow Industries set tangible goals and track its progress. Much of the data can be accessed through any of the 80 personal computers connected through a local area network. Systematic data cross-checking fosters reliability and consistency, and regular reviews ensure that the information supports effective management of the company.

Marlow uses a well-integrated, systematic approach for assuring the quality of its products and services. Extensive use of Design of Experiments Techniques has resulted in improved quality and stabilization of its major processes. In the last 3 years its yields have improved significantly while manufacturing costs have been reduced and cycle times improved. These improvements were accompanied by major reductions in waste stream environmental disposal.

Supplier partners figure prominently in Marlow's TQM system. The company continues to consolidate its list of suppliers, retaining only those key suppliers that score at the top of the Marlow Supplier Quality Index. By the end of 1991, it anticipates that 15 of its top 20 key suppliers will be certified to "ship to stock" without inspection. Marlow cultivates long-term partnerships and includes the technological expertise of valued suppliers at the start of its product and process improvement efforts. These suppliers often provide the small company with design and analytical expertise that is not available in-house.

Over 90 percent of the products produced by Marlow are custom designed to meet its customers' requirements. Because customer satisfaction is the overriding aim of its continuous improvement efforts, Marlow has developed an exhaustive system of feedback mechanisms—from several types of surveys to quarterly meetings with major clients. This information helps ensure that Marlow focuses on the principal needs of customers. When combined with the results of the company's benchmarking program, customer feedback points the way to strategic improvements in products and service.

Since 1988, Marlow has won six major quality awards from customers, and it passed on first inspection all 30 audits of its quality assurance system performed by defense industry customers. Over the last 10 years, Marlow has not lost a single major customer, and, in 1990, its top 10 customers rated the quality of Marlow TE coolers at 100 percent.

For more information, contact:
Raymond Marlow
President
10451 Vista Park Rd.
Dallas, TX 75238-1645
Phone: 214-340-4900
Fax: 214-341-5212

Zytec Corporation

From its beginning in 1984, the Zytec Corp. fixed its sights on quality, service, and value. By continuously improving these product and service attributes and working to establish a close partnership with customers, the Minnesota firm has risen to the top tier of the hundreds of manufacturers of power supplies for electronic equipment.

Organizing its quality improvement efforts around the concepts of W. Edwards Deming, Zytec has achieved double-digit annual growth in productivity over the last 3 years. New revenues have increased severalfold since 1984, making Zytec the fifth largest U.S. manufacturer of AC to DC power supplies. Sales per employee are approaching $100,000, as compared with an industry average of less than $80,000. Underlying these gains are, since 1988, a 50-percent improvement in manufacturing yields, a 26-percent reduction in manufacturing cycle time, a 50-percent reduction in the design cycle, and a 30- to 40-percent decrease in product costs—savings that are passed on to customers.

Building on these accomplishments and using the Baldrige award principles, Zytec is now realigning its continuous-improvement system, investing in computer-integrated manufacturing technology, and furthering employee training, all with the aim of advancing to a new threshold of quality performance—Six Sigma quality in most facets of its operations by 1995.

Zytec at a Glance　　Formerly a unit of Magnetic Peripherals, Inc., a joint venture subsidiary of four electronics firms, Zytec makes power supplies for original equipment manufacturers (OEMs) of computers as well as electronic office, medical, and testing equipment. Sales of the customized power supplies account for 90 percent of revenues. Zytec also repairs cathode-ray tube monitors and power supplies, including those of its manufacturing competitors. The company is headquartered in Eden Prairie, Minn., about 96 miles from its manufacturing and repair facilities, which employ 654 of its 748 workers.

When it began operating independently in 1984 following a leveraged buy out, Zytec depended almost entirely on orders from one of its former owners, which now account for less than 1.5 percent of revenues. In 1990, product sales to 20 customers—18 of which have made Zytec a sole-source supplier—totaled $50 million. The repair business, the largest of its kind in the United States, generated $5.8 million in additional revenues.

"Total Quality Commitment"　　As the foundation for continuous improvement, Zytec senior executives chose Deming's "14 points" for managing productivity and quality. Followed by many Japanese firms, the concepts defined the core values of quality improvement that executives sought to instill throughout the organization. Progress in achieving this cultural transformation is monitored through an annual survey of employees—one of several methods for assessing the quality commitment and the satisfaction of workers.

To foster a common quality focus and to ensure that all 33 of its departments move in step to meet ever more demanding customer requirements, Zytec has adopted an interactive ''Management By Planning'' (MBP) process that involves employees in setting long-term and annual improvement goals.

At an annual 2-day meeting, about 150 employees, representing all types of personnel, shifts, and departments, review and critique 5-year plans prepared by six cross-functional teams. Zytec executives then finalize the long-term strategic plan and set broad corporate objectives to guide quality planning in the departments, where teams develop annual goals to support each corporate objective. In face-to-face meetings with teams or representatives, Zytec CEO Ronald D. Schmidt first reviews departmental goals and, subsequently, action plans, including performance measures and monthly progress targets.

Concurrent with the internal process, the company invites selected customers and suppliers to scrutinize the long-range plan, leading to further refinement. Through these and other steps in the iterative planning process, Zytec helps ensure that it is setting the right goals and following up with the most appropriate actions, supported by adequate resources.

Coordination and integration also are hallmarks of the way Zytec carries out its plans. Design and development of new products, for example, are carried out by interdepartmental teams, which are assigned to projects from start to finish. Working closely with customers, the same cross-functional management teams review performance at four key stages: predesign initiation, design initiation, prototype delivery and testing, and preproduction certification. The teams are empowered to address all issues of suppliers and processes, including critical parameters for measurement and control.

Zytec is a data-driven company, developing meaningful, measurable criteria for evaluating performance at all levels. In addition, benchmarking competitors' products and services as well as the practices of acknowledged quality leaders in other industries provides Zytec with a clear picture of what it takes to achieve industry- or world-best status in key areas, from employee involvement to just-in-time manufacturing to supplier management.

To realize the full advantage of its employees, Zytec trains them in analytical and problem-solving methods—a major focus of the 72 hours of quality-related instruction received by most Zytec employees. Workers are expected to use this knowledge as their authority and responsibilities grow.

Several departments are directed by self-managed teams of workers. Zytec's production workers are encouraged to improve their knowledge and flexibility through an innovative employee evaluation and reward system called MFE—Multi-Functional Employee program. Through MFE, employees are rewarded for the number of job skills that they acquire.

By aligning all elements of quality-improvement—human, technological, and informational—with customer priorities, Zytec has made the most significant performance gains in the areas that count the most. Product quality, as derived from customer-supplied data on failures, has risen to the four-sigma range, putting it on track for Six Sigma quality by 1995. Since 1988, the mean-time-between-failure of a Zytec power supply has increased to over 1,000,000 hours as measured by actual field data and reliability testing, and from 1989 to 1990, the company's on-time delivery rate improved from 85 to 96 percent.

For more information, contact:
Ronald D. Schmidt
Chairman, President, and CEO
7575 Market Place Drive
Eden Prairie, MN 55344
Phone: 612-941-1100
Fax: 612-829-1837

Solectron Corporation

A leading independent provider of customized integrated manufacturing services to original equipment manufacturers (OEMs) in the electronics industry, Solectron specializes in the assembly of complex printed circuit boards and subsystems for makers of computers and other electronic products. Solectron also provides system-level assembly services, such as assembly of personal computers and mainframe mass storage subsystems, as well as turnkey materials management, board design, and manufacturability consultation and testing. The firm focuses its marketing efforts on value-added projects requiring a high level of reliability and quality, rapid turnaround time, and responsiveness to change.

By focusing on customer satisfaction, exploiting advanced manufacturing technology, and stressing continuous improvement in operations and services, Solectron has demonstrated that high quality and high efficiency translate into low total costs and timely delivery. Solectron competes successfully with both strong international competition and also with the internal production capabilities of its customers. Indeed, major computer firms known for manufacturing efficiency have closed internal assembly operations after determining that outsourcing the work to Solectron not only lowered costs but also improved quality. About 90 percent of new business is additional work from established customers. These customers have benefited from defect rates that have fallen to within the five-sigma range, or 233 parts per million, and on-time delivery rate of 97.7 percent over the last 2 years. Consistent with the goals of its major customers, Solectron has committed to achieving and then surpassing Six Sigma quality in critical processes over the next 5 years.

Solectron at a Glance   Founded in 1977, Solectron has grown from a small assembly job shop with annual revenues of several hundred thousand dollars to an employer of 2,100 people who work at five sites in San Jose and Milpitas, California.

Assembly of printed circuit boards accounts for about 80 percent of business, with the remainder divided among assembly of other electronic systems, subsystems, software packaging, disk duplication, remanufacture of customer products, and design and testing services. Solectron operates one of the world's largest surface mount facilities for the assembly of complex printed circuit boards and subsystems.

Among its some 60 customers are manufacturers of personal computers, workstations, disk and tape drives, and avionics, medical imaging, and telecommunication equipment. Some of these firms supply Solectron with all components for assembly into the finished product. An increasing number of customers, however, rely on Solectron to procure some or all components, thereby reducing their investment in inventory, facilities, and personnel.

Customer Needs Drive Results   As a contract manufacturing company, Solectron does not compete with its customers in designing and marketing products. Although it offers an original equipment design service, more often it manufactures a product designed by the customers. Solectron competes on the basis of service, quality, and cost, and the company goes to great lengths to determine how existing and prospective customers define superior performance. Besides conducting exhaustive searches for information on customers, competitors, and markets, Solectron has developed several mechanisms for ensuring direct and frequent feedback from customers. One of the most valuable is a weekly survey of all customers. The results are compiled into a customer satisfaction index, which CEO Dr. Winston Chen and other top executives review at one of their three weekly meetings on quality-related issues. The survey information also is used to grade the performance of each of Solectron's nine major divisions. Within the company, a similar system is used to evaluate the performance of specific work groups and departments in meeting the needs of their internal customers.

At Solectron, the concept of Continuous Improvement is a cultural strength. The company has a strong top management team on a crusade to revitalize American business through quality. The executive team sets corporate quality targets and then works with teams to set supporting goals in each functional area of the company. They have relied upon several strategies that give them a high-energy, customer-focused work force. These strategies, which include a strong "family" orientation, an effective communication system, and an innovative reward and recognition program, have held the organization together through rapid growth. The management style is participative with a high degree of coaching and autonomy. Solectron has a team-focused approach to employee involvement, which relies on training and mentorship to overcome barriers due to a multilingual work force composed of workers from over 20 cultures.

Each Solectron customer is supported by two teams that work to ensure quality performance and on-time delivery. A project planning team works with customers in planning, scheduling, and defining material requirements and lead time. A total quality control team meets weekly for monitoring and evaluating production with the aim of preventing potential problems and identifying ways to improve process yields.

"We Are the Best . . . and Getting Better"   Solectron's comprehensive information system, organized in a customized relational data base, enables regular—

often real-time—surveillance of internal quality performance and process control indicators. Key performance data are charted in all departments, and workers, most of whom are trained in statistical process control and problem-solving methods, are empowered to make process improvements and take corrective actions.

Statistical Process Control (SPC) is used regularly in all departments. SPC charts track performance of each machine with measurements recorded in an SPC data base. Division quality managers and the corporate quality director track and review results daily. Since 1987 the average product rejection rate has improved to better than 0.3 percent of shipments, a 50-percent improvement.

Upstream from its assembly operations, Solectron works with suppliers to improve the quality and reliability of their operations. As it does with its customers, the company views its suppliers as partners in pursuing Six Sigma quality, and it offers training and other technical assistance to help them continuously improve.

Investments in advanced technology are guided by Solectron's evaluation of its customers' future requirements and top management's emphasis on enhancing manufacturing capabilities. The company was quick to adopt "surface mount technology" (SMT) that, unlike the conventional method, permits integrated circuits and other components to be placed on both sides of a circuit board. Although requiring higher levels of capital investment and assembly expertise, SMT offers the advantages of increased packaging density and improved product performance. Solectron now has 19 surface mount assembly lines, and it is developing new bonding and soldering methods to exploit the advantages that SMT offers customers.

Solectron's quality improvement efforts are paying off, as indicated by its chief indicator: "customer satisfaction." It has won 37 superior performance awards over the last 10 years, 10 of those in 1990. After a recent quality audit, a major customer rated Solectron as the "best contract manufacturer of electronic assemblies in the U.S."

For more information, contact:
Dr. Thomas Kennedy
Vice President, Quality
2001 Fortune Drive
San Jose, CA 95131
Phone: 408-957-7031
Fax: 408-263-4150

1990 AWARD WINNERS

IBM Rochester

The concept of quality at IBM Rochester is linked directly to the customer. Detailed features are crafted by analyzing the needs and expectations of existing and potential owners of the computer hardware and software manufactured by the Rochester,

Minn., site of the International Business Machines Corporation. At every step, customers are directly involved in each aspect of the product from design to delivery—through advisory councils, global information systems, trials or prototypes, and numerous other feedback mechanisms.

The IBM Rochester quality culture has been transformed from reliance on technology-driven processes delivering products to market-driven processes directly involving suppliers, business partners, and customers delivering solutions. A 30 percent improvement in productivity occurred between 1986 and 1989. Product-development time for new mid-range computer systems has been reduced by more than half, while the manufacturing cycle has been trimmed 60 percent since 1983. Customers have benefited from a threefold increase in product reliability; an increase from 3 to 12 months in the product warranty period; and a cost of ownership that is among the lowest in the industry. IBM's share of the world market for intermediate computers increased in both 1988 and 1989.

IBM Rochester at a Glance   IBM Rochester manufactures intermediate computer systems—currently the AS/Entry Systems and the Application System/400 (AS/400). More than 400,000 IBM Rochester systems have been installed worldwide. This location also makes hard disk drives, which are electromechanical devices that store and retrieve information on magnetic disks. Sales of hard disk drives accounted for about a fifth of IBM Rochester's revenues in 1989.

IBM Rochester provides employment to more than 8,100 people and is responsible for product development and U.S. manufacturing. In addition, its processes are implemented in plants located in Japan, Mexico, United Kingdom, and Italy.

"Rochester Excellence . . . Customer Satisfaction"   IBM Rochester recently strengthened its strategic quality initiatives by formulating improvement plans based on six critical success factors: improved product and service requirements definition, an enhanced product strategy, a six-sigma defect elimination strategy, further cycle time reductions, improved education, and increased employee involvement and ownership. Each senior manager "owns" one of the six factors and assumes responsibility for plans and implementation. Progress toward achieving improvement goals is closely monitored. Support processes are a part of this network.

The continuous improvement of support processes at IBM Rochester rests on aggressive worldwide benchmarking, a process that analyzes products and services to determine the best of the breed in all industries. Over 350 teams are in place to work on opportunities. Scores of benchmarking studies have been completed.

Quality goals are established in five-year business plans and annual operating plans. Strategic targets are derived from its comprehensive benchmarking process. With the aid of financial planning models and mathematical decision-making tools, quality priorities are set, and the resources—human and capital—necessary to carry out these priorities are determined.

Most plans for achieving quality objectives originate with employees, and cross-functional teams identify needs for equipment, staffing, education, and process development. Each quality improvement plan has an owner—a managerial or non-managerial employee who heads the project team. With employee input, objectives and requirements are established for each employee, and a measurement system for monitoring progress is developed in advance of the project. Close coordination and efficient communication are ensured through regular planning meetings, in which key suppliers and customers participate.

IBM Rochester invests heavily in education and training, the equivalent of 5 percent of its payroll. Employees, supported by IBM's tradition of full employment, are encouraged to develop the skills and expertise for a variety of jobs. In 1989, about a third of the work force moved into new positions, and 13 percent were promoted. IBM Rochester is implementing a Management System for Education, which will offer skill planning, needs assessment, individual education plans, and education road maps on-line. Job flexibility and security, ample opportunity for advancement, and a well-developed recognition process are among factors contributing to rates of absenteeism and turnover that are well below national averages. Employee contributions to quality improvement are recognized in a variety of ways, including luncheons, receptions, and monetary and nonmonetary awards. Morale is high, as determined in IBM annual surveys, and by an independently conducted survey that compares levels of worker satisfaction at 34 U.S. companies.

Equipping workers with the tools and information they need to accomplish quality and customer satisfaction objectives is also a priority. Over 11,000 on-line terminals provide employees with worldwide access to extensive communication capabilities, databases, and design and analysis tools. For example, since 1986, IBM has invested more than $300 million in improving its processes and information systems. Such investments, many of them designed to improve problem-solving capabilities ensuring that defects are prevented rather than detected after they occur, have paid for themselves. Capital spending on equipment for defect detection declined 75 percent during the 1980s, and write-offs as a proportion of manufacturing output dropped 55 percent.

At the start of the product planning process, suppliers are included as partners to ensure that new hardware and software will achieve IBM goals for manufacturability, serviceability, reliability, performance, and cost. Accounting for about 30 percent of production output, IBM Rochester's approximately 700 production suppliers are expected to provide defect-free shipments and to keep pace with its progress in improving quality and reducing development and manufacturing cycles. Suppliers are trained, audited, and certified, and they are required to submit quality plans. IBM Rochester shares its own state-of-the-art technology with suppliers and, in turn, suppliers provide valuable expertise to IBM. Since 1984, IBM Rochester employees have instructed more than 1,000 supplier employees on continuous flow manufacturing, statistical process control, and design of experiments.

The Rochester quality process is a continuous loop that begins, ends, and begins again with the customer. Of the approximately 40 data sources analyzed to guide improvement efforts, most either provide information on customers' product and service requirements or guide steps to refine these expectations into detailed specifications for new IBM offerings. Customers are also active participants. For example, customers and business partners representing over 4,500 businesses worldwide participated on customer advisory councils throughout the development of the AS/400.

To strengthen its competitive quality position, IBM Rochester is aiming for a tenfold improvement in key quality areas by 1991, a hundredfold improvement by 1993, and a Six Sigma level of defects by 1994.

For more information, contact:
Roy A. Bauer 1-507-253-9000
IBM Rochester
Hwy. 52 North & 37th St. NW
Rochester, MN 55901

Federal Express Corporation

Seventeen years ago Federal Express Corporation launched the air-express industry. By constantly adhering to a management philosophy emphasizing people, service, and profit, in that order, the company achieved high levels of customer satisfaction and experienced rapid sales growth. Annual revenues topped $1 billion within 10 years of the company's founding, an exceptional achievement.

But past accomplishments do not ensure future success. That's why the management of Federal Express is setting ever higher goals for quality performance and customer satisfaction, enhancing and expanding service, investing heavily in advanced technology, and building on its reputation as an excellent employer. Company leaders are increasingly stressing management by fact, analysis, and improvement.

Through a quality improvement process focusing on 12 Service Quality Indicators (SQIs), all tied to customer expectations and articulated at all levels of its international business, the Memphis-based firm continues to set higher standards for service and customer satisfaction. Measuring themselves against a 100-percent service standard, managers and employees strive to improve all aspects of the way Federal Express does business.

Federal Express at a Glance   Conceived by Chairman and Chief Executive Officer Frederick W. Smith, Federal Express began operations in 1973. At that time a fleet of eight small aircraft was sufficient to handle demand. Five years later, the company employed 10,000 people, who handled a daily volume of 35,000 shipments. Today, approximately 90,000 Federal Express employees, at more than 1,650 sites process 1.5 million shipments daily, all of which must be tracked in a central information system, sorted in a short time at facilities in Memphis, Indianapolis, Newark, Oakland, Los Angeles, Anchorage, and Brussels, and delivered by a highly decentralized distribution network. The firm's air cargo fleet is now the world's largest.

Federal Express revenues totaled $7 billion in fiscal year 1990. Domestic overnight and second-day deliveries accounted for nearly three-fourths of the total, with the remainder being international deliveries. The company's share of the domestic market in 1989 was 43 percent, compared with 26 percent for its nearest competitor.

People-Service-Profit   Federal Express's "People-Service-Profit" philosophy guides management policies and actions. The company has a well-developed and thoroughly deployed management evaluation system called SFA (Survey/Feedback/Action), which involves a survey of employees, analysis of each work group's results by the work group's manager, and a discussion between the manager and the work group to develop written action plans for the manager to improve and become more effective. Data from the SFA process are aggregated at all levels of the organization for use in policymaking.

Training of front-line personnel is a responsibility of managers and "recurrency training" is a widely used instrument for improvement. Teams regularly assess training needs and a worldwide staff of training professionals devise programs to address those needs. To aid these efforts, Federal Express has developed an interactive video system for employee instruction. An internal television network, accessible throughout the company, also serves as an important avenue for employee education.

Consistently included in listings of the best U.S. companies to work for, Federal Express has a "no lay-off" philosophy, and its "guaranteed fair treatment procedure" for handling employee grievances is used as a model by firms in many industries. Employees can participate in a program to qualify front-line workers for management positions. In addition, Federal Express has a well-developed recognition program for team and individual contributions to company performance. Over the last five years, at least 91 percent of employees responded that they were "proud to work for Federal Express."

Service Quality Indicators   To spur progress toward its ultimate target of 100-percent customer satisfaction, Federal Express recently replaced its old measure of quality performance—percent of on-time deliveries—with a 12-component index that comprehensively describes how its performance is viewed by customers. Each item in the Service Quality Indicator (SQI) is weighted to reflect how significantly it affects overall customer satisfaction.

Performance data are gathered with the company's advanced computer and tracking systems, including the SuperTracker, a hand-held computer used for scanning a shipment's bar code every time a package changes hands between pick-up and delivery. Rapid analysis of data from the firm's far-flung operations yields daily SQI reports transmitted to workers at all Federal Express sites. Management meets daily to discuss the previous day's performance and tracks weekly, monthly, and annual trends. Analysis of data contained in the company's more than 30 major databases assists quality action teams (QATs) in locating the root causes of problems that surface in SQI reviews. Extensive customer and internal data are used by cross-functional teams involved in the company's new product introduction process.

To reach its aggressive quality goals, the company has set up one cross-functional team for each service component in the SQI. A senior executive heads each team and assures the involvement of front-line employees, support personnel, and managers from all parts of the corporation when needed. Two of these corporatewide teams have a network of over 1,000 employees working on improvements.

The Service Quality Indicator measurements are directly linked to the corporate planning process, which begins with the CEO and COO and an executive planning committee. SQIs form the basis on which corporative executives are evaluated. Individual performance objectives are established and monitored. Executive bonuses rest upon the performance of the whole corporation in meeting performance improvement goals. And, in the annual employee survey, if employees do not rate management leadership at least as high as they rated them the year before, no executive receives a year-end bonus.

Employees are encouraged to be innovative and to make decisions that advance quality goals. Federal Express provides employees with the information and technology they need to continuously improve their performance. An example is the Digitally Assisted Dispatch System (DADS), which communicates to some 30,000 couriers through screens in their vans. The system enables quick response to pick-up and delivery dispatches and allows couriers to manage their time and routes with high efficiency.

Since 1987, overall customer satisfaction with Federal Express's domestic service has averaged better than 95 percent, and its international service has rated a satisfaction score of about 94 percent. In an independently conducted survey of air-express industry customers, 53 percent gave Federal Express a perfect score, as compared with 39 percent for the next-best competitor. The company has received 195 awards over the last 13 years, and representatives of nearly 600 businesses and organizations have visited its facilities.

For more information, contact:
Daniel N. Copp
Managing Director, Public Relations
Federal Express Corporation
P.O. Box 727
Memphis, TN 38194-2605
Phone: 901-395-3460
Fax: 901-346-1013

Cadillac Motor Car Company

To many car buyers, the Cadillac nameplate symbolizes the highest level of quality. But during the 1980s, competitors made determined efforts to wrest that reputation away and, until 1988, gained market share at Cadillac's expense.

But the maker of luxury automobiles has risen to the challenge. Over the last several years, its cars have improved markedly in quality, reliability, durability, and performance. Through its greatly expanded warranty coverage and unique new service offerings, including a nationwide Roadside Service program, Cadillac has intensified its commitment to the customer. And it has become a nimbler competi-

tor, the result of a simultaneous engineering process guided by a finely tuned information system that helps translate buyer preferences and expectations into new
product features and new services.

By effectively integrating quality into all endeavors—from product planning to
personnel practices—Cadillac has reversed its decline in market share, attracting
new buyers while boasting the highest percentage of repeat buyers in the car
industry.

Cadillac at a Glance   Founded in 1902, Cadillac is the flagship division of the
General Motors (GM) North American Automotive Operations. It manufactures or
directs the production of nine car models—including two (Reatta and Riviera) mar-
keted by the GM Buick division and one (Toronado) by the Oldsmobile division—
that compete in the luxury segments of the automobile market. Cadillac models are
the Allante, Brougham, Seville, Eldorado, DeVille, and Fleetwood.

Directed by General Manager John O. Grettenberger, Cadillac employs about
10,000 people at its Detroit-area headquarters, four Michigan-based manufacturing
plants, and 10 sales and service zone offices in the United States. In the domestic
market, which accounts for nearly 99 percent of sales, cars are sold through a network of 1,600 franchised dealerships, partners in the division's quality improvement efforts.

Customer Satisfaction at the Master Plan   Cadillac's turnaround began in 1985.
That's when top management started implementing simultaneous engineering
(SE). SE contrasts sharply with the traditional serial approach to automobile development and manufacturing, in which individual departments functioned largely in
isolation from the others.

Product design and development now begin with integrated knowledge of all
essential elements, including performance targets, product features, systems and
parts, processes, and maintenance requirements. Thus, SE anticipates how changes
in one functional area will affect the others, making it easier to prevent problems
and bottlenecks, to determine in advance how to monitor and control production
processes, and to identify opportunities for quality improvement.

The effectiveness of SE, however, hinges critically on carefully orchestrated teamwork. More than 700 employee and supplier representatives now participate on
SE teams responsible for defining, engineering, marketing, and continuously
improving all Cadillac products. Their coordinated efforts on three recent major
styling changes trimmed 50–85 weeks from what typically had been a 175-week
process.

Successes achieved by SE teams were the springboard to a complete transformation in Cadillac's quality culture. Its partnerships with the United Auto Workers
(UAW) have been a catalyst in this transformation. Along with Cadillac executives
and plant managers, union leaders serve on the Divisional Quality Council, which
is part of the UAW/GM Quality Network. At Cadillac, the Quality Network also
includes plant councils at each of its seven major facilities, which are supported by

the efforts of nearly 600 work teams and cross-functional teams, each composed of between 10 and 15 hourly and salaried employees.

Pledging to involve its employees "in the running of the business," Cadillac solicits the views of all employee teams during the preparation of its annual business plans, which embody short- and long-term quality improvement goals. The open, yet disciplined, planning process, guided by analyses of information in more than 50 databases, culminates with the completion of detailed quality plans for plants and staff units. These plans translate business objectives into discrete measurable actions carried out by teams and individuals. Progress is closely monitored, and feedback is provided in weekly team meetings. Feedback is also provided through individual and team recognition awards.

A comprehensive program of competitive analyses—of products; product features; services; and planning, development, and manufacturing processes—provides Cadillac management and employees with a clear picture of what the division must do to maintain or achieve world-class status in each category.

Thorough planning is also a hallmark of Cadillac's "people strategy" for improving the effectiveness and job satisfaction of hourly and salaried employees' efforts. Especially close attention is paid to educational needs. Each plant and staff unit has a Training Priorities Committee to determine what skills and knowledge workers must have to accomplish quality goals, and training programs are crafted to individual needs. In 1990, for example, skilled hourly personnel will receive a minimum of 80 hours of formal instruction in such areas as quality improvement, leadership skills, process modeling, statistical methods, and health and safety.

Suppliers and dealers also are fully integrated into Cadillac's customer-focused quality improvement efforts. Three-fourths of the division's 55 Product Development and Improvement Teams have suppliers as members. External suppliers must demonstrate continuous improvement in meeting "targets for excellence" in five key areas: quality, cost, delivery, technology, and management. A well-developed assessment and part qualification process assures conformance, eliminating the need for regular inspection of shipments.

In reliability and durability tests equivalent to 100,000 miles of customer use and 10 years of corrosion exposure, all models have improved markedly, as determined from measures of the "number of things gone wrong" during the test. For all nine models, the number of such problems decreased between 27 percent and 71 percent since 1986 or, for new models, since production began. In tests of 1990 and 1991 cars, nearly all models met or exceeded world-class levels for reliability and durability.

For the customer, these product improvements and Cadillac's commitment to improving service have resulted in expanded warranty coverage—to a minimum of four years or 50,000 miles, as compared with one year or 12,000 miles in 1988. Improved product quality, however, has resulted in a 29-percent drop in warranty-related costs during the first year or 12,000 miles, from 1986 to 1989.

In step with service and product quality, customer satisfaction has risen, as measured through extensive surveys and analyses of complaints handled by its 24-hour

Customer Relations Center, for instance. On three key measures—satisfaction with cars, service, and total ownership experience—1985 customers rated Cadillac at about 70 percent. In 1989, Cadillac's scores in all three categories were 86 percent or better.

For more information, contact:
Rosetta M. Riley
Director, Customer Satisfaction
Cadillac Motor Car Company
2860 Clark St.
Detroit, MI 48232
Phone: 313-554-5700
Fax: 313-554-7789
or
Bill O'Neill
Director of Public Relations
Cadillac Motor Car Company
2860 Clark St.
Detroit, MI 48232
Phone: 313-554-5065
Fax: 313-554-5074

Wallace Co., Inc.

Wallace Co., Inc., a Houston-based industrial distribution company, bucked the conventional business wisdom during the mid-1980s. With the Gulf Coast economy in the doldrums and new construction activity—its primary source of revenues—at a standstill, Wallace avoided short-term remedies, and pursued a long-term strategy of Continuous Quality Improvement.

In only a few years, Wallace has distinguished itself from its competitors by setting new standards for service. It has emerged as a stronger firm with a rapidly growing sales volume, steadily increasing market share, and better profit performance.

Now entering the final stage of the three-phase quality program it initiated in 1985, Wallace has effectively merged business and quality goals, built new partnerships with customers and suppliers, and instilled associates with a commitment to one overriding aim: total customer satisfaction.

Wallace at a Glance   Founded in 1942, Wallace is a family-owned distribution company primarily serving the chemical and petro-chemical industries. Its 10 offices, located in Texas, Louisiana, and Alabama, distribute pipe, valves, and fittings, as well as value-added specialty products such as actuated valves and plastic-lined pipe. Wallace distributes directly in the Gulf Coast area but serves international markets as well.

In tandem with its move to Continuous Quality Improvement, Wallace shifted its marketing focus from engineering and construction activities to maintenance and repair operations, now the source of 70 percent of its sales. In 1989, sales totaled $79 million. The company employs 280 associates, all of whom have been trained in quality improvement concepts and methods.

"Continuous Quality Improvement"   The seeds of the Wallace quality process were sown and cultivated by the company's five top leaders, directed by John W. Wallace, Chief Executive Officer, and C. S. Wallace, Jr., President. Comprising the Quality Management Steering Committee, each of the five has undergone more than 200 hours of intensive training on the methods and philosophy of Continuous Quality Improvement. Their hands-on involvement is typified by the participation of at least one senior leader in all quality activities, including on-the-job training for associates.

Leadership drafted the company's Quality Mission Statement, which was circulated throughout the company. Embodying input from all associates, the final document serves as Wallace's public commitment to Continuous Quality Improvement. It is distributed to all associates, customers, and suppliers. Furthermore, Wallace developed 16 Quality Strategic Objectives—nine of which focus on improving customer satisfaction—to guide business decision making. In fact, business and quality aims are one and the same, formulated in Wallace's Quality Business Plan.

Associates are responsible for devising and carrying out plans to accomplish objectives under the company's cooperative, yet centralized, approach to quality improvement. Since 1985, participation on teams, whose membership is voluntary and cuts across departmental and district office boundaries, has increased sixfold. Team planning and decision making are greatly aided by an extensive set of customer-focused databases, accessible to all associates through the company's computer system. Teams are assisted by 12 statistical process control (SPC) coordinators, who chart trends, conduct failure mode effects analysis to isolate real and potential problems, and evaluate progress in accomplishing quality objectives. Each district office has at least one SPC coordinator on staff, and one day a week at all sites is devoted to evaluating and planning quality improvements.

Wallace has fixed its sights on providing the products and services that best meet the needs of its regional market, but the scope of its quality improvement efforts is truly worldwide. Measurable quality benchmarks are identified in global searches for the top-performing companies in each category of service or business operation, from on-time delivery to safety performance.

Not only does Wallace comprehensively monitor its activity—it has identified and now measures 72 discrete processes that contribute to on-time delivery and accurate invoicing—but it invites the scrutiny of customers. Customers receive computer-generated reports that document how well the company has been servicing its accounts. Customer feedback is ensured through four types of surveys, "partnering" meetings, frequent contacts by sales representatives, and a Total Customer Response Network that must respond to all inquiries and complaints within 60 minutes.

Moreover, customers have access to some of Wallace's databases. Wallace also has led the way in converting customers to Electronic Data Interchange. Both

Wallace and its customers reap the advantages of better inventory management, time savings, error reduction, and more accurate data. About 40 percent of Wallace's sales orders are now handled electronically, compared with less than 5 percent in 1988.

Wallace holds suppliers to its same high standards, requiring firms to provide statistical evidence of the quality of their shipments and to guarantee their products for a minimum of 12 months. Based on its quality surveillance measures, the distributor has trimmed the number of its suppliers to 325, down from more than 2,000 in 1987. To ensure that suppliers consistently provide products meeting the expectations of customers, Wallace provides training in Continuous Quality Improvement, a first in the industry. Last year, 15 suppliers initiated processes based on the Wallace model. In another pioneering initiative spawned by a committee of Wallace, customer, and supplier representatives, the company has implemented a vendor certification process, in which Wallace and its major customers will jointly assess the quality processes of suppliers.

Because associates drive quality improvement, Wallace has invested about $2 million in formal training between 1987 and the end of 1990. Teams of associates closest to a specific area targeted for improvement are charged with identifying the steps necessary to accomplish a quality objective, with standardizing the methods to assure consistent performance, and with conducting the necessary training at all departments and offices.

"Quality wins" are reported in the company's monthly newsletter, acknowledged in congratulatory letters from the CEO, and rewarded with dinners for the responsible associates and their families or with team picnics.

Simultaneous with management's efforts to increase associate involvement in Continuous Quality Improvement, rates of absenteeism, turnover, and work-related injuries have dropped sharply. New associate-led projects are intended to foster greater dedication and higher levels of job satisfaction. For example, teams are studying ways to enhance career development opportunities. In a newly begun program, each associate will visit at least one customer site to discuss service performance.

These and other initiatives have paid numerous dividends. Since 1987, Wallace's market share has increased from 10.4 percent to 18 percent. Its record of on-time deliveries has jumped from 75 percent in 1987 to 92 percent in 1990. By July 1991, the distributor has committed to guarantee all customers an on-time delivery rate of 98 percent. Its customer base has grown, while existing clients have increased their business. As a result, sales volume has grown 69 percent and, because of greater efficiency, operating profits through 1989 have increased 7.4 times. Wallace has earned numerous awards from customers in recent years, verifying its high and improving status as a quality supplier.

For more information, contact:
Michael E. Spiess
Vice President
Wallace Co., Inc.

P.O. Box 2597
Houston, TX 77252-2597
Phone: 713-685-4670
Fax: 713-672-5848

1989 AWARD WINNERS

Xerox Corporation Business Products and Systems

For its first 15 years, Xerox was without equal, best in an industry whose products were synonymous with its name. But challenges did come in the mid-1970s from foreign and U.S. competitors that surpassed Xerox reprographic products in both cost and quality.

Not even second best in some product categories, Xerox launched an ambitious quality improvement program in 1984 to arrest its decline in the world market it created. Today, the company can once again claim the title as the industry's best in nearly all copier-product markets. As a result, Xerox has not only halted loss of world market share, but also reversed it.

Xerox Business Products and Systems (BP&S), headquartered in Stamford, Connecticut, attributes the turnaround to its strategy of "Leadership Through Quality." The company defines quality through the eyes of the customer. Xerox BP&S knows what customers want in products and services.

Analyses of a wide variety of data, gathered with exhaustive collection efforts that include monthly surveys of 55,000 Xerox equipment owners, enable the company to identify customer requirements. The company uses this information to develop concrete business plans with measurable targets for achieving quality improvements necessary to meet customers' needs.

Xerox at a Glance   One of two Xerox Corporation businesses, Business Products and Systems employs 50,200 people at 83 U.S. locations. BP&S makes more than 250 types of document-processing equipment, generating $6 billion in 1988 U.S. sales, or 54 percent of the company's domestic revenues. Copiers and other duplicating equipment account for nearly 70 percent of BP&S revenues. The remainder is divided among sales of electronic printers and typing equipment, networks, workstations, and software products.

Leadership Through Quality   Directed by CEO David T. Kearns and his senior management team, the "Leadership Through Quality" thrust has made quality improvement and, ultimately, customer satisfaction the job of every employee. All have received at least 28 hours of training in problem-solving and quality improvement techniques. The company has invested more than four million manhours and $125 million in educating employees about quality principles.

Workers are vested with authority over day-to-day work decisions. And they are expected to take the initiative in identifying and correcting problems that affect the quality of products or services. Both salaried and hourly personnel have embraced these added responsibilities.

For example, the company's 1989 labor contract with the Amalgamated Clothing and Textile Workers' Union pledges employee support to "continuous quality improvement while reducing quality costs through teamwork and the tools and processes of Leadership Through Quality." This partnership with the union is considered a model by other corporations.

The phrase "Team Xerox" is not an empty slogan. It accurately reflects the firm's approach to tackling quality issues. Xerox BP&S estimates that 75 percent of its workers are members of at least one of more than 7,000 quality improvement teams. In 1988, teams in manufacturing and development were credited with saving $116 million by reducing scrap, tightening production schedules, and devising other efficiency- and quality-enhancing measures.

Teamwork also characterizes the company's relationship with many of its 480 suppliers. Suppliers are "process qualified" through a step-by-step procedure to analyze and quantify suppliers' production and control processes. Suppliers receive training and follow-up in such areas as statistical process control and total quality techniques; firms credit Xerox with improving their products and operations. For BP&S, increasing reliance on qualified suppliers over the last five years has reduced the number of defective parts reaching the production line by 73 percent.

Planning new products and services is based on detailed analyses of data organized in 375 information management systems, including 175 specific to planning, managing, and evaluating quality improvement. Much of this wealth of data has been amassed through an extensive network of market surveillance and customer feedback, all designed to support systematic evaluation of customer requirements. Over one-half of the company's marketing-research budget is allocated for this purpose, and each year its Customer Service Measurement System tracks the behavior and preferences of about 200,000 owners of Xerox equipment.

Benchmarking System   In its quest to elevate its products and services to world-class status, Xerox BP&S devised a benchmarking system that has, in itself, become a model. The company measures its performance in about 240 key areas of product, service, and business performance. Derived from international studies, the ultimate target for each attribute is the level of performance achieved by the world leader, regardless of industry.

Returns from the company's strategy for continuous quality improvement have materialized quickly. Gains in quality over the last five years include a 78 percent decrease in the number of defects per 100 machines; greatly increased product reliability, as measured by a 40 percent decrease in unscheduled maintenance; increasing copy quality, which strengthened the company's position as world leader; a 27 percent drop (nearly two hours) in service response time; and significant reductions in labor and material overhead. These improvements have enabled Xerox BP&S to take additional steps to distinguish itself from the competition; for instance, it was the first in the industry to offer a three-year product warranty.

The thrust of "Leadership Through Quality" is ongoing with Xerox BP&S. The process of continuous quality improvement, directed toward greater customer satisfaction and enhanced business performance, is currently targeting by 1993 a 50 percent reduction in unit manufacturing cost and four-fold improvement in reliability. Such goals illustrate the commitment contained in the Xerox Quality Policy, which states that "quality is the basic business principle at Xerox."

For more information, contact:
James E. Sierk
Vice President, National Quality Award Office
Xerox Corporation
Business Products and Systems
1387 Fairport Road
Fairport, NY 14450

Milliken & Company

Ten years ago, Milliken, a major textile manufacturer long-recognized for quality products and its use of state-of-the-art technology, asked why some Japanese competitors achieved higher quality, less waste, greater productivity, and fewer customer complaints while using technology less advanced than Milliken's. The reasons, company executives found, lay in management approaches and in personnel practices that, along with technology, drive improvements in quality and efficiency.

In 1981, senior management set in motion Milliken's Pursuit of Excellence (POE), a commitment to customer satisfaction that pervades all company levels at all locations. The results are impressive, providing improvements in what had already been an enviable record of quality and performance. In independently conducted surveys, Milliken tops the competition in all 15 measures of customer satisfaction.

Milliken at a Glance   Headquartered in Spartanburg, South Carolina, the 124-year-old privately-owned company employs 14,300 workers, or what the company terms "associates," most at Milliken's 47 manufacturing facilities in the United States. Its 28 businesses produce more than 48,000 different textile and chemical products—ranging from apparel fabrics and automotive fabrics to specialty chemicals and floor coverings—for more than 8,500 customers worldwide. Annual sales exceed $1 billion.

Pursuit of Excellence   Commitment to quality and customer satisfaction begins at the company's highest levels, with Roger Milliken, chief executive officer, and Thomas J. Malone, chief operating officer, devoting more than half their time to Milliken's POE process.

Through the Policy Committee and Quality Council, top management creates the environment and provides the leadership for quality improvement, and it closely monitors the progress of each company unit toward quality goals.

Milliken has achieved a flat management structure in which associates, working primarily in self-managed teams, exercise considerable authority and autonomy. Production work teams, for example, can undertake training, schedule work, and establish individual performance objectives. Moreover, any Milliken associate can halt a production process if that person detects a quality or safety problem.

The approach has worked so well that Milliken has reduced the number of management positions by nearly 700 since 1981, freeing up a large portion of the workforce for assignment as process improvement specialists. There has been a 77 percent increase in the ratio of production to management associates.

Teams are a hallmark of what observers now call the Milliken Quality Process. In 1988, 1,600 Corrective Action Teams were formed to address specific manufacturing or other internal business challenges, and about 200 Supplier Action Teams worked to improve Milliken's relationships with its suppliers. In addition, nearly 500 Customer Action Teams were formed to respond to the needs and aims of customers, including development of new products. Besides demonstrating a commitment to customer satisfaction, these teams created marketing opportunities that generated substantial additional sales revenue.

Complementing its many activities to extend the capabilities of its workforce, Milliken invests heavily in training. The company spent about $1,300 per associate in 1988. Training is also extended to Milliken's suppliers and customers. Each year since 1984, more than 7,500 visitors have received training in quality principles at Milliken's dedicated training facilities.

The recognition process, for both teams and individuals, is a highly visible, motivating force throughout the company. Recognition in many forms occurs with a wide variety of activities at all levels of the company. Participation by senior leadership is commonplace and extensive. Supplier recognition activities are a natural extension of those used within the company.

All quality improvement efforts are solidly based on factual information, contained in an array of standardized databases accessible from all Milliken facilities. Most manufacturing processes are under the scrutiny of real-time monitoring systems that detect errors and help pinpoint causes. The resultant data, some analyzed with the aid of computerized expert systems, support process improvement efforts to predict and prevent the causes of errors.

To speed progress in this area, process improvement specialists—the reassigned production managers—analyze and improve processes, including those in such non-manufacturing areas as billing and customer service. A substantial decrease in errors has been realized. Since 1981, a 60 percent reduction has been effected in the cost of non-conformance, which includes discounts for off quality, payment for freight on customer returns, and other cost items.

Milliken also maintains extensive databases on environmental and safety variables, suppliers, and customers, including the results of its extensive annual surveys on customer satisfaction. In addition, the company "benchmarks" the products and services of about 400 competitors, providing concrete measures for assessing its performance and for identifying marketing opportunities. Through this surveillance, Milliken determined, for example, that it trailed some competitors in meeting delivery targets. As a result, Milliken improved its record for on-time delivery from 75 percent in 1984 to an industry best of 99 percent in 1988.

Suppliers play an important role in Milliken's quality success. Through extensive efforts in developing supplier partnerships, the company has been able to reduce the number of its suppliers by 72 percent since 1981.

Customer Responsiveness   A key element of Milliken's approach to quality is customer responsiveness—providing what its customers need when they need it. Advanced technology developed by Milliken provides customers access to the company's state-of-the-art computer automated design system, which dramatically reduces the cycle time for new product development. Another critical element for textile users is the time to deliver sample material. Milliken's performance is considered the best in the textile business.

Roger Milliken has personally played a key role in pioneering quick response as an important strategy for American industry.

The company has been well recognized for achieving success for its customers. Milliken has received 41 major customer quality awards in the past five years, including a record five General Motors Mark of Excellence manufacturing awards. In addition, Milliken was voted the outstanding residential carpet manufacturer in the United States in 1988.

At Milliken, the Pursuit of Excellence is an evolving process that continuously yields new ideas for enhancing quality, increasing customer satisfaction, and improving business performance. Building on its quality successes, Milliken has established ambitious new objectives, called "Ten-Four" objectives, as a focus for future advances.

The company intends to achieve a ten-fold improvement in key customer-focused quality measures over the next four years. Each advance brings the innovative company closer to its long-range goal of a production system that is fully responsive to customer needs, providing, as Milliken says, "products that customers want, in the quantity they want, when they want them."

For more information, contact:
Newt Hardie
Vice President, Quality
Milliken & Company
P.O. Box 1926-M-181
Spartanburg, SC 29304

1988 AWARD WINNERS

Commercial Nuclear Fuel Division Westinghouse Electric Corporation

When electric utilities operating nuclear power plants install fuel-rod assemblies made by the Westinghouse Commercial Nuclear Fuel Division (CNFD), they can be

99.995 percent certain that each of the thousands of rods supplied will perform flawlessly. Realizing that future business depends on continued excellence in product performance, CNFD is pushing its all-important dependability rating even higher.

Prior to the early 1980's, the CNFD quality goals were geared toward satisfying regulatory requirements for fuel-rod assemblies. Then, motivated by stiff competition and demanding customer requirements, it raised its sights with the objective of being recognized as the world's highest-quality supplier of commercial nuclear fuel.

The Commercial Nuclear Fuel Division of Westinghouse is building a quality culture that asks employees to do "the right things right the first time." This philosophy makes every action by every employee a quality initiative. Customer satisfaction is the guiding principle, whether it is the ultimate customer or the next person in the process.

CNFD uses a "Total Quality" approach built upon four imperatives for continuous quality improvement: management leadership, product and process leadership, human resource excellence, and customer satisfaction. Progress is measured by a unique system called "Pulse Points." The system tracks improvements in over 60 key performance areas identified with statistical techniques and other evaluative tools, and it helps set measurable goals within each unit of CNFD, down to the jobs of hourly workers.

Product and service improvements attributable to the seven-year old program have paid business dividends. The value of new orders in 1987 was the highest in the decade.

CNFD at a Glance   Begun in 1969 and now part of the Westinghouse Nuclear Fuel Business Unit, one of 26 such units in the company, CNFD currently employs nearly 2,000 people at three sites. The Specialty Metals Plant, near Pittsburgh, produces the zircalloy tubes that encase pellets of uranium dioxide fuel processed at CNFD's Columbia, South Carolina plant. Final fabrication of fuel-rod assemblies is also done at the Columbia Plant. Headquarters Operations and Nuclear Engineering activities are located in Monroeville, Pennsylvania.

The CNFD currently supplies about 40 percent of the U.S. market for fuel-rod assemblies and about 20 percent of the world market. Fuel assemblies supplied by the Columbia Plant accounted for nearly seven percent of U.S. electrical needs in 1987.

"Total Quality"   CNFD uses state-of-the-art technology, such as robotics and other automated processing equipment, supercomputer simulations, expert systems and laser-diagnostics, and laser welding. It estimates that quality-related decisions have dictated 75 percent of its capital allocations during recent years. Management, however, attributes CNFD's substantial improvements in quality and efficiency not so much to advanced technology as it does to a "turned on" work force and to CNFD's Total Quality approach to operations.

Rather than having a chief quality officer, CNFD assigns responsibility for directing and coordinating quality improvements to the general manager and his various staff functions. These managers form the CNFD's Quality Council, which sets policies, plans and strategies, and directs the quality improvement process. Management's rationale is that quality concerns must be fully integrated into all design, production, and customer service activities.

In strategic planning, top management develops formal quality initiatives and Pulse Points that are deemed most critical to improving performance and customer satisfaction. Supporting measurable goals, all aimed at accomplishing divisional objectives, are developed in each of the departments and then for each worker. Progress is monitored through an extensive data-collection and trend-analysis system. Pulse Point trends are reviewed each month in a teleconference that includes top management at each division site.

Workers directly address quality improvement opportunities and help devise initiatives through their participation in project-oriented teams. Nearly 1,400 employees were members of 175 such teams in 1987. About 90 percent of all workers have undergone quality awareness or quality-related training during the past three years.

CNFD maintains close—usually daily—contact with its utility customers and regularly collects technical data to evaluate the performance of its fuel assemblies. Customer service plans are created for each client and are jointly reviewed each quarter. A customer's Fuel Users Group meets twice a year to share information and discuss needs for new products. Consistently high scores in surveys and customer-conducted audits reflect high levels of satisfaction. A more significant indicator, however, is repeat business. Existing customers accounted for more than 90 percent of the orders placed in 1987.

Although its eye is on the bottom line, CNFD management deliberately did not include cost concerns in its quality improvement program, believing that gains in quality would spawn cost-reductions through increases in efficiency. Results achieved between 1984 and 1987 confirm this belief. For example, first time through yields in the manufacture of fuel rods increased from less than 50 percent to 87 percent, substantially reducing scrap, product reworking, and manufacturing cycle time. This helped CNFD achieve over three years of 100 percent on-time delivery of high-quality products.

For more information contact:
James A. Fici
Manager, Total Quality Planning
Commercial Nuclear Fuel Division
Westinghouse Electric Corporation
P.O. Box 3912
Pittsburgh, PA 15230-3912

Globe Metallurgical Inc.

In a tailspin like most other firms in the nation's "smokestack industries," Globe Metallurgical Inc. refused to retreat from the rising tide of imported cheap, commodity-grade metals. While many U.S. makers of ferroalloys (iron-based metals) were closing plants, the Ohio-based company stated its refusal in the most convincing of terms. It initiated a quality-improvement program that has made its products the standards of excellence in the metals industry.

Globe set out in 1985 to become the lowest-cost, highest-quality producer of ferroalloys and silicon metal in the United States. At the same time, the firm shifted its focus from commodity markets, such as steel manufacturing, to the higher value-added markets represented by the foundry and chemical industries and certain segments of the aluminum industry.

Three years later, Globe occupies a quality niche above the competition. Not coincidentally, its share of the U.S. market for high-quality foundry alloys has risen dramatically, sales in Canada and Europe have increased significantly, and profitability has returned.

In quality audits by General Motors, Ford, Intermet, John Deere, and other customers, the firm's scores have set records, resulting in certified supplier status for Globe. Foreign buyers also recognize Globe's commitment to quality. When many European traders place an order for magnesium forrosilicon alloy they specify that the material must be "Globe quality," a standard that other suppliers must match.

Company History   A privately held company since 1987, when Moore McCormick Resources sold all of its metal-related businesses, Globe employs 210 people at plants in Beverly, Ohio, and Selma, Alabama. The plants produce about 100,000 tons of alloys annually for more than 300 customers. Annual sales totalled less than $100 million in 1987, but are projected to increase by approximately 30 percent in 1988.

The firm's drive for quality began two years before the leveraged buy out of Globe's current management. In 1985, Globe's managerial staff was trained in statistical process control and, by the year's end, the foundation of a company-wide quality-improvement system—termed Quality, Efficiency, and Cost (QEC)—was laid.

Elements of QEC   Globe's QEC program permeates the entire company, and goals for quality improvement are integrated into strategic planning and research and development activities. Quality committees exist at every level within the company, and rapid communication scales the distance between top officials, who make up Globe's QEC steering committee, and workers, who participate in "quality circles" that meet weekly. In between in each plant is the QEC committee, composed of the plant manager and department heads, that assembles each morning to review the previous day's performance.

The QEC committee assesses the causes of out of control conditions, reviews corrective measures, evaluates suggestions made by quality circles, and addresses broader quality issues that might be raised by the steering committee.

Now three years into its QEC program, Globe has found no surfeit of good ideas for improving product quality and reducing cost, many of them originating with workers. Improvement measures are carefully tracked, and the results—successes and failures—are published monthly.

In fact, Globe attempts to monitor and quantify every factor that influences product quality, making extensive use of computer-controlled systems that continually advise workers on whether target values for important processing variables are being met. Key variables are identified through a number of means, including failure mode effects analyses, statistical evaluations that identify production steps that are most prone to failure. Color control charts derived from a system developed in-house document each product's processing history. The charts provide workers, who are trained in statistical process control, with a performance appraisal and customers with important information for their manufacturing processes.

Significant improvements in achieving the targeted grade of metal have been realized since the implementation of the computer-controlled systems, with corresponding reductions in the amount of scrap or reclassified product produced. Today, only about 3 percent of the heats—including initial batches of new products— require reclassification. Similarly, greater consistency in final products, achieving specifications that fall within ranges more demanding than those imposed by customers, has significantly lowered the chance of an out-of-specification shipment. The improved consistency of the operation has increased the production rates on the furnaces, while significantly reducing energy consumption, a major cost item for Globe. At the same time Globe has realized improvements in manpower efficiency of over 50% in certain areas.

Customer complaints have decreased by 91 percent, from 44 in 1985, when 49,000 pounds of product were returned for replacement, to 4 in 1987, when no product was returned.

Among workers, who have flexible job assignments and whose quality-improvement efforts are recognized through personal letters from management and small gifts, Globe's QEC program is paying dividends. The accident rate, near the average for the ferroalloy industry in 1985, has fallen, while the industry average has risen. The Globe absenteeism rate has also decreased since 1985.

For more information contact:
Kenneth E. Leach
Vice President, Administration
Globe Metallurgical Inc.
P.O. Box 157
Beverly, OH 45715

Motorola Inc.

Like an olympic athlete seeking to score better than determined world rivals, Motorola Inc. seeks sales victories in world markets for electronic components and equipment by improving the quality of its own performance. For Motorola, quality improvement leading to total customer satisfaction is the key.

In 1981, Motorola launched an ambitious drive for a tenfold improvement in the quality of its products and services. Motorola succeeded. Now, the company has evidence that many of its products are the best in their class. Looking ahead, Motorola intends to top its achievements—further gains in quality for 1989, yet another leap in 1991, and near perfection a year later. The company's quality goal is simply stated: "Zero defects in everything we do."

Motorola's managers literally carry with them the corporate objective of "total customer satisfaction." It's on a printed card in their pockets. Corporate officials and business managers wear pagers to make themselves available to customers, and they regularly visit customers' businesses to find out their likes and dislikes about Motorola products and services. The information, along with data gathered through an extensive network of customer surveys, complaint hotlines, field audits, and other customer feedback measures, guides planning for quality improvement and product development.

Company at a Glance   Employing 99,000 workers at 53 major facilities worldwide and based in Schaumburg, Illinois, 60-year old Motorola is an integrated company that produces an array of products, distributing most through direct sales and service operations. Communication systems—primarily two-way radios and pagers—account for 36 percent of annual sales, and semiconductors account for 32 percent. The remaining revenues come from sales of cellular telephones and equipment for defense and aerospace applications, data communications, information processing, and automotive and industrial uses. Sales in 1987 totalled $6.7 billion.

Responding to the rapid rise of Japanese firms in world markets for electronics, Motorola's management began an almost evangelical crusade for quality improvement; addressing it as a company issue and, through speeches and full-page ads in major publications, as a national issue.

The company's most persuasive messages, however, are the results of its quest for quality. Most products have increased their market share, here and abroad. In Japan, for example, Motorola pagers, supplied to Nippon Telegraph and Telephone, were introduced in 1982 and now claim a major share of that market. Over the past two years alone, Motorola has received nearly 50 quality awards and certified supplier citations, tops among the 600 electronics firms responding to a survey published in March 1987.

Key Quality Initiatives   To accomplish its quality and total customer satisfaction goals, Motorola concentrates on several key operational initiatives. At the top of the list is "Six Sigma Quality," a statistical measure of variation from a desired result. In concrete terms, Six Sigma translates into a target of no more than 3.4 defects per million products, customer services included. At the manufacturing end, this requires designs that accommodate reasonable variation in component parts but production processes that yield consistently uniform final products. Motorola employees record the defects found in every function of the business, and statistical technologies are increasingly made a part of each and every employee's job.

Reducing the "total cycle time"—the time from when a Motorola customer places an order until it is delivered—is another vital part of the company's quality initiatives. In fact, in the case of new products, Motorola's cycle-time reduction is even more ambitious; the clock starts ticking the moment the product is conceived. This calls for an examination of the total system, including design, manufacturing, marketing, and administration.

Motorola management demonstrates its quality leadership in a variety of ways, including top-level meetings to review quality programs with results passed on through the organization. But all levels of the company are involved. Nonexecutive employees contribute directly through Motorola's Participative Management Program (PMP). Composed of employees who work in the same area or are assigned to achieve a specific aim, PMP teams meet often to assess progress toward meeting quality goals, identify new initiatives, and work on problems. To reward high-quality work, savings that stem from team recommendations are shared. PMP bonuses over the past four years have averaged about 3 percent of Motorola's payroll.

To ensure that employees have the skills necessary to achieve company objectives, Motorola has set up its own training center and spent in excess of $170 million on worker education between 1983 and 1987. About 40 percent of the worker training the company provided last year was devoted to quality matters, ranging from general principles of quality improvement to designing for manufacturability.

Motorola knows what levels of quality its products must achieve to top its competitors. Each of the firm's six major groups and sectors have "benchmarking" programs that analyze all aspects of a competitor's products to assess their manufacturability, reliability, manufacturing cost, and performance. Motorola has measured the products of some 125 companies against its own standards, verifying that many Motorola products rank as best in their class.

For more information contact:
Richard C. Buetow
Corporate Vice President and
    Director of Quality
Motorola Inc.
1303 East Algonquin Road
Schaumburg, IL 60196

Total Quality Management The European Model for Self-Appraisal 1992

An Introduction

In the 1980s organizations began to realize that their only way of surviving in business was to pay much greater attention to quality. In many markets, quality has already become the competitive edge.

This is not only confined to the quality of a product or a service. It now applies to delivery, administration, customer service and every other aspect of the organization's activities.

Quality now encompasses all the ways in which the organization meets the needs and expectations of its customers, its people, its financial stakeholders, and society at large.

Realizing this emerging requirement for Total Quality Management, many of the major business organizations in Europe have embarked on programs to improve their management and business processes. Evidence of significant benefits has already been seen—increased competitiveness, reduced costs, and greater satisfaction among all their interested parties.

THE EUROPEAN FOUNDATION FOR QUALITY MANAGEMENT

In recognition of the potential for competitive advantage through application of Total Quality, fourteen of the leading Western European businesses took the initiative of forming the European Foundation for Quality Management (E.F.Q.M.) in 1988. By the beginning of 1992, membership had grown to nearly 200 members from most Western European countries and most business sectors.

E.F.Q.M. has an important role to play, enhancing the position of Western European businesses in the world market. This will be achieved in two ways:

- accelerating the acceptance of quality as a strategy for global competitive advantage:
- stimulating and assisting the deployment of quality improvement activities.

TOTAL QUALITY MANAGEMENT

The Need for Self-Appraisal

Essentially, self-appraisal involves the regular and systematic review of the organization's activities and results. This process allows the organization to clearly discern its strengths and the areas in which improvements can be made. The aim of this booklet is to encourage, facilitate, and optimize self-appraisal, by providing guidelines on:

- the organizational activities, processes, resources, and results that should be appraised.
- the areas, within those organizational aspects, that should be addressed.

Despite the fact that every organization is unique, the following model provides a framework for self-appraisal that is applicable to virtually every business organization.

The European Model

Processes are the means by which the organization harnesses and releases the talents of its people to produce results. In other words, the processes and the people are the ENABLERS which provide the RESULTS.

Expressed graphically, the principle looks like this:

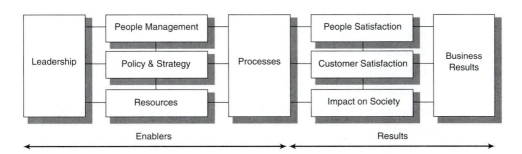

This model was developed as a framework for The European Quality Award, jointly sponsored by the European Commission, the European Foundation for Quality Management and the European Organization for Quality. Essentially the model tells us that:

Customer Satisfaction, People (employee) Satisfaction and *Impact on Society**

*In the 1990s it is vital that the organization achieves positive results in terms of the community at large. The criterion "Impact on Society" is included in the Model for this reason.

are achieved through
Leadership driving,
Policy and Strategy, People Management, Resources and *Processes,*
leading ultimately to excellence in
Business Results.

Each of the nine elements shown in the model is a criterion that can be used to appraise the organization's progress towards Total Quality Management.

The Results aspects are concerned with *what* the organization has achieved and is achieving.

The Enablers aspects are concerned with *how* results are being achieved.

The objective of a comprehensive quality management self-appraisal and self-improvement program is to regularly review each of these nine criteria and, thereafter, to adopt relevant improvement strategies.

ENABLERS

1. Leadership

The behavior of all managers in driving the organization towards Total Quality.

How the executive team and all other managers inspire and drive Total Quality as the organization's fundamental process for continuous improvement.

A Total Quality approach should demonstrate:

1a. *Visible involvement in leading quality management.*
Areas to address could include how managers:

- communicate with staff

- act as role models

- make themselves accessible and listen to staff

- assist in training staff

1b. *A consistent Total Quality culture.*
Areas to address could include how managers:

- are involved in assessing awareness of Total Quality

- are involved in reviewing progress in Total Quality

- include commitment to and achievement in Total Quality in appraisal and promotion of staff at all levels

1c. *Recognition and appreciation of the efforts and successes of individuals and teams.*
Areas to address could include the role of managers in recognition:

- at local

- at division

- at organization level
- of groups outside the organization e.g., suppliers or customers

1d. Support of Total Quality by provision of appropriate resources and assistance.
Areas to address could include how managers provide support through:

- funding facilitation
- funding improvement activity
- "championing"

1e. Involvement with customers and suppliers.
Areas to address could include how managers take positive steps to:

- meet customers and suppliers
- establish and participate in "partnership" relationships
- establish and participate in joint improvement teams

1f. Active promotion of quality management outside the organization.
Areas to address could include how managers promote quality management outside the organization through:

- membership of professional bodies
- publication of booklets, articles
- lectures at conferences and seminars
- assistance to local community

2. Policy and Strategy

The organization's values, vision and strategic direction and the ways in which the organization achieves them.

How the organization incorporates the concept of Total Quality in the determination, communication, implementation, review and improvement of its policy and strategy.

A Total Quality approach should demonstrate:

2a. How policy and strategy are based on the concept of Total Quality.
Areas to address could include how Total Quality is reflected in the organization's:

- values
- vision
- mission statements
- strategy statements

2b. How policy and strategy are determined using relevant information.
Areas to address could include the use of:

- feedback from customers and suppliers
- feedback from the organization's staff

- competitive and benchmark data
- forecasting methods and data on societal issues

2c. *How policy and strategy are the basis of business plans.*
   Areas to address could include:

- how key plans are tested and changed to align with the organization's policy

2d. *How policy and strategy are communicated.*
   Areas to address could include:

- the use of newsletters, posters, videos
- prioritizing initiatives
- how the organization evaluates the awareness of staff to its policy

2e. *How policy and strategy are regularly reviewed and improved.*
   Areas to address could include:

- how the organization evaluates the effectiveness and relevance of its policy
- how the organization reviews and improves its policy

3. People Management

The management of the organization's people.

How the organization releases the full potential of its people to improve its business continuously.

A Total Quality approach will demonstrate:

3a. *How continuous improvement in people management is effected*
   Areas to address could include how managers:

- review and improve human resources management
- improve human resources planning
- improve communications
- use surveys of staff perceptions of the organization

3b. *How the organization preserves and develops core skills through the recruitment, training and career progression of its people.*
   Areas to address could include how managers:

- define peoples' skills and compare them with the organization's requirements
- plan recruitment and advancement
- establish and implement training plans
- review the effectiveness of training
- continue to develop people after training

3c. *How the organization's performance targets are agreed and are reviewed continuously with staff.*
   Areas to address could include how managers:

- negotiate and assign objectives
- appraise and review staff

3d. *How the organization promotes the involvement of all its people in quality and continuous improvement.*
Areas to address could include how the organization:

- uses suggestion schemes
- uses quality organizations: quality circles, corrective action teams
- uses in-house conferences and meetings
- empowers its people to take action

4. Resources

The management, utilization and preservation of resources.
   How the organization improves its business continuously, by optimization of its resources.
   A Total Quality approach will cover:

4a. *Financial Resources*
Areas to address could include:

- management of cash flow, working capital, cost
- how strategies are evaluated financially
- management of shareholder value
- criteria for financial decision making
- the definition and use of "quality cost" concepts

4b. *Information Resources*
Areas to address could include:

- assurance and improvement of: data validity, integrity, accessibility and scope
- convenience and availability of data and information to customers and suppliers, management and staff involved in improvement
- how Information Technology strategies have been evaluated and improved

4c. *Material Resources*
Areas to address could include:

- management of raw material sources and supplies
- how material inventories are optimized
- how fixed assets are utilized to maximum effect

4d. *Application of Technology*
Areas to address could include:

- how alternative and emerging technologies are evaluated according to their business impact

- how technology has been exploited to secure competitive advantage
- how the introduction of technology has been integrated with human resource planning

5. Processes

The management of all the value-adding activities within the organization.

How key and support processes are identified, reviewed and, if necessary, revised to ensure continuous improvement of the organization's business.

Self-appraisal should indicate:

5a. *How key processes are identified*
Areas to address could include:

- how key processes* are defined: what processes are currently on the list
- the method of identification used:
- how interface issues are resolved
- how "impact on the business" is evaluated

*key processes could include:

- provision of raw materials and supplies
- manufacturing
- engineering
- reception of orders
- delivery of product or service
- invoicing and collection of debt
- determination of customer and people satisfaction
- new product and service development
- budgeting and planning

5b. *How the organization systematically manages its key and support processes.*
Areas to address could include:

- how process ownership and standards of operation are established
- how and by whom standards are monitored
- the role of performance measures in process management
- the role of ISO 9000 certification in process management

5c. *How process performance parameters, along with all relevant feedback are used to review key processes and to set targets for improvement.*
Areas to address could include:

- how feedback from customers, suppliers and external bodies and benchmarking are used in setting standards of operation and targets for improvement

- examples of measurement that show how current targets for improvement are related to past achievement
- the process for reviewing key processes

5d. How the organization stimulates innovation and creativity in process improvement.
Areas to address could include:

- how new principles of design, new technology and new operating philosophies are discovered and utilized
- how the creative talents of employees are brought to bear

5e. How the organization implements process changes and evaluates the benefits.
Areas to address could include:

- how and to whom process changes are communicated
- training of staff prior to implementation
- process for piloting new or changed procedures and for controlling implementation
- process for audit and review of changes and verification that the predicted results have been achieved

RESULTS

CUSTOMER SATISFACTION
PEOPLE SATISFACTION
IMPACT ON SOCIETY
BUSINESS RESULTS

The Results Criteria are concerned with what the organization has achieved and is achieving. These can be expressed as discrete results, but ideally as trends over a period of years.

The organization's results and trends for all Results Criteria should be assessed in terms of:

a—the organization's own targets
b—the relevance of the results to each group with an interest in the organization: customers, people, financial stakeholders and society at large.
c—the organization's actual performance

and where appropriate:

d—the performance of competitors

and/or

e—the performance of 'best in class' organizations

6. Customer Satisfaction

What the perception of external customers, direct and indirect, is of the organization and of its products and services.

A Total Quality approach will satisfy the needs and expectations of customers.

Areas to address could include customers perceptions of the organization with respect to:

Product and service quality:

- capability of meeting specifications
- defect, error, rejection rates
- consistency, reproducibility
- maintainability
- durability
- reliability
- on-time delivery
- in-full delivery
- logistics information
- delivery frequency
- responsiveness and flexibility
- product availability
- accessibility of key staff
- product training
- sales support
- product literature
- technical support
- simplicity, convenience and accuracy of documentation
- awareness of customer problems
- complaint handling
- warranty and guarantee provisions
- spare part availability
- innovation in service quality
- product development
- payment terms and financing

Indirect measures of Customer Satisfaction:

- complaint levels
- customer returns (by value and quantity)

- warranty payments
- re-work levels
- accolades and awards received

7. People Satisfaction

What the people's feelings are about their organization.
A Total Quality approach will satisfy the needs and expectations of its people. Areas to address could include:

- working environment: location, space, amenities
- health and safety provisions
- communication at local and organization level
- appraisal, target setting and career planning
- training, development, retraining
- awareness of requirements of job
- awareness of organization values, vision and strategy
- awareness of Total Quality process
- involvement in Total Quality process
- recognition schemes
- reward schemes
- organization (line management)
- organization for Total Quality
- perception of management style
- job security

Indirect measures of People Satisfaction:

- absenteeism and sickness
- staff turnover
- ease of recruitment

8. Impact on Society

What the perception of the organization is among society at large. This includes views of the organization's approach to quality of life, the environment and to the preservation of global resources.
A Total Quality approach will satisfy the needs and expectations of the community at large.
Areas to address could include:

The organization's active involvement in the community:

- charity
- education and training
- medical and welfare
- sports and leisure
- environment and ecology

The organization's activities to assist the preservation of global resources in terms of:

- energy conservation
- usage of raw materials and other inputs
- usage of recycled materials
- reduction of waste

The organization's activities to reduce and prevent nuisance and harm to neighbors as a result of operations, business related transportation and products:

- effluents and pollution
- hazards
- noise
- health risks

Indirect measures of impact on society:

- number of general complaints
- number of infringements of statutory limits
- incidents
- accolades and awards received by the organization

9. Business Results

What the organization is achieving in relation to its planned business performance. Areas to address could include some of the following:

- profit
- cash
- value of sales
- value added

- working capital
- liquidity
- shareholder returns
- long-term "value for shareholders"

(Several of the above can be expressed in absolute terms or as ratios per unit of capital or per employee.)

Non-Financial Measures   These will relate to achievement of other business targets and objectives and will include internal efficiency and effectiveness measures that are vital to the organization's continuing success.
   Areas to address could include some of the following:

- market share
- waste
- defects per unit of output or activity
- variability of product or service
- cost of non-quality

Cycle times such as:

- order processing time
- product delivery time
- batch processing time
- time to bring new products and services to the market
- time to break-even on new development
- inventory turnover time

Appendix II

Database of Authors
and Organizations

This list includes information on authors and organizations contacted directly by the editor. Organizations and authors from other previously published sources are not included.

Michael Brower
President
Michael Brower & Associates
32 Alpine St.
Cambridge, MA 02138
(617) 492-8893
Fax: (617) 492-6441

L. Edwin Coate
Vice Chancellor
Business & Administrative Services
University of California Santa Cruz
217 Venetian Rd.
Aptos, CA 95003
(408) 459-3778
Fax: (408) 459-3895

Harry Costin
President
Harry Costin & Associates
P.O. Box 15619
Boston, MA 02215
(617) 738-5059
Fax: (617) 277-9140

Joann De Mott
The J. De Mott Company
31347 Cougar Lane
Philomath, OR 97370
(503) 929-6785
Fax: (503) 929-6757

Ellen R. Domb
The PQR Group
399 N. Central Ave.
Upland, CA 91786
(714) 949-0857
Fax: (714) 949-4824

European Foundation for Quality Management
Building "Reaal" Fellenoord 47A
5612 AA Eindhoven
The Netherlands
+ 31 40 461075
Fax: + 31 40 432005

Armand Feigenbaum
General Systems Co.
Berkshire Common, South St.
Pittsfield, MA 01201
(413) 499-2880
Fax: (413) 443-7548

Helene Fine
55 Lake St.
New Bedford, MA 02740
(508) 992-6106

Harold Gilmore
Professor of Management
Univ. of Massachusetts Dartmouth
47 South Rd.
Falmouth, MA 02540
(508) 548-4556

GOAL QPC
13 Branch St.
Methuen, MA 01844-1953
(508) 685-3900
Fax: (508) 685-6151

Barry A. Goff
The Research Center for
Organizational Learning
Univ. of Connecticut
114 Ridgewood Rd.
Glastonbury, CT 06033
Phone & Fax: (203) 659-8743

Thomas J. Higginson
Professor of Management
Univ. of Massachusetts Dartmouth
145 Brayton Point Rd.
Westport, MA 02790
(508) 999-8862
Fax: (508) 999-8901

Jan C. Knakal
New Acropolis
852 W. Armitage 3rd Floor R
Chicago, IL 60614
(312) 929-9673

Ronald D. Mc Neil
Dean, College of Business & Industry
Univ. of Massachusetts Dartmouth
North Dartmouth, MA 02747
(508) 999-8432
Fax: (508) 999-8776

John Moran
Organizational Dynamics
Twenty-five Mall Rd.
Burlington, MA 01803-4100
(617) 221-5460
Fax: (617) 273-2558

Malcolm Baldrige Award
NIST
Route 270
Quince Orchard Rd.
Build. 101 Room A-537
Gaithersburg, MD 20899
(301) 975-2000
Fax: (301) 948-3716

Elizabeth Powers
Elizabeth Powers & Associates
P.O. Box 2346
Brentwood, TN 37024-2346
(615) 353-0352
Fax: (615) 327-4204

Mary Lou Roberts
Professor of Marketing
Univ. of Massachusetts Boston
4 Fox Lane
Milford, MA 01757
(617) 287-7733
Fax: (617) 287-7725

Robert P. Waxler
Professor
Univ. of Massachusetts Dartmouth
25 Strathmore Rd.
North Dartmouth, MA 02747
(508) 999-8752
Fax: (508) 999-8901

Madelyn Yucht
7 Buena Vista Park
Cambridge, MA 02140
(617) 497-5778

Index

___

Notes

———